Cyber Security of Industrial Control Systems in the Future Internet Environment

Mirjana D. Stojanović
University of Belgrade, Serbia

Slavica V. Boštjančič Rakas
University of Belgrade, Serbia

A volume in the Advances in Information Security,
Privacy, and Ethics (AISPE) Book Series

Published in the United States of America by
    IGI Global
    Information Science Reference (an imprint of IGI Global)
    701 E. Chocolate Avenue
    Hershey PA, USA 17033
    Tel: 717-533-8845
    Fax: 717-533-8661
    E-mail: cust@igi-global.com
    Web site: http://www.igi-global.com

Library of Congress Cataloging-in-Publication Data

Names: Stojanović, Mirjana D., editor. I Bostjancic Rakas, Slavica V.,
   1978- editor.
Title: Cyber security of industrial control systems in the future internet
   environment / Mirjana D. Stojanovic and Slavica V. Bostjancic Rakas,
   editors.
Description: Hershey, PA : Information Science Reference, 2020. I Includes
   bibliographical references and index. I Summary: ""This book provides
   research on current security risks in critical infrastructure schemes
   with the implementation of information and communication technologies.
   While highlighting topics such as intrusion detection systems, forensic
   challenges, and smart grids, this publication explores specific security
   solutions within industrial sectors that have begun applying internet
   technologies to their current methods of operation"--Provided by
   publisher"-- Provided by publisher.
Identifiers: LCCN 2019045655 (print) I LCCN 2019045656 (ebook) I ISBN
   9781799829102 (hardcover) I ISBN 9781799829119 (paperback) I ISBN
   9781799829126 (ebook)
Subjects: LCSH: Process control--Security measures. I Computer security.
Classification: LCC TS156.8 .C93 2020 (print) I LCC TS156.8 (ebook) I DDC
   658.5--dc23
LC record available at https://lccn.loc.gov/2019045655
LC ebook record available at https://lccn.loc.gov/2019045656

This book is published in the IGI Global book series Advances in Information Security, Privacy, and Ethics (AISPE) (ISSN: 1948-9730; eISSN: 1948-9749)

British Cataloguing in Publication Data
A Cataloguing in Publication record for this book is available from the British Library.

For electronic access to this publication, please contact: eresources@igi-global.com.

Advances in Information Security, Privacy, and Ethics (AISPE) Book Series

Manish Gupta
State University of New York, USA

ISSN:1948-9730
EISSN:1948-9749

Mission

As digital technologies become more pervasive in everyday life and the Internet is utilized in ever increasing ways by both private and public entities, concern over digital threats becomes more prevalent.

The **Advances in Information Security, Privacy, & Ethics (AISPE) Book Series** provides cutting-edge research on the protection and misuse of information and technology across various industries and settings. Comprised of scholarly research on topics such as identity management, cryptography, system security, authentication, and data protection, this book series is ideal for reference by IT professionals, academicians, and upper-level students.

Coverage

- Technoethics
- Cyberethics
- Cookies
- Internet Governance
- Security Information Management
- Electronic Mail Security
- Device Fingerprinting
- Risk Management
- IT Risk
- Global Privacy Concerns

IGI Global is currently accepting manuscripts for publication within this series. To submit a proposal for a volume in this series, please contact our Acquisition Editors at Acquisitions@igi-global.com or visit: http://www.igi-global.com/publish/.

Titles in this Series

For a list of additional titles in this series, please visit:
https://www.igi-global.com/book-series/advances-information-security-privacy-ethics/37157

Applied Approach to Privacy and Security for the Internet of Things
Parag Chatterjee (National Technological University, India) Emmanuel Benoist (Bern University of Applied Sciences, France) and Asoke Nath (St. Xavier's College Kolkata, University of Calcutt, India)
Information Science Reference • © 2020 • 315pp • H/C (ISBN: 9781799824442) • US $235.00

Internet Censorship and Regulation Systems in Democracies Emerging Research and Opportunities
Nikolaos Koumartzis (Aristotle University of Thessaloniki, Greece) and Andreas Veglis (Aristotle University of Thessaloniki, Greece)
Information Science Reference • © 2020 • 200pp • H/C (ISBN: 9781522599739) • US $185.00

Quantum Cryptography and the Future of Cyber Security
Nirbhay Kumar Chaubey (Gujarat Technological University, India) and Bhavesh B. Prajapati (Education Department, Government of Gujarat, India)
Information Science Reference • © 2020 • 320pp • H/C (ISBN: 9781799822530) • US $235.00

Impact of Digital Transformation on Security Policies and Standards
Sam Goundar (The University of the South Pacific, Fiji) Bharath Bhushan (Sree Vidyanikethan Engineering College, India) and Vaishali Ravindra Thakare (Atria Institute of Technology, India)
Information Science Reference • © 2020 • 300pp • H/C (ISBN: 9781799823674) • US $215.00

Handbook of Research on Intelligent Data Processing and Information Security Systems
Stepan Mykolayovych Bilan (State University of Infrastructure and Technology, Ukraine) and Saleem Issa Al-Zoubi (Irbid National University, Jordan)
Engineering Science Reference • © 2020 • 434pp • H/C (ISBN: 9781799812906) • US $345.00

Security and Privacy Issues in Sensor Networks and IoT
Priyanka Ahlawat (National Institute of Technology, Kurukshetra, India) and Mayank Dave (National Institute of Technology, Kurukshetra, India)
Information Science Reference • © 2020 • 323pp • H/C (ISBN: 9781799803737) • US $195.00

Modern Principles, Practices, and Algorithms for Cloud Security
Brij B. Gupta (National Institute of Technology, Kurukshetra, India)
Information Science Reference • © 2020 • 344pp • H/C (ISBN: 9781799810827) • US $195.00

701 East Chocolate Avenue, Hershey, PA 17033, USA
Tel: 717-533-8845 x100 • Fax: 717-533-8661
E-Mail: cust@igi-global.com • www.igi-global.com

Table of Contents

Section 1
General ICS Security Aspects: Architectures, Platforms, and Technologies

Mirjana D. Stojanović, Faculty of Transport and Traffic Engineering, University of Belgrade,
Serbia
Slavica V. Boštjančič Rakas, Mihailo Pupin Institute, University of Belgrade, Serbia

Jasna D. Marković-Petrović, Public Enterprise "Electric Power Industry of Serbia", Serbia

Gordana Gardašević, Faculty of Electrical Engineering, University of Banja Luka, Bosnia
and Herzegovina
Lazar Berbakov, Mihailo Pupin Institute, University of Belgrade, Serbia
Aleksandar Mastilović, Communications Regulatory Agency BH, Bosnia and Herzegovina

Luis Rosa, Department of Informatics Engineering, University of Coimbra, Portugal
Miguel Borges de Freitas, Department of Informatics Engineering, University of Coimbra,
Portugal
João Henriques, Department of Informatics Engineering, University of Coimbra, Portugal
Pedro Quitério, Department of Informatics Engineering, University of Coimbra, Portugal
Filipe Caldeira, Polytechnic Institute of Viseu, Portugal
Tiago Cruz, Department of Informatics Engineering, University of Coimbra, Portugal
Paulo Simões, Department of Informatics Engineering, University of Coimbra, Portugal

Section 2
Attack Models, Security Analysis, and Security Evaluation

Section 3
Security Considerations in Specific Industrial Sectors

Detailed Table of Contents

Section 1
General ICS Security Aspects: Architectures, Platforms, and Technologies

Chapter 1
Mirjana D. Stojanović, Faculty of Transport and Traffic Engineering, University of Belgrade,
Serbia
Slavica V. Boštjančič Rakas, Mihailo Pupin Institute, University of Belgrade, Serbia

This chapter explores challenges in securing industrial control systems (ICS) and Supervisory Control And Data Acquisition (SCADA) systems using Future Internet technologies. These technologies include cloud computing, fog computing, Industrial internet of things (IIoT), etc. The need to design specific security solutions for ICS/SCADA networks is explained. A brief overview of cyber vulnerabilities and threats in industrial control networks, cloud, and IoT environments is presented. The security of cloud-based SCADA systems is considered, including benefits and risks of SCADA migration to the cloud, challenges in securing such systems, and migration toward fog computing. Challenges in securing IIoT are addressed, including security risks and operational issues, key principles for securing IIoT, the functional security architecture, and the role of fog computing. Authors point out current standardization activities and trends in the area, and emphasize conclusions and future research directions.

Chapter 2
Jasna D. Marković-Petrović, Public Enterprise "Electric Power Industry of Serbia", Serbia

The evolution of architecture of contemporary SCADA systems follows trends in industry sector. Today, SCADA systems imply the application of smart grid and artificial intelligence concepts, the use of IP-based technologies, new mobile devices, as well as the use of private and public cloud computing services. Security risk assessment of contemporary SCADA systems needs to include new security aspects. This chapter analyzes information security in contemporary SCADA systems. Focus is then directed to SCADA network architecture and recommended security mechanisms for mitigating the security risk that assumes the use of Defense in Depth concept. Special attention is paid to SCADA-specific intrusion detection and intrusion prevention technologies. A case study outlines recommendations for security risk mitigation of SCADA system in a hydropower plant.

Chapter 3

Gordana Gardašević, Faculty of Electrical Engineering, University of Banja Luka, Bosnia and Herzegovina

Lazar Berbakov, Mihailo Pupin Institute, University of Belgrade, Serbia

Aleksandar Mastilović, Communications Regulatory Agency BH, Bosnia and Herzegovina

The Internet of Things (IoT) is an emerging and even revolutionary technology with an immense impact on our everyday life. The Industrial Internet of Things (IIoT) is a fast-growing technology that increases productivity and efficiency by combining the IoT platform with an existing industrial environment. IIoT networks are one of the main pillars for the success of the future Industry 4.0 and Cyber-Physical System (CPS) paradigm. The IIoT ecosystem represents a network of connected industrial devices that exchange and analyze collected data to enable new insights into industrial processes. Recently, intensive research activities have focused on cybersecurity issues for the IIoT. This chapter addresses the critical components of the IIoT security framework by analyzing the relevant aspects and providing an overview of state-of-the-art activities in this field. This chapter also discusses the IIoT architectural structure, applications, and underlying networking technologies, with a particular focus on security challenges and standardization activities.

Chapter 4

Luis Rosa, Department of Informatics Engineering, University of Coimbra, Portugal

Miguel Borges de Freitas, Department of Informatics Engineering, University of Coimbra, Portugal

João Henriques, Department of Informatics Engineering, University of Coimbra, Portugal

Pedro Quitério, Department of Informatics Engineering, University of Coimbra, Portugal

Filipe Caldeira, Polytechnic Institute of Viseu, Portugal

Tiago Cruz, Department of Informatics Engineering, University of Coimbra, Portugal

Paulo Simões, Department of Informatics Engineering, University of Coimbra, Portugal

In recent years, IACS (Industrial Automation and Control Systems) have become more complex, due to the increasing number of interconnected devices. This IoT (internet of things)-centric IACS paradigm, which is at the core of the Industry 4.0 concept, expands the infrastructure boundaries beyond the aggregated-plant, mono-operator vision, being dispersed over a large geographic area. From a cybersecurity-centric perspective, the distributed nature of modern IACS makes it difficult not only to understand the nature of incidents but also to assess their progression and threat profile. Defending against those threats is becoming increasingly difficult, requiring orchestrated and collaborative distributed detection, evaluation, and reaction capabilities beyond the scope of a single entity. This chapter presents the Intrusion and Anomaly Detection System platform architecture that was designed and developed within the scope of the ATENA H2020 project, to address the specific needs of distributed IACS while providing (near) real-time cybersecurity awareness.

Chapter 5

Branka Mikavica, Faculty of Transport and Traffic Engineering, University of Belgrade, Serbia

Aleksandra Kostić-Ljubisavljević, Faculty of Transport and Traffic Engineering, University of Belgrade, Serbia

Future internet environment is affected by permanent and rapid changes, triggered by the emergence of high bandwidth-demanding services, applications, and contents. Cloud computing might be considered as the prelude of the future internet. Additionally, the concept of elastic optical networks is a widely accepted promising solution for the future internet. This chapter addresses the security aspects of the content provisioning process with cloud migration over elastic optical networks in the future internet environment. Key characteristics of the cloud computing and elastic optical networks relevant to the content provisioning process are presented. Major threats in each segment of the observed process, including vulnerabilities in the cloud computing and security issues in elastic optical networks, are considered.

Section 2
Attack Models, Security Analysis, and Security Evaluation

Chapter 6

The production processes of critical infrastructures (CIs) are managed and monitored by Industrial Control Systems (ICS) such as SCADA (Supervisory Control and Data Acquisition). The resulting CIs networks are huge and complex, which have inadvertently called for the integration of other technologies such as the internet for efficiency. The integration of such unsecured technologies and the advent of new computing paradigms such as IoT (internet of things) and Cloud computing which are being integrated into current industrial environments, giving rise to Industry 4.0 have further expanded the attack surface. This chapter considers a new breed of security attacks, crypto-viral attacks (crypto mining and crypto ransomware attacks), which target both the production and control networks of CIs. The authors model these attacks and evaluate their impacts. Such modeling is crucial in understanding the extent of the scope and detection capabilities of the first line of defense (intrusion detection and prevention systems), and possible avenues for mitigation strategies are suggested.

Chapter 7

This chapter provides a complex data analysis of critical infrastructure SCADA vulnerabilities and exploits using fuzzy-decision algorithms. These algorithms are presented in two case studies describing possible scenarios of the cyber attack on two vital multi-parameter remote monitoring systems. The main objects of the cyber attack analysis are data obtained from their common SCADA system. The main focus is on multiparameter remote monitoring systems for monitoring electricity production and water traffic processes in the lock of hydropower plant. Newly developed fuzzy decision algorithms for comprehensive data analysis are presented to recognize the cyber attack. The results of the fuzzy modeling are directly dependent on the complex choice of the if-then rules on the basis of which decisions are made. In addition, two fuzzy logic systems (FLS-T1 and FLS-T2) are used for modeling several cyber attack scenarios.

Artificial intelligence is making significant changes in industrial internet of things (IIoT). Particularly, machine and deep learning architectures are now used for cybersecurity in smart factories, smart homes, and smart cities. Using advanced mathematical models and algorithms more intelligent protection strategies should be developed. Hacking of IP surveillance camera systems and Closed-Circuit TV (CCTV) vulnerabilities represent typical example where cyber attacks can make severe damage to physical and other Industrial Control Systems (ICS). This chapter analyzes the possibilities to provide better protection of video surveillance systems and communication networks. The authors review solutions related to migrating machine learning based inference towards edge and smart client devices, as well as methods for DDoS (Distributed Denial of Service) intelligent detection, where DDoS attack is recognized as one of the primary concerns in cybersecurity.

Chapter 9

Cyber-Physical Systems (CPSs) are systems which integrate computational, networking, and physical components within a single functional environment. They play an important role in critical infrastructure, government, and everyday life. CPSs encumber many requirements, such as robustness, safety and security, Quality of Service (QoS), and trust. In addition, CPSs combine a variety of digital and analog technologies. Consequently, their analysis, verification, and control can be challenging. The science of protecting CPSs from blended attacks, those combining cyber and physical attack vectors, is yet to be developed. A much-needed tool on this front is a suitable test environment in which to pursue lines of experimentation and exploration. This chapter describes a testbed that allows researchers to experiment on blended attack and defense scenarios in CPSs through gamification. The testbed features many different systems, both cyber and physical, that are fully instrumented for data analysis and assessment.

Power Grid, Water/Sewage control system, and Industrial automation are some examples of critical infrastructures. They are critical because malfunctioning of any of these may lead to severe industrial accidents. It may also have severe implications for the national economy and security. Nation-states are gearing up for potential cyber warfare, signs of which are already visible in various incidents such as

Stuxnet, BlackEnergy, and many other recent attacks. As a result, research in cyber defense for such critical systems is an urgent need for all countries. IIT Kanpur has established the National Interdisciplinary Center for Cyber Security and Cyber Defense of Critical Infrastructures (C3i Center) to engage in research in this crucial area. In the past, the authors carried out a lot of cybersecurity experiments on co-Simulator-based platforms. These experiments show that they do not allow us to penetrate at the granularity required to defend real systems and therefore, physical test-beds are to be constructed. In this chapter, the authors describe how to build various test-beds.

Section 3
Security Considerations in Specific Industrial Sectors

Chapter 11

The concept of "Cloud computing" became very interesting in recent years because it enables optimization of resources used and costs paid for it. Considering all advantages, this approach is applied widely in business systems of general purpose. In recent years, in literature it is possible to find considerations related to application of this approach in corporate systems as electric power utilities. Having in mind that such types of systems represent infrastructure ones that have great impact to the security of people and utilities, a very important question related to information security should be seriously considered. This chapter discusses advantages and disadvantages of application of cloud computing in electric power utility systems.

Chapter 12

This chapter presents the development of the Energy Internet throughout the history as an evolutionary solution based on modern technological development and needs, with the respect of its architecture, key features, and key concepts, such as energy router, prosumer, and virtual power plant. The architecture of modern IT support for the electric power sector is considered, including its basic characteristics, the integration of contemporary information and communication technologies, such as cloud and fog computing, as well as the security and quality of service issues that arise with the application of these technologies. This chapter provides an overview of recent research related to the concept of Energy Internet and identifies gaps and directions for further research.

Chapter 13

Internet of energy (IoE) is the natural evolution of Smart Grid incorporating the paradigm of internet of things (IoT). This complicated environment has a lot of threats and vulnerabilities, so the security challenges are very complex and specialized. This chapter contains a compilation of the main threats, vulnerabilities, and attacks that can occur in the IoE environment and the critical structure of the electrical grid. The objective is to show the best cybersecurity practices that can support maintaining a safe, reliable, and available electrical network complying with the requirements of availability, integrity, and confidentially of the information. The study includes review of countermeasures, standards, and specialized intrusion detection systems, as mechanisms to solve security problems in IoE. Better understanding of security challenges and solutions in the IoE can be the light on future research work for IoE security.

Chapter 14

Introduction of the Dynamic Line Rating (DLR) concept has an important role in implementing smart grids in the power utility's transmission network. DLR assumes real-time control of the overhead transmission line, based on the continuous evaluation of the actual thermal and other operating conditions, and further estimation of the maximum transmission line's load and other relevant parameters that determine operational limitations. This chapter presents cloud-based DLR systems in terms of architecture, cloud services, and cyber security issues. DLR systems are explored with regards to cloud computing in industry, applicable cloud services and infrastructures, and communication system's performance. Security and privacy of cloud-based DLR systems have been addressed in terms of public and private services. A secure hybrid cloud-based architecture to support DLR is proposed.

Chapter 15

Cyber security in Healthcare is a growing concern. Since it has been a proliferation of IoT devices, data breaches from the healthcare industry are increasing the concern about how cyber security can protect data from connected medical devices. Recent years have seen numerous hacking and IT security incidents. Many healthcare organizations are facing problems to defend their networks from cybercriminals. In the current digital era, the physical world has a cyber-representation. Both the real and virtual worlds are connected in areas, such as informatics and manufacturing. Health 4.0 (H4.0) refers to a group of initiatives aiming to improve medical care for patients, hospitals, researchers, and medical device suppliers. Increasing collaboration in terms of medical equipment, artificial organs, and biosensors is a way to facilitate H4.0. As a result, cyber security budgets have increased, new technology has been purchased, and healthcare organizations are improving at blocking attacks and keeping their networks secure.

Preface

Industrial control system (ICS) is a general term that describes the interconnected equipment used to monitor and control physical equipment and processes in industrial environments. ICS technologies include supervisory control and data acquisition (SCADA), distributed control systems (DCS), industrial automation and control systems (IACS), programmable logic controllers (PLCs), intelligent electronic devices (IEDs), sensors, etc. They are widely applied in manufacturing, electric utilities, oil and gas industry, water and wastewater treatment, transportation, healthcare, etc. Destruction, breakdowns of objects and systems, failures and limitations in providing vital services and access to critical resources may have serious consequences due to their strategic importance for national critical infrastructures.

Industrial control systems have a rich and long history (Hayden, Assante, & Conway, 2014). At present, ICS physical and cyber security are converging; however, that is a relatively recent phenomenon that appeared a few decades ago, when Internet technologies started to be gradually introduced to these systems.

The information and communication ICS infrastructure follows the development of technologies originally intended for general-purpose information systems. This means that the growing trend of ICS internetworking will continue toward Future Internet environments, with inherent and increased issues regarding cyber security (Knapp & Langill, 2015). The evolving threats are continuously challenging and reminding security professionals as well as corporations to come up with interconnected and integrated approach to ICS security.

MIGRATION OF INDUSTRIAL CONTROL SYSTEMS TOWARD THE FUTURE INTERNET

In the broadest sense, the Future Internet refers to simplifying people's usage of Internet and integrating its application in a way that allows incorporating the Internet into the personal, professional and societal life. Future Internet technologies include, but are not limited to, information centricity, cloud computing, fog computing, software-defined networking, elastic optical networks, 5G wireless technology, sensor networks, the use of nanotechnologies, mobile computing, big data processing and analytics, machine-to-machine (M2M) communications and artificial intelligence. Thus, the Internet of Things (IoT) concept describes the idea of everyday physical objects (things) being connected to the Internet and being able to identify themselves to other devices. The concept is evolving in several directions, such as the industrial IoT, consumer IoT, Energy Internet, Internet of nano-things, toward the paradigm of interconnected people, data, processes and things, which is called "Internet of Everything" (Miraz, Ali, Excell, & Picking, 2018).

In the past few years, cloud computing has progressively shifted its focus from consumer applications toward corporate control systems. The cloud-based services, provided through the public, private, or hybrid infrastructures, contribute to cost-effectiveness and simplification of the manufacturing processes. The world's leading cloud service providers are beginning to offer cloud solutions that will meet the needs of organizations with business operations in industries; this paradigm is known as "Industry cloud" or "Manufacturing cloud" (Devare, 2019; Sanders, 2019). Industry cloud is not restricted to public clouds; hybrid and private industry cloud infrastructures can be built with the assistance of professional system integration companies. Cloud computing is also one of the pillars of the Internet of Things and its applications in different areas of human activities.

Industrial IoT (IIoT) is a model of smart sensors, actuators and other industry devices, connected to the Internet and networked with the industrial applications. It is a fundamental building block of the Industry 4.0 program (also known as the fourth industrial revolution), which assumes complete digitalization of industrial production lines and application of Future Internet technologies in engineering products, organization of production, process control and provision of industrial services (Lu, 2017). IoT (and IIoT) devices generate massive amount of data, thus putting enormous pressure on the Internet infrastructure. Cloud computing together with big data assists in data storage, transmission, processing and analysis.

When delay, network bandwidth and security requirements are critical, fog computing bridges the gap between cloud and the operational edge by enabling computing, storage, networking, mobility and location awareness, as well as data management on network nodes within the close vicinity of end devices. Due to its distributed and localized operation, fog computing allows for the use of the same security policies, controls and procedures as in traditional industrial control systems, and also represents a powerful middleware solution for IIoT systems.

RESEARCH ISSUES AND CHALLENGES

Threats to industrial control systems can originate from outside sources, such as terrorists, hackers, industrial espionage, or from insiders, such as current and former employees, a contractor, a third-party vendor, or any other business associate that has access to the organization's data and computer systems.

The research published by the SANS Institute, in 2017, showed that the amount of external threats affecting vital, mission-critical systems was growing annually (Gregory-Brown, 2017). Another report by the same source, in June 2019, focused more broadly on the operational technology domain inside organizations, because "industrial control systems are interwoven and interdependent, while also actively exchanging information with a myriad of other systems and processes" (Filkins & Wylie, 2019, p. 2).

Now, the question arises why are Future Internet technologies so vulnerable to different kinds of cyber security threats? Apart from evolving threats, the main reason is certainly the heterogeneity of physical objects, networking technologies and applications that should be able to communicate and collaboratively provide immutable and verifiable data. Therefore, security risk factors involve: real-time and complex interactions; security flaws in particular parts of the system; flawed integration of security systems; insecure network connections; insecure communication protocols; shared technology issues; multiple points of entry and failure; the use of open software platforms; the use of commercial off-the-shelf hardware and software components; and the lack of protection for legacy systems with long operational life (Nazir, S. Patel, & D. Patel, 2017).

When searching for solutions to the problem, it is essential to understand the security objectives and requirements of ICS. According to the U.S. National Institute of Standards and Technology (NIST), "ICS security objectives typically follow the priority of availability and integrity, followed by confidentiality" (Stouffer, Pillitteri, Lightman, Abrams, & Hahn, 2015, p.1). Moreover, security issue of a continual real-time system assumes a comprehensive analysis and holistic understanding of network security, control theory, and physical systems. This establishes the need for solutions that are tailored to the industry and its individual cyber security risk profiles. Layered approaches to ICS cyber security are commonly used and applied to people, processes, technology and adversarial awareness (Aydos, Vural, & Tekerek, 2019). Defense in depth is a good example of a holistic, layered approach that often deploys specific controls to counter and neutralize security risks related to all assets (Tariq, Asima, & Khan, 2019).

The main research challenges can be classified into the following areas:

- **Systems Aspects**: Several frameworks for cyber security of ICS in the Future Internet environment have been developed by the leading standards organizations and consortia. Actually, they provide roadmaps for securing ICS information and communication infrastructure by specifying policies, procedures and standards necessary to ensure data availability, integrity and confidentiality. Research challenges include, but are not limited to: development of advanced functional and implementation security architectures; information security management and risk management; development of security standards, especially specific standards, recommendations and directions concerning particular industrial sectors; security requirements for service level agreements in cloud computing, etc.
- **Attack Models:** New attacks are being developed to exploit the vulnerabilities of industrial control systems based on Future Internet technologies. Understanding attack models provides more meaningful insight into ICS vulnerability, which can further be used to protect the system from future attacks. However, it is difficult (or even impossible) to predict/recognize potential attacks without knowledge of system vulnerabilities. For that reason, techniques for network analysis are of the key importance to identify vulnerabilities; they can help to gain an idea of how to protect the network. Also, attack models are useful for designing security mechanisms and techniques such as ICS-specific intrusion detection and prevention.
- **Security Mechanisms:** There are a variety of tools and techniques that are used to implement security services, such as mechanisms for access control, cryptographic mechanisms, firewalls and security filters, intrusion detection and prevention, protocol protection, etc. As already mentioned, specific security objectives dictate the need for ICS-specific security solutions. This is particularly true for the defense against ICS-specific cyber security threats and for securing application-specific protocols in such systems. Still, the question is whether some of general-purpose security solutions are applicable, either original or upgraded to meet the requirements of industrial networks.
- **Security Evaluation:** Continuous security evaluation of ICS is crucial for mitigating the cyber risk. However, pen-testing activities, which are typical for non-industrial environments, are unacceptable for industrial control systems, because they must maintain the operational continuity. It is unfeasible to perform security experiments on a real system due to cost of scale, downtime and risk of failure. Hence, realistic and comprehensive security testbeds are needed that allow for

experimentation with different solutions. In the context of Future Internet technologies, physical testbeds, i.e., testbeds equipped with real hardware components, are of particular interest.

- **Security Issues in Specific Industrial Sectors:** This research area is related to specific cyber security issues, standards and solutions related to application of Future Internet technologies in different industrial sectors, and their associated operational technologies and services.

OBJECTIVES OF THE BOOK AND TARGET AUDIENCE

The main objective of this book is to provide an in-depth insight into migration of advanced industrial control systems to Future Internet environments, with focus on cyber security as a prevailing risk factor for deployment of emerging information and communication technologies to the critical industry infrastructure. Besides a comprehensive state-of-the art review, it covers most of the up-to-date research topics regarding cyber security of industrial control systems. Equal emphases are placed upon the architectural view, specific security solutions and their applications, development of appropriate testbeds, and the standardization efforts in the field. The book also explores the possibilities of securing public network and service infrastructure to be utilized by industrial control systems.

The target audience will be composed of researchers, engineers, postgraduate and doctoral students, professionals and managers in the areas of industrial engineering and manufacturing systems, networking and telecommunications, as well as the cyber and network security.

ORGANIZATION OF THE BOOK AND CONTRIBUTIONS

The book is organized into three sections with a total of 15 chapters written by a group of 38 authors from eight worldwide countries. The group includes experienced and internationally recognized researchers and specialists in the area, and a number of young researchers.

The authors' contributions are achieved in different fields of this multidisciplinary area, from the system's level (security architectures, security and risk management), through attacks modeling and analysis, technology considerations, development of specific security solutions and test environments, to applications such as smart grids, video surveillance and healthcare. In addition, comprehensive surveys of relevant standards and practices have been presented throughout the book. The book provides an exhaustive list of references (more than 500 references) as well as more than 120 recommendations for additional reading. A brief description of each section and its associated chapters follows:

Section One is composed of the first five chapters and addresses general security aspects of ICS in the Future Internet environment including security architectures, platforms and technologies.

Chapter 1 identifies the challenges in securing industrial control systems in the Future Internet environment. The chapter sets the scene for discussions presented in the following chapters of this book. In particular, the chapter considers security of cloud-based SCADA systems, taking into account different migration scenarios. Next, cyber security of IIoT is addressed, including security risks and operational issues, key principles for securing IIoT and the functional security architecture. The role of fog computing is highlighted as a prospective middleware for different industrial scenarios. Finally, standardization activities and trends in the area are pointed out.

Chapter 2 emphasizes the role of cyber security risk assessment in next generation SCADA systems. The author focuses on SCADA network architecture and recommends defense-in-depth approach to mitigate the security risk. Next, SCADA-specific intrusion detection and prevention technologies are considered. The presented case study summarizes policies and procedures for security risk mitigation on the example of a hydropower plant SCADA system.

Chapter 3 presents a comprehensive survey of IIoT cyber security issues and solutions. The authors describe the IIoT architectural structure, applications, and the underlying networking technologies. They provide a thorough overview of state-of-the-art activities in the field and address the critical components of the IIoT security framework. Next, standardization activities, taxonomy of IIoT-specific cyber attacks and the strategy for achieving the IIoT cyber security have been explained in details.

Chapter 4 deals with cyber security of industrial automation and control systems in the context of IoT and Industry 4.0. The authors argue that the distributed nature of modern IACS makes it hard to understand the nature of incidents, to assess their progression and to create threat profile. They present the platform architecture for intrusion and anomaly detection system, which has been developed to fulfill the specific requirements of distributed IACS, while providing near real-time cyber security awareness.

Chapter 5 addresses the security aspects of the content provisioning process with cloud migration over elastic optical networks. The authors emphasize rapid changes in the Future Internet environment as a main characteristic that has a significant impact on industrial systems. In such a context, vulnerabilities, threats and security solutions for cloud-ready optical transport networks have been surveyed and discussed.

Section Two encompasses Chapters 6 to 10 focusing on attack models, security solutions and security evaluation.

Chapter 6 considers crypto-viral attacks on both the production and control networks of critical infrastructure systems in cloud environments. The authors model two forms of such attacks, namely the crypto mining and crypto ransomware attacks, and evaluate their impacts on ICS networks. They emphasize the importance of proper attack modeling for development of security mechanisms such as ICS-specific intrusion detection and prevention systems.

Chapter 7 proposes fuzzy-decision algorithms for comprehensive data analysis of SCADA systems vulnerabilities. The inputs for analysis are data obtained from the common SCADA system. Fuzzy models have been developed to detect anomalies in the data, in different cyber attack scenarios, with the aim of early detection of attacks and prevention of emergency situations. The proposed algorithms are demonstrated on two case studies concerning multi-parameter remote monitoring of electricity production and water traffic processes in hydropower plant lock, respectively.

Chapter 8 analyzes the possibilities to improve protection of video surveillance systems, such as closed-circuit television (CCTV), and their associated communication networks in IIoT environments. Distributed denial of service (DDoS) attacks are recognized as primary concerns in cyber security of such systems. The authors review solutions related to implementing machine and deep learning techniques in the edge and smart client devices, as well as the methods for intelligent detection of DDoS attacks.

Chapter 9 presents a testbed for cyber-physical systems (CPS) that is intended for experiments on blended attacks (the attacks that combine cyber and physical attack vectors) and defense scenarios, through gamification. The authors start from general description of the CPS testbed components such as robotic cars, gameplay arena, situational awareness platform, as well as hardware and software integration. Next, they describe the instrumentation strategy that feeds an "analytical engine" within the situational awareness platform, gamification principles and application in various research experiments.

Chapter 10 tackles cyber security experimentation testbeds for critical infrastructures. The authors argue that cyber security experiments on co-simulator based platforms are not sufficient for real systems, and emphasize the need to build physical testbeds. They present architecture of a national center for cyber security consisting of several testbeds developed for different industry sectors, including power utilities, water treatment and industrial automation, and also describe experimental setups for vulnerability assessment and testing machine learning-based intrusion detection techniques.

Section Three is composed of Chapters 11 to 15 and considers security of control systems and operational technologies in specific industrial sectors.

Chapter 11 discusses advantages and disadvantages of application of cloud computing in electric power utility systems, with the focus on information security risk. The author presents a brief overview of relevant security standards, emphasizes cloud computing risks and vulnerabilities, and recommends the steps for transition of power utilities' information infrastructure from classical to the cloud computing environment.

Chapter 12 reviews the Energy Internet (also known as Internet of Energy) concept with the respect to its architecture, emerging technologies and security issues. The author pays special attention to the integration of the advanced information and communication technologies, such as cloud and fog computing, with the electric power sector, as well as the security and quality of service issues that arise from such integration.

Chapter 13 compiles the main threats, vulnerabilities and attacks that may occur in the Internet of Energy environment and the critical infrastructure of the electrical grid. The authors present best practices that may contribute to maintain a safe, reliable and available electrical network that complies with the requirements for data availability, integrity and confidentially. The chapter also includes a review of countermeasures, standards and specific intrusion detection systems.

Chapter 14 addresses dynamic line rating (DLR) systems as an important part of smart grids in power utilities. DLR systems are analyzed with respect to application of cloud computing in industry, related cloud services and infrastructures, and communication system's performance. Public and private cloud services have been considered to explain security and privacy requirements of cloud-based DLR systems. A secure architecture based on hybrid cloud infrastructure has been proposed to support DLR applications.

Chapter 15 addresses cyber security issues in healthcare with respect to utilization of IoT in e-health. The Health 4.0 has been considered which represents the extension of the Industry 4.0 standard to the healthcare. Next, the authors focus on assistive technologies that are developed to help people with disabilities, and present the reconfigurable platform of assistive technology, built upon the computer integrated manufacturing (CIM) approach. The proposed platform establishes a solid foundation for deployment of various security mechanisms and for updating them over time.

In conclusion, the editors believe that this book will be valuable and inspiring for researchers, practitioners and managers who wish to keep up to date in the field and to better understand the essential issues concerning deployment of new information and communication technologies to critical infrastructure systems.

Mirjana D. Stojanović
University of Belgrade, Serbia

Slavica V. Boštjančič Rakas
University of Belgrade, Serbia
Belgrade, November 2019

REFERENCES

Aydos, M., Vural, Y., & Tekerek, A. (2019). Assessing risks and threats with layered approach to Internet of Things security. *Measurement and Control, 52*(5-6), 338–353. doi:10.1177/0020294019837991

Devare, M. H. (2019). Convergence of manufacturing cloud and Industrial IoT. In G. Kecskemeti (Ed.), *Applying integration techniques and methods in distributed systems and technologies* (pp. 49–78). Hershey, PA: IGI Global. doi:10.4018/978-1-5225-8295-3.ch003

Filkins, B., & Wylie, D. (2019). *State of OT/ICS cybersecurity survey*. SANS Institute & OWL Cyber Defense. Retrieved November 16, 2019, from https://owlcyberdefense.com/resource/sans-institute-2019-state-of-ot-ics-cybersecurity-survey/

Gregory-Brown, B. (2017). *Securing industrial control systems—2017*. SANS Institute. Retrieved November 16, 2019, from https://www.sans.org/reading-room/whitepapers/analyst/securing-industrial-control-systems-2017-37860

Hayden, E., Assante, M., & Conway, T. (2014). An abbreviated history of automation & industrial controls systems and cybersecurity. SANS Institute. Retrieved October 31, 2019, from https://ics.sans.org/media/An-Abbreviated-History-of-Automation-and-ICS-Cybersecurity.pdf

Knapp, E. D., & Langill, J. T. (2015). *Industrial network security: Securing critical infrastructure networks for smart grid, SCADA, and other industrial control systems* (2nd ed.). Waltham, MA: Syngress.

Lu, Y. (2017). Industry 4.0: A survey on technologies, applications and open research issues. *Journal of Industrial Information Integration, 6*, 1–10. doi:10.1016/j.jii.2017.04.005

Miraz, M. H., Ali, M., Excell, P. S., & Picking, R. (2018). Internet of Nano-Things, Things and Everything: Future growth trends. *Future Internet, 10*(8), Article 68.

Nazir, S., Patel, S., & Patel, D. (2017). Assessing and augmenting SCADA cyber security: A survey of techniques. *Computers & Security, 70*, 436–454. doi:10.1016/j.cose.2017.06.010

Sanders, J. (2019, August 1). Guide to industry cloud: What businesses need to know. *ZDNet*. Retrieved November 16, 2019, from https://www.zdnet.com/article/guide-to-industry-cloud-what-businesses-need-to-know/

Stouffer, K., Pillitteri, V., Lightman, S., Abrams, M., & Hahn, A. (2015). *Guide to industrial control systems (ICS) security (NIST Special Publication 800-82 Rev. 2)*. Gaithersburg, MD: U.S. National Institute of Standards and Technology. doi:10.6028/NIST.SP.800-82r2

Tariq, N., Asima, M., & Khan, F. A. (2019). Securing SCADA-based critical infrastructures: Challenges and open issues. *Procedia Computer Science, 155*, 612–617. doi:10.1016/j.procs.2019.08.086

Acknowledgment

The editors would like to express their gratitude to all the people involved in this project and, more specifically, to the authors, Editorial Advisory Board, reviewers, and the Publisher. Without their support, this book would not have become a reality. It is our hope that this collection of interesting and timely chapters will give inspiration and new ideas to researchers and practitioners in all areas of critical infrastructure protection.

First, the editors would like to thank the authors for their insightful contributions, their responsiveness to suggestions for changes, and the care they took in preparing their works.

Second, the editors wish to acknowledge the efforts of the Editorial Advisory Board and the reviewers, some of whom did double duty as authors and reviewers, for their role in crafting this book. The valuable contributions of the reviewers helped in the improvement of quality, coherence, and content presentation of chapters.

Finally, special thanks go to IGI Global for giving us the opportunity to publish this book.

Mirjana D. Stojanović
University of Belgrade, Serbia

Slavica V. Boštjančič Rakas
University of Belgrade, Serbia
Belgrade, November 2019

Section 1
General ICS Security Aspects: Architectures, Platforms, and Technologies

Chapter 1
Challenges in Securing Industrial Control Systems Using Future Internet Technologies

Mirjana D. Stojanović
https://orcid.org/0000-0003-1073-5804
Faculty of Transport and Traffic Engineering, University of Belgrade, Serbia

Slavica V. Boštjančič Rakas
https://orcid.org/0000-0002-0551-3070
Mihailo Pupin Institute, University of Belgrade, Serbia

ABSTRACT

This chapter explores challenges in securing industrial control systems (ICS) and Supervisory Control And Data Acquisition (SCADA) systems using Future Internet technologies. These technologies include cloud computing, fog computing, Industrial internet of things (IIoT), etc. The need to design specific security solutions for ICS/SCADA networks is explained. A brief overview of cyber vulnerabilities and threats in industrial control networks, cloud, and IoT environments is presented. The security of cloud-based SCADA systems is considered, including benefits and risks of SCADA migration to the cloud, challenges in securing such systems, and migration toward fog computing. Challenges in securing IIoT are addressed, including security risks and operational issues, key principles for securing IIoT, the functional security architecture, and the role of fog computing. Authors point out current standardization activities and trends in the area, and emphasize conclusions and future research directions.

DOI: 10.4018/978-1-7998-2910-2.ch001

INTRODUCTION

Over the past thirty years information and communication technologies (ICT) have been introduced in the Industrial Control Systems (ICSs) and particularly Supervisory Control and Data Acquisition (SCADA) networks. This implied adoption of open communication standards like Ethernet, Transmission Control Protocol/Internet Protocol (TCP/IP) suite and a variety of wireless standards. Consequently, the problem of increased susceptibility to different forms of cyber security threats appeared, which was verified by a number of successful attacks on worldwide ICS/SCADA systems (Stouffer, Pillitteri, Lightman, Abrams, & Hahn, 2015; Ogie, 2017; Schwab & Poujol, 2018). The need for specific security solutions, tailored to the requirements of industrial control networks, has been recognized as a critical issue from the very beginning.

Nowadays, we are facing with proliferation of the Future Internet technologies, including cloud computing, fog computing, Internet of Things (IoT), mobile computing, big data processing and analytics. The IoT concept is rapidly evolving in different directions. Thus, the Industrial Internet of Things (IIoT) encompasses interconnected sensors, actuators, and other devices networked together with computers' industrial applications, and it represents an essential building block of the Industry 4.0 model (H. Xu, Yu, Griffith, & Golmie, 2018). Energy Internet, also known as the Internet of Energy (IoE) represents a wide area network (WAN), which integrates different types of energy resources, storage and loads, and enables peer-to-peer energy delivery on a large scale (Cao et al., 2018; Bostjancic Rakas, 2020). Heterogeneous IoT (HetIoT) extends the IoT concept to support a variety of heterogeneous wireless technologies and many different applications in daily life and industry (Qiu, Chen, Li, Atiquzzaman, & Zhao, 2018).

Although these technologies bring substantial benefits for the industry regarding information and economic efficiency, cyber security remains a crucial risk factor, which is even more distinct than when using traditional Internet technologies.

Apart from industry efforts (Howard, 2015; Nugent, 2017; Byers, 2018; Aleksandrova, 2019), only a few academic research papers systematically surveyed security issues in ICS/SCADA systems using Future Internet environments (Sadeghi, Wachsmann, & Waidner, 2015; Sajid, Abbas, & Saleem, 2016; Stojanovic, Bostjancic Rakas, & Markovic-Petrovic, 2019).

There are many open issues regarding cyber security of industrial control systems in the Future Internet environments, from the system's level (network security architectures, risk management, security policy implementation), through specific solutions (intrusion detection and prevention systems, encryption, authentication mechanisms), development of dedicated test environments, to definition of security policies that are applied during operational lifecycle. The main objective of this chapter is to emphasize challenges in securing ICS/SCADA systems in such new environments, particularly cloud computing, fog computing and/or IIoT.

The rest of the chapter is structured as follows. The background section explains the reasons for designing specific security solutions for ICS/SCADA networks and presents a brief overview of cyber vulnerabilities and threats in industrial control networks, cloud and IoT environments. In the following section, security of cloud-based SCADA systems is considered, including benefits and risks of SCADA migration to the cloud environment, challenges in securing such systems and migration toward fog computing environment. Further, challenges in securing IIoT are analyzed, including a brief comparison of IoT and IIoT requirements, security risks and operational issues, key principles for securing IIoT, the functional IIoT security architecture and the role of fog computing. The next section addresses standardization efforts in the area. The chapter ends with emphasizing the future research directions and concluding remarks.

BACKGROUND

Although the incorporation of the Internet technologies in industrial networking has reduced the boundary between ICS/SCADA and enterprise networks, they still have basically different requirements, which naturally cause differences in network design as well as security objectives and solutions (Galloway & Hancke, 2013; Markovic-Petrovic, Stojanovic, & Bostjancic Rakas, 2019). Namely, for general-purpose infrastructures, primary focus is the balanced protection of the confidentiality, integrity and availability of data (the so-called CIA triad), which gives the highest priority to data confidentiality. The infrastructure of industrial control systems assumes the same triad, but with the reversed order of priorities (AIC), which means that the most important item is availability. This difference is essential in terms of defining security policies and selecting security mechanisms, with the key objective to preserve availability of all systems that constitute critical infrastructure 24 hours, 7 days a week (24/7 service). The ultimate goal is to achieve required performance of a real-time system, operating on the 24/7 basis under conditions in which regular behavior coexists with system failures, environmental conditions, human errors, and cyber attacks.

ICS/SCADA networks are characterized by regular traffic patterns and a limited set of telecommunication protocols (Galloway & Hancke, 2013; Mantere, Sailio, & Noponen, 2013). The most important features that affect design of specific security solutions are discussed below.

Traffic Properties: ICS/SCADA network traffic is characterized by throughput stability, periodic patterns, clear statistics of packet size, predictable flow direction, and expected connection lifetime. Significant increase of throughput may point to some forms of cyber attacks, failures, or operating errors. Periodic traffic prevails in control networks due to transmission of data samples in regular intervals. Aperiodic events may occur due to change of state or alarm conditions, but may also indicate some forms of attacks. Most of the systems at the fieldbus level send packets without buffering due to severe delay requirements. A clear packet size statistics is created, and the average packet size represents a good indicator of regular behavior or anomaly. Flow direction indicates which system initiates the connection. After connection establishment, data amount sent from one system to another is predictable with large probability.

Delay Requirements: Packet transfer delay and packet inter-arrival times from all network nodes are meaningful data for anomaly detection in ICS/SCADA networks. This is a consequence of real-time operating requirements. Response time should typically be less than the sample time of collected data. The most stringent requirements are at the fieldbus and controller network levels. Response time requirements are usually in the range of 250 microseconds to 1 millisecond whereas less stringent processes require response times in the range of 1 to 10 milliseconds. Application layer poses lower delay requirements, typically up to 1 second.

Updates and Order of Events: Updates should be performed on a regular basis, because the data is only valid in its assigned time period. The order of updating is important for sensor data concerning monitoring of the same process or correlated processes. The order of data arrival to the control center plays an important role in presentation of process dynamics and influences decision making.

Protocols: Each industrial control network implements a precisely defined set of protocols. The appearance of new protocols indicates serious changes in the network. Protocols are typically configured statically, in a way that guarantees the best network performance. Among a range of standard and vendor-specific communication protocols the most widespread are Modbus, Distributed Network Protocol (DNP3), International Electrotechnical Commission (IEC) 60870-5 series, IEC 60870-6 series and IEC 61850 series. The majority of protocols are created or extended to operate over TCP/IP networks. In addition, most of the current fieldbus protocols are Ethernet-based. A comprehensive survey and taxonomy of ICS/SCADA protocols can be found in the literature (Gao et al., 2014; Galloway & Hancke, 2013).

Cyber Vulnerabilities and Threats in Industrial Control Networks

Cyber vulnerabilities in industrial control networks can be exploited from outside sources, such as terrorists, hackers, competitors, or industrial espionage, or from inside attacks, frequently caused by dissatisfied employees, third-party vendors, or site engineers (Yang et al., 2014). Human errors, negligence equipment failures and natural disasters may also affect ICS/SCADA vulnerabilities.

One of the most common sources of vulnerabilities refers to *resource limitations*. Physical devices are simple and designed to efficiently perform limited operations. For that reason, they often do not have memory and processing resources to carry out security functions. Real-time control systems typically suffer from poor authorization and authentication mechanisms, and they neither record login attempts nor make distinction between human users (Goldenberg & Wool, 2013).

Legacy systems represent another source of vulnerabilities. For example, former SCADA systems were isolated from public networks; for that reason only physical security was a concern rather than cyber security.

Attacks on ICS/SCADA systems can be classified in several ways. Moris and W Gao (2013) identify four classes of ICS attacks, namely reconnaissance, response and measurement injection, command injection and denial of service (DoS). *Reconnaissance attacks* aim to discover information about a network and to identify the equipment characteristics. *Response and measurement injection* refer to attacks where packets which contain sensor reading values are being captured, modified and forwarded. Similarly, *command injection attacks* insert false control and configuration commands into a control system. *Denial of Service* (DoS) attacks attempt to stop the proper functioning of some portion of the ICS or to disable the entire system. These attacks may target the cyber system or the physical system.

Maglaras et al. (2019) also distinguish four categories of ICS cyber attacks: key-based attacks, data-based attacks, impersonation-based attacks and physical-based attacks. *Key-based attacks* denote grabbing secret keys that are used by consumers and suppliers for registration and authentication. *Data-based attacks* refer to unauthorized change of data, and include a number of attacks such as modification attack, data integrity attack, repudiation attack, etc. *Impersonation-based attacks* try to impersonate a trusted individual or company in an attempt to gain access to sensitive data. Examples of such attacks are man-in-the-middle (MITM) attack, eavesdropping attack, replay attack and redirection attack. *Physical-based attacks* manipulate the physical properties of devices to cause sensors and embedded devices to malfunction. Examples of such attacks are differential attack, malware attack, collusion attack, and inference attack.

Ghosh and Sampalli (2019) emphasize the fact that attacks can occur at all layers of SCADA network, from the supervisory level to the field instrumentation level. They classify cyber attacks on SCADA systems into *attacks on hardware*, *attacks on software*, and *attacks on network connections*, and present a comprehensive review of the most widespread attacks on SCADA networks.

Cyber Vulnerabilities and Threats in Cloud Environment

Besides cyber security threats that are present in the traditional computing platforms and networks, cloud computing copes with a number of additional vulnerabilities (Hari Krishna, Kiran, Murali, & Pradeep Kumar Reddy, 2016). They include:

- Attacks by other customers.
- Shared technology issues.
- Malfunctions of provider's or customer's security systems.
- Flawed integration of provider's and customer's security systems.
- Insecure application programming interfaces.
- Data loss or leakage.
- Insider attacks.
- Account or service hijacking.
- Legal and regulatory issues.

Besides, vulnerabilities depend on the type of cloud service. For example, Infrastructure as a Service (IaaS) is susceptible to most of the threats that are well known from the traditional information and communication systems (Chavan, Patil, Kulkarni, Sutar, & Belsare, 2013). Besides, customers are responsible for securing their applications, because all of them are running on the virtual machines, which act like "black boxes" for the provider. Platform as a Service (PaaS) is particularly susceptible to shared technology issues, because of different security settings for various kinds of resources and potential data leakage (Sandikkaya & Harmanci, 2012). On the other side, Software as a Service (SaaS) typically requires only a web browser and the Internet connection. Similarly to web service, it is predominantly susceptible to data security and confidentiality (Soufiane & Halima, 2017). The other common issues refer to data backup, data access, storage locations, availability, authentication, etc.

Cyber Vulnerabilities and Threats in IoT Environment

The general architecture of IoT can be structured into three layers, namely the perception layer, network layer and application layer. Each of these layers is susceptible to different forms of cyber attacks (Kamble & Bhutad, 2018).

Perception layer is responsible for perceiving the physical properties of things and relies on several sensing technologies such as wireless sensor networks (WSNs), radio frequency identification (RFID), near field communication (NFC), etc. This layer is susceptible to cyber threats such as unauthorized access to tags, node capture attacks, tag cloning and false data injection attacks.

Network layer processes the data received from the perception layer and forwards processed data to the application layer through various wireless and wired network technologies. The most common cyber security threats encompass spoofing attack, sinkhole attack, sleep deprivation attack, different forms of DoS attacks and insecure protocols.

Application layer uses the data obtained from the underlying layer and provides the required tools for developers to implement a variety of IoT applications. It mainly relies on cloud computing and big data analytics; hence, it is susceptible to all threats that are typical for the cloud computing environment.

SECURITY OF CLOUD-BASED SCADA SYSTEMS

There are two main ways to support SCADA applications in cloud computing environment, as indicated in Figure 1 (Stojanovic et al., 2019).

The first way assumes that SCADA application is executed on company's premises. Control functions of SCADA application are isolated in the controller network, while SCADA application is connected to public cloud services that allow visualization of processes, reports and remote access at corresponding work stations (Human Machine Interface, HMI).

The second way, which is suitable for distributed applications, assumes that SCADA application is executed in the cloud, and is remotely connected (using WAN links) to the control center. Such applications are typically implemented on private and hybrid cloud infrastructures.

Re-hosting, refactoring and revising are the three migration scenarios of SCADA system to the cloud, with respect to service selection (Church et al., 2017). Re-hosting is the fastest and the simplest scenario,

Figure 1. Support of SCADA applications in cloud computing environment

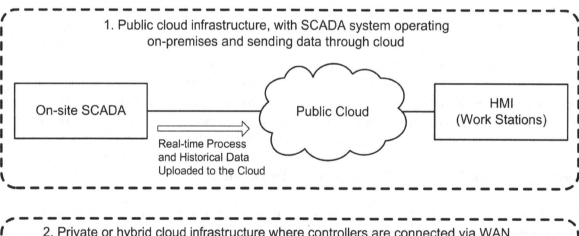

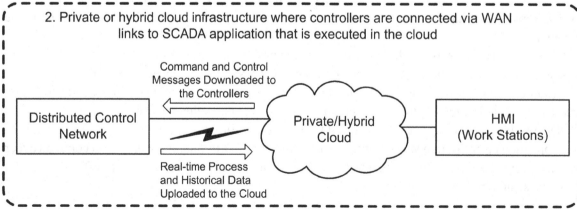

which assumes installing the existing SCADA applications in the cloud, based on IaaS. Refactoring and revising assume re-engineering to take benefit of cloud computing capabilities, primarily scalability and reliability. Refactoring refers to simple modification of particular features. For example, implementation of resource control allows adding resources when the application is intensively used and releasing resources when they are not needed. Revising assumes larger modifications at the application core. For example, PaaS database can be used for modification of application to provide multiple contracts for the offered SaaS. This requires replacement of the existing SCADA applications with cloud-based SaaS solutions.

Benefits and Risks

When discussing benefits and risks of cloud-based SCADA systems, a distinction should be made between public and private cloud infrastructures.

With public cloud, benefits mainly refer to improving economic efficiency. On-demand access and lease of resources allows for savings in purchasing, installing and maintaining ICT equipment, as well as technical staff, needed for ICT resource maintaining. Other benefits include:

- Enhanced scalability, because users can simply purchase additional resources on a virtual cloud server, with no need of installing and maintaining the additional hardware.
- Ubiquitous access to information located on a cloud server, which makes the collaboration on projects more efficient.
- Simplified upgrade of the existing applications and deployment of new ones through re-hosting, refactoring and revising.

The use of public cloud services increases risks regarding quality of service (QoS) and cyber security. The user cannot control the network performance; even servers' locations are unknown to their users. Hence, there is a risk that QoS requirements will not be met. Probably the most challenging issue is increased and/or unpredictable delay, since it can obstruct the real-time SCADA operation and cause serious consequences to the industrial process. Besides, the problems of availability and reliability exist in every system in the public cloud.

SCADA systems using public cloud services suffer from the same cyber security risks as the other systems integrated into cloud. Still, there are a number of threats in the public cloud environment that might make SCADA systems more vulnerable:

- Due to sharing an infrastructure with unknown outside parties, such systems are more exposed to cyber threats such as command/response injection, DoS and distributed DoS (DDoS) attacks, as well as MITM attacks.
- Insecure network connections between SCADA systems and the cloud increase the risk of jeopardizing the whole industrial process by outside attackers.
- Some of widespread SCADA-specific application layer protocols lack protection, particularly in terms of authentication and encryption mechanisms.
- The use of commercial off-the-shelf solutions potentially increases the cyber security risk.

The situation is different with private cloud infrastructure, which may bring technical benefits in addition to cost reduction and improving the overall economic efficiency. Experimental results from a study on private cloud-based electric power SCADA system indicated technical feasibility of the professional private cloud solution (Chen, Chen, & Gan, 2015). Such a system meets the requirements of power grid operations, while some QoS parameters such as network load rate are even better than those of the traditional, non-cloud solution. Similarly, it is easier to secure private cloud, by applying proper security architecture, which is completely managed by the cloud owner.

Challenges in Securing Cloud-Based SCADA Systems

According to Stojanovic et al. (2019), security solutions concerning public cloud infrastructure should address the challenges related to:

- Information input/output.
- Shared storage and computational resources.
- Shared physical infrastructure.

Information Input/Output: The main requirement is to avoid exposing the critical control infrastructure to the Internet. When using public cloud services, push technology should be exploited to move data to the cloud rather than pull technology. Push technology (also known as server push) is a method of Internet-based communication where the sender or central server initiates transaction request. In contrast, pull/get technology assumes that the transaction request is initiated by the receiver or client. With push technology, there are no open network ports on the control infrastructure, and SCADA applications stay isolated in the controller network.

Shared Storage and Computational Resources: SCADA owner cooperating with a cloud service provider (CSP) should be informed how the computational resources are managed for different cloud-based applications, including QoS guarantees, guarantees for network access, fault-tolerance strategy, etc.

Shared Physical Infrastructure: There is a need to secure cloud infrastructure locations, as well as communication links that connect the cloud infrastructure to the rest of the communications infrastructure. Besides, SCADA owner should be able to inspect and audit the locations from which SCADA application will be served.

When selecting the CSP and assessing maturity of the offered cloud service, a number of criteria should be taken into account, including service identification and specification, technical characteristics, business conditions, etc. It should be noted that the leading cloud service providers are working toward the "Industry cloud", i.e., cloud solutions that will meet the needs of industrial systems in terms of QoS and security requirements.

The most efficient way to protect SCADA system connected to the public cloud is to establish precise service level agreement (SLA) that fulfills the required criteria. Different approaches are possible to establish end-to-end SLA-based communication services (Bostjancic Rakas & Stojanovic, 2019). A possible SLA structure, derived from generic templates presented in works of Stojanovic et al. (2010) and Stojanovic et al. (2013), is illustrated in Figure 2. The SLA encompasses the following parts: service identification, service specification, business part, technical part and reporting.

Service identification refers to the service package offered by the CSP.

Service specification encompasses detailed service description, QoS level and security level.

Business part includes contact information, the level of user's control regarding changes of the CSP infrastructure, service renegotiation capabilities, accounting information (pricing, charging and bill-

Figure 2. A possible structure of the SLA between SCADA owner and CSP

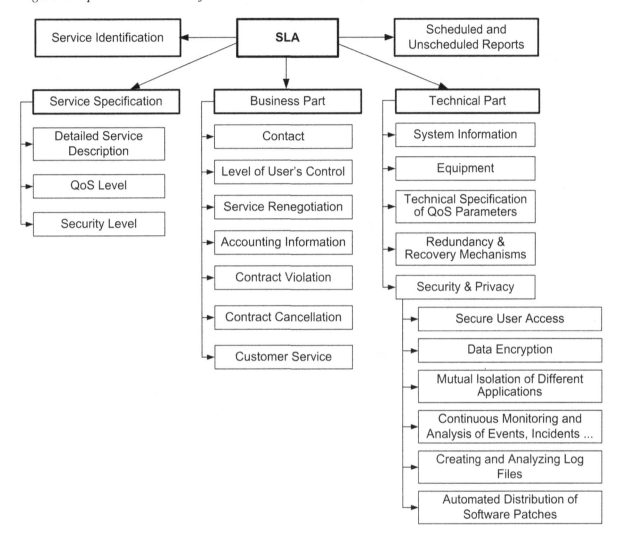

ing), consequences for both the user and the CSP in the case of contract violation, contract cancellation conditions, and customer service. Taking into account real-time operation of SCADA utility, consistent and reliable customer service should assure readiness to take immediate corrective actions of all vulnerabilities identified.

Technical part includes all relevant technical characteristics of the service such as system information, equipment specification, QoS parameters, redundancy and recovery mechanisms, as well as security and privacy. Security and privacy may refer to: secure user access; data encryption; mutual isolation of information originating from different applications; continuous real-time monitoring and analysis of events, incidents, suspicious activities and anomalies; capabilities to create and analyze log files; means to detect intrusions in real-time; ability to generate responses to detected attacks; and automated distribution of software patches.

Reporting part assumes provisioning scheduled and unscheduled reports that satisfy business needs.

Securing the private cloud infrastructure is much simpler, since all solutions are responsibility of the network owner. Defense-in-depth strategy is recommended, i.e., "Layering security mechanisms such that the impact of a failure in any one mechanism is minimized" (Stouffer et al., 2015, p. 3). This strategy includes appropriate security policies, employing demilitarized zone (DMZ) network architecture to prevent direct traffic between the corporate and SCADA networks, as well as security mechanisms such as smart access control, firewalls, intrusion detection and prevention systems, antivirus software, deploying security patches on a regular basis, etc.

Migration to Fog Computing Environment

Principally, fog computing extends cloud computing and services to the edge of network. Therefore, end users, fog and cloud together constitute a three layer system architecture (Mouradian et al., 2018).

Stojanovic et al. (2019) propose a fog-based architecture that includes ICS/SCADA components. Hence, the end users layer includes field devices, smart energy meters, line sensors, and may also include IIoT devices. This layer is connected with the fog layer by means of wired or wireless local area networks (LANs). The fog layer consists of one or more fog domains, each comprised of fog nodes, i.e., industrial controllers, switches, routers, embedded servers, etc. Fog nodes provide integration with the cloud layer, routing and switching, data storage and sharing, real-time analytics, outage management, controller functions, wireless access, etc. The fog layer and the cloud layer communicate via WAN connections.

Tom and Sankaranarayanan (2017) propose an IoT-based SCADA integrated with fog for power distribution automation system. Fog computing is used to perform real-time streaming analysis, in order to control consumer utilization, manage outages, control power quality and to maintain pole transformers. At the same time, low bandwidth utilization and delay are preserved when taking immediate control actions.

In terms of ICS/SCADA requirements, fog computing introduces the following benefits in comparison to cloud computing (Byers, 2018; Stojanovic et al., 2019):

- Distributed network architecture.
- LAN-based communication with ICS/SCADA components.
- Large number of server nodes.
- Low delay.
- Low bandwidth cost.
- Mobility and location awareness.
- High security.

With fog computing, security operates locally, using the same corporate ICT policy, controls, and procedures as in traditional ICS/SCADA system. Such a concept inherently improves cyber security in comparison to cloud computing environment. Yet, fog computing includes the virtualization and can still be affected by the similar threats like cloud. This implies that security solutions for fog-based and cloud-based SCADA systems are basically similar. The emphasis is on the techniques such as authentication, access control in fog nodes, intrusion detection and protecting privacy (Khan, Parkinson, & Qin, 2017).

CHALLENGES IN SECURING INDUSTRIAL IoT SYSTEMS

The starting point for securing IIoT is a comparison with the IoT technology, because IoT and IIoT are two parallel technologies with the same standard protocols, interfaces and intelligence. However, they have different operational processes, principles, users, and goals. The main novelties that IIoT introduces in comparison to IoT are as follows:

- IIoT aims to achieve maximum efficiency and seamless workflow in any industrial process, while IoT focuses on optimizing consumption, personal comfort, and control of expenses.
- IIoT is mainly focused on monitoring production and business environmental parameters, while IoT is used to automate everyday household processes.
- IIoT architecture is designed to meet requirements of hard real-time industrial applications, with very high reliability and availability. Besides, IIoT equipment must be able to cope with extreme environmental conditions such as high variations of temperature, volume pressure, harmonic motions, at distant locations.
- Multidimensional interoperability assumes open standards which allow creating a cooperative environment with various protocols, data sets, enterprise resource planning (ERP) systems, and integration with the existing legacy operational technologies.
- High scalability assumes a widespread IIoT network of controllers, robots, and other equipment, thousands of new sensors and putting in place non-IoT devices.

Cyber Security Threats and Risks

IIoT needs robust security and privacy mechanisms, such as encrypted and agile system architectures, specialized chipsets, authentication and real-time intrusion detection. The following threats are particularly relevant in view of IIoT: insecure web, mobile and cloud interfaces, privacy concerns, poor physical security, insecure software/firmware, insufficient authentication and authorization, insecure network connections, lack of encryption at the transport layer, etc.

Sajid et al. (2016) identify specific threats to the SCADA systems in IoT-cloud environments as follows: advanced persistent threats, lack of data integrity, MITM attacks such as spoofing and sniffing, replay attacks and various forms of DoS attacks. Cyber attacks on the IIoT system may cause not only performance deterioration and uncertainty, but also safety issues for persons, the environment, and the equipment, as well. In addition, the data collected during industrial manufacturing and production is often highly confidential, which makes IIoT systems attractive targets for attackers.

Similarly to IoT, the concept of IIoT assumes a layered hierarchy together with related security risks at each layer:

- Local area networks collect and locally process data from connected objects at the lowest layer. The main security risks refer to lack of authentication and security in sensors equipment.
- Data is transmitted to the cloud via gateways. The main security risks include lack of security in protocols and gateways.
- Data is stored and processed in the cloud. Appropriate platforms are used as well as specific algorithms such as big data analytics. The main risk factor is lack of data security.

- Interfacing between platforms and end users for monitoring may cause security risks due to lack of secure communication protocols.

The consequences of successful attack reflect in a number of operational issues such as: equipment damage, unforeseen operational concerns, endangered personal safety and regulatory issues. Security risks and operational issues in IIoT are summarized in Figure 3.

Key Principles of IIoT Security

Key principles for securing IIoT rely on currently available good practices and the existing security standards. Following is a brief description of those principles.

Securing All IIoT System's Parts before Integration: Since IIoT applications are usually built with the existing ICS devices, they inherit security flaws or even the lack of security of such devices. Many of interconnected devices still use customized protocols or gateways (developed without sufficient security care) instead of universal protocols such as Open Platform Communications Unified Architecture (OPC UA). The OPC UA security architecture includes concepts such as trusted information (AIC triad) and access control (Foundation, O.P.C., 2018).

Network Segregation: This method has been a best practice in networking for a long time. It assumes dividing large networks into several separate logical networks, as well as developing and enforcing policies for controlling the communications between specific hosts and servers. Security tools that surround each network efficiently isolate and monitor network activities, thus preventing policy violations. An example of IIoT network segregation is implementation model based on layered databuses (Industrial Internet Consortium [IIC], 2019), as illustrated in Figure 4. Databus is a logically connected space, which implements a common set of templates (data models, protocols, security) for communication between endpoints. At the lowest layer, smart machines use databus for local control, automation and real-time analytics. Second layer encompasses systems, which use another databus for supervisory control and

Figure 3. Security risks and operational issues in IIoT

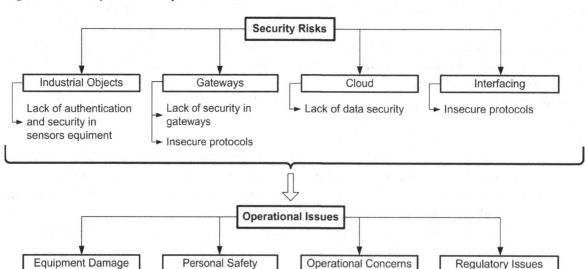

monitoring. Merging such systems into a "system of systems", at the third layer, enables complex and scalable applications for control, monitoring and analysis. The highest layer of this model, industrial Internet, is based on cloud computing.

Continuous Monitoring and Analysis: This process assumes permanent monitoring and analysis of the network activities, in order to detect and identify anomalies and suspicious activities (Sajid et al., 2016). Analysis of log records plays an important role in troubleshooting, anomaly detection, network forensics, etc. Memory dump analysis enables detection of known and unknown malicious activities that

Figure 4. An example of IIoT network segregation by layered databuses (adapted from IIC, 2019)

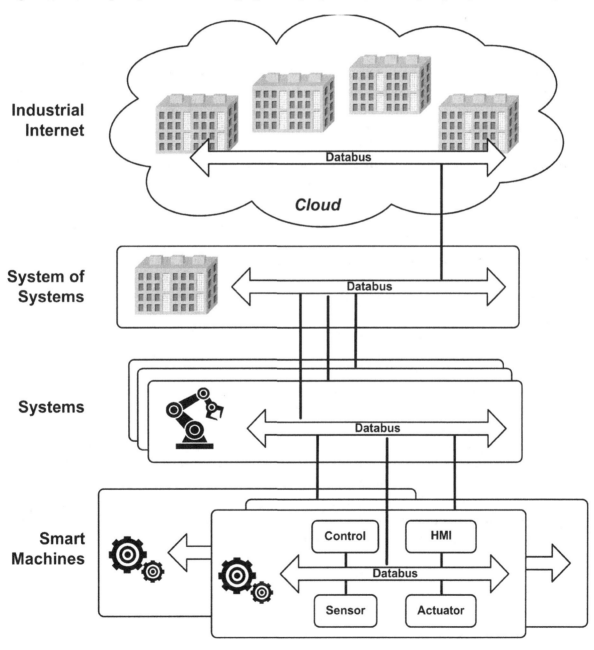

are present within the memory of an operating system. Network traffic analysis is performed in order to detect network traffic anomalies, including malicious activities. It may encompass behavioral analysis (e.g., protocol procedures, traffic intensity, etc.) and/or traffic pattern analysis, which can be performed on per-packet basis or per-flow basis.

Attribution of Cyber Attacks: Disclosure of the attacker's identity and/or location directly concerns regulatory issues, particularly when attacks are launched from another country, because it poses questions concerning the authority to investigate and prosecute the cyber crime (Cook, Nicholson, Janicke, Maglaras, & Smith, 2016; Maglaras et al., 2019).

Application of Tools for Detecting Malicious Activities and Proxy Solutions: Detecting tools encompass firewalls, intrusion detection and prevention systems, antivirus software, etc. Proxy solutions, such as packet filtering and access control, are used to build a protection layer around vulnerable or legacy components.

System's Maintenance: The quality of system design predominantly influences its security level. Vulnerability tests are useful in detecting, e.g., unknown errors in cloud systems. They should be performed in regular intervals, because new threats are being revealed through analysis over time. Besides, distribution of software updates and patches on a regular basis is mandatory, particularly for the third-party software, which is typically used by IoT-cloud SCADA systems.

Functional IIoT Security Architecture

The functional architecture of IIoT security is illustrated in Figure 5 (IIC, 2016). It encompasses the following building blocks:

- **Endpoint Protection:** This block implements security on edge and cloud devices. Its main functions encompass physical and cyber security, as well as an authoritative identity.
- **Communications and Connectivity Protection:** This block uses the endpoint authoritative identity to implement authentication and authorization mechanisms, by means of strong cryptographic techniques and the information flow control techniques.
- **Security Monitoring and Analysis:** This block is responsible for keeping the system secure by permanent monitoring and analyzing its state.
- **Security Configuration and Management:** New vulnerabilities and threats call for updates of policies, firmware and software; therefore, the security features of an IIoT system must be configurable and manageable.
- **Data Protection:** The common data protection function supports previously described building blocks, by protecting all types of data, i.e., inactive data at the endpoints (data-at-rest), data that is processed and transmitted at communication layer (data-in-motion), data collected in monitoring and analysis, as well as the system configuration and management data.
- **Security Model and Policy:** Security model coordinates the work of all functional elements and determines the way of implementation of security and the associated policies.

Figure 6 presents a detailed functional structure of endpoint protection block, as well as communications and connectivity protection block.

Figure 5. The functional IIoT security architecture: building blocks (adapted from IIC, 2016)

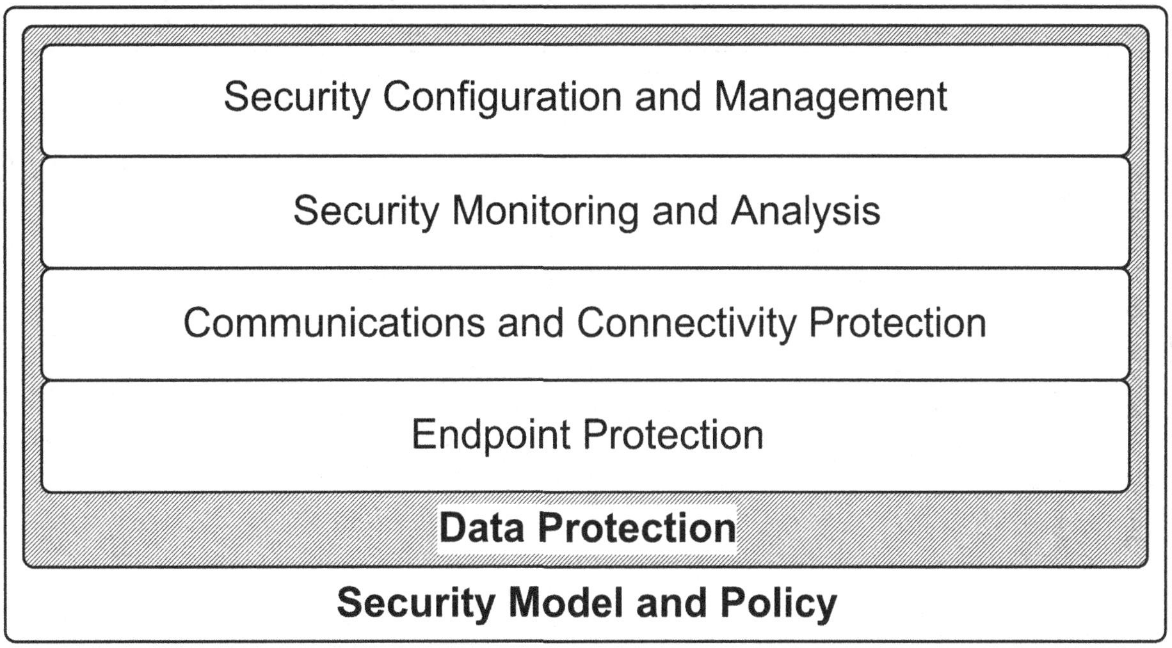

```
┌────────────────────────────────────────────────────────────┐
│  ┌──────────────────────────────────────────────────────┐  │
│  │        Security Configuration and Management          │  │
│  └──────────────────────────────────────────────────────┘  │
│  ┌──────────────────────────────────────────────────────┐  │
│  │          Security Monitoring and Analysis             │  │
│  └──────────────────────────────────────────────────────┘  │
│  ┌──────────────────────────────────────────────────────┐  │
│  │      Communications and Connectivity Protection       │  │
│  └──────────────────────────────────────────────────────┘  │
│  ┌──────────────────────────────────────────────────────┐  │
│  │              Endpoint Protection                      │  │
│  └──────────────────────────────────────────────────────┘  │
│                  **Data Protection**                        │
└────────────────────────────────────────────────────────────┘
                  **Security Model and Policy**
```

Apart from physical security, the endpoint protection includes definition of the root of trust, definition of the unified endpoint identity, integrity protection, access control, monitoring and analysis, as well as endpoint configuration and management.

Communications and connectivity protection includes physical security of connections, protection of communicating endpoints, cryptographic protection, information flow protection, network monitoring and analysis (intrusion detection, network access control, protocol analysis, log analysis), as well as network configuration and management (network segregation, cryptographic protection of communication parameters, configuration of gateways and firewalls).

The Role of Fog Computing in Securing IIoT

Middleware support is needed between the industrial environment and cloud services, because most of industrial processes have stringent delay and security requirements. Fog can be observed as a prospective middleware for different industrial scenarios such as mining, smart grid and power industry, transportation, waste management, food industry, agriculture, etc. (Aazam, Zeadally, & Harras, 2018).

The benefits of fog computing for IIoT encompass delay reduction, agile response (in terms of data analysis and decision making), cost effectiveness and the increased security (Butun, Sari, & Österberg, 2019). Securing fog nodes, which act as gateways between IIoT network and the cloud, should encompass access control, authentication, AIC triad and protection of privacy.

Zhou et al. (2019) have shown that fog computing can provide efficient DDoS mitigation in the IIoT network. They propose a distributed attack mitigation scheme that assumes traffic analysis at multiple dispersed locations and assigns the appropriate virtualized network computation functions. The scheme has a three-level architecture (field, fog and cloud levels), where each level performs the functions cor-

Figure 6. Functional structure of endpoint protection and communications & connectivity protection

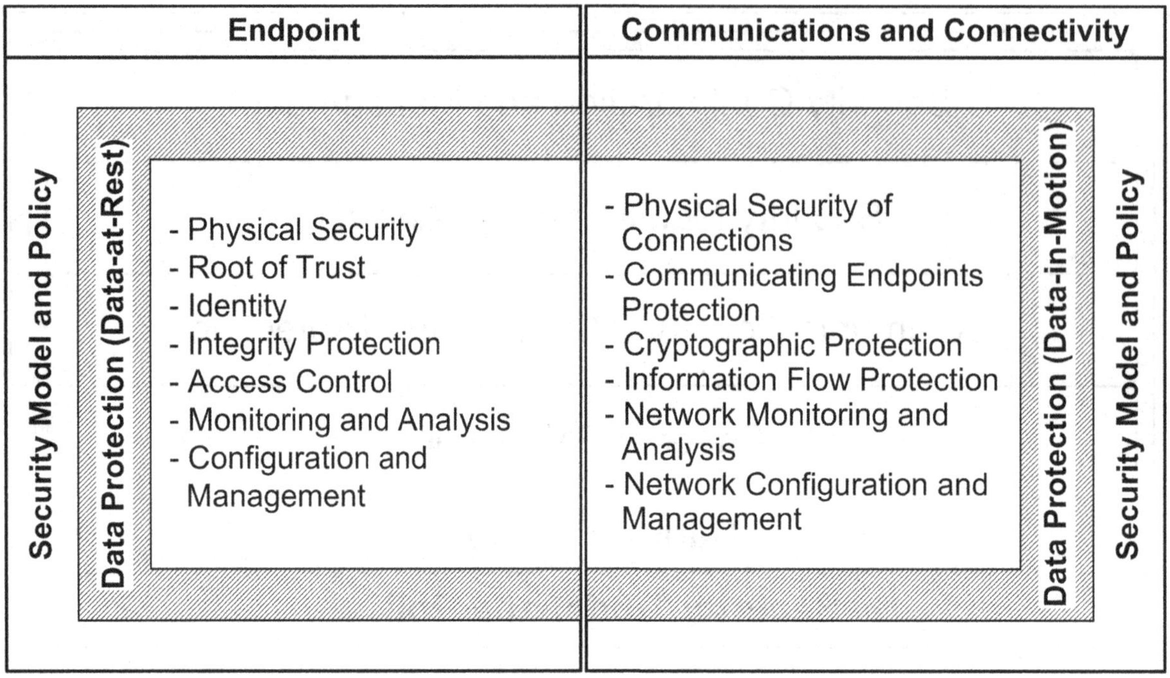

Endpoint	Communications and Connectivity
Security Model and Policy / **Data Protection (Data-at-Rest)** - Physical Security - Root of Trust - Identity - Integrity Protection - Access Control - Monitoring and Analysis - Configuration and Management	- Physical Security of Connections - Communicating Endpoints Protection - Cryptographic Protection - Information Flow Protection - Network Monitoring and Analysis - Network Configuration and Management **Data Protection (Data-in-Motion)** / **Security Model and Policy**

responding to its processing capabilities. Performance evaluation has demonstrated advantages of such a method in terms of detection accuracy and timeliness.

STANDARDIZATION EFFORTS

The importance of critical infrastructure protection resulted in intensive efforts of national and international standardization bodies to adopt standards, recommendations, directives and guidelines concerning security of industrial control systems. The objective of this section is to point to current standardization activities and trends regarding application of the Future Internet technologies in ICS/SCADA networks, rather than to provide a comprehensive review of standards. Surveys of current security standards and recommendations for ICS/SCADA systems can be found in the literature (Gao et al., 2014; Zhou, Xu, Wang, & Chen, 2017; Ghosh & Sampalli, 2019).

Relevant documents can be broadly classified into three groups:

1. General standards concerning cyber security of ICT systems.
2. Common standards and guidelines for ICS/SCADA protection.
3. Specific directives concerning ICS/SCADA in particular industrial sectors.

Table 1 summarizes the most representative standards and other documents with respect to the indicated classification.

General standards concerning cyber security of ICT systems must be taken into account when designing and developing each security system. There are many general standards and recommendations, which are being approved by leading international standardization bodies such as International Organization for Standardization (ISO), International Telecommunication Union - Telecommunication Standardization Sector (ITU-T), Internet Engineering Task Force (IETF), American National Standards Institute (ANSI), European Telecommunications Standards Institute (ETSI), etc.

The ISO/IEC 27000-series comprises information security standards, published jointly by the ISO and the IEC, which provide best practice recommendations on information security management. The ISO/IEC 27001 is an information security management system standard (the last revision was published

Table 1. Representative standards and other documents concerning ICS/SCADA cyber security

Type of Standard		Publisher & Document ID	Title	Year
General-purpose standard concerning cyber security		• ISO/IEC 27001	Information security management systems - Requirements	2013
		• ISO/IEC 27002	Code of practice for information security controls	2013
		• ISO/IEC 270017 • ITU-T X.1631	Code of practice for information security controls based on ISO/IEC 27002 for cloud services	2015
		• ITU-T X.1361	Security framework for the Internet of things based on the gateway model	2018
		• ITU-T X.1362	Simple encryption procedure for Internet of things (IoT) environments	2017
		• ETSI TS 103 645	Cyber security for consumer Internet of Things	2019
		• IETF RFC 8576 (Informational)	Internet of Things (IoT) security: State of the art and challenges	2019
Common standard for ICS/SCADA protection		• NIST SP 800-82 Rev. 2 (Stouffer et al., 2015)	Guide to industrial control systems (ICS) security	2015
		• NIST SP 500-299	NIST cloud computing security reference architecture (draft)	2013
		• ISA/IEC 62443 series	Security for industrial automation and control systems	Multi-part
		• IIC:PUB:G4:V1.0:PB: 20160926 (IIC, 2016)	Industrial Internet of Things volume G4: Security framework	2016
Specific standard concerning ICS/SCADA in:	Electric power industry	• IEC 62351 series	Security for industrial automation and control systems	Multi-part
		• IEEE 1402-2000	IEEE guide for electric power substation physical and electronic security	2000
		• IEEE P2023	Standard for digital transformation architecture and framework	Up-coming
	Oil and gas industry	• API 1164	Pipeline SCADA Security	2009
		• AGA-12 series	Cryptographic protection of SCADA communications	Multi-part
	Water and wastewater treatment	• ANSI/AWWA G430-14	Security practices for operation & management	2014

in October 2013), which specifies a systematic approach to managing sensitive company information so that it remains secure. Certification to ISO/IEC 27001 is possible but not mandatory; some organizations implement the standard in order to benefit from the best practice it contains. In addition, ISO/IEC 27002 is a popular, internationally-recognized standard of good practice for information security. It is relevant to all types of organization, i.e., any organization that uses information technologies. ISO/IEC 27017 standard complements the ISO/IEC 27002 by providing guidelines on the information security of cloud computing. This standard is also adopted by the ITU-T (recommendation X.1631).

The ITU-T approves recommendations in all areas of cyber security, including security architectures, models and frameworks; security management, security policy and policy mechanisms; security assessment and evaluation criteria; intrusion detection; security services; security mechanisms; layered network security; security protocol standards; next generation networks; service-specific security standards, etc. Security related work is covered by the ITU-T X-series and Y-series of recommendations. Thus, cloud computing security is addressed by the X-1600 series of recommendations. IoT security is covered by recommendations X.1361 and X.1362, which specify security framework for the IoT based on the gateway model and encryption procedure for IoT environments, respectively.

The IETF work on the Internet cyber security is organized into 22 active working groups, which cover all relevant areas of network and protocol security, as well as security management. The work on IoT security is still in the research phase. In April 2019, the IETF issued the Request for Comments (RFC) document, which presents an overview of important IoT security aspects (Garcia-Morchon, Kumar, & Sethi, 2019).

The ANSI partnered with the Internet Security Alliance (ISAlliance) and others to coordinate the work in the area of ICT cyber security.

The main areas of ETSI's work related to security cover mobile/wireless communications, emergency telecommunications, information technology infrastructure, smart cards, fixed communications, and security algorithms. In December 2012, the European Commission (EC) and the ETSI launched the Cloud Standardization Coordination (CSC) initiative, which includes cloud computing interoperability and security. In February 2019, ETSI released the first globally applicable standard for consumer IoT security (ETSI TS 103 645).

Among organizations that adopt or will adopt common standards and guidelines for ICS/SCADA protection, the most relevant are the U. S. National Institute of Standards and Technology (NIST), the International Society of Automation (ISA) and the IIC.

The NIST provides standards for the wide spectrum of technologies, from the smart electric power grid and electronic health records to atomic clocks, advanced nanomaterials, and computer chips. The NIST special publication (SP) 800-82 (Stouffer et al., 2015) provides guidelines on how to secure ICS/SCADA and other control systems, regarding their performance, reliability and safety requirements. The "NIST Cloud Computing Program" was launched in November 2010, and includes Cloud Computing Security Working Group, which works on defining the cloud computing security reference architecture (NIST SP 500-299). The work on IoT security is conducted within the "NIST Cybersecurity for IoT Program", which started in November 2016, and includes cybersecurity framework, cybersecurity framework profile for manufacturing, security systems engineering, cloud security, etc.

The ISA99 standards development committee approves standards for industrial automation and control systems security. This original and ongoing ISA99 work is adopted by the IEC in producing the IEC 62443 series of standards. The IIoT security challenges have led to the establishment of the ISA99 Working Group 9, which is focused on the IIoT cybersecurity. The objective of this working group is to explore the applicability of the well known IEC 62443 series of industrial standards to IIoT systems, including general categories of IIoT devices within industrial automation and control systems (Leander & Causevic, 2019).

The IIC has been founded in 2014 as a global non-profit partnership of industry, government and academia. It aims to help the organizations to utilize technologies that are necessary to speed up the deployment of the industrial Internet by identifying, assembling, testing and promoting best practices. The IIC's Security Working Group is responsible for a common security framework for the industrial Internet, comprising security model and policy, data protection, endpoint protection (edge-cloud), communications and connectivity protection, security monitoring and analysis, as well as security configuration and management. The first document describing the IIoT security framework has been published in 2016 (IIC, 2016). It should be noted that standard security certifications and measures still do not exist for the fog computing. The IIC will also address this issue, since it has merged with the former OpenFog Consortium in 2019.

Specific directives concerning ICS/SCADA security refer to particular industrial sectors such as the electric power industry, oil and natural gas industry, water and wastewater treatment. Most standardization efforts are carried out in the electric power sector.

IEC 62351 is a standard developed for handling the security of multiple IEC series of ICS/SCADA protocols, including IEC 60870-5 series, IEC 60870-6 series, IEC 61850 series, etc. The main security objectives include authentication of data transfer through digital signatures, authenticated access, prevention of eavesdropping, playback and spoofing, and intrusion detection capabilities.

The Institute of Electrical and Electronics Engineers (IEEE) defines a guide for electric power substation physical and electronic security (IEEE 1402-2000), which identifies and discusses security issues related to human intervention during the construction, operation, and maintenance of electric power supply substations. In 2019, the IEEE has initiated the work on the IEEE P2023, standard for digital transformation, which poses new and complex challenges in information systems and technology, process automation, cloud computing, robotics, and artificial intelligence. The standard aims to provide architecture and framework, which address scalability, systems and interfaces, security and privacy challenges for digital transformation applications.

The American Petroleum Institute (API) has issued the standard API 1164, which refers to pipeline SCADA security and addresses access control, communication security (including encryption), information distribution classification, physical issues (including disaster recovery and business continuity plans), operating systems, network design, data interchange between enterprise and third-party support/customers, management systems, and field devices configuration and local access. Additionally, the API has issued two documents related to security issues in oil and gas industry. The first document represents security guidance for the oil and gas facilities, and covers operational regulations, standards, and recommended practices, which relate to facility design and safety, environmental protection, emergency response, and protection from theft and vandalisms. The second document describes security vulnerability assessment methodology for the petroleum and petrochemical industries and contains a methodology for evaluating the probability and consequences of terrorist attacks against refineries and petrochemical facilities.

The American Gas Association (AGA) has issued standard AGA-12, which provides cryptographic protection for SCADA communications, including encryption policy; retrofit link encryption for asynchronous serial communications; protection of networked systems; and protection embedded in SCADA components.

American Water Works Association (AWWA), in cooperation with the ANSI, published the ANSI/AWWA G430-14 standard, concerning security practices for operation and management. This standard describes critical requirements for establishing and operating a protective security program for a water, wastewater, or reuse utility. Topics covered include commitment to security, security culture, defined security roles and employee expectations, vulnerability assessment, resources dedicated to security and security implementation, access control and intrusion detection, contamination detection, monitoring and surveillance, and information protection and continuity.

FUTURE RESEARCH DIRECTIONS

Securing ICS/SCADA systems in the Future Internet environment is an open research topic. When deciding to utilize Future Internet technologies, each company/organization should provide answers to the following questions:

1. How are models and dynamics of migration toward Future Internet environments affected by cyber security risk?
2. How industrial control systems can be secured in these new environments, i.e., what security solutions are right with respect to aforementioned priorities concerning availability, integrity and confidentiality?
3. How will investments in security affect the overall company's costs?
4. Are all security solutions ICS/SCADA-specific or solutions for general-purpose information systems can be used to some extent?

The answer to the first question is that gradual migration will probably be the best choice for most of the companies. The second question poses a number of problems that should be solved at different levels: starting from the system's level (network security architectures, definition and implementation of security policies), through multi-pronged approach that combines mechanisms such as access control, protocol analysis, endpoint security and encryption, to particular security mechanisms like intrusion detection and prevention systems, secure protocols or live forensics. The third question calls for consistent application of security risk management and the associated cost-benefit analysis. Although different qualitative and quantitative approaches, methods and tools for risk assessment in industrial control environment can be found in the literature, only a few of them deals with the Future Internet environment. The fourth question is related to the previous one, regarding security investments. This applies especially for the defense against ICS/SCADA-specific cyber security threats and securing specific communication protocols in such systems. Still, a number of general-purpose security solutions may be applicable, original or upgraded to suit the requirements of industrial networks.

Among many open leads in the area, the following are the most important:

- A precise taxonomy of cyber vulnerabilities and threats in industrial control networks is needed, particularly related to cloud, fog and IIoT environments. Additional work is also needed on the attribution of cyber attacks on critical infrastructures.

- All IIoT participants must design and integrate security into their components and systems before building them. In other words, chips, boards and software should have security built in from the beginning, and attested to the right level of security before implementation.
- One of the key features of IIoT is the integration between the machines and the humans who run them. New entry points will be introduced into the reference model to increase connectivity. These new capabilities introduce cyber security considerations that will need to be addressed.
- Special attention should be paid to development of appropriate test environments for new security solutions, including testbeds, datasets and attack models.
- Significant research efforts are needed to address risk assessment, because risk management takes the outputs of the risk assessment process to consider the options for risk mitigation and finding the trade-offs among overall costs, benefits, and risks of using Future Internet technologies in the industrial environment.
- The ongoing work on cyber security standardization should be intensified. In particular, there is a need for developing specific security standards for the other industrial sectors apart from electric power industry.

CONCLUSION

Future Internet technologies bring a lot of benefits to the industrial sector, particularly in terms of seamless connectivity, improved scalability, efficient system configuration and maintenance, and improving the overall economic efficiency. However, cyber security problems may pose limitations to the migrations of ICS/SCADA systems toward Future Internet environments.

First, public and private cloud architectures can both be the right choice for ICS/SCADA. Although the use of public cloud services brings a number of economic benefits, it requires a careful risk analysis and gradual migration. Another issue concerns the choice of cloud service provider. A properly defined SLA represents a starting point for provisioning of secure public cloud services with the required QoS level. Migration to fog computing can mitigate risks regarding cyber security and fulfillment of stringent delay requirements. The private cloud infrastructure may bring substantial technical benefits in terms of QoS and security, in addition to cost savings and increased business opportunities.

Second, different operational processes, principles, users, and objectives of the IoT and IIoT cause the need for different security solutions. The main issue comes from the fact that IIoT applications are usually assembled with the existing ICS/SCADA equipment; hence, they bring in security issues of such equipment. For that reason, one of the key requirements for IIoT participants concerns integrating security solutions into their components and systems. Besides, introducing new entry points to the IIoT system, in order to increase connectivity, may increase cyber security risk.

Finally, intensive standardization efforts are needed in the area, including the work toward specific standards concerning particular industrial sectors as well as the cross-cut standards and guidelines.

ACKNOWLEDGMENT

This research was supported by the Ministry of Education, Science and Technological Development of Serbia [grant number TR 32025 and grant number TR 36002].

REFERENCES

Aazam, M., Zeadally, S., & Harras, K. A. (2018). Deploying fog computing in Industrial Internet of Things and Industry 4.0. *IEEE Transactions on Industrial Informatics*, *14*(10), 4674–4682. doi:10.1109/TII.2018.2855198

Aleksandrova, M. (2019). Industrial IoT security: How to protect smart manufacturing. Retrieved October 8, 2019, from https://easternpeak.com/blog/industrial-iot-security-how-to-protect-smart-manufacturing/

Boštjančič Rakas, S. (2020). Energy Internet: Architecture, emerging technologies and security issues. In M. Stojanovic, & S. Bostjancic Rakas (Eds.), *Cyber security of industrial control systems in the Future Internet environment*. Hershey, PA: IGI Global.

Boštjančič Rakas, S., & Stojanović, M. (2019). A centralized model for establishing end-to-end communication services via management agents. *Promet – Traffic & Transportation, 31*(3), 245-255.

Butun, I., Sari, A., & Österberg, P. (2019). Security implications of fog computing on the Internet of Things. In *Proceedings of the International Conference on Consumer Electronics* (pp. 1-6). New York: IEEE. 10.1109/ICCE.2019.8661909

Byers, C. (2018). Fog computing for industrial automation. Retrieved October 8, 2019, from https://www.controleng.com/articles/fog-computing-for-industrial-automation/

Cao, Y., Li, Q., Tan, Y., Li, Y., Chen, Y., Shao, X., & Zou, Y. (2018). A comprehensive review of Energy Internet: Basic concept, operation and planning methods, and research prospects. *Journal of Modern Power Systems and Clean Energy*, *6*(3), 399–411. doi:10.100740565-017-0350-8

Chavan, P., Patil, P., Kulkarni, G., Sutar, R., & Belsare, S. (2013). IaaS cloud security. In *Proceedings of the 2013 International Conference on Machine Intelligence and Research Advancement* (pp. 549-553). New York: IEEE.

Chen, Y., Chen, J., & Gan, J. (2015). Experimental study on cloud computing based electric power SCADA system. *ZTE Communications*, *13*(3), 33–41.

Church, P., Mueller, H., Ryan, C., Gogouvitis, S. V., Goscinski, A., & Tari, Z. (2017). Migration of a SCADA system to IaaS clouds – a case study. *Journal of Cloud Computing: Advances, Systems, and Applications*, *6*(11), 1–12.

Cook, A., Nicholson, A., Janicke, H., Maglaras, L., & Smith, R. (2016). Attribution of cyber attacks on industrial control systems. *EAI Transactions on Industrial Networks and Industrial Systems*, *3*(7), 1–15.

Foundation, O. P. C. (2018). *Practical security recommendations for building OPC UA applications* (White Paper). Retrieved August 1, 2019, from https://opcfoundation.org/wp-content/uploads/2017/11/OPC-UA-Security-Advise-EN.pdf

Galloway, B., & Hancke, G. P. (2013). Introduction to industrial control networks. *IEEE Communications Surveys and Tutorials*, *15*(2), 860–880. doi:10.1109/SURV.2012.071812.00124

Gao, J., Liu, J., Rajan, B., Nori, R., Fu, B., Xiao, Y., ... Chen, C. L. P. (2014). SCADA communication and security issues. *Security and Communication Networks*, *7*(1), 175–194. doi:10.1002ec.698

Garcia-Morchon, O., Kumar, S., & Sethi, M. (2019). Internet of things (IoT) Security: State of the Art and Challenges. *IETF RFC 8576 (Informational)*. Retrieved October 8, 2019, from https://www.rfc-editor.org/search/rfc_search.php

Ghosh, S., & Sampalli, S. (2019). A survey of security in SCADA networks: Current issues and future challenges. *IEEE Access: Practical Innovations, Open Solutions, 7*. doi:10.1109/ACCESS.2019.2926441

Goldenberg, N., & Wool, A. (2013). Accurate modeling of Modbus/TCP for intrusion detection in SCADA systems. *International Journal of Critical Infrastructure Protection, 6*(2), 63–75. doi:10.1016/j.ijcip.2013.05.001

Hari Krishna, B., Kiran, S., Murali, G., & Pradeep Kumar Reddy, R. (2016). Security issues in service model of cloud computing environment. *Procedia Computer Science, 87*, 246–251. doi:10.1016/j.procs.2016.05.156

Howard, P. D. (2015). *A security checklist for SCADA systems in the cloud*. Retrieved October 8, 2019, from https://gcn.com/articles/2015/06/29/scada-cloud.aspx

Industrial Internet Consortium (IIC). (2016). Industrial Internet of Things Volume G4: Security Framework. Document IIC:PUB:G4:V1.0:PB:20160919. Retrieved October 8, 2019, from https://www.iiconsortium.org/pdf/IIC_PUB_G4_V1.00_PB.pdf

Industrial Internet Consortium (IIC). (2019). The Industrial Internet of Things Volume G1: Reference Architecture, Version 1.9. Retrieved October 8, 2019, from https://www.iiconsortium.org/pdf/IIRA-v1.9.pdf

Kamble, A., & Bhutad, S. (2018). Survey on Internet of Things (IoT) – security issues & solutions. In *Proceedings of the Second International Conference on Inventive Systems and Control (ICISC 2018)*, (pp. 307-312). New York: IEEE. 10.1109/ICISC.2018.8399084

Khan, S., Parkinson, S., & Qin, Y. (2017). Fog computing security: A review of current applications and security solutions. *Journal of Cloud Computing: Advances, Systems, and Applications, 6*(19), 1–22.

Leander, B., & Causevic, A. (2019). Applicability of the IEC 62443 standard in Industry 4.0/IIoT. In *Proceedings of the 14th International Conference on Availability, Reliability and Security*, (Article 101, pp. 1-8). Canterbury, UK: ACM. 10.1145/3339252.3341481

Maglaras, L., Ferrag, M. A., Derhab, A., Mukherjee, M., & Janicke, H. (2019). Cyber security: From regulations and policies to practice. In A. Kavoura, E. Kefallonitis, & A. Giovanis (Eds.), *Springer Proceedings in Business and Economics. Strategic innovative marketing and tourism* (pp. 763–770). Cham, Switzerland: Springer International Publishing. doi:10.1007/978-3-030-12453-3_88

Mantere, M., Sailio, M., & Noponen, S. (2013). Network traffic features for anomaly detection in specific industrial control system network. *Future Internet, 5*(4), 460–473. doi:10.3390/fi5040460

Markovic-Petrovic, J. D., Stojanovic, M. D., & Bostjancic Rakas, S. V. (2019). A fuzzy AHP approach for security risk assessment in SCADA networks. *Advances in Electrical and Computer Engineering, 19*(3), 69–74. doi:10.4316/AECE.2019.03008

Morris, T., & Gao, W. (2013). Classifications of industrial control system cyber attacks. In *Proceedings of the 1st International Symposium for ICS & SCADA Cyber Security Research* (pp. 22-29). Leicester, UK: British Computer Society.

Mouradian, C., Naboulsi, D., Yangui, S., Glitho, R. H., Morrow, M. J., & Polakos, P. A. (2018). A comprehensive survey on fog computing: State-of-the-art and research challenges. *IEEE Communications Surveys and Tutorials, 20*(1), 416–464. doi:10.1109/COMST.2017.2771153

Nugent, E. (2017, November/December). How cloud and fog computing will advance SCADA systems. *Manufacturing Automation, 32*(7), 22–24.

Ogie, R. I. (2017). Cyber security incidents on critical infrastructure and industrial networks. In *Proceedings of the 9th International Conference on Computer and Automation Engineering* (pp. 254-258). New York: ACM. 10.1145/3057039.3057076

Qiu, T., Chen, N., Li, K., Atiquzzaman, M., & Zhao, W. (2018). How can heterogeneous Internet of Things build our future: A survey. *IEEE Communications Surveys and Tutorials, 20*(3), 2011–2027. doi:10.1109/COMST.2018.2803740

Sadeghi, A.-R., Wachsmann, C., & Waidner, M. (2015). Security and privacy challenges in industrial Internet of Things. In *Proceedings of the 52nd ACM/EDAC/IEEE Design Automation Conference* (pp. 1-6). New York: IEEE. 10.1145/2744769.2747942

Sajid, A., Abbas, H., & Saleem, K. (2016). Cloud-assisted IoT-based SCADA systems security: A review of the state of the art and future challenges. *IEEE Access: Practical Innovations, Open Solutions, 4*, 1375–1384. doi:10.1109/ACCESS.2016.2549047

Sandikkaya, M. T., & Harmanci, A. E. (2012). Security problems of Platform-as-a-Service (PaaS) clouds and practical solutions to the problems. In *Proceedings of the IEEE 31st Symposium on Reliable Distributed Systems* (pp. 463-468). New York: IEEE. 10.1109/SRDS.2012.84

Schwab, W., & Poujol, M. (2018). The state of industrial cybersecurity 2018. Retrieved October 8, 2019, from https://ics.kaspersky.com/media/2018-Kaspersky-ICS-Whitepaper.pdf

Soufiane, S., & Halima, B. (2017). SaaS cloud security: Attacks and proposed solutions. *Transactions on Machine Learning and Artificial Intelligence, 5*(4), 291–301. doi:10.14738/tmlai.54.3194

Stojanovic, M., Bostjancic Rakas, S., & Acimovic-Raspopovic, V. (2010). End-to-end quality of service specification and mapping: The third-party approach. *Computer Communications, 33*(11), 1354–1368. doi:10.1016/j.comcom.2010.03.024

Stojanovic, M., Kostic-Ljubisavljevic, A., & Radonjic-Djogatovic, V. (2013). SLA-controlled interconnection charging in next generation networks. *Computer Networks, 57*(11), 2374–2394. doi:10.1016/j.comnet.2013.04.013

Stojanović, M. D., Boštjančič Rakas, S. V., & Marković-Petrović, J. D. (2019). SCADA systems in the cloud and fog environments: Migration scenarios and security issues. *FACTA UNIVERSITATIS Series: Electronics and Energetics, 32*(3), 345–358.

Stouffer, K., Pillitteri, V., Lightman, S., Abrams, M., & Hahn, A. (2015). *Guide to industrial control systems (ICS) security (NIST Special Publication 800-82 Rev. 2)*. Gaithersburg, MD: U.S. National Institute of Standards and Technology. doi:10.6028/NIST.SP.800-82r2

Tom, R. J., & Sankaranarayanan, S. (2017). IoT based SCADA integrated with fog for power distribution automation. In *Proceedings of the 12th Iberian Conference on Information Systems and Technologies* (pp. 1-4). New York: IEEE. 10.23919/CISTI.2017.7975732

Xu, H., Yu, W., Griffith, D., & Golmie, N. (2018). A survey on Industrial Internet of Things: A cyber-physical systems perspective. *IEEE Access: Practical Innovations, Open Solutions, 6,* 78238–78259. doi:10.1109/ACCESS.2018.2884906

Yang, Y., McLaughlin, K., Sezer, S., Littler, T., Im, E. G., Pranggono, B., & Wang, H. F. (2014). Multi-attribute SCADA-specific intrusion detection system for power networks. *IEEE Transactions on Power Delivery, 29*(3), 1092–1102. doi:10.1109/TPWRD.2014.2300099

Zhou, L., Guo, H., & Deng, G. (2019). A fog computing based approach to DDoS mitigation in IIoT systems. *Computers & Security, 85,* 51–62. doi:10.1016/j.cose.2019.04.017

Zhou, X., Xu, Z., Wang, L., & Chen, K. (2017). What should we do? A structured review of SCADA system cyber security standards. In *Proceedings of the 4th International Conference on Control, Decision, and Information Technologies* (pp. 605-614). New York: IEEE. 10.1109/CoDIT.2017.8102661

ADDITIONAL READING

Bellavista, P., Berrocal, J., Corradi, A., Das, S. K., Foschini, L., & Zanni, A. (2019). A survey on fog computing for the Internet of Things. *Pervasive and Mobile Computing, 52,* 71–99. doi:10.1016/j.pmcj.2018.12.007

Campos, J., Sharma, P., Jantunen, E., Baglee, D., & Fumagalli, L. (2016). The challenges of cybersecurity frameworks to protect data required for the development of advanced maintenance. *Procedia CIRP, 47,* 222–227. doi:10.1016/j.procir.2016.03.059

Cherdantseva, Y., Burnap, P., Blyth, A., Eden, P., Jones, K., Soulsby, H., & Stoddart, K. (2016). A review of cyber security risk assessment methods for SCADA systems. *Computers & Security, 56,* 1–27. doi:10.1016/j.cose.2015.09.009

Dotson, C. (2019). *Practical cloud security*. Sebastopol, CA: O'Reilly Media.

Hariri, R. H., Fredericks, E. M., & Bowers, K. M. (2019). Uncertainty in big data analytics: Survey, opportunities, and challenges. *Journal of Big Data, 6,* article 44, 1-10.

Kamal, M. (2019). ICS layered threat modeling. SANS Institute – Information Security Reading Room. Retrieved October 8, 2019, from https://www.sans.org/reading-room/whitepapers/ICS/ics-layered-threat-modeling-38770

Knowles, W., Prince, D., Hutchison, D., Disso, J. F. P., & Jones, K. (2015). A survey of cyber security management in industrial control systems. *International Journal of Critical Infrastructure Protection*, *9*, 52–80. doi:10.1016/j.ijcip.2015.02.002

Lamba, V., Simková, N., & Rossi, B. (2019). Recommendations for smart grid security risk management. *Cyber-Physical Systems*, *5*(2), 92–118. doi:10.1080/23335777.2019.1600035

Lin, H., Yan, Z., Chen, Y., & Zhang, L. (2018). A survey on network security-related data collection technologies. *IEEE Access: Practical Innovations, Open Solutions*, *6*, 18345–18365. doi:10.1109/ACCESS.2018.2817921

Stojanovic, M., Acimovic-Raspopovic, V., & Bostjancic Rakas, S. (2013). Security management issues for open source ERP in the NGN environment. In M. Khosrow-Pour (Ed.), *Enterprise resource planning: Concepts, methodologies, tools, and applications* (Vol. II, pp. 789–804). Hershey, PA: IGI Global. doi:10.4018/978-1-4666-4153-2.ch046

KEY TERMS AND DEFINITIONS

Cloud Computing: A method of using remote servers hosted on the Internet to store, manage, and process data.

Cloud Service Provider (CSP): A third-party company that offers cloud services (software as a service, platform as a service, infrastructure as a service, etc.) to business and/or residential customers.

Cyber Security Risk: Exposure to harm or loss resulting from data breaches or attacks on information and communication systems.

Endpoint: In the context of Industrial Internet of Things, a component that has computational capabilities and network connectivity.

Fog Computing: An architecture that uses edge devices to perform a large amount of computation, storage and communication, locally and routed over the Internet.

Gateway: In the context of Industrial Internet of Things, a device that bridges the edge of an IIoT system to the cloud.

Industrial Internet of Things (IIoT): A system of interconnected sensors, actuators, and other devices networked together with computers' industrial applications.

Service Level Agreement (SLA): A contract between the service provider and the customer, which defines provider's responsibilities in the sense of quality of service guarantees, performance metrics, measurement methods, tariffs and billing principles, as well as penalties for both the user and the provider in the case of contract violation.

Chapter 2
Methodology for Cyber Security Risk Mitigation in Next Generation SCADA Systems

Jasna D. Marković-Petrović

https://orcid.org/0000-0002-0373-8022

Public Enterprise "Electric Power Industry of Serbia", Serbia

ABSTRACT

The evolution of architecture of contemporary SCADA systems follows trends in industry sector. Today, SCADA systems imply the application of smart grid and artificial intelligence concepts, the use of IP-based technologies, new mobile devices, as well as the use of private and public cloud computing services. Security risk assessment of contemporary SCADA systems needs to include new security aspects. This chapter analyzes information security in contemporary SCADA systems. Focus is then directed to SCADA network architecture and recommended security mechanisms for mitigating the security risk that assumes the use of Defense in Depth concept. Special attention is paid to SCADA-specific intrusion detection and intrusion prevention technologies. A case study outlines recommendations for security risk mitigation of SCADA system in a hydropower plant.

INTRODUCTION

Supervisory Control and Data Acquisition (SCADA) systems are widely used in industrial sector, primarily in production, transmission and distribution of electrical energy, oil and gas refining, telecommunications, transportation, as well as water and wastewater control. These industrial sectors are a part of critical infrastructure. Therefore, SCADA systems are a target for cyber attacks, since the malfunction or failure of such systems can cause serious consequences, due to their strategic importance for critical infrastructure of every country. This problem rises with the introduction of new generation SCADA systems that are no longer isolated and are not using only proprietary protocols and software.

Next generation SCADA systems assume deployment of smart grids, artificial intelligence concept and remote control of complex systems, the use of the Internet Protocol (IP) technology, the rise in the

DOI: 10.4018/978-1-7998-2910-2.ch002

number of remote users, the use of public and private cloud and fog computing services, the emergence of new mobile devices and the Industrial Internet of Things (IIoT). From stand-alone, isolated systems, these systems have evolved into those connected with other SCADA and corporate IT systems. This has caused a rise in the number and type of connections to SCADA systems, and consequently, a rise in the number and variety of attacks to the telecommunication networks of industrial control systems. Several successfully performed attacks on the SCADA systems' infrastructure have been registered and reported worldwide, producing ill effects of varying degrees.

In order to reduce the security risk, it is necessary to take large-scale, comprehensive measures, which include adopting an appropriate security policy for information infrastructure, staff informing and training on the adopted policy, establishing the adopted policy and conducting continuous information security risk management.

This chapter starts from the premise that the application of conventional security mechanisms is not always a proper solution for telecommunication networks of SCADA systems. The reasons for this are the different requirements regarding availability and quality of service, as well as the applied information and communication technologies in comparison with the business information systems. Hence, the implementation of the specific security mechanisms designed for SCADA systems is of high importance for achieving the efficient protection. The rest of the chapter is structured as follows. The literature review is presented in the background section.

In the following section, performance requirements of SCADA networks are presented, considering the differences between general-purpose and industrial information systems. Further, security aspects of SCADA systems have been analyzed, including the cyber threats directed towards the infrastructure of the next generation SCADA systems and the infrastructure's vulnerability. The next section presents the evolution of the SCADA systems architecture, with the emphasis on next generation SCADA systems. The chapter continues with the consideration of secure SCADA network architecture in the future Internet environment. The basis for defining such an architecture is the functional and logical architecture describing the structure and basic functions of SCADA systems. The next section considers security mechanisms, namely the firewall and intrusion detection and prevention systems (IDPS), which are specific for the design and application in next generation SCADA systems. In the following section, based on the previous observations, a case study is presented, which proposes the network architecture and technology for reducing the information security risk of SCADA system in a hydropower plant. The chapter ends with emphasizing the future research directions and concluding remarks.

BACKGROUND

The strategic role of critical infrastructure and technological progress causes the need for contemporary information and communication systems. All systems have to provide high reliability, availability, and transmission of correct and timely information in order to plan production, efficient resource utilization, remote control of production facilities, reporting and successful operation of industrial system.

IP technology is widely adopted as a base for the integration of operational and business services in contemporary industrial telecommunication networks. Such networks have flaws and vulnerabilities known to malicious users. Particularly, potential migration of SCADA systems towards cloud computing environment needs to be considered. Such a realization contributes to cost reduction and business efficiency improvement, but sets additional security requirements (Stojanovic, Bostjancic Rakas, & Markovic-Petrovic, 2019).

In past years, a number of successful attacks on the SCADA system infrastructure, with less or more serious consequences, have been reported (Derbyshire, Green, Prince, Mauthe, & Hutchison, 2018; Hemsley & Fisher, 2018; Nicholson, Webber, Dyer, Patel, & Janicke, 2012). However, the number of reported incidents does not reflect the real picture about the frequency and nature of such attacks, since the system users are often not aware of these attacks, and often they don't even report the incidents due to fear of losing reputation. Considering the importance of industrial processes, where the remote control is accomplished through SCADA system, each information about newly discovered vulnerabilities and flaws, as well as reporting attacks, help in improving the measures to reduce security risk. Since 2010, there is a significant growth in vulnerabilities of SCADA systems (Industrial Control Systems Cyber Emergency Response Team [ICS CERT], 2016a). Therefore, analyses conducted in testbed and simulation environments are very important, since they can help with determining the way of how the cyber attacks affect the informational and physical infrastructure of SCADA system.

Simulation analysis of industrial control systems performances in the context of simultaneous, distributed attacks on IP-based SCADA network infrastructure is presented in (Markovic-Petrovic & Stojanovic, 2013). Distributed denial of service (DDoS) attacks on SCADA infrastructure of a hydropower plant was simulated. A simulation model is developed to analyze the performances of remote control under such attacks. Simulation results show degradation of performances (availability, delay, packet loss ratio, processor resources utilization) and malfunction of the remote monitoring and control service.

Li et al. (2016) analyzed the influence of false sequential logic attack on SCADA system. The authors first model the attack, and then analyze in detail the impact of such attacks on a physical system. Simulation results show that this type of attacks can cause financial losses, but it can also damage the equipment and hurt people.

Due to frequent attacks on SCADA infrastructure and apparent impact of these attacks to degradation of system's performance, the research should focus on information security risk management. Important steps in such a process are security risk analysis and assessment (NIST, 2012). The result of these steps is assessed risk measure, which is taken into account for decision making regarding dealing with risk as well as assessed financial impact of the implemented security mechanisms. Specific requirements of industrial information system regarding reliability, quality of service and applied protocols, cause development of dedicated security risk assessment methods for SCADA systems. Markovic-Petrovic and Stojanovic (2014) proposed a security risk assessment method, which is focused on attack consequences and identification of conditions that influence the degree of risk. Special attention is paid to selection of parameters for quantification of losses due to successful cyber attack, while the parameters' values are determined based on statistical analysis of relevant SCADA historical data. Another method (Markovic-Petrovic, Stojanovic, & Bostjancic Rakas, 2019) takes into account subjective opinions of relevant SCADA experts, in addition to the analysis of historical data. The proposed method is based on fuzzy analytic hierarchy process (AHP) to quantify the appropriate experts' opinions. It takes into account their expertise, working experience, field of work, and other parameters. The particular advantage of this method is that it can also be used in a design phase of industrial control systems, when historical data is not available. In such cases, risk assessment is carried out based on only subjective experts' opinions.

Risk analysis and assessment are followed by the selection of security measures and mechanisms. Measures for security risk mitigation encompass a number of different activities. The most important is to define general security measures with the adoption of continuity policy that defines in detail the procedures in case of a failure of industrial control system's vital functions. It is recommended to create a backup control center as well as other redundant measures, depending on particular system. Other important measures are: (1) to inform and continually educate employees about the security policy and security mechanisms and (2) to perform continual internal and occasionally external control regarding the right implementation of adopted control measures.

The second group of activities is focused on access control, which assumes assigning privileges for accessing a particular network segment, applications and data, as well as provisioning of physical access control to remote control system's locations. In the context of security mechanisms, password management and biometrics are of particular importance. Password management is imposed by a higher management level with requirements for more complex passwords and authorization mechanisms. When passwords are sent over network infrastructure it is necessary to use encryption. Biometrics assumes methods for unique person recognition based on one or more physical characteristics. The use of such a technology is becoming increasingly widespread in contemporary authentication mechanisms in SCADA systems.

The third group of security measures refers to discovery of malicious software and its elimination. They are of particular importance for security of SCADA systems, but there is a problem regarding processing requirements that slow down system performance. Activities such as running the antivirus software, updating the databases with definitions of particular viruses, system scanning to find malicious code and similar actions, require processor resources that are often unavailable to every SCADA system's component.

In SCADA systems, different techniques and technologies are used for detection and prevention of attacks, such as firewalls, IDPS, honeypots, etc.

Baker et al. (2015) proposed security concept for cloud-SCADA systems based on Service Oriented Architecture in order to improve integrity of such systems. They defined a set of security measures that need to be implemented to provide an acceptable security risk. This concept is verified with a case study that describes a smart grid system.

Lei et al. (2018) also analyzed security of a smart grid. Authors pointed out the differences regarding security and reliability in cyber-physical systems and set boundaries for research in these two areas. Degradation of cyber security can cause financial losses, denial of service or equipment damage. Therefore, the authors give guidelines for the vulnerability and threat analysis, selection of appropriate security mechanisms and security strategies.

Sajid et al. (2016) deal with the security of SCADA systems in IoT environment, pointing out vulnerability increase in Internet environment and the most important threats to these systems. The authors give the following recommendations to improve security:

1. Network segregation.
2. Continuous monitoring and analysis.
3. Log analysis.
4. File integrity monitoring.
5. Network traffic analysis.
6. Memory dump analysis.
7. Updating and patching regularly.
8. Testing vulnerability regularly.
9. Proxy solutions.
10. Tools for detecting malicious activity.

Nazir et al. (2017) proposed SCADA architecture based on autonomic computing. The concept is based on hierarchy of autonomous managers that help operator with decision making. Authors advocate that final decision should be made by a human due to exceptional importance of SCADA systems and risks caused by potential false alarms.

Mackintosh et al. (2019) propose the combination of orthogonal methods with the existing strategies of multilayer defense to improve security mechanisms in the case of adaptive and frequently asymmetrical attacks. They propose a concept that introduces more functional and security control for every layer of SCADA system with necessary real-time maintenance of traffic flows.

The main focus of this chapter is network architecture of SCADA system and to propose measures for reducing of information security risk caused by infrastructural attacks on SCADA system.

PERFORMANCE REQUIREMENTS OF THE SCADA NETWORK

Information security on the global Internet has reached a certain level of maturity. Although experiences in the sphere of global Internet security are often applicable to other IT systems as well, the security requirements of SCADA systems in terms of their reliability, service quality and applied protocols differ from those of general-purpose IT systems. The solutions implemented in general-purpose IT systems cannot be straightforwardly introduced to SCADA systems; instead, in most cases, it is necessary to find new security solutions adapted to the control environment. Considering the role of SCADA systems in industrial processes, it can be concluded that the requirements of these systems are significantly different from the requirements of general-purpose IT systems.

Table 1 presents the main differences regarding the requirements of general-purpose IT systems and SCADA systems (ICS CERT, 2016b; Stouffer, Pillitteri, Lightman, Abrams, & Hahn, 2015; Tuptuk & Hailes, 2018).

An important difference refers to the potential adverse effects of a successful cyber-attack. In general-purpose IT systems, the hazardous impact may involve the loss of data and the violation of privacy, whereas in SCADA systems, not only can the production and/or service provision be interrupted, but the consequences can also have major ill-effects on the environment, equipment security and public health and safety.

Risk management is an ongoing process, which should enable secure access to information and network resources by ensuring information confidentiality and integrity, user authentication, access control, service availability and action integrity. For general-purpose infrastructure, CIA (Confidentiality, Integrity, Availability) security principle applies, i.e., a triplet that gives priority to confidentiality, then integrity and at last the data availability. In the case of SCADA infrastructure, safety is an additional aspect with the greatest priority, i.e., safety and protection of the people and the environment, followed by the same triplet, but in the reverse order, with data availability of the highest priority, followed by data integrity and availability. Therefore, security principle in SCADA systems can be defined as quadruplet SAIC. This difference is crucial regarding the safety policy and directions in the implementation of security mechanisms, where 24/7 availability of such systems is most important, as well as protection of human safety, health and the environment.

SECURITY ASPECTS OF SCADA SYSTEMS

A prerequisite for developing an efficient strategy for SCADA security improvement is to identify vulnerabilities and threats to these systems. SCADA vulnerabilities come from applying open standards and protocols with known deficiencies, the use of insecure protocols designed for control systems, interconnection of control network to other networks, limitations of existing security technologies, the increasing usage of remote access, availability of technical information about control systems, etc. (Gao et al., 2014). On the other hand, different motives and groups of potential attackers are evident, that aim to threaten security of SCADA systems (Nicholson et al., 2012). Finally, the diversity of cyber attacks increases the vulnerability of SCADA system (Lei, Chen, Butler-Purry, & Singh, 2018; Mackintosh, et al., 2019).

Attacks can be classified according to different criteria such as goal, purpose, source and target. In the case of the attack goal, there are attacks that jeopardize availability (communication link jamming, software modification, data erasure), integrity (control signal modification, sensor data modification) and confidentiality (eavesdropping, fiber tapping, packet sniffing, traffic monitoring). The purpose of the attack can be impact on system operation (modification, interruption, fabrication) or recording the state and parameters of system's components (interception).

Taking into account the attack sources, there are internal and external attacks. Internal attacks are a consequence of employees' activities and they can be intentional, executed by unsatisfied employees or unintentional attacks that come from random activities leading to system's errors. External attacks are executed by hackers, organized groups, competing firms, terrorists, etc. Sometimes, the goals of such attacks are financial gain, harming and ruining the reputation, revenge, etc.

Regarding target, attacks can be classified into three categories. In the first category are attacks on remote units and edge devices. Remote access to these devices can jeopardize the whole system because these devices are used for the control of the entire infrastructure. In the second category are attacks on

Table 1. Typical differences between business and industrial IT systems

	Business IT Systems	SCADA Systems
Risk impact	• Data loss.	• Production disruption. • Impact on the environment. • Human health and safety. • Equipment safety.
Safety awareness	• High.	• Not enough, but increasing.
Order of priorities	• CIA	• Safety. • AIC.
Real-time operation	• Delay tolerant.	• Time critical.
Availability	• Disruption tolerant.	• 24/7 service.
Performances	• High throughput.	• Medium throughput.
Software update	• Automated.	• Needs planning. • Incremental.
Antivirus software	• Usual.	• Hard to implement.
Processor resources to support security	• Enough resources.	• Limited resources.
Components lifecycle	• 3-5 years.	• 15-20 years.

SCADA protocols, where attacker uses the protocol vulnerabilities to get the data about remote units and SCADA system. In the third group are attacks on the infrastructure, such as DoS attacks.

ARCHITECTURE EVOLUTION

General configuration of SCADA system encompasses three subsystems (Stouffer et al., 2015):

- **Subsystem of Remote Terminal Units (RTUs):** Programmable logic controllers (PLCs), and intelligent electronic devices (IEDs). This subsystem performs local control of actuators and sensors monitoring that are used to collect various analog and digital data, as well as to issue digital commands or to write analog values.
- **Central Subsystem**: Represents a local area network (LAN) at control center that connects SCADA server (MTU), historian server, data visualization server such as virtual network computing (VNC), human machine interface (HMI) server and consoles, as well as communication devices, such as routers and/or switches. Control center gathers and analyses information from remote stations (at different locations), presents them on HMI and generates action based on detected events. Control center is also in charge for general alarms, trend analysis and report generation.
- **Communication Subsystem:** Connects control center with remote stations subsystem and allows for operators to remotely access stations over fieldbus, for diagnostic purposes and repairing failures.

Most contemporary SCADA systems are implemented in a dedicated subnet, which is connected to enterprise network, so that the engineering workstations can be implemented in the clients of the business network, through web applications.

SCADA architecture has changed in accordance with the development and change of contemporary computer and communication technologies; hence, four generations of SCADA systems can be differentiated: monolithic, distributed, networked and Internet-based (Figure 1).

First generation SCADA systems had a central computer with a mainframe computer platform that was connected to remote terminal units through dedicated network built exactly for that purpose. There were no connections with other networks, with system redundancy provided with dual central computers. Only proprietary protocols were used and connectivity with other SCADA systems was limited.

Second generation SCADA system used the benefits of development and progress of computer techniques and LAN technologies/architectures. Functions of SCADA central computer are divided between multiple computers in one network. Some of these computers have the role of communication server and establish connections with RTUs; others have implemented databases or have the role of historian or HMI. In this way, system efficiency is increased; redundancy and availability are achieved more easily. Still communication with RTUs remained the same as in monolithic architecture, i.e., limited regarding implemented protocols and equipment vendors.

Third generation SCADA systems support open architecture, standards and protocols. Functions are still divided between interconnected servers, but LAN is extended to wide area network (WAN). The use of open standards provides an independency from equipment manufacturers, which brings new quality, since the SCADA system manufacturers can make a greater contribution to development in this field. Third generation SCADA systems also use IP-based communication between central and remote

Figure 1. Evolution of SCADA architecture

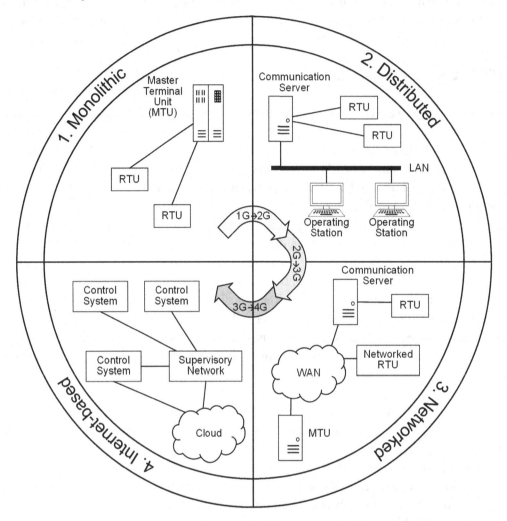

subsystems, which creates possibility for dividing functions of communications server among multiple computers. The second advantage is that SCADA system functionalities can be divided among not only multiple computers, but also on geographically dispersed locations, which increases system's security and reliability.

The fourth generation SCADA systems are Internet-based. Contemporary SCADA systems use advanced technologies, such as cloud computing and IIoT. These systems improve business capabilities; primarily they decrease implementation costs and improve system's scalability. Depending on which functions are moved to the cloud environment, two concepts arise. In the first one, SCADA application is executed on servers that are directly connected to control network, while data is transferred to the cloud where they can be stored and distributed to different users. In the second concept, SCADA application is completely executed in the cloud, and is remotely connected to control network. The cloud infrastructure can be private, public or hybrid. From security point of view, it is more convenient to use private cloud infrastructure. When migrating the SCADA system to cloud environment, it is very important to consider, apart from evident advantages, also risk factors of fourth generation SCADA systems. Key risks refer to information security, system's performances, availability, and reliability (Stojanovic et al., 2019).

SECURE SCADA NETWORK ARCHITECTURE

Taking into account the importance of SCADA systems and their role in critical infrastructure, numerous national institutions worldwide considered security of new generation SCADA systems and proposed measures for security risk limitations. The results of such activities are standards, frameworks and directions for design and improvement of SCADA networks. Tuptuk and Hailes (2018) provided a detailed overview of standards and regulations in the area. This chapter focuses primarily to network architecture of communication subsystem to support SCADA, starting from the analysis of available literature, which provides guidelines for implementing secure architecture of such systems (ICS CERT, 2016b; Mahan et al., 2011; Obregon, 2015; Stouffer et al., 2015). A common recommendation is to use Defense-in-Depth model that is a security concept based on multilayered protection. Such a security concept provides redundancy and multiple in-depth security layers by applying appropriate measures and mechanisms. These measures encompass the use of firewalls, creation of industrial demilitarized zone (IDMZ), implementation of IDPSs, installation of software patches, as well as implementation of security procedures and policies.

Logical architecture of industrial control system, presented in Figure 2, describes the structure and basic functions of such a system. This model presents an upgrade of enterprise network architecture, a Purdue Enterprise Reference Architecture (PERA), which is adapted for SCADA systems. In the model, devices and equipment are separated by hierarchical functions. Enterprise network and SCADA network

Figure 2. A layered architecture of SCADA network

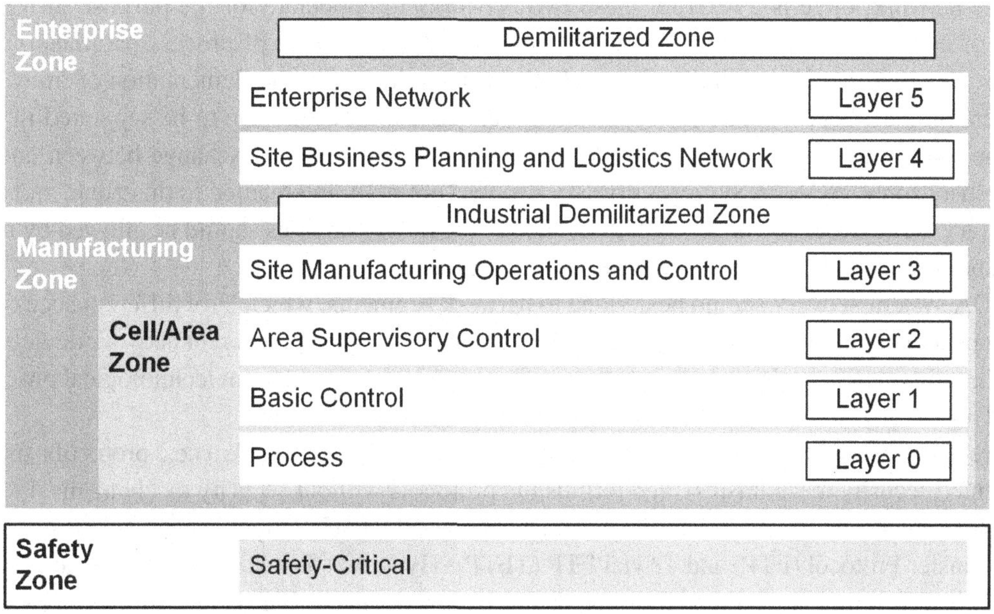

are divided into logical segments (zones and layers) that encompass equipment and services with similar functions and requirements.

Enterprise zone encompasses two layers, namely layers 4 and 5. The highest, fifth layer represents the enterprise network. Business applications run at this layer, which provides Internet access and virtual private network (VPN) connections via enterprise demilitarized zone (DMZ), where web services are provided. Layer 4 is in charge of planning, e-mail services, print servers, and management of corporate IT resources maintenance.

IDMZ is located between the enterprise and production zone. Users from enterprise network can access reports, archives, process visualization through this zone's services. Direct traffic flow from enterprise network to SCADA system's network is forbidden.

Production zone encompasses layers 0–3. Third layer services and systems are in charge of process control and management to provide an optimal and reliable production and/or services. Typical systems, services and applications at this layer are storage, reporting, remote access, engineering workstations, IT services, active directory and time synchronization. This layer provides control and management of the whole production process that can include several production locations. Each location is a special zone made of three layers, namely layers 0–2. Layer 2provides local control and management and encompasses HMI, alarm systems and operators' workstations. Layer 1 represents main control and encompasses RTUs, PLCs and IEDs. This layer provides local control of actuators and sensors on the lowest layer (layer 0). These elements collect analog and digital data and issue digital commands or write analog values.

Systems in safety zone represent ultimate prevention measure. At this layer, process' parameters are monitored; in the case of danger, secure stop of a process is initiated to prevent material damage and people's injuries. Due to mission critical role of such systems, it is not safe to connect them to SCADA network. However, due to existing need for monitoring of parameters in this zone, networking of these systems becomes a practice, but it is necessary to create special security zones in the SCADA network. Based on such hierarchy a secure SCADA network architecture is designed, which is connected to enterprise network (Figure 3) (Obregon, 2015).

Even though the telecommunication network of the SCADA system should be separated from the enterprise network, there is a need for these two networks to cooperate for the purpose of reporting, analysis of events at clients of the enterprise network, and monitoring of process parameters. In this case, it is very important to minimize the number of connections, with implementation of firewalls and IDPS technologies. Servers that are accessed from enterprise network have to be separated in IDMZ. This zone represents an additional security layer for secure information exchange between enterprise and industrial zones. SCADA system's primary services are not implemented in this zone, and all data is temporary. Remote access for configuration and maintenance purposes should be allowed by opening only the predefined port for the appropriate service/protocol.

SCADA system network should be divided to network segments, which have different access rights, with independent administration and handling the data originating from different network devices. Definition of communication rules between the segments should take into account technological process and it should allow only necessary, authenticated and authorized traffic flows.

Secure architecture assumes communication only via secure protocols (i.e., protocols that have implemented security mechanisms), and forbids the protocols without security mechanisms. Examples are the use of Secure Shell (SSH) instead of Telnet, Secure FTP (SFTP) and Secure Copy (SCP) instead of File Transfer Protocol (FTP) and Trivial FTP (TFTP), Hypertext Transfer Protocol Secure (HTTPS) instead of HTTP protocols. Industrial protocols, such as Modbus/TCP, Ethernet, Inter-Control Center

Figure 3. Secure SCADA network architecture

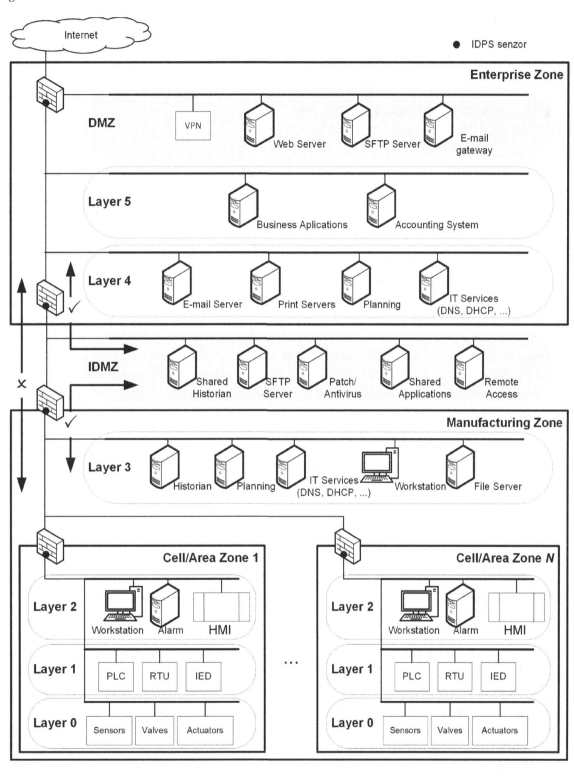

Communications Protocol (ICCP) and Distributed Network Protocol (DNP3) are critical for communication, because they are designed without security mechanisms and usually do not require authentication for remote control. Therefore, industrial protocols should be applied only in the control network; their use is forbidden outside the control network.

APPLICATION OF FIREWALL ANDIDPS TECHNOLOGIES IN SCADA NETWORKS

The role of firewall devices is domain separation, monitoring, gathering and storing log events, user authentication, ingress/egress traffic supervision and blocking of unauthorized traffic. There are two main types of firewalls: host-based and network-based.

Host-based firewalls are usually used for servers with multiple network interfaces. However, such a connection between network segments is very vulnerable; therefore, such solutions are not recommended to be used in contemporary SCADA security architectures.

Network-based firewalls use different techniques depending on the protocol layer. At the transport layer, unawareness of the protocols applied to SCADA systems presents a limitation for implementing firewalls. For this reason, firewalls designed for general-purpose IT networks are inadequate for industrial systems.

Today, firewall products for SCADA systems can be found on the market. Performance analysis of industrial firewalls, primarily regarding the introduced delay in time critical systems, can be found in (Cheminod, Durante, Seno, & Valenzano, 2018). The authors analyze dedicated devices that recognize industrial application layer protocols, primarily Modbus/TCP.

Due to limited number of applications in SCADA network, the use of proxy servers brings some benefits, but there are also limitations regarding the introduced delay. The prerequisites for efficient protection are well-positioned firewalls and the implementation of adequate configuration rules. The network-based firewalls should be implemented between neighboring security zones (Figure 3), as well as towards the wireless network. Each firewall should implement the rules for control of ingress/egress traffic. Firewalls are inefficient in the case of infrastructure attacks because the verification of every malicious traffic packet introduces an unacceptable delay into the time-critical SCADA systems. The implementation of IDPS is therefore necessary.

The IDPS technologies are mainly classified according to by the types of events that they can recognize and the methodologies that they use to identify incidents (Scarfone & Mell, 2007, p.2-2).

According to the type of event, IDPS classification encompasses the following four types:

- **Network-Based**: Monitors traffic in network segments and analyzes activities of network and application protocols in order to identify suspicious activities.
- **Host-Based**: Monitors characteristics of a host and events in the hosts in order to detect incidents.
- **Wireless**: Monitors traffic in wireless network and analyzes appropriate medium access control (MAC) protocols.
- **Network Behavior Analysis**: Analyzes network traffic in order to identify threats that are generated by unusual traffic flows, such as DDoS attacks, some forms of malicious software or violation of security policies.

According to methodology for incident detection, IDPS can be: (1) signature-based; (2) anomaly-based and (3) specification-based.

Signature-based methods compare monitored events with signatures (samples that correspond to known threats) in order to identify possible incidents. These methods are very efficient in detection of known threats, but completely inefficient in detection of new or unknown threats, as well as modified attacks.

Anomaly-based methods compare monitored events to a list of activities that are predefined as normal, in order to identify significant deviations. IDPS has static and dynamic profiles that represent normal behavior of users, hosts, network connections, or applications. Initial profile is generated during the learning phase that lasts for a couple of days or weeks. A large number of anomaly detection methods have been developed, including statistical-based, data mining-based, knowledge-based and machine learning-based (García-Teodoro, Díaz-Verdejo, Maciá-Fernández, & Vázquez, 2009). The main advantage of anomaly-based methods is a high efficiency in detecting unknown threats. A typical problem of these methods is wrong inclusion of malicious activities into profiles. Another problem with generating profiles is a question of accuracy, which is a consequence of complex activities in network.

Specification-based methods compare monitored events to predefined profiles generated based on definitions of protocol activities for every state of protocol machine. In other words, they use universal profiles that are defined by standardization organizations and/or software vendors. These methods can identify irregular series of messages, such as replication of the same command, or setting a command that is not preceded by a command specified by a protocol. Their main disadvantage is intensive utilization of process and memory resources due to recording the states of large number of simultaneous sessions and complex analysis of these states.

Most of the IDPS technologies use multiple detection methodologies, separated or integrated, in order to detect wide range of attacks as accurate as possible.

Attack prevention represents a response to detected threats and actions to preclude their realization. There are a few response techniques. The first one stops the attack by terminating the network connection or user session that are used for the attack, by blocking the access to the attack target from the account or IP address belonging to the attacker, or by completely blocking access to the target. The second technique assumes that the attack is disrupted by changing configurations, changing control parameters or generating software patches. In the third technique, IDPS changes the content of the attacks by removing or replacing malicious parts.

System response time, timely delivery of all relevant data and up-to-date information are very important in SCADA-specific IDPS, because data is valid only for a specified time interval. Order of packets (from sensors) arrival is also very important, especially if they are used for the control of the same or correlated processes. The order of data arrival to control center has an important role in the presentation of process dynamics and influences right decision making, whether it is control algorithm in question or an operator that monitors industrial process.

The network traffic within a SCADA system is predictable, since the applications and services are known, and only a limited number of predetermined protocols are used. Therefore, anomaly-based detection methodology is suitable to be used in SCADA-specific IDPS.

Like firewalls, IDPS systems used in industrial control networks need to have a possibility of monitoring the SCADA-specific protocols. A review of typical IDPS architectures, designed for SCADA networks, can be found e.g., in (Colbert & Hutchinson, 2016).

In secure network architecture of SCADA system, IDPS systems have to be located at points of intensive traffic, on the borders of security zones and towards the networks with sensitive information.

Potential drawbacks of the prevention capabilities implementation reveal when normal traffic is flagged as malicious and as such discarded, which can cause the absence of alarms and configuration messages. For that reason, numerous industrial organizations use only intrusion detection capabilities.

CASE STUDY

A run-off-river hydropower plant with total installed power of 270 MW is assumed. The production of electrical energy is provided with ten equal generators, each producing 27 MW.

There are two network segments in the network architecture of power plant's SCADA system. One is supervisory network for the control and management of the whole power plant, where of key importance are servers and engineering workstations, while the second segment is the process network, which encompasses controllers for control and management of generators and auxiliary systems.

The connection of these two segments is possible with the implementation of two network interfaces on key acquisition data servers, and with the installed firewall with IDPS towards the process network.

There are multiple connections between the supervisory and process networks and other networks:

- **Connection with the enterprise network, which is further connected to the Internet**. This link has the firewall installed.
- **Connections with regional and national dispatching centers**. These connections are established via the process network.
- **Connection with the system for production control at the level of national power company**. This connection is also established via the supervisory network.
- **Connection with SCADA partner power plant**. This connection allows online exchange of key parameters important for mutual operation of the two power plants. The connection is established via server with dual network interfaces. Host-based firewall is installed on this server.

By comparing the contemporary network architecture of a particular SCADA system with the guidelines for secure architecture, several weaknesses that increase security risk can be identified. Weaknesses/vulnerabilities and recommendations for their removal or mitigation are as follows:

- There is no IDMZ in the production zone; hence, traffic form enterprise zone towards the third layer that provides control and management of the whole power plant is allowed. To overcome this weakness implementation of another firewall and migration of server that is accessed from clients in enterprise network to IMDZ are needed. These are servers for supporting reporting and process visualization (Web server and HMI server).
- The communication with partner power plant's SCADA system and communication with National dispatching centers and National energy management system, should take place through IDMZ servers and using the associated services.
- Key acquisition data servers couple the two network segments. Such a solution increases network vulnerability. Acquisition data server has to be a part of the network that implements the third SCADA layer, while communication with other network segments should be achieved by appropriate routing schemes.

Figure 4. Architecture of the SCADA system in a hydropower plant

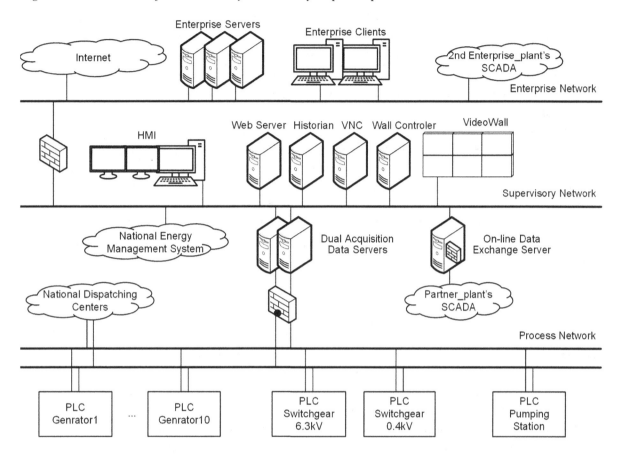

This case study confirmed that security of SCADA network requires continual care, and security risk analyses have to be executed on a regular basis, as well as after new system configuration and settings. Initial SCADA network architecture satisfied, during the design phase, security requirements of that time. New connections and introduction of new remote users increased security risk and violated the overall security. The use of recommended measures regarding secure SCADA network architecture provides mitigation of security risk.

FUTURE RESEARCH DIRECTIONS

The use of contemporary technologies in SCADA systems changes the security awareness of such systems. Due to the components' long-life cycle, initial SCADA network architecture should evolve during the operation in accordance with continual security risk assessment and appropriate security mechanisms.

In recent decades, awareness of both the vulnerability of SCADA systems to cyber-attacks and the number and variety of threats to these systems has increased significantly. Nowadays the trend of cyber-attacks to SCADA systems is continued. Also, the evolution of the architecture of SCADA systems and the new connections with other industrial and enterprise information systems causes new vulnerabilities in these systems. Therefore, research in this area should be continued in three directions.

Industrial control systems operate in real time and monitor critical infrastructure processes. For that reason, it is impossible to conduct penetrating tests on a real system. Therefore, it is necessary to develop simulation models and test-bed environments that will enable the performances' analysis in terms of cyber-attacks to next generation SCADA systems. The simulation and test-bed environments should also provide an analysis of SCADA system vulnerabilities and their detection.

The second direction of research should be focused to the development and design of SCADA specific firewalls and IDPS technologies. Development of these systems should be continuous, according the emergence of new threats and modifications of attacks to SCADA systems.

The third area of research should comprise the development of risk assessment methods for next generation SCADA systems. These methods should include all aspects of information security risk in the new environment, as well as the consequences that result from a successful cyber-attack. An important result of these methods should be cost-benefit analysis of the adopted security mechanisms.

Finally, efforts should be made to collect data of real incidents and security breaches, and to analyze the consequences of these attacks. The experience in real industrial control environments could contribute to the quality of scientific research

CONCLUSION

In order to mitigate security risk in next generation SCADA networks there is a need to take extensive and comprehensive measures, which assume adoption of the appropriate information security policy and continuous security risk management. Secure network infrastructure is a prerequisite for meeting the specific security requirements of SCADA systems.

The secure network architecture relies on the Defense-in-Depth model, which represents a security concept based on multi-layered protection. A special emphasis is placed on network segmentation, whereby the segments of the networked architecture correspond to the functional layers of the logical architecture. Every segment is isolated and the communication between individual network segments is strictly controlled. The network segments are given different access rights, with the provision of independent administration and the use of data from various networked devices. The definition of inter-segment communication rules should respect the technological process and enable only the necessary, authenticated and authorized network traffic.

Security based on this method ensures redundancy and multiple protections by implementing adequate security mechanisms. Success of such a concept depends on the implementation of appropriate SCADA-specific technologies and proper configuration of the installed equipment. Based on the proposed secured SCADA network architecture, directions for enhancement of overall security infrastructure have been emphasized and discussed on a case study of a run-off-river hydropower plant.

REFERENCES

Baker, T., Mackay, M., Shaheed, A., & Aldawsari, B. (2015). Security-oriented cloud platform for SOA-based SCADA. In *Proceedings of the 15th IEEE/ACM International Symposium on Cluster, Cloud and Grid Computing* (pp. 961-970). New York: IEEE. 10.1109/CCGrid.2015.37

Cheminod, M., Durante, L., Seno, L., & Valenzano, A. (2018). Performance evaluation and modeling of an industrial application-layer firewall. *IEEE Transactions on Industrial Informatics*, *14*(5), 2159–2170. doi:10.1109/TII.2018.2802903

Colbert, E. J., & Hutchinson, S. (2016). Intrusion detection in industrial control systems. In E. J. Colbert, & A. Kott (Eds.), *Cyber-security of SCADA and other industrial control systems* (pp. 209–237). Cham, Switzerland: Springer. doi:10.1007/978-3-319-32125-7_11

Derbyshire, R., Green, B., Prince, D., Mauthe, A., & Hutchison, D. (2018). An analysis of cyber security attack taxonomies. In *Proceedings of the IEEE European Symposium on Security and Privacy Workshops* (pp. 153-161). New York: IEEE. 10.1109/EuroSPW.2018.00028

Gao, J., Liu, J., Rajan, B., Nori, R., Fu, B., Xiao, Y., ... Chen, C. L. P. (2014). SCADA communication and security issues. *Security and Communication Networks*, *7*(1), 175–194. doi:10.1002ec.698

García-Teodoro, P., Díaz-Verdejo, J., Maciá-Fernández, G., & Vázquez, E. (2009). Anomaly-based network intrusion detection: Techniques, systems, and challenges. *Computers & Security*, *28*(1-2), 18–28. doi:10.1016/j.cose.2008.08.003

Hemsley, K. E., & Fisher, R. E. (2018). *History of industrial control system cyber incidents* (Idaho National Laboratory Technical Report INL/CON-18-44411-Revision-2). Retrieved October 15, 2019, from https://www.osti.gov/servlets/purl/1505628

Industrial Control Systems Cyber Emergency Response Team (ICS-CERT). (2016a). *ICS-CERT annual vulnerability coordination report*. Retrieved November 10, 2019, from https://www.hsdl.org/?abstract&did=804703

Industrial Control Systems Cyber Emergency Response Team (ICS-CERT). (2016b). *Recommended practice: Improving industrial control system cybersecurity with Defense-in-Depth strategies*. Retrieved November 10, 2019, from https://www.hsdl.org/?abstract&did=797585

Lei, H., Chen, B., Butler-Purry, K. L., & Singh, C. (2018). Security and reliability perspectives in cyber-physical smart grids. In *Proceedings of the IEEE Innovative Smart Grid Technologies-Asia (ISGT Asia)* (pp. 42-47). New York: IEEE. 10.1109/ISGT-Asia.2018.8467794

Li, W., Xie, L., Deng, Z., & Wang, Z. (2016). False sequential logic attack on SCADA system and its physical impact analysis. *Computers & Security*, *58*, 149–159. doi:10.1016/j.cose.2016.01.001

Mackintosh, M., Epiphaniou, G., Al-Khateeb, H., Burnham, K., Pillai, P., & Hammoudeh, M. (2019). Preliminaries of orthogonal layered defence using functional and assurance controls in industrial control systems. *Journal of Sensor and Actuator Networks*, *8*(1), 14. doi:10.3390/jsan8010014

Mahan, R. E., Fluckiger, J. D., Clements, S. L., Tews, C., Burnette, J. R., Goranson, C. A., & Kirkham, H. (2011). *Secure data transfer guidance for industrial control and SCADA systems*. Richland, WA: Pacific Northwest National Lab. doi:10.2172/1030885

Markovic-Petrovic, J., & Stojanovic, M. (2013). Analysis of SCADA system vulnerabilities to DDoS attacks. In *Proceedings of the 11th International Conference on Telecommunications in Modern Satellite Cable and Broadcasting Services - TELSIKS 2013* (vol. 2, pp. 591-594). New York: IEEE. 10.1109/TELSKS.2013.6704448

Markovic-Petrovic, J., & Stojanovic, M. (2014). An improved risk assessment method for SCADA information security. *Elektronika ir Elektrotechnika, 20*(7), 69–72. doi:10.5755/j01.eee.20.7.8027

Markovic-Petrovic, J. D., Stojanovic, M. D., & Bostjancic Rakas, S. V. (2019). A fuzzy AHP approach for security risk assessment in SCADA networks. *Advances in Electrical and Computer Engineering, 19*(3), 69–74. doi:10.4316/AECE.2019.03008

National Institute of Standards and Technology (NIST). (2012). *Guide for conducting risk assessments (NIST Special Publication 800-30 Rev. 1)*. Gaithersburg, MD: U.S. NIST.

Nazir, S., Patel, S., & Patel, D. (2017). Autonomic computing architecture for SCADA cyber security. *International Journal of Cognitive Informatics and Natural Intelligence, 11*(4), 66–79. doi:10.4018/IJCINI.2017100104

Nicholson, A., Webber, S., Dyer, S., Patel, T., & Janicke, H. (2012). SCADA security in the light of cyber-warfare. *Computers & Security, 31*(4), 418–436. doi:10.1016/j.cose.2012.02.009

Obregon, L. (2015). *Secure architecture for industrial control systems*. SANS Institute. Retrieved November 16, 2019, from https://www.sans.org/reading-room/whitepapers/ICS/secure-architecture-industrial-control-systems-36327

Sajid, A., Abbas, H., & Saleem, K. (2016). Cloud-assisted IoT-based SCADA systems security: A review of the state of the art and future challenges. *IEEE Access: Practical Innovations, Open Solutions, 4*, 1375–1384. doi:10.1109/ACCESS.2016.2549047

Scarfone, K., & Mell, P. (2007). *Guide to intrusion detection and prevention systems (IDPS) (NIST Special Publication 800-94)*. Gaithersburg, MD: U.S. National Institute of Standards and Technology.

Stojanović, M. D., Boštjančič Rakas, S. V., & Marković-Petrović, J. D. (2019). SCADA systems in the cloud and fog environments: Migration scenarios and security issues. *FACTA UNIVERSITATIS Series: Electronics and Energetics, 32*(3), 345–358.

Stouffer, K., Pillitteri, V., Lightman, S., Abrams, M., & Hahn, A. (2015). *Guide to industrial control systems (ICS) security (NIST Special Publication 800-82 Rev. 2)*. Gaithersburg, MD: U.S. National Institute of Standards and Technology. doi:10.6028/NIST.SP.800-82r2

Tuptuk, N., & Hailes, S. (2018). Security of smart manufacturing systems. *Journal of Manufacturing Systems, 47*, 93–106. doi:10.1016/j.jmsy.2018.04.007

ADDITIONAL READING

Alguliyev, R., Imamverdiyev, Y., & Sukhostat, L. (2018). Cyber-physical systems and their security issues. *Computers in Industry*, *100*, 212–223. doi:10.1016/j.compind.2018.04.017

Coffey, K., Maglaras, L. A., Smith, R., Janicke, H., Ferrag, M., & Derhab, A. … Yousaf, A. (2018). Vulnerability assessment of cyber security for SCADA systems. In S. Parkinson, A. Crampton, & R. Hill (Eds.), Guide to Vulnerability Analysis for Computer Networks and Systems (pp. 59-80). Cham, Switzerland: Springer.

Ding, D., Han, Q.-L., Xiang, Y., Ge, X., & Zhang, X.-M. (2018). A survey on security control and attack detection for industrial cyber-physical systems. *Neurocomputing*, *275*, 1674–1683. doi:10.1016/j.neucom.2017.10.009

Qassim, Q., Jamil, N., Daud, M., & Che Hasan, H. (2019). Towards implementing scalable and reconfigurable SCADA security testbed in power system environment. *International Journal of Critical Infrastructures*, *15*(2), 91–120. doi:10.1504/IJCIS.2019.098834

Rubio, J. E., Alcaraz, C., Roman, R., & Lopez, J. (2019). Current cyber-defense trends in industrial control systems. *Computers & Security*, *87*, 1–12. doi:10.1016/j.cose.2019.06.015

Sun, C.-C., Hahn, A., & Liu, C.-C. (2018). Cyber security of a power grid: State-of-the-art. *International Journal of Electrical Power & Energy Systems*, *99*, 45–56. doi:10.1016/j.ijepes.2017.12.020

Tsuchiya, A., Fraile, F., Koshijima, I., Órtiz, A., & Poler, R. (2018). Software defined networking firewall for industry 4.0 manufacturing systems. *Journal of Industrial Engineering and Management*, *11*(2), 318–333. doi:10.3926/jiem.2534

Volkova, A., Niedermeier, M., Basmadjian, R., & De Meer, H. (2018). Security challenges in control network protocols: A survey. *IEEE Communications Surveys and Tutorials*, *21*(1), 619–639. doi:10.1109/COMST.2018.2872114

KEY TERMS AND DEFINITIONS

Defense-in-Depth: Strategy of using multiple security measures in several layers to protect the information system.

Firewall: A hardware/software capability that limits access between networks and/or systems in accordance with a specific security policy.

Intrusion Detection System: A hardware and/or software product that monitors network traffic for possible security breaches and issues alerts when suspicious activity is discovered. Possible security breach can be either attacks from outside the organization or attacks or malfeasance from within organizations.

Intrusion Prevention System: A hardware and/or software product that block suspicious activity attempting to stop detected possible incidents. Basically, this system is extension of intrusion detection system.

Risk Assessment: The process of identifying, estimating, and prioritizing risks. This process comprises threat and vulnerability analyses and considers risk mitigation.

Risk Management: The processes to manage information security risk to organizational functionality and assets, individuals, other organizations, etc. Risk management includes risk analysis, assessing risk, risk strategy choosing, security measurements implementation and monitoring risk over time.

Security Zone: A collection of information systems connected by one, or more, internal networks under the control of a single authority and one security policy. The systems may be structured by physical proximity or by function and may be independent of location.

Chapter 3
Cybersecurity of Industrial Internet of Things

Gordana Gardašević
Faculty of Electrical Engineering, University of Banja Luka, Bosnia and Herzegovina

Lazar Berbakov
https://orcid.org/0000-0002-9628-2967
Mihailo Pupin Institute, University of Belgrade, Serbia

Aleksandar Mastilović
https://orcid.org/0000-0002-9130-619X
Communications Regulatory Agency BH, Bosnia and Herzegovina

ABSTRACT

The Internet of Things (IoT) is an emerging and even revolutionary technology with an immense impact on our everyday life. The Industrial Internet of Things (IIoT) is a fast-growing technology that increases productivity and efficiency by combining the IoT platform with an existing industrial environment. IIoT networks are one of the main pillars for the success of the future Industry 4.0 and Cyber-Physical System (CPS) paradigm. The IIoT ecosystem represents a network of connected industrial devices that exchange and analyze collected data to enable new insights into industrial processes. Recently, intensive research activities have focused on cybersecurity issues for the IIoT. This chapter addresses the critical components of the IIoT security framework by analyzing the relevant aspects and providing an overview of state-of-the-art activities in this field. This chapter also discusses the IIoT architectural structure, applications, and underlying networking technologies, with a particular focus on security challenges and standardization activities.

DOI: 10.4018/978-1-7998-2910-2.ch003

INTRODUCTION

The Internet of Things (IoT) refers to a global phenomenon that provides technology to support emerging applications in every single part of the worldwide society. Approaching the 21st century, many accessible technology buzzwords, besides the IoT, find a way to create their own space in the engineering community, such as Big Data, Artificial Intelligence (AI), Machine Learning (ML), Smart Industry 4.0, etc. (Institute of Electrical and Electronics Engineers [IEEE], 2017). Humanity has decided to collect data on everything, to correlate them, thus achieving in-depth and hidden knowledge on every parameter, process, or behavior. The Deep Knowledge unlocks possibilities to analyze, predict, and optimize processes and services at homes, cities, in an industrial environment, etc. It creates artificial smartness in the ambiance of conventional decision makings and non-optimized resource usage. Not only are all these technologies and solutions related to the IoT, but also many aspects of modern lifestyles and regular services (e.g., smart cities and local urban services). These opportunities enable the Digitalization and even more extensive - Digital Transformation, which affects not only the engineering aspect but also the social aspect of everyday life. These cumulative results of existing modern solutions create the new industrial and business environment. The 4th industrial revolution or Industry 4.0 launches the transition from automated manufacturing toward an intelligent manufacturing concept (Hermann, Pentek, & Otto, 2015). The Industry 4.0 concept envisions that Industries of the Future will rely on a network of connecting factories, machines, and other parts of the value chain. Such a network is used to effectively exchange information among different parts of the system, which results in improved industrial processes and reduced waste. Nowadays, assembled products enhanced with, e.g., Radio-Frequency Identification (RFID) tags, provide additional functionalities so that they can easily be identified and localized across the manufacturing line. In this way, an original product forwards information to the production line and to different parts of the production processes depending on their current status. This approach is particularly suitable for Small and Medium-sized Enterprises (SMEs), thus providing increased flexibility and the capability to produce smaller batches that adhere to the customer's preferences.

For practical applications and scenarios, the IoT architecture enables massive sensors deployment within the measurement and detection network, which can sense the environment (Gardašević et al., 2017). From that perspective, the next step is an ability to create a proper mechanism for an automated reaction for predefined and learned triggers that mimics the reflex response of a living being. Systems with these abilities are named "responsive" and represent an advanced level of "smart" systems. From the telecommunications' perspective and depending on the type of application and its technical requirements, two types of sensors deployment may be distinguished: Massive Machine-to-Machine (mM2M) communications and Critical Machine-to-Machine communications (cM2M). The most promising applications and scenarios for the IoT are in the industrial and finance sectors. In these sectors, there is a strong need for optimization and high investment prospect for advanced research and new applications.

The Industrial Internet of Things (IIoT) is a fast-growing technology that increases productivity and efficiency by combining the IoT platform with an existing industrial environment. IIoT networks are one of the main pillars for the success of the future Industry 4.0 and Cyber-Physical System (CPS) paradigm. The IIoT ecosystem represents a network of connected industrial devices that exchange and analyze collected data to enable new insights into industrial processes. As a result, it provides significant cuts in operational costs, reduces waste, improves quality, and increase the overall safety of industrial systems. Also, predictive maintenance, on its own, can bring significant benefits in terms of reduction of operation costs while also ensuring smooth and uninterrupted operation of critical infrastructure.

Individually, by optimizing operations among a large number of increasingly autonomous control systems and devices, the IIoT can achieve a profound impact on many industry domains, where smart factories, smart supply chain, critical urban infrastructures, and logistics are among the most notable cases (Xu, Yu, Griffith, & Golmie, 2018). On the other side, the expansion of the IIoT brings new security concerns and makes the risk assessment more difficult. The IIoT takes an essential role in the business processes in the industry, which are more sensitive or even critical for industrial production. By introducing the more values and more money in the process, more criminal activities appear, thereby increasing the cybersecurity risk at all levels of the industrial system. Apart from threats of losing revenue, brand impact and liability, in some IoT applications like healthcare and autonomous driving, even human lives can be at risk.

With the increase of connected objects, the availability of mass-produced sensors and devices, and by the proliferation of M2M services, the potential cyber-attack risks become more significant than before. If the security policy in the IIoT does not assume and implement well all possible threats and dangers, that can have a substantial impact on cybersecurity. It allows hackers to access the core of the industrial systems. Previously, communication networks that are responsible for monitoring and controlling industrial systems were completely separate from the rest of the ICT infrastructure.

New frontiers in communication technologies, such as 5G and beyond 5G, Software Defined Networking (SDN), edge and cloud computing, ML and AI, play a crucial role in the architectural design of future IIoT framework. The Internet Protocol version 6 (IPv6) is becoming a de facto enabling protocol for the global IoT connectivity. For a successful implementation of an IIoT network, there is an urgent need for a standardized, layered architecture and protocol suite explicitly designed to meet the requirements of IIoT applications and security models. Relevant bodies, such as International Telecommunication Union - Telecommunication Standardization Sector (ITU-T), Institute of Electrical and Electronics Engineers (IEEE), European Telecommunications Standards Institute (ETSI), World Economic Forum, National Institute of Standards and Technology (NIST), Industrial Internet Consortium (IIC), Global System for Mobile communication (GSM) Association, IoT Security Foundation (IoTSF), Internet Engineering Task Force – IPv6 over the Time Slotted Channel Hopping mode (IETF 6TiSCH) group, have recently intensified their activities in this field.

The objective of this chapter is to address the critical components of the IIoT security framework by analyzing the relevant aspects and providing an overview of state-of-the-art activities in this field. This chapter discusses the IIoT architectural structure, applications, and underlying networking technologies, with a particular focus on security challenges and standardization activities.

BACKGROUND

Traditional industrial systems, such as Supervisory Control and Data Acquisition (SCADA), have played a significant role in industrial environments for decades. Typical industrial applications exploit fieldbus systems, each having its ecosystem and therefore not supporting the interoperability. In the last decade, standards that are based on wireless technologies, such as Wireless Sensor and Actuator Network (WSAN) and purposely designed for the industry (e.g., WirelessHART, ISA100.11a, ZWave), have been released (Rodenas-Herraiz, Garcia-Sanchez, Garcia-Sanchez, & Garcia-Haro, 2013). However, these systems are not designed to provide the "end-to-end" Internet Protocol (IP) connectivity and scalability, which is a prerequisite for the convergence of Operational Technology (OT, i.e., traditional hardware and software systems) and Information Technology (IT, i.e., advanced computing, data aggregation/analysis and ubiquitous communication systems).

The IIoT is a broad paradigm, but the most common definition is that the IIoT refers to interconnected sensors, actuators, and other devices to provide industrial applications, including manufacturing and energy management. This connectivity allows for data collection, exchange, and analysis, potentially facilitating improvements in productivity and efficiency as well as other economic benefits (Boyes, Hallaq, Cunningham, & Watson, 2018). In an IIoT system, the working and industrial environments experience characteristics (e.g., dust, heat, water) that make reliable operations challenging. Such operations require taking various aspects of real-time wireless communications into account (e.g., packet delay, throughput requirements of each flow, heterogeneity of wireless channels, security, and privacy guarantees). Wireless links are also affected by surrounding electromagnetic interference from other wireless devices. Therefore, these phenomena should be taken into consideration while designing the overall security framework.

Gartner, Inc. (2017) predicts that by 2020, 25% of identified attacks on enterprises will involve IoT systems. Moreover, Gartner reports a total of 5 billion IoT devices today with the potential to grow up to 500% in the next 5 years. The growing presence of the IoT, and specifically the IIoT, caused the growing size of the attacks, but this trend means both a threat and an opportunity (Johnson, 2017). The past decade has launched the rapid development of critical technologies, such as IoT, AI, Big Data, and Blockchain. Advanced attack techniques, such as distributed attacks, ML-based and AI-based protection mitigating and evolving, make cybersecurity personnel incapable of defending the most of systems including critical ones. The evolution of the cyber defense and the usage of advanced ML and AI algorithms, which can detect the most attack patterns including zero-day threats, have changed the context of cybersecurity, in parallel with the evolution of cyber-threats based on AI and ML techniques (IEEE, 2017).

A significant barrier to successful IIoT adoption lies in cybersecurity issues that make it extremely difficult to harness its full potential. The IIoT systems dramatically increase the cyber-attack risk (by introducing new security threats due to newly connected devices and protocols, thus making them more vulnerable to interference), the disruption of process controls, the theft of intellectual property, the loss of corporate data, and the industrial espionage. IIoT systems are not only possible targets for cyber-attacks; the system architecture and full deployment is a perfect tool for building distributed zombie networks - the botnet platforms for launching intense and unpredictable cyber-attacks to the third-party targets. One of the relevant examples was the Mirai Botnet in 2016 when a few thousands of IoT devices were infected by converting into zombies, which later deploy a massive Distributed Denial-of-Service (DDoS) attack to a designated target. As a consequence, world-famous online services such as Netflix, CNN, Twitter, and many others were significantly affected. After this event, also confirmed by Gartner in a few its surveys and reports in 2018, cybersecurity issues and risks remain the top barrier to successful IoT implementation. The classification of cyber-threats in IIoT systems can be performed by the IIoT Organization Layers (according to a physical location, device type or component type), by the IIoT Operational Level (according to functions and functionalities, benefits and logical operations), or by communications and applications protocols. Most of the cyber-threats types are related to the Internet or internal Transmission Control Protocol/Internet Protocol (TCP/IP) based systems, which means that all well-known cyber-attacks in TCP/IP protocol stack result in affecting some of the IIoT system's components, in a direct or indirect way.

In the context of vulnerability, the cyber-threat can cause issues in one or more fundamental cyber-security models, such as the Confidentiality, Integrity, and Availability (CIA) model. Various attacks differ in their goals; some of them aim at stealing information, while others aim at disturbing the system operations, or they cause stopping all operations, thus targeting the availability. The most common cyber-threat from this group is Denial-of-Services (DoS) and its advanced version DDoS. The IIoT ecosystem integrates heterogeneous networking technologies to provide the interconnection among various devices; therefore, the protection of the IIoT system from cyber-attacks is crucial. Moreover, cyber-attacks may cause not only information transmission delay and uncertainty, but also safety issues for humans, environment, and machines, as well.

The IIoT is still in its early stage, but with an enormous market potential. The lack of finalized standardization frameworks and the fact that companies often ship products to the market too fast usually results in poorly implemented security. Besides, security researchers often identify security vulnerabilities late, when the IoT devices are compromised in large quantities. Devices usually require a manual software update which makes the process of software update slow and in some cases even not feasible. Once the security mechanisms are implemented, a security subsystem monitors and analyzes all sensing, communications, and operations processes continuously in the (pseudo) real-time. Its main goal is to monitor the overall state of the industrial system and analyze the collected data to detect possible security violations and potential security threats. If such events are detected, predefined actions such as revoking device access can be performed automatically to prevent further damage promptly. The data collected during industrial manufacturing and production is valuable and privacy-sensitive, and as a consequence, IIoT systems are becoming valuable targets for attackers. To answer all these issues, it is crucial to understand interconnections between all components that form an IIoT environment and to design an overall cybersecurity framework.

INDUSTRIAL INTERNET OF THINGS (IIoT): ARCHITECTURE, TECHNOLOGIES, AND APPLICATIONS

The IIoT represents a natural step towards smart manufacturing and production, as well as an evolution from the distributed control systems thus introducing a higher level of automation, independence, self-regulation, and self-optimization to refine the process control. These benefits stem from the availability of real-time data obtained by connecting all the parts across the value chain, thus effectively enabling self-organization without explicit human intervention.

As previously mentioned in the Introduction, the Industry 4.0 leverage on advancements of IT and its symbiosis with operational and communication processes to improve the production automation and digitalization, which results in the more efficient production of improved quality and lower price. Although digitalization of industry has started well before the term Industry 4.0 is coined, the advances in cloud computing and availability of on-demand big data analysis along with 3D printing and augmented reality have enabled this new form of industrial process automation. Industry 4.0 is targeted in manufacturing industries, but its principles can also be applied to other types of industries. Industry 4.0 aims to increase business competitiveness by leveraging on the cooperation of different companies. Besides, productivity is expected to increase as a result of the reduction of operational costs and increasing efficiency. The cooperation among different stakeholders in the value chain can help to optimize the manufacturing processes.

Consequently, new job opportunities emerge since there is a strong need for highly valued jobs in engineering and data science that covers the existing gap found in traditional industries. Nevertheless, a portion of the currently existing jobs will be lost, since machines and artificial intelligence are going to replace them. Finally, the customer experience is expected to be significantly enhanced, since decision-makers can respond to the market needs faster, delivering products of better quality with lower costs.

IIoT Architecture

The IIoT describes a very complex system that combines automation, robotics, sensors, networking technologies and cloud-computing for analysis, optimization, and decision-making. The IIoT exists as a cumulative result of many advanced technologies, such as advanced robotics and CPS, ML and AI, big data, control theory, advanced distributed systems, cloud and edge computing, cognitive computing, semantic modeling, cybersecurity, machine-to-machine, and others. For simplification purposes and motivated by the protocol organization in computer networks, the IIoT architecture can be designed as the multi-layer stack structure (Hylving & Schultze, 2013):

- **Content Layer:** User interface devices (e.g., screens, tablets).
- **Service Layer**: Applications and middleware.
- **Network Layer:** Communication technologies, protocols.
- **Device Layer:** Hardware (e.g., CPS, sensors, actuators).

Similarly, Figure 1 illustrates the three-tier architecture of an IIoT system. It consists of the *Edge*, *Platform*, and *Enterprise* tier that are in charge of different functionalities related to data and control flows.

The *Edge* tier is responsible for collecting data from the edge nodes towards the edge gateway, and vice versa. The architecture of the edge tier is highly dependent on the specific use case that impacts the decision regarding the distribution and nature of the network. In simple scenarios, the Edge tier may contain only basic sensing or actuating devices, while in most IIoT use cases it represents the complex combinations of different sensors, actuators, as well as interfaces towards the legacy equipment.

The *Platform* tier serves the purpose of receiving, processing, and control from the enterprise tier towards the edge tier. It is used for the consolidation of the processes and the data coming from the edge tier. Furthermore, it provides management functionalities for various devices as well as general services, such as data access control, querying, and data analysis.

The *Enterprise* tier provides the domain-specific functionalities, such as those related to, e.g., energy sector, logistics, process industry, and healthcare. It is aimed to enable the interface towards the end-users, such as managers, operators, and specialists. The enterprise tier receives the data from the edge and platform tier, while also generating the control actions based on different rules specific to the given domain.

Communication Technologies for IIoT

Communication requirements for various IIoT domains and applications have to be carefully studied and designed, particularly in terms of Quality of Service (QoS) parameters, such as latency, throughput, packet loss, determinism, availability, reliability, security, and privacy. Industrial applications span a broad range of domains and services: industrial automation, connected factories, smart logistics management, production facilities, retail services, manufacturing, and transportation systems. Each particular

Figure 1. Three-tier IIoT system architecture

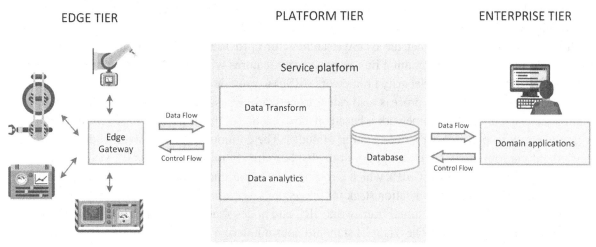

application has different networking design requirements. Some applications require reliable low latency communications, while others demand low power consumption or long-range wireless communication.

The *Physical layer* of an IIoT protocol stack includes various devices such as sensors and actuators, manufacturing equipment, gateways, and storage/control devices. The *Network layer* should provide a reliable communication platform based on wireless networking technologies: Bluetooth Low Energy (BLE), RFID, WSAN, IEEE 802.11ah (Wi-Fi Low Power), Low Power Wide Area Network (LPWAN), 5G and Beyond 5G networks. Moreover, the increasing demand for Machine-Type Communications (MTC) has resulted in many emerging communication architectures, such as SDN, Network Function Virtualization (NFV), Network Slicing (as part of 5G networking), that can provide the necessary support for industrial applications (Lu & Xu, 2018).

IEEE 802.15.4 standard is designed mainly for low power and Low Rate Wireless Personal Area Networks (LR-WPANs) and covers functionalities of physical (PHY) and Media Access Control (MAC) layers (IEEE, 2011; Kushalnagar, Montenegro, & Schumacher, 2015). The IETF group has developed several IP-based protocols on the top of IEEE 802.15.4: IPv6 over Low-Power WPANs (6LoWPAN) (IEEE, 2011), Routing Protocol for Low Power and Lossy Network (RPL) (Winter et al., 2012), Constrained Application Protocol (CoAP) (Shelby, Hartke, & Bormann, 2014). ZigBee is one of the most popular solutions, particularly for home automation and smart city applications (Buratti et al., 2016). LPWAN technologies, such as Long Range WAN (LoRaWAN), Narrowband-IoT (NB-IoT) and Long Term Evolution – Machine type communication (LTE-M), are becoming promising solutions for IIoT applications due to low complexity, energy efficiency, robustness, higher device density, and excellent coverage. For ultra-reliable and high-performance IIoT applications, such as process monitoring and automotive applications, 5G New Radio (NR) architecture can provide enhanced mobile broadband (eMBB) and ultra-reliable and low-latency communication (URLLC).

Recently, the IETF IPv6 over the TSCH mode of the IEEE 802.15.4e (6TiSCH) working group has standardized a set of protocols to support low power industrial-grade IPv6 networks (Vilajosana, Watteyne, Vučinić, Chang, & Pister, 2019). The 6TiSCH is rooted in the Time Slotted Channel Hopping (TSCH) mode of the IEEE 802.15.4-2015 standard and provides high immunity against multipath fading and external interference. This model provides determinism, reduces power consumption, and increases reliability. The 6TiSCH supports various multi-hop topologies where the RPL protocol performs routing, while the IPv6 connectivity is provided through 6LoWPAN functionalities (Vasiljević & Gardašević, 2019). Figure 2 illustrates the 6TiSCH reference protocol stack.

It should be emphasized that the 6TiSCH architecture provides security mechanisms and secure lightweight join processes combining link-layer security features with a secure joining procedure using the CoAP. It defines Minimal Security Framework (MSF) to provide support for a new device to securely join a 6TiSCH network. This process also refers to network access authentication, authorization, and parameter distribution. The framework is based on the existence of the Join Registrar/Coordinator (JRC), a central entity responsible for authentication of nodes. The communication between nodes and JRC is carried out via Join Proxy (JP), a neighbor node that has already joined the network. MSF also defines the Constrained Join Protocol (CoJP), which is responsible for parameter distribution needed to configure the rest of the 6TiSCH communication stack for the secure association. Additional security mechanisms may be added on top of this minimal framework. JRC and nodes share the symmetric cryptographic key called pre-shared key (PSK). The 6TiSCH standard does not define the provisioning of PSK and leaves it to designers for implementation.

IIoT Applications

As discussed in the previous section, the IIoT is expected to be one of the main pillars for the successful adoption of IoT benefits in various industrial areas, as shown in Figure 3. The next section presents some typical applications where the IIoT can bring significant benefits and increase their efficiency.

Figure 2. 6TiSCH protocol stack

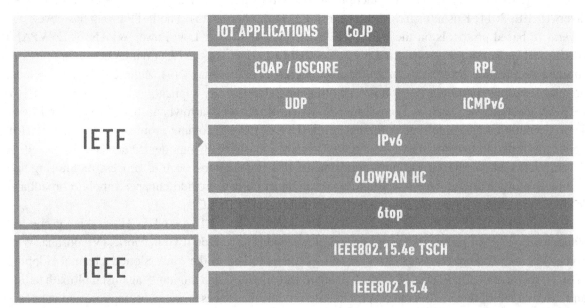

Energy Sector and Utilities

The domain of energy and utilities, which is strongly related to other industry domains and everyday lives, has a particular interest in implementing IIoT principles to provide more reliable service prone to external threats. The peaks of energy consumption are known to harm energy production, distribution management, and environment, in particular, if thermal power plants need to be constructed to satisfy the peak demands. Furthermore, renewable energy sources have energy generation patterns that do not match the energy demand in time, making them unsuitable for dealing with this issue. One of the solutions is to adopt a more intelligent demand-side energy management using the demand-response (DR) programs (Bahrami & Sheikhi, 2016). This approach, which employs energy load curtailment and rescheduling, allows decreasing the energy consumption during peak periods. To stimulate the end-users to reschedule or decrease their consumption, economic benefits such as energy price reduction, which energy service companies (ESCOs) offer to their customers. This type of peak management provides considerable benefits to ESCOs, which now do not need to buy additional energy with high prices on the open energy market and use additional capacity of the distribution networks. The large industries already applied the Demand-Response model, but its application in the residential sector, which can be characterized by a large number of users with low energy consumption, is still to be deployed. The application requests a smart meter's deployment in the residential sector in households, which would

Figure 3. Applications of IoT in industries

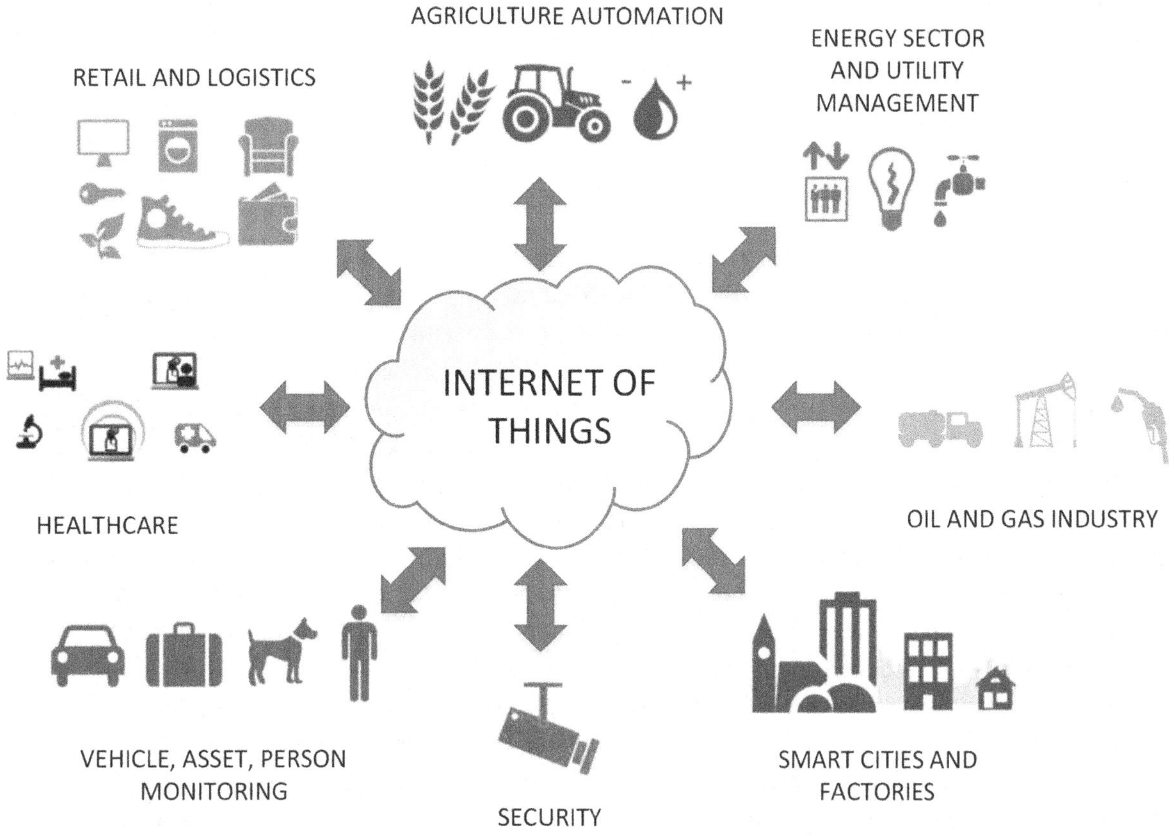

allow the precise and more frequent measurements of total energy consumption. The possibility to automatically control the household equipment and reschedule of their operation to non-peak periods requires devices, such as the so-called smart plugs to be installed and controlled through a suitable web or mobile applications. Nevertheless, these new types of smart meters and actuators are expected to have even lower prices in the future, making such connectivity between energy production and consumption points more appealing and cost-effective.

Oil and Gas Industry

Oil and Gas industry is highly dependent on advanced technology and data analysis for exploration as well as for the regular operation of drilling machines and related equipment (Li, Wan, Zhang, Li, & Jiang, 2018). It requires a vast number of sensors, actuators, as well as collaborative data collection (Berbakov, Anton-Haro, & Matamoros, 2014) and processing tools and software which allow more efficient monitoring and process automation. Previously, before the advent of cloud computing and due to the limited availability of data storage and processing power, a vast amount of collected data was dropped since there was no processing power capable of analyzing it on time. Now, since the costs of renting storage and processing have decreased significantly, such data can be processed, and more informed decisions can be made based on intelligent machine learning algorithms. This capability, in addition to wireless sensors and high throughput communication links, has resulted in more predictable exploration, thus reducing the costs and enabling more efficient fieldwork.

In addition to improving the efficiency of exploration, such a large amount of data collected from the machinery allow predictive maintenance algorithms to be run to reduce potential downtimes and outage periods. The interconnection of heterogeneous devices, machines, and sensors enables new ways of interaction among different system components, resulting in a more reliable operation with self-configuration capabilities.

Logistics and Retail Industry

Before the introduction of the IoT paradigm, a sector of logistics was one of the first which has adopted the principles of IIoT. Before the development of RFID tags, the barcodes were used to track the current location of packages. Nevertheless, using barcode scanners still required manual work, and further development in this field was necessary. On the other hand, by embedding RFID tags into packages, RFID readers were able to track multiple packages and stacks simultaneously, which improved the accuracy and processing speed. This approach enables automatic storage of information related to items, as well as updating their location, making all this information available to other parts of a logistics service provider on time (Zhang, 2018). Also, by embedding additional sensors, such as those capable of measuring temperature and humidity, critical information regarding an unsuitable storage environment can be sent before the sensitive stock is damaged. Due to possibly large number of sensor nodes, which are usually battery operated, energy efficiency of communication schemes becomes one of the main challenges to solve (Berbakov, Anton-Haro, & Matamoros, 2013).

For the efficient operation of forklift vehicles in large warehouses, IIoT capabilities promise considerable benefits in the reduction of accidents and reduced times for the transfer of selected packages. By using a collection of location beacons, RFID tags, RFID readers and data stored in warehouse ERP software, it is possible to employ intelligent routing algorithms to instruct the drivers to take the optimal route from the actual location. Besides, by using radar and laser sensors on the forklift, it is possible to detect the presence of obstacles and pedestrians and prevent possible collisions, thus reducing the number of accidents.

Similar to the logistics industry, the retail sector can benefit from significant savings by incorporating IIoT principles into its processes and organization. Personal advertising and adaptive in-store experience powered by RFID tags and Bluetooth beacons represent one of the main benefits for the retail sector, where both retailers and customers can gain from the application of IIoT concepts. By implementing such an approach, retailers achieve more sales, whereas the customer has a better user experience and less time needed for shopping.

Healthcare

In recent years, many countries in the world have experienced an increase in the aging population, and a rise in life expectancy. These trends have significantly contributed to disabilities and increased incidence rate of chronic diseases. In the past, doctors needed to visit personally the disabled and elderly people that cannot make their way to the hospitals, which puts additional burden on the already limited healthcare budget. Nevertheless, recent advances in wireless communications and the development of inexpensive miniature sensors paved the way for the development of IoT solutions for personalized remote healthcare (Rodrigues et al., 2018). Sensors, such as heart rate, blood pressure, oxygen concentration, electrocardiogram (ECG) and inertial sensors (Berbakov et al., 2019), can be provided to the patients with the associated wireless communication hub. These devices are then used by the patients to take their daily measurements after what the remote services collect the data, where can be automatically analyzed and sent to the doctors if anomalous behavior is detected.

This approach, sometimes referred to as Ambient Assisted Living (AAL), allows the elderly and disabled to live independently for as long as possible in their own homes, thus having a better quality of life. At the same time, it results in the reduction of hospitalization costs and provides support for doctors to serve a more significant number of patients at the same time.

The previous examples of the application of IIoT in a different domain demonstrate how the collected data may be classified as highly private (e.g., customer's behavior in retail industry and healthcare records) and of critical importance (e.g., energy and utility provider). Unauthorized access to such data can have unprecedented consequences, which may not be even envisioned nowadays since the industries mentioned above often rely on legacy systems that cannot be accessed outside of the organization.

SECURITY AND PRIVACY ISSUES IN IIoT

IIoT solutions may have constrained system resources and it is a challenging task to provide support for system safety and real-time execution. These factors may not allow the implementation of all security measures and controls to their fullest extent (as required by the "Defense-in-Depth" strategy). The security program implementation should take into account all required functional and non-functional aspects of the system behavior, also including their relative priorities. In order to analyze and discuss different security issues, it is necessary to define the essential components of information assurance. These are: *confidentiality, integrity, authentication, availability,* and *non-repudiation*, although not all of them have to be provided to satisfy the information security of a particular organization. The security issues may appear in various forms: from the physical device attacks perspective including wired and wireless scanning, protocol attacks, authentication attacks, DoS, to the application layer attacks including the manipulation of operating system vulnerabilities, access control, and application-level attacks. Depending on the particular application, some of the perspectives may be more relevant than the others. Therefore, a careful analysis of the IIoT architectural design is required. The secure boot approach, which employs cryptographic code signing techniques, ensures that a device can only execute code deployed by the device manufacturer, or other trusted party. In such a way, it prevents hackers from replacing the original code with the malicious one. Nevertheless, not all IIoT manufacturers employ this approach.

Another critical aspect of security is a *mutual authentication*, which ensures that the IoT device is the legitimate member of the system before it can start transmitting or receiving the data from the network, thus preventing the situation where data may come from the fraudulent source. In addition to authentication, secure communication is the main prerequisite for any successful IIoT implementation. The encryption of data sent over the networks, through various layers of the IIoT protocol stack, ensures that only those with the valid decryption key can access the data.

It is important to emphasize that the majority of IIoT devices (and IoT devices, in general) are small and low power devices, with constrained processing and memory resources. That limits the capability to use regular crypto-algorithms and protocols within the TCP/IP stack, to protect communications and devices. The IIoT uses a limited version of the public key infrastructure (PKI), cryptographic protocols and crypto keys makes a considerable cybersecurity risk and unwanted opportunity for attackers. The IIoT security policy has to be even more strictly compared to the computer network's security policy. For some applications, the security policy makes eliminatory requirements for the deployment technologies (e.g., the IIoT system for nuclear power plants). That means a redefinition of the security policy by requesting the convergence of IT and OT trustworthiness into the IIoT trustworthiness, and precise verification on security (Mouratidis & Diamantopoulou, 2018), privacy, reliability, resilience, and safety.

Numerous security challenges in the development of the IIoT have led to the proposal of various mitigation strategies. A major security challenge in the IIoT is providing the systematic approach while taking into account all connections between IIoT components and accompanying ecosystem, both at the physical and cyber level. In responding to this challenge, the IIoT security framework must be designed in a proactive manner.

The factory, which is enhanced by advanced sensors, communications systems, and data storage, has to raise the industrial production and level of productivity to the advanced level, thus introducing the operational excellence. The term "operational excellence" involves a few important aspects and benefits. However, these benefits could be targeted by cyber-threats, thus disturbing the regular working regime in the factory or any other complex industrial production system.

Operational excellence is based on the following:

1. Overall equipment effectiveness.
2. Sales and growth.
3. Data-driven improvements.
4. Performance benchmarking.
5. Maximization of returns on IIoT investment and revenue.

Standardization

The IIoT commercial use is in an early stage, and the standardization process is still running. IIoT end-point devices and architectures play a crucial role in the complete cybersecurity policy and strategy for the IIoT-based applications and the industrial system as a whole. This becomes even more true with the increased level of IIoT-based applications in the conventional industrial systems. The IIoT environment carries an increased risk for cyber-attacks, and this risk rises together with new deployments. In parallel, IIoT systems with a massive number of devices could create zombie networks for the deployment of very intensive DDoS attacks on third-party systems. The risk becomes even bigger if it assumes the future development of IIoT systems, including CPSs, Cloud/Edge/Fog computing, and other functionalities.

Many international organizations, such as the ITU, the IEEE, the IETF, the IIC, the OpenFog Consortium, and many other international, regional and national engineering associations, working groups and standardization institutions, work intensively on purpose-specific solutions to establish cybersecurity framework for the IIoT applications based on modern techniques and technologies.

The IIoT cybersecurity framework is a multilayer framework which interoperates with existing solutions and technologies, particularly with the TCP/IP stack (including both, IPv4 and IPv6). It also includes modification and upgrade of existing communications protocols for the specific working regime (e.g., low-duty cycle, low bit rate needs), design of new applications layer protocols for specific operations, and many others. The fundamental challenge for these activities is the design of efficient cryptographic algorithms that are applicable in the context of various constraints associated with the IIoT and largely heterogeneous end-point devices and their applications. Finding appropriate solutions and incorporating them into standards and protocols is essential for the IIoT matching their massive deployment in industrial processes (Wollschlaeger, Sauter, & Jasperneite, 2017). Therefore, traditional cybersecurity techniques might fail. The IIoT cybersecurity techniques should be reliable, IIoT application-specific, power, energy and hardware limitation-aware. The cryptography algorithms might delay the handling of core industrial function which is not allowed in time-critical industrial processes. The future vision for the Fog Computing-based IIoT systems aims to provide the real-time analysis and sensors reading by moving data acquisition, transfer, storing, analyzing and control closer to the network edge where the sensors and actuators, as well as the observed industrial process are located (Tang et al., 2017).

IIoT Cyber-Attacks Classes

IIoT cybersecurity shares the part of the same or very similar threats as the conventional TCP/IP communication system, but other threats are particularly related to the industrial environment and the IIoT architecture. From the perspective of industrial structure and possible targets in intelligent industrial systems, the cyber-threats are organized in classes:

1. Industrial Control Systems (ICS).
2. Distributed Control Systems (DCS).
3. Programmable Logic Controllers (PLC).
4. Supervisory Control and Data Acquisition (SCADA).
5. Human-Machine Interface (HMI).

Additional adoption of the TCP/IP-based connectivity for establishing communications between various industrial systems and devices has increased the entire cybersecurity risk. From the conventional perspective, the cyber-threats can be organized in classes depending on targeting layer and protocols, which describes the following section.

IIoT-Specific Cyber-Attacks

The structural organization of an IIoT system is used for the cyber-threats segmentation. Figure 4 illustrates a three-layer organization (Atzori, Iera, & Morabito, 2010). There are other multi-layers approaches, but in general, they share the same functional organization and operations.

The Device or *Sensing layer* is responsible for sensing data and objects, including a wide range of hardware nodes: sensors, actuators, processors, data storage. This layer has its specific functions and operation, which influence the preferred cyber-attack types and techniques. At this layer, the attackers focus primarily on confidentiality trying to steal the data and collect the added value. There are some examples of cyber-attacks targeting aspects of integrity and availability, but in general, at this layer, these issues are not common.

Sensing layer prevalent cyber-threats are: *Replay attacks*, *Timing attacks*, *Node capture attacks*, *Malicious Data attacks*, and *Side-Channel attacks* (Lu & L. D. Xu, 2018).

The Replay attack is the attack on the (Industrial) IoT system where an attacker eavesdrops secured communications channel, intercepts data streams. An attacker could delay original messages or resends them to misdirect receivers, thus passively using the data stream copy keeping the original stream untouched or blocking the designated receiver to get stream. This cyber-attack is similar to the conventional "Man-in-the-Middle" attack, but consequences and effects could be very different. The prevention and defense techniques are based on the mutual authentication operation using the proper session key, which is randomly generated on both sides of the communications channel. The generated keys are only valid

Figure 4. Three-layer model for the (Industrial) Internet of Things architecture

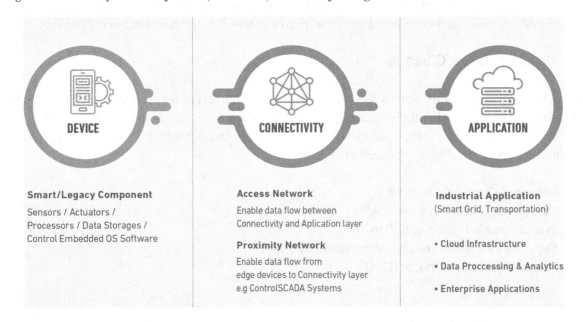

Smart/Legacy Component

Sensors / Actuators / Processors / Data Storages / Control Embedded OS Software

Access Network

Enable data flow between Connectivity and Aplication layer

Proximity Network

Enable data flow from edge devices to Connectivity layer e.g ControlSCADA Systems

Industrial Application
(Smart Grid, Transportation)

• Cloud Infrastructure

• Data Proccessing & Analytics

• Enterprise Applications

for one transmission and cannot be used again (e.g., for resending to additional or completely new fake destinations). Additional prevention measure is the implementation of the Timestamp techniques, thus reducing the time window which defines a certain length of time for the message transmitting and receiving. An attacker cannot eavesdrop and resend message for the same time as planned for the regular operation. The proper level of the cybersecurity against the Replay attack in the IIoT systems may assume some additional techniques, but these two and their combination are considered as adequate levels of prevention.

In the *Time attack,* an attacker tries to compromise a communication's crypto-keys by analyzing the time taken to execute cryptographic algorithms (Sicari, Rizzardi, Grieco, & Coen-Porisini, 2015). The time attack exploits the data-depended behavioral characteristics rather than the mathematical properties of the algorithm. Modern cryptographic algorithms have the property to hide or reduce the visibility of its implementation. The attacker focuses the time of execution of some subroutines on every authorized input. The time attack can be applied to any data-depended algorithm which includes time variation (e.g., multiplication on a CPU varies on the input). This attack in combination with crypto analysis can increase the rate of information leakage.

The Node control or Device hijacking is a cyber-attack where the attacker assumes the control of a device. This threat is very often, and it is usually the first step for more advanced attacks, for scenarios when the attacker only takes control of a single device to infect other devices. This attack is usually combined with the Malicious Data attack, where an attacker injects additional fake information to the system to create an additional node (Farooq, Waseem, Khairi, & Mazhar, 2015). The implementation of this attack type is very depended on device type and targeting its authentication procedure and sometimes involving authorization steps.

The Side Channel Attack (SCA) is a cyber-attack based on collecting side information which could be used later for launching another type of cyber-attack. Information, such as power consumption, hardware configuration, and cryptographic computations abilities, are typical examples of this cyber-attack type. This cyber-attack type involves some other cyber-attack types with the most important difference that the target is not the data channel but the control channel which could be used indirectly for information leakage.

The Proximity network shown in Figure 4 enables the data flow between sensors, devices, actuators through dedicated gateways. Next, the access network serves the purpose of connecting the edge gateway to the platform tier. Finally, the service network provides connectivity between various services in the platform and enterprise tiers, as well as between the services in each tier. It is usually implemented as a private network over the public Internet, thus enabling secure communication between the end-users and services offered by the IIoT platform.

The Connectivity or *Network layer* is responsible for establishing and maintaining the communication channel, parameters' setting, data routing information and receiving verification. All system nodes, including gateways, switching and routing devices, sensors, cloud/fog/edge computing nodes, communicate over the established channels for data transfer, synchronization, and signaling messages. This layer defines the communication technology used for each particular system, e.g., Wi-Fi, ZigBee, Bluetooth, LoRaWAN, Sigfox, NB-IoT, LTE, or even combining them using the proper interfaces called gateways. Gateways act in the system to establish the bridge between separated subsystems based on different communications techniques and protocol stacks, with additional functionalities, e.g., aggregating, filtering and forwarding existing traffic. This layer is a platform for a broad scope of cyber-attacks that target confidentiality, integrity, and availability. Besides conventional cyber-attacks, such as Spoofing, "Man-in-the-Middle" and others, there is a specific one called *Sybil attack*.

The Sybil attack targets integrity, where an attacker places a random node at multiple locations in the system at the same time. This technique helps an attacker to spread malware across the system quickly. Intercepting the routing data and creating a routing loop is a widespread scenario for attacks at this layer.

The Application layer is responsible for establishing a connection between an application and IIoT system operation and the Network layer. This layer also contains Data centers, which store collected data for future analysis and related operations. Cyber-attacks at this layer mainly target data, trying to steal them, sometimes even to destroy them or change some values to influence on the final analysis. The data protection becomes a critical problem for prevention and protection at the Application layer. The cybersecurity challenges for this layer are data access permissions and related policies, authentication mechanisms, and data recovery.

TCP/IP-Like Cyber-Attacks in the IIoT Systems

"Man-in-the-Middle" is a conventional cyber-threat well-known from the TCP/IP networks, where the attacker breaches, interrupts or spoofs communications between two nodes or systems. Specifically, for the IIoT system, the attacker could assume control of the industrial process, smart actuator or an industrial robot, knocking it out of its designated line or speed what could damage an assembly line, injure or even kill the human operator. This perspective also defines a new approach for the risk assessment, because this cyber-attack could be lethal as well as, e.g., automated (self-driving) cars. One practical example of this cyber-threat in the IIoT system is that the attacker assumes the control of a smart meter and uses that device to launch a *ransomware* attack against the Energy Management System (EMS) when a smart meter is not the real target for the cyber-attack.

DoS and DDoS attacks are also well-known concepts, but this class of the cyber-attack has an entirely new meaning in the context of the IIoT. This class of cyber-threat has the goal to make a machine, network or industrial process unavailable to its intended users on temporary or indefinitely based disrupting service. The prevention or defense is almost unavailable because incoming traffic is flooding a targeted device(s) from multiple sources. It makes it difficult stopping this attack by merely blocking a single source or source group, or at least it is almost impossible without disruption the industrial process or stopping it completely.

"Permanent Denial-of-Service" (PDoS) is the IIoT-specific cyber-threat, which is also known as the *Phlashing* and it is not common in the conventional TCP/IP based systems. This class of attack takes into account hardware limitations for numerous IIoT devices. Its purpose is to attack the device so severely that the replacement or reinstallation of hardware is required (an example is the *BrickerBot*) in order to exploit hard-coded passwords in IoT devices, which causes PDoS.

Examples of IoT Cyber-Attacks

The general concept of the IoT is a broader perspective for the IIoT, and most of the cyber-threats are common, where only a few of them are IIoT-specific. It is recommended to analyze the problem from the general perspective at the beginning and then to move to an application-specific threat. This approach is essential in order to understand threats and to plan a proper defense and prevention approach.

The Mirai Botnet (Dyn Attack)

In October 2016, the most massive DDoS attack ever was launched on service provider Dyn. The platform for zombie network creation was the IoT Botnet. The IoT Botnet was created using the Mirai malware, and the infected device continues to search the Internet for other vulnerable IoT devices using known default usernames and passwords to log in and infecting them with the malware. The Mirai malware was very successful and preferred devices for attacks were digital cameras and DVR players (Kilpatrick, 2018).

Hackable IoT Smart Healthcare Cardiac Device

Attacks on medical IoT devices are the worst nightmares for the future commercial IoT market penetration. The weakness of a medical device was a huge step back for the massive adoption of the IoT smart devices in the eHealth services. In the USA, the FDA (U.S. Food and Drug Administration) confirmed that medical's implantable cardiac devices have vulnerabilities that could open backdoors for illegal access. If a device is controlled by the hacker once, he could deplete the battery or change incorrect pacing, thus creating shocks or misuse of the device in another way. It is evident that medical healthcare applications are very critical and cyber-attack on these devices could cause significant health issues or even deaths. The officials said that the vulnerability occurred in the transmitter that reads data and shares them remotely, and hackers used them to access the transmitter. A similar case happened later on with the Owlet Wi-Fi baby heart monitor (IoT Solutions World Congress, 2018).

Cybersecurity Strategy for the IIoT

Like any other system, the IIoT has to achieve the CIA defined goals: *Confidentiality, Integrity, and Availability*. These goals may vary from system to system, but this is a fundamental checklist to verify efficiency for any established cybersecurity. Cyber-threats to the IoT and IIoT devices and systems are more likely than attacks to the embedded systems, including PCs and smartphones. Massive deployment of IIoT devices creates an ideal platform for cyber-attacks to the third-party targets.

The cybersecurity rules for prevention are as follows:

1. Devices, which do not update their firmware, software, and passwords periodically, should never be implemented. Regular update of both firmware and software is necessary to mitigate vulnerabilities.
2. All devices have to change their default username and password before the installation and connection to the Internet.
3. Even if the system employs a lot of IoT devices, each single IoT device should be unique on the Internet, having a unique password.
4. For Cloud, Fog, and Edge-based services, as an authentication process, users' credentials must be sent in encrypted form and never in the plain text. It is strongly recommended to establish and keep secure communications not only for starting the authentication process but also for all other types of communication if the device's CPU capabilities allow that.
5. Companies, which are system integrators, usually ignore the security of peripheral devices, components, or networks, which can cause severe consequences to the system. Every single component, device, and network must be security tested and verified before the integration. After the installation process, testing and verification of the system are obligatory.

6. Firmware Integrity and Secure Boot means the application of the cryptographic code which ensures that a device only executes the code generated by the device OEM or another trusted party (if necessary – avoid, if possible). The secure boot procedure prevents illegal insertion of malicious code which replaces the original firmware. Chipsets of many existing IIoT devices do not have capabilities for advanced computations for a secure boot, which causes the general issue. That is an additional argument for emergent standardization for all IIoT products before the market deployment.

7. Mutual Authentication is a critical procedure to integrate any device in the system. The device authentication is a necessary and critical operation and should take place before receiving or transmitting data. This procedure can stop spreading the malicious code to the rest of the system when the already hacked device is present. The procedure of Mutual Authentication means that both entities (devices, servers) must prove their identity to each other before any other interaction. For this purpose, there are many options based on symmetric or asymmetric crypto keys for the two-way authentication. The Secure Hash Algorithm (SHA-x) along with for symmetric keys-based Hash Authentication Code (HMAC) or asymmetric keys-based Elliptic Curve Signature Algorithm (ECDSA) are possible solutions.

8. Real-Time Performance and Security Monitoring means to establish permanent and real-time service for monitoring all communications and processes in the industrial system, with advanced functions to identify all anomalies in the system. Moreover, this procedure can set the alarm state for additional analysis, also using AI or ML cyber-threats identification techniques. This approach is critical for endpoints security in order to avoid incorrect reporting of events and reactions.

FUTURE RESEARCH DIRECTIONS

The security of IIoT systems has to cover a broad spectrum of applications in diverse environments and based on heterogeneous communications techniques. One of the most important challenges relates to standardization and interoperability issues. Moreover, there are many research and standardization efforts in order to achieve high-standard confidentiality, integrity, and availability, especially for some sensitive IIoT applications with a high-risk level assessment.

The complex architecture and heterogeneity of applications makes the IIoT very difficult to standardize, therefore the cybersecurity issues are even more complex and challenging. The IEEE and IETF make the most significant progress in this direction by creating the IEEE 802.15.4 and IEEE 802.15.4e standards and specifications. These standards implement the IPv6 packet fragmentation and reassembly mechanisms and provide security mechanisms and secure light-weight join processes combining link-layer security features with a secure joining procedure using the CoAP at the application level.

Future research directions in the cybersecurity field identify the following trends: cloud-based services cybersecurity, 5G cybersecurity, QoS-based design, fault tolerance mechanisms, and others.

CONCLUSION

The current manufacturing industry is undergoing a new technology-driven change known as Industry 4.0 and Cyber-Physical System paradigm. Advanced networking and information processing technologies, as well as a new generation of sensor devices, are having a significant impact on the ICT sector and industrial systems. A significant barrier to successful IIoT adoption lies in cybersecurity issues that make it extremely difficult to harness its full potential. IIoT systems dramatically increase the attack variations (by introducing new security threats), the disruption of process controls, the theft of intellectual property, the loss of corporate data, and the industrial espionage. Therefore, each component of an IIoT system must follow relevant protocols/procedures to detect, mitigate, verify, and manage IIoT security risks and vulnerabilities throughout the entire life cycle of the IIoT system. Many challenging issues still need to be addressed in order to achieve a required level of IIoT cybersecurity, particularly in terms of confidentiality, scalability, data integrity, accessibility, and interoperability. Research and standardization activities in this field are of primary interest in the coming years.

REFERENCES

Atzori, L., Iera, A., & Morabito, G. (2010). The Internet of Things: A survey. *Computer Networks: The International Journal of Computer and Telecommunications Networking*, *54*(15), 2787–2805. doi:10.1016/j.comnet.2010.05.010

Bahrami, S., & Sheikhi, A. (2016). From demand response in smart grid toward integrated demand response in smart energy hub. *IEEE Transactions on Smart Grid*, *7*(2), 650–658.

Berbakov, L., Anton-Haro, C., & Matamoros, J. (2013). Optimal transmission policy for cooperative transmission with energy harvesting and battery operated sensor nodes. *Signal Processing*, *93*(11), 3159–3170. doi:10.1016/j.sigpro.2013.04.009

Berbakov, L., Anton-Haro, C., & Matamoros, J. (2014). Joint optimization of transmission policies for collaborative beamforming with energy harvesting sensors. *IEEE Transactions on Wireless Communications*, *13*(7), 3496–3509. doi:10.1109/TWC.2014.2323268

Berbakov, L., Jovanović, Č., Svetel, M., Vasiljević, J., Dimić, G., & Radulović, N. (2019). Quantitative assessment of head tremor in patients with essential tremor and cervical dystonia by using inertial sensors. *Sensors (Basel)*, *19*(19), 1–16. doi:10.339019194246 PMID:31574913

Boyes, H., Hallaq, B., Cunningham, J., & Watson, T. (2018). The Industrial Internet of Things (IIoT): An analysis framework. *Computers in Industry*, *101*, 1–12. doi:10.1016/j.compind.2018.04.015

Buratti, C., Stajkic, A., Gardasevic, G., Milardo, S., Abrignani, M., Mijovic, S., ... Verdone, R. (2016). Testing protocols for the Internet of Things on the EuWIn platform. *IEEE Internet of Things Journal*, *3*(1), 124–133. doi:10.1109/JIOT.2015.2462030

Farooq, M. U., Waseem, M., Khairi, A., & Mazhar, S. (2015). A Critical analysis of the security concerns of Internet of Things (IoT). *International Journal of Computers and Applications*, *111*(7), 1–6. doi:10.5120/19547-1280

Gardašević, G., Veletić, M., Maletić, N., Vasiljević, D., Radusinović, I., Tomović, S., & Radonjić, M. (2017). The IoT architectural framework, design issues and application domains. *Wireless Personal Communications*, *92*(1), 127–148. doi:10.100711277-016-3842-3

Gartner, Inc. (2017). *Gartner says worldwide IoT security spending to reach $348 million in 2016.* Retrieved November 10, 2019, from https://www.gartner.com/en/newsroom/press-releases/2016-04-25-gartner-says-worldwide-iot-security-spending-to-reach-348-million-in-2016

Hermann, M., Pentek, T., & Otto, B. (2015). *Design principles for Industrie 4.0 scenarios: A literature review.* Retrieved November 10, 2019, from http://www.snom.mb.tu-dortmund.de/cms/de/forschung/Arbeitsberichte/Design-Principles-for-Industrie-4_0-Scenarios.pdf

Hylving, L., & Schultze, U. (2013). Evolving the modular layered architecture in digital innovation: The case of the car's instrument cluster. In *Proceedings of the International Conference on Information Systems (ICIS 2013): Reshaping Society Through Information Systems Design* (vol. 2, article 13). Red Hook, NY: Curran Associates.

Institute of Electrical and Electronics Engineers (IEEE). (2011). IEEE Standard for local and metropolitan area networks - Part 15.4: Low-rate wireless personal area networks (LR-WPANs). *Standard 802.15.4-11.*

Institute of Electrical and Electronics Engineers (IEEE). (2017). *Artificial intelligence and machine learning applied to cybersecurity.* Retrieved November 10, 2019, from https://www.ieee.org/content/dam/ieee-org/ieee/web/org/about/industry/ieee_confluence_report.pdf?utm_source=lp-link-text&utm_medium=industry&utm_campaign=confluence-paper

Johnson, B. D. (2017). *A widening attack plain.* West Point, NY: Army Cyber Institute.

Kilpatrick, H. (2018). *Five infamous IoT hacks and vulnerabilities.* Retrieved November 10, 2019, from https://www.iotsworldcongress.com/5-infamous-iot-hacks-and-vulnerabilities/

Kushalnagar, N., Montenegro, G., & Schumacher, C. (2015). IPv6 over low-power wireless personal area networks (6LoWPANs): Overview, assumptions, problem statement, and goals. *IETF RFC 4919 (Informational).* Retrieved November 10, 2019, from https://datatracker.ietf.org/doc/rfc4919/

Li, X., Wan, P., Zhang, H., Li, M., & Jiang, Y. (2018). The application research of Internet of Things to oil pipeline leak detection. In *Proceedings of the 2018 15th International Computer Conference on Wavelet Active Media Technology and Information Processing (ICCWAMTIP)* (pp. 211-214). New York: IEEE. 10.1109/ICCWAMTIP.2018.8632561

Lu, Y., & Xu, L. D. (2018). Internet of Things (IoT) cybersecurity research: A review of current research topics. *The Internet of Things Journal, 6*(2), 2103–2115. doi:10.1109/JIOT.2018.2869847

Mouratidis, H., & Diamantopoulou, V. (2018). A security analysis method for Industrial Internet of Things. *IEEE Transactions on Industrial Informatics, 14*(9), 4093–4100. doi:10.1109/TII.2018.2832853

Rodenas-Herraiz, D., Garcia-Sanchez, A., Garcia-Sanchez, F., & Garcia-Haro, J. (2013). Current trends in wireless mesh sensor networks: A review of competing approaches. *Sensors (Basel), 13*(5), 5958–5995. doi:10.3390130505958 PMID:23666128

Rodrigues, J., De Rezende Segundo, D., Junqueira, H., Sabino, M., Prince, R., Al-Muhtadi, J., & De Albuquerque, V. H. C. (2018). Enabling technologies for the Internet of Health Things. *IEEE Access: Practical Innovations, Open Solutions, 6,* 13129–13141. doi:10.1109/ACCESS.2017.2789329

Shelby, Z., Hartke, K., & Bormann, C. (2014). The constrained application protocol (CoAP). *IETF RFC 7252 (Standards Track)*. Retrieved November 10, 2019, from https://datatracker.ietf.org/doc/rfc7252/

Sicari, S., Rizzardi, A., Grieco, L. A., & Coen-Porisini, A. (2015). Security, privacy and trust in Internet of Things: The road ahead. *Computer Networks*, *76*, 146–164. doi:10.1016/j.comnet.2014.11.008

Tang, B., Chen, Z., Hefferman, G., Pei, S., Wei, T., He, H., & Yang, Q. (2017). Incorporating intelligence in fog computing for big data analysis in smart cities. *IEEE Transactions on Industrial Informatics*, *13*(5), 2140–2150. doi:10.1109/TII.2017.2679740

Vasiljević, D., & Gardašević, G. (2019). Packet aggregation scheduling in 6TiSCH networks. In *Proceedings* of the *IEEE EUROCON 2019: 18th International Conference on Smart Technologies* (pp. 1-5). New York: IEEE.

Vilajosana, X., Watteyne, T., Vučinić, M., Chang, T., & Pister, K. (2019). TiSCH: Industrial performance for IPv6 Internet-of-Things networks. *Proceedings of the IEEE*, *107*(6), 1153–1165. doi:10.1109/JPROC.2019.2906404

Winter, T., Thubert, P., Brandt, A., Hui, J., Kelsey, R., & Levis, P. … Alexander, R. (2012). RPL: IPv6 routing protocol for low-power and lossy networks. *IETF RFC 6550 (Standards Track)*. Retrieved November 10, 2019, from https://datatracker.ietf.org/doc/rfc6550/

Wollschlaeger, M., Sauter, T., & Jasperneite, J. (2017). The future of industrial communication: Automation networks in the era of the Internet of Things and Industry 4.0. *IEEE Industrial Electronics Magazine*, *11*(1), 17–27. doi:10.1109/MIE.2017.2649104

Xu, H., Yu, W., Griffith, D., & Golmie, N. (2018). A survey on Industrial Internet of Things: A cyber-physical systems perspective. *IEEE Access: Practical Innovations, Open Solutions*, *6*, 78238–78259. doi:10.1109/ACCESS.2018.2884906

Zhang, N. (2018). Smart logistics path for cyber-physical systems with Internet of Things. *IEEE Access: Practical Innovations, Open Solutions*, *6*, 70808–70819. doi:10.1109/ACCESS.2018.2879966

ADDITIONAL READING

Cherepanov, A., & Lipovsky, R. (2017*). Industroyer: Biggest threat to industrial control systems since Stuxnet*. Retrieved November 10, 2019, from https://www.welivesecurity.com/2017/06/12/industroyer-biggest-threat-industrial-control-systems-since-stuxnet/

Chirgwin, R. (2018). *IT 'heroes' saved Maersk from NotPetya with ten-day reinstallation bliz*. Retrieved November 10, 2019, from https://www.theregister.co.uk/2018/01/25/after_notpetya_maersk_replaced_everything/

Condliffe, J. (2016). Ukraine's power grid gets hacked again, a worrying sign for infrastructure attacks. Retrieved November 10, 2019, from https://www.technologyreview.com/s/603262/ukraines-power-grid-gets-hacked-again-a-worrying-sign-forinfrastructure-attacks/

Forrest, C. (2017). *NotPetya ransomware outbreak cost Merck more than $300M per quarter*. Retrieved November 10, 2019, from https://www.techrepublic.com/article/notpetya-ransomware-outbreak-cost-merck-more-than-300m-per-quarter/

ICS-CERT. (2017). *Alert (ICS-ALERT-17-102-01A): BrickerBot permanent Denial-of-Service attack*. Retrieved November 10, 2019, from https://www.us-cert.gov/ics/alerts/ICS-ALERT-17-102-01A

Kaspersky Lab. (2017). *More than 50% of organizations attacked by ExPetr (Petya) cryptolocker are industrial companies*. Retrieved November 10, 2019, from https://ics-cert.kaspersky.com/alerts/2017/06/29/more-than-50-percent-of-organizations-attacked-by-expetr-petya-cryptolocker-are-industrial-companies/

Ng, A. (2018). *US: Russia's NotPetya the most destructive cyberattack ever*. Retrieved November 10, 2019, from https://www.cnet.com/news/uk-said-russia-is-behind-destructive-2017-cyberattack-in-ukraine/

Perlroth, N., Scott, M., & Frenkel, S. (2017). *Cyberattack hits Ukraine then spreads internationally*. Retrieved November 10, 2019, from https://www.nytimes.com/2017/06/27/technology/ransomware-hackers.html

Sentryo. (2018). *Analysis of Triton industrial malware*. Retrieved November 10, 2019, from https://www.sentryo.net/analysis-triton-malware/

Stoler, N. (2018). *Anatomy of the Triton malware attack*. Retrieved November 10, 2019, from https://www.cyberark.com/threat-research-blog/anatomy-triton-malware-attack/

KEY TERMS AND DEFINITIONS

Authentication: A set of procedures for identifying individuals or groups and check their data or system access rights.

Availability: A set of principles and metrics that assures the reliability and constant access to data for the authorized individuals or groups.

Confidentiality: A set of principles and metrics that control information access.

Cybersecurity: A set of techniques and algorithms to protect computers, networks, programs, and data from unauthorized access or exploitation, on criteria for maintaining usability, reliability, confidentiality, integrity, and availability.

Industrial Internet of Things: A system that transforms traditional industrial control systems into smart, digital and connected industrial platforms, thus introducing a higher level of automation, independence, self-regulation, and self-optimization to refine the process control.

Industry 4.0: A collective term for technologies and concepts of value chain organization that aims at providing the development of smart factories with fully integrated production systems.

Integrity: A set of principles and metrics that assures the sensitive data is trustworthy and accurate.

IoT Device: An endpoint component of the IIoT system that interacts with the physical world through sensing or actuating.

Chapter 4
Evolving the Security Paradigm for Industrial IoT Environments

Luis Rosa
ⓘ https://orcid.org/0000-0002-8230-4045
*Department of Informatics Engineering,
University of Coimbra, Portugal*

Miguel Borges de Freitas
ⓘ https://orcid.org/0000-0002-4939-1773
*Department of Informatics Engineering,
University of Coimbra, Portugal*

João Henriques
ⓘ https://orcid.org/0000-0001-7380-9511
*Department of Informatics Engineering,
University of Coimbra, Portugal*

Pedro Quitério
ⓘ https://orcid.org/0000-0003-1004-6574
*Department of Informatics Engineering,
University of Coimbra, Portugal*

Filipe Caldeira
ⓘ https://orcid.org/0000-0001-7558-2330
Polytechnic Institute of Viseu, Portugal

Tiago Cruz
ⓘ https://orcid.org/0000-0001-9278-6503
*Department of Informatics Engineering,
University of Coimbra, Portugal*

Paulo Simões
ⓘ https://orcid.org/0000-0002-5079-8327
Department of Informatics Engineering, University of Coimbra, Portugal

ABSTRACT

In recent years, IACS (Industrial Automation and Control Systems) have become more complex, due to the increasing number of interconnected devices. This IoT (internet of things)-centric IACS paradigm, which is at the core of the Industry 4.0 concept, expands the infrastructure boundaries beyond the aggregated-plant, mono-operator vision, being dispersed over a large geographic area. From a cybersecurity-centric perspective, the distributed nature of modern IACS makes it difficult not only to understand the nature of incidents but also to assess their progression and threat profile. Defending against those threats is becoming increasingly difficult, requiring orchestrated and collaborative distributed detection, evaluation, and reaction capabilities beyond the scope of a single entity. This chapter presents the Intrusion and Anomaly Detection System platform architecture that was designed and developed within the scope of the ATENA H2020 project, to address the specific needs of distributed IACS while providing (near) real-time cybersecurity awareness.

DOI: 10.4018/978-1-7998-2910-2.ch004

INTRODUCTION

In recent years, Industrial Automation and Control Systems (IACSs) have experienced an increase in their complexity, due to the growing number of attached devices, sensors and actuators. Quite often, these components are spread out in the field – this is the case for micro-generation, smart metering, oil and gas distribution or smart water management, among others. This Internet of Things (IoT)-centric IACS paradigm, which is at the core of the Industry 4.0 concept, blurs the infrastructure boundaries, expanding them beyond the single or aggregated-plant, vertical silo perspective, being dispersed over a widespread geographic area, with increasingly small areas of coverage as we progress towards its periphery.

However, IoT-centric IACS pose several challenges. As the boundaries of the IACS expand towards households, they involve several third-party entities, such as telecommunications or utility providers, in a scenario that naturally demands the introduction of multi-tenancy mechanisms for supporting Machine-to-Machine (M2M) communications and infrastructure orchestration. Specifically, and from a cybersecurity-centric perspective, the distributed nature of modern IACS makes it difficult not only to understand the nature of incidents but also to assess their progression and threat profile. Dealing with such threat profiles is a difficult task, furthermore if considering the need to involve several different entities in developing coordinated and collaborative distributed detection, analysis and reaction mechanisms. Hence, this situation constitutes an opportunity to rethink the current approach of cybersecurity for IACS, resorting to new tools and models providing a comprehensive level of coverage for the whole value chain of a Critical Infrastructure (CI) in increasing sophisticated and networked scenarios.

This situation calls for a different approach to cyber threat detection, which was one of the most relevant contributions of the ATENA H2020 project (ATENA Consortium, 2016). The main objective of ATENA project (Vitali et al., 2017) is to *improve the efficiency and resilience capabilities of modernized Critical Infrastructures against a wide variety of cyber-physical threats, being those malicious attacks or unexpected faults which may affect the IACS, corporative or simple ICT devices. (…) Every element of the IACS Trusted Control Chain* (Figure 1) *could be impacted by incident (natural or malicious). The ATENA prototype will demonstrate the capabilities to detect the incident, to identify the problem, to assess the risk for the overall CI and to provide solution to restore the reliability of the CI behavior i.e., to restore a Trusted Control Chain all over the CI network.*

Quite unsurprisingly, the ATENA project objectives statement explicitly describes a reference scenario where a chain of trust traverses a multi-tenant environment, precisely one of the main concerns of modern IoT-centric IACS. For this purpose, the ATENA architecture included an Intrusion and Anomaly Detection System (IADS) subsystem, which was designed from the ground up to deal with the challenges such complex environments.

This chapter intends to present and describe the ATENA IADS architecture, designed from the ground up to address the specific needs of distributed IACS, while providing (near) real-time cybersecurity awareness. The IADS is built around a data-driven security concept, aimed at providing a considerable degree of flexibility in terms of IACS security management, monitoring and configuration, while preventing risks, both from operational errors and from cyber-attacks, intrusions or malware.

The rest of this chapter, which departs from prior published work (Rosa et al., 2017) is structured as follows. The *Background and Related Work* section provides a state-of-the-art overview about event processing techniques and solutions for security applications, also encompassing a description of a distributed intrusion detection system (IDS) implementation from the same authors of this chapter, which is considered to be representative of a more conventional solution. Afterwards, the *Proposed Architecture*

Figure 1. IACS trusted control chain

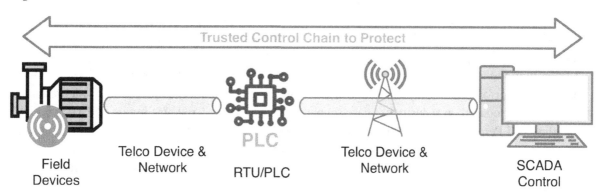

section describes the IADS architecture and its main components, being followed by a section dedicated evaluating its Event Processing capabilities. This chapter will be closed with a section focused on *Future Research Directions,* followed by the final *Conclusions.*

BACKGROUND AND RELATED WORK

Once cybersecurity awareness started to grow among the automation community (partially due to several security incidents), organizations in industry, researchers, and governments began working towards improving security in such systems. For example, organizations such as the National Institute of Standards and Technology (NIST), the International Society of Automation (ISA) (published by the American National Standards Institute [ANSI]), the North American Energy Reliability Committee (NERC) or the European Agency for Cybersecurity (ENISA) have published several documents with recommendations and policies to deal with IACS threats and vulnerabilities (ANSI/ISA, 2018; ENISA, 2017; NERC, 2010; Stouffer, Lightman, Pillitter, Abrams, & Hahn, 2015). Such issues were also addressed within the scope of European projects such as VIKING (VIKING Consortium, 2011), MICIE (MICIE Consortium, 2011), CRISALIS (CRISALIS Consortium, 2015), PRECYSE (PRECYSE Consortium, 2015), CockpitCI (CockpitCI Consortium, 2012) or ATENA (ATENA Consortium, 2016).

Moreover, research on intrusion and anomaly detection for IACS have been undertaken on several related topics, including IDSs (Ghaeini & Tippenhauer, 2016; Han, Xie, Chen, & Ling, 2014; Moon, Im, Kim, & Park, 2017) device-level anomaly detection and classification (Karri & Rajendran, 2010; Raposo, Rodrigues, Sinche, Sá Silva, & Boavida, 2019; Zaddach, Bruno, & Balzarotti, 2014) detection based on traffic and protocol models (Goldenberg & Wool, 2013; Kalluri, Mahendra, Kumar, & Prasad, 2017) and approaches based on machine-learning techniques (Junejo & Goh, 2016; Yang, Cheng, & Chuah, 2019) among others.

Over the last years, different anomaly detection systems have been proposed leveraging the new advancements in the Big Data and IACS cyber-security fields. Several authors suggest the usage of Big Data and Event Streaming processing techniques to cope with modern Industrial IoT (IIoT) environments. One of the promising strategies includes combining streaming and batch processing techniques into so-called lambda architecture (Marz & Warren, 2015). This allows to have near real-time data processing, providing low latencies as well as handle large volumes of data. For instance, in a cyber-security context we want to immediately process and report a known security incident but at the same time we might want to apply more complex anomaly detection algorithms on the top of massive amounts of events. This section discusses some of the recent advances and scenarios referred in the literature on how such strategies are being applied.

Concerning the topics of event processing tools and techniques, one of the earliest studies provides a comparative performance analysis of several correlator engines (namely Esper, SEC, Nodebrain and Drools), mostly focused on security use case scenarios (Rosa, Alves, Cruz, & Simões, 2015). Later on, Dayarathna and Perera (2018) undertook a comprehensive survey about Event Processing techniques, tools and languages, including a discussion of the recent advancements in several areas such as IoT, Streaming Machine Learning and Distributed Stream Computing Platforms (DSCPs). Ariyaluran Habeeb et al. (2019) provide a survey on big data anomaly detection technologies and discussed several research challenges of real-time big data processing. They collected information about the most used software tools (i.e., Hadoop, Spark, Kafka, etc) in each domain (i.e., network traffic, healthcare or safety critical scenarios, etc.) and how the different machine learning algorithms and techniques are being used. At the end, they identified several shortcomings and challenges of the existing approaches, providing a recommendation list for future research.

Inoubli et al. (2018) detailed an experimental evaluation study of the 5 most used Big Data processing frameworks (Hadoop, Spark, Flink, Storm and Samza) by recreating a word count example over several different datasets. The authors compared not only the performance and features of each tool, but they also discussed how they perform in batch and stream processing. Zou et al. (2019) used Apache Spark and Hadoop to analyze the flow data of a large smart city environment (up to 5500 heterogeneous sensor nodes from 30 different networks) having achieved better results using Apache Spark. Rettig et al. (2015) introduced an anomaly detection framework based on Pearson correlation and entropy in the Swisscom telecommunication network. They used both Apache Kafka and Spark to build a solution capable to detect both, network failures or anomalies resulted from large-scale human activity. They also conducted several experiments to demonstrate the scalability of the platform in terms of the number of the nodes and the volume of data.

Regarding IACS-specific studies, Iturbe et al. (2017) undertook a survey more focused on Industrial Networks including their characteristics and constrains, presenting a taxonomy to classify existing anomaly-based systems for Industrial Networks, also discussing the open gaps in the literature. While similar approaches might be borrowed from other domains, the authors of that study highlight the fact that a few proposals exist exclusively for Industrial Networks. Similarly, a recent survey by Awad et al. (2018) on digital forensics applied to Supervisory Control And Data Acquisition (SCADA), identified a significant gap in the available tools focused on SCADA environments in terms of complexity, generality, and versatility.

Menon et al. (2019) proposed a stream processing framework using Apache Spark and Spark Streaming, capable of processing data directly from Phasor Measurement Units (PMUs) in a smart grid domain at a high rate (60/120 frames per second per each PMU). They successfully recreated a scenario with over 120 PMUs. Waagsnes & Ulltveit-moe (2018) described a platform used to recreate a virtualized environment with SCADA network traffic using the IEC 60870-5-104 protocol. Then, a Security Information and Event Management (SIEM) module developed on top of the Elasticsearch stack was developed to monitor the performance of two Open-source Network IDSs (NIDSs), Snort and Suricata. Such research is valuable to understand how the multiple components might coexist in a network anomaly detection solution within the context of a SCADA environment. Similarly, Singh et al. (2019) compared

Snort with Bro, using the DNP3 protocol, another SCADA protocol. They tested both against different types of attacks, being both solutions capable to handle the attacks. Nevertheless, they obtained lower latencies using Bro.

Designing for Conventional ICS: the CockpitCI PIDS as a Modern SIEM

The Perimeter Intrusion Detection System (PIDS), developed in the context of the European CockpitCI project was designed to address the protection of CI infrastructures against cyber-physical events providing a situation awareness to the SCADA operators (CockpitCI Consortium, 2012). The reference architecture (Figure 2) included a multi-level processing framework fed by several specialized detection probes strategically deployed across the infrastructure within a CI, allowing to detect complex cyber-attacks (Cruz et al., 2016). This way, the framework was able to collect and aggregate evidences from several assets across the infrastructure, allowing to detect and correlate complex attacks that might spread over several domains.

Nevertheless, the CockpitCI was built around the notion of a single-tenant CI, limited in a geographical space (such as an industrial plant). With the advent of the IIoT this required a redesign of the entire architecture. Moreover, apart from the One-Class Support Vector Machine (Maglaras, 2014) – that allowed to analyze network flows but that was not suitable for distributed scenarios, the analytics capabilities of the platform were mainly focused on signature-based detection mechanisms and a limited number of correlation techniques. The component provisioning was also limited to static deployments and customized configurations that, in worst-case scenarios, required direct configuration of each device. It was not possible to deploy on-demand probes that are particularly useful for load-balancing within elastic scenarios, such as IIoT that might have different requirements over the time.

As the move towards IIoT became evident, the need to diversify event sources to improve security context information, as well as the scale requirements imposed by such scenarios anticipated serious problems for the CockpitCI SIEM. Specifically, correlation – the core SIEM functionality that makes it possible to relate several events together to detect anomalies – requires fine-tuning to successfully be able extract meaningful results from diversified event sources. Despite the fact the CockpitCI SIEM was designed to provide a scalability advantage over monolithic solutions by means of a hierarchical correlator arrangement, it would not be enough, as the increased number of events flowing at growing rates, together with complex correlation task sand the need to process rules within a limited time window would eventually pose a considerable burden for the correlator engines, implying high latencies or even event loss.

Proposed Architecture

As illustrated in Figure 3, the IADS reference architecture is focused on Critical Infrastructures and Essential Services (ES) and aims to detect and report cyber-physical issues. As a result of complete redesign of the PIDS, the IADS is also focused on more distributed scenarios and the flexibility to adjust to heterogeneous environments. The following sections, describe its main components, including the data streaming platform, the Big Data SIEM, the probes, as well as the forensics and auditing compliance module (FCA). The main idea behind such architecture is to have a scalable solution to detect, aggregate and correlate cyber-physical events and timely report them to the CI operator. Such events might

Figure 2. The CockpitCI PIDS reference architecture

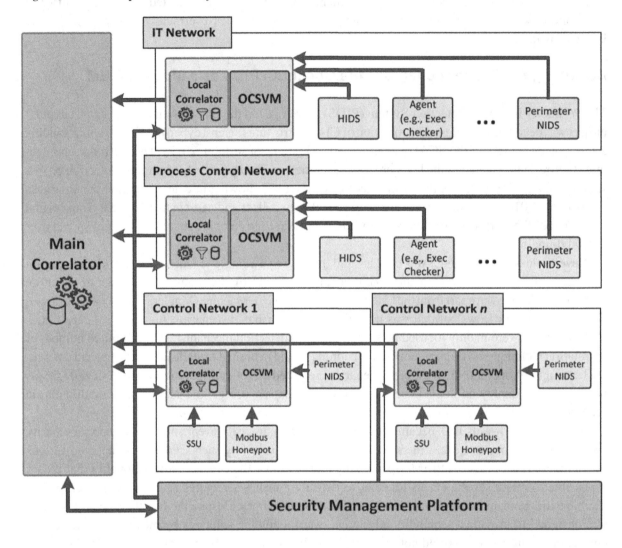

come from the output of a security detection probe as well as the result of any of the event processing algorithms deployed in the upper levels.

The IACS design decouples evidence-gathering, event transport and processing capabilities in a multi-layer model. It is divided into three vertical subsystems: Distributed IDS (DIDS), Management and Forensics and Compliance Auditing. The core DIDS includes the following subsystems (from bottom to top):

- **Probes:** Represent the lowest level of the DIDS, providing detection capabilities (collecting evidence and providing event feeds regarding suspicious activities) or simply forwarding activity events for further processing. Events are generated using an established format and associated data models, further discussed next. Third-party data sources are integrated as probes by means of adaptors, whose purpose is to normalize data feeds.

Figure 3. Intrusion and anomaly detection system (IADS)

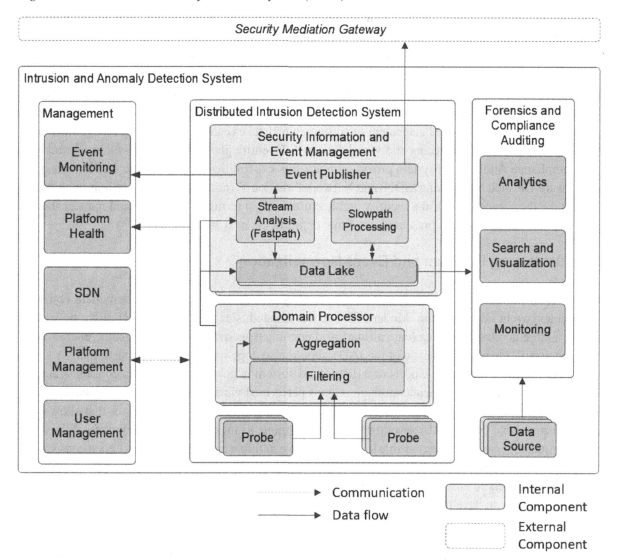

- **Domain Processors:** Pre-process the information feeds from the probes, in order to reduce noise and aggregate events before being sent to analysis. Domain processors are ideally deployed near to the collection points – despite its capabilities, they are not full-featured analysis components, rather providing the means to reduce and mitigate some of the data streaming noise, with a minimum overhead.
- **The Big Data Security Information and Event Manager (SIEM):** Implements the main analytics capabilities for the IADS, comprising two types of data modules: streaming (fast path, for online event stream processing) and batch processing (slow path, for slow jobs that may take time to complete).

The Domain Processors and Big Data SIEM subsystems are designed from the ground up to be horizontally scalable, in such a way that it becomes possible to create several service instances to deal with reliability or scalability requirements which my span different infrastructure points-of-presence. For instance, the Big Data SIEM components may be deployed on different data centers, available in geographically distinct locations. Also, Domain processors can be instanced on edge computing points-of-presence (such as nano data centers), providing the means to leverage upcoming solutions such as 5G verticals to improve event collection and transport capabilities, providing service instances closer to the peripheral branches of the protected infrastructure. For IIoT scenarios, these capabilities are instrumental to comply with one of the main IADS objectives: being able to keep up with the protected infrastructure.

The IADS also includes a Management subsystem, which takes care of the configuration, authentication and authorization, monitoring and visualization of the entire platform state, as well as a Forensics and Compliance Auditing subsystem providing black-box capabilities. Moreover, the IADS makes use of Software-Defined Networking (SDN) and Network Function Virtualization (NFV) to improve service support for the components of the security architecture, both in terms of flexibility and manageability. All these components will be presented into more detail in the next subsections.

Data Streaming Platform and Event Normalization

This section introduces the IADS Data Streaming subsystem describing all inter-component communication and event normalization. Modern CIs are not isolated islands as before, they might be spread among a large geographical area (e.g., a smart grid encompasses multiple domains from generation to consumption). This way, the design of the IADS should also cope with those new constraints.

One of the most important aspects of a distributed system is how its components communicate. In the IADS, all the inter-component communication is performed via a dedicated messaging system. The authors adopted a hybrid approach between queuing and publish-subscribe mechanisms that allow data to be consumed and processed by several distributed components in parallel. At each domain of the CI, a cluster of message brokers is responsible to store and serve multiple topics, from / where each component can produce / consume messages. Depending on the deployment scenario, each topic might be replicated over several brokers to ensure fault-tolerance or partitioned to obtain an increased performance. Such abstraction allows to have multiple probes producing events in the same manner multiple independent components might consume and process each of those events concurrently. For instance, it is possible to apply different anomaly detection algorithms to the same event in parallel. Moreover, each domain contains a domain processor component used to pre-process all the events coming from the probes, allowing to segregate and implement an intermediate processing logic that may range from simple event filtering to more complex aggregations (e.g., sliding time windows for network packet flows analysis).

The authors used Apache Kafka for the messaging system. The domain processors were developed on top of the Apache Kafka Streams API, enabling the usage of multiple and flexible topologies from small to medium use cases without need to have a dedicated processing framework at each domain while having *exactly-once* processing guarantees and a tight integration with the remaining streaming platform.

On the other hand, since the possibility of existing of an infinite number of heterogeneous probes, each one producing different kinds of events, it is also important to have a strategy to normalize their outputs. The authors replaced the XML based format used in the CockpitCI, the IDMEF, with a dedicated data serialization system, Apache Avro, combined with a custom data-model. This way, it was achieved a better performance and flexibility. Each message, as illustrated in Figure 4, is composed of 3 main parts: an *uuid* that uniquely identifies the message across the entire system, a *metadata* part that contains a list of all the components that produced or processed the message, and a *payload* containing a list of the events referring to the message.

In the IADS data-model, a message might represent several events, for instance as a result of an aggregation step. Each of those events has its own type and schema.

Big Data SIEM

The IADS combines the strengths of the classic SIEM, typically limited to simple event management and correlation techniques, with all the possibilities of the Big Data and machine learning approaches. The Big Data SIEM represents the core analytics component of the IADS, combining two types of data

Figure 4. Example of an unserialized Avro/JSON formatted message using the ATENA/IADS data model

```
{
  "uuid": "99e01a19-87be-4e27-9fd4-b100afd32f57",
  "Metadata": {
    "Origins": [
      {
        "URI" : "IADS-GenericProbe",
        "UserAgent" : "IADSGenericProbe",
        "Timestamp": "2018-10-12T17:18:39.412586811-04:00"
      }
    ],
    "Checksum": "..."
  },
  "Payload": {
    "Events": [
      {
        "URIofType": "schema.json",
        "Type": "Network",
        "Severity": "emerg",
        "Data": {
          "Subtype": "Attack",
          "Entities": { […] },
          "Items": { […] }
        }
      }
    ]
  }
}
```

processing techniques: streaming (fast path) and batch processing (slow path). Fast path processing is focused on near real-time analysis that may be implemented using stream processing or even micro-batch techniques (using micro time-windows), while slow-path processing allows for sifting through available evidence using techniques which are not time-constrained. Combined, the two types of processing strategies resemble a lambda pattern allowing to cope with different kinds of threat analysis.

Either based on a previous classified event, a signature or by inference from other events, the Big Data SIEM is responsible to ultimately report (or discard) an event as a cyber-physical incident. Like the remaining components of the architecture, the Big Data SIEM was developed as a distributed, scalable and fault-tolerant component. Not all deployments will have the same computation needs. Therefore, one of the important features of the SIEM is the flexibility to transparently scale-in-out depending on the requirements of the deployed computation algorithms.

Both types of analysis mechanisms were implemented using the Apache Spark framework. This has the advantage of reducing the code complexity by abstracting approaches with same base code. Moreover, by relying on the top of high-profile open-source projects, a third party can easily develop additional anomaly detection algorithms to extend the support of the platform. Moreover, Apache Spark not only provides out-of-the-box integration with Apache Kafka, allowing to access Kafka messages directly as data streams using their *Spark Streaming* API but also already contains a significant number of machine learning algorithms in their *MLib* portfolio.

The idea is to avoid creating a closed framework, limiting the diversity of anomaly detection techniques that can be effectively deployed, providing instead an open and flexible approach that can be used to integrate multiple algorithms. One of the first strategies the authors pursued was analyzing network-based indicators and features such as timestamps, inter-packet packet arrival times, sources/destinations and specific application layer fields against classical machine learning algorithms such as Support Vector Machines (SVMs) and Random Forests in order to flag network-based attacks, one of critical issues in SCADA systems.

The Big Data SIEM also includes a dedicated component, the *Event Publisher*, used to push the results of the event analysis to the upper layers via a *Security Mediation Gateway (SMGW),* and a *Data Lake* component, using Apache Cassandra, a distributed NoSQL database used not only as a persistent storage for all the events but also as an integration point for the forensics and audit compliance module.

Security Probes

The security probes constitute the lowest level of the IADS architecture, providing a continuous event feed which is used by the upper processing layers to correlate and infer about the security of the CI.

Below are described some of the most relevant probes used, including not only classical security probes (such as IDS or Information Technology (IT) Honeypots) but also innovative components such as the Shadow Security Unit (SSU) or the SCADA Honeypot specifically developed for SCADA environments.

- **Network IDS**: Strategically deployed in the perimeter of each network domain, a NIDS can monitor deviations in network flows and match each network packet against a set of known rules. The authors assessed the SCADA support of different existing open-source NIDS such as Snort and Suricata as well as developed new specific SCADA rules (Rosa et al., 2019).

- **Host IDS:** Acting at a host-level, a HIDS can detect local anomalous activities (e.g., file tampering) or even monitor logs (e.g., Windows events). They are useful not only for reporting deviations in real-time but they might also be useful during a forensics investigation.

- **Honeypots:** Honeypots are dedicated devices used to detect unauthorized communications such as network scans or SCADA requests. The IADS platform is also composed of specialized SCADA Honeypots, capable to detect unauthorized field requests by emulating the behavior of several Power-Line Communication (PLC) devices with support for multiple SCADA protocols (Simões, Cruz, Proença, & Monteiro, 2015).

- **Shadow Security Unit:** The Shadow Security Unit is a dedicated component capable of detecting deviations by comparing both the SCADA network communications and the physical I/O values of a field controller (i.e., PLC or a Remote Terminal Units (RTU)). The IADS SSU represents an evolution of the concept proposed in the scope of the CockpitCI project (Cruz et al., 2015; Graveto, Rosa, Cruz, & Simões, 2019), a low-cost device, deployed in parallel with a controller requiring minimal changes to the existing control networks yet capable of modeling a physical process and detect subtle variations based on simple machine learning techniques (limited by its computational power capabilities).The SSU development effort encouraged further research on the modeling of physical systems to provide a reference for anomaly detection (the so-called *digital twins*). As a result, some structural conditions were identified, which not only determine the detectability and identifiability of attacks targeting IACS networks, but also suggest adequate ways of reacting to cyber-physical attacks.

- **Statistical and Instrumentation Probes**: Finally, statistical and instrumentation probes are important to provide several kinds of information, such as field process telemetry or network communications values and statistics, that are used as input of algorithms and machine learning techniques deployed at the upper layers. As an example, the authors developed a custom probe to extract statistics and Domain Name System (DNS) headers used by the upper layers to infer about potential data exfiltration based on DNS tunneling techniques.

Besides of the security probes main role, collecting evidences from both, physical processes and communication infrastructure, each was also constituted by a configuration agent and event normalization adaptor. The configuration agent provides a simple and uniform strategy that allows to specify all the probe configurations via a configuration file, a YAML file with a custom scheme that can be dynamically updated via a custom management protocol on top of MQTT protocol. This way, it was possible to orchestrate multiple and heterogeneous security probes using a common user interface and protocol.

On the other hand, the event normalization adaptor was used to ensure all the messages produced by different components were properly normalized into the IADS custom data model. Moreover, the event adaptor, based on another configuration YAML file, was designed to easily convert the output of a component into the IADS format (e.g., based on a set of regular expressions it can convert the output of syslog message into an IADS event).

By abstracting both management and event production from the core detection mechanism, the authors are pursuing an open platform where third-party components can be easily integrated without the need of changing their code. The idea behind IADS is not to replace all the existing detection components in the market but to combine their strengths into a common platform.

Software-Defined Networking (SDN) and Network Function Virtualization (NFV)

When combined, Software-Defined Networking (SDN) and Network Function Virtualization (NFV) provide not only a separation between control and data plane as well as an abstraction from the hardware to enable an improved network orchestration. The IADS platform goes beyond and explores those technologies to create SDN-assisted probes and services. Note that the use of these technologies is limited to SDN environments that, given SCADA constrains, certifications or standards compliance reasons might not always be possible.

Several probes were developed as virtualized probes allowing to deploy then in a simple and flexible way using SDN mechanisms. This is especially useful for multi-tenancy scenarios where several probes and instances can be provisioned on-demand and associated to network segments. This way, it is also easier when to cope with network changes where all the virtualized probes can be easily reconfigured in centralized user interface.

As an example, the authors developed an SDN-assisted virtual NIDS (vNIDS) to overcome the shortcomings of the classical NIDS deployments. Traditionally, this requires a mirroring port manually configured in each to monitor the remaining ports and network flows. Nevertheless, leveraging SDN and NFV it is possible to redirect network flows on-demand to multiple vNIDS instances (by associating them to monitoring ports). Such a strategy is also useful to address the network contention problem where as soon as we approach the maximum bandwidth of a monitoring port, it is possible to seamless span additional vNIDS instances.

Another SDN-assisted service developed in the context of the IADS explores the SDN flow mechanisms to create unidirectional network paths, Figure 5 (Freitas, Rosa, Cruz, & Simões, 2019). Such approach is valuable for SCADA environments as allows to block all the unwanted communications to a restricted domain (the field devices) while it allows the SCADA values to reach SCADA control stations in a unidirectional communication.

Moreover, the SDN controller values and statistics are also an extremely useful data source that might be push to the upper processing layers enabling all sort of anomaly detection mechanisms on top of the SDN data.

Forensics and Compliance Auditing (FCA)

More than ever, the complexity of recent attacks, the exponential growth of available raw data as well as the business policies creates the need for a flexible tool that can be used to easily auditing with all the regulations as well as to help during a forensics investigation to search for evidences from large volumes of data and assets across multiple domains.

The IADS FCA subsystem was designed to record and persist digital evidences obtained from the cyber-analysis layer as well as other sources (such as service logs, Authentication Authorization and Accounting (AAA) sessions or physical access control systems, among others), both for forensics and compliance auditing purposes. Moreover, the FCA offers a convenient interface for semi-automatic feature identification and extraction, designed to ease forensics analysis tasks, as well as for detection of non-conformities regarding the established organization policies (both for internal processes and for assessment of the third-party supplier value chain).

For the development of the FCA module (Figure 6), the authors used the Elasticsearch stack (Elasticsearch, Logstash, and Kibana) together with several data sources such as Microsoft Windows events

Figure 5. NFV assisted SDN virtual data diode (from Freitas et al., 2019)

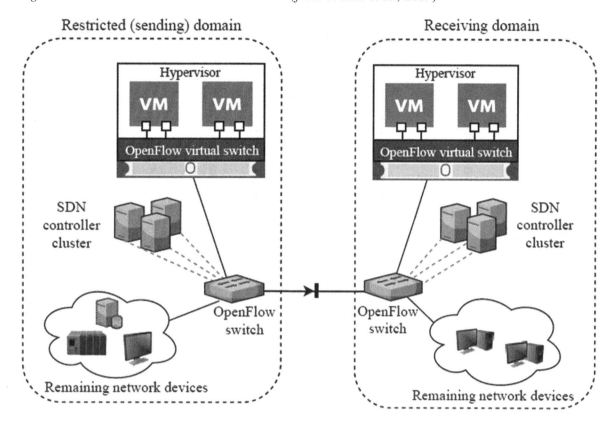

or web log accesses to create a flexible but powerful tool for manual and semi-automatic search of evidences. This module was integrated with the remaining IADS architecture by linking both data-lakes of the SIEM and FCA, so that all the IADS events can be easily searchable across the forensics tool. Moreover, the FCA module also included a semi-automatic mechanism to detect anomalies within the forensics evidences using a gradient boosting decision tree algorithm developed using the Dask framework and XGBoost library.

IADS Event Processing subsystem Evaluation

An evaluation of the event throughput for the IADS platform was undertaken, in order to better understand how the multiple components affect the overall framework performance. All the tests were conducted within a VMware ESXi 6.5 virtualized environment hosted on a Dell R710 server with an Intel(R) Xeon(R) CPU X5660 @ 2.80 Ghz and 4 Linux CentOS 6.4 virtual machines, each one using 8 virtual CPUs, 8 GB RAM and 20 GB of persistent storage. The tests consisted in producing, processing and consuming a variable number of Avro-encoded messages following the IADS data model, as illustrated in Figure 4.

First the messages were produced using a single custom probe (Figure 7) and published to a Kafka topic. Then, a domain processor (based on the Kafka Streams API) with a forwarding topology was used to push the messages to a different topic. Each of those messages were later consumed, inspected and filtered by a Spark task. Finally, all the messages were pushed to another topic and ultimately consumed

Figure 6. FCA subsystem reference architecture

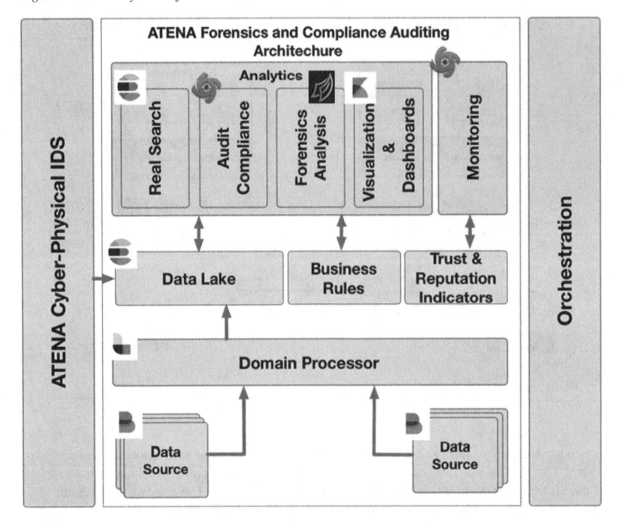

by the event publisher. A vanilla Kafka cluster (0.10.2.0 version) with three brokers was used among all the tests. Nevertheless, four scenarios using different topics configurations were derived. In the first scenario all the topics were created using only one partition and no replication (i.e., replication factor 1). In the second scenario, the replication factor was increased to two. In the third scenario, the partition number was increased to three while keeping the replication factor 1. In the fourth scenario, both, replication and partition number were increased, to two and three, respectively.

Figure 8 and Figure 9 show the overall number of messages both produced and consumed measured at the probe and event publisher level respectively in each of the four scenarios. Even without specific Kafka client configurations, the platform already shows promising results as majority of the scenarios it was surpassed the 10K messages per second rate for both producing and consuming. The other tests, the ones with smaller batches of messages did not achieve those numbers, probably as a result of the cold-start effect since several tests last less than a second. More, contrary to what was expected the four different scenarios configurations did not reveal significant differences. The event producer was config-

Figure 7. Event processing evaluation scenario

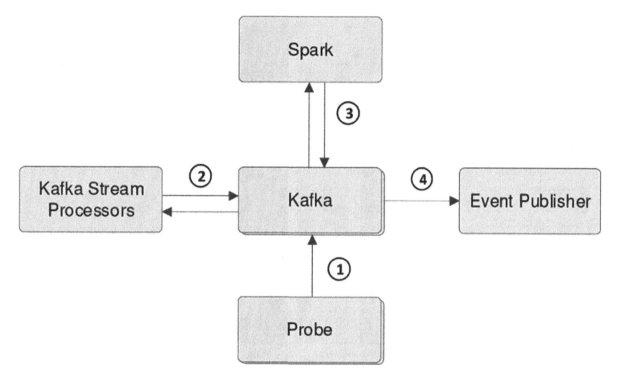

ured with an acknowledgment level of 1 (i.e., a tradeoff between asynchronous writes and full in-sync replicas). This way, the number of replicas did not significantly affect the results.

For fully synchronized writes, a decrease in the message rate production should be expected as the replication factor increases since the Kafka partition leader needs to wait for the acknowledgment of the replicas. On the other hand, the number of partitions is used as unit of parallelism, allowing to have multiple consumers, each one assigned to a partition. More, since the partitions of a given topic might spread across several brokers, it is possible to achieve better results by load-balancing the write operations. Nevertheless, for the evaluated scenarios neither the probe nor the event publisher reveals significant gains.

Future Research Directions

Future developments will include research on innovative anomaly detection strategies as well as a detailed evaluation of the entire solution against different use cases, including additional intrusion scenarios and SCADA-specific scenarios. Additionally, it will be also interesting to compare how different SCADA anomaly detection mechanisms proposed in the literature behave in a highly distributed computation model and how the entire event processing approach envisioned in the IADS can help to improve the anomaly detection models. For instance, by adding a near-time event processing layer, one can leverage a flow-based analysis (e.g., at a network level) that might help to reduce the number of false positives as opposed to a packet-based analysis. Similar, it could also be interesting to explore how other types of information sources such SDN packet flows or even the platform monitoring input might be useful for intrusion and anomaly detection purposes.

Figure 8. Single probe event production results

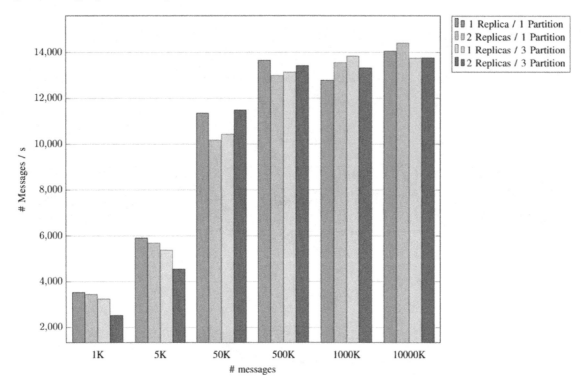

Figure 9. Event publisher event consumption results

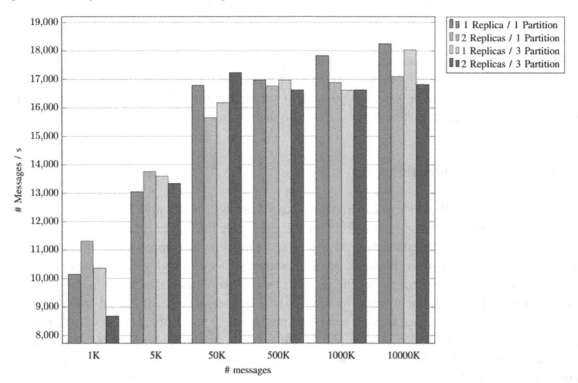

Moreover, once IIoT becomes pervasive, a significant effort will also be required to protect users' privacy, while providing efficient cybersecurity capabilities. While most of the existing solutions do not take such issues into consideration, going against privacy and data protection regulations might simply make it impossible for them to be deployed into production. As such, mechanisms providing users with awareness about the operators' actions or the means to access and manage their profile data will be of paramount importance. In this perspective, some of the next developments will also focus on dispelling the myth that effective analytics do not necessarily imply intrusive data collection. For this purpose, an effort will be made towards improving the evidence collection mechanisms, enforcing anonymity as much as possible, both for data used in training/modeling and for detection tasks.

CONCLUSION

The IADS platform, designed from the beginning as a flexible and distributed solution, represents a significant improvement of its predecessor, the CockpitCI PIDS, allowing to fulfill the recent advances in IIoT environments. Not only can the entire IADS scale-in horizontally to meet different infrastructure requirements but it allows to include different types of anomaly detection strategies that range from batch processing using machine learning algorithms to stream processing that is capable of handling streams of events in (near) real-time. More, a significant effort was also devoted to the probe provisioning where several heterogeneous probes can be easily configured and deployed on-demand to fulfill the needs of elastic scenarios. Future developments will include a research of more innovative anomaly detection strategies as well as a detailed evaluation of the entire solution.

ACKNOWLEDGMENT

This work was partially funded by the ATENA H2020 [H2020-DS-2015-1 Project 700581] and Mobiwise P2020 SAICTPAC/0011/2015 Projects.

REFERENCES

American National Standards Institute/International Society of Automation (ANSI/ISA). (2018). *Security for industrial automation and control systems. ANSI/ISA-62443 Series of standards*. Washington, DC: ANSI.

Ariyaluran Habeeb, R. A., Nasaruddin, F., Gani, A., Targio Hashem, I. A., Ahmed, E., & Imran, M. (2019). Real-time big data processing for anomaly detection: A survey. *International Journal of Information Management, 45*, 289–307. doi:10.1016/j.ijinfomgt.2018.08.006

ATENA Consortium. (2016). A European H2020 Project – ATENA. Retrieved November 10, 2019, from https://www.atena-h2020.eu/

Awad, R. A., Beztchi, S., Smith, J. M., Lyles, B., & Prowell, S. (2018). Tools, techniques, and methodologies: A survey of digital forensics for SCADA systems. In *Proceedings of the Annual Industrial Control System Security (ICSS) Workshop*. New York, NY: ACM. 10.1145/3295453.3295454

Cockpit, C. I. Consortium. (2012). A European FP7 Project – CockpitCI. Retrieved November 10, 2019, from https://cockpitci.itrust.lu/

CRISALIS Consortium. (2015). *CRISALIS - CRitical Infrastructure Security AnaLysIS*. Retrieved October 15, 2019, from https://cordis.europa.eu/project/rcn/103538/factsheet/en

Cruz, T., Barrigas, J., Proenca, J., Graziano, A., Panzieri, S., Lev, L., & Simoes, P. (2015). Improving network security monitoring for industrial control systems. In *Proceedings of the IFIP/IEEE International Symposium on Integrated Network Management, IM 2015* (pp. 878-881). New York: IEEE. 10.1109/INM.2015.7140399

Cruz, T., Rosa, L., Proenca, J., Maglaras, L., Aubigny, M., Lev, L., ... Simões, P. (2016). A cybersecurity detection framework for supervisory control and data acquisition systems. *IEEE Transactions on Industrial Informatics*, *12*(6), 2236–2246. doi:10.1109/TII.2016.2599841

Dayarathna, M., & Perera, S. (2018). Recent advancements in event processing. *ACM Computing Surveys*, *51*(2), 1–36. doi:10.1145/3170432

European Union Agency for Cybersecurity (ENISA). (2017). *Communication network dependencies for ICS/SCADA systems*. Retrieved November 10, 2019, from https://www.enisa.europa.eu/publications/ics-scada-dependencies

Freitas, M. B., Rosa, L., Cruz, T., & Simões, P. (2019). SDN-enabled virtual data diode. In S. K. Katsikas & ... (Eds.), Lecture Notes in Computer Science: Vol. 11387. *Computer Security* (pp. 102–118). Cham, Switzerland: Springer. doi:10.1007/978-3-030-12786-2_7

Ghaeini, H., & Tippenhauer, N. (2016). Hamids: Hierarchical monitoring intrusion detection system for industrial control systems. In *Proceedings of the 2nd ACM Workshop on Cyber-Physical Systems Security and Privacy (CPS-SPC'16)* (pp. 103-111). New York, NY: ACM. 10.1145/2994487.2994492

Goldenberg, N., & Wool, A. (2013). Accurate modeling of Modbus/TCP for intrusion detection in SCADA systems. *International Journal of Critical Infrastructure Protection*, *6*(2), 63–75. doi:10.1016/j.ijcip.2013.05.001

Graveto, V., Rosa, L., Cruz, T., & Simões, P. (2019). A stealth monitoring mechanism for cyber-physical systems. *International Journal of Critical Infrastructure Protection*, *24*, 126–143. doi:10.1016/j.ijcip.2018.10.006

Han, S., Xie, M., Chen, H.-H., & Ling, A. Y. (2014). Intrusion detection in cyber- physical systems: Techniques and challenges. *IEEE Systems Journal*, *8*(4), 1052–1062. doi:10.1109/JSYST.2013.2257594

Inoubli, W., Aridhi, S., Mezni, H., Maddouri, M., & Mephu Nguifo, E. (2018). An experimental survey on big data frameworks. *Future Generation Computer Systems*, *86*, 546–564. doi:10.1016/j.future.2018.04.032

Iturbe, M., Garitano, I., Zurutuza, U., & Uribeetxeberria, R. (2017). Towards large-scale, heterogeneous anomaly detection systems in industrial networks: A survey of current trends. *Security and Communication Networks, 2017*, 1–17. doi:10.1155/2017/9150965

Junejo, K., & Goh, J. (2016). Behaviour-based attack detection and classification in cyber physical systems using machine learning. In *Proceedings of the 2nd ACM International Workshop on Cyber-Physical System Security (CPSS'16)* (pp. 34-43). New York, NY: ACM. 10.1145/2899015.2899016

Kalluri, R., Mahendra, L., Kumar, R. K., & Prasad, G. L. (2017). Simulation and impact analysis of denial-of-service attacks on power SCADA. In *Proceedings of the National Power Systems Conference (NSPC)*. New York: IEEE.

Karri, R., Rajendran, A. J., Rosenfeld, K., & Tehranipoor, M. (2010). Trustworthy hardware: Identifying and classifying hardware trojans. *Computer, 43*(10), 39–46. doi:10.1109/MC.2010.299

Maglaras, L. A., Cruz, T., & Jiang, J. (2014). Integrated OCSVM mechanism for intrusion detection in SCADA systems. *Electronics Letters, 50*(25), 1935–1936. doi:10.1049/el.2014.2897

Marz, N., & Warren, J. (2015). *Big Data: Principles and best practices of scalable realtime data systems.* New York: Manning Publications

Menon, V. K., Sajith Variyar, V., Soman, K. P., Gopalakrishnan, E. A., Kottayil, S. K., Almas, M. S., & Nordström, L. (2019). A Spark™ based client for synchrophasor data stream processing. In *Proceedings of the Conference on the Industrial and Commercial Use of Energy, ICUE* (pp. 1-9). New York: IEEE.

MICIE Consortium. (2011). *MICIE - Tool for systemic risk analysis and secure mediation of data exchanged across linked CI information infrastructures.* Retrieved October 15, 2019, from https://cordis.europa.eu/project/rcn/88359/factsheet/en

Moon, D., Im, H., Kim, I., & Park, J. (2017). DTB-IDS: An intrusion detection system based on decision tree using behavior analysis for preventing APT attacks. *The Journal of Supercomputing, 73*(7), 2881–2895. doi:10.100711227-015-1604-8

North American Energy Reliability Committee (NERC). (2010). *NERC-CIP Reliability Standards (CIP-002 through CIP-009).* Retrieved November 2019, from https://www.nerc.com/pa/Stand/Pages/CIP0024RI.aspx

PRECYSE Consortium. (2015). *PRECYSE - Prevention, protection and REaction to CYber attackS to critical infrastructures.* Retrieved October 2019, from https://cordis.europa.eu/project/rcn/102446/factsheet/en

Raposo, D., Rodrigues, A., Sinche, S., Sá Silva, J., & Boavida, F. (2019). Security and fault detection in In-node components of IIoT constrained devices. *IEEE Local Computer Networks Conference (LCN).* New York: IEEE.

Rettig, L., Khayati, M., Cudre-Mauroux, P., & Piorkowski, M. (2015). Online anomaly detection over Big Data streams. In *Proceedings of the IEEE International Conference on Big Data* (pp. 1113-1122). New York: IEEE. 10.1109/BigData.2015.7363865

Rosa, L., Alves, P., Cruz, T., & Simões, P. (2015). A comparative study of correlation engines for security event management. In *Proceedings of the 10th International Conference on Cyber Warfare and Security (ICCWS 2015)*. Kruger National Park, South Africa: ACPI Press.

Rosa, L., Freitas, M., Mazo, S., Monteiro, E., Cruz, T., & Simoes, P. (2019). A comprehensive security analysis of a SCADA protocol: From OSINT to mitigation. *IEEE Access: Practical Innovations, Open Solutions, 7*, 42156–42168. doi:10.1109/ACCESS.2019.2906926

Rosa, L., Proença, J., Henriques, J., Graveto, V., Cruz, T., Simões, P., ... Monteiro, E. (2017). An evolved security architecture for distributed industrial automation and control systems. In *Proceedings of the 16th European Conference on Information Warfare and Security, ECCWS 2017*. Dublin, Ireland: ACPI.

Simões, P., Cruz, T., Proença, J., & Monteiro, E. (2015). Specialized honeypots for SCADA systems. In M. Lehto, & P. Neittaanmäki (Eds.), Intelligent Systems, Control and Automation: Science and Engineering: Vol. 78. Cyber Security: Analytics, Technology, and Automation (pp. 251-269). Cham, Switzerland: Springer. doi:10.1007/978-3-319-18302-2_16

Singh, V. K., Ebrahem, H., & Govindarasu, M. (2019). Security evaluation of two intrusion detection systems in smart grid SCADA environment. In *Proceedings of the 2018 North American Power Symposium, NAPS 2018*. New York: IEEE.

Stouffer, K., Pillitteri, V., Lightman, S., Abrams, M., & Hahn, A. (2015). *Guide to industrial control systems (ICS) security (NIST Special Publication 800-82 Rev. 2)*. Gaithersburg, MD: U.S. National Institute of Standards and Technology. doi:10.6028/NIST.SP.800-82r2

VIKING Consortium. (2011). *VIKING - Vital Infrastructure, networKs, INformation and control systems manaGement*. Retrieved October 15, 2019, from https://cordis.europa.eu/project/rcn/88625/factsheet/en

Vitali, T., David, T., Ofer, B., Michal, F., Aubigny, M., Panzieri, S., & Simões, P. (2017). *D7.1 – Validation plan*. ATENA Project Document.

Waagsnes, H., & Ulltveit-moe, N. (2018). Intrusion detection system test framework for SCADA systems. In *Proceedings of the 4th International Conference on Information Systems Security and Privacy* (pp. 275-285). Madeira, Portugal: ScitePress. 10.5220/0006588202750285

Yang, H., Cheng, L., & Chuah, M. C. (2019). Deep-learning-based network intrusion detection for SCADA systems. In *Proceedings of the IEEE Conference on Communications and Network Security (CNS)*. New York: IEEE. 10.1109/CNS.2019.8802785

Zaddach, J., Bruno, L., Francillon, A., & Balzarotti, D. (2014). Avatar: A framework to support dynamic security analysis of embedded systems' firmwares. In *Proceedings of the Network and Distributed System Security (NDSS) Symposium*. Internet Society.

Zou, X., Cao, J., Sun, W., Guo, Q., & Wen, T. (2019). Flow data processing paradigm and its application in smart city using a cluster analysis approach. *Cluster Computing, 22*(2), 435–444. doi:10.100710586-018-2839-y

ADDITIONAL READING

International Society of Automation (ISA). (2015). *ISA-62443-1-1 security for industrial automation and control systems part 1: Terminology, concepts, and models draft 5.* Research Triangle Park, NC: International Society for Automation.

Khraisat, A., Gondal, I., Vamplew, P., & Kamruzzaman, J. (2019). Survey of intrusion detection systems: Techniques, datasets and challenges. *Cybersecurity, 2*(1), 20. doi:10.118642400-019-0038-7

Knapp, E. D., & Langill, J. T. (2014). *Industrial network security: Securing critical infrastructure networks for smart grid, SCADA, and other industrial control systems.* Waltham, MA: Syngress.

Krutz, R. L. (2005). *Securing SCADA systems.* Hoboken, NJ: John Wiley & Sons, Inc.

Nazir, S., Patel, S., & Patel, D. (2017). Assessing and augmenting SCADA cyber security: A survey of techniques. *Computers & Security, 70,* 436–454. doi:10.1016/j.cose.2017.06.010

Rosa, L., Cruz, T., Simões, P., Monteiro, E., & Lev, L. (2017). Attacking SCADA systems: A practical perspective. In *Proceedings of the 2017 IFIP/IEEE Symposium on Integrated Network and Service Management (IM)* (pp. 741-746). New York: IEEE. 10.23919/INM.2017.7987369

Volkova, A., Niedermeier, M., Basmadjian, R., & De Meer, H. (2018). Security challenges in control network protocols: A survey. *IEEE Communications Surveys and Tutorials, 21*(1), 619–639. doi:10.1109/COMST.2018.2872114

KEY TERMS AND DEFINITIONS

Anomaly Detection: Analysis techniques which try to identify deviations regarding an established normal behavior or operational pattern of a system.

Critical Infrastructure (CI): Systems whose incapacity or destruction would have a debilitating effect on the economic security of an enterprise, community or nation.

Forensics and Compliance Auditing (FCA): A set of analysis capabilities to retrieve insights from persisted data. Two kinds of actors interact with these capabilities: Operators and Security Analysts. Operators receive continuous information from the processes performing rule assessment, evaluating the critically of events and preparing a set of responsive actions to minimize their impact. Security Analysts are responsible for extracting insights from the interpretation of stored events, performing ad hoc queries to understand related thread event paths and preparing improvement measures.

Industrial Automation and Control Systems (IACS): Systems that ensure the supervision and control of a series of processes involved in the production and delivery of goods and services, from assembly lines to power plants. In fact, several universal and essential services, such as utility or telecommunications infrastructures, which are crucial to maintain the social, industrial, economic and security status of a modern country, depend on IACS.

Industrial IoT (IIoT): The result of the evolution of industrial automation technologies towards assimilating the IoT paradigm. The outcome is a new generation of automation infrastructures which are highly distributed and interconnected, spawning large coverage areas.

LAMBDA Architecture: An architecture designed to deal with immutable data sets that grow over time (which is the nature of the security events being generated from the probes). The Lambda architecture encompasses both stream techniques for fast, time-window based event processing and batch processing techniques, which constitute a slow path for event processing, sifting through large volumes of data (stored in a large repository, such as a data lake) to search for trends or anomalous patterns.

Security Information and Event Management (SIEM): This term is typically used to refer to systems oriented towards performing log/event storage and processing (typically filtering and correlation).

Security Probe: Security agents whose role is to capture relevant evidence from several strategic points and components of the protected infrastructure, which is to be streamed and pre-processed before being sent to a security analytics platform.

Software-Defined Networking (SDN): Consists of an architecture that decouples forwarding functions (data plane) from network control (control plane), enabling network programmability. It constitutes a flow-oriented virtualization mechanism for networks, allow for the flexible creation and management of network overlays on top of existing physical infrastructures, while also enabling significant security and reliability benefits.

Chapter 5
Security Issues of Cloud Migration and Optical Networking in Future Internet

Branka Mikavica

Faculty of Transport and Traffic Engineering, University of Belgrade, Serbia

Aleksandra Kostić-Ljubisavljević

Faculty of Transport and Traffic Engineering, University of Belgrade, Serbia

ABSTRACT

Future internet environment is affected by permanent and rapid changes, triggered by the emergence of high bandwidth-demanding services, applications, and contents. Cloud computing might be considered as the prelude of the future internet. Additionally, the concept of elastic optical networks is a widely accepted promising solution for the future internet. This chapter addresses the security aspects of the content provisioning process with cloud migration over elastic optical networks in the future internet environment. Key characteristics of the cloud computing and elastic optical networks relevant to the content provisioning process are presented. Major threats in each segment of the observed process, including vulnerabilities in the cloud computing and security issues in elastic optical networks, are considered.

INTRODUCTION

Continuous and rapid change, cost-saving aspects and the need for flexibility affect the industrial systems in Future Internet environment. Additional improvements in networking are required to tackle these challenges. Nowadays, cloud computing is recognized as a widespread networking approach with extensive acceptance and deployment. The concept of cloud computing along with the flexible network access and the scalable distributed computing provides a promising solution for many business challenges in the Future Internet environment. Due to numerous advantages, both business and public customers are gradually migrating to the cloud. Virtualization, as a key characteristic of cloud computing, enables flexible management of computing resources, distributing them as needed for a certain service into a

DOI: 10.4018/978-1-7998-2910-2.ch005

data center, or spreading them across several data centers connected to the network (Contreras et al., 2012). The computing resources can be provided on demand, upon customers' requests. Such elasticity in resource utilization provides agile adaptation to the business requirements. In this multitenant model, the sharing of resources among numerous customers reduces costs and maximizes utilization, thus leveraging the economy of scale. Additionally, due to the possibility of resource allocation in different data centers, the provisioning of services, contents and applications to the customers become independent of where either the resource or the customer is located.

The versatile utilization of resources and the distinct requirements of the applications running can produce variable traffic patterns on the connections to the data centers. The flexibility provided by cloud computing dynamically changes the traffic demand, thus affecting network planning and dimensioning. The network utilization is time-varying and less predictable. Furthermore, various applications running on cloud systems lead to new traffic patterns including anycast flows. Those traffic flows can be described as one-to-one-of-many flows. Additionally, the concentration of processing in a relatively small number of data centers increases the volume of traffic on network links adjacent to these data centers. A new network concept is needed to support challenges emerged with cloud computing introduction. Such a concept should be capable of providing the required capacity on demand through automatic elastic connectivity services in a scalable and cost-efficient manner. Therefore, the new capacity demands require evolution to optical-transport-based solutions (Develder et al., 2012). A transport network is an indispensable segment of the cloud computing model and provides the connectivity among distributed computing resources. The cloud-ready transport network should meet requirements in terms of flexibility (the ability to guarantee the required capacity on demand), multilayer oriented network management and joint optimization of the resources of both the cloud-based applications and the underlying network providing connectivity (Klinkowski & Walkowiak, 2013).

Optical networks have an essential role in communication systems since they provide a reliable infrastructure for the transport of aggregated IP traffic. Recently, significant research advances emerged in optical networking, including developments of spectrally efficient modulation techniques and new optical components (Klinkowski & Walkowiak, 2013). These networking capabilities have led to the introduction of an elastic optical network (EON) infrastructure (Jinno et al., 2012). The newly introduced optical transport networks can utilize network resources more efficiently and concurrently, enable network connectivity adaptively to bandwidth demands. The capacity of a lightpath can be adjusted by allocating enough spectrum that satisfies traffic demand. Thus, resource utilization in EONs is vastly improved compared to conventional fixed-grid optical networks.

Due to the increasing number of threats in the optical networks, data security gains significant research interest. Since EON is the key development direction of the optical transport network, it is crucial to improve the defense capability of EON against the possible attacks. In this chapter, the cloud migration over elastic optical networks in the context of the content provisioning process is going to be addressed, with special reference on the security aspect of provisioning of services, contents and applications.

BACKGROUND

Future Internet environment is characterized by rapid changes. Major transitions are induced by the introduction of cloud computing and the emergence of the new optical network infrastructure, i.e., elastic optical networks. The continuous growth of Internet traffic is mainly caused by provisioning of the high bandwidth-demanding contents. Significant improvements in the content provisioning process are possible to achieve by enabling cloud migration. The term cloud migration refers to the possibility of replication of the original contents provided by content and application provider (Kostic-Ljubisavljevic & Mikavica, 2018).The determination of the cloud storage size to be occupied mainly depends on the number of requests for content provisioning that are going to be served by the cloud, as well as the size of the contents migrated to the cloud storage. Appropriate cloud migration strategy minimizes costs, i.e., minimizes occupied cloud storage, and minimizes rejection of requests for content provisioning. The rejection occurs when the content provider's capacity is exceeded and concurrently the required content is not migrated to the cloud (Mikavica & Kostic-Ljubisavljevic, 2016). Enhanced virtualization, standardization and automation of cloud data centers provide performances' improvement, greater capacity and bandwidth. However, the concentration of the processing and storage capacity in a relatively small number of data centers significantly increases traffic volumes on the network links adjacent to the data centers. Enormous traffic volumes demand implementation of network topologies capable to support ever-increasing requirements. Elastic optical network topology is considered as a promising solution for an effective and cost-efficient cloud-ready transport network (Mikavica, Markovic, & Kostic-Ljubisavljevic, 2018).Some key characteristics of cloud computing and elastic optical networking in the Future Internet environment are presented below.

Cloud computing represents the paradigm for enabling network access to a scalable and elastic pool of shareable physical or virtual resources with self-service provisioning and administration on-demand (International Telecommunication Union – Telecommunication Standardization Sector [ITU-T], 2014). Cloud resources can be rapidly provisioned and terminated with minimal management effort or providers' interaction. Key characteristics of cloud computing are the following: on-demand self-service, broad network access, resource pooling, rapid elasticity and scalability, and measured service (Mell & Grance, 2011). A cloud customer can unilaterally provision computer capabilities including server time and network storage automatically, without necessary interaction with the provider. Physical and virtual resources in a cloud computing model are available over a network and accessed through standard mechanisms. Cloud customers can access cloud resources regardless of their location. The cloud provider's resources are pooled to serve multiple tenants, with different physical and virtual resources dynamically allocated depending on traffic demand. In general, cloud customers do not have control or knowledge over the exact location of the cloud provider's resources. Thus, there is a sort of location independence. However, cloud customers can specify location at a higher level of abstraction, for example, country or data center. Cloud resources comprise storage, processing, memory and network bandwidth. Cloud resources can be elastically initiated and terminated to scale rapidly according to demand. From the cloud customers' perspective, cloud resources available for provisioning often appear to be unlimited, with the possibility of quantity adjustment at any time. Cloud resources can automatically control and optimize utilization by leveraging a metering capability at some level of abstraction. Therefore, cloud services can be monitored, controlled, reported and billed, while transparency is provided for both cloud provider and cloud customer. The main advantage of the measured-service cloud feature is that cloud customers pay only for the resources they use.

Depending on the resources used, there are three cloud capabilities types: application, infrastructure and platform capabilities type. These types have minimal overlapping functionalities (ITU-T, 2014). It is important to emphasize the difference between cloud capabilities types and cloud service categories. There are only three cloud capabilities types, while cloud service category presents a group of cloud services with a common set of qualities and includes capabilities from one or more cloud capabilities types. Some representative categories of cloud service are Communication as a Service (CaaS), Compute as a service (CompaaS), Data Storage as a Service (DSaaS), Infrastructure as a Service (IaaS), Network as a Service (NaaS), Platform as a Service (PaaS) and Software as a Service (SaaS). The number of emerging cloud service categories is increasing.

Depending on the control and sharing of physical or virtual cloud resources, cloud computing can be organized in several cloud deployment models: public cloud, private cloud, community cloud and hybrid cloud. These deployment models differ in terms of ownership, management and operation of cloud resources.

One of the most important aspects of cloud computing that needs to be coordinated across roles and implemented consistently is security. It ranges from physical security to application security and comprises authentication, authorization, availability, confidentiality, integrity, incident response, security monitoring and security policy management (ITU-T, 2014). Since cloud resources are connected using an internal network, an attack on the network may induce delays in communication or disable network access (Ahmad Khan, 2016).Additionally, attacks on virtual machines (VM), which host the required software for the service and are deployed on the virtualization of the cloud provider, can significantly impact the security for malicious purposes (Liu, Zhang, Xin, & Wang, 2014). Furthermore, cloud services are also vulnerable to security threats, which potentially may lead to the violation of data protection or even unavailability of services for all cloud customers (Gruschka & Iacono, 2009). Since the cloud relies on traditional architecture, it is even more vulnerable to security threats. Along with the increasing number of threats, the corresponding countermeasures are also developed. For example, various countermeasures are proposed for attacks emerging due to network, such as botnet and stepping-stone attacks (Kourai, Azumi, & Chiba, 2012). Some cryptographic techniques are proposed for mitigation the risk of violation of data protection attacks (Ahmad Khan, 2016). Different authentication mechanisms can be used for vulnerabilities in VM migration (Godfrey & Zulkernine, 2013). Additionally, the intrusion detection systems can tackle the attacks related to denial or theft-of-service (Hay, Cid, & Bray, 2008). Security issues significantly affect cloud system performance. In Xu, Qiu, Sheng, Luo, & Xiang (2018), two critical security factors are observed, i.e., malicious attacks and the security protection mechanism. The relations between security and cloud service performance are modeled using a hierarchical approach. The results show that the importance of security in the modeling and evaluation of the Quality of Service (QoS) is significant and requires comprehensive analysis. Several studies provide a classification of attacks and corresponding countermeasures (Hashizume, Rosado, Fernandez-Medina, & Fernandez, 2013).Depending on cloud capabilities types, in Subashini & Kavita (2011) is presented a layer-wise categorization of security attacks. The scalability of cloud and compliance regulations as major cloud security issues are described by Carlin & Curran (2013).

Optical networking technology experienced pertinent progress to meet the rapid increasing of IP centered services such as cloud computing, big data applications etc. It was necessary to create a new standardized grid, allowing the best spectral efficiency for the increased diversity of the spectrum requirements. Therefore, International Telecommunication Union (ITU) proposed a finer grid associating a variable frequency slot to a lightpath, named flexible frequency grid, i.e., flex-grid. Such flex grid allows allocation of a variable number of fixed-sized slots to an optical channel as a function of its requirements. In the literature, the terms flex-grid, gridless, or elastic optical networks are used interchangeably to classify systems not complied with ITU's fixed-grid channel spacing (Velasco et al., 2016).

The most important issue in elastic optical networking, along with the design, network planning and operation, is routing and spectrum allocation (RSA). Traffic demand needs to be routed over the network and a portion of the spectrum should be allocated to the given traffic demand, thus creating a lightpath. The RSA problem is a specific optimization problem that needs to be solved. Two key constraints must be satisfied while solving RSA problem, the continuity constraint and the contiguity constraint. The continuity constraint ensures that the allocated spectrum slots are the same along the links in the route. The contiguity constraint guarantees that allocated resources are contiguous in the spectrum. The problem of content provision over EON with possible cloud migration is addressed by Mikavica et al. (2018). The analysis encompasses the problem of content placement into cloud data centers along with the RSA problem. A mixed integer linear programming model is formulated to optimize cloud migration, spectrum utilization and lightpath length, simultaneously. The RSA problem is NP-complete (Christodoulopoulos, Tomkos, & Varvarigos, 2011). Therefore, efficient methods able to solve real problem instances in reasonable time are needed. Considering the relevance of the security aspects, addressing the RSA problem along with network security is crucial. A study analyzing these issues is performed by (Xuan et al., 2016). The proposed optimization model determines an optimal routing and allocation scheme with the guaranteed security level by minimizing the maximum sequence number of spectrum slices. A hybrid algorithm is used to solve the observed problem efficiently. The first stage of the analysis is the determination of the candidate paths with guaranteed required security level for connection requests using a heuristic algorithm. Afterwards, the genetic algorithm with a tailor-made crossover operator and a well-designed mutation operator is formulated. Experimental results indicate that the proposed algorithm is more efficient than the compared ones. However, connection requests need to be sorted in advance, which constraints the application of the proposed algorithm on static routing and allocation problem.

Since heterogeneous technologies of multi-vendor network elements can be found in backbone networks, it is important to address the multi-domain scenario of EONs (J. Zhu, Zhao, Lu, & Z. Zhu, 2016). Thus, it is possible to accommodate the interoperability issues, improve network scalability and extend service coverage when using network elements of different vendors. Security threats in a multi-domain EON scenario can be mitigated using opaque domains (providing exclusively optical-to-electrical-to-optical conversions in-between domains). However, this solution increases both capital expenditure and operational expenditure. Therefore, it is necessary to design an attack-aware service provisioning scheme in transparent multi-domain EONs. Vulnerabilities of optical components along with RSA in EONs are analyzed by (J. Zhu et al., 2016) in both intra-domain and inter-domain scenarios. A multi-domain attack-aware RSA algorithm is proposed to improve the overall security in EON. An integer linear programming model is formulated to obtain optimal solutions. In addition, a heuristic algorithm is proposed to reduce the time complexity. The results show that the proposed algorithms are satisfying in terms of effectiveness.

Confidential issues in EONs are analyzed by Bai et al. (2018). The problem of eavesdropping attacks in RSA is solved by an eavesdropping-aware RSA algorithm to guarantee information security. Additionally, for further security improvements, an eavesdropping-aware multi-flow virtual concatenation-based secure RSA algorithm is proposed. The results show that the proposed algorithms provide enhanced security against eavesdropping and improve network performance efficiently.

Various survivability schemes are analyzed by Stapleton et al. (2018), and an approach to implementing protection and restoration in EON is proposed. Thus, the flexibility and granularity of EONs are efficiently exploited. An overview of physical-layer attacks in elastic optical networks is provided by (Skorin-Kapov, Furdek, Zsigmond, & Wosinska, 2016). Different attack scenarios with possible entry point attackers along with their consequences are observed. Furthermore, a general security framework is proposed to reduce the overall network vulnerability.

SECURITY ISSUES IN A CLOUD ENVIRONMENT

Security and privacy are considered as a major architectural component of the cloud. Hence, security responsibilities require a comprehensive analysis of different cloud service and deployment models. It is important to emphasize that security is a cross-cutting aspect and extends through all layers of the reference model, ranging from physical to application security. Security concerns affect not only cloud providers, but also cloud customers and other relevant participants.

Cloud service categories require different types of service management operations. Furthermore, cloud service categories use various entry points into cloud systems. Consequently, there are numerous different attacking possibilities for adversaries. Therefore, cloud security design and implementation need to consider the impact of different cloud service categories and corresponding issues.

The analysis of cloud security should also comprise the impact of different cloud deployment models. There are two possible aspects of cloud security analysis from the perspective of cloud deployment model. The first one is based on the different level of exclusivity of tenants in a deployment model. For example, security issues differ in a private and public cloud environment. A private cloud is dedicated to a single organization, while a public cloud can have unpredictable tenants concurrently. Therefore, workload isolation is less of a security concern in a private cloud compared to a public cloud. The second aspect uses the concept of access boundaries (F. Liu et al., 2011). For example, a private cloud does not necessarily require additional boundary controllers at the cloud boundary if the private cloud is hosted within the corresponding organization boundary. However, an outsourced private cloud requires the establishment of additional protection at the boundary.

In a cloud environment, cloud provider and cloud customer have different degrees of control over the computing resources and collaboratively design, build, deploy and operate cloud resources. Shared control triggers shared responsibilities in providing appropriate protection against security threats. It is important to determine which party should implement certain protective measures since different service models imply different degrees of control between the cloud provider and cloud customer. For example, the cloud provider typically performs account management controls in IaaS scenarios, while management of application customer account in an IaaS environment is not the providers' responsibility.

Security attacks can be classified depending on the cloud component under attack, i.e., network-based attacks, VM based attacks, storage-based attacks and application-based attacks, as shown in Figure 1.

The cloud resources are connected through a network, which simultaneously provides connections outside the cloud. An intruder may disrupt data privacy and confidentiality by network attacks. There are three possible network attacks: port scanning, botnets and spoofing attacks. The port scanning is used to

Figure 1. Classification of security attacks in cloud environment

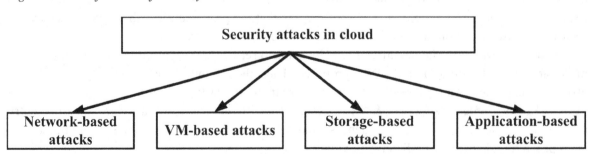

investigate the status of a service provisioning on a targeted machine. It requires access to the network hosting the targeted machine. The result of this attack may be a denial of service. A botnet may be used to steal data from a host machine. A control system can be established by a bot-master, while several machines can act as a stepping-stone to steal private data. The spoofing attacks are used to impersonate entities for malicious purposes. Such attacks replace the IP address of a packet with a forged one. Furthermore, a DNS spoofing attack may cause a DNS server to redirect traffic to an attacker's system.

Data protection can also be violated through VM based attacks. Various phases in VM management can be exploited to undertake a large number of attacks. In the scope of the VM based attacks, several types of attacks can be distinguished by Ahmad Khan (2016): cross VM side-channel attacks, VM creation attacks, VM migration and rollback attacks and VM scheduler-based attacks. The VM side-channel attacks can extract resource usage data or cryptographic keys from a targeted VM, which is placed on the same physical machine as the attacker's VM. During the creation of VMs, malicious code can be inserted into a VM image. In this case, a virtual image management system providing filters and scanners for detecting and recovering need to be used (Wei, Zhang, Ammons, Bala, & Ning, 2009). Additionally, the contents of the VM become vulnerable during VM migration from one physical machine to another. Thus, the log of execution state being maintained for implementing a rollback may become accessible during VM migration. Furthermore, VM scheduler is also prone to vulnerabilities, causing resource stealing or theft-of-service (Zhou, Goel, Desnoyers, & Sundaram, 2011). Some modified schedulers may improve security and maintain fairness and efficiency.

Private data stored on a cloud storage device can be stolen by an attacker from outside or by a malicious insider (Li, Yu, Ren, Lou, & Hou, 2013). Without the implementation of a strict monitoring mechanism, access to sensitive information may occur. Two storage-based attacks may be distinguished: data scavenging and data deduplication (Ahmad Khan, 2016). Data scavenging presents malicious recovering of removed data from a storage device (Jansen, 2011). Data deduplication may occur while minimizing storage and bandwidth requirements when it becomes possible to identify the files and their contents (Harnik, Pinkas, & Shulman-Peleg, 2010). This situation may be mitigated by ensuring that there is only a specific number of file copies (Kaaniche & Laurent, 2014).

The applications running on a cloud are prone to various attacks by injecting code to trace execution paths and exploit this information for malicious purposes. Moreover, protocols implemented to provide services on a cloud system are vulnerable to attacks and any running applications may use them as a source of the intrusion. Shared architectural components may also be used by an application as a source for malicious activities. There are three application-based attacks: malware injection and steganography attacks, shared architectures and web services and protocol-based attacks (Ahmad Khan, 2016). If a cloud platform allows for an insecure interface for application development, malicious code may be injected. In the case of a steganography attack, the malicious code is embedded within files, which are transmitted over the network (Mazurczyk & Szczypiorski, 2011). In the case of a shared architecture, the execution path of the application can be traced and used to detect activities and seize account (Zhang, Juels, Reiter, & Ristenpart, 2014). Another variant of application-based attack occurs if the message headers of the protocols implemented by web servers are manipulated (Gruschka & Iacono, 2009). The security policies and validation mechanisms should be implemented to enable uninterrupted service provisioning.

SECURITY ISSUES IN CLOUD-READY OPTICAL TRANSPORT NETWORKS

Due to the significant increase in network usage and accessibility of optical networks, the provisioning of properly secured communications is of great importance. The first step for securing communication is employing cryptographic protocols at higher layers of the protocol stack. However, it is necessary to provide a secure physical layer against threats. The physical layer of an optical network is vulnerable to a variety of attacks, comprising jamming, physical infrastructure attacks, eavesdropping and interception. Security mechanisms at the physical layer of an optical network should operate at real-time to augment security procedures employed at the higher layers of the protocol stack (Fok, Wang, Deng, & Prucnal, 2011). Thus, overall system security is enhanced. Optical communication systems have less risk of side-channel attacks, as optical devices do not generate electromagnetic interference and are less vulnerable to electromagnetic-based side-channel eavesdropping.

In general, the threats in optical networks can be classified into several categories (as shown in Figure 2):

- Threats where an adversary tries to attack confidentiality.
- Threats where an unauthorized entity tries to communicate (authentication issues).
- Threats where an entity alerts or manipulates communication (integrity issues).
- Threats where an adversary tries to subvert the communications (availability issues).
- Privacy risks related to adversary observing the existence of communications (privacy and traffic analysis).

Although optical networks are not prone to electromagnetic interferences, an attacker can eavesdrop on an optical system using physically tapping into the optical fiber or by listening to the residual crosstalk from an adjacent channel while impersonating a legitimate customer (Furdek, Skorin-Kapov, Bosiljevac, & Sipus, 2010). Tapping optical fiber occurs if the fiber is exposed and without physical protection. A fiber can be tapped by peeling off the protective material and cladding of the fiber, while the light leaves the fiber. By placing a second fiber adjacent to the place where light leaves from the fiber, it is possible to seize the desired optical signal. The eavesdropper must operate at a very low signal-to-noise ratio to perform tapping without noticing. Since the majority of optical fibers in communication systems are bundled together and have multiple layers of protective material and cabling, so the physical tapping is not easy to perform. Another way of eavesdropping is to sense the residual adjacent channel crosstalk while impersonating one of the customers. Confidentiality can be improved using optical encryption and optical coding. Encryption is a promising approach to secure the signal in the physical layer. Without the knowledge of the encryption key, the data cannot be recovered by the eavesdropper. Since there is no electromagnetic interference in the fiber-optical transmission, the eavesdroppers cannot retrieve any useful information without knowledge of the encryption key. Optical code-division multiple access (OCDMA) can enhance information security since it allows the confidential information hidden in the optical layer based on optical encoding (Huang, Wang, Wang, Zhang, & Dai, 2017). OCDMA provides originates from the encoding/decoding process and its multiplexing properties. Each data stream is encoded by a certain code that can be identified using the corresponding decoder. Optical coding is less efficient compared to optical encryption. However, it introduces an additional layer of protection from eavesdropping.

A specific coding/decoding scheme between the given counterparts of customers is required to improve authentication. Such a coding scheme forms an identity for the customer. A unique OCDMA

Figure 2. Classification of security threats in optical networks

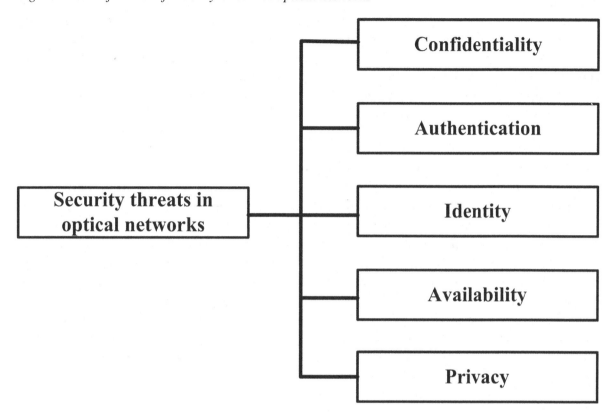

coding/decoding scheme can provide a certain level of authentication if the given code is agreed upon between the sender-receiver pair of customers. The OCDMA signal in the presence of other OCDMA traffic is not possible to be decoded by an unauthorized customer. Therefore, along with the multi-access capability, OCDMA codes support authentication issues between two customers. The procedure of coding/decoding is the following. Each customer encodes the data by a unique OCDMA code that serves as the sender's identity. To receive the data from an authorized sender, the receiver should use the corresponding decoder. Data encoded by other encoder are considered as unauthorized data. In that case, the data are blocked due to the inconsistency between the encoders and decoders. An unauthorized customer cannot impersonate the authenticated sender without knowledge of the code, and hence, it is not possible to compromise the OCDMA system.

The privacy of communication systems can be significantly improved by steganography. Messages are hidden in plain sight so that only the sender and the corresponding receiver are aware of the transmission. Optical steganography provides the transmission of a secret data channel, namely, the stealth channel, which can be hidden in the presence of the public channels (Fok et al., 2011). However, the data rate of the stealth channel must be lower compared to the public channel. This approach is based on the generation of a series of short optical pulses (stealth pulses) which are temporally stretched using a dispersive optical element with high group-velocity dispersion. Those short optical pulses have a wide spectral width, while the high dispersion element provides that each wavelength component propagates at different speeds. High group-velocity dispersion causes that stealth pulses are stretched sufficiently to reduce the peak amplitudes to a level below the system noise. In the presence of the public signals, the stretched stealth pulses are hidden under both the ambient noise in the network and the public signal. In the spectral domain, the stealth signal can be immersed below the background noise, or it can share the same spectrum as the public channel. The main reason for this procedure is to make the stealth signal invisible in the spectral domain. At the reception, the public channel is recovered by a conventional optical receiver. The stealth signal causes minimal performance degradation due to low amplitude. A match group-velocity dispersion is needed to enable stealth pulses recovering. The public signal must be distinguished from the received signal before the stealth signal can be identified.

Signal jamming attacks are also possible in optical networks. In some situations, a denial of service can occur. The denial of service does not always cause the theft of information. However, it may subtract network resources, such as bandwidth, or can result in financial losses to the network provider. Physical damage to an optical fiber can happen intentionally or unintentionally. An attacker can cut off an exposed segment of the unprotected fiber, or damage can occur negligently during digging. Regardless of the intent, optical networks are usually configured with redundant paths, thus minimizing disruption of services. Based on the self-healing ring architectures, survivability and availability in optical networks are enabled. Due to large code cardinality and soft-blocking, the OCDMA technique represents effective protection and increases service availability under physical infrastructure attack while minimizing the bandwidth usage (Fok et al., 2011). Thus, the OCDMA-based backup channel can be used to implement a bandwidth-efficient bidirectional OCDMA ring network. Detection, localization and prevention of jamming attacks in optical networks can be performed by machine learning solutions since machine learning is recently recognized as an efficient statistical method to address the issues of attack detection and prevention in real-time (Natalino, Schiano, Di Giglio, Wosinska, & Furdek, 2018).

SOLUTIONS AND RECOMMENDATIONS

Various systems for intrusion detection and prevention are proposed to tackle the challenges in the cloud migration over an elastic optical network. An Intrusion Detection System (IDS) analyzes the packet header and payload and compares any anomalies found with the normal traffic. If the anomalous traffic is detected, this system identifies the pattern against common threats and alerts the network administrator. A system for prevention, i.e., an Intrusion Prevention System (IPS), operates by the same algorithm as the IDS but also provides rejection of packets and terminates the connection. Considering that the network supporting cloud migration is a high-speed network, such a system requires a completely automated intrusion detection/prevention system. A Network Intrusion Detection/Prevention System (NIDS/NIPS) is a promising solution for provisioning a secure environment for all computing systems in a network. The security issues of a single host can be treated by a Host-based Intrusion Detection/Prevention System (HIDS/HIPS). It is worth noting that scalability of the IDS is of crucial importance for efficient utilization of the cloud architectures and optical networking in the Future Internet environment. The trusted cloud computing environment is necessary to provide a secure and confidential execution environment while maintaining data integrity. Different mechanisms for enabling a trusted computing environment are proposed (Ahmad Khan, 2016). Furthermore, strict regulation is necessary to ensure secure cloud migration over elastic optical networks. Various regulatory bodies have set rules encompassing a wide range of applications and practices (Ahmad Khan, 2016).

In the context of the elastic optical networking in the content provisioning process, several challenges need to be solved. Different communication requests in elastic optical networks share common fiber links must be separated in the spectrum domain by a guard band to prevent interference or satisfy the security requirement, due to physical impairments or attacks in the optical layer. To satisfy different interference or security levels, the size of the guard band should be adapted, instead of fixed guard bands (Wu, Zhou, Z. Zhu, & Chen, 2016).The security challenge in elastic optical networks can also be mitigated by data scrambling in the code, time and frequency domains (F. Liu, Ren, & Bai, 2014). Data scrambling can be used to randomize the spectrum allocation to improve security and prevent the attacker to decode the data (Singh, Bziuk, & Jukan, 2016).Thus, the security is improved, but at the cost of the increased blocking probability. This issue needs to be appropriately tackled.

FUTURE RESEARCH DIRECTIONS

Along with the expansion of cloud services, the number of vulnerability incidents in the context of content provisioning over elastic optical networks is on the rise. Despite the appropriate countermeasures proposed in numerous studies, many security issues and challenges require a comprehensive approach and present a subject for future research directions, as described below.

Firstly, a trusted environment is a prerequisite for efficient and reliable communications. Data stored in the cloud should only be accessible to authentic customers. Regarding this issue, trusted execution technologies provide reliable verification of the system integrity, which affects management and security policies. It is essential to identify all necessary measures to protect the system. Protocols defined for communication between cloud providers and cloud customers are vulnerable to various attacks. For example, protocol messages can be manipulated to violate data protection. Additionally, the insecure interfaces used to interact with cloud systems are considered to the major threats. It is crucial to mitigate the vulnerability of the existing protocols, to provide a secure implementation of these protocols and to incorporate highly efficient encryption mechanism. The identity and access management support control of the cloud customers' access to the shared pool of physical and virtual cloud resources. The diversity of protocols, conformance requirements and architectures make the access management even more complex. Therefore, new models of controlled access are required. Although major threats and vulnerabilities in the cloud environment are recognized, the development of open standards is necessary for the improvement of security. The assessment of cloud security from different perspectives, including services, deployment and interoperability needs to be comprehensively performed.

Developing new attack-aware methods for elastic optical networks in the content provisioning process involves different challenges and poses new research opportunities in terms of novel latency-aware and attack-aware anycast protection and improved RSA algorithms. Furthermore, secure authentication and access are still great challenges and require a comprehensive approach to solving. Advances in optical encryption methods can support the development of new authentication schemes and improve data privacy.

CONCLUSION

Cloud computing provides access to a sharable and elastic pool of physical or virtual resources. Main advantages of cloud computing are on-demand self-service, broad network access, rapid elasticity, scalability and measured service. Despite its effectiveness and the widespread adoption, some constraints affect its prevalence. One of the most important challenges that need to be appropriately analyzed and tackled is data security. Security issues affect not only cloud providers, but also cloud customers and other relevant participants in the Future Internet environment. In general, security concerns range from physical security to application security and include authentication, authorization, availability, confidentiality, integrity, incident response, security monitoring and security policy management. Due to a significant increase in optical networks deployment, the provisioning of thoroughly secured communications is essential. Optical networks are vulnerable to a variety of attacks, including jamming, physical infrastructure attacks, eavesdropping and interception. This chapter presents an overview of the issues and research contributions aiming at data security in the content provisioning process with the possibility of cloud migration over elastic optical networks. Data security threats are categorized and countermeasures suggested in the literature are presented.

ACKNOWLEDGMENT

This research was supported by the Ministry of Education, Science and Technological Development of Serbia [grant number TR 32025].

REFERENCES

Ahmad Khan, M. (2016). A survey of security issues for cloud computing. *Journal of Network and Computer Applications*, *71*, 11–29. doi:10.1016/j.jnca.2016.05.010

Bai, W., Yang, H., Yu, A., Xiao, H., He, L., Feng, L., & Zhang, J. (2018). Eavesdropping-aware routing and spectrum allocation based on multi-flow virtual concatenation for confidential information service in elastic optical networks. *Optical Fiber Technology*, *40*, 18–27. doi:10.1016/j.yofte.2017.10.004

Carlin, S., & Curran, K. (2013). Cloud computing security. In K. Curran (Ed.), *Pervasive and Ubiquitous Technology Innovations for Ambient Intelligence Environment* (pp. 12–17). Hershey, PA: IGI Global. doi:10.4018/978-1-4666-2041-4.ch002

Christodoulopoulos, K., Tomkos, I., & Varvarigos, E. (2011). Elastic bandwidth allocation in flexible OFDM based optical networks. *Journal of Lightwave Technology*, *29*(9), 1354–1366. doi:10.1109/JLT.2011.2125777

Contreras, L. M., Lopez, V., Gonzalez de Dios, O., Tovar, A., Munoz, F., Azanon, A., & Fernandez-Palacios, J. P. (2012). Toward cloud-ready transport network. *IEEE Communications Magazine*, *50*(9), 48–55. doi:10.1109/MCOM.2012.6295711

Develder, C., De Leeheer, M., Dhoedt, B., Pickavet, M., Colle, D., De Turck, F., & Demeester, P. (2012). Optical networks for grid and cloud computing applications. *Proceedings of the IEEE*, *100*(5), 1149–1167. doi:10.1109/JPROC.2011.2179629

Fok, M. P., Wang, Z., Deng, Y., & Prucnal, P. R. (2011). Optical layer security in fiber-optic networks. *IEEE Transactions on Information Forensics and Security*, *6*(3), 725–736. doi:10.1109/TIFS.2011.2141990

Furdek, M., Skorin-Kapov, N., Bosiljevac, M., & Sipus, Z. (2010). Analysis of crosstalk in optical couplers and associated vulnerabilities. In *Proceedings of the 33rd International Convention MIPRO* (pp. 461-466). New York: IEEE.

Godfrey, M., & Zulkernine, M. (2013). A server-side solution to cache-based side-channel attacks in the cloud. In *Proceedings of the International Conference on Cloud Computing (CLOUD)* (vol. 6, pp. 163-170). New York: IEEE. 10.1109/CLOUD.2013.21

Gruschka, N., & Iacono, L. (2009). Vulnerable cloud: SOAP message security validation revisited. In *Proceedings of the International Conference on Web Services* (pp. 625-631). New York: IEEE. 10.1109/ICWS.2009.70

Harnik, D., Pinkas, B., & Shulman-Peleg, A. (2010). Side channels in cloud services: Deduplication in cloud storage. *IEEE Security and Privacy*, *8*(6), 40–47. doi:10.1109/MSP.2010.187

Hashizume, K., Rosado, D. G., Fernandez-Medina, E., & Fernandez, E. B. (2013). An analysis of security issues for cloud computing. *Journal of Internet Services and Applications*, *4*(1), 1–13. doi:10.1186/1869-0238-4-5

Hay, A., Cid, D., & Bray, R. (2008). *OSSEC host-based intrusion detection guide*. Burlington, MA: Syngress Publishing.

Huang, Y., Wang, X., Wang, K., Zhang, D., & Dai, B. (2017). A novel optical encoding scheme based on spectral phase encoding for secure optical communication. In *Proceedings of the International Conference on Optical Communications and Network (ICOCN)* (vol. 16, pp. 1-3). New York: IEEE. 10.1109/ICOCN.2017.8121476

International Telecommunication Union – Telecommunication Standardization Sector (ITU-T). (2014). *Information technology – Cloud computing – Overview and vocabulary. ITU-T Recommendation Y.3500*. Geneva, Switzerland: ITU-T.

Jansen, W. A. (2011). Cloud hooks: Security and privacy issues in cloud computing. In *Proceedings of the 44th International Conference on System Science* (vol. 44, pp. 1-10). New York: IEEE. 10.1109/HICSS.2011.103

Jinno, M., Takara, H., Kozicki, B., Tsukisima, Y., Sone, Y., & Matsuoka, S. (2009). Spectrum-efficient and scalable elastic optical path network: Architecture, benefits, and enabling technologies. *IEEE Communications Magazine*, *47*(11), 66–73. doi:10.1109/MCOM.2009.5307468

Kaaniche, N., & Laurent, M. (2014). A secure client side deduplication scheme in cloud storage environments. In *Proceedings of the International Conference on New Technologies, Mobility, and Security (NTMS)* (vol. 6, pp. 1-7). New York: IEEE. 10.1109/NTMS.2014.6814002

Klinkowski, M., & Walkowiak, K. (2013). On the advantages of elastic optical networks for provisioning of cloud computing Traffic. *IEEE Network*, *27*(6), 44–51. doi:10.1109/MNET.2013.6678926

Kostic-Ljubisavljevic, A., & Mikavica, B. (2018). Vertical integration between providers with possible cloud migration. In M. Khosrow-Pour (Ed.), *Encyclopedia of Information Science and Technology* (Vol. II, pp. 1164–1173). Hershey, PA: IGI Global. doi:10.4018/978-1-5225-2255-3.ch100

Kourai, K., Azumi, T., & Chiba, S. (2012). A self-protection mechanism against stepping-stone attacks for IaaS clouds. In *Proceedings of the International Conference on Ubiquitous Intelligence Computing and International Conference on Autonomic Trusted Computing* (vol. 9, pp. 539-546). New York: IEEE. 10.1109/UIC-ATC.2012.139

Li, M., Yu, S., Ren, K., Lou, W., & Hou, Y. (2013). Toward privacy-assured and searchable cloud data storage services. *IEEE Network*, 27(4), 56–62. doi:10.1109/MNET.2017.1600280

Liu, B., Zhang, L., Xin, X., & Wang, Y. (2014). Physical layer security in OFDM-PON based on dimension-transformed chaotic permutation. *IEEE Photonics Technology Letters*, 26(2), 127–130. doi:10.1109/LPT.2013.2290041

Liu, F., Ren, L., & Bai, H. (2014). Mitigating cross-VM side channel attack on multiple tenants cloud platform. *Journal of Computers*, 9(4), 1005–1013. doi:10.4304/jcp.9.4.1005-1013

Liu, F., Tong, J., Mao, J., Bohn, R., Messina, J., Badger, L., & Leaf, D. (2011). *NIST cloud computing reference architecture (NIST Special Publication 500-292)*. Gaithersburg, MD: U.S. National Institute of Standards and Technology.

Mazurczyk, W., & Szczypiorski, K. (2011). Is cloud computing steganography-proof? In *Proceedings of the International Conference on Multimedia Information Networking and Security* (vol. 3, pp. 441-442). New York: IEEE.

Mell, P., & Grance, T. (2011). *The NIST definition of cloud computing (NIST Special Publication 800-145)*. Gaithersburg, MD: U.S. National Institute of Standards and Technology.

Mikavica, B., & Kostic-Ljubisavljevic, A. (2016). Interconnection contracts between service and content provider with partial cloud migration. *Elektronika ir Elektrotechnika*, 22(6), 92–98. doi:10.5755/j01.eie.22.6.17230

Mikavica, B., Markovic, G., & Kostic-Ljubisavljevic, A. (2018). Lightpath routing and spectrum allocation over elastic optical networks in content provisioning with cloud migration. *Photonic Network Communications*, 36(2), 187–200. doi:10.100711107-018-0788-2

Natalino, C., Schiano, M., Di Giglio, A., Wosinska, L., & Furdek, M. (2018). Field demonstration of machine-learning-aided detection and identification of jamming attacks in optical networks. In *Proceedings of the 2018 European Conference on Optical Communication (ECOC)* (pp. 1-3). New York: IEEE. 10.1109/ECOC.2018.8535155

Singh, S. K., Bziuk, W., & Jukan, A. (2016). Balancing Data Security and Blocking Performance with Spectrum Randomization in Optical Networks. In *Proceedings of the IEEE Global Communications Conference (GLOBECOM)* (pp. 1-7). New York: IEEE. 10.1109/GLOCOM.2016.7841622

Skorin-Kapov, N., Furdek, M., Zsigmond, S., & Wosinska, L. (2016). Physical layer security in evolving optical networks. *IEEE Communications Magazine*, 54(8), 110–117. doi:10.1109/MCOM.2016.7537185

Stapleton, M., Maamoun, K., & Mouftah, H. T. (2018). Implementing CoS in EON protection and restoration schemes to preserve network resources. In *Proceedings of the 20th International Conference on Transparent Optical Networks (ICTON)* (pp. 1-4). New York: IEEE. 10.1109/ICTON.2018.8473666

Subashini, S., & Kavita, V. (2011). A survey on security issues in service delivery models of cloud computing. *Journal of Network and Computer Applications, 34*(1), 1–11. doi:10.1016/j.jnca.2010.07.006

Velasco, L., Riuz, M., Christodoulopoulos, K., Varvarigos, M., Zotkiewicz, M., & Pioro, M. (2016). Routing and spectrum allocation. In V. Lopez, & L. Velasco (Eds.), *Elastic optical networks: Architecture, technologies, and control* (pp. 55–81). Cham, Switzerland: Springer.

Wei, J., Zhang, X., Ammons, G., Bala, V., & Ning, P. (2009). Managing security of virtual machine images in a cloud computing. In *Proceedings of the ACM Workshop on Cloud Computing Security (CCSW '09)* (pp. 91-96). New York: ACM.

Wu, H., Zhou, F., Zhu, Z., & Chen, Y. (2016). Interference-and-security-aware distance spectrum assignment in elastic optical networks. In *Proceedings of the 21st European Conference on Networks and Optical Communications (NOC)* (vol. 21, pp. 100-105). New York: IEEE. 10.1109/NOC.2016.7506993

Xu, H., Qiu, X., Sheng, Y., Luo, L., & Xiang, Y. (2018). A QoS-driven approach to the cloud service addressing attributes of security. *IEEE Access: Practical Innovations, Open Solutions, 6*, 34477–34487. doi:10.1109/ACCESS.2018.2849594

Xuan, H., Wang, Y., Hao, S., Xu, Z., Li, X., & Gao, X. (2016). Security-aware routing and core allocation in elastic optical network with multi-core. In *Proceedings of the International Conference on Computational Intelligence and Security (CIS)* (vol. 12, pp. 294-298). New York: IEEE. 10.1109/CIS.2016.0073

Zhang, Y., Juels, A., Reiter, M. K., & Ristenpart, T. (2014). Cross-tenant side-channel attacks in PaaS clouds. In *Proceedings of the ACM SIGSAC Conference on Computer and Communications Security* (pp. 990-1003). New York: ACM.

Zhou, F., Goel, M., Desnoyers, P., & Sundaram, R. (2011). Scheduler vulnerabilities and coordinated attacks in cloud computing. In *Proceedings of the International Symposium on Network Computing and Applications (NCA)* (vol. 10, pp. 123-130). New York: IEEE. 10.1109/NCA.2011.24

Zhu, J., Zhao, B., Lu, W., & Zhu, Z. (2016). Attack-aware service provisioning to enhance physical-layer security in multi-domain EONs. *Journal of Lightwave Technology, 34*(11), 2645–2655. doi:10.1109/JLT.2016.2541779

ADDITIONAL READING

Bacis, E., De Capitani di Vimercati, S., Foresti, S., Paraboschi, S., Rosa, M., & Samarati, P. (2020). Securing resources in decentralized cloud storage. *IEEE Transactions on Information Forensics and Security, 15*, 286–298. doi:10.1109/TIFS.2019.2916673

Bauer, E., Schluga, O., Maksuti, S., Bicaku, A., Hofbauer, D., & Ivkic, I., … Wohrer, A. (2017). Towards a security baseline for iaas-cloud back-ends in Industry 4.0. In *Proceedings of the International Conference for Internet Technology and Secured Transactions (ICITST-2017)* (vol. 12, pp. 427-432). New York: IEEE. 10.23919/ICITST.2017.8356438

Cheng, J., Jiang, R., & Shen, J. (2018). Elastic optical networks for Future Internet and new defragment scheme by extending the maximal unoccupied spectrum blocks. In *Proceedings of the Advanced Information Technology, Electronic and Automation Control Conference (IAEAC 2018)* (vol. 3, pp. 485-489). New York: IEEE. 10.1109/IAEAC.2018.8577711

Colombo, M., Asal, R., Hieu, Q., El-Moussa, F. A., Sajjad, A., & Dimitriakos, T. (2019). Data protection as a service in the multi-cloud environment. In *Proceedings of the International Conference on Cloud Computing (CLOUD)* (vol. 12, pp. 81-85). New York: IEEE. 10.1109/CLOUD.2019.00025

Kowalski, M., & Zyczkowski, M. (2016). Data encryption of optical fibre communication using pseudo-random spatial light modulation. *Opto-Electronics Review*, *24*(2), 75–81. doi:10.1515/oere-2016-0012

Kunz, F., & Man, Z. A. (2019). Finding risk patterns in cloud system models. In *Proceedings of the International Conference on Cloud Computing (CLOUD)* (vol. 12, pp. 251-255). New York: IEEE. 10.1109/CLOUD.2019.00051

Nguyen, M., & Khorev, P. B. (2019). Information risks in the cloud environment and cloud-based secure information system model. In *Proceedings of the International Youth Conference on Radio Electronics, Electrical and Power Engineering (REEPE)* (pp. 1-6). New York: IEEE. 10.1109/REEPE.2019.8708845

Tanash, R., Khalifeh, A. F., & Darabkh, K. A. (2019). Communication over cloud computing: A security survey. In *Proceedings of the 42nd International Convention on Information and Communication Technology, Electronics and Microelectronics (MIPRO)* (vol. 42, pp. 496-501). New York: IEEE. 10.23919/MIPRO.2019.8756926

Thakur, S., & Breslin, J. G. (2019). A robust reputation management mechanism in the federated cloud. *IEEE Transactions on Cloud Computing*, *7*(3), 625–637. doi:10.1109/TCC.2017.2689020

KEY TERMS AND DEFINITIONS

Cloud Customer: End customer or another provider requiring access to cloud resources.

Cloud Migration: Storing a portion of the content and application provider's original contents into the cloud resources to improve performances in the content provisioning process.

Cloud Provider: The provider which owns cloud resources with certain computational and storage capacities and provides cloud services.

Cloud Resources: Physical or virtual resources of the cloud provider which are accessible to cloud customers.

Content and Application Provider: The provider which creates and aggregates all original contents in the content provisioning process.

Content Provisioning Process: The process of delivering contents to the customers.

Data Security: Issues related to physical and application security comprising authentication, authorization, availability, confidentiality, integrity, incident response, security monitoring and security policy management.

Elastic Optical Networks: Optical network architecture providing data transmission with spectrum allocation depending on traffic demands.

Section 2
Attack Models, Security Analysis, and Security Evaluation

Chapter 6
Modeling of ICS/SCADA Crypto-Viral Attacks in Cloud-Enabled Environments

Aaron Zimba

https://orcid.org/0000-0002-2587-106X

Mulungushi University, Zambia

Douglas Kunda

Mulungushi University, Zambia

ABSTRACT

The production processes of critical infrastructures (CIs) are managed and monitored by Industrial Control Systems (ICS) such as SCADA (Supervisory Control and Data Acquisition). The resulting CIs networks are huge and complex, which have inadvertently called for the integration of other technologies such as the internet for efficiency. The integration of such unsecured technologies and the advent of new computing paradigms such as IoT (internet of things) and Cloud computing which are being integrated into current industrial environments, giving rise to Industry 4.0 have further expanded the attack surface. This chapter considers a new breed of security attacks, crypto-viral attacks (crypto mining and crypto ransomware attacks), which target both the production and control networks of CIs. The authors model these attacks and evaluate their impacts. Such modeling is crucial in understanding the extent of the scope and detection capabilities of the first line of defense (intrusion detection and prevention systems), and possible avenues for mitigation strategies are suggested.

INTRODUCTION

Critical infrastructure (CI) networks have traditionally been separated from networks. This has been mainly because of the prevalent use of proprietary protocols (Rubio, Alcaraz, Roman, & Lopez, 2019). Most of the devices in these networks ran unsecure protocols and little attention was paid since the systems thereof were "air-gapped" and inherently secure from cyber-attacks (Zimba, Wang, & Chen, 2018). As

DOI: 10.4018/978-1-7998-2910-2.ch006

such, in as far as security was concerned; much effort was channeled towards physical security. However, nowadays, critical infrastructures no longer operate in closed environments but are rather being integrated into public technologies such as the Internet and cloud computing. This integration has been fostered due to the standardization of CI devices and protocols as well as the costs associated with outsourcing various services from cloud computing (MacKay, Baker, & Al-Yasiri, 2012). The integration of CIs to public networks has exposed the traditionally unsecure CI devices and networks. This has broadened the attack surface in the CI landscape.

The attack surface has further dramatically increased with the advent of new paradigms such as Internet of Things (IoT) and Cloud computing which are being integrated into current industrial environments, giving rise to Industry 4.0 (Khan & Turowski, 2016). Since most CI networks comprise the production networks, which encompasses networked CI devices and the control networks which comprise Industrial Control System/Supervisory Control and Data Acquisition Systems (ICS/SCADA), the target in these networks is twofold. CIs have been further exposed to cyber-attacks due to the outsourcing of technical services from the cloud. In some cases, both production devices and SCADA systems of some CIs are directly reachable from the Internet (Alcaraz & Zeadally, 2015), which in itself presents a severe security threat. In light of this, it is important to protect both the CI devices and the systems that control them. The diagram in Figure 1 shows a typical ICS/SCADA system and the associated susceptible points to cyber-attacks.

Tier 0 is the Production Network layer which is similar to the physical world and includes input/output (I/O) devices such as sensors, actuators, Programmable Logic Controllers (PLCs) and Distributed Control Systems (DCSs), Remote Terminal Units (RTUs) for remote access, and general Wi-Fi and radio frequency (RF) networks. In some network design patterns, low level devices in this tier are directly connected to the Internet (Zimba et al., 2018) which exposes the network to the attacker (attacker').

Tier 1 is the SCADA Network layer which houses among other things the Human Machine Interface (HMI), the Engineering Workstation (EW), the Tier 1 Data Historian (D. Hist1), Central Object Repository (COR), and Application Servers (AS). They are used to configure, monitor and control the devices in Tier 0 while feeding information to the upper tier. Equally, some network design patterns expose the SCADA network directly to the Internet and such systems are easily discoverable (Anton et al., 2018) on IoT search engines such as Shodan (Matherly, 2016) and Censys (Arnaert & Antipolis, 2016). This exposes the SCADA network to attackers from the Internet (attacker❺) if vulnerabilities are discovered. Alternatively, the attacker can traverse through Tier 2 and compromise the system at this layer.

In most CI network design patterns, Tier 2 is the network exposed to the public Internet. It is at this layer where the Tier 2 Data Historian is found. The corporate or enterprise network is usually interconnected at this layer. The attacker (attacker❹) at this layer can compromise the system either from the corporate network by phishing benign users or exploit vulnerabilities directly from the Internet since this is an Internet-facing layer.

Another source of attack is the Cloud Trusted Third Party (Cloud/TTP) where the CI is outsourcing technical services through cloud computing. The attacker (attackerŽ) can exploit the trust relationship between the CI and the technical service provider. The integration of remote access support further increases the attack surface. Other sources of attacks include infection through legitimate remote system users (attackerŒ) and arbitrary Internet attacks from cyber-crime groups (attacker❷). The cyber-attacks assumed thus far are generic. However, with the advent of digital money (crypto currencies), there has been a shift towards attacks that are more rewarding and those that make the acquisition of crypto currencies simpler.

Figure 1. An overview of a typical ICS/SCADA system

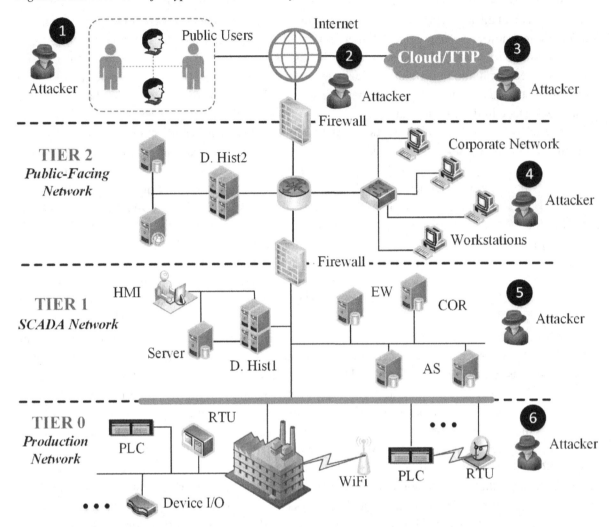

In light of the aforementioned, a new breed of security attacks, crypto-viral attacks, which target both the production and control networks of critical infrastructures have emerged in the past decade. These attacks have been documented (Lundbohm, 2017) incapacitate critical infrastructures worldwide, the most prominent being health and energy sector (G. Martin, P. Martin, Hankin, Darzi, & Kinross, 2017; Wueest, 2014). As such, it is imperative to model crypto-viral attacks in CIs as well as ICS/SCADA systems for formulation and enforcement of better security policies and mechanisms. In this chapter, crypto-viral attacks were modeled, i.e., crypto mining and crypto ransomware attacks in CIs, and the impacts thereof were evaluated. These attacks leverage the cryptographic primitives of devices and protocols present in most networks (Palisse, Le Bouder, Lanet, Le Guernic, & Legay, 2017; Zimba, Wang, Mulenga, & Odongo, 2018).

BACKGROUND

Cyber criminals have always sought secure ways of obtaining proceeds of cybercrime. However, conventional transfers of money leave a trail which makes it easy to track criminals. Crypto currencies on the other hand offer the anonymity and privacy so desired by the criminals. Cyber criminals now demand payment in crypto currencies such as Bitcoin (Nakamoto, 2008). Furthermore, cyber criminals prefer to attack inherently vulnerable systems, i.e., vulnerable systems which require less effort to attack. Most of the critical infrastructure systems fall in this category due to the fact that most of the devices in CI are not secure (Brown, Carlyle, Salmerón, & Wood, 2005) despite being connected to the public Internet. Vulnerabilities in ICS/SCADA which impact critical infrastructure organizations which in turn manage complex networks continue to emerge at an alarming rate. This is shown in Figure 2 according to the ICS-CERT 2017 report (CISA - Cyber+Infrastructure, 2017).

Since CI serve almost every sector of the society, no industry is spared from these cyber-attacks as a result of exploitation of the vulnerabilities exhibited in the products shown Figure 2.

Devices that are used in production networks in ICS use special protocols to communicate. Most of these protocols are not secure. These ICS protocols are broadly deployed in four major critical infrastructure

Figure 2. Vulnerabilities exhibited in various CI products in different industries 2017

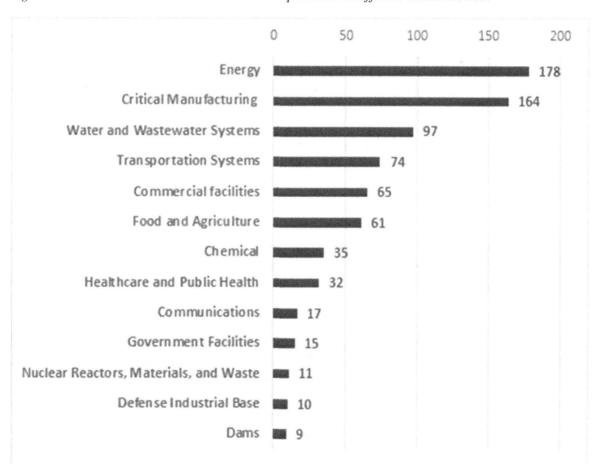

application areas (Mirian et al., 2016): (i) smart grids including power plants, ii) process automation, (iii) building management, and (iv) metering infrastructures. Vulnerable devices and protocols are associated with various CVEs (Common Vulnerabilities and Exposures) (MITRE, 2019). Such devices are easily found using public ICS/SCADA search engines such as Shodanor Censys. The attention is focused to Shodan and Censys because they are amongst the three main Internet-wide scanning projects, the other one being ZoomEye (O'Hare, MacFarlane, & Lo, 2019). Table 1 shows documented ICS protocols, their CI application areas, and the number of associated CVEs.

Most of the common ICS protocols used in CI lack protection by design and are thus susceptible to MITM attacks such as eavesdropping and traffic manipulation. It's however worth noting that Niagara Fox shown in Table 1 provides authentication. Nonetheless, authentication alone as a security measure is insufficient.

In order to mitigate these vulnerabilities in ICS, an effective vulnerability assessment methodology is needed. The process of vulnerability assessment is general implemented in the following steps (SecureWorks, Inc., 2015):

1. Compilation of assets and resources in the system.
2. Assignment of value and importance to the compiled resources.
3. Identification of security vulnerabilities in each asset and resource.
4. Proposition of mitigation by prioritization of the most severe vulnerabilities.

As such, it is important to understand how the vulnerabilities in an ICS are exploited by the attacker to materialize a cyber-attack. Generally, the attacker will scan and discover vulnerabilities in ICS devices. He then leverages the interdependencies amongst the vulnerabilities to reach the goal. CVEs give details on how these vulnerabilities can be exploited. In the case of cryptoviral attacks, the attacker finally selects which devices will be used in crypto ransomware attacks or crypto mining attacks. As such, ICS/SCADA systems present an attractive target for cyber criminals. One type of attacks that has gained notoriety is cryptoviral attacks in the form of crypto mining and crypto ransomware attacks.

Table 1. Common ICS protocols and associated CVEs

Protocol	Port #	Application Area	No. of CVEs	ICS Search Engine
DNP3	20000	Smart Grids	39	Shodan & Censys
Modbus	502	Process Automation	23	Shodan & Censys
Codesys	2455	Smart Grids	20	Shodan
EthernetIP	2221, 2222, 44818	Process Automation	9	Shodan
BACnet	47808-47823	Building Management	7	Shodan & Censys
Siemens S7	102	Process Automation	7	Shodan & Censys
GE-SRTP	18245, 18246	Process Automation	7	Shodan
OMRON FINS	9600	Process Automation	7	Shodan
HART IP	5094	Process Automation	6	Shodan
Niagara Fox	1911, 4911	Building Management	5	Shodan & Censys

Crypto-mining attacks effectuate an attack on availability in which the target devices are maliciously used to generate crypto currencies such as Bitcoin for the attacker. The result is a slowed down network which might result in a catastrophe depending on the vitality of the time factor in the targeted CI. In other instances, overused devices have even caused devastating fires (Roberts, 2018; Zimba, Wang, Chen, & Mulenga, 2018). On the other hand, crypto-ransomware attacks take hostage of some part or the whole of the critical infrastructure and bring to a halt the production network. Such attacks on the energy sector have caused huge blackouts on targeted countries or cities (Lee, Assante, & Conway, 2016). It is worth noting that some crypto-ransomware that are state-sponsored such as advanced persistent threats (APTs) are not interested in ransom payments but rather seek to incapacitate the targeted CI.

Crypto-viral attacks on CI and ICS/SCADA are not always direct. If they target a cloud system that is outsourced by the CI, the corresponding CI may be affected. As such, an attack on an Internet Service Provider (ISP) might not only affect traditional clients but also CI corporations ascribed to such. Therefore, when modeling attacks in CIs, it is important to consider a myriad of attack vectors even not those directly associated with the CI production and control networks. In this chapter, a modeling technique that takes into consideration the various infection vectors from third party sources as well is adopted.

Heritage (2019) presents the challenges faced in Protecting Industry 4.0 and propose solutions as information technology (IT), operational technology (OT) and intellectual property (IP) converge. The author explains how the convergence of IT and OT, especially via the IoT, presents new risks as well as potential gains. The author further explains how the advent of the smart factory and Industry 4.0 represents a new front in the war on cyberthreats in this new computing paradigm. He shows how malicious threat actors have many opportunities to sabotage and hijack processes as well as steal lucrative data. Pramod and Sunitha (2018) present attacks on SCADA communication protocols and show how the use of standard technologies and interconnections between the systems leads to variety of security attacks. They argue that one can provide security and safety to the system by identifying possible sources of threats and objectives of attackers and continuous monitoring of the operations of the system. They present detailed attack incidents that occurred on command and control systems in a certain domain (from the year 1982 to 2017). Furthermore, they discuss the general attacker goals on SCADA, and analyzed the behavior of normal/abnormal SCADA protocols using the Wireshark tool. Ibarra et al. (2019) use an explicit case of the effects of crypto ransomware attacks on SCADA systems. They explain how the migration of traditional SCADA systems to modern information and communication technologies (ICT)-based systems named cyber-physical systems is causing security challenges. They analyzed the risk impact of ransomware attacks on SCADA systems and suggested countermeasures to protection SCADA systems and the components therein from ransomware attacks.

Modeling Crypto-Viral Attacks

To better understand which modeling technique will be the most appropriate for a given cryptoviral attack, it is important to understand the various categories of these attacks. To this effect, a cryptoviral taxonomy based on various factors is formulated. There are several factors that affect the categorization of cryptoviral attacks. Using the amount of input resources required to actualize the attack, a categorization of cryptoviral attacks into two broad categories is made: cryptoviral extortion (crypto ransomware) and crypto mining (crypto-jacking). Figure 3 shows the taxonomy of cryptoviral attacks which is deduced from literature.

Crypto ransomware is basically categorized as based on symmetric or asymmetric encryption. The latest variants used in crypto ransomware attacks use a combination of both symmetric and asymmetric encryption, hence hybrid. It is worth noting that most crypto ransomware attacks utilize the crypto functions provided by the operating system to effectuate the attack. Most ICS devices run on legacy operating systems such Windows. When the crypto ransomware attack is successful, it encrypts the target files such they only become useable in the presence of the corresponding cryptographic keys, which are in the hands of the attacker regardless of the attack model. At this point is it important to note that for maximum impact, the target devices in an ICS/SCADA system under a crypto ransomware attack are the devices on the SCADA network. If the supervisory and control network is attack, then the whole lot of the CI enters a critical stage as this would could severe damage, even endanger not only the lives of the operators but the surrounding areas as well as places connected to the attacked system. This is so because there would be no means of controlling the processes and avoiding accidents. In cases where human lives are at high risks, such as hospitals, some hospital management has been documented to

Figure 3. A taxonomy of cryptoviral attacks

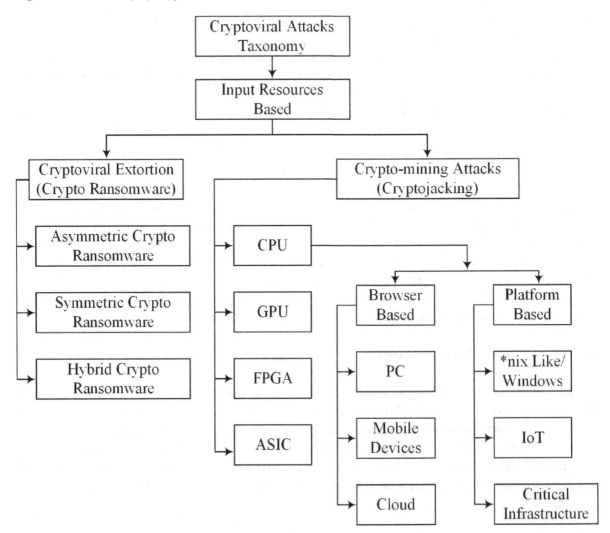

have paid the ransoms in order to restore the system. However, there are no guarantees after paying the ransom because all depends on the word of the attacker. In some cases, the attackers demand more ransom after paying them, and other keeping dragging the victims in circles when in the actual fact they do not have the capability of restoring the system. The diagram in Figure 4 shows a typical asymmetric-based crypto ransomware attack on a generic system.

Crypto mining attacks on the other hand can be categorized based on the target processing unit used in mining the crypto currencies. The broad classes are GPU (graphics processing unit), CPU (central processing unit), FPGA (field-programmable gate array), and ASIC (application-specific integrated circuit) based mining process. The reader is referred to (Zimba et al., 2019) for more details on this. Since most devices found in ICS/SCADA systems use CPUs, most crypto mining attacks are tailored to CPU generated crypto currencies. It is worth noting that some crypto currencies are only mineable by a certain type of processing unit. In this regard, Monero is mineable using local CPUs. The major challenge, however, is that a single CPU-based device cannot mine substantial crypto currencies. As such, there needs to be consented efforts of pooling multiple CPU-based devices to mine a given crypto

Figure 4. A typical asymmetric-based crypto ransomware attack

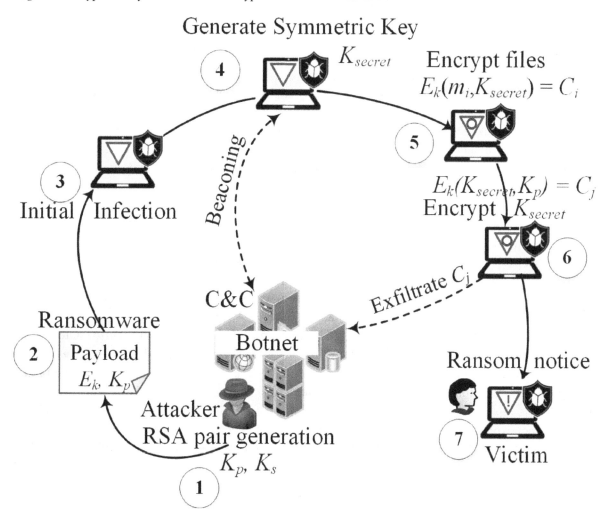

currency. Attackers achieve this by pooling victim devices to a botnet which is in turn used to generate crypto currencies for the attacker. Therefore, the attacker's task is to identify vulnerable ICS devices whose CPU can be leveraged to mine the crypto currencies. The diagram in Figure 5 shows a generic browse-based crypto mining attack.

There are many modeling techniques employed when addressing cyber-attacks in various environments (Ding, Han, Xiang, Ge, & Zhang, 2018; Mahmoud, Hamdan, & Baroudi, 2019; Ten, Manimaran, & Liu, 2010). However, not all of them are applicable when addressing crypto-viral attacks. This is due to the fact crypto-viral attacks present a new dimension of Availability attack techniques in the CIA (Confidentiality, Integrity, Availability) triad. Traditionally, network denial of service (DoS) attacks have characterized attacks on Availability but crypto-viral attacks present a subset of DoS attacks, DoR (Denial of Resource) (Al-rimy, Maarof, & Shaid, 2017). This calls for modeling technique that is different from traditional models. In this chapter, the use of dynamic Bayesian networks that are representative of a complex network are employed and integrated with the use of dynamic attack graphs (Poolsappasit, Dewri, & Ray, 2012). Such a fusion of modeling approaches is effective in that it addresses the dynamic nature of evolving crypto-viral attacks which evolve with time. Furthermore, the use of dynamic attack graphs provides for the identification of pivot nodes in the generated attack graphs. Pivot nodes are very useful when formulating mitigation strategies because they tell which nodes ought to be prioritized when implementing security solutions.

Complex Network Characteristics of the Attack Network Model

When an attacker gains entry into the ICS network by exploiting a vulnerable node, he uses it as a stepping stone to reach other devices of interest. It could be that the initially compromised device is not the end-goal of the attack as it could be residing in Tier 2 or above. As such, using this device as a pivot node to discover other vulnerable nodes and traverse the network according. Therefore, the attacker forms a sub-network of compromised devices is denominated as Attack Network (AN). Since the attacker moves from one device to the other in the attack network, the vulnerabilities in nodes in the attack network are said to be related.

As such, the discovery of a vulnerable node in the ICS and its subsequent addition to the AN leads to the dynamic growth of the AN. Conversely, if a vulnerable node is discovered by the security analyst and secured, this leads to the subsequent deletion of a node from the AN. From this, it is clear that as time progresses, the AN is bound to grow or shrink dynamically with the addition or deletion of nodes. The growth of this attack network can be illustrated as a time-dependent multi-slice network. The diagram in Figure 6 shows the growth of an AN network with time.

As shown in Figure 6, the evolution of an AN can be modeled into different security states in the time domain depicting the severity of the attack. In state S_0. the system is considered to be secure as no breach has occurred. In this state, the nodes in a potential AN are discrete and the attacker can not traverse any node. After time t_1. the attacker implements a reconnaissance attack and discovers vulnerable nodes, a state representative of S1. In this state the nodes in the AN are only susceptible but the attacker has not exploited any vulnerability. After time t_2. the attacker via node n_1 is able to exploit and traverse nodes adjacent to this root node. This is represented by the state S_2. After time t_3. the attacker is able to carry out the attack after having reached the required nodes. This is representative of the state

Figure 5. A typical crypto mining attack

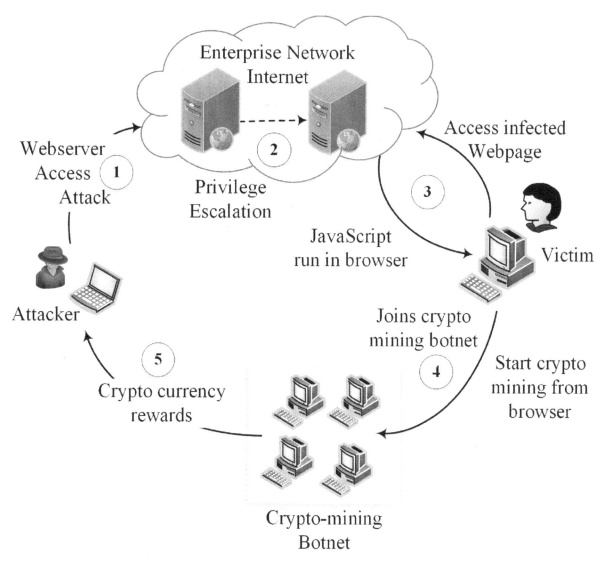

S_3.where the red nodes denote a crytoviral attack in the ICS/SCADA network. As such, the graph representative of the AN can equally be modeled as a Bayesian attack network (BAN):

$$BAN^{AN} = \left(G^{AN}, \alpha_i^{AN}, St^{AN} \right).$$ (1)

where:

- $G^{AN} = (N_i, E_i)$.is a graph of discrete random variables representative of the presence exploitable vulnerabilities in the nodes N_i.and the corresponding attack edges or arcs E_i.
- α_i^{AN}.is a collection of network parameters ω_i. i.e., $\omega_i . \hat{I} \ \alpha_i^{AN}$..
- St^{AN}.is an attack step denoting the feasibility of attack traversal from one node to the other.

Figure 6. Dynamic growth of an AN sub-network in a compromised ICS

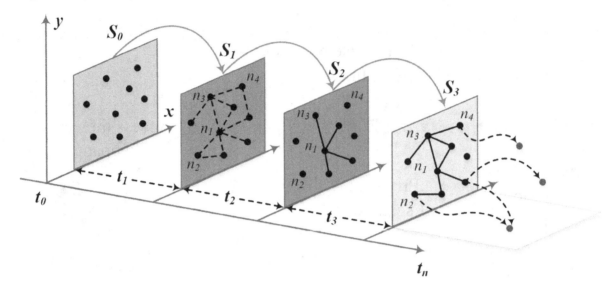

Bayesian attack networks are used in order to take advantage of the conditional dependability exhibited by the vulnerabilities in adjacent nodes. As previously stated, the AN dynamically grows with time as nodes tend to be added or deleted depending on the attack action or the mitigation thereof. This calls for modeling of this Bayesian attack network as a multi-edge graph with respect to time. Therefore, the BAN representative of the attack graph in Equation (1) can generally be expressed with respect to time as:

$$G_t^{AN} = \left(N_t, E_t\right).$$ (2)

where $N_t = \{n_x | x = 1,2,3,\ldots h_t\}$. is a set of nodes taking participating in the attack up to time t and $E_t = \{e_y | y = 1,2,3,\ldots k_t\}$. is the set of the associated attack edges. This dynamicity of the attack network exhibits properties of a Scale-Free complex network. The state of the graph after time t+1 can thus be expressed as a complex Bayesian attack network:

$$G_{t+1}^{AN}(N,E) : \begin{cases} N_{t+1} = \left(N_t \cup \{n_+^{t+1}\}\right) - \{n_-^{t+1}\} \\ E_{t+1} = \left(E_t \cup \{e_+^{t+1}\}\right) - \{e_-^{t+1}\} \end{cases}.$$ (3)

where $\{n_+^{t+1}\}$.denotes node addition and $\{n_-^{t+1}\}$.is the failure node removed from the attack network upon failure of the preceding attack. In the same manner, $\{e_+^{t+1}\}$.enotes emerging of an attack edge associated-with the added attack node whereas $\{e_-^{t+1}\}$.denotes removal of the attack edge.

However, the addition of new vulnerable nodes is dependent on the initially exploited vulnerabilities of the other devices. This dependability echoes the properties of Bayesian networks. Therefore, the probability of reaching the targeted goal can be found by computing the probability of exploiting a node. The probability of exploiting a vulnerable node where the vulnerability is present and exploitable can be computed from CVEs. To achieve this, the CVSS Base Score (Forum of Incident Response and Security

Teams [FIRST], 2015) value of a vulnerability is first determined. This base score is then converted to a probability. Such computation of conditional probability is not uncommon and the reader is referred to (Zimba, Chen, & Wang, 2019) for more details. Given the base score of a vulnerability exhibited in a vulnerable ICS component, the probability of exploiting it can be expressed as:

$$Pr_{AN}(N_i | \forall c \in R_i) = {BS_i}/{10}. \qquad (4)$$

where Pr_{AN} .is the probability of exploiting the node, and R_i .and c are the characteristics features of the base score need for exploiting the vulnerability exhibited by the node.

Illustrative Attack Graph Models for Cryptoviral Attacks in ICS/SCADA Networks

Having modeled the AN as dynamic complex Bayesian network model, now cryptoviral attacks are illustrated, using these models. In the illustration, the public facing network (Tier 2) as the entry point into the network is used. The public facing network in Tier 2 is directly connected to the Internet. As such, it presents a larger attack surface unlike Tier 1 or Tier 0 which might be segmented by firewalls.

Two attack scenarios are defined: one depicting a crypto ransomware attack and another one depicting a crypto mining attacking, since these two are sub-classes of cryptoviral attacks. An attack graph is generated that maps to the different abstraction layers of Figure 1. The resultant is a Bayesian attack graph shown in Figure 7.

The attack graph presents four target nodes, namely N_2 .nd N_{v1} .on the SCADA network, and N_3 .and N_{v2} .on the production network. It is clear that in order to reach these nodes, the attacker has to traverse the network via the exploitable pivot node N_1 . The infiltration sources denoted as N_{0i} .represent the various attack sources through which the attacker enters the ICS infrastructure as echoed Figure 1 as attacker Œ, attacker ❷, attacker Ž, and attacker ❹. It is worth noting that the nodes N_{v1} .and N_{v2} .have two incoming edges. As such the conditional probability of reaching those nodes depends on the relationships shared by the vulnerabilities at this node. If complete exploitation of such a node requires the exploitation of both vulnerabilities, then the final conditional probability is computed as an intersection of events:

$$\Pr(N_i) = \Pr(N_j \cap N_k), where\, i, j, k \in \mathbb{R} .$$

$$= \Pr(N_j) \cdot \Pr(N_k). \qquad (5)$$

As such, the conditional probability of exploiting N_{v1} .or intersection of events is computed as:

$$\Pr(N_{v1} | N_1, N_2) = \Pr(N_1) \cdot \Pr(N_2). \qquad (6)$$

Similarly, the conditional probability of exploiting N_{v2} .or intersection of events is computed as:

Figure 7. An illustrative attack graph of cryptoviral attacks in ICS/SCADA network

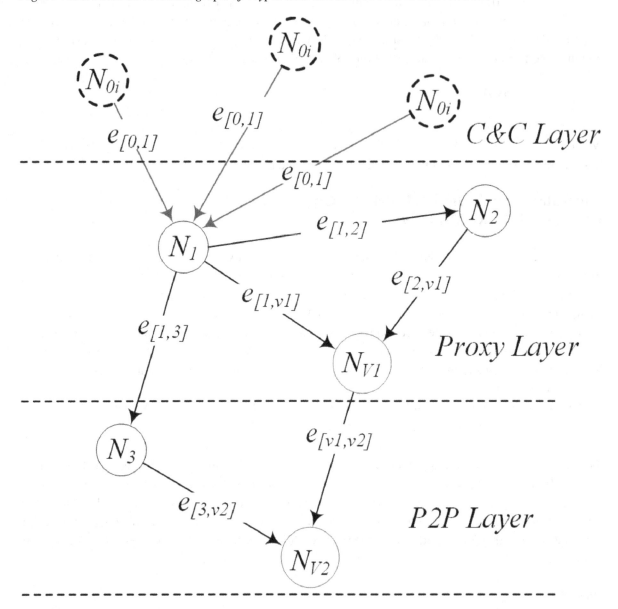

$$\Pr\left(N_{v2} \mid N_{v1}, N_3\right) = \Pr\left(N_{v1}\right) \cdot \Pr\left(N_3\right)$$

$$\Pr\left(N_{v2} \mid N_{v1}, N_3\right) = \Pr\left(N_1\right) \cdot \Pr\left(N_2\right) \cdot \Pr\left(N_3\right) \tag{7}$$

If the complete exploitation of the target node only needs either of the exhibited vulnerabilities to be exploited, then the conditional probability of reaching such a node is computed as union of probability events:

$$\Pr(N_i) = \Pr(N_j \cup N_k), where\, i, j, k, \in \mathbb{R}$$

$$= \Pr(N_j) + \Pr(N_k) - \Pr(N_j) \cdot \Pr(N_k) \tag{8}$$

As such, the conditional probability of exploiting N_{v1} for union of events is computed as:

$$\Pr(N_{v1} \mid N_1, N_2) = \Pr(N_1) + \Pr(N_2) - \Pr(N_1) \cdot \Pr(N_2) \tag{9}$$

Similarly, the conditional probability of exploiting N_{v2} for union of events is computed as:

$$\Pr(N_{v2} \mid N_{v1}, N_3) = \Pr(N_{v1}) + \Pr(N_3) - \Pr(N_{v1}) \cdot \Pr(N_3) \tag{10}$$

The Equations (5) – (10) are only valid when a vulnerability is not only present in a node but also exploitable from the adjacent node. As such, a way to determine the reachability of a vulnerable node from an initially compromised node needs to be devised. An adjacency matrix to determine this reachability is used. The adjacency matrix of the attack graph in Figure 7 is computed as shown below. The connectivity matrix representative of the adjacency matrix of the graph. Using graph theory, the connectivity matrix is denoted by a |N| X |N| matrix, where the matrix element is a binary variable; 1 if there exists an edge between the nodes, and 0 if the edge is absent between any two given nodes.

$$CM = \begin{bmatrix} 0 & 1 & 0 & 0 & 0 & 0 \\ 1 & 0 & 1 & 1 & 1 & 0 \\ 0 & 1 & 0 & 0 & 1 & 0 \\ 0 & 1 & 0 & 0 & 0 & 1 \\ 0 & 1 & 1 & 0 & 0 & 1 \\ 0 & 0 & 0 & 1 & 1 & 0 \end{bmatrix}$$

From the adjacency matrix, it is clear that node N_1 has the highest vertex degree. This node is the central pivot node that holds the success of the attack in both the SCADA layer and subsequently the production layer. As such, when mitigating security in ICS/SCADA systems, it is imperative to identify the central pivot node and turn it into a failure node. This is so because eliminating this node from the attack graph thwarts the attack process on both tiers. Using the adjacency matrix, attack instances for target nodes on the SCADA network and the production network can be deduced. The two target nodes on the SCADA networks are N_2 and N_{v1}, and the corresponding attack paths P_i to these nodes are:

$$P_1: N_0 \rightarrow N_1 \rightarrow N_2$$

$$P_2: N_0 \rightarrow N_1 \rightarrow N_2 \rightarrow N_{v1}$$

$$P_3: N_0 \rightarrow N_1 \rightarrow N_{v1}$$

The other two nodes on the production network are N_2 and N_{v1} and their corresponding attack paths are:

$P_4 : N_0 \rightarrow N_1 \rightarrow N_3$

$P_5 : N_0 \rightarrow N_1 \rightarrow N_3 \rightarrow N_{v2}$

$P_6 : N_0 \rightarrow N_1 \rightarrow N_{v1} \rightarrow N_{v2}$

$P_7 : N_0 \rightarrow N_1 \rightarrow N_2 \rightarrow N_{v1} \rightarrow N_{v2}$

It is visible from the attack paths that in other attack instances such as P_6 and P_7, the target node under certain attack instances (P_2 and P_3) act as pivot nodes. Equally during mitigation, elimination of such nodes should be prioritized.

In crypto ransomware attacks, the goal of the attacker is usually to infect and encrypt as many files as possible in the shortest possible timeframe. The target devices in the case of ICS systems would be the control network or the SCADA networks. Clearly, shorter attack paths such as P_1 in the SCADA network and P_4 in the production networks present optimal paths for the attacker. However, such a requirement is not entirely valid for crypto mining attacks. In crypto mining attacks, the attacker seeks to compromise devices that are continually running for longer hours. These might not necessarily be reflected under crypto ransomware attacks. Indicators of Compromise (IOCs) for cryptoviral attacks are explained in the following section.

Indicators of Compromise (IOCs)

When an attack ensues in a network, the actions thereof generate noise as the threat actor (human or software) interacts with the system files and network. Such noise in the form of network traffic and operating system's system calls indicate the high likelihood of a compromise. Hence, the presence of such characteristics in a network, form the basis of IOCs. Different attacks have different actions and they thus generate different IOCs. The focus is on those indicators that are reflective of cryptoviral attacks. The IOCs can generally be classified either as host-based or network-based IOCs.

Crypto Mining IOCs

In order to understand and detect crypto mining IOCs, the anatomy of a crypto mining attack needs to be considered, as depicted in Figure 5. Crypto mining attacks can be either memory based or browser based. In the case of the former, an executable crypto mining malware runs in memory and facilities for the addition of the victim device to the mining pool. In the case of the latter, there is no execution in memory but the web-browser is leverage via JavaScript code to mining the appropriate crypto currency. In both cases, the number one IOC is the presence of crypto mining executable or JavaScript mining code. The executable can be verified with reputed sources such as VirusTotal for cryptographic hashes such as MD5, SHA1, or SHA256. VirusTotal maintains a database of malware cryptographic hashes which a security analyst or administrator can compare with the cryptographic hashes derived from files captured from their compromised network. A positive match of these hashes values for files found on the system is a high IOC. Such files find their way into systems via various infection vectors such as social engineering, vulnerability exploitation, watering hole attacks, just to mention a few. In the case of social engineering, the entry point into the network would be corporate users if the SCADA network is connected to the enterprise network. Alternatively, using computers in the SCADA network to directly access the network can facilitate the propagation of these files via infection vectors such as emails.

When a device is infected with crypto mining code, the malware payload is usually downloaded from a command and control (C&C) infrastructure domain. The malware is said to beacon back to the C&C to register the infection and download appropriate instructions and directives for crypto mining. Among other things, the malware reports the operating system platform of the victim, whether the CPU architecture is 32-bit or 64-bit, and so on. Some downloaded directives include instruction to which mining pool to enlist the new victim, the crypto mining protocol, the crypto mining algorithm to use and so on. These features can easily be captured over the network as raw traffic since communications to the C&C servers at this stage is mostly in clear text. As such, an intrusion detection that looks for these files and directives detects the associated IOCs with a high true-positive rate.

Another type of IOCs is physically observing the performance of the affected device. This is more of a host-based approach. Crypto mining attacks seek to use as much processing power of the victim as possible. Such overhead has been documented to even cause fires due to overheating of the CPU (Stewart, 2018). As such, monitoring the CPU usage via a centralized system and comparing it with past performances for the same condition will detect abnormal usage of the CPU. In the case of browser-based crypto mining, the browser is the resource that is leveraged to do the actual mining. As such, a continuous abnormal usage of the CPU by the browser in the presence of an Internet connection could be an IOC. In such cases, it is prudent to check what domains the browser subprocesses are connecting. The presence of connections to blacklisted domains of C&C and crypto mining pools is a sure case of an IOC. The probable victim devices at this stage could either be in Tier 0 or Tier 1 layer of the ICS system.

Crypto Ransomware IOCs

Host-based IOCs

Unlike in crypto mining attacks, IOCs in crypto ransomware attacks present a big challenge. This is due to the fact that the effects of ransomware attacks are usually seen after the attack has occurred. The attackers usually achieve this by employing symmetric encryption which is way faster at encrypting targeted files than asymmetric encryption. To achieve the resilience provided by asymmetric encryption, attackers usually employ hybrid cryptosystems where the symmetric key used to encrypt the targeted files is further encrypted by an embedded public key in the ransomware payload. Common symmetric and asymmetric encryption algorithms include Advanced Encryption Standard (AES) and Rivest, Shamir, and Adleman (RSA) encryption.

However, there are some host-based and network-based features that point to an ensuing ransomware attack. Host-based features include excessive access and use of the operating system's Crypto application programming interface (API). Since an average computer user cannot tell whether access to the operating system's Crypto API, a host-based intrusion detection system is more realistic. Furthermore, since some ransomware families such as WannaCry used separate advanced encryption standard (AES) key for encryption of each files, subsequently, excessive generation of encryption keys via the pseudorandom number generator (PRNG) could be an indicator of compromise. The number of encryption keys used by a normal system is way smaller compared to those generated by ransomware malware in a short period of time (Genç, Lenzini, & Ryan, 2018). It is worth noting at this point that unlike browser-based crypto mining attacks, crypto ransomware attacks are operating system dependent. This is because the POSIX API used in Unix-like systems is incompatible with the Win32 API. As such, host-based IOCs of this nature will largely depend on the underlying operating system.

Network-Based IOCs

Just like in crypto mining attacks, the attacker gains entry into the network via some specified infection vectors. Upon infection of an ICS device, the malware likewise beacons and contacts the C&C server for further directives. It also communicates to the C&C server to inform the server-end about the properties of the victimized system such as the operating system and the architecture of the system whether it is a 64-bit or 32-bit system. In certain attack structures where the public key is not embedded in the payload of the ransomware, it is at this stage that the key is downloaded from the C&C server. This was a typical feature of the CryptWall ransomware. The ransomware downloads other directives that would help it propagate if it has worm capabilities like the WannaCry malware. The network-based IOCs generated at this point are clearer than host-based IOCs. These IOCs include the IP addresses of the C&C, the Bitcoin address where the ransom demand is to be paid, a kill-switch domain for sandbox evasion, and other files. For tangible files that can be captured from the raw network traffic, their corresponding cryptographic hash values serve as effective IOCs whose cryptographic hashes can be counter-checked on VirusTotal. The IP addresses of the C&C servers and the domains captured from the network traffic generated by the ransomware can also be used as blacklist entries for IOCs. Additionally, publicly blacklisted IP addresses that are not contacted by the ransomware should also included as IOC should they be observed in the network.

Mitigation Strategies

Mitigation strategies in any environment should not be done in isolation, and as such, our proposed mitigation strategies stem from the applied modeling techniques. Using the characteristics of the crypto-viral attacks propagation in a complex network as a scale-free network model (Barabási, Albert, & Jeong, 2000), it is possible to infer which features are leveraged by the attacker and optimize them when formulating a secure network structure. These features utilized by the attacker have been discussed as IOCs in the previous section. As such, the best mitigation strategies are best built from these IOCs.

Mitigating Crypto Mining Attacks

Some network structures interconnect the corporate, control, and production network in a cascaded manner (Marrone, 2017). Consequently, some crypto-viral attacks take advantage of such a design pattern (Kao & Hsiao, 2018) but having modeled the propagation model of the attack, it is possible to design a network structure that does not foster the propagation of such an attack. A network model that does not foster the propagation of an attack from one layer to the other is best achieved by explicitly segmenting the tier subnets and using strong network access control lists. This calls for whitelisting which hosts or devices from which tier have access to SCADA and production devices. Connecting SCADA and production networks directly to the Internet should be avoided whenever possible. In cases where it's imperative to connect some devices in these layers to the public Internet, strict VPNs with host-based access control should be implemented. Such an approach ensures that if a host is compromised, it will be easily isolated and would be very unlikely to propagate the infection to other devices, let alone in another tier.

Additionally, for browser-based crypto mining which is on the rise, it is important to install mine-blockers on all browser-capable devices. Similarly, it is imperative to centrally monitor CPU usage by different processes since extensive CPU usage is a typical characteristic feature of crypto mining attacks. Furthermore, addition of an IDS that is able to effectively detect the IOCs discussed in the previous section would also be effective. Since critical infrastructure is not a place to mine crypto currencies at any time, it is imperative to block access to crypto mining pools and set up alarms for any requests to such a domain or IP address. A device in Tier 0 or Tier requesting to access any of these blocked destinations should be isolated and investigated further as this is another IOC.

Users present the weakest link in cyber-attacks. As such, user awareness via training and sensitization on the dangers and the way in which crypto mining attacks find their way into ICS systems is equally important. The security of a well secured ICS system can easily be breached by a reckless user who does not understand the implications of their actions. In the same manner, the need-to-know and least-privilege rule should be applied to avoid privilege escalations upon a successful infection from the attacker.

Mitigating Crypto Ransomware Attacks

Unlike crypto mining attacks that can be remedied, crypto ransomware attacks on critical infrastructure are more fatal. This is because some crypto ransomware attacks virtually impossible to undo and this would cost a lot of money. A typical example is the crypto ransomware attack of Erebus on Nayana in South Korea (Cimpanu, 2019) where the victim had to pay more than $1 million because it was impossible to decrypt the victimized files without the attacker's keys. Similarly, the NotPetya (Zimba & Chishimba, 2019) attack costed victim companies millions of dollars because the attack was irreversible. All this implies that in as far as crypto ransomware attacks are concerned, prevention is better than cure.

One of the best ways to prevent crypto ransomware attacks is to block it at the entry point into the network. This calls for the reduction of Internet-facing connections to the very minimum and implementing effective web-bases filters for emails that are not only signature-based but also heuristics-based. This should be supplemented with an effective user awareness approach. Another technique to employ is to digitally sign application running in Tiers 0 and 1, and to check the signature of every application that seeks to access the Crypto API or the PRNG for generation of encryption keys. Only trusted applications should be permitted to carry out such operations. This can be achieved by integrating a MAC and DAC access models to form hybrid access control models with strong access control and capability lists.

Another way to prevent an ensuing crypto ransomware attack is to block connections to the C&C server. This calls for blacklisting known crypto ransomware C&C servers and frequently updating such a database to capture new ransomware domains and C&C servers. In the same light, kill-switch domains which are used when trying to evade detection should be included in the blacklist entries. These domains can be obtained from trusted public repositories or via static malware analysis.

Cryptoviral attacks are drastically evolving. They were practically not present in the past decade and neither were they substantial threat to critical infrastructure not until a few years ago. It is expected that the complexity of cryptoviral attacks will increase. This means that it is anticipated that sophisticated attacks on how to mine crypto currencies from benign users might emerge soon. Similarly, crypto ransomware attack paradigms are expected to evolve. Therefore, this calls for a flexible and extensible approach to modeling these attacks.

FUTURE RESEARCH DIRECTIONS

The insights of this chapter may help in the implementation of a long-term monitoring system to detect cryptoviral activities in critical infrastructure and industrial control systems. The modeling brought forth in this chapter may also be helpful finding susceptible and unprotected SCADA/ICS systems and devices and which can be used by responsible stakeholders to improve the security mitigation process. Furthermore, the approach in presented in this chapter may be specifically extended to cryptoviral attacks in Internet of Things and smart technologies. In future works, the presented modeling approach and incorporate additional data sources will be extended, in order to devise a fine-grained clustering and classification detection methodology.

CONCLUSION

There has been significant progress in the development of security models in tradition networks against conventional cyber-attacks. However, such research should extend to security models for non-traditional works which are representative of the new computing paradigms such as IoT and Cloud computing, which are being integrated into current industrial environments, giving rise to Industry 4.0. This chapter looked at modeling of cryptoviral attacks in critical infrastructure and ICS/SCADA networks. A threat model was presented which showed the susceptibility of critical infrastructure Tier networks to different attacks. Two cryptoviral attacks were considered namely crypto mining attacks and crypto ransomware attacks. The two were modeled as dynamic Bayesian network where the underlying sub-network (AN) was modeled as a Scale-Free network whose vertex degree increased dynamically as the progresses. Conditional probability was then used to express the likelihood of compromising ICS devices from within the Tier layer or across Tiers. Base score parameters were adopted to find the probabilities of exploiting the vulnerable nodes. The generated attack graph showed the attack paths which an attacker can use to traverse the SCADA network upon successfully compromising a host in Tier 1 or Tier 2. Indicators of compromise features were drawn from the noise generated by both types of the attack. The IOCs were generally classified as host-based and network-based. It was clear that network-based IOCs are more effective as they were not host-dependent nor were operating system dependent. The proposed mitigation strategies were based on the formulated IOCs. Similarly, network-based mitigation was seen to be more effective.

Since cryptoviral attacks exhibit complex network characteristics, this called for a different approach in modeling non-conventional cyber-attacks in critical infrastructure networks. As such, the complexity of these new computing paradigms and the associated new breed of cyber-attacks should not be left to lag behind owing to how devastating cryptoviral attacks can be to critical infrastructure. As such, this chapter concludes with a vivid summary, a well-balanced assessment of crypto-viral attacks in CIs, and a roadmap for future directions of security of ICS in the Future Internet.

REFERENCES

Al-rimy, B. A. S., Maarof, M. A., & Shaid, S. Z. M. (2017). A 0-day aware crypto-ransomware early behavioral detection framework. In F. Saeed et al. (Eds.), Lecture Notes on Data Engineering and Communications Technologies: Vol. 5. Recent Trends in Information and Communication Technology (pp. 758-766). Cham, Switzerland: Springer.

Alcaraz, C., & Zeadally, S. (2015). Critical infrastructure protection: Requirements and challenges for the 21st century. *International Journal of Critical Infrastructure Protection, 8*, 53–66. doi:10.1016/j.ijcip.2014.12.002

Anton, S. D., Fraunholz, D., Lipps, C., Pohl, F., Zimmermann, M., & Schotten, H. D. (2018). Two decades of SCADA exploitation: A brief history. In *Proceedings of the IEEE Conference on Applications, Information and Network Security* [New York: IEEE.]. *Anästhesiologie, Intensivmedizin, Notfallmedizin, Schmerztherapie, 2017*, 98–104.

Arnaert, M., & Antipolis, S. (2016). Modeling vulnerable Internet of Things on SHODAN and CENSYS: An ontology for cyber security. In *Proceedings of the Tenth International Conference on Emerging Security Information, Systems and Technology SECURWARE 2016* (pp. 299-302). Wilmington, DE: IARIA.

Barabási, A. L., Albert, R., & Jeong, H. (2000). Scale-free characteristics of random networks: The topology of the world-wide web. *Physica A, 281*(1-4), 69–77. doi:10.1016/S0378-4371(00)00018-2

Brown, G. G., Carlyle, W. M., Salmerón, J., & Wood, K. (2005). Analyzing the vulnerability of critical infrastructure to attack and planning defenses. *Tutorials in Operations Research,* 102-123.

Cimpanu, C. (2019, March 9). Georgia county pays a whopping $400,000 to get rid of a ransomware infection. *ZDNet.* Retrieved November 10, 2019, from https://www.zdnet.com/article/georgia-county-pays-a-whopping-400000-to-get-rid-of-a-ransomware-infection/

CISA - Cyber+Infrastructure. (2017). *ICS Archive Information Products* [Number of vulnerable products used in different industries]. Retrieved, November 10, from https://www.us-cert.gov/ics/ics-archive

Ding, D., Han, Q. L., Xiang, Y., Ge, X., & Zhang, X. M. (2018). A survey on security control and attack detection for industrial cyber-physical systems. *Neurocomputing, 275*, 1674–1683. doi:10.1016/j.neucom.2017.10.009

Forum of Incident Response and Security Teams (FIRST). (2015). *Common vulnerability scoring system v3.0: Specification document.* Retrieved November 01, 2019, from https://www.first.org/cvss/v3.0/specification-document

Genç, Z. A., Lenzini, G., & Ryan, P. Y. A. (2018). No random, no ransom: A key to stop cryptographic ransomware. In C. Giuffrida, S. Bardin, & G. Blanc (Eds.), *Vol: 10885. Detection of Intrusions and Malware, and Vulnerability Assessment* (pp. 234–255). Lecture Notes in Computer Science. Cham, Switzerland: Springer. doi:10.1007/978-3-319-93411-2_11

Heritage, I. (2019). Protecting Industry 4.0: Challenges and solutions as IT, OT and IP converge. *Network Security, 2019*(10), 6–9. doi:10.1016/S1353-4858(19)30120-5

Ibarra, J., Javed Butt, U., Do, A., Jahankhani, H., & Jamal, A. (2019). Ransomware impact to SCADA systems and its scope to critical infrastructure. In *Proceedings of 12th International Conference on Global Security, Safety, and Sustainability, ICGS3 2019* (pp. 1-12). New York: IEEE. 10.1109/ICGS3.2019.8688299

Kao, D. Y., & Hsiao, S. C. (2018). The dynamic analysis of WannaCry ransomware. In *Proceedings of 20th International Conference on Advanced Communication Technology ICACT* (pp. 159-166).New York: IEEE

Khan, A., & Turowski, K. (2016). A survey of current challenges in manufacturing industry and preparation for Industry 4.0. In A. Abraham, S. Kovalev, V. Tarassov, & V. Snášel (Eds.), *Advances in Intelligent Systems and Computing: Vol 450. Proceedings of the First International Scientific Conference "Intelligent Information Technologies for Industry (IITI' 16)* (pp. 15-26). Cham, Switzerland: Springer.

Lee, R., Assante, M., & Conway, T. (2016). Analysis of the cyber attack on the Ukrainian power grid. Washington, DC: Electricity Information Sharing and Analysis Center (E-ISAC).

Lundbohm, E. (2017). Understanding nation-state attacks. *Network Security, 2017*(10), 5–8. doi:10.1016/S1353-4858(17)30101-0

MacKay, M., Baker, T., & Al-Yasiri, A. (2012). Security-oriented cloud computing platform for critical infrastructures. *Computer Law & Security Review, 28*(6), 679–686. doi:10.1016/j.clsr.2012.07.007

Mahmoud, M. S., Hamdan, M. M., & Baroudi, U. A. (2019). Modeling and control of cyber-physical systems subject to cyber attacks: A survey of recent advances and challenges. *Neurocomputing, 338*(21), 101–115. doi:10.1016/j.neucom.2019.01.099

Marrone, S. (2017). Towards a unified definition of cyber and physical vulnerability in critical infrastructures. In *Proceedings of 2nd IEEE European Symposium on Security and Privacy Workshops, EuroS and PW 2017*. New York: IEEE 10.1109/EuroSPW.2017.67

Martin, G., Martin, P., Hankin, C., Darzi, A., & Kinross, J. (2017, July 6). Cybersecurity and healthcare: How safe are we? *BMJ (Online)*. Retrieved November 10, 2019, from https://www.bmj.com/content/358/bmj.j3179

Matherly, J. (2016). *Complete guide to Shodan: Collect. Analyze. Visualize. Make Internet intelligence work for you*. British Columbia, Canada: Leanpub.

Mirian, A., Ma, Z., Adrian, D., Tischer, M., Chuenchujit, T., Yardley, T., … Bailey, M. (2016). An Internet-wide view of ICS devices. In *Proceedings of the 14th Annual Conference on Privacy, Security, and Trust, PST 2016* (pp. 96-103). New York: IEEE. 10.1109/PST.2016.7906943

MITRE. (2019). *Common vulnerabilities and exposures (CVE)*. Retrieved November 10, 2019, from https://cve.mitre.org/data/downloads/index.html

Nakamoto, S. (2008). *Bitcoin: A peer-to-peer electronic cash system* [White Paper]. Retrieved November 10, 2019, from https://bitcoin.org/bitcoin.pdf

O'Hare, J., MacFarlane, R., & Lo, O. (2019). Identifying vulnerabilities using internet-wide scanning data. In *Proceedings of the 12th International Conference on Global Security, Safety and Sustainability, ICGS3 2019*. New York: IEEE. 10.1109/ICGS3.2019.8688018

Palisse, A., Le Bouder, H., Lanet, J. L., Le Guernic, C., & Legay, A. (2017). Ransomware and the legacy crypto API. In F. Cuppens, N. Cuppens, J.-L. Lanet, & A. Legay (Eds.), Lecture Notes in Computer Science: Vol. 10158. *Risks and Security of Internet and Systems* (pp. 11–28). Cham, Switzerland: Springer. doi:10.1007/978-3-319-54876-0_2

Poolsappasit, N., Dewri, R., & Ray, I. (2012). Dynamic security risk management using Bayesian attack graphs. *IEEE Transactions on Dependable and Secure Computing, 9*(1), 61–74. doi:10.1109/TDSC.2011.34

Pramod, T. C., & Sunitha, N. R. (2018). SCADA: Analysis of attacks on communication protocols. In *Proceedings of the International Symposium on Sensor Networks, Systems and Security* (pp. 219-234). Cham, Switzerland: Springer. 10.1007/978-3-319-75683-7_17

Roberts, P. (2018, March/April). This is what happens when bitcoin miners take over your town. *Politico Magazine*. Retrieved November 10, 2019, from https://www.politico.com/magazine/story/2018/03/09/bitcoin-mining-energy-prices-smalltown-feature-217230

Rubio, J. E., Alcaraz, C., Roman, R., & Lopez, J. (2019). Current cyber-defense trends in industrial control systems. *Computers & Security, 87*, 1–12. doi:10.1016/j.cose.2019.06.015

SecureWorks, Inc. (2015, April 8). Vulnerability assessments versus penetration tests [Web log comment]. Retrieved June 23, 2019, from https://www.secureworks.com/blog/vulnerability-assessments-versus-penetration-tests

Stewart, W. (2018, February 9). Illegal Bitcoin mining factory sparks massive blaze thanks to overheating computers used to create cryptocurrency. *The Sun*. Retrieved November 10, 2019, from https://www.thesun.co.uk/news/5538526/bitcoin-mining-factory-cryptocurrency-illegal-russia-fire-overheating-computers/

Ten, C. W., Manimaran, G., & Liu, C. C. (2010). Cybersecurity for critical infrastructures: Attack and defense modeling. *IEEE Transactions on Systems, Man, and Cybernetics. Part A, Systems and Humans, 40*(4), 853–865. doi:10.1109/TSMCA.2010.2048028

Wueest, C. (2014). *Targeted attacks against the energy sector*. San Diego, CA: Symantec Corporation.

Zimba, A., Chen, H., & Wang, Z. (2019). Bayesian network based weighted APT attack paths modeling in cloud computing. *Future Generation Computer Systems, 96*, 525–537. doi:10.1016/j.future.2019.02.045

Zimba, A., & Chishimba, M. (2019). On the economic impact of crypto-ransomware attacks: The state of the art on enterprise systems. *European Journal for Security Research, 4*(1), 3–31. doi:10.100741125-019-00039-8

Zimba, A., Wang, Z., & Chen, H. (2018). Multi-stage crypto ransomware attacks: A new emerging cyber threat to critical infrastructure and industrial control systems. *ICT Express, 4*(1), 14–18. doi:10.1016/j.icte.2017.12.007

Zimba, A., Wang, Z., Chen, H., & Mulenga, M. (2019). Recent advances in cryptovirology: State-of-the-art crypto mining and crypto ransomware attacks. *Transactions on Internet and Information Systems (Seoul), 13*(6), 3258–3279.

Zimba, A., Wang, Z., Mulenga, M., & Odongo, N. H. (in press). Crypto mining attacks in information systems: An emerging threat to cyber security. *Journal of Computer Information Systems.*

ADDITIONAL READING

Butt, U. J., Abbod, M., Lors, A., Jahankhani, H., Jamal, A., & Kumar, A. (2019, January). Ransomware Threat and its Impact on SCADA. In *Proceedings of the 12th International Conference on Global Security, Safety and Sustainability (ICGS3)* (pp. 205-212). New York: IEEE. 10.1109/ICGS3.2019.8688327

Kumar, C. O., & Bhama, P. R. S. (2019). Detecting and confronting flash attacks from IoT botnets. *The Journal of Supercomputing, 75*(12), 8312–8338. doi:10.100711227-019-03005-2

KEY TERMS AND DEFINITIONS

Censys: A search engine that scans the Internet searching for devices and return aggregate reports on how resources.

Command and Control (C&C): A network of servers controlled by the attacker from where instructions are obtained by an agent on a compromised host.

Common Vulnerabilities and Exposures (CVE) System: A system that provides a reference method for publicly known information security vulnerabilities and exposures.

Critical Infrastructure (CI): A basic system necessary for survival of a nation.

Indicators of Compromise (IOC): Pieces of forensic data, such as data found in system log entries or files that identify potentially malicious activity on a system or network.

Industrial Control System (ICS): A collective of different types of control systems and associated instrumentation, which include the devices, systems, networks, and controls used to operate and/or automate industrial processes.

Man-In-The-Middle (MITM) Attack: A common type of cybersecurity attack that allows attackers to eavesdrop on the communication between two targets.

Pseudo Random Number Generator (PRNG): Refers to an algorithm that uses mathematical formulas to produce sequences of random numbers.

Shodan: A search engine that lets the user find specific types of devices connected to the Internet using a variety of filters.

Supervisory Control And Data Acquisition (SCADA): An automation control system that is used in industries such as energy, oil and gas, water, power, and many more.

Chapter 7

Fuzzy–Decision Algorithms for Cyber Security Analysis of Advanced SCADA and Remote Monitoring Systems

Saša D Milić

(iD) https://orcid.org/0000-0001-5757-3430

Electrical Engineering Institute Nikola Tesla, Serbia

ABSTRACT

This chapter provides a complex data analysis of critical infrastructure SCADA vulnerabilities and exploits using fuzzy-decision algorithms. These algorithms are presented in two case studies describing possible scenarios of the cyber attack on two vital multi-parameter remote monitoring systems. The main objects of the cyber attack analysis are data obtained from their common SCADA system. The main focus is on multiparameter remote monitoring systems for monitoring electricity production and water traffic processes in the lock of hydropower plant. Newly developed fuzzy decision algorithms for comprehensive data analysis are presented to recognize the cyber attack. The results of the fuzzy modeling are directly dependent on the complex choice of the if-then rules on the basis of which decisions are made. In addition, two fuzzy logic systems (FLS-T1 and FLS-T2) are used for modeling several cyber attack scenarios.

INTRODUCTION

World economy faces unprecedented challenges, whether from soaring population growth, energy resource constraints, or warming climate and myopic financial markets. Today's trends and financial climate in the electricity market dictate the constant need for improving operations in the power system. Market liberalization and market operations in the electricity sector have set new requirements to improve the strategies of maintenance and electricity production in power plants. Consumers have a major impact on the market, mostly through companies that are involved in trade with electricity. There are also several

DOI: 10.4018/978-1-7998-2910-2.ch007

powerful strategic weapons used by market and industry leaders to leverage their positional advantages (Lin, Chen, & Chu, 2015).

Sustainable technology and sustainable development are different facets of the same approach. Despite of the rising awareness of the urgency in finding more efficient and effective ways to achieve sustainable development, comprehensive and consistent meaning is still elusive both in theory and practice (Jakšić, Rakićević, & Jovanović, 2018; Ritala, Olander, Michailova, & Husted, 2015).

Supervisory Control and Data Acquisition (SCADA) system is a computer-based monitor and control system. In other words, SCADA is a main networked system for monitoring and controlling all technical systems and processes in the power facilities. The older SCADA systems were isolated and localized from conventional networks having specialist protocols such as Modbus, Profibus, etc. for interfaces with devices on the basic level. These protocols are a commonly available means of connecting industrial electronic devices such as smart sensors, programmable logic controllers (PLCs), microprocessor-controlled electronic devices, remote terminal units (RTUs), and industrial computers.

The end of the 20th century was marked by a rapid expansion of the Internet. The expansion of the Internet is accompanied by a widespread application of the Transmission Control Protocol/Internet Protocol (TCP/IP). It is a communication protocol used to interconnect network devices on the internet, intranet, and extranet.

Today we have gone a step further. The need for connecting devices over the Internet has required new communication concepts. Internet of Things (IoT) encompasses everything connected to the internet. Industrial Internet of Things (IIoT) is the network of multitude of smart electronic devices (smart sensors, PLCs, monitoring systems, alarm and warning units) connected by communications technologies. IIoT enables better monitoring of technological processes, the use of cloud technology, comprehensive multiparametric analysis, better fault and aging prediction and timely decision making. The growth of the IIoT is drastically changing how experts, engineers and managers of power plants interact with multiparameter remote monitoring systems, smart sensors, alarm and warning units, and different kind of RTUs (Boyes, Hallaq, Cunningham, & Watson, 2018; Sisinni, Saifullah, Han, Jennehag, & Gidlund, 2018). Today, a large number of embedded devices, RTUs, smart sensors, and complex monitoring systems are used in safety and security-critical applications such as SCADA systems and Machine to Machine (M2M) communication in power plants and traffic infrastructure (Babić, Milić, & Rakić, 2017; Milić & Srećković, 2008; Milić, Žigić, & Ponjavić, 2013; Misović, Milić, & Đurović, 2016). SCADA systems are used in many critical infrastructure applications (Falco, Caldera, & Shrobe, 2018). These applications are increasingly becoming the targets of cyber attacks. The IIoT changes in the power system and traffic by creating a new imperative to share data from smart sensors and monitoring systems managed by SCADA with alarm, warning and control systems. This data sharing concept brings many benefits. Some of these benefits are: energy savings, timely maintenance, condition based maintenance, prediction based maintenance, maintenance based on risk assessment, better assessment of fault probability, better investment planning, more reliable production, staff reduction, etc. A detailed economic analysis shows even greater benefits when taking into account the savings from production and traffic optimization.

Improving maintenance and increasing energy efficiency by reducing unplanned outages involves the continuous introduction of new monitoring systems and modernization of old ones. With the constant introduction of new monitoring systems and smart sensors, the number of observed parameters increases, which significantly complicates the existing SCADA systems. In addition to the many benefits that are achieved by analyzing the data obtained from the SCADA system, there are also serious risks associated with possible attacks on the SCADA. The most common attacks are external attacks that can occur due to their internet connection.

Nowadays, a modern SCADA system has the key role to improve the following areas in a power plant, such as early fault detection, defect tracking and warning and alarming. Based on online data obtained from the SCADA system it is possible to implement the following strategies, and long-term and short-term activities:

- Introducing new measurement methodologies and methods.
- Simultaneously monitoring important parameters of several different industrial processes.
- Giving expert opinions and proposals (repair, replacement or new equipment).
- Making proposals and suggestions for maintenance and investment planning.
- Comprehensive and multi-parametric analysis.
- Reports and conclusions.
- Reduce the overhaul duration by choosing appropriate measurement methods and repair actions.
- Implementation of strategies:
    ◦ Risk analysis.
    ◦ Risk assessment.
    ◦ Reliability assessment.
    ◦ Maintenance management.
    ◦ Outage management.
    ◦ Asset management.
    ◦ Operational excellence.
    ◦ Life cycle management.

Cyber attacks on SCADA systems with "hidden" intent to attack strategic multi-parameter monitoring systems can cause unexpected consequences in different areas (electricity sector, traffic sector, industrial sector, environment). In the narrower sense, at the level of the production facility, the cyber attack can cause great damage.

BACKGROUND

Present trends such as market deregulation, business liberalization, competition and market conditions require continuous business improvement of the power sector. Implementation of new models of risk management and improving decision making processes are essential conditions for sustainable development and energy efficiency. It seems that existing strategies have not paid enough attention to the damage that can be caused by successful cyber attacks. The efficiency of these models, among other things, depends on the implemented strategies for analyzing the consequences of cyber attacks.

This chapter presents some novel aspects of IT engineering, which include management, monitoring and maintenance of two independent processes in a hydropower plant. A multi-layered organized management structure of hydropower plant should be protected against cyber attack.

Consequently, it is necessary to continuously improve and modernize the methods of defense against cyber attacks. Investing in the protection of SCADA systems are often considered unnecessary expense, because these attacks so far have been very rare. However, the consequences of these attacks can be catastrophic and it is very difficult to determine the financial and economic consequences of these attacks. Investing in the protection of cyber attacks itself has been viewed and managed as a cost-center where stick to a budget is of the highest priority. The novel types of cyber attacks can bypass bad data detection mechanisms in the SCADA systems (Mohammadpourfard, Sami, & Seifi, 2017). Due to the emerging threat of cyber attacks, defense methodologies and algorithms are rapidly evolving to protect strategic power systems (Ntalampiras, 2016).

The complex challenges of energy and sustainable development were highlighted at the United Nations Conference, which was about Environment and Development, held in Rio de Janeiro in 1992. Over the last twenty years, we can notice that the number of theories has grown in order to improve operations in the field of management, maintenance, monitoring and control of electrical power systems. Entire scientific and technical areas have expanded researching about these issues. Systems engineering and project management are two complementary disciplines that aim at achieving a common goal.

On the management level, it is very important to integrate knowledge sharing with management and maintenance strategies in order to improve the timely decision making (Ritala et al., 2015). This can be achieved only by means of reliable and timely data obtained from the operational and SCADA levels.

Figure 1 shows three hierarchical levels: operational, SCADA and management level. The place and interconnection of SCADA level with management (executive) and operational levels are clearly visible.

Data storage and associated processing are performed on SCADA level in the power plant (traditional concept, see Figure 1) or at the IIoT platform hosted in the cloud. Implementation of IIoT strategies is illustrated in Figure 2.

From a strategic point of view, it is very important to recognize the need to integrate several management theories with the aim to improve the maintenance of capital equipment of electric power system as well as to improve the process of corporate governance. The practical application of these theories must also involve the analysis of the risk of cyber attacks. Asset management, risk management and maintenance management theories are related, as it is shown by the international standard (International Organization for Standardization [ISO], 2014).

Risk Management

Information and data are important assets of any organization. Data security represents protection against a wide range of threats to operational and business risk. There are several standards that have been prepared for establishing, implementing, operating, monitoring, reviewing, maintaining and improving data and information security. Some of them are closely related to the electric power industry and include a requirement to adopt the risk assessment and treatment processes.

Generally speaking, the risk is the impact of uncertainty on the achievement of the objectives. Risk identification, analysis, and mitigation are areas in which knowledge, adherence to procedures, excellence, and compliance with regulations and standards are imperative. The risk management process consists of five basic steps:

- **Determining the Context**: Establish the context by identifying the objectives of the water traffic through a ship's lock, electricity production, and maintenance and then consider the internal and external parameters within which the risk must be managed.
- **Risk Identification**: Identify the risk that might have an impact on the water traffic through a ship's lock, electricity production and maintenance.

Figure 1. Place and role of the SCADA in the hydro power plant

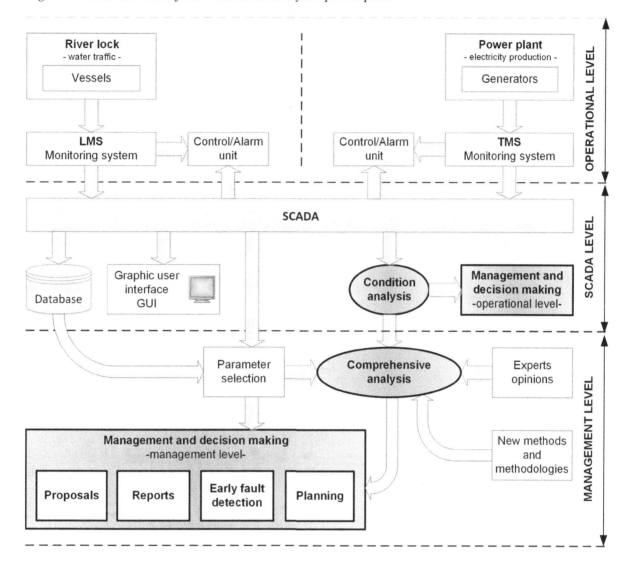

- **Risk Analysis**: This step deals with the analysis of the structure of cyber attacks. This step has to offer clear answers to two key questions: What can happen? & How can it happen?
- **Risk Assessment (Evaluate the Risk):** Decide whether the risk is acceptable or unacceptable and then to make decisions about future actions.
- **Risk Treatment**: The final step "risk treatment" should represent one or a combination of the following four solutions: risk avoidance, risk transfer, risk acceptance and risk reduction.

The risk treatment process, illustrated in Figure 3, can be divided into several time phases.

Defining risk is the most important step in the risk management process. A large number of methods basically come down to a methodological concept for risk assessment and risk management that identifies and prevents problems before they occur. Risk management is preceded by risk assessment and analysis.

Figure 2. Implementation of Industrial Internet of Things (IIoT) strategy: comprehensive concept (synergy) of linking SCADA of a power plant to the cloud and its host applications

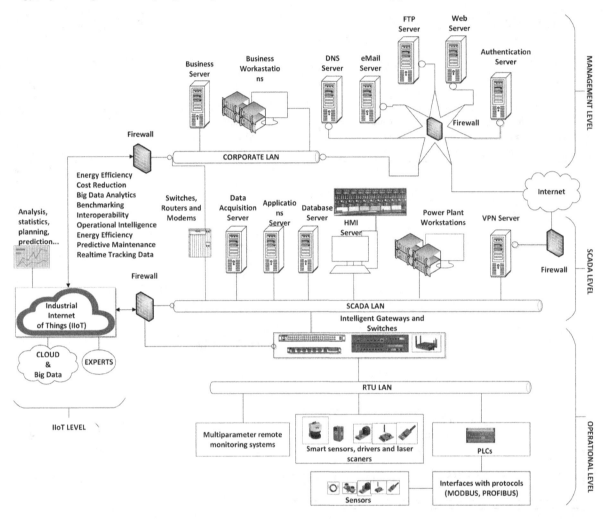

Figure 3. Time phases of risk treatment

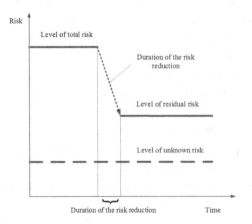

The control systems are a part of organizational information system. There are a few risk assessment models for cyber attacks on information systems of power plants (Patel & Zaveri, 2010). The hydropower and water traffic systems are complex systems with multi-layered hierarchical structures. For the purposes vessel passages and electricity production, identifying, analyzing, monitoring and reduction of risk are imperative in these sectors. Mentioned previously is the main reason why it was necessary to develop a practically usable and integrated strategy of risk treatment in a decision making. Integrated strategy of risk assessment and risk management is illustrated in Figure 4.

Risk assessment is preceded by the risk management, but in practical terms, they are inseparable processes. Risk management has to coordinate activities to direct and control an organization with regard to risk. A risk analysis is a formal, systemized process to anticipate the future, including the means and the likelihood of detecting incipient symptoms in time to prevent or minimize the occurrence and/or consequences of an actual cyber attack.

Adapted Asset Management Strategy

Cyber security threats could potentially impact the asset management. Asset management (AM) has been defined as follows (IEEE Technology Navigator): "Asset management is a systematic process of deploying, operating, maintaining, upgrading, and disposing of assets cost-effectively." One of the first questions to be asked in constructing the practically applicable defensive strategy based on AM is what is important to the power plants. There are many answers, and only issues related to attacks on SCADA systems are considered here. Based on a review of CIGRE TB 541, asset management can be classed as follows:

- Condition assessment and asset monitoring.
- End of life issues (Aging) and life cycle management.
- Asset management decision making and risk management.
- Asset development.
- Maintenance processes and decision making.

Figure 4. Integrated strategy of risk assessment and risk management

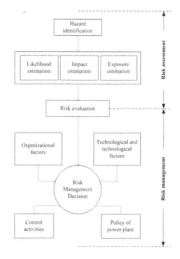

- Collection of asset data and information.

Figure 5 shows the newly developed AM strategy which main aim is to implement all the previously mentioned. This algorithm is an improved conception of AM strategy that is adapted and extended to the cyber crime requirements of hydro power plant and its river lock.

Fuzzy Decision Making

According to Vanier (2001), the quality of a decision made is directly proportional to reliability of information, so that correct and timely decisions cannot be expected without reliable information. In recent times, the decision-making process has evolved into a theory that deals with researchers of different disciplines. It is a complex and demanding process that is based on a large number of heterogeneous data and information. The complexity of the decision making process is growing with the involvement of different attitudes of the experts and the subjectivity of the decision makers. When taking into account the situations described by insufficient information or situations described by information obtained from unreliable sources, then the whole process is further complicated. There are several types of cyber attacks that degrade the quality of information.

The main development framework for fuzzy algorithms will be in line with the main framework of the decision making process. When making decisions, there are many steps that can be taken; but when making good decisions there are really only five steps that need to be considered. These steps are as follows:

1) State the problem or stating the goal.
2) Gather information for weighing the options.
3) Consider the consequences.
4) Make the decision.
5) Evaluate the decision.

Figure 5. Adapted and extended framework of AM strategy

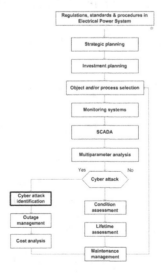

Hydro power plants and their river locks are very complex systems. Decision making based on a large number of heterogeneous data and information is a complex and demanding process. This process is further complicated when different attitudes and opinions of experts are taken into account. The decision-making process using fuzzy logic is also useful in the cases where there is insufficient information or the existing information is unreliable. Conventional system theory relies on crisp mathematical models of systems. However, for a large number of practical problems, which are described by linguistic forms, fuzzy logic theory is more suitable. The pioneer and founder of the fuzzy logic theory is Lotfi A. Zadeh (Zadeh, 1965, 1999). He introduced fuzzy sets for describing ambiguity and fuzziness of the linguistic representation of certain physical phenomena and technological processes. Fuzzy sets are convenient mathematical apparatus for treating subjectivity, versatility and uncertainty.

In fuzzy logic, which is also sometimes called diffuse logic, there are not just two alternatives but a whole continuum of truth values for logical propositions. Often in practice, the same set of fuzzy rules can use different fuzzy logic systems. Many of them could be processed via fuzzy logic system type-1 (FLS-T1) which has crisp and precise membership values. However, crisp membership values of FLS-T1 can in some cases be a disadvantage, e.g., when opinions of measurement experts differ. In such cases, it is recommended to use fuzzy logic systems type-2 (FLS-T2). A FLS−T2 is characterized by a fuzzy membership function, that is, the membership value for each element is in itself a fuzzy set in [0,1]. The membership functions of FLS-T2 are three dimensional and include a footprint of uncertainty. There are at least two reasons for considering the applications of FLS-T2. The first is the uncertainty of results obtained from SCADA, and the second is the differing expert opinions and operational conditions in creating fuzzy rules. This chapter shows the use of both types of FLS. FLS-T1 will be used for fuzzy modeling system with multiple inputs, but also in case of a simultaneous cyber attack on both monitoring systems. A special emphasis is placed on the application of FLS-T2 which can reduce the numerical and linguistic uncertainties associated with the inputs and outputs of FLS-T1. FLS-T2 is used for fuzzy modeling specific cases of cyber attack.

Fuzzy Logic System Type-1 (FLS-T1)

The first step in FLS is the fuzzification. Fuzzification is the process of changing a crisp value into a fuzzy value. The first step is to form sets of input variables based on linguistic forms (e.g., small, medium, large) and selected membership functions (triangular, trapezoidal, Gaussian, bell...). Fuzzy sets of output variables are similarly formed. The step of forming fuzzy rules requires the involvement of a knowledge base, expert opinions, and/or knowledge from the literature. There are several ways of defining fuzzy rules (AND, OR...), and those that best define a particular phenomenon or a particular situation are applied. This case study used the if-then form of fuzzy rules. Fuzzy decision making within the fuzzy logic system (FLS) implies the three phases: implication, aggregation and defuzzification.

There are many different algorithms and methods for fuzzy inference, fuzzy approximate reasoning and fuzzy decision making (Mamdani, 1977; Mamdani & Gaines, 1981; Milic, Vulevic, & Stojic, 2019; Takagi & Sugeno, 1985). From the application point of view, two most important and most widely used fuzzy logic controllers (FLCs) are the Mamdani-type FLC and the Takagi-Sugeno FLC (Sugeno & Takagi, 1983). For example, Mamdani's method of fuzzy control uses minimization for implication, maximization for aggregation, and center of mass for defuzzification. Aggregation is the process of obtaining the final consequence, i.e., consequences based on the individual consequences obtained as a result of the application of individual rules applying the implication method. After the aggregation process, an output fuzzy set is obtained, which is translated into a crisp value by a defuzzification process (e.g., using the "centre of mass" method), which can be a numerical value or some selected action.

The FLS-T1 was first proposed by Mamdani (1977) and then has been widely applied in many practical applications in which there are many uncertainties. In addition to the Mamdani FLS, today the most commonly used system is Takagi-Sugeno FLS-T1 (TS-FLS-T1) (Takagi & Sugeno, 1985). FLS-T1 is composed of four main components: fuzzifier, fuzzy rules, inference engine, and defuzzifier (Milic et al., 2019).

In this chapter, for the needs of fuzzy modeling, the following membership functions are used (1)-(5):

1. Triangular-shaped membership function:

$$f(x;a,b,c) = \begin{cases} 0, & x \le a \\ \dfrac{x-a}{b-a}, & a \le x \le b \\ \dfrac{c-x}{c-b}, & b \le x \le c \\ 0, & c \le x \end{cases} \tag{1}$$

2. Trapezoidal-shaped membership function:

$$f(x;a,b,c,d) = \begin{cases} 0, & x \le a \\ \dfrac{x-a}{b-a}, & a \le x \le b \\ 1, & b \le x \le c \\ \dfrac{d-x}{d-c}, & c \le x \le d \\ 0, & d \le x \end{cases} \tag{2}$$

3. Z-shaped membership function:

$$f(x;a,b) = \begin{cases} 1, & x \le a \\ 1 - 2 \cdot (\dfrac{x-a}{b-a})^2, & a \le x \le \dfrac{a+b}{2} \\ 2 \cdot (\dfrac{x-b}{b-a})^2, & \dfrac{a+b}{2} \le x \le b \\ 0, & x \ge b \end{cases} \tag{3}$$

4. S-shaped membership function:

$$f(x;a,b) = \begin{cases} 0, & x \le a \\ 2 \cdot (\dfrac{x-a}{b-a})^2, & a \le x \le \dfrac{a+b}{2} \\ 1 - 2 \cdot (\dfrac{x-b}{b-a})^2, & \dfrac{a+b}{2} \le x \le b \\ 1, & x \ge b \end{cases} \tag{4}$$

5.   Gaussian curve membership function:

$$f(x;\sigma,c) = e^{\frac{-(x-c)^2}{2\sigma^2}}$$

(5)

Fuzzy Logic System Type-2 (FLS-T2)

FLS-T2 are particularly useful when it is difficult to determine the exact membership function (MF), or in modeling the diverse expert opinions. FLS-T2s have a wide range of applications due to their abilities to handle uncertainties compared to FLS-T1s. FLS-T2 involves the operations of fuzzification, inference, and output processing. The FLS-T2 contains all basic elements of the FLS-T1 with the addition of two more elements. FLS-T2 is composed of six main components: fuzzifier, fuzzy rules, inference engine, expert opinions, type reducer and defuzzifier (Milic et al., 2019).

This chapter presents the practical application of fuzzy logic based on the complex structure of FLS-T2. The application of FLS-T2, similar to FLS-T1, involves a fuzzifier, if-then rules, inference engine and an output processing unit, which in this case consists of a type reducer and a defuzzifier. In contrast to the standard known structure of FLS-T2, a modified structure is presented here that emphasizes the influence of expert opinion. Figure 6 illustrated the concept of FLS-T2. This additional block represents the expert opinions with the intention of indicating their importance in the decision-making process modeled using the FLS-T2. It is important to emphasize that the main difference between FLS-T1 and FLS-T2 is the type reducer whose output is a fuzzy set. To get a crisp value like true/false, yes/no, 0/1… a deffuzifier is used. The type reducer generates a fuzzy output (output is a fuzzy set type 1). That fuzzy output is then transformed into crisp value.

With regard to the three-dimensional structure of fuzzy sets type 2, the term *"footprint of uncertainty"* (FOU) was introduced for their two-dimensional graphical representation. FOU provides a very convenient verbal description of the entire domain of support for all the secondary grades of a type-2 membership function (John & Mendel, 2009; Karnik, Mendel, & Liang, 1999; Mendel, 2014; Mendel, Hagras, Tan, Melek, & Ying, 2014; Mendel & John, 2002).

For fuzzy modeling a few cyber attack scenarios in both case studies, a generic fuzzy model structure Takagi-Sugeno-Kang (TSK) was used. This generic structure is characterized by high accuracy and a small number of fuzzy rules. The TSK fuzzy model is defined by the rules (6):

Figure 6. Fuzzy Logic System Type-2 (FLS-T2)

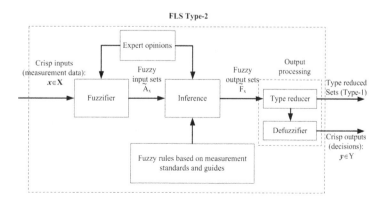

$$R^n : \textit{If } x_1 \textit{ is } \tilde{X}_1^n \textit{ and } ... \textit{ and } x_I \textit{ is } \tilde{X}_I^n \textit{ then } Y^n \tag{6}$$

The TSK phase model is defined by rules (6) where the input logic assumptions are given to fuzzy sets (fuzzy numbers) $\tilde{X}_i^n$ $(i = 1,...,I)$ and the consequences are the output membership function $Y^n = [\underline{y}^n, \overline{y}^n]$ at the specified interval with boundaries $\underline{y}^n$ and $\overline{y}^n$. These boundaries can be either just numerical values (crisp) or linear upper and lower functions (7), (8).

$$\underline{y}^n = \underline{a}_1^n \cdot x_1 + ... + \underline{a}_I^n \cdot x_I + \underline{b}^n \tag{7}$$

$$\overline{y}^n = \overline{a}_1^n \cdot x_1 + ... + \overline{a}_I^n \cdot x_I + \overline{b}^n \tag{8}$$

The aggregation of all the fuzzy rules defines the fuzzy set (9):

$$F^n(\mathrm{x}') \equiv \left[\underline{f}^n, \overline{f}^n \right], \; n = 1,...,N \tag{9}$$

where the products of the individual membership functions for each numerical input $(x_1, ..., x_I)$ according to the lower or upper membership functions for T2 intervals are defined as (10), (11):

$$\underline{f}^n = \left[\underline{\mu}_{\tilde{X}_1^n}(x_1') \times ... \times \underline{\mu}_{\tilde{X}_I^n}(x_I') \right] \tag{10}$$

$$\overline{f}^n = \left[\overline{\mu}_{\tilde{X}_1^n}(x_1') \times ... \times \overline{\mu}_{\tilde{X}_I^n}(x_I') \right] \tag{11}$$

The output of the type reducer according to "center of the set" are the values of y_l and y_r (12), (13) that define the interval of the output fuzzy set $Y(x')=[y_l, y_r]$:

$$y_l = \frac{\sum_{n=1}^{L} \underline{y}^n \overline{f}^n + \sum_{n=L+1}^{N} \underline{y}^n \underline{f}^n}{\sum_{n=1}^{L} \overline{f}^n + \sum_{n=L+1}^{N} \underline{f}^n} \tag{12}$$

$$y_r = \frac{\sum_{n=1}^{R} \overline{y}^n \underline{f}^n + \sum_{n=R+1}^{N} \overline{y}^n \overline{f}^n}{\sum_{n=1}^{R} \underline{f}^n + \sum_{n=R+1}^{N} \overline{f}^n} \tag{13}$$

The crisp value of y is given as the arithmetic mean (14):

$$y = \frac{y_l + y_r}{2} \tag{14}$$

REMOTE MONITORING SYSTEMS IN THE ELECTRIC POWER SYSTEM

The efficient operation of power plants or any energy facility for electricity production depends on the reliability of SCADA systems and operational readiness of capital equipment. Good condition monitoring reduces the number of failures and maintenance costs and is a basic requirement for good predictive maintenance planning. It should be noted that electricity generation often depends on some processes that are not directly involved in it. A good example of this is a railway transport of coal (fossil energy for thermal power plant) (Milić & Srećković, 2008). Also, the process of electricity generation should not disturb some other processes. A good example of this is a water transport through the ship's lock (the locks are integral parts of hydropower plants) (Misović et al., 2016).

This chapter presents two case studies describing possible scenarios of the attack on two vital multi-parameter monitoring systems and their common SCADA system: 1) Systems for remote temperature monitoring of ten hydrogenerators (TMS) (Milić et al., 2013), and 2) Laser monitoring system of the lock gate zones (LMS) (Misović et al., 2016). Both monitoring systems have been installed in the same hydroelectric power plant. They have been developed to monitor several parameters of completely different processes, and it is possible to analyze the scenario of a simultaneous cyber attack on them. Endangering the work of one of these systems indirectly affects the work of another. Therefore, it is very important to monitor the operation of all systems and maintain them in the operating mode.

In both case studies, the developed fuzzy-decision algorithms and modeled fuzzy logic systems to cyber threat are analyzed. This approach allows two types of analysis. The first one refers to the analysis of known types of cyber attacks such as: replay, spoofing, denial of service, control message modification, write to MTU, RTU response alteration, write to RTU, etc. The second one refers to the logical data analysis. A special methodology of logical analysis of the results obtained from the monitoring systems is presented. Special parts of algorithms are used to SCADA data analysis based on logical assumptions related to the characteristics of processes monitored by these monitoring systems. These analyses are carried out in real time based on a set of criteria that relate to the specificity of the process of passage of a vessel through the lock, and to the specific characteristics of the water-cooled poles of hydrogenator. A detailed consideration will be given to each criterion from a set of criteria that serve to reveal hidden illogicalities that could threaten the mentioned processes in the power plant and cause more serious damage such as: temporary interruption of electricity generation, generator outage, damage to the generator, ship damage, the lock's door damage... The aforementioned consequences of SCADA cyber attack can be classified into short-term or temporary. Much more danger is from damage that threatens the operation of all ten generators or stops the passage of the vessels through the lock for a long period of several months.

The hardest thing is to detect a cyber attack that changes process parameters while keeping those changes within expected limits. Both case studies have provided algorithms and fuzzy models that successfully recognize this type of cyber attack.

In order to make the right decisions, it is very important to develop the ability to analyze the complex dependencies between cyber security and management actions.

The Consequences of the Cyber Attack on the Monitoring Systems

The cyber attack on the SCADA directly threatens the operation of all systems that are connected or networked with it. The cyber attacks that modify and fake data (measured parameters) are extremely dangerous on all hierarchical levels.

At the operational level, as a result of the cyber attack on SCADA, the major failures could be occurred in a power plant and in its lock. These failures could be an outage of the one or more generators and/or interruption of the vessel passage through the lock.

At the alarm level, false alarm or warning cold be generated. The consequences of the cyber attack could be false alarm level settings, so that alarm (fake) signals are continuously generated (fake low level), or that alarms are not generated despite the fact they should be generated (fake high level).

At the managerial level, erroneous information can cause poor investment planning and endangering the company's position on the market.

In any case, the emergence of modified data from SCADA systems is absolutely unacceptable. For the above reasons, this chapter presents several fuzzy-decision algorithms (FDAs) that validate the data obtained from the SCADA system (from two monitoring systems) in order to identify the cyber attack. With the application of FLS-T1 and FLS-T2, several scenarios were modeled in which the logical accuracy of the data was assessed. FLS-T2s were used because they handle rule uncertainties.

Fuzzy-decision algorithms for cyber security analysis of advanced SCADA and remote monitoring systems are presented in two following case studies.

Case Study #1: A Fuzzy Decision Algorithm for Temperature Monitoring System

An online temperature remote monitoring system of the hydrogenator (TMS) is composed of two measurement subsystems. The first one is based on the measuring of emission of infrared radiation from the rotor poles in motion and the second one is based on the measuring from stationary temperature sensors (Resistive Temperature Detectors - RTDs) mounted on the stator. The system is connected to SCADA and it is very useful for online temperature monitoring without work interruption. TMS has key roles in the monitoring of capital equipment in a power plant such as fault detection, avoidance of unplanned outage, condition-based maintenance, etc. Figure 7 illustrates ten independent TMS systems for all ten generators.

A Fuzzy Modeling for Temperature Monitoring System

A cyber attack scenario involves an attack on the measurement parameters. The main parameters of the monitoring system are temperature of rotor poles of hydrogenator, generator power, temperature of coolant and number and type of SCADA alarms.

A fuzzy model is based on seventy-two carefully selected if-then rules. Fuzzy numbers with different membership functions (*triangle, Gauss, Gauss2, Z* and *S* shaped membership function) are used in the fuzzy models. A brief explanation of the selected parameters is given in Table1, and results of fuzzy modeling are given in the Figure 8.

Figure 7. Temperature monitoring systems connected to SCADA

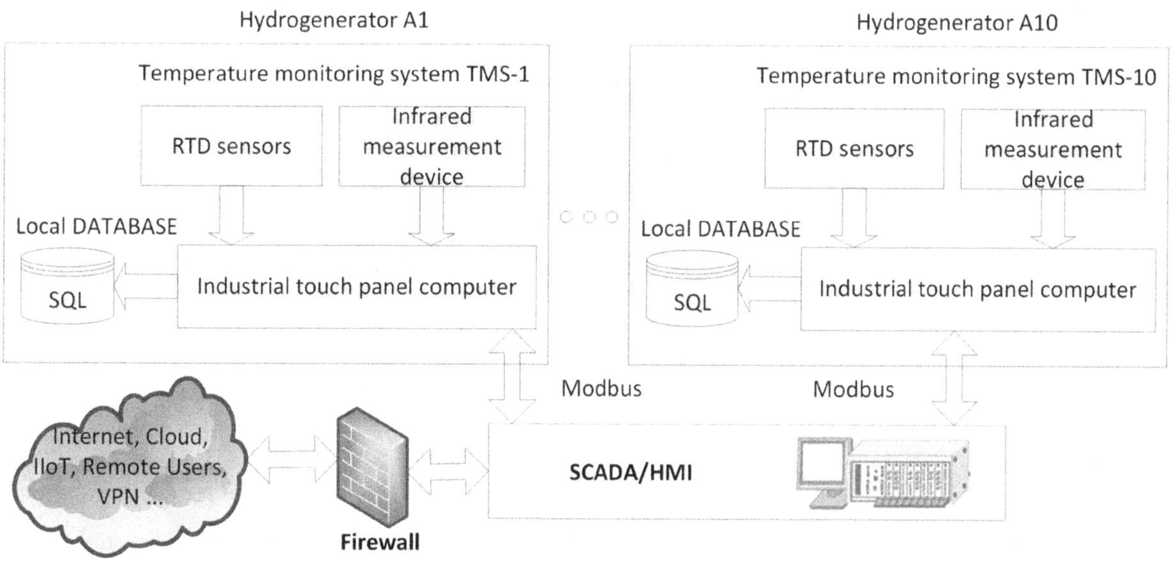

Table 1. Membership functions of FLS-T1 for TMS

Membership Functions	Group/Class	Fuzzy Intervals
Overheated poles [°C] (*input 1*)	Low.	Z [0; 30].
	Medium.	Gauss2 [7; 20; 7; 40].
	High.	S [40; 60].
Generator power [MW] (*input 2*)	Low	Z [0; 15]
	Rated	Gauss2 [5; 15; 5; 25]
	High	S [25; 40]
Coolant [°C] (*input 3*)	Cold	Z [0; 15]
	Low-normal	Gauss [5; 15]
	High-normal	Gauss [5; 25]
	High	S [25; 40]
SCADA alarm (*input 4*)	No	Triangle [0; 0; 1]
	Yes	Triangle [0; 1; 1]
Cyber attack (*output*)	No	Triangle [0; 0; 0.5]
	Further analysis	Triangle [0; 0.5; 1]
	Yes	Triangle [0.5; 1; 1]

Figure 8. Probability of cyber attack as a function of SCADA alarm and overheated poles

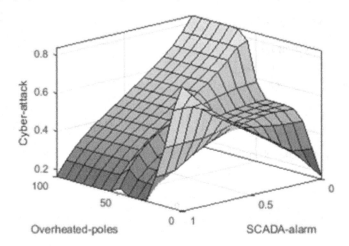

The different expert opinions and simultaneous SCADA alarms are treated in fuzzy model using FLS-T2. The membership functions based on fuzzy sets type-2 (Table 2) are used for describing realistic cyber attack scenarios but with the different expert opinions and different number of simultaneous SCADA alarms.

Figure 9 shows the result of the fuzzy type-2 modeling. The three-dimensional surface represents a set of solutions for all cases of two input parameters.

Table 2. Membership functions of FLS-T2 for TMS

Membership Functions	Group/Class	Fuzzy Intervals
Alarm number [%] (*input 1*)	Small number	Upper MF: triangle [0; 0; 20; 1]
		Lower MF: triangle [0; 0; 15; 0.8]
	Middle number	Upper MF: triangle [5; 20; 35; 1]
		Lower MF: triangle [10; 20; 30; 0.8]
	Big number	Upper MF: triangle [20; 35; 50; 1]
		Lower MF: triangle [25; 35; 45; 0.8]
	Very big number	Upper MF: trapezoid [35; 50; 100; 100; 1]
		Lower MF: trapezoid [40; 50; 100; 100; 0.8]
Expert opinions [%] (*input 2*)	Low agreement level	Upper MF: triangle [0; 0; 40; 1]
		Lower MF: triangle [0; 0; 30; 0.5]
	Medium agreement level	Upper MF: triangle [10; 50; 90; 1]
		Lower MF: triangle [20; 50; 80; 0.5]
	High agreement level	Upper MF: triangle [60; 100; 100; 1]
		Lower MF: triangle [70; 100; 100; 0.5]
Cyber attack (*output*)	No	[0]
	Further analysis	[0.5]
	Yes	[1]

Figure 9. Probability of cyber attack as a function of a number of simultaneous SCADA alarms and expert opinions

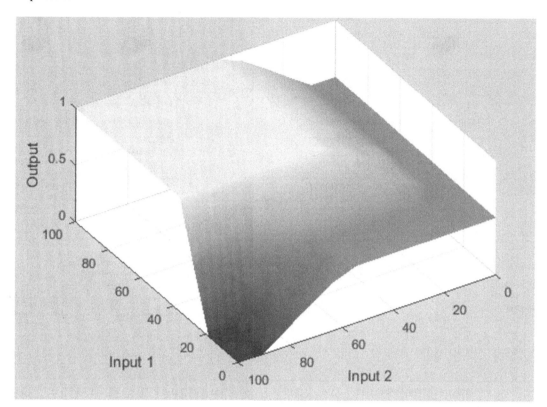

Case Study #2: A Fuzzy Decision Algorithm for Laser Monitoring System

LMS has been developed with the aim of preventing the wrong manipulation of the lock doors in situations where there is a risk of collision between the vessel and the door (Figure 10).

LMS consists of four laser scanners (two scanners per gate), four DSP controllers and a few servers (Figure 10). LMS is connected to the SCADA of the power plant and has to monitor the following processes: gate manipulation, chamber filling, chamber emptying, vessel passage, arrival time and the time of the vessel's stay in the chamber. At the application level, an algorithm for detecting interference and undesirable objects was implemented. The algorithm should reject the following objects as interference: floating debris, heavy rain, snow, fog, high waves, engine smoke, etc.

A Fuzzy Modeling for Laser Monitoring System

A cyber attack scenario involves an attack on the measurement parameters. The main parameters of the monitoring system are position of the upper and bottom lock doors, the state of being filled with water into a chamber, the presence of a ship in the vicinity of the door and the type and number SCADA alarms. A fuzzy model is based on twenty-one carefully selected if-then rules. Fuzzy numbers with triangle membership functions are used in the fuzzy models (Table 3). The following Figures (11–13) show the results of fuzzy modeling. The three-dimensional surfaces represent a few sets of solutions for all input

Figure 10. Laser monitoring systems connected to SCADA

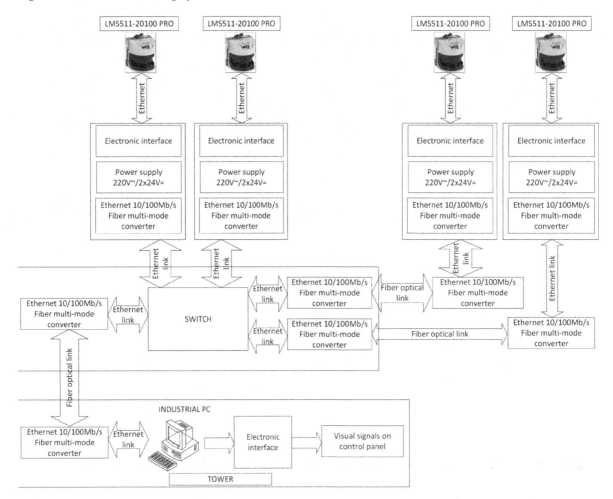

parameters. Table 4 lists two input and one output parameters that were used to model the FLS-T2 for detecting cyber attack on LMS.

Figure 14 shows the result of the fuzzy type-2 modeling. The three-dimensional surface represents a set of solutions for all cases of two input parameters.

FUTURE RESEARCH DIRECTIONS

There is a number of complex multi-parameter monitoring and expert systems connected to SCADA systems in hydro and thermal power plants. All of these systems are compromised by possible cyber attacks. The development of defense algorithms represents a large research field in the near future. This chapter presents the good directions for future researching. One of the major challenges in future research is the choice of the most vulnerable parameters that may be the target of cyber attacks. The application of the FLS-T2 fuzzy system in defense algorithms should minimize the effects of subjectivity and expert opinion disagreement on decision making processes related to cyber attack assessment. The introduction

Table 3. Membership functions of FLS-T1 for LMS

Membership Functions	Group/Class	Fuzzy Intervals
Upper door (*input 1*)	Opened	Triangle [0; 0; 1]
	Closed	Triangle [0; 1; 1]
Bottom door (*input 2*)	Opened	Triangle [0; 0; 1]
	Closed	Triangle [0; 1; 1]
Chamber (*input 3*)	Empty	Triangle [0; 0; 1]
	Full	Triangle [0; 1; 1]
Vessel presence (*input 4*)	No	Triangle [0; 0; 1]
	Yes	Triangle [0; 1; 1]
SCADA alarm (*input 5*)	No	Triangle [0; 0; 1]
	Yes	Triangle [0; 1; 1]
Cyber attack (*output*)	No	Triangle [0; 0; 0.5]
	Further analysis	Triangle [0; 0.5; 1]
	Yes	Triangle [0.5; 1; 1]

Figure 11. Probability of cyber attack as a function of SCADA and upper doors

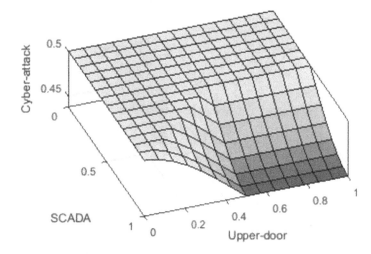

of new protection methods and strategies of cyber attack should be aligned with the protection strategies of SCADA systems, as well as with new management theories at the management level in power plants.

CONCLUSION

About two decades ago, when the rapid development of decision-making theories began, their divisions were not strictly defined. This chapter presents a synthesis of a few management and decision-making theories, practical application of fuzzy logic and a newly developed concept of detection of cyber attacks on SCADA and monitoring systems. Fuzzy models have been developed to analyze cyber attacks with

Figure 12. Probability of cyber attack as a function of SCADA and bottom doors

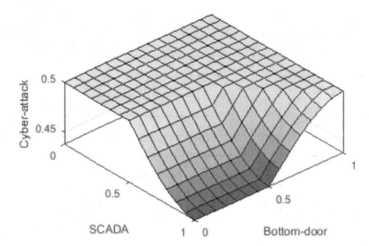

Figure 13. Probability of cyber attack as a function of SCADA and lock chamber

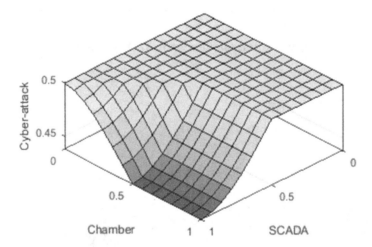

the aim of early detection of attacks and prevention of emergency situations. In other words, this chapter presents a novel fuzzy measurement algorithm for cyber attack detection in the hydropower plant with the aim to combine the advantages of two fuzzy logic systems with the advantages of parameter selection on SCADA system. The last part of the chapter is addressed to the validation of the proposed fuzzy algorithms, as well as fuzzy modeling, that were carried out using appropriate software (MATLAB) and results obtained in real scenarios.

Although the mentioned theories offer many solutions, it was nevertheless necessary to develop and modify individual algorithms of decision making. A lot of current scenarios were discussed with the aim of developing a detailed and practical implementation of the strategy and comprehensive concept of protection of cyber attacks on two strategic monitoring systems in hydropower plant. The basis of security strategies is to find parameters that have been violently altered by cyber attacks.

Hydrogenerators are capital production units in hydropower plants. The river lock is a part of river dam within hydropower plant and has key role for regulating water traffic. Cyber attacks on the monitor-

Figure 14. Probability of cyber attack as a function of a vessels distance from the lock door and lock door position

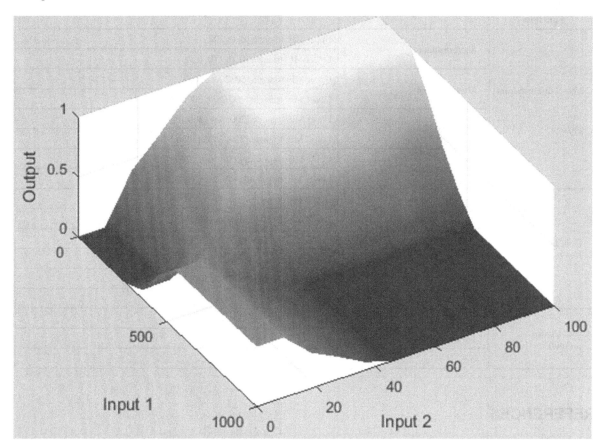

ing systems of generators and river lock can have unprecedented consequences in electricity generation and water (river) traffic.

The establishment of novel decision-making algorithms of monitoring and SCADA systems is especially important if one takes into consideration the on-line (real-time operation) defense against cyber attacks. The presented algorithms should be an upgrade of any SCADA and monitoring systems with the aim of reducing the number of outages, duration of the downtime, maintenance costs and cyber crime costs and consequences of more sophisticated cyber attacks. The establishment of these algorithms is useful to increase of reliability of electricity production and water traffic, and reduction of maintenance and management costs.

Table 4. Membership functions of FLS-T2 for LMS

Membership Functions	Group/Class	Fuzzy Intervals
Vessel distance from door [m] (*input 1*)	Short distance	Upper MF: triangle [0; 0; 200; 1]
		Lower MF: triangle [0; 0; 150; 0.5]
	Mean distance	Upper MF: triangle [50; 200; 350; 1]
		Lower MF: triangle [100; 200; 300; 0.5]
	Long distance	Upper MF: triangle [200; 350; 500; 1]
		Lower MF: triangle [250; 350; 450; 0.5]
	Very long distance	Upper MF: trapezoid [350; 500; 1000; 1000; 1]
		Lower MF: trapezoid [400; 500; 1000; 1000; 0.5]
Door position[%] (*input 2*)	Locked	Upper MF: triangle [0; 0; 40; 1]
		Lower MF: triangle [0; 0; 30; 0.5]
	Intermediate position	Upper MF: trapezoid [10; 30; 70; 90; 1]
		Lower MF: trapezoid [20; 35; 65; 80; 0.5]
	Unlocked	Upper MF: triangle [60; 100; 100; 1]
		Lower MF: triangle [70; 100; 100; 0.5]
Cyber attack (*output*)	No	[0]
	Further analysis	[0.5]
	Yes	[1]

REFERENCES

Babić, B. M., Milić, S. D., & Rakić, A. Ž. (2017). Fault detection algorithm used in a magnetic monitoring system of the hydrogenerator. *IET Electric Power Applications*, *11*(1), 63–71. doi:10.1049/iet-epa.2016.0232

Boyes, H., Hallaq, B., Cunningham, J., & Watson, T. (2018). The Industrial Internet of Things (IIoT): An analysis framework. *Computers in Industry*, *101*, 1–12. doi:10.1016/j.compind.2018.04.015

Falco, G., Caldera, C., & Shrobe, H. (2018). IIoT cybersecurity risk modeling for SCADA systems. *IEEE Internet of Things Journal*, *5*(6), 4486–4495. doi:10.1109/JIOT.2018.2822842

International Organization for Standardization (ISO). (2014). Asset management – Overview, principles and terminology. *Standard ISO*, *55000*, 2014.

Jakšić, M., Rakićević, J., & Jovanović, M. (2018). Sustainable technology and business innovation framework: A comprehensive approach. *Amfiteatru Economic*, *20*(48), 418–436. doi:10.24818/EA/2018/48/418

John, R. I., & Mendel, J. M. (2009). Fuzzy logic, type-2 and uncertainty. In R. A. Meyers (Ed.), *Encyclopedia of Complexity and System Science*. New York: Springer. doi:10.1007/978-0-387-30440-3_235

Karnik, N. N., Mendel, J. M., & Liang, Q. (1999). Type-2 fuzzy logic systems. *IEEE Transactions on Fuzzy Systems*, *7*(6), 643–658. doi:10.1109/91.811231

Lin, B., Chen, W., & Chu, P. (2015). Mergers and acquisitions strategies for industry leaders, challengers, and Niche players: Interaction effects of technology positioning and industrial environment. *IEEE Transactions on Engineering Management*, *62*(1), 80–88. doi:10.1109/TEM.2014.2380822

Mamdani, E. H. (1977). Application of fuzzy logic to approximate reasoning using linguistic synthesis. *IEEE Transactions on Computers*, *C-26*(12), 1182–1191. doi:10.1109/TC.1977.1674779

Mamdani, E. H., & Gaines, B. (Eds.). (1981). *Fuzzy reasoning and its applications*. New York: Academic Press.

Mendel, J. M. (2014). General type-2 fuzzy logic systems made simple: A tutorial. *IEEE Transactions on Fuzzy Systems*, *22*(5), 1162–1182. doi:10.1109/TFUZZ.2013.2286414

Mendel, J. M., Hagras, H., Tan, W.-W., Melek, W. W., & Ying, H. (2014). *Introduction to type-2 fuzzy logic control: Theory and applications*. Hoboken, NJ: John Wiley & Sons. doi:10.1002/9781118886540

Mendel, J. M., & John, R. I. B. (2002). Type-2 fuzzy sets made simple. *IEEE Transactions on Fuzzy Systems*, *10*(2), 117–127. doi:10.1109/91.995115

Milić, S., & Srećković, M. (2008). A stationary system of non-contact temperature measurement and hot box detecting. *IEEE Transactions on Vehicular Technology*, *57*(5), 2684–2694. doi:10.1109/TVT.2008.915505

Milic, S., Vulevic, B., & Stojic, Dj. (2019). A fuzzy-measurement algorithm for assessing the impact of EMF on health. *Nuclear Technology & Radiation Protection*, *34*(2), 129–137. doi:10.2298/NTRP190121018M

Milić, S., Žigić, A., & Ponjavić, M. (2013). On-line temperature monitoring, fault detection and a novel heat run test of water-cooled rotor of hydrogenerator. *IEEE Transactions on Energy Conversion*, *28*(3), 698–706. doi:10.1109/TEC.2013.2265262

Misović, D., Milić, S., & Đurović, Ž. (2016). Vessel detection algorithm used in a laser monitoring system of the lock gate zone. *IEEE Transactions on Intelligent Transportation Systems*, *17*(2), 430–440. doi:10.1109/TITS.2015.2477352

Mohammadpourfard, M., Sami, A., & Seifi, A. R. (2017). A statistical unsupervised method against false data injection attacks: A visualization-based approach. *Expert Systems with Applications*, *84*, 242–261. doi:10.1016/j.eswa.2017.05.013

Ntalampiras, S. (2016). Automatic identification of integrity attacks in cyber-physical systems. *Expert Systems with Applications*, *58*, 164–173. doi:10.1016/j.eswa.2016.04.006

Patel, S., & Zaveri, J. (2010). A risk-assessment model for cyber attacks on information systems. *Journal of Computers*, *5*(3), 352–359. doi:10.4304/jcp.5.3.352-359

Ritala, P., Olander, H., Michailova, S., & Husted, K. (2015). Knowledge sharing, knowledge leaking and relative innovation performance: An empirical study. *Technovation*, *35*, 22–31. doi:10.1016/j.technovation.2014.07.011

Sisinni, E., Saifullah, A., Han, S., Jennehag, U., & Gidlund, M. (2018). Industrial Internet of Things: Challenges, opportunities, and directions. *IEEE Transactions on Industrial Informatics, 14*(11), 4724–4734. doi:10.1109/TII.2018.2852491

Sugeno, M., & Takagi, A. (1983). A new approach to design of fuzzy controller. In P. P. Wang (Ed.), *Advances in fuzzy sets, possibility theory and applications* (pp. 325–334). New York: Plenum Press. doi:10.1007/978-1-4613-3754-6_20

Takagi, T., & Sugeno, M. (1985). Fuzzy identification of systems and its applications to modeling and control. *IEEE Transactions on Systems, Man, and Cybernetics, 15*(1), 116–132. doi:10.1109/TSMC.1985.6313399

Vanier, D. J. (2001). Why industry needs management tools. *Journal of Computing in Civil Engineering, 15*(1), 35–43. doi:10.1061/(ASCE)0887-3801(2001)15:1(35)

Zadeh, L. A. (1965). Fuzzy sets. *Information and Control, 8*(3), 338–353. doi:10.1016/S0019-9958(65)90241-X

Zadeh, L. A. (1999). From computing with numbers to computing with words. From manipulation of measurements to manipulation of perceptions. *IEEE Transactions on Circuits and Systems, 46*(1), 105–119. doi:10.1109/81.739259

ADDITIONAL READING

Aazam, M., Zeadally, S., & Harras, K. A. (2018). Deploying fog computing in Industrial Internet of Things and Industry 4.0. *IEEE Transactions on Industrial Informatics, 14*(10), 4674–4682. doi:10.1109/TII.2018.2855198

Al Ghazo, A. T., Ibrahim, M., Ren, H., & Kumar, R. (2019). A2G2V: Automatic attack graph generation and visualization and its applications to computer and SCADA networks. [early access]. *IEEE Transactions on Systems, Man, and Cybernetics. Systems, §§§,* 1–11. doi:10.1109/TSMC.2019.2915940

Bruce, A. G. (1998). Reliability analysis of electric utility SCADA systems. *IEEE Transactions on Power Systems, 13*(3), 844–849. doi:10.1109/59.708711

Carcano, A., Coletta, A., Guglielmi, M., Masera, M., Fovino, I. N., & Trombetta, A. (2011). A multi-dimensional critical state analysis for detecting intrusions in SCADA systems. *IEEE Transactions on Industrial Informatics, 7*(2), 179–186. doi:10.1109/TII.2010.2099234

Fang, S., Xu, L. D., Zhu, Y., Ahati, J., Pei, H., Yan, J., & Liu, Z. (2014). An integrated system for regional environmental monitoring and management based on Internet of Things. *IEEE Transactions on Industrial Informatics, 10*(2), 1596–1605. doi:10.1109/TII.2014.2302638

Hajipour, V., Kazemi, A., & Mousavi, S. M. (2013). A fuzzy expert system to increase accuracy and precision in measurement system analysis. *Measurement, 46*(8), 2770–2780. doi:10.1016/j.measurement.2013.04.015

Hou, W., Guo, L., & Ning, Z. (2019). Local electricity storage for blockchain-based energy trading in Industrial Internet of Things. *IEEE Transactions on Industrial Informatics*, *15*(6), 3610–3619. doi:10.1109/TII.2019.2900401

Long, H., Wang, L., Zhang, Z., Song, Z., & Xu, J. (2015). Data-driven wind turbine power generation performance monitoring. *IEEE Transactions on Industrial Electronics*, *62*(10), 6627–6635. doi:10.1109/TIE.2015.2447508

Machado, T. G., Mota, A. A., Mota, L. T. M., Carvalino, M. F. H., & Pezzuto, C. C. (2016). Methodology for identifying the cybersecurity maturity level of smart grids. *IEEE Latin America Transactions*, *14*(11), 4512–4519. doi:10.1109/TLA.2016.7795822

Puttgen, H. B., & Jansen, J. F. (1988). An expert system for the design of a power plant electrical auxiliary system. *IEEE Transactions on Power Systems*, *3*(1), 254–261. doi:10.1109/59.43208

KEY TERMS AND DEFINITIONS

Alarm Number: This parameter describes the number of simultaneous SCADA number. In the real production of electricity and the day-to-day process of transporting ships through the river lock, it is not possible to have multiple simultaneous alarms.

Asset Management (AM): It is one of many management theories relating to the process of managing and disposing of assets and goods.

Fuzzy Logic Controller (FLC): It is controller based on fuzzy logic principles.

Generator Power: Power parameters describe the operation mode of the generator.

Laser Monitoring System (LMS): LMS is online laser remote monitoring system of the river lock.

SCADA Alarms: This parameter describes the number of simultaneous alarms that occur on SCADA.

Temperature Monitoring System (TMS): TMS is online temperature remote monitoring system of the hydrogenerator.

Upper and Bottom Door Position: The process of starting the lock door takes some time and the current position of the door at the time of alarm generation is very important. By analyzing this parameter, cyber attack can be detected.

Vessel Presence: This parameter shows the distance of the vessel from the lock door (the vessel is located near the lock door).

Vessels Distance: This parameter shows the distance of the vessel from the lock (the approach of the vessel to the lock).

Chapter 8
Intelligent Automation Using Machine and Deep Learning in Cybersecurity of Industrial IoT:
CCTV Security and DDoS Attack Detection

Ana Gavrovska

(iD) https://orcid.org/0000-0003-2740-2803

School of Electrical Engineering, University of Belgrade, Serbia

Andreja Samčović

(iD) https://orcid.org/0000-0001-6432-2816

Faculty of Transport and Traffic Engineering, University of Belgrade, Serbia

ABSTRACT

Artificial intelligence is making significant changes in industrial internet of things (IIoT). Particularly, machine and deep learning architectures are now used for cybersecurity in smart factories, smart homes, and smart cities. Using advanced mathematical models and algorithms more intelligent protection strategies should be developed. Hacking of IP surveillance camera systems and Closed-Circuit TV (CCTV) vulnerabilities represent typical example where cyber attacks can make severe damage to physical and other Industrial Control Systems (ICS). This chapter analyzes the possibilities to provide better protection of video surveillance systems and communication networks. The authors review solutions related to migrating machine learning based inference towards edge and smart client devices, as well as methods for DDoS (Distributed Denial of Service) intelligent detection, where DDoS attack is recognized as one of the primary concerns in cybersecurity.

DOI: 10.4018/978-1-7998-2910-2.ch008

INTRODUCTION

Web connectivity and application of artificial intelligence in automation and relevant sensor data exchange in industry and smart manufacturing have opened the door for fourth industrial revolution (Industry 4.0) (Boyes, Hallaq, Cunningham, & Watson, 2018; Lu, 2017; Tuptuk & Hailes, 2018). System architectures for Supervisory Control and Data Acquisition (SCADA) have been developed for direct control and smart monitoring, based on computers and communication networks (Jiang, Yin, & Kaynak, 2018). The growth of Internet of Things (IoT) and internet-based solutions has led to web SCADA and advanced Industrial Control Systems (ICSs) which employ web platforms and user interfaces. Physical processes are monitored in cyber-physical systems. Networked computers and other devices (sensors, actuators,...) are connected usually with distributed ICS/SCADA systems, where there is a control hierarchy: from direct Industrial IoT (IIoT) or device control (usually real-time control), to computer-based high-level control dedicated to: supervisory control of particular sets of devices, coordination and scheduling. A typical hierarchy in remote control systems is presented in Figure 1. Smart cities and smart factories use decentralized decision making. HMI (Human-Machine Interface) enables visualizing the control events and monitoring processes for authorized operators (Dawson, Lamb, & Carbajal, 2018; Hurttila, 2019; Qiu, Chen, Li, Atiquzzaman, & Zhao, 2018).

Artificial intelligence (AI) needs to be used to intelligently react to both user input and environmental parameters. Machine and deep learning should be integrated to IoT and IIoT, having in mind system requirements and low-power equipment (Awad, Beztchi, Smith, Lyles, & Prowell, 2018; Dogaru & Dumitrache, 2019; Pacheco, Cano, Flores, Trujillo, & Marquez, 2018; Tang, Sun, Liu, & Gaudiot, 2017; Teixeira et al., 2018). Intelligent control relies on cognitive systems, making a job-losing concern. It is believed that use of I(IoT) by utilizing AI makes efficient and cost-effective solutions, incorporates knowledge for advanced processing and reasoning, Figure 2. Also, using IoT and AI, multi-agent systems can contribute in executing tasks efficiently compared to individual solving issues.

Figure 1. A typical hierarchy in remote control systems (SCADA)

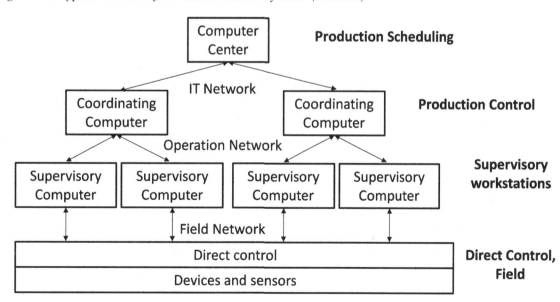

Even though industrial facilities and machines can be easily operated using web based architectures, (cyber-) security, privacy and safety issues still remain, where high economic costs and business models, designs (know-how) and information are in stake. Besides ethical and legal issues, there are also compatibility issues or issues of inappropriate AI usage. Computer and network attacks and AI errors may seriously affect the physical and other ICS processes. Software malware may control ICS/SCADA devices and change the control processes, or steal and/or modify valuable information. Information security is considered in order to prevent or reduce unauthorized access and use of IIoT (Dogaru & Dumitrache, 2019; Pacheco et al., 2018; Thames & Schaefer, 2016). The combination of balanced protection of the confidentiality, integrity and availability of data is the key in industrial security, where proposed standards and regulations, protocols, policies, antivirus and encryption are used with rising security awareness, and should not affect productivity in any way. Protocols such as Modbus are used to enable standard TCP/IP communication. Control products can use specific firewalls and virtual private networks.

Also, there are concerns regarding privacy and surveillance such as in CCTV (Closed-Circuit Television) systems. The typical example of a cyber-attack is Distributed Denial of Service (DDoS), which represents the famous threat to (I)IoT functions. Botnets, the nets of compromised devices, can be used to perform such attacks. Here, using machine and deep learning in cybersecurity of (I)IoT will be analyzed, having in mind DDoS as one of the primary concerns. Recent experiments and experimental setups with deep learning approaches for DDoS detection are considered in order to analyze the most relevant security issues.

VULNERABILITIES AND DDoS

In the age of Industry 4.0 there is a need to optimize production where IT protocols and personnel should be adapted to production access details, where every command for field component should be click away. Stable communication is needed to provide low latency services, as well as efficient big data analysis in order to provide meaningful information. Working with big data and analytics is illustrated in Figure 3.

Advanced processing and cognitive computing provide new possibilities for system and multimedia management, as well as failure and intrusion detection (alarming). Multimedia services and communication traffic models should be carefully analyzed and predicted (Marković, Gavrovska, & Reljin, 2016; Samčović, 2019). Particular abnormal behavior in packet size (e.g., particular singularities in time series) and other relevant traffic parameters should be detected (Gavrovska, Milivojević, Zajić, & I. Reljin, 2016; Gavrovska, Zajić, I. Reljin, & B. Reljin, 2013; Samčović, 2016). Cloud computing is usually applied in (I)IoT to effectively deal with information and resource sharing, data storage and on-demand services (Thames & Schaefer, 2016). Cloud-based storage enables keeping relevant data that can be easily reached without having to access local device storages. "Big data" is stored, and Internet Protocol (IP) enables

Figure 2. (I)IoT with the use of AI

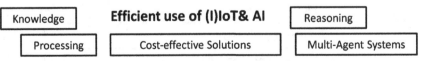

Figure 3. IP communication, big data storage and analytics

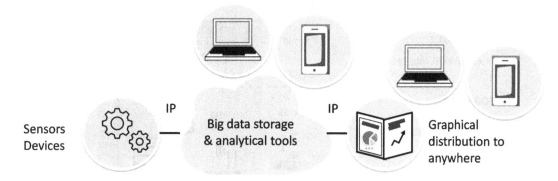

communication. Finally, graphical representations with relevant data are distributed and can be reached through HMI interface.

AI can be enabled for decision making, learning and automation and making digital twins for flexible system design. Even though making digital twins and dealing with different scenarios without tackling the real physical processes have its advantages, system vulnerabilities exist. The vulnerabilities for IIoT can be found on different levels, besides cyber-physical or cloud level. Thus, behavior-based anomaly detection and firewall devices can be considered having in mind different levels and concepts (Demertzis & Iliadis, 2019; Kannus & Ilvonen, 2018; X. Zhou et al., 2018). Due to IIoT architecture, it is possible to move data storage closer to the particular location at the edge of the network leading to both cloud and edge computing (Hu, Dhelim, Ning, & Qiu, 2017; L. Zhou, Guo, & Deng, 2019). Fog networking and computing also enable moving to the edge of the network with local resource pooling, reduction of latency and efficient bandwidth usage for more scalable performances avoiding centralized solutions (servers in data centers) or clouds. Edge and fog concepts allow IIoT to make processing locally with network traffic reduction since decisions are made locally. In other words, intelligent processing having in mind low-power is performed locally, whereas the edge concept is built on embedded automation controllers and the fog is a kind of LAN (Local Area Network) based processing which uses edge devices like sensors or client devices (e.g., smart phones) and gateways. The main system layers are illustrated in Figure 4.

Machine learning enables intelligent solutions and allows systems to be more efficient and accurate in decision making and making predictions. Since machine learning algorithms are popular in many fields, it is expected that they would be a part of the interconnected devices for industry – IIoT. The IIoT vulnerabilities can also be integrated with low-power products due to machine and deep learning. However, it is believed that intelligent automation will make crucial changes in cybersecurity of IIoT.

Widely spread (I)IoT objects are cameras, especially surveillance cameras, which are the main parts of a CCTV system (Costin, 2016; Cusack & Tian, 2017; Muthusenthil & Kim, 2018; Winkler & Rinner, 2013). Lack of privacy can be considered as an important issue since the systems are frequently parts of public networks. CCTV systems are attractive targets for professional attackers due to the relative network openness. Servers in a CCTV system store, manipulate and monitor visual information received from surveillance camera. Privacy protection or cryptography modules are parts of the CCTV systems. In order to protect data, blanking, obfuscation (making visual information unclear) and/or encryption are applied. Various approaches can be applied, such as pixelization, blurring, lossy compression, and mosaicking. Data hiding techniques, such as watermarking or steganography, can be used for additional

Figure 4. Fog and edge concepts

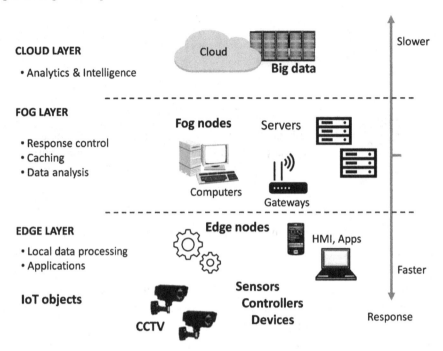

security. Hard cuts can also affect recorded visual data (Zajić, Gavrovska, I. Reljin, & B. Reljin, 2019). A single video frame can be sufficient to change video sequence information. CCTV camera collects data, as a device for video acquisition. A variety of facial algorithms have been implemented in CCTV systems. Facial detection and facial recognition units are common in advanced CCTV systems/servers, where important facial features are extracted. Usually, it is more important to be able to observe the behavior of a person. Privacy enforcement systems acquire video data only as a part of a surveillance task, which is primarily specified before the beginning of recording. Besides facial detection and recognition units, it is usually more important to be able to observe the particular behavior (of a person or network traffic). Contextual information, like location and time (timestamps) can be of great importance to analyze sensitive visual data.

The origin of video information is also of high importance (Zajić et al., 2019). Namely, the identity of camera used for video capture in video surveillance should be known. This can be achieved in the process of authentication the CCTV camera in a network and embedding that information into the video streams. Furthermore, updated visual data must be guaranteed, in order to prevent possible attacks when recorded video sequence is in the network. The CCTV cameras and their software stack are no more considered as trusted parties. However, it is not obvious what type of privacy protection is suitable at the sensor. Furthermore, privacy protection on a sensor level means that image analysis and processing on the CCTV camera must be adjusted to the preprocessed image data. An important question is the identification of an appropriate trade-off between privacy protection and security on the sensor level.

Data comes from different sources and contain a variety of information. The classification of data is based depending on their importance and the potential risk of unauthorized access. The next step is system classification, which is based also on a sensitivity level. The IIoT system should be divided into different sections and classified taking into account their level of vulnerability. The user access should be closely monitored. Based on the role of users, their access depends on certain levels of sensitive data. Furthermore, strategic plans need to be considered in any scenario where data can be corrupted or manipulated. Last, but not least, the whole IoT system needs to be continuously monitored, because different attacks can have a different impact on a system.

DDoS attacks represent one of the main cyber-attacks where a large number of devices can be comprised. It disrupts providing services in IP based communication network over a period of time. This was the case in 2016, when the Mirai botnet commanded 100,000 IoT devices to perform DDoS professional attack, where many of the websites were not accessible for several hours. The Mirai source code was publicly released and is available for experimental analysis (Cusack & Tian, 2017; De Donno, Dragoni, Giaretta, & Spognardi, 2017). Providing intelligent DDoS traffic detection solutions is an important topic today.

MOVING MACHINE AND DEEP LEARNING TO IIoT – SMART CCTV AT THE EDGE

High capacity servers are needed because of huge amounts of captured images/pictures, particularly in the case of high-resolution monitoring. Visual data can be modified in an attack during data transmission or in a database. Protection measures can be considered at the sensor level or at a higher abstraction level. For example, on-camera or server-side measures can be applied, even though it is well known that application level is mostly used. Therefore, it is important to detect manipulations of the software such as system libraries and the operating system. There is a potential risk of unauthorized access on different levels of sensitive data.

Enabling machine and deep learning to IoT or IIoT is not an easy task having in mind limitation in memory resources and computing power (Li, Ota, & Dong, 2018). Machine learning (ML) is a high-level processing and moving/migrating to the cloud seems to be a feasible solution. Traditionally, due to power capabilities, the cloud is often thought as the best choice for training and testing ML methods. In cloud-centric environment the collected data from I(IoT) is first sent to cloud for further processing, and the processing results are returned to the device from the IoT network. By increasing power of edge devices or by fog computing the delay and unnecessary transmissions may be appropriately solved. Deep-learning is often considered even more complex than traditional ML methods. The third-party libraries are called in available deep learning (DL) algorithms, such as the deep neural networks (DNNs) which are popular nowadays. With the reduction of power consumption there is also a significant increase in latency of a few seconds. The requirements for low-latency services go to approximately 500 ms, meaning the deep structures are still not suitable for cloud based real-time tasks in IIoT systems. Migrating machine learning based tasks to edge devices is possible by enabling intelligent decision making or inference engine on the target device. This continues to introduce decision making points for controlling multimedia network data and traffic. Thus, CCTV surveillance can be also considered as edge network service, where edge computing enables introducing intelligence in the system.

Facial recognition is an obvious capability for smart cities and factories to deploy in CCTV systems. The deployment of cameras is enormous for ensuring the safety and security of people and equipment. Privacy concerns still remain. Analytics is found both on the edge and control (higher) level, and statistical results make foundations for intelligence in CCTV. Software-enabled solutions make optimized and smart "vision", when sending relevant information or alerting someone is a result of the implemented artificial intelligence.

Intelligence is important since a combination of different attacks can occur in a distributed manner. A CCTV network should ensure certain guarantees about availability of services under different conditions. Moreover, reasonable resistance against Denial of Service (DoS) must be provided. One solution that can be applied regardless to protocol may be deep defense.

MACHINE AND DEEP LEARNING IN (I)IoT: DEEP DEFENSE FOR DDoS

When targeting the server, attacker can directly manipulate with sensitive data, or use I(IoT) network of compromised devices, as illustrated in Figure 5.

Service can be denied in this manner which is the result of DDoS attacks. DDoS traffic detection is significant since the availability of IIoT is generally prone to DDoS attacks besides available measures like the cryptographic ones. In a DDoS attack the incoming traffic can originate from different sources, like hundreds or even thousands of devices. It is not possible to prevent the attack by blocking a single IP address. DDoS is a malicious attempt to disrupt not only target server, but also multimedia or customer services and the network itself. Users using Internet Service Providers (ISPs) will not able to use the services like Netflix, because something is preventing regular network traffic. This is why this is a burning issue. (I)IoT devices and computers may be under the control of the attacker due to the malware infection. This is a group of bots or a botnet.

Big data is used to analyze the response behavior of such network by identification of the usual state of operations and unusual behavior caused by potential attacks. Typical DDoS attacks can be classified as application layer-based or can be interpreted from the aspect of the used infrastructure (volume-based or protocol-based attacks), as shown in Figure 6. Flooding attacks are common and can be described as attacker continuously sends packets with the aim of affecting victim's bandwidth (UDP – User Datagram

Figure 5. Using (I)IoT network of compromised devices

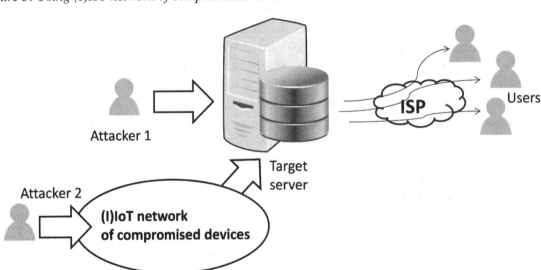

Protocol, ICMP – Internet Control Message Protocol) or systems resources (SYN/ACK flood). In the UDP attack, attacker sends UDP packets to random ports of the target. SYN flood attack is due to sending a large number of TCP (Transport Control Protocol) SYN packets with spoofed source IP addresses (TCP handshake). The target is unable to deal with requests and becomes overwhelmed. Traffic attacks are the ones where large volumes of TCP, UDP or ICMP packets are sent to the victim, whereas the junk data produce decrease of the network bandwidth. The application layer-based ones use application-layer data messages for making the denial of service effect. HTTP flood is similar to pressing the same web browser button over and over in order to send a huge volume of HTTP requests from thousands of devices. DNS attack can be made by making a request to a DNS server with spoofed IP address. The result is that the DNS server responds to the target with huge amount of data. Attack vectors are initially designed for legitimate users, and not for the attackers.

Traditional methods for security protection are not sufficient and potential vulnerabilities or security weaknesses are changing. In other words, attacks are adapting to the new circumstances and smart environments consisted of different sensors and devices. Thus, machine learning (ML) methods are applied to make the DDoS attack detection automatic and relying. ML-based detection implementation for particular tasks should still be tested in different circumstances. Real-time processing is one of the goals when dealing with high amount of data. Datasets used for training and testing can also affect the experimental results, and both data partitioning and feature selection should be taken into account (Gavrovska, Zajić, Milivojević, & I. S. Reljin, 2018). Deep learning (DL) (usually deep neural networks - DNNs), as a kind of ML is gaining increasing publicity today in many fields, especially in DDoS detection since there is a need for developing methods which give high accuracy in DDoS attack detection and intrusion detection generally. The term "deep learning" refers to multiple layers holding multiple levels of perception such that each layer receives input data from the previous layer and gives the result to following layer.

Besides the standard taxonomy related to the type of DDoS attacks and taxonomy of defense mechanisms in recent surveys (Bawany, Shamsi, & Salah, 2017; Miloslavskaya, & Tolstoy, 2019; Salim, Rathore, & Park, 2019; Vishwakarma & Jain, 2019) there is a little about the deep experimental setups from the recent literature which was the main motivation for this paper. If DL is IoT-based or network-based

Figure 6. DDoS and potential vulnerabilities

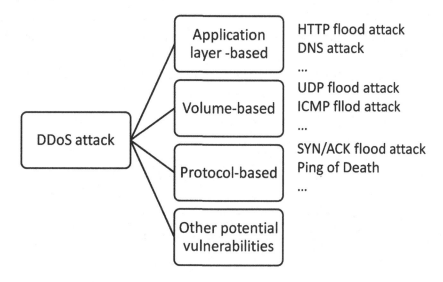

implemented, it can be used for DDoS detection and/or mitigation, as illustrated in Figure 7. Even though, the biggest issue is to resolve whether there are some indications of having attack related traffic or just normal regular traffic, mitigating is important. There are no exact measures of how to deal with DDoS, or just DoS attacks, but network monitoring is essential and logging mechanisms can make a barrier. So far, most deep defense approaches concentrate just on DDoS detection, and they are discussed here. An example of recent deep reinforcement learning based smart mitigation in software-defined networks (SDN) is presented in the recent work (Liu, Dong, Ota, Li, & Wu, 2018). The SDNs differentiate network control data from the rest of the data, for obtaining more control in comparison to traditional networks. In terms of packet streams the network can be more controlled using network operating systems.

As noted in the work of Vishwakarma and Jain (2019), there are a lot of surveys and works about traditional DDoS attack defending, but rarely concerning the IoT networks. In (Vishwakarma & Jain, 2019) popular malware gaining popularity is discussed like Mirai, which is responsible for DDoS attack in 2016 and represents a Linux-based malware comprising up to 15 million devices with a flood speed of 1Tbps. Others like Wirex, Reaper, Torri, and 3ve-2018 malware also exist. Prevention based defense mechanisms should be a strategic way to deal with malware, where mitigation methods tend to reduce the effect made by them, like flooding.

Table 1 shows methods and experiments performed in recent DDoS detection literature (2017-2019 period). Besides the main objective, the tested method(s), datasets and obtained results, oriented mostly towards the DL DDoS detection, are summarized. Recurrent deep neural networks (RNNs) are mostly used, as a supervised learning algorithm. It can be understood as a cascaded chain of decision units for solving the complex tasks.

DL methods can provide accurate DDoS attack detection. One of the proposed solutions is Deep-Defense, where a RNN is used to perform DDoS attack detection on the network (Liu et al., 2018). In the work of Yuan et al. (2017) four RNN models are used, relying on experiments with Convolutional Neural Network (CNN), Long Short-Term Memory Neural Network (LSTM), and Gated Recurrent Unit Neural Network (GRU). Also, it is shown that DL solution may give excellent result compared with conventional network monitoring based on statistical divergence. Error rate reduction was presented showing decrease from 7.517% to 2.103% for LSTM. Different attacks were a part of the dataset, mostly HTTP Web attacks, specifically frequent in Data15 as a part of the ISCX2012 dataset.

An overview of the TensorFlow application through the literature for deep RNN solution is given in the work of Bediako (2017). The author focuses on the use of LSTM based Recurrent Neural Network (RNN) and flooding attacks like UDP, Internet Control Message Protocol (ICMP) (Ping) and TCP SYN flood, obtaining error rate of 0.007% and accuracy of 99.993% for the collected dataset of 15,000 sample size. Evaluation is performed on both CPU and GPU compared with the work of Yuan et al. (2017).

Figure 7. Deep learning in DDoS detection and mitigation

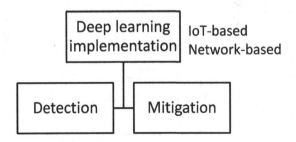

Five category classifications for identifying four attack types were performed by Yin et al. (2017). The authors worked with four attack types (DDoS, User to Root (U2R), Probe (Probing) and Root to Local (R2L)) and NSL-KDD dataset with a separate training and testing set. Comparison of the RNN method is made to J48 (decision tree), ANN (Artificial Neural Network), RF (Random Forest) and SVM (Support Vector Machines) approaches. Compared to KDD Cup 1999 dataset, this one has more appropriate training and testing set in order not to favor more frequent records.

Another TensorFlow ANN approach, also with DL, was presented in the work of Kim et al. (2017), where flooding attacks were analyzed. It is stated that placing the detection module within the system in right location is important for the detection performance, since e.g., low rate attacks are difficult to detect from the victim-end since it can be similar behavior to legitimate traffic. It was tested on the KD-DCup99 dataset developed by the Defense Advanced Research Projects Agency (DARPA) with both normal and abnormal connections on the network. The results provided low likelihood to detect normal as attack data.

Shone et al. (2018) proposed non-symmetric deep auto-encoder (NDAE) for unsupervised feature learning, and DL classification model constructed using stacked NDAEs. For the implementation GPU-enabled TensorFlow was used, as well as KDDCup99 and NSL-KDD datasets. KDDCup99 is consisted of 4,900,000 single connection vectors each of which contains 41 features, where here as in the work of Kim et al. (2017) only 10% was used as a suitable representation containing 494,021 training records and 311,029 testing records. With similar structure (22 attack patterns or normal traffic, and fields for 41 features) NSL-KDD dataset was tested. NDAE method is compared to DBN (Deep Belief Network) performance, obtaining a 5% improvement in accuracy and training time reduction of up to 98.81%. Both 5-class and 13-class classification using stacked NDAE (S-NDAE) were performed.

McDermott et al. (2018) had an aim to collect a dataset incorporating botnet traffic, attack vectors, and normal traffic. IoT scenario was made using the Mirai source code and Sricam AP009 IP cameras used as bots to attack a target Raspberry Pi. The Mirai botnet malware includes 10 DDoS attack types, including UDP flood (udp), Recursive DNS (dns), SYN packet flood (syn), ACK packet flood (ack), and GRE flood (greip).

Meidan et al. (2018) used deep auto-encoders to detect abnormal behavior. IoT environment was consisted of nine commercial IoT devices (doorbells, thermostat, baby monitor, security cameras, webcam), where it is observed that Philips B120N/10 baby monitor demonstrated the highest false positive rate. Two IoT-based botnets, Mirai and BASHLITE, were analyzed. The main idea was to collect data, extract features, train anomaly detector and continuously monitor traffic in order to analyze the IoT constraints related to traffic. The auto-encoder for each device captures snapshots of regular network traffic. They encode and compress data, and when the encoder is not able to reconstruct the snapshot a traffic deviation may occur.

Since large datasets are necessary to perform packet inspection and employ deep solution, ML approaches were analyzed within the smart home LAN in Doshi et al. (2018). It is assumed that the time range of DoS attacks is about 1.5 minutes. One of the aims was to generate a dataset in a consumer IoT environment (home camera, smart switch, android phone). It is said that each of the three IoT devices execute each of the three DoS attack classes (TCP SYN, UDP, and HTTP GET flood) once within a ten minute interval. For DDoS defense a gateway router (middlebox) was placed to monitor the traffic. Both stateless features (related to packet size, inter-packet interval, protocol), and important features (bandwidth, IP destination address cardinality) were captured/acquired.

Pajouh et al. (2018) used RNN method to analyze ARM-based IoT applications' execution operation codes (OpCodes), since ARM processors have been used in cloud edge devices as well as Raspberry Pi II. New dataset with new malware was gathered and tested using three LSTM configurations.

Hwang et al. (2019) examined real-time analysis due to the difficulties of delay of the flow-based data preprocessing in intrusion detection systems. The authors considered a packet level classification using the LSTM model. The evaluation was performed on ISCX2012, USTC-TFC2016, IoT dataset from Robert Gordon University (Mirai-RGU) and IoT dataset collected on their Mirai Botnet (Mirai-CCU).

L. Zhou et al. (2019) applied fog computing concept for DDoS detection. Real-time traffic filtering using firewall devices was performed. The experiment was made using industrial control system testbed.

Yang et al. (2019) proposed a deep belief network (DBN) with the multi-restricted Boltzmann machine (RBM) and the back propagation (BP) network. In particular, DBN-SVM model was proposed, where SVM was used for training. There are also other recent papers considering DDoS attack detection, made for particular purposes like vehicular ad-hoc network or smart grid (Ali & Li, 2019; Zeng et al., 2019).

SOLUTIONS AND RECOMMENDATIONS

Having in mind recent development, as presented in Table 1, potential vulnerabilities still exist in IIoT environment, and there is a lot of work ahead in the DDoS detection research. ML and DL-based methods for DDoS detection show high performance, and their capabilities are evident. It can be summarized from the recent literature that some of the main aspects can be significantly improved.

There are a lot of methods tested on the local datasets. Some of the available benchmarking datasets exist, but are not considered sufficient enough for employing big data and deep learning solutions for various attacks. This leads to the lack of possibility to compare the results in many cases for the same circumstances and IIoT environments. Both quantity and quality of data for experimental analysis should be considered.

New classification solutions should work with normal traffic, as well as old and new (unknown) malware. Thus, the ability to adapt to novel security issues is important. The datasets for testing deep defense methods should be capable to balance the existence of the well-known attacks. The ensemble of attacks can possibly decrease the method efficiency.

Features, like the stateless ones, should be extracted and tested according to their relevance. Even in the case of DL-based methods the choice of features can affect the accuracy and false alarm percentages. The number of made assumptions should be kept at minimum (e.g., protocol-based detection and protocol-agnostic approaches). There are issues in the cases of "unseen" attacks within the specific time period (low-rate attacks). Quality of Service (QoS) and Quality of Experience (QoE) measurements are valuable in anomaly network traffic monitoring.

Detection modules should be appropriately located having in mind the two-way traffic and possibilities of migrating learning-based engines (edge and fog concepts, cloud computing). Moreover, real-time filtering unwanted packets should be tested for both consumer and industrial IoT testbeds. Standards for IIoT environments should provide insight into available measures and possible security weaknesses.

Particular IoT devices or data can be more exposed to attacks than others. In some cases, knowing IoT-based constraints should be of vital importance for controlling packet streams and network traffic prediction. Different security levels should be tested both in real and lab environment.

Table 1. Methods and experiments performed in recent DDoS detection literature

Paper	Objective	Method (s)	Dataset (Train/Test Samples)	Results
Yuan et al. (2017)	DDoS attack detection on the network	Deep learning Four RNN models (LSTM, CNNLSTM,GRU, 3LSTM)	*Data14* includes 9,648,653 packets (6.85GB); *Data15* includes 34,983,043 packets (23.4GB). 20 network traffic fields from SCX2012 legitimate or attack network activities with corresponding information (e.g., name, time period, source IP, destination IP, source port, destination port, etc.). Total number of training samples: *Data14* -15,176; *Data15* - 233,450. Mostly HTTP web attacks.	LSTM shows 2.103% error rate (Accuracy 97.897%) for *Data15* and 2.004% error rate (Accuracy 97.996%) for *Data14*
Bedeiako et al. (2017)	DDoS flood network detection (CPU and GPU based experiments)	LSTM RNN limited to determining up to 20 different attack types.	Dataset composed of 22 different attacks out of which 6 were DDoS attacks and 16 were non-DDoS attack types. Flooding attacks analyzed (UDP, ICMP, TCP SYN).	0.007% error rate (Accuracy 99.993%) for dataset of 15,000 samples size
Yin et al. (2017)	RNN Deep learning for intrusion detection	RNN - five-class classification (Normal, DoS, R2L, U2R, Probe attack) compared to J48, ANN, RF and SVM.	NSL-KDD dataset; 41 features mapped into 122-dimensional features; 49,402 training samples (39,145 for DoS) and 31,104 testing samples (22,985 for DoS).	83.49% detection rate (false positive rate - FPR 2.06%) for DoS attack
Kim et al. (2017)	Intrusion detection	ANN with adaptive moment (Adam) optimizer	KDD Cup 99 dataset (both normal and abnormal connections on the network); field that shows 22 attack patterns or normal traffic, and fields for 41 other features; training set to include 10-90% attack data (10% of the KDDCup99), and testing set used the entire KDD Cup 99 dataset of 4,898,431 records.	High accuracy and detection rate averaging 99%. False alarm rate achieved 0.08%.
Shone et al. (2018)	Deep Learning Approach to Network Intrusion Detection	Non-symmetric deep auto-encoder (S-NDAE) method for five-class classification (Normal, DoS, R2L, U2R, Probe attack) and 13-class classification	KDD Cup99 (10%) and NSL-KDD datasets with Normal, DoS, R2L, U2R, Probe attack class. KDD Cup99 (494,021 training and 311,029 testing records). NSL-KDD (training for 5 classes: 125,973, for 13 classes: 125,881)	KDD Cup99 Performance (Accuracy 97.85%) NSL-KDD 5-class Performance (Accuracy 85.42%) NSL-KDD 13-class Performance (Acc 89.22%)
McDermott et al. (2018)	Botnet detection in the IoT using DNN representation of a Mirai infection	LSTM deep learning using a Bidirectional LSTM-RNN (BLSTM-RNN); Mirai botnet malware (10 DDoS attacks)	Train samples (387,060, 391,002, 391,622); Validation samples (208,418, 210,540, 210,874) for mirai, udp and dns	Results for mirai, udp, and dns: 99%, 98%, 98% validation accuracy and 0.000809, 0.125630, 0.116453 validation loss, respectively.
Meidan et al. (2018)	Network-based detection of IoT botnet attacks (nine IoT devices)	Trained deep auto-encoder (one for each device) to learn the IoT normal behaviors; compared to SVM, Isolation Forest, LOF - Local Outlier Factor approach)	Each auto-encoder with input layer size equal to the number of features in the dataset (i.e., 115). BASHLITE (Scan, junk, UDP, TCP, combo attacks), Mirai attacks (Scan, Ack, Syn UDP, UDP plain flood).	Detecting every single attack launched by every compromised IoT device; mean FPR of 0.007±0.01.
Doshi et al. (2018)	ML DDoS detection for consumer IoT	ANN, K nearest neighbors (KN), SVM with linear kernel (LSVM), Decision tree using Gini impurity scores (DT), Random Forest using Gini impurity scores (RF)	Dataset of 491,855 packets; 459,565 malicious and 32,290 benign packets. Training set with 85% of the combined normal and DoS traffic, and testing on the remaining traffic (TCP SYN flood, UDP flood, HTTP GET flood).	ANN provided 93.9% for stateless features and 98.9% for all features
Pajouh et al. (2018)	Deep RNN for IoT malware for analyzing ARM processors used in cloud edge devices (ARM-based IoT applications' execution operation codes (OpCodes))	Three different Long Short Term Memory configurations (LSTM-1,-2,-3)	281 malware and 270 benign data; final vector of 681 possible Opcode indices	LSTM-2 (depth2) of Accuracy of 98.18% (94% on new malware)
Hwang et al. (2019)	LSTM-Based DL for traffic classification at the Packet Level	Packet splitting and word embedding for the LSTM model	ISCX2012, USTC-TFC2016, Mirai-RGU and Mirai-CCU datasets	Evaluation results of the Mirai-CCU dataset validation on the Mirai-RGU training model: Accuracy 97.22%, FPR 0.36%
L. Zhou et al. (2019)	Fog computing-based approach in IoT systems (industrial control system testbed)	Firewall with Deep Packet Inspection	Two types of DDoS attacks (TCP attack and crashing the Modbus service)	99.84% and 88.02% detection rates for fog computing approach
Yang et al. (2019)	Detect wireless network intrusion behavior	DBN-SVM detection method	The DBN-SVM model was trained by sampling 20%, 40%, 60%, and 80% of the NSL-KDD training set.	Accuracy 97.45%

Cyber attacks should be efficiently detected, but the question whether to employ deep defense in every case still remains. Thus, both non-ML and traditional ML (like ANN, SVM, random forests, decision trees) methods are relevant. DL-based approaches should be selected depending on the set goals. Such deep defense solutions should have their place in smart environment. The efforts towards more secure CCTV system offer benefits for monitored infrastructure, even in smart environments.

FUTURE RESEARCH DIRECTIONS

Machine and deep learning methods implementation for network-based security are parts of future smart environments and CCTV systems. Having in mind future trends in intelligent automation and future trends in building new machine and deep learning solutions for network traffic control and simulation, it is expected that the ever-lasting combat between system attackers and securing vulnerable data and devices will continue.

Larger number of IIoT devices leads to more potential vulnerabilities and developing more advanced methods for DDoS detection. Known and unknown malware are changing feature selection and procedures in cybersecurity tasks. Both lab and real environments are expected to take part in future research.

CONCLUSION

Security (and privacy) issues still exist. Smart cities, smart factories and smart homes could be significantly improved by migrating learning-based engines to desired locations and by increasing anomaly detection accuracies in real-time. Future work should be oriented towards new machine and deep learning architectures, methods and solutions, and new benchmarking public datasets.

ACKNOWLEDGMENT

This research was partially supported by the Serbian Ministry of Education, Science and Technological Development [grant number TR 32048 and grant number TR 32025].

REFERENCES

Ali, S., & Li, Y. (2019). Learning multilevel auto-encoders for DDoS attack detection in smart grid network. *IEEE Access: Practical Innovations, Open Solutions*, 7, 108647–108659. doi:10.1109/ACCESS.2019.2933304

Awad, R. A., Beztchi, S., Smith, J. M., Lyles, B., & Prowell, S. (2018). Tools, techniques, and methodologies: A survey of digital forensics for SCADA systems. In *Proceedings of the Annual Industrial Control System Security (ICSS) Workshop*. New York, NY: ACM. 10.1145/3295453.3295454

Bawany, N. Z., Shamsi, J. A., & Salah, K. (2017). DDoS attack detection and mitigation using SDN: Methods, practices, and solutions. *Arabian Journal for Science and Engineering, 42*(2), 425–441. doi:10.100713369-017-2414-5

Bediako, P. K. (2017). *Long short-term memory recurrent neural network for detecting DDoS flooding attacks within TensorFlow implementation framework.* (Doctoral dissertation). Retrieved November 15, 2019, from http://urn.kb.se/resolve?urn=urn:nbn:se:ltu:diva-66802

Boyes, H., Hallaq, B., Cunningham, J., & Watson, T. (2018). The Industrial Internet of Things (IIoT): An analysis framework. *Computers in Industry, 101*, 1–12. doi:10.1016/j.compind.2018.04.015

Costin, A. (2016). Security of CCTV and video surveillance systems: Threats, vulnerabilities, attacks, and mitigations. In *Proceedings of the 6th international workshop on trustworthy embedded devices* (pp. 45-54). New York: ACM. 10.1145/2995289.2995290

Cusack, B., & Tian, Z. (2017). Evaluating IP surveillance camera vulnerabilities. In *Proceedings of the 15th Australian Information Security Management Conference* (pp. 25-32). Perth, Australia: Edith Cowan University.

Dawson, L. A., Lamb, C., & Carbajal, A. J. (2018). *Industrial control systems cyber security risk candidate methods analysis (No. SAND2018-7592).* Albuquerque, NM: Sandia National Lab. doi:10.2172/1463794

De Donno, M., Dragoni, N., Giaretta, A., & Spognardi, A. (2017). Analysis of DDoS-capable IoT malwares. In *Proceedings of the Federated Conference on Computer Science and Information Systems* (pp. 807-816). New York: IEEE.

Demertzis, K., & Iliadis, L. (2019). Cognitive web application firewall to critical infrastructures protection from phishing attacks. *Journal of Computations & Modelling, 9*(2), 1–26.

Dogaru, D. I., & Dumitrache, I. (2019). Cyber attacks of a power grid analysis using a deep neural network approach. *Journal of Control Engineering and Applied Informatics, 21*(1), 42–50.

Doshi, R., Apthorpe, N., & Feamster, N. (2018). Machine learning DDoS detection for consumer internet of things devices. In *Proceedings of the IEEE Security and Privacy Workshops (SPW)* (pp. 29-35). New York: IEEE. 10.1109/SPW.2018.00013

Gavrovska, A., Zajić, G., Reljin, I., & Reljin, B. (2013). Classification of prolapsed mitral valve versus healthy heart from phonocardiograms by multifractal analysis. *Computational and Mathematical Methods in Medicine, 2013*, 1–10. doi:10.1155/2013/376152 PMID:23762185

Gavrovska, A. M., Milivojević, M. S., Zajić, G., & Reljin, I. (2016). Video traffic variability in H. 265/ HEVC video encoded sequences. In *Proceedings of the 13th Symposium on Neural Networks and Applications (NEUREL)* (pp. 1-4). New York: IEEE. 10.1109/NEUREL.2016.7800130

Gavrovska, A. M., Zajić, G. J., Milivojević, M. S., & Reljin, I. S. (2018). Machine-learning based blind visual quality assessment with content-aware data partitioning. In *Proceedings of the 14th Symposium on Neural Networks and Applications (NEUREL)* (pp. 1-5). New York: IEEE. 10.1109/NEUREL.2018.8587018

Hu, P., Dhelim, S., Ning, H., & Qiu, T. (2017). Survey on fog computing: Architecture, key technologies, applications and open issues. *Journal of Network and Computer Applications*, *98*, 27–42. doi:10.1016/j.jnca.2017.09.002

Hurttila, A. (2019). *Cybersecurity in SCADA engineering*. Retrieved November 15, 2019, from https://www.theseus.fi/bitstream/handle/10024/170574/Hurttila%2C%20Antti.pdf?sequence=2&isAllowed=y

Hwang, R. H., Peng, M. C., Nguyen, V. L., & Chang, Y. L. (2019). An LSTM-based deep learning approach for classifying malicious traffic at the packet level. *Applied Sciences*, *9*(16), 3414. doi:10.3390/app9163414

Jiang, Y., Yin, S., & Kaynak, O. (2018). Data-driven monitoring and safety control of industrial cyber-physical systems: Basics and beyond. *IEEE Access: Practical Innovations, Open Solutions*, *6*, 47374–47384. doi:10.1109/ACCESS.2018.2866403

Kannus, K., & Ilvonen, I. (2018). Future prospects of cyber security in manufacturing: findings from a Delphi study. In *Proceedings of the 51st Hawaii International Conference on System Sciences* (pp. 4762-4771). Waikoloa Village, HI: Curran Associates. 10.24251/HICSS.2018.599

Kim, J., Shin, N., Jo, S. Y., & Kim, S. H. (2017). Method of intrusion detection using deep neural network. In *Proceedings of the IEEE International Conference on Big Data and Smart Computing (BigComp)* (pp. 313-316). New York: IEEE.

Li, H., Ota, K., & Dong, M. (2018). Learning IoT in edge: Deep learning for the Internet of Things with edge computing. *IEEE Network*, *32*(1), 96–101. doi:10.1109/MNET.2018.1700202

Liu, Y., Dong, M., Ota, K., Li, J., & Wu, J. (2018). Deep reinforcement learning based smart mitigation of DDoS flooding in software-defined networks. In *Proceedings of the IEEE 23rd International Workshop on Computer Aided Modeling and Design of Communication Links and Networks (CAMAD)* (pp. 1-6). New York: IEEE. 10.1109/CAMAD.2018.8514971

Lu, Y. (2017). Industry 4.0: A survey on technologies, applications and open research issues. *Journal of Industrial Information Integration*, *6*, 1–10. doi:10.1016/j.jii.2017.04.005

Marković, D. R., Gavrovska, A. M., & Reljin, I. S. (2016). 4K video traffic analysis using seasonal autoregressive model for traffic prediction. In *Proceedings of the 24th Telecommunications Forum (TELFOR)* (pp. 1-4). New York: IEEE. 10.1109/TELFOR.2016.7818885

McDermott, C. D., Majdani, F., & Petrovski, A. V. (2018). Botnet detection in the internet of things using deep learning approaches. In *Proceedings of the International Joint Conference on Neural Networks (IJCNN)* (pp. 1-8). New York: IEEE. 10.1109/IJCNN.2018.8489489

Meidan, Y., Bohadana, M., Mathov, Y., Mirsky, Y., Shabtai, A., Breitenbacher, D., & Elovici, Y. (2018). N-BaIoT – Network-based detection of IoT botnet attacks using deep auto-encoders. *IEEE Pervasive Computing*, *17*(3), 12–22. doi:10.1109/MPRV.2018.03367731

Miloslavskaya, N., & Tolstoy, A. (2019). Internet of Things: Information security challenges and solutions. *Cluster Computing*, *22*(1), 103–119. doi:10.100710586-018-2823-6

Muthusenthil, B., & Kim, H. S. (2018). CCTV surveillance system, attacks and design goals. *Iranian Journal of Electrical and Computer Engineering, 8*(4), 2072.

Pacheco, A., Cano, P., Flores, E., Trujillo, E., & Marquez, P. (2018). A smart classroom based on deep learning and osmotic IoT computing. In *Proceedings of the Congreso Internacional de Innovación y Tendenciasen Ingeniería (CONIITI)* (pp. 1-5). New York: IEEE. 10.1109/CONIITI.2018.8587095

Pajouh, H. H., Dehghantanha, A., Khayami, R., & Choo, K. K. R. (2018). A deep recurrent neural network based approach for Internet of Things malware threat hunting. *Future Generation Computer Systems, 85,* 88–96. doi:10.1016/j.future.2018.03.007

Qiu, T., Chen, N., Li, K., Atiquzzaman, M., & Zhao, W. (2018). How can heterogeneous Internet of Things build our future: A survey. *IEEE Communications Surveys and Tutorials, 20*(3), 2011–2027. doi:10.1109/COMST.2018.2803740

Salim, M. M., Rathore, S., & Park, J. H. (2019). Distributed denial of service attacks and its defenses in IoT: A survey. *The Journal of Supercomputing,* 1–44.

Samčović, A. (2016). Security Issues in Internet of Things Environment. In *Proceedings of the Eighth International Conference on Business Information Security* (pp. 59-65). Belgrade, Serbia: Metropolitan University.

Samčović, A. (2019). Multimedia Services in Cloud Computing Environment. In *Proceedings of the International Scientific Conference on Information Technology and Data Related Research - Sinteza 2019* (pp. 176-183). Belgrade, Serbia: Singidunum University.

Shone, N., Ngoc, T. N., Phai, V. D., & Shi, Q. (2018). A deep learning approach to network intrusion detection. *IEEE Transactions on Emerging Topics in Computational Intelligence, 2*(1), 41–50. doi:10.1109/TETCI.2017.2772792

Tang, J., Sun, D., Liu, S., & Gaudiot, J. L. (2017). Enabling deep learning on IoT devices. *Computer, 50*(10), 92–96. doi:10.1109/MC.2017.3641648

Teixeira, M., Salman, T., Zolanvari, M., Jain, R., Meskin, N., & Samaka, M. (2018). SCADA system testbed for cybersecurity research using machine learning approach. *Future Internet, 10*(8), 76. doi:10.3390/fi10080076

Thames, L., & Schaefer, D. (2016). Software-defined cloud manufacturing for industry 4.0. *Procedia CIRP, 52,* 12–17. doi:10.1016/j.procir.2016.07.041

Tuptuk, N., & Hailes, S. (2018). Security of smart manufacturing systems. *Journal of Manufacturing Systems, 47,* 93–106. doi:10.1016/j.jmsy.2018.04.007

Vishwakarma, R., & Jain, A. K. (2019). A survey of DDoS attacking techniques and defense mechanisms in the IoT network. *Telecommunication Systems,* 1–23.

Winkler, T., & Rinner, B. (2013). Privacy and security in video surveillance. In P. K. Atrey, M. S. Kankanhalli, & A. Cavallaro (Eds.), *Intelligent Multimedia Surveillance* (pp. 37–66). Berlin, Germany: Springer. doi:10.1007/978-3-642-41512-8_3

Yang, H., Qin, G., & Ye, L. (2019). Combined wireless network intrusion detection model based on deep learning. *IEEE Access: Practical Innovations, Open Solutions*, 7, 82624–82632. doi:10.1109/ACCESS.2019.2923814

Yin, C., Zhu, Y., Fei, J., & He, X. (2017). A deep learning approach for intrusion detection using recurrent neural networks. *IEEE Access: Practical Innovations, Open Solutions*, 5, 21954–21961. doi:10.1109/ACCESS.2017.2762418

Yuan, X., Li, C., & Li, X. (2017). DeepDefense: Identifying DDoS attack via deep learning. In *Proceedings of the IEEE International Conference on Smart Computing (SMARTCOMP)* (pp. 1-8). New York: IEEE. 10.1109/SMARTCOMP.2017.7946998

Zajić, G., Gavrovska, A., Reljin, I., & Reljin, B. (2019). A video hard cut detection using multifractal features. *Multimedia Tools and Applications*, 78(5), 6233–6252. doi:10.100711042-018-6420-8

Zeng, Y., Qiu, M., Zhu, D., Xue, Z., Xiong, J., & Liu, M. (2019). DeepVCM: A deep learning based intrusion detection method in VANET. In *Proceedings of the IEEE 5th Intl Conference on Big Data Security on Cloud (Big Data Security), IEEE Intl Conference on High Performance and Smart Computing (HPSC) and IEEE Intl Conference on Intelligent Data and Security (IDS)* (pp. 288-293). New York: IEEE. 10.1109/BigDataSecurity-HPSC-IDS.2019.00060

Zhou, L., Guo, H., & Deng, G. (2019). A fog computing based approach to DDoS mitigation in IIoT systems. *Computers & Security*, 85, 51–62. doi:10.1016/j.cose.2019.04.017

Zhou, X., Xu, Z., Wang, L., Chen, K., Chen, C., & Zhang, W. (2018). Behavior based anomaly detection model in SCADA system. In *Proceedings of the MATEC Web of Conferences* (*vol. 173, Article* 01011). EDP Sciences. 10.1051/matecconf/201817301011

ADDITIONAL READING

Bawany, N. Z., & Shamsi, J. A. (2019). SEAL: SDN based secure and agile framework for protecting smart city applications from DDoS attacks. *Journal of Network and Computer Applications*, 145, 1–17. doi:10.1016/j.jnca.2019.06.001

Hoque, N., Bhattacharyya, D. K., & Kalita, J. K. (2015). Botnet in DDoS attacks: Trends and challenges. *IEEE Communications Surveys and Tutorials*, 17(4), 2242–2270. doi:10.1109/COMST.2015.2457491

Kolias, C., Kambourakis, G., Stavrou, A., & Voas, J. (2017). DDoS in the IoT: Mirai and other botnets. *Computer*, 50(7), 80–84. doi:10.1109/MC.2017.201

Liu, G., Quan, W., Cheng, N., Zhang, H., & Yu, S. (2019). Efficient DDoS attacks mitigation for stateful forwarding in Internet of Things. *Journal of Network and Computer Applications*, 130, 1–13. doi:10.1016/j.jnca.2019.01.006

Lykou, G., Anagnostopoulou, A., & Gritzalis, D. (2019). Smart airportc: Threat mitigation and cyber resilience controls. *Sensors (Basel)*, 19(1), 19. doi:10.339019010019

McGlade, D., & Scott-Hayward, S. (2019). ML-based cyber incident detection for electronic medical record (EMR) systems. *Smart Health*, *12*, 3–23. doi:10.1016/j.smhl.2018.05.001

Monge, M. A. S., González, A. H., Fernández, B. L., Vidal, D. M., García, G. R., & Vidal, J. M. (2019). Traffic-flow analysis for source-side DDoS recognition on 5G environments. *Journal of Network and Computer Applications*, *136*, 114–131. doi:10.1016/j.jnca.2019.02.030

National Institute of Standards and Technology. (2018). *Interagency report on status of international cybersecurity standardization for the internet of things (IoT) (NIST 8200)*. Gaithersburg, MD: Interagency International Cybersecurity Standardization Working Group.

Patel, C., & Doshi, N. (2019). Security challenges in IoT Cyber World. In A. Hassanien, M. Elhoseny, S. Ahmed, & A. Singh (Eds.), *Lecture Notes in Intelligent Transportation and Infrastructure. Security in Smart Cities: Models, Applications, and Challenges* (pp. 171–191). Cham, Switzerland: Springer.

KEY TERMS AND DEFINITIONS

Attack Detection System: It is also known as intrusion detection system. It is a system that monitors network traffic for detection of unauthorized access or activity in a network-based environment. When anomalous event is detected, some attack/intrusion detection systems are capable of taking specific actions to prevent or weaken the impact of the attacks.

Closed-Circuit Television (CCTV): Also known as video surveillance system. It is a closed-circuit system consisted of video cameras which transmit visual information to a specific place found on the same network. It differs from broadcast television, where the signal is openly transmitted. The term is used for camera-based surveillance security systems where visual monitoring is needed (e.g., in stores, banks, airports, factories), and can have many industrial and non-industrial applications.

Cybersecurity: It is a general term which describes technologies, processes, methods, and practices for the purpose of protection of internet-connected information systems from attacks, i.e., cyberattacks. Cybersecurity can refer to security of data, software or hardware within information systems.

Deep Learning: It is a part of machine learning intended for learning form large amounts of data, as in the case of experience-based learning. It can be considered that feature engineering in deep learning-based models is partly left to the machine. In the case of artificial neural networks, deep neural networks are expected to have various layers within architectures for solving complex problems with higher accuracy compared to traditional machine learning. Moreover, high performance automatic results are expected without human intervention.

Distributed Denial of Service (DDoS): In DDoS attack, the incoming network traffic affects a target (e.g., server) from many different compromised sources. Consequently, online services are unavailable due to the attack. The target's resources are affected with different malicious network-based techniques (e.g., flood of network traffic packets).

Industrial Internet of Things: Sensors and devices which are internet-based interconnected for industrial applications and smart industrial environments are known as IIoT or Industrial Internet of Things. The connectivity of devices and information systems enable improvements in efficiency and productivity.

Machine Learning: It refers to an application of artificial intelligence focusing on algorithms which can be used for building models (e.g., based on statistics) from input data. Such automatic analytical models need to provide outputs based on the learning relations between input and output values. The algorithms are often categorized as supervised, semi-supervised or unsupervised.

Network Traffic: It is the amount of data, mostly encapsulated in network packets, transferring across a network at a point of time. Network monitoring and measurements enable network traffic control.

Chapter 9
A Cyber–Physical System Testbed for Security Experimentation

John Hale
University of Tulsa, USA

Abraham Habib
University of Tulsa, USA

Rujit Raval
University of Tulsa, USA

Ryan Irvin
University of Tulsa, USA

Peter Hawrylak
ⓘD https://orcid.org/0000-0003-3268-7452
University of Tulsa, USA

ABSTRACT

Cyber-Physical Systems (CPSs) are systems which integrate computational, networking, and physical components within a single functional environment. They play an important role in critical infrastructure, government, and everyday life. CPSs encumber many requirements, such as robustness, safety and security, Quality of Service (QoS), and trust. In addition, CPSs combine a variety of digital and analog technologies. Consequently, their analysis, verification, and control can be challenging. The science of protecting CPSs from blended attacks, those combining cyber and physical attack vectors, is yet to be developed. A much-needed tool on this front is a suitable test environment in which to pursue lines of experimentation and exploration. This chapter describes a testbed that allows researchers to experiment on blended attack and defense scenarios in CPSs through gamification. The testbed features many different systems, both cyber and physical, that are fully instrumented for data analysis and assessment.

DOI: 10.4018/978-1-7998-2910-2.ch009

INTRODUCTION

Cyber-physical systems (CPSs) integrate cyber with physical capabilities to include computation, networking and physical processes. They are used in various industries to operate critical functions and have requirements such as resilience, security, robustness, reliability, privacy, and Quality of Service (QoS). CPSs present a collection of challenges and requirements not always found in a classical business information system or embedded system. To construct a CPS, a combination of different engineering competencies is required. As a result, a new discipline of systems engineering that spans both the technical domains as well as the corresponding application sectors is formed.

Correspondingly, a new discipline and science must follow in the emerging field of CPS security. The challenges here are many. CPSs combine a variety of diverse technologies, resulting in a complex attack surface. Unforeseen interactions that span the cyber and physical domains confound analysis. Consequently, as described by Sha et al. (2008), the science of security remains one of the least understood topics in CPSs.

A deeper understanding of the nature of CPS security can only be achieved through direct experimentation and observation. To support such explorations, a gamified CPS testbed to allow researchers to design experiments exposing the fundamental principles of CPS security was created. The testbed is a fully instrumented collection of robotic vehicles driven wirelessly by computer and equipped with on-board process control elements. The vehicles interact with Near Field Communication (NFC) beacons placed in an arena in support of game tasks. A key element of the testbed is the collection of vulnerabilities and attack vectors associated with each CPS component. The testbed, its instrumentation and gamification, along with examples and approaches for applying attacks, are explained in this chapter.

BACKGROUND

One of the most significant advances in the development of computer science, information, and communication technologies is represented by the emergence of CPSs. CPSs are systems that link the physical world through sensors or actuators with the virtual world of information processing. They are composed from diverse constituent parts that collaborate to create some global behavior in the control of physical processes. These constituents include software systems, communications technology, and sensors/actuators that interact with the real world, often including embedded technologies.

CPSs are far more common in today's age then they were a quarter of a century ago. They are no longer limited to enterprise control systems but can now be found in day to day use by an average consumer. A few examples are cars, home alarm systems, building security systems, Internet of Things (IoT) devices, and more; even a connected coffee machine is a CPS. With the widespread adoption of internet connected CPSs (many with blatant flaws) security is more prevalent now than ever before.

To advance the state of the art in this field, researchers have developed CPS testbeds for experimentation. With these physical and virtual testbeds, researchers can now conduct investigations with real and simulated hardware, systematically exploring attack vectors and defense strategies.

Related Research

Security considerations for CPSs have accumulated over the past decade in a variety of industrial sectors. Advances in embedded wireless technology and pervasive computing have pushed research in CPS security forward even further. Numerous studies have explored distinct domains and domain specific applications of CPSs and consequential security issues and challenges.

Use of CPS in Industry Sectors

Gunes et al. (2014) summarize a number of research efforts that address key CPS application domains, namely smart manufacturing, emergency response, air transportation, critical infrastructure, healthcare and medicine, intelligent transportation, and robotics for service. Table 1 provides an overview on the CPS applications according to their functionality (Gunes et al., 2014).

Gupta et al. (2014) has informed the impact of research in the fields of biomedical and healthcare systems, next-generation air transportation systems and in the field of smart grid and renewable energy. Sha et al. (2008) and Sridhar et al. (2012) give details about the use of CPSs in the fields of medical device networks and the electric power grid. Humayed et al. (2017) summarize existing control mechanisms, and further identify the unsolved issues and challenges in different CPS applications such as Industrial Control Systems (ICSs), Smart Grid Systems, Medical Devices, and Smart Cars.

Giraldo et al. (2017) survey CPS domains, challenges, attacks, defenses, current research trends and security level implementation and identifies a variety of open problems on how to isolate and mitigate an attack once it is detected.

Dondossola et al. (2009) and Tung et al. (2014) address various issues by scanning web vulnerabilities of testbeds in power control systems and smart grids. Kwon et al. (2013) and Akella et al. (2010) deal with information flow security within a CPS and security against stealthy deception attacks. The complexity of the cyber-physical relationship can pose non-intuitive system dependencies. Performing accurate risk assessments requires the development of models that provide a basis for dependency analysis and quantifying impacts (Sridhar et al., 2012). It also states common weaknesses which can be present in any CPS and must be taken care of in the process of making a CPS more secure (Sridhar et al., 2012).

Table 1. Functionality of CPS domains (Gunes et al., 2014)

Types of Domains	Scale	Functionality
Smart Manufacturing	Medium Scale	Optimizing productivity in the manufacture of goods or delivery of services.
Emergency Response	Medium/Large Scale	Handling threats to public safety, protecting nature, and infrastructures.
Air Transportation	Large Scale	Operation and traffic management of aircraft systems.
Critical Infrastructure	Large Scale	Distribution of water, electricity, gas, and oil.
Health Care and Medicine	Medium Scale	Monitoring health conditions of patients.
Intelligent Transportation	Medium/Large Scale	Improving safety, and services in traffic management with real-time info sharing.
Robotics for Service	Medium/Large Scale	Performing services for the welfare of humans.

Competitive Learning Platforms

Competitive learning platforms in cyber security afford participants the opportunity to explore and experience different scenarios for education and training. Conklin (2006) and Fink et al. (2013) discuss various cyber defense competitions along with the necessity for laboratory experiments and field studies. The main goal of these competitions is to offer the participants an interesting challenge that prepares them for real-world situations and help them develop the necessary skills to be a successful professional. Gamification in a testbed is useful in boosting learner engagement, putting knowledge into practice, and motivating goal-oriented knowledge retention.

Cyber Security and CPS Testbeds

Cyber security testbeds, a combination of hardware, software, and networking components, are platforms for conducting rigorous and transparent testing of security theories, concepts, and implementations. As shown in Table 2, CPS research is currently segregated into isolated sub-disciplines and applications. Thus, CPSs are designed and analyzed using a variety of modeling tools and mechanisms depending on their end goal and application domain.

The most prominent example of a large isolated sub-discipline is the National SCADA Test Bed Program (NSTB). This program was created in partnership with the Department of Energy and the energy sector. Its purpose is to support efforts to enhance the cyber security of SCADA systems throughout the energy industry.

The NSTB has brought rise to multiple critical infrastructure (CI) testbeds from several research facilities. The NSTB Multi-Laboratory Team is made up of the Idaho Critical Infrastructure Test Range, SANDIA Center for SCADA Security, Pacific Northwest Electricity Infrastructure Operations Center, Oak Ridge, and Argonne. Between these five entities, they have developed testbeds covering SCADA, Cyber Security, Wireless, Powergrid, Control Systems, Distributed Energy Technology, Networking, Visualization and Analytics, and CI Protection Analysis.

The findings and achievements found in these different research testbeds are notable -- a few of their methodologies can be found in this paper. There is, however, little research which motivates or enhances a unified understanding of CPS security through gamified experimentation with blended attacks on a fully instrumented testbed.

CPS Testbed

This section describes various components of the CPS testbed. Additionally, it illustrates how the hardware and software are integrated to provide a rich environment for experimenters and operators, and also describes some limitations of the testbed.

Testbed Components

The CPS testbed incorporates a combination of wireless networking, digital processing, and process control technologies to create a competitive learning environment focused on driving and hacking robotic cars in the context of a game. Having a diverse mix of components and technologies in the testbed increases the variety of attack and defends scenarios for players.

Table 2. Cyber Security and CPS Testbeds

Testbed	Functionality
DeterLab (Benzel et al., 2006) (Benzel et al., 2009)	A testbed developed for creation and deployment of fundamentally transformational cyber security research methodologies. Designed with several hundred experimental nodes, the DeterLab testbed provides an intermediate point between small-scale and large-scale experiments.
Amigobot Robot (Sabaliauskaite, 2017)	A platform for performing vulnerability analysis, detecting attacks, and guidelines for conducting experimental studies in the context of cyber security.
Unmanned Vehicle (Wan et al., 2011)	The research explored the integration of an intelligent road and an unmanned vehicle in the form of CPSs. In these unmanned vehicles, they have used the vision navigation system to detect the physical environment, along with GPS and other sensors to locate and navigate.
VPST (Bergman et al, 2009)	Virtual Power System Testbed (VPST) is designed to integrate with testbeds across the country to explore performance and security of SCADA protocols and equipment. VPST combines large-scale simulation/emulation of networks of SCADA power devices with real power system hardware and software.
Sandia SCADA Testbed (Phillips et al., 2009)	A testbed developed to analyze the risks of cyber-attacks against US SCADA systems. The researchers designed and created the cyber-to-physical bridge (C2P) system; a system that links cyber-attack vectors to physical resulting events in the electric power grid. The research has been extended to study Reliability Impacts from Cyber Attack and Grid Dynamic Impacts from Cyber Attack.
CI VAPT (Negi et al., 2019)	Vulnerability Assessment and Penetration Testing (VAPT), more commonly known as pen testing, is an effective method of testing a CPS's security. As it is unrealistic to do this kind of testing on a live critical system, Negi et al. developed a modular CPS testbed that covered multiple prominent classes of attack in order to do VAPT.
IEC 60870-5-104 SCADA (Qassim et al., 2018)	The IEC-60870-5-104 protocol is an international standard for SCADA tele-control messages over a TCP/IP network. Research by Qassim et al. on its security vulnerabilities found that many of these control systems using the protocol lack any built-in security mechanisms at the application and data link layer for authentication and encryption. With this knowledge they built a SCADA testbed that uses the IEC protocol for command injection attack simulation and study.

Robotic Cars

The testbed includes two fully instrumented robotic cars within an arena, which can be operated wirelessly. The robotic cars are loaded with a small collection of hardware elements connected with each other to support their operation and control in a wireless environment through an operator interface.

Figure 1 shows the robotic car's hardware block diagram. The Seeed Studio BeagleBone Green Wireless (BBGW) unit is an open-source hardware design that includes a high-performance flexible Wi-Fi/Bluetooth interface to accommodate wireless communication, which runs on Debian Jessi version 8.5.

Teensy 3.2 microcontrollers and stepper motor drivers are used to operate the Nema 14 stepper motors. The Teensy is a complete USB-based microcontroller development system capable of implementing many types of projects. RFID cards on the robotic cars are accessed by the NFC Readers placed in the arenas, which are used to facilitate the scoring solution. Arduinos (Ardunio MEGA 2560) enable NFC communication between a card attached to the car and readers at fixed locations in the arena.

As shown in Figure 1, these robotic cars are powered by a set of three 3.7V batteries connected in series. The batteries provide sufficient power as required by the BeagleBone and Teensys. Two sets of Teensys are connected to the BeagleBone through USB ports. Each Teensy is connected to a stepper motor. Teensy accepts the input and operates the stepper motor, while the Arduino Mega connects to the NFC Reader and manages the NFC functions. Each of these platforms - the BeagleBone, the Teensy

Figure 1. Robotic car prototype hardware diagram

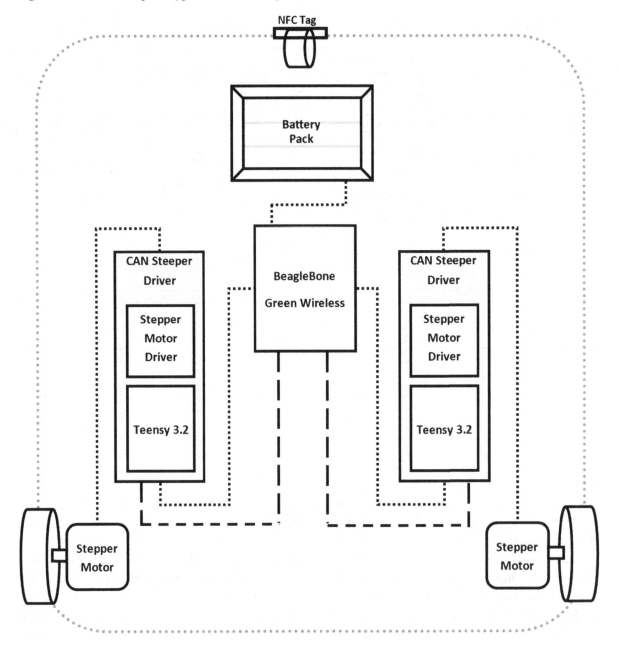

controllers, and the Arduinos -- have their own vulnerabilities and weaknesses that may be exploited by opponents during gameplay.

Operator Interface Software

The user interface used on a standard computing platform allows an operator to control the robotic car wirelessly. As seen on Figure 2, the keys that control the car's speed and direction are displayed on the interface.

Electron, an open-source framework engaging web technologies such as JavaScript, HTML, and CSSwas used to make the user interface. Electron is built on Node.js that runs on Mac, Windows, and Linux providing cross-platform functionality for the applications. The Electron operator interface has two primary elements: (1) the graphical user interface (GUI) and (2) a Python background script. The interface continuously listens for key press and release events, which are displayed graphically. Key presses trigger events (e.g., keyup and keydown), which are converted into codes transferred to the middleware Python file over a serial port. This file communicates with the BeagleBone resident on the car, which contains a Python file using socket communications. The BeagleBone sends key codes to the Teensy by using the PyUSB library in Python. The Teensy operates the stepper motors according to the received key codes.

Table 3 describes how the interface provides direction to the car on the basis of the keys pressed by operator.

To facilitate data acquisition for instrumentation of the testbed, each pressed key and converted codes are stored in log files along with the timestamp. These log files are transferred to the situational awareness platform after gameplay over Wi-Fi.

Gameplay Arena

The gameplay arena is a 6ft x 4ft enclosed perimeter in which both cars can be operated, and the game can be played. The dedicated space for gameplay is needed as a camera mounted on top of the arena tracks the car using color labels. The camera tracks the cars throughout the gameplay and stores various 'physical' information related to the cars, such as movement, direction, and location in the arena at a particular time. The camera is directly attached to a situational awareness platform feeding spatial information to it. Two color labels are located on the front and rear of the cars, which allows them to be more easily detected.

The arena has two NFC readers connected via Arduino to the situational awareness platform. The situational awareness platform is placed on top of the frame, which makes it easier for players to be updated with the score and get notifications about achievement of virtual cargo i.e., inventory. This arena is designed such a way that only two NFC readers will reside in the inner part of the frame.

Situational Awareness Platform (SAP)

The SAP is a dedicated machine that resides on the arena and presents information during the gameplay, collecting data from testbed components.

Two NFC readers and the camera are directly connected to the SAP. The SAP is connected with both BeagleBones' Wi-Fi access points on the robotic cars. This allows the SAP to store/retrieve data from

Figure 2. Operator interface GUI

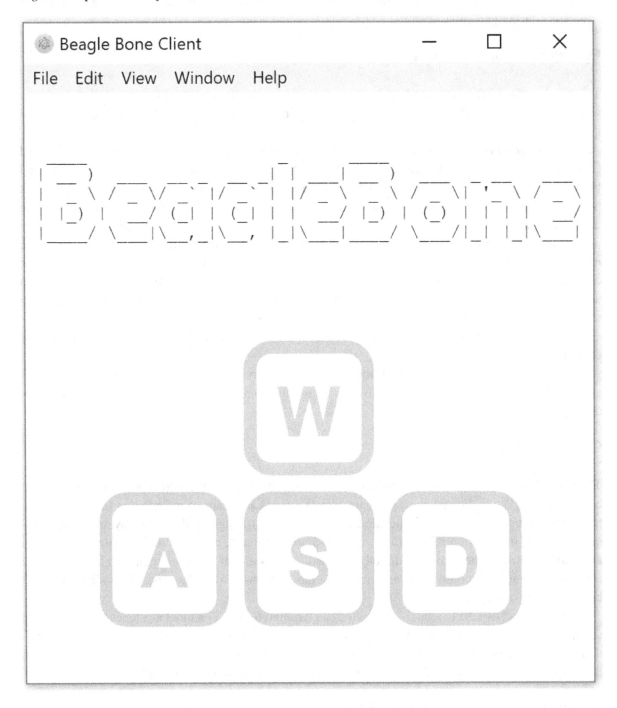

the other components. Figure 3 depicts the user interface for the SAP. The user interface provides data visualization for both robotic cars from collected cyber state and physical state information. Operators can view the status of inventory and score on the user interface. It displays a real-time graph for temperature

Table 3. Key input VS car direction

Key	Converted Code	Direction
W	W	Forward
S	S	Backward
WA	L	Forward Left
WD	R	Forward Right
SA	Q	Backward Left
SD	E	Backward Right

and battery voltage to notify major variation in the values. The video captured by the camera, path of the robotic cars, their movement, and directions are also shown in the user interface.

Hardware and Software Integration

Having multiple sets of hardware, this experimental testbed provides many functionalities. This section describes how the different hardware are connected in order to communicate with each other and fulfill their role in gameplay. Also, the logical connection behind the operation of these hardware is described.

Figure 4 shows the architecture integrating the hardware and software required to support gameplay and experimentation within the CPS testbed.

Figure 3. Situational awareness platform user interface

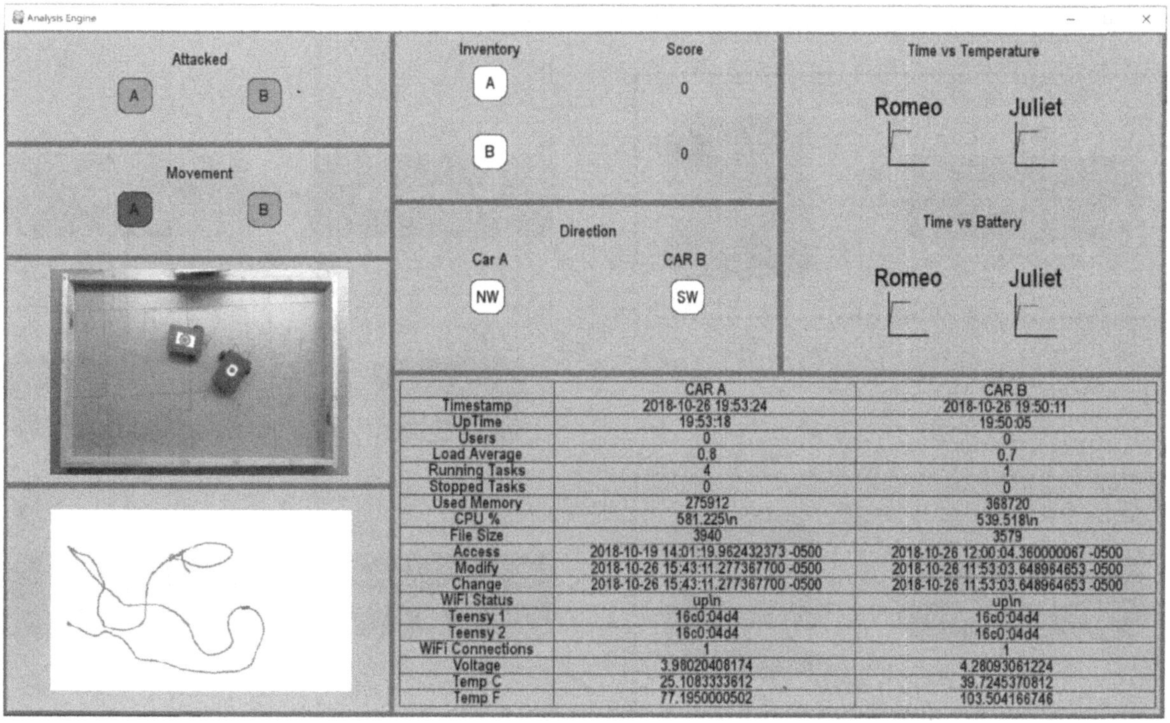

Both sets of robotic cars and operator laptops are connected with each other via the access points provided by BeagleBones. Thus, both networks are independent and never communicate with each other throughout the gameplay. This is to ensure that there is no network interference between the two sets of cars and their laptops during gameplay. Furthermore, it allows for cleaner network captures for the SAP. During boot up, both BeagleBones initiate wireless access points (SoftAp0). Once the boot process is completed, the files responsible for driving the robotic car run automatically in the background. An operator's laptop is connected to the BeagleBone Wi-Fi access point. The operator launches the user interface from their system to drive the car. Key presses trigger events (e.g., key-up and key-down) which are translated to the code and transferred to the middleware Python file over a serial port. These codes are sent to the BeagleBone resident on the car, which contains a Python file using socket communications. The BeagleBone sends retrieved key codes to the Teensy by using the PyUSB library in Python. The Teensy operates the stepper motors according to the received key codes.

The SAP is connected with *all* the devices/components of the arena to provide full instrumentation of the testbed. To facilitate this functionality, the SAP uses a TP-Link TL-WN725N N150 USB wireless Wi-Fi network adapter. Thus, the SAP connects to both of the operator networks via the dual NICS, and to the camera and two NFC Readers via two Arduinos over USB. The Python file on the SAP has various classes that connect and communicate with these devices through COM ports. The camera uses OpenCV2 in order to track the car and produce images from captured video at 30 frames per seconds (FPS).

Infrastructure Integration

The complete infrastructure diagram including hardware and software connections is shown in Figure 5. The SAP is designed to be the central information hub and is connected to every device in the testbed. It

Figure 4. Hardware architecture integration

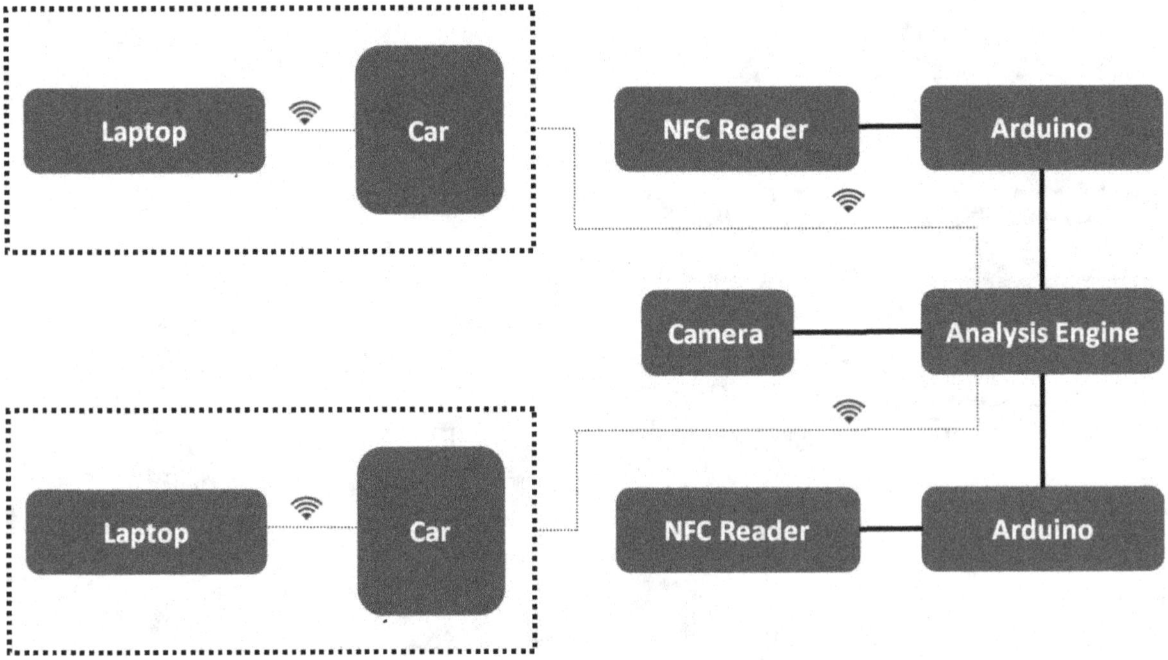

collects logs and data from all devices during gameplay. The SAP runs the physical tracking and scoring elements of the testbed. Using a threaded programming approach, it simultaneously runs the camera tracking, NFC tracking, log collecting, and updates the scoring GUI based off the collected data.

The SAP is connected to the Logitech camera via USB and uses it to run the CV image processing as a threaded process. Both NFC Arduino readers are connected via USB and transmit a '0' character to the SAP using the Arduino serial protocol if an NFC card was successfully scanned (scoring a point).

The SAP connects to both of the Laptop/Car networks via Wi-Fi. It collects the keypress and keysend events from the laptop, and the key strokes and key codes files from the BeagleBone via python sockets.

The BeagleBone is connected to the laptop via Wi-Fi and receives key stroke events via python sockets. It then converts the key strokes to key code events and sends them to the teensy via the Arduino serial protocol. All of these events are logged on both the laptops and BeagleBones in csv files and are sent to the SAP. The teensy receives the keypress events from the operator interface and translates them to movement via the stepper motors.

When a game is started the laptop/BeagleBone networks are initiated first. The analysis laptop is then connected to both networks and then the SAP is run. Instrumentation testing is done between every stage to ensure that all logging is working.

Limitations

The design and prototype implementation of the testbed suffer from a few limitations that are worth noting. These can be considered as transient constraints that future implementations and designs may overcome.

Limited Game Length

The game length is currently limited to 120 minutes due to continuous power consumption during gameplay. This limitation is a result of the Teensy and BeagleBone both requiring a continuous amount of 5V, while the cars are powered by three 3.7V batteries in series. After 120 minutes, the car's batteries must be changed.

Limited Number of Cars

At most only two cars can take part in the gameplay. This limitation exists because only two cards can be supported at a time due to how the NFC readers are configured.

NFC Communication Range

The technology used in NFC is based on the ISO/IEC 14443 and ISO/IEC 18000-3 Radio-frequency identification (RFID) communication protocols. The NFC technology used in this application has an operating range of approximately 4 to 5 cm which is common for NFC implementations. So, in order to pick up or deliver the virtual cargo, a car must be close enough to the NFC reader such that it can read the data on the NFC tag. (However, one may regard this "limitation" as more of a gameplay characteristic.)

Figure 5. Infrastructure integration

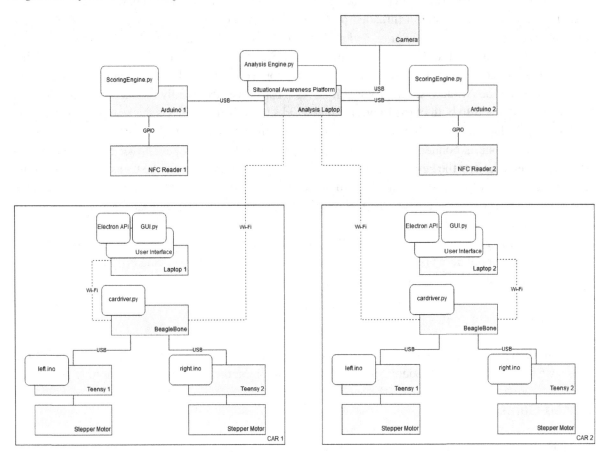

Instrumentation

In order to use the testbed as a basis for CPS security experimentation and training, it must incorporate a robust instrumentation strategy to capture its state at any given moment. This is crucial to identifying attack vectors and their effects on system elements. The instrumentation provides ground truth to validate the theories and practices. The testbed architecture adopts an integrated instrumentation strategy that feeds an analytical engine within the situational awareness platform. This section describes how the physical and the cyber state of the testbed are instrumented and also how the logs are generated by various components.

Data Acquisition

The situational awareness platform (SAP) is connected to all the components of the arena. This makes it easier to generate and share the information and/or logs generated by different components. The SAP gathers data from other network components from the beginning until the end of gameplay. Logs are also generated and stored within the systems operating the robotic cars and can be transferred to the SAP after gameplay.

The various types of data generated by system components and gathered by the SAP are shown in Figure 6.

Storing and sharing logs to the SAP is an important aspect of the testbed. With centralized logging, one can easily troubleshoot and identify the cause of an attack applied on the testbed environment. Logs created during the gameplay fulfill an important role in the testbed instrumentation scheme. The types of data that are generated and stored by different components of the arena can be divided into three categories: physical state, cyber state, and command and control.

Physical State

The instrumentation scheme must capture various elements of the physical system state, including the cars' location, movement, and direction.

Figures 5 and 6 shows the connection between the camera and SAP and what kind of data is shared between them. In the car tracking system, the reference point of the arena is predefined so that the current location of the cars within the arena can be accurately tracked. This establishes reference points from which to acquire the location of the cars.

Figure 6. Distribution of logs in the testbed

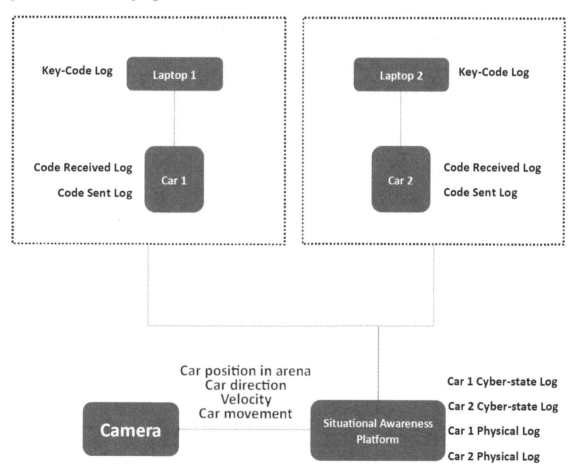

Figure 7 shows a physical log created and stored in the SAP. It stores the current location of the car in the arena in the X-Y plane, the direction of the car, and the movement for each timestamp. The testbed uses a Logitech c270 camera that communicates with the SAP over USB. The program uses the OpenCV2 API to interface with it via Python. Using CV2, the program captures a frame (or still image) from the camera and then runs it through a color processing method. The method works by detecting HSV values in the frame and compares them to established HSV color range values. When a color value is found to be in range, CV2 then draws a box around the color, labels it, and outputs a X, Y value of the location of the box. This capture process is done at 30 frames per second. Not only does this determine the location of the cars, it also helps determine the movement of the cars, their orientation, and the amount of movement in X and Y directions.

Another physical variable captured by the SAP is the temperature of the BeagleBones. Overheating a BeagleBone may be a viable objective in a blended attack vector. Log files of both the BeagleBones are generated which store the temperature through TMP36 sensor every 4 to 5 seconds. The TMP36 is a low voltage, precision centigrade temperature sensor.

Battery draining attacks motivate instrumenting battery life for each car as well. As each robotic car is powered by three 3.7V batteries, capturing the values of input voltage to the BeagleBone and making

Figure 7. Physical state log of the robotic car

Time	X	Y	Direction	Movement	dX	dY
20181026_15:26:51	360	207	South	yes	-5	-14
20181026_15:26:51	359	208	South-East	yes	-6	-14
20181026_15:26:51	360	209	South	yes	-5	-13
20181026_15:26:51	360	207	South	yes	-5	-14
20181026_15:26:51	360	209	South	yes	-5	-12
20181026_15:26:51	360	210	South	yes	-5	-12
20181026_15:26:51	360	209	South	yes	-5	-12
20181026_15:26:52	362	212	South	yes	-4	-10
20181026_15:26:52	362	213	South	yes	-3	-9
20181026_15:26:52	361	211	South	yes	-4	-10
20181026_15:26:52	363	215	South	yes	-2	-6
20181026_15:26:52	363	216		no	-2	-5
20181026_15:26:52	364	217		no	-1	-5
20181026_15:26:52	365	217		no	-1	-4
20181026_15:26:52	364	219		no	-2	-3
20181026_15:26:52	365	220		no	0	-1
20181026_15:26:52	365	221		no	0	0
20181026_15:26:52	365	221		no	0	0
20181026_15:26:52	365	222		no	0	0
20181026_15:26:52	365	222		no	0	0
20181026_15:26:52	365	221		no	0	0
20181026_15:26:52	365	222		no	0	0
20181026_15:26:52	365	222		no	0	1
20181026_15:26:52	365	221		no	0	0
20181026_15:26:52	365	221		no	0	0
20181026_15:26:52	365	221		no	0	0
20181026_15:26:52	366	222		no	0	0

Figure 8. Voltage divider circuit

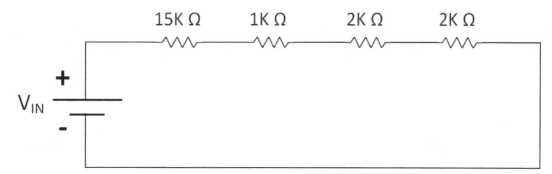

it available to the SAP is one important aspect of SAP. For calculating the voltage on the BeagleBone a voltage divider circuit with four resistors has been made, as seen in Figure 8. In this circuit, four resistors are connected in series to drop the battery voltage to a safe level that the BeagleBone can read. The value for output voltage (VOUT) is calculated by the input voltage (VIN) across the first resistor (15K).

Temperature and voltage information is stored in a single file along with the cyber state information on the SAP. Figure 9 shows the edited log file that is captured by the SAP during gameplay for temperature (in Celsius and Fahrenheit) and voltage (in Volts).

Figure 9. Temperature and voltage log

Timestamp	Voltage	Temp(Celsius)	Temp(Fahrenheit)
2018-10-25 14:07:19 PM	4.210171429	44.39444449	111.9100001
2018-10-25 14:07:23 PM	4.210171429	44.39444449	111.9100001
2018-10-25 14:07:28 PM	4.210171429	44.51574079	112.1283334
2018-10-25 14:07:33 PM	4.227861224	44.57638894	112.2375001
2018-10-25 14:07:38 PM	4.210171429	44.57638894	112.2375001
2018-10-25 14:07:44 PM	4.227861224	44.69768523	112.4558334
2018-10-25 14:07:49 PM	4.24555102	44.33379635	111.8008334
2018-10-25 14:08:02 PM	4.263240816	44.1518519	111.4733334
2018-10-25 14:08:08 PM	4.263240816	44.21250005	111.5825001
2018-10-25 14:08:11 PM	4.263240816	44.2731482	111.6916668
2018-10-25 14:08:33 PM	4.263240816	44.2731482	111.6916668
2018-10-25 14:08:37 PM	4.24555102	44.1518519	111.4733334
2018-10-25 14:08:40 PM	4.263240816	44.2731482	111.6916668
2018-10-25 14:08:54 PM	4.263240816	44.1518519	111.4733334
2018-10-25 14:08:58 PM	4.263240816	44.21250005	111.5825001
2018-10-25 14:09:02 PM	4.263240816	44.0305556	111.2550001
2018-10-25 14:09:07 PM	4.263240816	44.1518519	111.4733334
2018-10-25 14:09:12 PM	4.263240816	44.21250005	111.5825001
2018-10-25 14:09:15 PM	4.263240816	44.21250005	111.5825001
2018-10-25 14:09:18 PM	4.263240816	44.2731482	111.6916668

Cyber State

Major changes in hardware state, such as CPU usage percentage, occupied memory, the number of users connected to a robotic car, CPU load average, and OS and file system information are sent to the SAP.

Using commands through the terminal to eject the Teensys is a possible attack vector. The cars also send the vendor ID (16c0) and product ID (04d4) for the Teensys to the SAP on a regular interval. Figures10 and 11 show the log file created and stored by the SAP upon receiving data from one of the robotic cars. In the case of the attack where the intruder modifies/deletes the file driving the car stored on the BeagleBone, it is necessary to include file related information in the log so that one can identify if changes are made. Accordingly, file size, last access, modify, and change time are also stored in the logs.

The cars also share a network log, which includes the number of nodes connected to the network, the Wi-Fi status (up/down), teensy connections, and wireless state file changes. From this collection of acquired information, the SAP can compose the cyber state of the testbed.

Command and Control

Driving the robotic car through the operator interface is a multi-stage process. Once a connection is established, the operator interface reads the keystrokes, converts them to key codes, and sends them to the BeagleBone. After receiving the codes, the BeagleBone sends them to the Teensy, which directly controls the stepper motor.

During this process there are three phases where key codes are created and/or transferred: When the operating laptop reads and sends keystrokes (Figure 12); when the BeagleBone receives the key codes (Figure 13); and when the BeagleBone transfers the received code to the Teensy (Figure 14). As the SAP needs to receive the log files from both the individual networks, all the keystroke and key code logs are

Figure 10. Cyber state log 1

Timestamp	UpTime	Users	Load Average	Running Tasks	Stopped Tasks	Used Memory	CPU %	File Size	Access
2018-10-25 14:07:19 PM	14:07:12	0	0.4	4	0	289956	421.618\n	3575	2016-06-14 18:00:04.520000009 -0500
2018-10-25 14:07:23 PM	14:07:17	0	0.4	2	0	297248	428.718\n	3575	2016-06-14 18:00:04.520000009 -0500
2018-10-25 14:07:28 PM	14:07:23	0	0.4	2	0	311284	435.58\n	3575	2016-06-14 18:00:04.520000009 -0500
2018-10-25 14:07:33 PM	14:07:28	0	0.4	2	0	318396	442.253\n	3575	2016-06-14 18:00:04.520000009 -0500
2018-10-25 14:07:38 PM	14:07:33	0	0.4	2	0	325540	448.758\n	3575	2016-06-14 18:00:04.520000009 -0500
2018-10-25 14:07:44 PM	14:07:38	0	0.5	2	0	334416	455.497\n	3575	2016-06-14 18:00:04.520000009 -0500
2018-10-25 14:07:49 PM	14:07:52	0	0.5	2	0	354668	471.307\n	3575	2016-06-14 18:00:04.520000009 -0500
2018-10-25 14:08:02 PM	14:07:57	0	0.5	1	0	354916	470.279\n	3575	2016-06-14 18:00:04.520000009 -0500
2018-10-25 14:08:08 PM	14:08:03	0	0.5	1	0	354792	469.325\n	3575	2016-06-14 18:00:04.520000009 -0500
2018-10-25 14:08:11 PM	14:08:06	0	0.5	1	0	354916	470.292\n	3575	2016-06-14 18:00:04.520000009 -0500
2018-10-25 14:08:33 PM	14:08:28	0	0.5	1	0	354808	474.318\n	3575	2016-06-14 18:00:04.520000009 -0500
2018-10-25 14:08:37 PM	14:08:32	0	0.5	1	0	355040	475.238\n	3575	2016-06-14 18:00:04.520000009 -0500
2018-10-25 14:08:40 PM	14:08:46	0	0.5	1	0	355040	470.761\n	3575	2016-06-14 18:00:04.520000009 -0500
2018-10-25 14:08:54 PM	14:08:49	0	0.5	1	0	355040	471.682\n	3575	2016-06-14 18:00:04.520000009 -0500
2018-10-25 14:08:58 PM	14:08:53	0	0.5	1	0	354912	472.209\n	3575	2016-06-14 18:00:04.520000009 -0500
2018-10-25 14:09:02 PM	14:08:57	0	0.5	1	0	355164	472.889\n	3575	2016-06-14 18:00:04.520000009 -0500
2018-10-25 14:09:07 PM	14:09:02	0	0.5	1	0	355164	472.077\n	3575	2016-06-14 18:00:04.520000009 -0500
2018-10-25 14:09:12 PM	14:09:07	0	0.5	1	0	355164	472.131\n	3575	2016-06-14 18:00:04.520000009 -0500
2018-10-25 14:09:15 PM	14:09:10	0	0.5	1	0	355288	472.98\n	3575	2016-06-14 18:00:04.520000009 -0500

Figure 11. Cyber state log 2

Modify	Change	WiFi Status	Teensy 1	Teensy 2	WiFi Connections
2018-10-22 11:19:53.508571385 -0500	2018-10-22 11:19:53.508571385 -0500	up\n	16c0:04d4	16c0:04d4	1
2018-10-22 11:19:53.508571385 -0500	2018-10-22 11:19:53.508571385 -0500	up\n	16c0:04d4	16c0:04d4	1
2018-10-22 11:19:53.508571385 -0500	2018-10-22 11:19:53.508571385 -0500	up\n	16c0:04d4	16c0:04d4	1
2018-10-22 11:19:53.508571385 -0500	2018-10-22 11:19:53.508571385 -0500	up\n	16c0:04d4	16c0:04d4	1
2018-10-22 11:19:53.508571385 -0500	2018-10-22 11:19:53.508571385 -0500	up\n	16c0:04d4	16c0:04d4	1
2018-10-22 11:19:53.508571385 -0500	2018-10-22 11:19:53.508571385 -0500	up\n	16c0:04d4	16c0:04d4	1
2018-10-22 11:19:53.508571385 -0500	2018-10-22 11:19:53.508571385 -0500	up\n	16c0:04d4	16c0:04d4	1
2018-10-22 11:19:53.508571385 -0500	2018-10-22 11:19:53.508571385 -0500	up\n	16c0:04d4	16c0:04d4	1
2018-10-22 11:19:53.508571385 -0500	2018-10-22 11:19:53.508571385 -0500	up\n	16c0:04d4	16c0:04d4	1
2018-10-22 11:19:53.508571385 -0500	2018-10-22 11:19:53.508571385 -0500	up\n	16c0:04d4	16c0:04d4	1
2018-10-22 11:19:53.508571385 -0500	2018-10-22 11:19:53.508571385 -0500	up\n	16c0:04d4	16c0:04d4	1
2018-10-22 11:19:53.508571385 -0500	2018-10-22 11:19:53.508571385 -0500	up\n	16c0:04d4	16c0:04d4	1
2018-10-22 11:19:53.508571385 -0500	2018-10-22 11:19:53.508571385 -0500	up\n	16c0:04d4	16c0:04d4	1
2018-10-22 11:19:53.508571385 -0500	2018-10-22 11:19:53.508571385 -0500	up\n	16c0:04d4	16c0:04d4	1
2018-10-22 11:19:53.508571385 -0500	2018-10-22 11:19:53.508571385 -0500	up\n	16c0:04d4	16c0:04d4	1
2018-10-22 11:19:53.508571385 -0500	2018-10-22 11:19:53.508571385 -0500	up\n	16c0:04d4	16c0:04d4	1
2018-10-22 11:19:53.508571385 -0500	2018-10-22 11:19:53.508571385 -0500	up\n	16c0:04d4	16c0:04d4	1
2018-10-22 11:19:53.508571385 -0500	2018-10-22 11:19:53.508571385 -0500	up\n	16c0:04d4	16c0:04d4	1

stored. The operator machines log the keys being pressed, and the BeagleBone stores two separate logs for the key code received from the operator laptop and code sent to the Teensys.

Once gameplay is finished, the SAP will have one log file from each operator system and two log files from each robotic car. Inconsistencies therein may be indicators of compromise.

Gamification

The CPS testbed is designed with several game elements. Compromised of game-like controls and a scoring engine, and populated by inherently vulnerable systems, it allows for a gamified platform that can be used for security research and education on CPSs.

Game-Play

Game-Play Goals and Strategies

The variety of components working in combination on the testbed serves as a rich platform for CPS security gamification. Players can enter a game wherein a member of each team can operate their car in the arena with the purpose of outscoring their opponent. Other members of each team can try to hack the opponent's car or environment through blended attacks.

Figure 15 depicts gameplay in the testbed. The current testbed supports two robotic cars but could be extended to accommodate more.

Figure 12. Key stroke events sent from the laptop to the BeagleBone

```
Mon Oct 22 2018 12:46:50 GMT-0500 (Central Daylight Time)      Key(s): WA      Code Sent: L
Mon Oct 22 2018 12:46:50 GMT-0500 (Central Daylight Time)      Key(s): WA      Code Sent: L
Mon Oct 22 2018 12:46:50 GMT-0500 (Central Daylight Time)      Key(s): WA      Code Sent: L
Mon Oct 22 2018 12:46:50 GMT-0500 (Central Daylight Time)      Key(s): W       Code Sent: W
Mon Oct 22 2018 12:46:50 GMT-0500 (Central Daylight Time)      Key(s): WA      Code Sent: L
Mon Oct 22 2018 12:46:50 GMT-0500 (Central Daylight Time)      Key(s): WA      Code Sent: L
Mon Oct 22 2018 12:46:50 GMT-0500 (Central Daylight Time)      Key(s): WA      Code Sent: L
Mon Oct 22 2018 12:46:50 GMT-0500 (Central Daylight Time)      Key(s): WA      Code Sent: L
Mon Oct 22 2018 12:46:50 GMT-0500 (Central Daylight Time)      Key(s): WA      Code Sent: L
Mon Oct 22 2018 12:46:50 GMT-0500 (Central Daylight Time)      Key(s): WA      Code Sent: L
Mon Oct 22 2018 12:46:50 GMT-0500 (Central Daylight Time)      Key(s): WA      Code Sent: L
Mon Oct 22 2018 12:46:50 GMT-0500 (Central Daylight Time)      Key(s): WA      Code Sent: L
Mon Oct 22 2018 12:46:50 GMT-0500 (Central Daylight Time)      Key(s): WA      Code Sent: L
Mon Oct 22 2018 12:46:50 GMT-0500 (Central Daylight Time)      Key(s): WA      Code Sent: L
Mon Oct 22 2018 12:46:50 GMT-0500 (Central Daylight Time)      Key(s): WA      Code Sent: L
Mon Oct 22 2018 12:46:50 GMT-0500 (Central Daylight Time)      Key(s): WA      Code Sent: L
Mon Oct 22 2018 12:46:50 GMT-0500 (Central Daylight Time)      Key(s): WA      Code Sent: L
Mon Oct 22 2018 12:46:50 GMT-0500 (Central Daylight Time)      Key(s): WA      Code Sent: L
Mon Oct 22 2018 12:46:50 GMT-0500 (Central Daylight Time)      Key(s): WA      Code Sent: L
Mon Oct 22 2018 12:46:50 GMT-0500 (Central Daylight Time)      Key(s): W       Code Sent: W
Mon Oct 22 2018 12:46:50 GMT-0500 (Central Daylight Time)      Key(s): W       Code Sent: W
Mon Oct 22 2018 12:46:50 GMT-0500 (Central Daylight Time)      Key(s): W       Code Sent: W
Mon Oct 22 2018 12:46:51 GMT-0500 (Central Daylight Time)      Key(s): WA      Code Sent: L
```

Figure 13. Key code events received from the laptop

```
Mon Oct 22 2018 12:44:11      Host: ('192.168.8.115', 60089)      Code Recieved: l
Mon Oct 22 2018 12:44:11      Host: ('192.168.8.115', 60089)      Code Recieved: l
Mon Oct 22 2018 12:44:11      Host: ('192.168.8.115', 60089)      Code Recieved: l
Mon Oct 22 2018 12:44:11      Host: ('192.168.8.115', 60089)      Code Recieved: w
Mon Oct 22 2018 12:44:11      Host: ('192.168.8.115', 60089)      Code Recieved: l
Mon Oct 22 2018 12:44:11      Host: ('192.168.8.115', 60089)      Code Recieved: l
Mon Oct 22 2018 12:44:11      Host: ('192.168.8.115', 60089)      Code Recieved: l
Mon Oct 22 2018 12:44:11      Host: ('192.168.8.115', 60089)      Code Recieved: l
Mon Oct 22 2018 12:44:11      Host: ('192.168.8.115', 60089)      Code Recieved: l
Mon Oct 22 2018 12:44:11      Host: ('192.168.8.115', 60089)      Code Recieved: l
Mon Oct 22 2018 12:44:11      Host: ('192.168.8.115', 60089)      Code Recieved: l
Mon Oct 22 2018 12:44:11      Host: ('192.168.8.115', 60089)      Code Recieved: l
Mon Oct 22 2018 12:44:11      Host: ('192.168.8.115', 60089)      Code Recieved: l
Mon Oct 22 2018 12:44:11      Host: ('192.168.8.115', 60089)      Code Recieved: l
Mon Oct 22 2018 12:44:11      Host: ('192.168.8.115', 60089)      Code Recieved: l
Mon Oct 22 2018 12:44:11      Host: ('192.168.8.115', 60089)      Code Recieved: l
Mon Oct 22 2018 12:44:11      Host: ('192.168.8.115', 60089)      Code Recieved: l
Mon Oct 22 2018 12:44:11      Host: ('192.168.8.115', 60089)      Code Recieved: l
Mon Oct 22 2018 12:44:11      Host: ('192.168.8.115', 60089)      Code Recieved: l
Mon Oct 22 2018 12:44:11      Host: ('192.168.8.115', 60089)      Code Recieved: w
Mon Oct 22 2018 12:44:11      Host: ('192.168.8.115', 60089)      Code Recieved: w
Mon Oct 22 2018 12:44:11      Host: ('192.168.8.115', 60089)      Code Recieved: w
Mon Oct 22 2018 12:44:11      Host: ('192.168.8.115', 60089)      Code Recieved: l
```

Figure 14. Key Code events sent from the BeagleBone to the Teensy

```
Mon Oct 22 2018 12:44:11    Host: ('192.168.8.115', 60089)    Code Sent: l
Mon Oct 22 2018 12:44:11    Host: ('192.168.8.115', 60089)    Code Sent: l
Mon Oct 22 2018 12:44:11    Host: ('192.168.8.115', 60089)    Code Sent: l
Mon Oct 22 2018 12:44:11    Host: ('192.168.8.115', 60089)    Code Sent: w
Mon Oct 22 2018 12:44:11    Host: ('192.168.8.115', 60089)    Code Sent: l
Mon Oct 22 2018 12:44:11    Host: ('192.168.8.115', 60089)    Code Sent: l
Mon Oct 22 2018 12:44:11    Host: ('192.168.8.115', 60089)    Code Sent: l
Mon Oct 22 2018 12:44:11    Host: ('192.168.8.115', 60089)    Code Sent: l
Mon Oct 22 2018 12:44:11    Host: ('192.168.8.115', 60089)    Code Sent: l
Mon Oct 22 2018 12:44:11    Host: ('192.168.8.115', 60089)    Code Sent: l
Mon Oct 22 2018 12:44:11    Host: ('192.168.8.115', 60089)    Code Sent: l
Mon Oct 22 2018 12:44:11    Host: ('192.168.8.115', 60089)    Code Sent: l
Mon Oct 22 2018 12:44:11    Host: ('192.168.8.115', 60089)    Code Sent: l
Mon Oct 22 2018 12:44:11    Host: ('192.168.8.115', 60089)    Code Sent: l
Mon Oct 22 2018 12:44:11    Host: ('192.168.8.115', 60089)    Code Sent: l
Mon Oct 22 2018 12:44:11    Host: ('192.168.8.115', 60089)    Code Sent: l
Mon Oct 22 2018 12:44:11    Host: ('192.168.8.115', 60089)    Code Sent: l
Mon Oct 22 2018 12:44:11    Host: ('192.168.8.115', 60089)    Code Sent: l
Mon Oct 22 2018 12:44:11    Host: ('192.168.8.115', 60089)    Code Sent: l
Mon Oct 22 2018 12:44:11    Host: ('192.168.8.115', 60089)    Code Sent: l
Mon Oct 22 2018 12:44:11    Host: ('192.168.8.115', 60089)    Code Sent: w
Mon Oct 22 2018 12:44:11    Host: ('192.168.8.115', 60089)    Code Sent: w
Mon Oct 22 2018 12:44:11    Host: ('192.168.8.115', 60089)    Code Sent: w
Mon Oct 22 2018 12:44:11    Host: ('192.168.8.115', 60089)    Code Sent: l
```

Figure 15. CPS testbed capture the flag gameplay

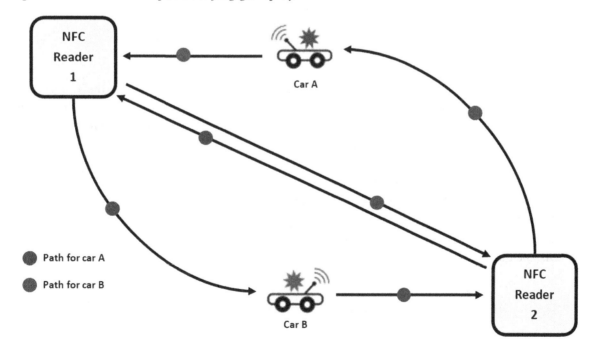

The basic objective in the game is for an operator to drive the car between depot stations outfitted with NFC readers, simulating the pick-up and drop-off of cargo. Teams score points for successfully delivering cargo from an opponent's home station to their home station. As explained in Figure 15, Car A will make contact with NFC Reader 1 to pick up the virtual cargo and make contact with NFC Reader 2 to drop it off, scoring a point. Conversely, Car B will visit NFC Reader 2 to pick up virtual cargo and then visit NFC Reader 1 for delivery, registering a score.

The goal of the game is to either reach the score limit first or have the most points once time expires. Cars can only carry one piece of virtual cargo at a time. Players cannot legitimately interact with the opponent's extraction zone or base; however, they still are able to drive into those zones to try and block the opponent from scoring.

Attack Vectors

The range of attack options available on targets in the CPS testbed can be generally categorized as: (1) network, (2) system, (3) hardware, and (4) operator interface. Attackers can chain individual exploits in these categories to build blended attack vectors disrupting an opponent's ability to control their car or interact with the testbed.

Network Attacks

Wireless networks, which are common in CPS domains, obviate an attacker's need for physical access to assets, expanding their attack surface. Accordingly, our testbed integrates NFC and Wi-Fi for operation and control, each wireless technology having its own risk profile. Vulnerabilities inherent in these technologies permit eavesdropping, data corruption, data modification, and man-in-the middle attacks during data transmission. An attack vector special to NFC is one that permits impersonation, wherein the NFC mode switching capability allows a vehicle to act as a base station. This could allow a team to either score bogus points or create a fake base station, fooling the other team.

System Attacks

System attacks exploit weaknesses in support software, including those found on the Linux-based Debian operating system running on the vehicle's BeagleBone -- or on the driver's operating system. The BeagleBone is a primary target, as it is a locus of communication and control for the robotic vehicle. An attacker that successfully gains control of it can:

- Modify operator command behavior, e.g., remapping action keys.
- Disable vehicle Wi-Fi, severing the operator's control channel.
- Reduce the speed of a vehicle or freeze it altogether.
- Inject commands to an opponent's vehicle.
- Disable the Teensys.

Hardware Attacks

Hardware-based attacks target the code base of microcontrollers, impacting the performance of the vehicle's motors or battery. Alternatively, they might pivot from a system attack and command the car's microcontrollers to deliver commands that degrade performance or damage components. One example of a hardware-based attack is to issue a rapid-fire sequence of commands to drain the battery of a vehicle.

Operator Interface Attacks

The operator interface is a collection of HTML, JavaScript, Node.js, and CSS, using port communication to exchange data with the vehicle's BeagleBone. The entire collection of language and system-level vulnerabilities associated with these interface technologies and protocols is available to the attacker.

The operator interface can be compromised in three basic steps: (1) locate/extract the app source code, (2) modify the source code, and (3) insert/execute the modified source code on the target. This process varies on different operating systems, but the general pattern remains constant.

For example, on Windows, the installer builds to the following:
"C:\Users\username\AppData\Local\hackable-beagle-bone-client"

In this directory, a folder named resources contains a file named app.asar holding the source code. Assuming Node.js has been installed in the PC, this can be done with following commands:

npm install asar –g or
asar extract app.asar app

This creates a directory with the full source code, in this case, consisting primarily of javascript and Python. The code can then be modified or completely rewritten before being executed or replacing the original app. On a MacOS, the contents are not stored in an archive. They can be viewed and modified directly by right clicking the app, selecting and navigating to Show Package Contents and Contents\Resources\app respectively.

APPLICATION: RESEARCH EXPERIMENTATION

This section motivates the use of the gamified CPS testbed as a platform for research and experimentation. It demonstrates one of many planned attacks for the robotic car and uses it as ground truth for evaluating a CPS attack modeling construct called a hybrid attack graph. The experimentation methodology, attack scenario, and experimental results are presented.

Research Experimentation Methodology

Attack graphs are a general tool that can be used to represent and analyze attacks against a variety of information systems -- corporate networks, mobile devices, electrical power grid systems, and even automobile networks (Bilar, Cybenko, & Murphy, 2013; Nagaraja, Mittal, Hong, Caesar, & Borisov, 2010;

Hawrylak, Louthan, Daily, Hal, & Papa, 2012; Hawrylak, Hartney, Haney, Hamm, & Hale, 2013).With respect to analysis of security properties, they hold substantial promise for providing insights into the vulnerabilities of cyber physical systems. Extensions to support cyber physical systems which exhibit hybrid behavior, force the consideration of continuous domain elements and state variables. Tools to generate and analyze attack graphs exist, but suffer from a lack of expressiveness and from the availability of a suitable platform against which to assess the merits of their foundations, designs and implementations – this is especially true where cyber physical systems are concerned. The gamified CPS testbed affords an opportunity to explore the application of attack graphs in a cyber physical domain.

An approach adopted in such an exploration is depicted in Figure 16 and calls for modeling the CPS test bed and an exploit portfolio in a format ingestible by an attack graph generation tool or usable by an expert (step 1 in Figure 16). Once an attack graph is generated, whether by hand or by an automated/ interactive tool, attack scenarios can be extracted from the graph. Each of these scenarios can be exercised (or at least attempted) by players in the testbed (step 2 in Figure 16). Alternatively, a "free play" exploration under the developed exploit portfolio can be pursued. In either case, the data pulled from the testbed can be yield useful insights that determine the viability of predicted scenarios, or reveal latent scenarios. Subsequent analysis may serve to validate or invalidate aspects of the network model, the exploit portfolio or the attack graph generation process itself (step 3 in Figure 16).

Car Halt Attack

The methodology described above is applied here driven by an attack scenario that mounts a denial of service attack on a car in the testbed. Recall that the two Teensys connected to the BeagleBone's USB

Figure 16. Research experimentation methodology for exploring and validating attack graphs

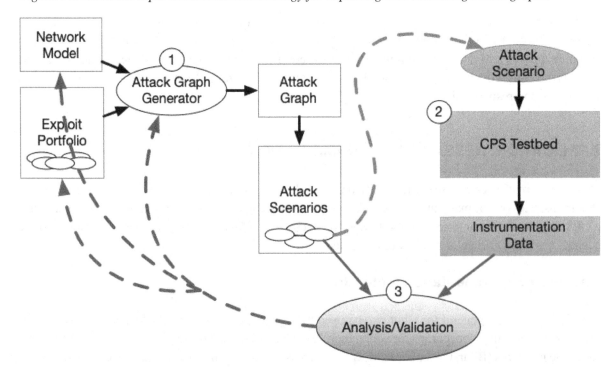

ports drive the car's stepper motors. The attack scenario is predicated on the fact that one can make a car halt in place by disconnecting the Teensys from the Debian operating system (OS).

In order to model this attack, a simple network model and attack graph was created to supplement the planning phase. The network model lists the assets of the CPS and their qualities as seen in Figure 17. The attack graph, Figure 18, shows the states of the cyber-physical cars before, during, and after the attack in terms of post- and pre-conditions. State A, a pre-condition state, is the initial state of the cars as gameplay begins. State C, a post-condition state, is the goal the attacker wants to obtain. The exploits and states in between comprise the attack paths that the attacker will take to get to the goal state. In this example, an extraneous post-condition state, State D, illustrates that a different post-condition can be obtained by following a different attack path. Rather than halt the car, an attacker can give themselves control of it thus opening up many new branches to the attack graph.

After determining the scope and attack methods, the assets needed to prove that the attack occurred were added into the instrumentation system watch list for logging.

For the sake of testbed simplicity and ease of applying attacks, several assumptions were adopted for the configuration of the CPS. A major assumption is that the Wi-Fi access point (AP) the BeagleBone hosts is open with no password. This provides a trivial exploit vector that allows players to execute attacks quickly and efficiently.

The two Teensys are connected to the BeagleBone via its USB ports. Once inserted into the hardware, USB devices are managed by the operating system (OS). Upon insertion, the OS identifies peripheral device through a simple handshake on the USB protocol and decides if it needs drivers for it. If not, it

Figure 17. Network model for the car halt attack

```
Network Model
        Assets:
                BeagleBone
                Teensy
        Facts:
                Quality: BeagleBone, "Debian 9"
                Quality: BeagleBone, serial_py_version,
1.2.5
                Quality: BeagleBone, antri-virus, false
                Quality: BeagleBone, root, false
                Quality: BeagleBone, password, false
                Quality: BeagleBone, wifi-ap-security,
open
                Quality: BeagleBone, compromised, false
                Quality: Teensy, "serial_reader_X"
                Quality: Teensy,
serial_reader_X_version, 1
                Quality: Teensy, compromised, false
                Topology: BeagleBone, Teensy,
connected
```

Figure 18. Attack graph for the car halt attack

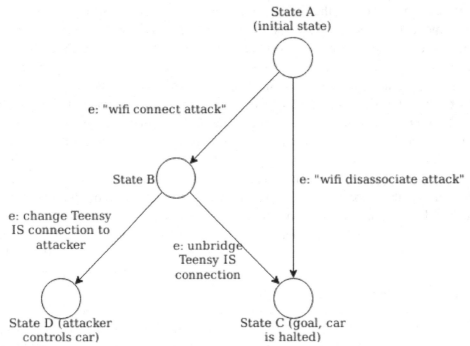

mounts it; otherwise it initializes and starts talking to the device. In the case of the robotic cars, the OS in BeagleBone is Debian Jessie.

This attack begins with the attacking player connecting to the BeagleBone's insecure access point (AP). From there they are able to elevate their shell to root. The attackers know that the OS is Debian. Therefore, they will know that all the drivers for attached USB devices are stored at the /sys/bus/usb/ drivers/usb location. Then they execute lsusb in order to find devices connected to the USB ports. Executing this command in the terminal is shown in Figure 19.

The output shows a list of USB host controllers (the lines starting with "Bus") and their connected devices on a tree structure. It has the bus number, device number, and unique pair of vendor and product IDs. Vendor ID and Product ID are two key pieces of information as they represent a connected device. In the attacker's case, they want the vendor and product IDs that represent the Teensy.

The attacker infers that the two devices that share the same product and vendor IDs are the two Teensys. From lsusb they know that the Teensys are connected on Bus 001 and are Devices 003 and 004 respectively.

By executing the ls command on /sys/bus/usb/drivers/usb the attacker sees multiple system directories. The directories of interest are bind and unbind. The former stores the list of connected devices which are enabled and active and, conversely, the latter has the list of disabled or removed peripheral devices. The attacker then changes directory (cd) between the different folders (1-1, 1-1.1, 1-2, etc.) where they find various files and directories representing the different devices. In order to identify which directory represents the Teensys, the attackers execute the catidVendor command. This command returns the vendor id of the represented directory. They execute this on each directory until they find the id 16c0, which is the Teensy's vendor id. In this case, the directory belonging to the Teensy is 1-1.

Figure 19. Output of car halt attack

```
root@juliet:/var/lib/cloud9# lsusb
Bus 001 Device 003: ID 16c0:04d4 Van Ooijen Technische Informatica
Bus 001 Device 004: ID 16c0:04d4 Van Ooijen Technische Informatica
Bus 001 Device 002: ID 05e3:0610 Genesys Logic, Inc. 4-port hub
Bus 001 Device 001: ID 1d6b:0002 Linux Foundation 2.0 root hub
root@juliet:/var/lib/cloud9# cd /sys/bus/usb/drivers/usb
root@juliet:/sys/bus/usb/drivers/usb# ls
1-1  1-1.1  1-1.3  bind  uevent  unbind  usb1
root@juliet:/sys/bus/usb/drivers/usb# echo "1-1" > /sys/bus/usb/drivers/usb/unbind
root@juliet:/sys/bus/usb/drivers/usb# lsusb
Bus 001 Device 002: ID 05e3:0610 Genesys Logic, Inc. 4-port hub
Bus 001 Device 001: ID 1d6b:0002 Linux Foundation 2.0 root hub
root@juliet:/sys/bus/usb/drivers/usb# █
```

Finally, the attacker creates an entry for the directory 1-1 in the unbind file by using the echo command. By executing echo "1-1">/sys/bus/usb/drivers/usb/ubind, as shown in Figure 13, the Teensys will be deactivated and the OS will no longer see them connected to the USB ports. This brings the CPS into the post-condition of State C. The car will no longer drive until the driver remotes into the system and undoes these changes.

Instrumentation and Validation of the Car Halt Attack

After performing this experiment, the logical connections of the Teensys are removed. Executing the command echo "1-1">/sys/bus/usb/drivers/usb/ubind appends devices connected on '1-1' to the unbind list. The effect of executing the command logically disconnects both Teensys and stops the movement of the car.

Figure 20 shows the cyber state logs stored by the situational awareness platform that has major variations. At 'UpTime' 15:23:17, number of users logged into the BeagleBone changes from 0 to 1 and number of Wi-Fi connections becomes 3. This indicates that there is a connection from an external user. Going further, fluctuation in the number of running processes can be identified.

Logs of the cyber state have two columns, which indicate the Host ID and Product ID of the Teensys. The Host ID and Product ID for Teensys are 16c0 and 04d4 respectively. As shown in Figure 20, the values for Teensy1 and Teensy2 are 16c0:04d4 at 'UpTime' 15:26:43. At 'UpTime' 15:26:49, the values for Teensy1 and Teensy2 changes to 05e3:0610 and 1d6b:0002 respectively. The 'Timestamp' value was 15:26:55 at this time. This indicates that the Teensys were removed from the system between timestamp 15:26:49 and 15:26:55.

Furthermore, the bind and ubind files are logged via the kernel level Audit Daemon or Audit.d. Any modifications to these files including when the file was edited, what was edited, and who made the edit is logged via the daemon and piped to the SAP.

The SAP also stores logs for the physical state of the robotic cars. Figure 21 shows the change in the movement from yes to no. Movement is seen in the car at timestamp 15:26:51 but not after 15:26:52.

Figure 20. Changes detected in the cyber log during car halt attack

Timestamp	UpTime	Users	Load Average	Running Tasks	Stopped Tasks	Used Memory	CPU %	File Size	Access	Modify	Change	WiFi Status	Teensy 1	Teensy 2	WiFi Connections
2018-10-26 15:23:13 PM	15:23:07	0	0.7	1	0	388704	427.387\n	3936	2018-10-1	2018-10-22	2018-10-2	up\n	16c0:04d4	16c0:04d4	2
2018-10-26 15:23:16 PM	15:23:10	0	0.7	1	0	389480	427.911\n	3936	2018-10-1	2018-10-22	2018-10-2	up\n	16c0:04d4	16c0:04d4	2
2018-10-26 15:23:20 PM	15:23:14	0	0.7	1	0	389720	428.257\n	3936	2018-10-1	2018-10-22	2018-10-2	up\n	16c0:04d4	16c0:04d4	3
2018-10-26 15:23:24 PM	15:23:17	1	0.7	1	0	391256	428.843\n	3936	2018-10-1	2018-10-22	2018-10-2	up\n	16c0:04d4	16c0:04d4	3
2018-10-26 15:23:27 PM	15:23:21	1	0.7	1	0	391364	429.248\n	3936	2018-10-1	2018-10-22	2018-10-2	up\n	16c0:04d4	16c0:04d4	3
2018-10-26 15:23:31 PM	15:23:24	1	0.7	1	0	392248	429.797\n	3936	2018-10-1	2018-10-22	2018-10-2	up\n	16c0:04d4	16c0:04d4	3
2018-10-26 15:23:34 PM	15:23:28	1	0.7	1	0	392356	430.152\n	3936	2018-10-1	2018-10-22	2018-10-2	up\n	16c0:04d4	16c0:04d4	3
2018-10-26 15:23:37 PM	15:23:31	1	0.7	1	0	392232	430.532\n	3936	2018-10-1	2018-10-22	2018-10-2	up\n	16c0:04d4	16c0:04d4	3
2018-10-26 15:23:40 PM	15:23:34	1	0.7	1	0	392356	430.95\n	3936	2018-10-1	2018-10-22	2018-10-2	up\n	16c0:04d4	16c0:04d4	3
2018-10-26 15:23:44 PM	15:23:37	1	0.7	1	0	393048	431.526\n	3936	2018-10-1	2018-10-22	2018-10-2	up\n	05e3:0610	1d6b:0002	3
2018-10-26 15:23:47 PM	15:23:41	1	0.7	1	0	392168	431.965\n	3936	2018-10-1	2018-10-22	2018-10-2	up\n	05e3:0610	1d6b:0002	3
2018-10-26 15:23:50 PM	15:25:45	1	0.7	3	0	399896	424.364\n	3936	2018-10-1	2018-10-22	2018-10-2	up\n	16c0:04d4	16c0:04d4	3
2018-10-26 15:25:58 PM	15:25:51	1	0.7	2	0	400416	425.755\n	3936	2018-10-1	2018-10-22	2018-10-2	up\n	16c0:04d4	16c0:04d4	3
2018-10-26 15:26:03 PM	15:25:57	1	0.7	1	0	397832	426.906\n	3936	2018-10-1	2018-10-22	2018-10-2	up\n	16c0:04d4	16c0:04d4	3
2018-10-26 15:26:09 PM	15:26:02	1	0.7	1	0	397956	428.151\n	3936	2018-10-1	2018-10-22	2018-10-2	up\n	16c0:04d4	16c0:04d4	3
2018-10-26 15:26:14 PM	15:26:08	1	0.7	1	0	398080	429.444\n	3936	2018-10-1	2018-10-22	2018-10-2	up\n	16c0:04d4	16c0:04d4	3
2018-10-26 15:26:20 PM	15:26:14	1	0.8	1	0	398328	430.819\n	3936	2018-10-1	2018-10-22	2018-10-2	up\n	16c0:04d4	16c0:04d4	3
2018-10-26 15:26:26 PM	15:26:20	1	0.8	3	0	399368	432.231\n	3936	2018-10-1	2018-10-22	2018-10-2	up\n	16c0:04d4	16c0:04d4	3
2018-10-26 15:26:32 PM	15:26:26	1	0.8	1	0	401128	433.608\n	3936	2018-10-1	2018-10-22	2018-10-2	up\n	16c0:04d4	16c0:04d4	3
2018-10-26 15:26:38 PM	15:26:31	1	0.8	3	0	401252	434.884\n	3936	2018-10-1	2018-10-22	2018-10-2	up\n	16c0:04d4	16c0:04d4	3
2018-10-26 15:26:43 PM	15:26:37	1	0.8	1	0	401376	436.021\n	3936	2018-10-1	2018-10-22	2018-10-2	up\n	16c0:04d4	16c0:04d4	3
2018-10-26 15:26:49 PM	15:26:43	1	0.8	3	0	401376	437.395\n	3936	2018-10-1	2018-10-22	2018-10-2	up\n	16c0:04d4	16c0:04d4	3
2018-10-26 15:26:55 PM	15:26:49	1	0.8	1	0	401392	438.787\n	3936	2018-10-1	2018-10-22	2018-10-2	up\n	05e3:0610	1d6b:0002	3
2018-10-26 15:27:02 PM	15:26:56	1	0.8	1	0	397212	439.332\n	3936	2018-10-1	2018-10-22	2018-10-2	up\n	05e3:0610	1d6b:0002	3

Thus, applying the cross-referencing analysis on the data proves that the Teensys were removed at 15:26:52. This demonstrated the viability of the attack.

Input Reversal Attack

This attack path models an attack on the driver python file integrity. It is a proof of concept for the key stroke, and key code instrumentation. An option a player may take after gaining root shell on the car is to modify the driver python file to sabotage the key code inputs from being sent to the teensy. If they were to add a delay or invert the key codes, the attacking player could sabotage the opposing team's car's operation.

This attack, similar to the previous one, begins with the attacking player connecting to the Beagle-Bone's AP. Their next step is to gain a root shell. From there they change directory to the projects folder. This folder hosts all off the BeagleBone's working files. As seen in Figure 22, in this folder pyserial. py can be found. Pyserial.py is the python program that accepts key code input from the laptop and transfers it to the Teensy.

The attacking player can modify this working file by making the edits in Nano and then restarting the execution. As shown in Figure 23, the attacking player can insert logic to invert all the key codes and cause the car to drive in the opposite manner.

By saving this file and restarting the Python execution, the BeagleBone uses the latest iteration of this file. There are a few seconds of downtime where the car does not move, and then upon executing the modified file, the car starts moving in inverse of what the operator is pressing.

Figure 21. Changes Detected in the Physical Log during Car Halt Attack

Time	X	Y	Direction	Movement	dX	dY
20181026_15:26:51	360	207	South	yes	-5	-14
20181026_15:26:51	359	208	South-East	yes	-6	-14
20181026_15:26:51	360	209	South	yes	-5	-13
20181026_15:26:51	360	207	South	yes	-5	-14
20181026_15:26:51	360	209	South	yes	-5	-12
20181026_15:26:51	360	210	South	yes	-5	-12
20181026_15:26:51	360	209	South	yes	-5	-12
20181026_15:26:52	362	212	South	yes	-4	-10
20181026_15:26:52	362	213	South	yes	-3	-9
20181026_15:26:52	361	211	South	yes	-4	-10
20181026_15:26:52	363	215	South	yes	-2	-6
20181026_15:26:52	363	216		no	-2	-5
20181026_15:26:52	364	217		no	-1	-5
20181026_15:26:52	365	217		no	-1	-4
20181026_15:26:52	364	219		no	-2	-3
20181026_15:26:52	365	220		no	0	-1
20181026_15:26:52	365	221		no	0	0
20181026_15:26:52	365	221		no	0	0
20181026_15:26:52	365	222		no	0	0
20181026_15:26:52	365	222		no	0	0
20181026_15:26:52	365	221		no	0	0
20181026_15:26:52	365	222		no	0	0
20181026_15:26:52	365	222		no	0	1
20181026_15:26:52	365	221		no	0	0
20181026_15:26:52	365	221		no	0	0
20181026_15:26:52	365	221		no	0	0
20181026_15:26:52	366	222		no	0	0

Instrumentation and Validation of the Attack

After performing the attack, the key codes that the BeagleBone sends to the Teensy should be inverse of what it receives from the laptop. Figure 24 shows the key presses and key codes sent from the laptop to the BeagleBone. Figure 25 shows the key codes received from the laptop. And Figure 26 shows the key codes that the BeagleBone sent to the Teensy.

The logs of the key codes show that between 15:35:19 and 24 there is no code being sent or logged. Furthermore, the key codes being sent from the laptop and received by the BeagleBone continue to be the same, however after 15:35:25 the key codes being received by the Teensy are opposite of what is

Figure 22. Output of input reversal attack (projects folder)

Figure 23. Output of input reversal attack (logic)

```
while True:
    #c = getch.getch()
    (data,addr) = mySocket.recvfrom(SIZE)

    Timestamp = str(datetime.datetime.now().strftime('%a %b %d %Y %X'))
    Code = str(data)
    Host = str(addr)
    with open('RomeoCodeRcvd.txt','a') as f:
        f.write("%s \t Host: %s \t Code Recieved: %s" % (Timestamp , Host, Code))

    # this is the attack
    if data == 'w':
        data = 's'
    elif data == 's':
        data = 'w'
    elif data == 'l':
        data = 'r'
    elif data == 'r':
        data = 'l'
    # this is the attack

    device[0].write(0x02,'\0x09,\0x0,\0x0,\0x0,\0x0,\0x0,\0x0,\0x0'+data)
    device[1].write(0x02,'\0x09,\0x0,\0x0,\0x0,\0x0,\0x0,\0x0,\0x0'+data)
    with open('RomeoCodeSent.txt','a') as f:
        f.write("%s \t Host: %s \t Code Sent: %s" % (Timestamp , Host, Code))
```

being sent by the BeagleBone. This indicates that the pyserial.py file was reloaded between timestamp 15:35:19 and 15:35:24. The Cyber Log would show the file's modification date, if any.

FUTURE RESEARCH DIRECTIONS

- **Intrusion Detection System:** Dynamic logs about the cyber state and physical state of the robotic cars can help identifying intrusions in real-time. For example, an increase in the number of Wi-Fi connection indicates an unusual activity which increases the probability of the attack. Using this intelligence, an attack detection tool can be developed to provide real-time notification of attack probability. In a similar manner, the CPS testbed can be used to verify the soundness and completeness of hybrid attack graph generation and analysis software. An attack graph provides a global view of all possible sequences of exploits which an intruder may use to penetrate a network. Hybrid attack graphs (HAGs) extend this concept to the Cyber-Physical domain, incorporating continuous value model elements and variables, such as temperature and velocity (Cook, Shaw, Hawrylak, & Hale, 2016).

- **Testbed Simulator:** A companion computer simulation can be constructed for creating, testing, and refining testbed and gameplay features entirely in software. Using the simulation is a great way to test hacks that are possible on the physical system and see if they make a good addition to the game and to hypothesize and cross-validate system behavior. Linking a simulation with the

Figure 24. Input reversal attack log (keys pressed)

```
1    Sat Oct 26 2019 15:35:01 GMT-0500 (Central Daylight Time)Key(s): W    Code Sent: W
2    Sat Oct 26 2019 15:35:02 GMT-0500 (Central Daylight Time)Key(s): W    Code Sent: W
3    Sat Oct 26 2019 15:35:03 GMT-0500 (Central Daylight Time)Key(s): W    Code Sent: W
4    Sat Oct 26 2019 15:35:04 GMT-0500 (Central Daylight Time)Key(s): W    Code Sent: W
5    Sat Oct 26 2019 15:35:05 GMT-0500 (Central Daylight Time)Key(s): W    Code Sent: W
6    Sat Oct 26 2019 15:35:06 GMT-0500 (Central Daylight Time)Key(s): W    Code Sent: W
7    Sat Oct 26 2019 15:35:07 GMT-0500 (Central Daylight Time)Key(s): W    Code Sent: W
8    Sat Oct 26 2019 15:35:08 GMT-0500 (Central Daylight Time)Key(s): W    Code Sent: W
9    Sat Oct 26 2019 15:35:09 GMT-0500 (Central Daylight Time)Key(s): W    Code Sent: W
10   Sat Oct 26 2019 15:35:10 GMT-0500 (Central Daylight Time)Key(s): W    Code Sent: W
11   Sat Oct 26 2019 15:35:11 GMT-0500 (Central Daylight Time)Key(s): W    Code Sent: W
12   Sat Oct 26 2019 15:35:12 GMT-0500 (Central Daylight Time)Key(s): WD       Code Sent: R
13   Sat Oct 26 2019 15:35:13 GMT-0500 (Central Daylight Time)Key(s): WD       Code Sent: R
14   Sat Oct 26 2019 15:35:14 GMT-0500 (Central Daylight Time)Key(s): WD       Code Sent: R
15   Sat Oct 26 2019 15:35:15 GMT-0500 (Central Daylight Time)Key(s): WD       Code Sent: R
16   Sat Oct 26 2019 15:35:16 GMT-0500 (Central Daylight Time)Key(s): WD       Code Sent: R
17   Sat Oct 26 2019 15:35:17 GMT-0500 (Central Daylight Time)Key(s): W    Code Sent: W
18   Sat Oct 26 2019 15:35:18 GMT-0500 (Central Daylight Time)Key(s): W    Code Sent: W
25   Sat Oct 26 2019 15:35:25 GMT-0500 (Central Daylight Time)Key(s): S    Code Sent: S
26   Sat Oct 26 2019 15:35:26 GMT-0500 (Central Daylight Time)Key(s): S    Code Sent: S
27   Sat Oct 26 2019 15:35:27 GMT-0500 (Central Daylight Time)Key(s): S    Code Sent: S
28   Sat Oct 26 2019 15:35:28 GMT-0500 (Central Daylight Time)Key(s): S    Code Sent: S
29   Sat Oct 26 2019 15:35:29 GMT-0500 (Central Daylight Time)Key(s): S    Code Sent: S
30   Sat Oct 26 2019 15:35:30 GMT-0500 (Central Daylight Time)Key(s): W    Code Sent: W
31   Sat Oct 26 2019 15:35:31 GMT-0500 (Central Daylight Time)Key(s): W    Code Sent: W
32   Sat Oct 26 2019 15:35:32 GMT-0500 (Central Daylight Time)Key(s): W    Code Sent: W
33   Sat Oct 26 2019 15:35:33 GMT-0500 (Central Daylight Time)Key(s): W    Code Sent: W
34   Sat Oct 26 2019 15:35:34 GMT-0500 (Central Daylight Time)Key(s): WD       Code Sent: R
35   Sat Oct 26 2019 15:35:35 GMT-0500 (Central Daylight Time)Key(s): WD       Code Sent: R
36   Sat Oct 26 2019 15:35:36 GMT-0500 (Central Daylight Time)Key(s): WD       Code Sent: R
```

testbed in a tightly coupled manner affords the opportunity to consider the development of attack playback, reconstruction, and alternative path exploration capabilities.

- **Testbed for CPS Education:** The CPS testbed represents a valuable tool for experimentation and exploration. As a formative effort, to engage the CPS testbed in the education, a sequence of interconnected CPS security laboratory experiences can be created. With these exercises, students can become proficient with risk assessment methodologies, gain experience with vulnerability analysis tools, security controls, and exposure to exploit development, all within the special context of cyber physical systems.

CONCLUSION

The CPS testbed presented in this paper is an instrumented and gamified environment in which to improve our understanding of CPS security. Having heterogeneity in its components, the testbed serves as a model platform for research of and learning CPS security concepts. Centralizing all the logs on a dedicated machine provides a higher degree of confidence in resolution of blended attacks in future applications. This makes it easier to determine the effects of attacks and extract more actionable information.

Figure 25. Input reversal attack log (key presses received)

```
Sat Oct 26 2019 15:35:01    Host: ('192.168.8.115', 52194)    Code Recieved: w
Sat Oct 26 2019 15:35:02    Host: ('192.168.8.115', 52194)    Code Recieved: w
Sat Oct 26 2019 15:35:03    Host: ('192.168.8.115', 52194)    Code Recieved: w
Sat Oct 26 2019 15:35:04    Host: ('192.168.8.115', 52194)    Code Recieved: w
Sat Oct 26 2019 15:35:05    Host: ('192.168.8.115', 52194)    Code Recieved: w
Sat Oct 26 2019 15:35:06    Host: ('192.168.8.115', 52194)    Code Recieved: w
Sat Oct 26 2019 15:35:07    Host: ('192.168.8.115', 52194)    Code Recieved: w
Sat Oct 26 2019 15:35:08    Host: ('192.168.8.115', 52194)    Code Recieved: w
Sat Oct 26 2019 15:35:10    Host: ('192.168.8.115', 52194)    Code Recieved: w
Sat Oct 26 2019 15:35:11    Host: ('192.168.8.115', 52194)    Code Recieved: w
Sat Oct 26 2019 15:35:12    Host: ('192.168.8.115', 52194)    Code Recieved: r
Sat Oct 26 2019 15:35:13    Host: ('192.168.8.115', 52194)    Code Recieved: r
Sat Oct 26 2019 15:35:14    Host: ('192.168.8.115', 52194)    Code Recieved: r
Sat Oct 26 2019 15:35:15    Host: ('192.168.8.115', 52194)    Code Recieved: r
Sat Oct 26 2019 15:35:16    Host: ('192.168.8.115', 52194)    Code Recieved: r
Sat Oct 26 2019 15:35:17    Host: ('192.168.8.115', 52194)    Code Recieved: w
Sat Oct 26 2019 15:35:18    Host: ('192.168.8.115', 52194)    Code Recieved: w
Sat Oct 26 2019 15:35:25    Host: ('192.168.8.115', 52194)    Code Recieved: s
Sat Oct 26 2019 15:35:26    Host: ('192.168.8.115', 52194)    Code Recieved: s
Sat Oct 26 2019 15:35:27    Host: ('192.168.8.115', 52194)    Code Recieved: s
Sat Oct 26 2019 15:35:28    Host: ('192.168.8.115', 52194)    Code Recieved: s
Sat Oct 26 2019 15:35:29    Host: ('192.168.8.115', 52194)    Code Recieved: s
Sat Oct 26 2019 15:35:30    Host: ('192.168.8.115', 52194)    Code Recieved: w
Sat Oct 26 2019 15:35:31    Host: ('192.168.8.115', 52194)    Code Recieved: w
Sat Oct 26 2019 15:35:32    Host: ('192.168.8.115', 52194)    Code Recieved: w
Sat Oct 26 2019 15:35:33    Host: ('192.168.8.115', 52194)    Code Recieved: w
Sat Oct 26 2019 15:35:34    Host: ('192.168.8.115', 52194)    Code Recieved: r
Sat Oct 26 2019 15:35:35    Host: ('192.168.8.115', 52194)    Code Recieved: r
Sat Oct 26 2019 15:35:36    Host: ('192.168.8.115', 52194)    Code Recieved: r
```

Consisting of a diverse array of digital and analog components, the CPS testbed will catalyze research in CPS security, creating a much-needed link between theory, simulation, and experimentation. It will help researchers and students by creating a unified view and give shape to the science of CPS security.

ACKNOWLEDGMENT

This material is based on work supported by the National Science Foundation under Grant No.1524940. Any opinions, findings, and conclusions or recommendations expressed in this material are those of the author(s) and do not necessarily reflect the views of the National Science Foundation.

Figure 26. Input reversal attack log (key presses processed)

```
Sat Oct 26 2019 15:35:01    Host: ('192.168.8.115', 52194)    Code Sent: w
Sat Oct 26 2019 15:35:02    Host: ('192.168.8.115', 52194)    Code Sent: w
Sat Oct 26 2019 15:35:03    Host: ('192.168.8.115', 52194)    Code Sent: w
Sat Oct 26 2019 15:35:04    Host: ('192.168.8.115', 52194)    Code Sent: w
Sat Oct 26 2019 15:35:05    Host: ('192.168.8.115', 52194)    Code Sent: w
Sat Oct 26 2019 15:35:06    Host: ('192.168.8.115', 52194)    Code Sent: w
Sat Oct 26 2019 15:35:07    Host: ('192.168.8.115', 52194)    Code Sent: w
Sat Oct 26 2019 15:35:08    Host: ('192.168.8.115', 52194)    Code Sent: w
Sat Oct 26 2019 15:35:10    Host: ('192.168.8.115', 52194)    Code Sent: w
Sat Oct 26 2019 15:35:11    Host: ('192.168.8.115', 52194)    Code Sent: w
Sat Oct 26 2019 15:35:12    Host: ('192.168.8.115', 52194)    Code Sent: r
Sat Oct 26 2019 15:35:13    Host: ('192.168.8.115', 52194)    Code Sent: r
Sat Oct 26 2019 15:35:14    Host: ('192.168.8.115', 52194)    Code Sent: r
Sat Oct 26 2019 15:35:15    Host: ('192.168.8.115', 52194)    Code Sent: r
Sat Oct 26 2019 15:35:16    Host: ('192.168.8.115', 52194)    Code Sent: r
Sat Oct 26 2019 15:35:17    Host: ('192.168.8.115', 52194)    Code Sent: w
Sat Oct 26 2019 15:35:18    Host: ('192.168.8.115', 52194)    Code Sent: w
Sat Oct 26 2019 15:35:25    Host: ('192.168.8.115', 52194)    Code Sent: w
Sat Oct 26 2019 15:35:26    Host: ('192.168.8.115', 52194)    Code Sent: w
Sat Oct 26 2019 15:35:27    Host: ('192.168.8.115', 52194)    Code Sent: w
Sat Oct 26 2019 15:35:28    Host: ('192.168.8.115', 52194)    Code Sent: w
Sat Oct 26 2019 15:35:29    Host: ('192.168.8.115', 52194)    Code Sent: w
Sat Oct 26 2019 15:35:30    Host: ('192.168.8.115', 52194)    Code Sent: s
Sat Oct 26 2019 15:35:31    Host: ('192.168.8.115', 52194)    Code Sent: s
Sat Oct 26 2019 15:35:32    Host: ('192.168.8.115', 52194)    Code Sent: s
Sat Oct 26 2019 15:35:33    Host: ('192.168.8.115', 52194)    Code Sent: s
Sat Oct 26 2019 15:35:34    Host: ('192.168.8.115', 52194)    Code Sent: l
Sat Oct 26 2019 15:35:35    Host: ('192.168.8.115', 52194)    Code Sent: l
Sat Oct 26 2019 15:35:36    Host: ('192.168.8.115', 52194)    Code Sent: l
```

REFERENCES

Akella, R., Tang, H., & McMillin, B. M. (2010). Analysis of information flow security in cyber-physical systems. *International Journal of Critical Infrastructure Protection*, 3(3-4), 157–173. doi:10.1016/j.ijcip.2010.09.001

Benzel, T. V., Braden, B., Faber, T., Mirkovic, J., Schwab, S. J., Sollins, K. R., & Wroclawski, J. (2009). Current developments in DETER cybersecurity testbed technology. In *Proceedings of the Cybersecurity Applications & Technology Conference for Homeland Security* (pp. 57-70). New York: IEEE. 10.1109/CATCH.2009.30

Benzel, T. V., Braden, R., Kim, D., Neuman, C., Joseph, A. D., & Sklower, K. (2006). Experience with DETER: A testbed for security research. In *Proceedings of the 2nd International Conference on Testbeds and Research Infrastructures for the Development of Networks and Communities, 2006. TRIDENTCOM 2006* (pp. 379-388). New York: IEEE. 10.1109/TRIDNT.2006.1649172

Bergman, D. C., Jin, D., Nicol, D. M., & Yardley, T. M. (2009). The virtual power system testbed and inter-testbed integration. In *Proceedings of the 2nd Conference on Cyber Security Experimentation and Test*. New York: ACM.

Bilar, D., Cybenko, G., & Murphy, J. P. (2013). Adversarial dynamics: The conficker case study. In S. Jajodia et al. (Eds.), Advances in Information Security: Vol. 100. Moving Target Defense II (pp. 41-71). New York: Springer.

Conklin, W. A. (2006). Cyber defense competitions and information security education: An active learning solution for a capstone course. In *Proceedings of the 39th Annual Hawaii International Conference on System Sciences (HICSS'06)* (vol. 9, pp. 220b-220b). New York: IEEE. 10.1109/HICSS.2006.110

Cook, K., Shaw, T., Hawrylak, P. J., & Hale, J. (2016). Scalable attack graph generation. In *Proceedings of the 11th Annual Cyber and Information Security Research Conference* (Article 21). New York: ACM. 10.1145/2897795.2897821

Dondossola, G., Garrone, F., Szanto, J., Deconinck, G., Loix, T., & Beitollahi, H. (2009). ICT resilience of power control systems: experimental results from the CRUTIAL testbeds. In *Proceedings of the IEEE/IFIP International Conference on Dependable Systems & Networks* (pp. 554-559). New York: IEEE. 10.1109/DSN.2009.5270292

Fink, G. A., Best, D. M., Manz, D. O., Popovsky, V., & Endicott-Popovsky, B. (2013). Gamification for measuring cyber security situational awareness. In D. D. Schmorrow, & C. M. Fidopiastis (Eds.), Lecture Notes in Computer Science: Vol. 8027. *Foundations of Augmented Cognition*. Berlin, Germany: Springer. doi:10.1007/978-3-642-39454-6_70

Giraldo, J., Sarkar, E., Cardenas, A. A., Maniatakos, M., & Kantarcioglu, M. (2017). Security and privacy in cyber-physical systems: A survey of surveys. *IEEE Design Test*, *34*(4), 7–17. doi:10.1109/MDAT.2017.2709310

Gunes, V., Peter, S., Givargis, T., & Vahid, F. (2014). A survey on concepts, application, and challenges in cyber-physical systems. *Transactions on Internet and Information Systems (Seoul)*, *8*, 4242–4268.

Gupta, A., Kumar, M., Hansel, S., & Saini, A. K. (2013). Future of all technologies - The cloud and cyber physical systems. *International Journal of Enhanced Research in Management & Computer Applications*, *2*(2), 1–6.

Hawrylak, P. J., Hartney, C., Haney, M. A., Hamm, J. K., & Hale, J. (2013). Techniques to model and derive a cyber-attacker's intelligence. In B. Igelnik, & J. M. Zurada (Eds.), *Efficiency and Scalability Methods for Computational Intellect* (pp. 162–180). Hershey, PA: IGI Global. doi:10.4018/978-1-4666-3942-3.ch008

Hawrylak, P. J., Louthan, G., Daily, J. S., Hale, J. W., & Papa, M. (2012). Attack graphs and scenario driven wireless computer network defense. In M. Khosrow-Pour (Ed.), *Crisis Management: Concepts, Methodologies, Tools, and Applications* (pp. 774–791). Hershey, PA: IGI Global.

Humayed, A., Lin, J., Li, F., & Luo, B. (2017). Cyber-physical systems security – A survey. *IEEE Internet of Things Journal*, *4*(6), 1802–1831. doi:10.1109/JIOT.2017.2703172

Kwon, C., Liu, W., & Hwang, I. (2013). Security analysis for Cyber-Physical Systems against stealthy deception attacks. In *Proceedings of the 2013 American Control Conference* (pp. 3344-3349). New York: IEEE. 10.1109/ACC.2013.6580348

Nagaraja, S., Mittal, P., Hong, C., Caesar, M., & Borisov, N. (2010). BotGrep: Finding P2P bots with structured graph analysis. In *Proceedings of the 19th USENIX conference on Security*. New York: ACM.

Negi, R., Kumar, P., Ghosh, S., Shukla, S. K., & Gahlot, A. (2019). Vulnerability assessment and mitigation for industrial critical infrastructures with cyber physical test bed. In *Proceedings of the IEEE International Conference on Industrial Cyber Physical Systems (ICPS)* (pp. 145-152). New York: IEEE. 10.1109/ICPHYS.2019.8780291

Phillips, L. R., Richardson, B. T., Stamp, J. E., & LaViolette, R. A. (2009). Final report: impacts analysis for cyber attack on electric power systems (National SCADA Test Bed FY08) (Technical Report No. SAND2009-1673). Albuquerque, NM: Sandia National Laboratories.

Qassim, Q. S., Jamil, N., Daud, M., Ja'affar, N., Yussof, S., Ismail, R., & Kamarulzaman, W. A. (2018). Simulating command injection attacks on IEC 60870-5-104 protocol in SCADA system. *IACSIT International Journal of Engineering and Technology*, 7(2), 153–159. doi:10.14419/ijet.v7i2.14.12816

Sabaliauskaite, G., Ng, G. S., Ruths, J., & Mathur, A. (2017). A comprehensive approach, and a case study, for conducting attack detection experiments in cyber-physical systems. *Robotics and Autonomous Systems*, 98, 174–191. doi:10.1016/j.robot.2017.09.018

Sha, L., Gopalakrishnan, S., Liu, X., & Wang, Q. (2008). Cyber-physical systems: A new frontier. In *Proceedings of the IEEE International Conference on Sensor Networks, Ubiquitous, and Trustworthy Computing* (pp. 1-9). New York: IEEE.

Sridhar, S., Hahn, A., & Govindarasu, M. (2012). Cyber-physical system security for the electric power grid. *Proceedings of the IEEE*, 100(1), 210–224. doi:10.1109/JPROC.2011.2165269

Tung, Y., Tseng, S., Shih, J., & Shan, H. (2014). W-VST: A testbed for evaluating web vulnerability scanner. In *Proceedings of the 14th International Conference on Quality Software* (pp. 228-233). New York: IEEE. 10.1109/QSIC.2014.50

Wan, J., Suo, H., Yan, H., & Liu, J. (2011). A general test platform for cyber-physical systems: Unmanned vehicle with wireless sensor network navigation. *Procedia Engineering*, 24, 123–127. doi:10.1016/j.proeng.2011.11.2613

ADDITIONAL READING

Cárdenas, A. A., Amin, S., Lin, Z., Huang, Y., Huang, C., & Sastry, S. S. (2011). Attacks against process control systems: Risk assessment, detection, and response. In *Proceedings of the 6th ACM Symposium on Information, Computer and Communications Security, ASIACCS 2011* (pp. 355-366). New York: ACM. 10.1145/1966913.1966959

Cook, A. (2018). *Establishing cyber situational awareness in industrial control systems*. (Doctoral dissertation). Retrieved from De Montfort University e-theses. (https://www.dora.dmu.ac.uk/xmlui/handle/2086/17463)

Gredler, M. E. (2013). Games and simulations and their relationships to learning. In D. Jonassen & M. Driscoll (Eds.), *Handbook of Research on Educational Communications and Technology*. Abingdon, Oxfordshire, UK: Taylor & Francis Group.

Hahn, A., Kregel, B., Manimaran, G., Fitzpatrick, J., Adnan, R., Sridhar, S., & Higdon, M. (2010). Development of the PowerCyber SCADA security testbed. In *Proceedings of the Sixth Annual Workshop on Cyber Security and Information Intelligence Research, CSIIRW'10* (Article 21). New York: ACM. 10.1145/1852666.1852690

Li, M., Hawrylak, P., & Hale, J. (2019). Concurrency strategies for attack graph generation. In *Proceedings of the 2nd International Conference on Data Intelligence and Security (ICDIS)* (pp. 174-179). New York: IEEE.

Liljenstam, M., Liu, J., Nicol, D. M., Yuan, Y., Yan, G., & Grier, C. (2005). RINSE: the real-time immersive network simulation environment for network security exercises. In *Proceedings of the Workshop on Principles of Advanced and Distributed Simulation (PADS'05)* (pp. 119-128). New York: IEEE. 10.1109/PADS.2005.23

Sridhar, S., & Manimaran, G. (2010). Data integrity attacks and their impacts on SCADA control system. In *Proceedings of the IEEE PES General Meeting* (pp. 1-6). New York: IEEE. 10.1109/PES.2010.5590115

Ten, C., Manimaran, G., & Liu, C. (2010). Cybersecurity for critical infrastructures: Attack and defense modeling. *IEEE Transactions on Systems, Man, and Cybernetics. Part A, Systems and Humans*, 40(4), 853–865. doi:10.1109/TSMCA.2010.2048028

KEY TERMS AND DEFINITIONS

Audit Daemon (Audit.d): Audit.d is a linux subsystem that can do access control monitoring and auditing. It is able to monitor and log any aspect of the linux system is running on.

Beaglebone: A low-power open-source single-board computer produced by Texas Instruments designed with open source software development in mind.

Competitive Learning Platform: A platform in computer science that gives participants the opportunity to explore and experience different challenging scenarios for education and training.

Cyber Physical System (CPS): A system which integrates computational, networking, and physical components within a single functional environment.

Domain: A sphere of knowledge, influence, or activity.

Gamification: The process of adding games or game-like elements to something to encourage user testing participation.

Instrumentation: The use or application of instruments (as for observation, measurement, or control).

OpenCV: A library of programming functions mainly aimed at real-time computer vision.

Stepper Motor: A stepper motor is an electric motor that divides a full rotation into a number of equal 'steps'. The motor can then be controlled to precisely turn a certain amount of steps.

Teensy: The Teensy is a complete USB-based microcontroller development system, in a very small footprint, capable of implementing many types of projects.

Testbed: Any facility or means for testing something in development.

APPENDIX

The car's build of materials can be found below in Table 4. It is designed using parts from Adafruit, Pololu, McMaster Carr, and SeedStudio. Several parts and boards were fabricated by hand and laser cut.

Table 4. Car Build of Materials

CAR BOM					
Name	**Spec**	**Manufacturer**	**Vendor**	**Part No**	**QTY**
Car Body	Custom acrylic plate	N/A	N/A	N/A	1
Beaglebone Green Wireless		SeedStudio	SeedStudio	N/A	1
Motors	Nema 14	Nema	Pololu	1209	2
Wheels			Pololu	3272	2
Wheel Adapters			Pololu	2673	
Caster Wheel			Adafruit	2942	1
8020 aluminum bar short	7" -1010 profile		McMaster Carr	N/A	2
8020 aluminum bar long	7.5" -1010 profile		McMaster Carr	N/A	2
1/4-20 screws			McMaster Carr	N/A	21
1/4-20 t-nuts			McMaster Carr	N/A	10
12mm m3 standoff			McMaster Carr	N/A	11
10mm m3 screw			McMaster Carr	N/A	11
8mm m3 screw			McMaster Carr	N/A	19
Motor Driver Assembly	Custom PCB Assembly	N/A	N/A	N/A	2
Motor Bracket	Custom Laser Printed	N/A	N/A	N/A	2
BeagleBone Cape	Custom PCB Assembly	N/A	N/A	N/A	1
Caster Bracket	Custom 3D Printed	N/A	N/A	N/A	1
Battery Pack	Custom PCB Assembly	N/A	N/A	N/A	2
Cable Covers	Custom 3D Printed	N/A	N/A	N/A	1
Motor Driver	Custom PCB Assembly	N/A	N/A	N/A	2

Chapter 10

Building Industrial Scale Cyber Security Experimentation Testbeds for Critical Infrastructures

Rohit Negi

https://orcid.org/0000-0002-4211-5637

C3i Center, Indian Institute of Technology, Kanpur, India

Anand Handa

C3i Center, Indian Institute of Technology, Kanpur, India

Sandeep Kumar Shukla

C3i Center, Indian Institute of Technology, Kanpur, India

ABSTRACT

Power Grid, Water/Sewage control system, and Industrial automation are some examples of critical infrastructures. They are critical because malfunctioning of any of these may lead to severe industrial accidents. It may also have severe implications for the national economy and security. Nation-states are gearing up for potential cyber warfare, signs of which are already visible in various incidents such as Stuxnet, BlackEnergy, and many other recent attacks. As a result, research in cyber defense for such critical systems is an urgent need for all countries. IIT Kanpur has established the National Interdisciplinary Center for Cyber Security and Cyber Defense of Critical Infrastructures (C3i Center) to engage in research in this crucial area. In the past, the authors carried out a lot of cybersecurity experiments on co-Simulator-based platforms. These experiments show that they do not allow us to penetrate at the granularity required to defend real systems and therefore, physical test-beds are to be constructed. In this chapter, the authors describe how to build various test-beds.

DOI: 10.4018/978-1-7998-2910-2.ch010

INTRODUCTION

In this chapter, the authors describe the various industrial-scale testbeds that are built from scratch at National Interdisciplinary Center for Cyber Security and Cyber Defense of Critical Infrastructures, IIT Kanpur (Negi, Kumar, Ghosh, Shukla, & Gahlot, 2019). Besides describing the architectures of power distribution, transmission, and generation testbeds, a multi-stage water treatment plant testbed, and industrial automation testbed, authors also briefly outline various experimental setup like vulnerability assessment and penetration activities undertaken, and machine learning-based intrusion detection techniques. The authors believe that capturing their set up in this chapter would help others to build similar facilities for research and education around the world. Each country should develop its own facilities for this kind of research and education. Given that the cybersecurity of critical infrastructure is now closely associated with the national security of a country (Alcaraz & Zeadally, 2015; Nicholson, Webber, Dyer, Patel, & Janicke, 2012), sooner than later – skill development, creation of tools for protecting against cyber-attacks against infrastructure, and ability to analyze threats to such systems will be required by every country in the world. To the best of the authors' knowledge C3i center is the first in India to develop such a wide-range cybersecurity experimentation framework and laboratory for critical infrastructure security.

The first well-known incident happened in the 1990s, where a cyber-attack happened on Siberian Gas Pipeline Explosion ("Repository of industrial security incidents [RISI] online incident database," 2015). More recently, the authors witness the attacks on the power grids of Ukraine ("December 2015 Ukraine power grid cyberattack," 2015) several times in the past few years. Therefore, this kind of facility is the need of the hour. With this kind of facility, one can perform experiments with the vulnerabilities, and the threats faced by various automation systems engaged in critical infrastructure. Also, one can experiment on the protective software and hardware systems designed to thwart such attacks.

Most critical infrastructures starting from the water and sewage treatment plants to power grid – are cyber-physical systems. This means that there is a physical plant – whose dynamics is based on laws of physics and computationally best captured with partial differential equations. The physical dynamics needs to be governed and controlled – otherwise the safety of the plant would be violated. This control is possible if one knows the physical state of the plant, and the current inputs to the system. That is where sensors come into play. Measurements of various physical parameter values are taken by sensors at the plant and sent to the controller(s) through communication network(s). The controller estimates the state of the system and accordingly decides on what governance needs to be applied and sends relevant instructions to the actuators. The actuation allows the physical plant to remain or be attracted back to its intended trajectory. This cycle of measurement-control-actuation must be done often enough so that in the intervening period the plant does not get too far away from the intended safe trajectory. Even though the preceding characterization of a cyber-physical system might give an impression of a centralized control – but, for large scale cyber-physical systems, there are many local controls, as well as hierarchical control. For example, local controls might be enforced through a programmable logic controller or even simple control device, whereas a higher-level control may be exerted by human operators at the control center, with the help of Supervisory Control And Data Acquisition (SCADA) systems. Similarly, the communication network is not necessarily just a single network, but possibly hierarchical. At the field level, the sensors might be interfaced with various industrial control protocols such as Modbus RTU, Proðbus, DeviceNet, etc., but for a remote control center, Transmission Control Protocol/Internet Protocol (TCP/IP) network is used, and hence protocol translation/encapsulation through Remote Terminal Units (RTUs) are required. Having summarized the structure of a critical cyber-physical system above, it is not difficult to imagine that cyber-attack surfaces are abound in such systems ("2017 cyberattacks on Ukraine," 2017; Cimpanu, 2016; Frost & Tajitsu, 2017; Lee, Assante, & Conway, 2014; Mayne, 2018; Posirca, 2017; Steitz & Auchard, 2016). The sensors and actuators themselves are possible targets for attacks because many of these field devices such as digital relays, Phasor Measurement Units (PMUs) are all full-fledged computing devices. The industrial control protocols such as DNP3, Modbus, etc., are neither encrypted, nor authenticated, leading to a huge scope for man-in-the-middle attacks including false data injection. The RTUs and PLCs are also computing devices with real-time operating systems and various applications – and so are the control center computers, SCADA software and hardware, and the entire associated network infrastructure. Another attack path has arisen in plants where the field/plant control infrastructure is connected to the enterprise network for real-time monitoring the plant state and performance. Although, in most cases, such connections are mediated by multiple layers such as Demilitarized Zone (DMZs) and firewalls, attacks at the enterprise network have often found its way all the way to the control devices. Other than the operational network architectural weaknesses, there are also software and hardware bugs in most industrial control devices such as PLCs, RTUs, SCADA, including their firmware, operating environment, run-time systems, and applications. Bugs often get introduced while patching and upgrading as well. To be sure that devices that are going into critical infrastructure, one must have a good setup for penetration testing and vulnerability assessment. Further, the setup should allow for hardware-in-the-loop or software-in-the-loop testing of new or modified devices plugged into the set up so that any new product in the market can also be assessed. Also, architectural assessment is needed as it is often the network and overall architecture, access control plan, firewall and intrusion detection system positioning that makes the difference between a secure and a vulnerable system. Despite of all kinds of preventive mechanisms – attacks will still happen as there might be insider attacks induced by social engineering, or exploitation of vulnerabilities in the perimeter defense, one must also build continuous monitoring and surveillance mechanism in such systems. As part of this continuous monitoring and surveillance system, one must apply machine learning techniques – i.e. data-driven AI techniques for intrusion detection and prevention. The C3i center therefore experiments with all these different aspects of modern critical infrastructures grounded in center's real industry scale testbeds of various infrastructure sectors. Sectors for which the authors have built testbeds so far are: Power distribution, transmission and generation, water treatment process control, and industrial manufacturing process control. In the rest of this chapter, the authors describe details and illustrations of the design of the various testbeds and outline briefly how they have used them so far in cyber security research and education. The authors believe that even though they are not presenting a novel methodology or algorithm for cyber-physical system control, safety or security, but they are providing a valuable pointer to carry out similar research and build similar training facilities around the world. Authors' designs and the mode of usage of the testbeds for further research may help researchers to build successful research programs, as well as security testing/certification facilities.

BACKGROUND

Vulnerability assessment and penetration testing (VAPT) of live industrial systems might invite some unfavorable situations. Frameworks like SCADASiM (Mahoney & Gandhi, 2011); SCADASim (Queiroz, Mahmood, & Tari, 2011); MALsim (Sui, Wu, Yin, Zhou, & Gong, 2010); VSCADA (Dayal, Deng, Tbaileh, & Shukla, 2015); the framework proposed by Aragó et al. (2014), etc. Simulated SCADA testbeds presented in works of Chabukswar et al. (2010) and Almalawi et al. (2013) are located to put the SCADA systems under observation. Researchers are conducting experiments using the Tennessee Eastman chemical process control system (Li, Zhou, Tian, & Qin, 2018) with a simple discrete PI algorithm and a second-order plant (Long, Wu, & Hung, 2005).

With physical testbeds, users can research with real hardware, and all attack surfaces can be explored. However, it is quite expensive and time-consuming to set up a real environment. In the last few years, cybersecurity research has picked up significantly, which resulted in the installation and commissioning of various physical SCADA testbeds. The Indian Institute of Technology, Kanpur (2019) lists 17 different environmental research and testing facilities, which include testbeds at Idaho National Lab, the Pacific Northwest National Laboratory, SANDIA Center for SCADA Security, etc. Many of these have been sources of high-quality data for anomaly detection benchmarking for intrusion detection research.

Three Layers in Cyber-Physical Systems

Most cyber-physical systems comprise of three major layers – namely Information Technology (IT) layer, Operational Technology (OT) layer and Industrial Control System (ICS) layer. In the past, OT environments used to be air gaped and isolated from the IT layer. However, with the increasing trend of IP-convergence these layers are being connected albeit via the mediation demilitarized zone (DMZ) with firewalls and Intrusion Detection Systems (IDS), as demonstrated in Figure 1.

Threat Vectors

As depicted in Figure 2, the lowest layer, i.e., the ICS layer is tightly coupled with the physical system using hardwired signals and serial communication. This layer is majorly vulnerable to physical attacks and requires physical access to the devices. Further, both the Original Equipment Manufacturers (OEMs) and end-users can become victims and the supply chain gets compromised, and logic bombs and Trojans

Figure 1. Three major layers of cyber-physical system

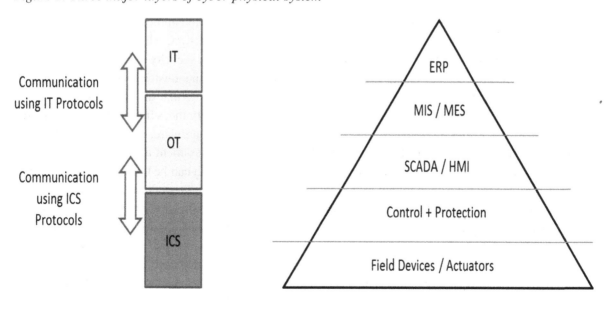

can be injected inside the components of this layer. Insider attacks are also major threat to this layer. In between ICS layer and OT layer, the communication between PLC/RTU/Intelligent Electronic Device (IEDs) (from the ICS layer) to the SCADA/Human Machine Interface (HMI) (OT layer) usually resorts to data-link layer protocols. The two layers share information with each other using client-server or publisher-subscriber mechanism. The various communication ports enabled at the ICS layer devices become the first point to become targets as they get exposed to the network-borne adversaries. Devices used in the ICS are communicating using industrial communication protocols such as Modbus TCP, ProðNet, Ethernet IP, IEC 61850, IEC 60870-5-104, etc. As the safety/security requirements of the ICS is the SAIC triad (safety, availability, integrity and confidentiality), availability took precedence over confidentiality. Therefore, these protocols are not designed considering integrity/confidentiality. Other protocol applications running on the controllers such as Simple Network Management Protocol (SNMP), File Transfer Protocol (FTP), HyperText Transfer Protocol (HTTP), etc., may also provide intrusion paths to adversaries. The OT layer has a number of application software running. Of these, SCADA/HMI software (I/O server, report server, trend server, alarm server, clients for visualization, etc.) are tightly coupled with the ICS. On the other side, these OT layer applications are communicating with other application software like MES, MIS, etc. Vulnerabilities in this software again enhance the attack surface (ICS Computer Emergency Response Team [CERT], 2019). The IT layer consists of ERP and other IT software and they acquire data from the OT layer and use the information to optimize the resources and increase the profit of the organization. These are often directly connected to the enterprise network which in turn is connected to the Internet. Phishing based attacks at the enterprise IT system have been found the root cause of many cyber incidents in the recent past. Moreover, there is always maintenance, changes, and updates which are applied by the OEMs to the devices in the ICS and OT layer. These updates and patches could provide direct exposure of OT/ICS layer to the Internet as OEMs often do these remotely.

Need for Cyber-Physical Test-Beds

In the past, the researchers have created co-simulation framework such as VSCADA (Dayal et al., 2015) to do cyber security experiments where the field and control is simulated using a domain-specific simulation (such as a power system simulator), communications with the Network Simulator version 2 (NS-2), and the SCADA environment with a real SCADA software – the authors found that the threat vectors mostly target vulnerabilities in the devices, protocols, and software which are not modeled in such virtual co-simulation environment. Thus, to experiment with cyber security vulnerabilities in sector specific cyber-physical system, and to test the mitigation techniques, real industrial scale testbeds are the best even though they require significant financial investments. It is true that the co-simulation is cost effective and easy to deploy. Simulation also does not require any safety measures as they do not result in any loss of person and property. However, in the absence of real hardware, vulnerabilities become assumptions and it does not fulfill the objective of Vulnerability Assessment and Penetration Testing (VAPT). Further, a real system facilitates us to develop solutions which can be tightly coupled with the existing infrastructure and tested. One may argue that such testing can be done on live systems in the utilities – but the authors feel that the most utilities would not agree to allow cyber security experiments on their operational systems. In case, the VAPT causes any harm to the hardware and software, it might be very expensive to get them changed. Also, zero downtime requirements may not even allow rebuilding the complete setup. Also, since cyber threats are evolving and utilities need to test any upgrades for cyber-attack exposure before procurement, a replica of the existing system can help by hardware-in-the-

Figure 2. Threat vector

Devices / Layer	Control and Protection Devices			Network Devices	Supervisory Devices	
	PLC	**RTU**	**Numerical Relay**	**Switch, Router etc.**	**HMI**	**SCADA**
Application	Web: CSRF, RFI, XSS, Weak Password Management, Insecure communication (HTTP), DoS	Web: CSRF, Weak Password Management, Insecure communication (HTTP), DoS	Web: Insecure communication (HTTP), DoS	Network related attack in general (if any)	X11 server	
	Modbus TCP: DoS, MITM, Malicious command execution	Modbus TCP: DoS, MITM, Malicious command execution				Credentials theft
		IEC-60870-5-104: DoS, MITM, Malicious command execution				
Operating System	TCP/IP	TCP/IP	TCP/IP		TCP/IP	*Any vulnerability exclusive of SCADA systems
	Hash Collision	Hash Collision				
Firmware	Hardcoded FTP credentials	Hardcoded FTP credentials				

loop testing. They may also get security solutions developed and thoroughly tested on such industrial scale testbeds without any downtime.

Experimental Setup at the C3i Center

The experimental setup at the center is extensive, granular and facilitates research on VAPT methodology and tool development; intrusion detection algorithms and tools; malware analysis (MA); honeypots; blockchain based security solutions; and other cyber security related problems. The setup shown in Figure 3 also facilitates researchers by providing industry vertical specific testbeds so that research can be more focused. Testing setup includes the power supply of the center; process automation testbed, manufacturing automation testbed; and power automation testbed. Devices used in the setup are commercial off-the-shelf industrial devices majorly used in water industry, power industry, oil, gas and chemical industry, consumer packaged goods industry, transportation industry, material handling, etc. Working philosophy and behavior of different industry verticals is different. To design and develop the industry-specific best fit solution requires testbed of each type. By adding a few more domains like health care and transportation, testing setup will become a replica of a smart city. These testbeds also help produce data sets for OT and ICS of each industrial segment, which will be made available to researchers worldwide. Researchers who do not have access to such testbeds can use center's data sets for developing new algorithms for intrusion detection with higher accuracy. It is quite expensive to replicate an industry scale testbed. The investment required for the infrastructure and its equipment and raw material used in the testbed could be prohibitive.

C3i Power Generation and Distribution System to Run the Testbeds

C3i center is designed as a prosumer (producer-consumer). The researchers have set up Distributed Energy Resources (DER) with solar power generation and diesel power generation as depicted in Figure 4.

Figure 3. System configuration of the C3i experimental setup

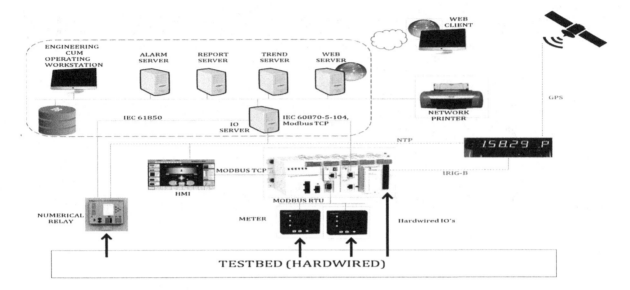

These DER are synchronized with the power coming from the campus distribution grid. There are total 8 incoming and 5 outgoing connectors in the system. All these outgoings are used to feed the critical and non-critical loads of the center. Critical load includes PC, Server, network devices, control panel, etc. Non-critical load includes the light, fan and other auxiliary supply of the center. During normal operations, the complete load of the center is running on the generated solar power. In case the total load of the center exceeds the power generated by solar panels installed, then excess power is imported from the campus distribution system. During the blackout / shutdown / scheduled power-cut, excess power will be generated locally using diesel generators.

This power generation & distribution setup is monitored and controlled at the top by a SCADA system. Operations can be performed in both local and remote mode to ensure all loads are satisfied at the center. SCADA system is continuously monitoring the load requirements of the center to optimize the generation, auto mains failure, auto load sharing, synchronization, etc.

Synchronization is monitoring of the measurements associated with Diesel Generator (DG), and the common bus bar is the main purpose of the panel in Figure 5.

Initially, the DG are in the switched off mode and common bus bar has power coming from the solar and campus grid. When there is a power cut, and the center load demands more power which moves to emergency power on power cut due to the UPS installed, the PLC needs to start the master DG. It takes around 20 seconds for the master DG to start supporting the load. If the power generated by the master DG is not sufficient to feed the load, then the PLC will send command to start the other DG and balance the load among them. The percentage loading of a particular DG can be input by an operator using the SCADA interface. In case the DG engines fails to start in the first cranking then two or more auto commands will be given in proper intervals. If the engine fails to start, indication will appear and logs will be created in the SCADA system for the same. For load management, whenever the DG sets being overloaded (more than 80%), the PLC will start the next DG sets after a predefined time delay. After starting the DG set, the PLC will take care of the synchronization and proper load sharing as per the DG ratings. In case running a DG set is being under loaded (less than 40%), then PLC will stop the DG set after

Figure 4. Single line diagram of power generation and distribution panel

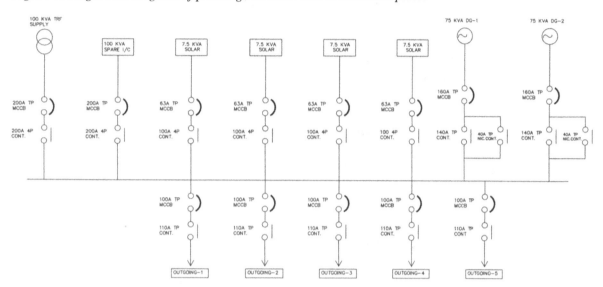

transferring the load onto the other DG set. During VAPT and other cyber security attack experiments, this system is isolated from the campus grid to launch several attacks on the system without affecting the campus distribution system in anyway. During this kind of penetration testing, complete lab load is transferred to the solar and diesel generation. However, a separate power generation, transmission and distribution setup has also been setup to perform attacks without affecting the activities of the laboratory.

Figure 5. Power distribution and synchronization panel at C3i

Process Automation Testbed in the Form of a Water Treatment Plant

Process automation testbed is a replica of multi stage water treatment plant comprising of pumps, solenoid valves, motorized valves, level transmitters, pressure transmitters, flow meters, temperature sensors, PLC, SCADA, etc. The stages of the plant are as mentioned below:

- Intake section which is used to intake and collect the raw water for treatment.
- **Coagulation Using Chemical Dosing**: Alum dosing in the raw water.
- **Flocculation**: Stirring of water.
- **Sedimentation**: Settling of heavy particles at the base of the clarifier.
- **Aeration**: Pushing air bubbles into the water.
- **Filtration**: Multi-layer sand filters.
- **Chlorination**: To disinfect the water.
- **Clean in Process**: Backwash of the filters.

Figure 6 shows the piping diagram of the various stages of the testbed and Figure 8 shows a picture of the actual water treatment plant testbed at the C3i center. The goal of building this testbed is to experiment with multi-stage process automation, coordination of multiple PLCs and SCADA monitoring & control.

This process automation testbed is equipped with SCADA based monitoring and operator control which is used for continuous monitoring of all the vital parameters of the water (level, pH, turbidity, pressure, flow, etc.) at the different stages. Figure 7 shows the system configuration of the water treatment plant. The PLCs at the intake stage monitors the level of intake tank and actuates inlet valve to fill the tank up to an upper set point input via SCADA interface. The same PLC is used to operate outlet valve and boost the water up to the clarifier if the level of water in intake tank is within the defined limits. If the clarifier is already full and does not require water, then intake section stops feeding it. Clarifier collects water and doses it using chemical (alum). The water from the top of the clarifier is transferred to filter-bed. Clarifier has a lot of waste settled down at its bottom which will discharge to recycling/sewage tank. From sewage tank that water can be recycled to clarifier using mechanical filters. Fitter-bed takes in the water and filters the water using standard sand filters. This filtration process limits the impurities and clean water is stored for chlorination. This treated water is used in backwash tank for cleaning the filter. Treated water is supplied to different tanks.

Testbed for Discrete Automation

A discrete automation testbed is designed and implemented to mimic a discrete manufacturing control system as shown in Figure 9.

The goal is to find cyber vulnerabilities in the architectures and equipment in such system as industry standard sensors, controllers, and actuators are integrated in the replica of a fully automated manufacturing pipeline. This testbed replicates the development of a work piece which goes through a multi-stage pipeline of workstations for different types of processing. The actual work on the work piece is just to move it from stage to stage without making any changes to the piece, and finally sort the pieces based on color. There are 5 stages in the pipeline. The five stages are as follows:

Figure 6. Piping and instrumentation diagram of the water treatment plant

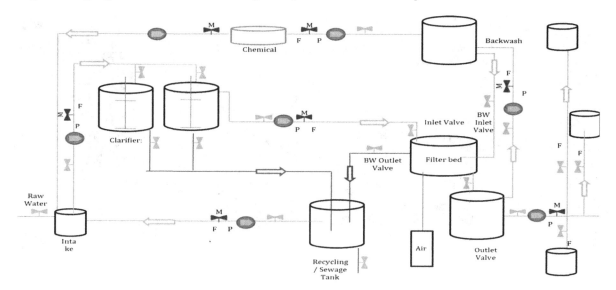

- **Feeder Station:** The feeder station mimics the functionality of bunkering, sorting and feeding components to the manufacturing process – as if raw material is being fed to the pipeline. Initially, the job is stacked in a magazine barrel. The controller detects the availability of jobs by means of a through-beam sensor. The jobs are in two separate cylinders. The cylinder pushes the lowest work piece from the gravity-feed magazine up to the mechanical stop. From that position the job is transferred to next stage.

- **Inspection Station:** Major role of the inspection station is to acquire the actual job to check whether it is inline with set points and results in deciding whether the work piece is acceptable/

Figure 7. System configuration of water treatment plant

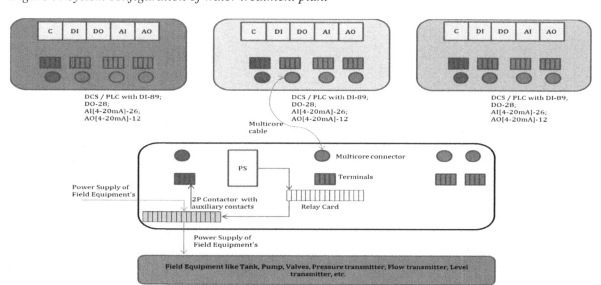

Figure 8. Water treatment plant at C3i

rejected. The inspection station inspects the height and weight of the job arrived and if it passes inspection, it lifts the job with a mechanical arm to transfer the work piece by a slide to the next station. It also sends faulty rejected work pieces to the rejection bay.

- **Buffer Station:** Buffer station is a First In First Out (FIFO) store, where the order of parts is not changed. The work pieces are separated out at the output of the buffer zone prior to being passed on to the subsequent station. Buffer station ensures steady flow of components to the next station by allowing one component at a time for processing. It stores up to 5 work pieces at a time and if

Figure 9. States of modular manufacturing set

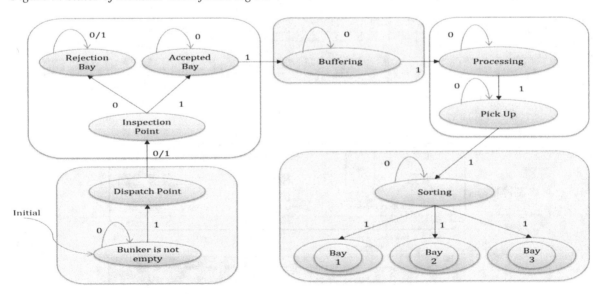

the count has exceeded 5, it communicates with the upstream stations to hold the supply of the job until there is a demand from the downstream station.

- **Process Station:** The process station demonstrates drilling operation on a work piece available on top of pneumatically driven rotary indexing table and transfers the work piece via pick and place module to downstream station. It senses the presence of the incoming work piece in order to proceed with drilling operation. Drilling module consists of a drilling machine along a pneumatic linear drive module which moves the drill unit up and down. The rotary indexing table is driven by a DC motor to index the jobs at an angle of 60 degrees/each time. The transfer of work piece to the subsequent station done by a linear pick and place unit.

- **Sorting Station:** The sorting station sorts the incoming work pieces based on color and material characteristics and sends them to appropriate bays. The sorting station has 3 slides to sort the incoming jobs. A conveyor module is fitted with sensors to sense the presence of jobs at the start of the conveyor. Inductive sensors and color sensors are used to detect whether the material is metallic, non-metallic and what its color is. Based on that, it is diverted to the appropriate slides. A pneumatically actuated sorting arrangement is provided which extends for pushing the work pieces onto the appropriate slides. Networking and signaling the subsequent stations for further processing should be done by establishing I/O communication between the PLCs of subsequent stations. The PLCs used in this station should be capable of handling various digital inputs/ outputs, and it should have Ethernet interface to communicate with PC for programming and SCADA monitoring. Major items used in the system are filter regulators and lubricator units with pressure gauge, solenoid valves, one touch fittings mounted with suitable mountings, etc., for easy assembly and disassembly. Figure 10 shows a snapshot of the discrete process control testbed in the form of a pipelined manufacturing replica.

Testbed for Power Automation

The C3i Power automation testbed, besides the power supply panel that authors described earlier, also comprises of power generation, transmission and distribution. This power generation setup includes DC motor coupled with 3 phase AC motor, intelligent protection devices, step-up transformers, etc., as shown in Figure 11.

Power transmission setup includes 100 km long conductor with fault injector units, differential protection relays, distance protection relays, etc. Power distribution includes distribution substation with step-down transformers, distance protection relay, differential protection relay, RLC load, etc. All the sections have field instruments integrated with PLC/RTU based SCADA system. The generator is operated in both lead and lag mode. This generator system has DC motor coupled with a three-phase AC motor. The DC motor acts as a prime mover and AC motor as a three-phase synchronous generator. Excitation voltage for the rotor field winding is given by controllable digital voltage regulator. The Controller controls the power generated by regulating the speed of the DC motor. This setup is integrated with various IEDs which are protecting the generation setup from failure and sending measurements up to control the center. Generated power is transmitted after a step-up up to 1100 V using a 415/1100 V, 50 Hz, three-phase power transformer. An experimenter can induce symmetrical and asymmetrical faults in the transmission system. The user can select phase(s) and ground involved in the induced faults, along with a provision for creating faults with varying fault resistance. The capacitive/inductive effects

Figure 10. Modular manufacturing testbed

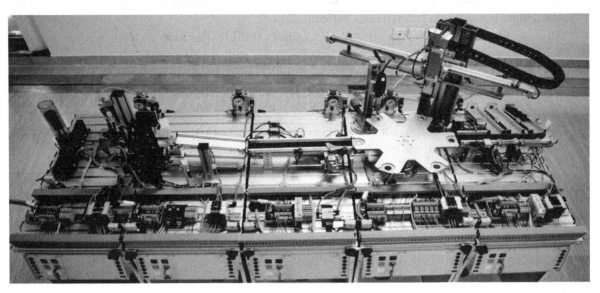

of transmission lines are also present by design. The loading section consists of distributed load banks. There is flexibility of remote/manual control for balanced/unbalanced three-phase resistive, inductive, and capacitive load. More details of this can be found in Negi et al. (2019).

Current Uses of the C3i Test-beds

C3i Center at IIT Kanpur offers a wide range of services using the installed test beds which includes Vulnerability and Penetration Testing, Intrusion Detection System, Malware Analysis, etc. In the domain of vulnerability and penetration testing, C3i center engineers are engaging this infrastructure to study vulnerabilities present in the industrial components. Already the center has discovered and disclosed the vulnerabilities, among which 7 have been assigned Common Vulnerabilities and Exposures (CVE) numbers and corresponding security advisories attributed to C3I center have been published by the vendors. One more CVE has been assigned but until the vendor sends the security advisories, they will not be put in the National Vulnerability Database (NVD) database. More than 15 vulnerabilities have been disclosed by C3i center to multiple ICS vendors with proof-of-concept videos. These are being validated by the vendors upon completion of which CVEs will be assigned. Several penetration testing, industrial

Figure 11. Power testbed

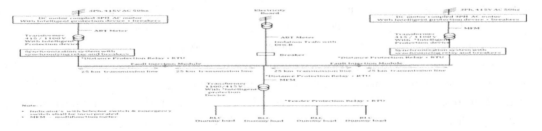

network traffic capture and analysis tools have been developed which are being further developed. Based on the testbed generated data, several intrusion detection alert generation tools have also been developed.

The indigenous Web based Malware Analysis tool developed at center is capable of detecting and classifying malware in near real time with a high accuracy of 99% and a low False Positive Rate less than 1%. The tool does various types of analysis for various kinds of binaries such as Windows, Linux, Android, etc. It uses an ensemble of machine learning models. The tool uses different kinds of approaches to detect and classify malware such as static analysis, dynamic analysis, and memory forensics.

A completely homegrown threat intelligence monitoring and analytics framework is built to monitor all cyber events incident upon the center. Machine learning based detection of threats with high accuracy (above 95%) and with low false positive rate (less than 5%) is implemented and integrated with the threat intelligence monitoring system. It may help any SOC (Security Operation Center) to obtain full visibility, situational awareness and actionable threat intelligence. This system can be customized for other facilities outside the center as well.

FUTURE RESEARCH DIRECTIONS

Here are some of the areas that need further research in the context of cyber security test-beds for critical infrastructures. First, while vulnerability assessment and penetration testing has been an art so far – with invention of a few tools to help the VAPT testers – further automation is necessary to achieve more scalable VAPT methodologies. Furthermore, vulnerability assessment of upcoming upgrades/patches is something that is often overlooked. Easing the validation of patches and upgrades before they are put into production environment needs to be efficient and effective – further tools and methodologies are required. Second, integration of these testbeds with learning management platforms to provide lab as a service would be a good direction to pursue as scalable training of engineers and operators in the various industrial plants, utilities, etc., are growing in importance. Third, design and development of several security technologies like Honeypots, real-time intrusion detection, malware analysis and screening for ICS and OT environments need further investment in research. Fourth, extension of testbeds to emulate emerging trends of industry 4.0 should be simulated with integration of autonomous robotic environment and automated storage and retrieval systems. Finally, further work is required in threat analysis and mitigation planning and in the development of more effective and efficient risk-based approaches to cyber security of ICS systems.

CONCLUSION

In this chapter, the authors argue that developing physical industrial-scale testbed for critical cyber-physical systems is very crucial for cyber security research in this domain. The authors describe the design and function of several testbeds the researchers have developed at C3i center which are being used for discovering and disclosing vulnerabilities, developing penetration testing tools, developing intrusion-detection tools, etc. The researchers also plan to create sector-specific cyber-attack data-set and make them available for researchers to use for further machine learning based tools for attack detection. The authors also are developing various mitigation techniques and experimenting with architectural techniques to thwart various threat vectors. The authors hope that the content of this chapter will help others to develop similar testbeds for further research in cyber security of critical infrastructures.

ACKNOWLEDGMENT

This research was supported by the Science and Engineering Research Board (SERB), Department of Science and Technology (DST), Government of India and the UI ASSIST.

REFERENCES

Alcaraz, C., & Zeadally, S. (2015). Critical infrastructure protection: Requirements and challenges for the 21st century. *International Journal of Critical Infrastructure Protection*, *8*, 53–66. doi:10.1016/j. ijcip.2014.12.002

Almalawi, A., Tari, Z., Khalil, I., & Fahad, A. (2013). SCADAVT – A framework for SCADA security testbed based on virtualization technology. In *Proceedings of the 38th Conference on Local Computer Networks (LCN 2013)* (pp. 639-646). New York: IEEE. 10.1109/LCN.2013.6761301

Aragó, A. S., Martinez, E. R., & Clares, S. S. (2014). SCADA laboratory and test-bed as a service for critical infrastructure protection. In *Proceedings of the 2nd International Symposium on ICS & SCADA Cyber Security Research* (pp. 25-29). New York: ACM. 10.14236/ewic/ICSCSR2014.4

Chabukswar, R., Sinópoli, B., Karsai, G., Giani, A., Neema, H., & Davis, A. (2010). Simulation of network attacks on SCADA systems. *First Workshop on Secure Control Systems. Cyber Physical Systems Week*. Retrieved November 05, 2019, from https://ptolemy.berkeley.edu/projects/truststc/pubs/693/SCS%20Paper.pdf

Cimpanu, C. (2016, March 9). *Korean energy and transportation targets attacked by OnionDog APT*. Retrieved November 01, 2019, from https://news.softpedia.com/news/korean-energy-and-transportation-targets-attacked-by-oniondog-apt-501534.shtml

2017 . *cyberattacks on Ukraine*. (n.d.). In Wikipedia. Retrieved November 01, 2019, from https://en.wikipedia.org/wiki/2017_cyberattacks_on_Ukraine

Dayal, A., Deng, Y., Tbaileh, A., & Shukla, S. (2015). VSCADA: A reconfigurable virtual SCADA test-bed for simulating power utility control center operations. In *Proceedings of the IEEE Power & Energy Society General Meeting* (pp. 1-5). New York: IEEE. 10.1109/PESGM.2015.7285822

December 2015 Ukraine power grid cyberattack. (n.d.). In Wikipedia. Retrieved October 08, 2019, from https://en.wikipedia.org/wiki/December_2015_Ukraine_power_grid_cyberattack

Frost, L., & Tajitsu, N. (2017, May 15). Renault-Nissan is resuming production after a global cyberattack caused stoppages at 5 plants. *Reuters*. Retrieved November 01, 2019, from https://www.businessinsider.com/renault-nissan-production-halt-wannacry-ransomeware-attack-2017-5?IR=T

Indian Institute of Technology. Kanpur. (2019). *Interdisciplinary center for cyber security and cyber defense of critical infrastructures*. Retrieved, November 02, 2019, from https://security.cse.iitk.ac.in

Industrial Control Systems Cyber Emergency Response Team (ICS-CERT). (2019). *ICS advisory* (ICSA-19-150-01). Retrieved, November 02, 2019, from https://www.us-cert.gov/ics/advisories/ICSA-19-150-01

Lee, R. M., Assante, M. J., & Conway, T. (2014). *Cyber attack on German steel mill* (Case Study Paper). SANS Institute. Retrieved November 01, 2019, from https://ics.sans.org/media/ICS-CPPE-case-Study-2-German-Steelworks_Facility.pdf

Li, X., Zhou, C., Tian, Y.-C., & Qin, Y. (2018). A dynamic decision-making approach for intrusion response in industrial control systems. *IEEE Transactions on Industrial Informatics*, *15*(5), 2544–2554. doi:10.1109/TII.2018.2866445

Long, M., Wu, C.-H., & Hung, J. Y. (2005). Denial of service attacks on network-based control systems: Impact and mitigation. *IEEE Transactions on Industrial Informatics*, *1*(2), 85–96. doi:10.1109/TII.2005.844422

Mahoney, W., & Gandhi, R. A. (2011). An integrated framework for control system simulation and regulatory compliance monitoring. *International Journal of Critical Infrastructure Protection*, *4*(1), 41–53. doi:10.1016/j.ijcip.2011.03.002

Mayne, M. (2018, February 15). First confirmed cryptocurrency attack on SCADA network [Web log comment]. Retrieved October 31, 2019, from https://www.immuniweb.com/blog/first-confirmed-cryptocurrency-attack-on-scada-network.html

Negi, R., Kumar, P., Ghosh, S., Shukla, S. K., & Gahlot, A. (2019). Vulnerability assessment and mitigation for industrial critical infrastructures with cyber physical test bed. In *Proceedings of the IEEE International Conference on Industrial Cyber Physical Systems (ICPS)* (pp. 145-152). New York: IEEE. 10.1109/ICPHYS.2019.8780291

Nicholson, A., Webber, S., Dyer, S., Patel, T., & Janicke, H. (2012). SCADA security in the light of cyber-warfare. *Computers & Security*, *31*(4), 418–436. doi:10.1016/j.cose.2012.02.009

Posirca, O. (2017, May 13). Dacia production in Romania, partially crippled by cyber-attack | WannaCry infection suspected. *Business Review*. Retrieved, November 02, 2019, from http://business-review.eu/news/dacia-production-in-romania-partially-crippled-by-cyber-attack-wannacry-infection-suspected-137678

Queiroz, C., Mahmood, A., & Tari, Z. (2011). SCADASim – A framework for building SCADA simulations. *IEEE Transactions on Smart Grid*, *2*(4), 589–597. doi:10.1109/TSG.2011.2162432

Repository of industrial security incidents (RISI) online incident database. (2015). Retrieved October 08, 2019, from https://www.risidata.com/Database/event_date/asc

Steitz, C., & Auchard, E. (2016, April 26). German nuclear plant infected with computer viruses, operator says. *Reuters*. Retrieved October 08, 2019, from https://www.reuters.com/article/us-nuclearpower-cyber-germany/german-nuclear-plant-infected-with-computer-viruses-operator-says-idUSKCN0XN2OS

Sui, X., Wu, J., Yin, W., Zhou, D., & Gong, Z. (2010). MALsim: A functional-level parallel simulation platform for CMPs. In *Proceedings of the 2nd International Conference on Computer Engineering and Technology (ICCET):* Vol. 2. New York: IEEE.

ADDITIONAL READING

Aghamolki, H. G., Miao, Z., & Fan, L. (2015). A hardware-in-the-loop SCADA testbed. In *Proceedings of the North American Power Symposium (NAPS)* (pp. 1-6). New York: IEEE.

Ahmed, I., Roussev, V., Johnson, W., Senthivel, S., & Sudhakaran, S. (2016). A SCADA system testbed for cybersecurity and forensic research and pedagogy. In *Proceedings of the 2nd Annual Industrial Control System Security Workshop* (pp. 1-9). New York: ACM. 10.1145/3018981.3018984

Korkmaz, E., Dolgikh, A., Davis, M., & Skormin, V. (2016). Industrial control systems security testbed. In *Proceedings of the 11th Annual Symposium on Information Assurance* (pp. 13-18). University at Albany, State University of New York.

Mallouhi, M., Al-Nashif, Y., Cox, D., Chadaga, T., & Hariri, S. (2011). A testbed for analyzing security of SCADA control systems (TASSCS). In *Proceedings of the Innovative Smart Grid Technologies (ISGT)* (pp. 1-7). New York: IEEE. 10.1109/ISGT.2011.5759169

Mathur, A. P., & Tippenhauer, N. O. (2016). SWaT: A water treatment testbed for research and training on ICS security. In *Proceedings of the International Workshop on Cyber-physical Systems for Smart Water Networks (CySWater)* (pp. 31-36). New York: IEEE. 10.1109/CySWater.2016.7469060

Metzger, M. (2016, July 13). SFG malware discovered in European energy company. *SC Media*. Retrieved November 01, 2019, from https://www.scmagazineuk.com/sfg-malware-discovered-european-energy-company/article/1476686

Morris, T. H., Vaughn, R. B., & Dandass, Y. S. (2011). A testbed for SCADA control system cybersecurity research and pedagogy. In *Proceedings of the 7th Annual ACM Cyber Security and Information Intelligence Research Workshop (CSIIRW)* (Article 27). New York: ACM. 10.1145/2179298.2179327

KEY TERMS AND DEFINITIONS

Industrial Control System (ICS): A general notion that refers to several types of control systems and associated tools used for the industrial process control.

MODBUS TCP: It is simply the Modbus RTU protocol with a TCP interface that runs on Ethernet.

Operational Technology (OT): An artifact used to communicate with industrial control system to monitor and control the plant floor with highly interactive user interface.

Programmable Logic Controller (PLC): A general notion that refers to an industrial computer adapted for controlling the manufacturing, batching, processing, etc., automation in industries.

Remote Terminal Unit (RTU): RTU is an industrial computer adapted for acquiring the manufacturing, batching, processing, etc., automation data in industries and transmitting telemetry data up to the master system.

Supervisory Control and Data Acquisition (SCADA): These systems are used to monitor and control a plant or equipment in industries such as telecommunications, water and waste control, energy, oil and gas refining and transportation.

Vulnerability Assessment and Penetration Testing (VAPT): Vulnerability assessment and penetration testing (VAPT) is the key to address the security loop holes in any system – IT or industrial control system. Penetration testing emphasizes on gaining as much access as possible while a vulnerability assessment emphasizes on identifying components that are vulnerable to a cyber-attack.

Section 3
Security Considerations in Specific Industrial Sectors

Chapter 11
Application of Cloud Computing in Electric Power Utility Systems:
Advantages and Risks

Radoslav M. Raković

Energoprojekt Entel plc, Belgrade, Serbia

ABSTRACT

The concept of "Cloud computing" became very interesting in recent years because it enables optimization of resources used and costs paid for it. Considering all advantages, this approach is applied widely in business systems of general purpose. In recent years, in literature it is possible to find considerations related to application of this approach in corporate systems as electric power utilities. Having in mind that such types of systems represent infrastructure ones that have great impact to the security of people and utilities, a very important question related to information security should be seriously considered. This chapter discusses advantages and disadvantages of application of cloud computing in electric power utility systems.

INTRODUCTION

Cloud computing concept has sparked great interest in recent years because it enables optimization of the resources engaged and pricing mechanism applied on a pay-per-use basis. This "on-demand oriented service" approach offers a number of advantages (Mell & Grance, 2011). First, computer configuration could become simpler, and therefore less expensive. Then, the services are charged per scope of use only, no more and no less. Also, a wide range of applications is provided, data storage and backup capacity is practically unlimited, almost all services are available to users irrespective of their location, data can be shared among multiple users working together, these data are not available to other users in the case of the computer theft, etc. Taking into account all the above-mentioned advantages, it stands to reason why the cloud computing approach is widely applied, particularly in general-purpose business systems.

However, there are still some disadvantages of cloud computing in practice. Initially, cloud computing assumes permanent connection to an external network, which may pose a problem in the environment

DOI: 10.4018/978-1-7998-2910-2.ch011

with poor Internet connection quality, or the lack thereof. Secondly, significant part of resources engaged, as well as data and information used, are not fully controlled by the user. Despite the fact that mutual obligations between a cloud service user and a cloud service provider are defined by some rules in the form of Service Level Agreement (SLA), practical experience shows that rules of user's behavior in any system do not ensure sufficient level of guarantee for their observance i.e. that data and information will be properly secured. In the real life, one thing are rules, another thing is observance or violation of these rules. It follows that the information security issue is the most critical one in such type of arrangements.

The objective of this chapter is to classify and discuss the information security risks with respect to cloud computing application, with particular focus on electric power utility systems. The chapter deals with four main topics. First, a brief overview of the Information Security Management System standards is given, principally ISO 27001:2013 as the general standard, as well as ISO 27019:2017 and ISO 27017:2015 as the sector-specific standards, with special reference to information security controls, suited for electric power utility and cloud computing environment. Then, the main characteristics of service models in cloud computing are discussed. Based on these considerations, advantages and information security risks of cloud computing application in EPUs systems are addressed. Finally, steps for transition from classical to cloud computing environment are presented, with a particular emphasis on information security aspects within electric power utility systems.

BACKGROUND

Considerations related to cloud computing application in corporate systems, such as Electric Power Utilities, have been discussed in literature by a number of authors in recent years. Some of authors consider possibility of cloud computing application in traditional SCADA (Supervisory Control And Data Acquisition) systems (Y. Chen, J. Chen, & Gan, 2015; Church et al., 2017; Wilhoit, 2013), others discuss application in modern smart grid systems (Bitzer, 2015; Chaichi, Lavoie, Zarrin, Khalifa, & Sue, 2015; Parthasarathy & Karthika, 2017; Popeanga, 2012), etc. Generally, all authors agree that application of the cloud computing has a number of advantages. At the same time, it is evident that an important issue of information security must be seriously addressed, having in mind that these types of systems represent an infrastructure that has a great impact to security of people and utilities.

Generally, information security deals with protection of three main properties of information - confidentiality, integrity and availability (CIA triad). Confidentiality means that data and information are not made available or disclosed to unauthorized individuals, entities or processes. Integrity relates to completeness and accuracy of information. Availability means that the information is accessible and usable upon demand by an authorized entity. These information security properties are covered by general ISO 27001:2013 (International Organization for Standardization [ISO], 2013) standard for Information Security Management System (ISMS) requirements and vocabulary (ISO, 2018). The central idea of the standard is that different threats from environment can endanger or cause harm to information assets due to their vulnerability that represents certain degree or level of risks to which the main information security properties might be exposed. Specific requirements related to some areas of application initiated development and publication of particular, Electric Power Utility-specific standard such as ISO 27019:2017 (ISO, 2017), as well as cloud computing-specific ISO 27017:2015 (ISO, 2015) standard.

Brief Overview of ISO 27001

The unified structure of all management system standards, issued by the ISO, is defined in the document titled Annex SL (ISO, 2012). The ISO 27001:2013 standard was one of the first standards harmonized with this Annex, including basic information security requirements, related to information security risk assessment and treatment, information security incident management and business continuity management. In comparison with other management standards, it could be noted that the ISO 27001:2013 standard has a separate Annex A, dedicated to specific security controls, and aimed at eliminating or reducing the said risks to an acceptable level. The Annex covers 14 areas of information security, 35 control objectives and 114 security controls. An overview of this Annex is given in Table 1. The table shows that areas of security cover a wide range of information security issues, each of which is typically focused on either technical or organizational actions, while others combine both of them. Generally speaking, these security areas, including security objectives and specified controls, represent global guidelines for holistic approach to information security and some kind of reminder for an organization with respect to its main activities. These activities should be implemented to ensure a level of information security adequate to the risk.

However, the application of general-purpose standard (that represents "the key to every door") in particular areas, shows that the existing controls should be modified or the new specific controls should be defined. The scope of these modifications affected the issuance of new sector-specific standards in the ISO 27000 family.

Brief Overview of ISO 27019

The specifics of information security within electric power utility (EPU) systems arises from specifics of process control (usually in real-time conditions), as well as from consequences to security at the level of system as a whole, to people and to facilities in any case of information security breach. Nowadays, these types of systems are exposed to threats from various terrorist groups because any disturbance in electricity supply has serious consequences and enables these groups to achieve their target goals.

The first specifics of ISO 27019 (ISO, 2017) standard, when compared to ISO 27001:2013, is that the acronym "CIA" was inverted to "AIC". In fact, the main information security properties, namely "Confidentiality – Integrity – Availability", in case of electric power utility systems, have a reversed order of importance and priority. These types of systems consider the "Availability" of information as the most important property for the implementation of basic system function. The second important component is the "Integrity", serving to ensure the completeness and accuracy of information, in particular for real-time decisions. Finally, the "Confidentiality" represents the third property, whose importance here is not as high as is in other types of systems.

Additional specifics of EPU are legacy systems. It means that the system "history" is visible across the system components, with facilities and equipment belonging to different technology generations, where some of them are state-of-the art, computer-oriented and remotely controllable, while others are obsolete without any possibility of accessing them remotely. This resulted from the fact that EPUs are large-scale systems, requiring substantial investments and a long time to develop and implement.

List of specific information security controls in EPU systems is given in Table 2. It can be seen from the table that there are 14 new controls (added to 114 standard ones), 5 of them are grouped into 3 new security objectives (added to 35 standard ones) and 9 of them represent an extension to scope of con-

Table 1. Information security controls as per Annex A of ISO 27001:2013

	Area of Security	Number of Objectives	Number of Controls
A5	Information security policy.	1	2
A6	Organization of information security.	2	7
A7	Human resource security.	3	6
A8	Asset management.	3	10
A9	Access control.	4	14
A10	Cryptography.	1	2
A11	Physical and environmental security.	2	15
A12	Operations security.	7	14
A13	Communications security.	2	7
A14	System acquisition, development and maintenance.	3	13
A15	Supplier relationships.	2	5
A16	Information security incident management.	1	7
A17	Information security aspects of business continuity management.	2	4
A18	Compliance.	2	8
	TOTAL	35	114

trols within 5 existing security objectives. The emphasis of the new EPE specific controls is placed on protection of control centers, from the point of view of buildings, hardware and software components of equipment, supporting systems such as electricity supply, air conditioning, etc., protection of communications with peripheral equipment, particularly in the case when such equipment is located in the third-party premises (other EPU organization or consumers).

Brief Overview of ISO 27017

Cloud computing also requires modification of existing information security controls, as well as the application of new, specific ones. List of specific information security controls in cloud computing environment is given in Table 3. As can be seen from the table below, there are 7 new controls (added to 114 standard ones), 3 of them are grouped into 2 new security objectives (added to 35 standard ones) and 4 of them represent an extension to scope of controls within 4 existing security objectives. The emphasis of the new controls is placed on allocation of responsibilities of a service provider and a service customer, as well as the network security control and monitoring of cloud services.

As per ISO 27017 (ISO, 2015) clauses, the cloud service customer should agree with the cloud service provider on an appropriate allocation of information security roles and responsibilities and confirm that it can fulfill its allocated roles and responsibilities. The information security roles and responsibilities of both parties should be stated in an agreement. The cloud service customer should identify and manage its relationship with the customer support and care function of the cloud service provider. The cloud service provider should agree and document an appropriate allocation of information security roles and responsibilities with its cloud service customers, its cloud service providers, and its suppliers.

Table 2. EPU sector-specific controls, as per ISO 27019:2017

	Security Objective / Control
6.1	Internal organization.
6.1.6 ENR	Identification of risks related to external parties.
6.1.7 ENR	Addressing security when dealing with customers.
11.1	Secure areas.
11.1.7 ENR	Securing control centers.
11.1.8 ENR	Securing equipment rooms.
11.1.9 ENR	Securing peripheral sites.
11.3	Security of equipment sited at the premises of the third party (NEW OBJECTIVE).
11.3.1 ENR	Equipment sited at the premises of other energy utility organizations.
11.3.2 ENR	Equipment sited at customer's premises.
11.3.3 ENR	Interconnected and communication systems.
12.8	Legacy systems (NEW OBJECTIVE).
12.8.1 ENR	Treatment of legacy systems.
12.9	Safety functions (NEW OBJECTIVE).
12.9.1 ENR	Integrity and availability of safety functions.
13.1	Network security management.
13.1.4 ENR	Securing process control data communication.
13.1.5 ENR	Logical connection of external process control systems.
14.2	Security in development and support processes.
14.2.10 ENR	Least functionality.
17.2	Redundancies.
17.2.2 ENR	Emergency communication.

CLOUD COMPUTING SERVICES AND DEPLOYMENT MODELS

As per the official definition of the National Institute of Standards and Technology (NIST) within U.S. Department of Commerce (Mell & Grance, 2011), a cloud infrastructure is the collection of hardware and software that enables the five essential characteristics of cloud computing – on-demand self-service, broad network access, resource pooling, rapid elasticity and measured service. There are three cloud computing service models (Mell & Grance, 2011; Raković, 2017), as illustrated in Figure 1:

- **Software as a Service – SaaS**: The customer accesses to different provider's applications running on a cloud infrastructure, using its device through web browser or a program interface. Some of these applications are free of charge, while others are billed, commonly on a monthly or annual subscription basis. In such a model, the customer has no possibility to adapt this application to his/her specific needs, but it eliminates the expenses associated with license agreement, maintenance or investment into hardware or software improvement.
- **Platform as a Service – PaaS**: Development environment is available to the customer with a possibility of creating customer-specific or acquired applications using servers, network infrastruc-

Table 3. Cloud computing sector specific controls, as per ISO 27017:2015

	Security Objective / Control
6.3	Information security roles and responsibilities (NEW OBJECTIVE).
6.3.1 CLD	Shared roles and responsibilities within a cloud computing environment.
8.1	Responsibility for assets.
8.1.5 CLD	Removal of cloud service customer assets.
9.5	Access control to user data in cloud in shared virtual computer environment (NEW OBJECTIVE).
9.5.1 CLD	Segregation in virtual computing environments.
9.5.2 CLD	Virtual machine hardening.
12.1	Operational procedures and responsibilities.
12.1.5 CLD	Administrator's operational security.
12.4	Logging and monitoring.
12.4.5 CLD	Monitoring of cloud services.
13.1	Network security management.
13.1.4 CLD	Alignment of security management for virtual and physical networks.

ture, operating systems, programming languages, storage etc., supported by the provider. In such an arrangement, customer has a control over its application, and the allocated resources are under control of a provider.

- **Infrastructure as a Service – IaaS**: The customer can use computer infrastructure as a virtual platform and can manage processing, storage, networking and other computer resources and can also run a support at the level of both operation system and application. It means that the customer uses servers, software, and storage space or network equipment as a virtual platform, instead of buying them.

Two additional types of cloud computing are recognized by the International Telecommunication Union – Telecommunication Standardization Sector (ITU-T), 2015:

- **Communications as a Service – CaaS**: Represents a combination of SaaS and PaaS solutions.
- **Network as a Service – NaaS**: In such an arrangement, connection and relevant network characteristics are provided to the customer.

Depending on the cloud computing resource customers, NIST (Mell & Grance, 2011) recognizes several types of deployment models. The cloud infrastructure is provisioned for exclusive use by a single organization (private cloud), or group of organizations (community cloud), can be available for open use by general public (public cloud) or can be a combination of the two options (hybrid cloud). These models differ from each other with respect to resources and services used, level of services provided, information security level provided, costs related to it, etc. Certainly, it is not possible to generally declare which of these models is the best one. It is only possible to discuss the optimal solution for each particular case, which is directly associated with the criteria used.

Figure 1. Cloud computing basic service models

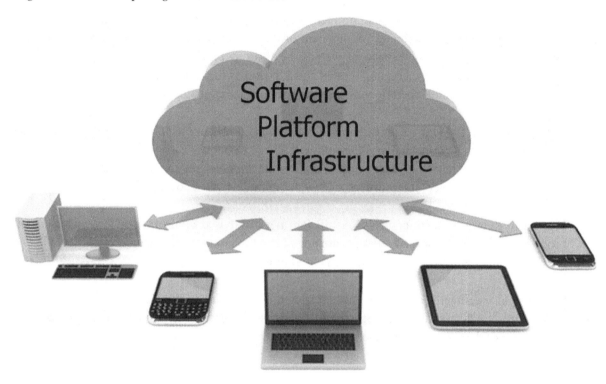

CLOUD COMPUTING RISKS AND VULNERABILITIES

Information security essence and terms used in this area are given in Figure 2 (Raković, 2017). The information asset is exposed to different threats, both external and internal, which can cause some form of harm. Whether it will happen or not depends on the level at which this asset is resistant to impact of threats, described as its vulnerability. Combination of undesired event likelihood (probability that a threat will exploit asset vulnerability) and consequences of the impact on information security represent the information security risk. General-purpose information security management standard ISO 27001 (ISO, 2013) is based on information security risks assessment, as well as on application of security controls to treat them, depending on their acceptability (avoiding, elimination, mitigation, transfer, etc.).

It is evident that cloud computing environment makes certain changes in approach to information security issues, by modifying some of the existing elements and adding the new ones. As per the cited references (Grobauer, Walloschek, & Stocker, 2011), in cloud computing environment the "consequences"

Figure 2. Information security essence and terms

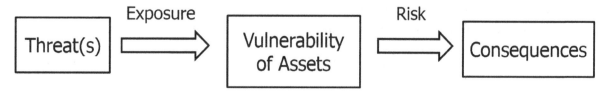

as the risk component have not been changed at all from a cloud customer perspective, but only from a cloud service provider perspective, and are incorporated into a risk assessment. However, a significant change happens in the "likelihood" component of the risk i.e. the cloud computing has changed the attacker's access level and motivation, as well as the effort and the risk. In such circumstances, the "vulnerability" as a resistance to a certain type of attack becomes the key point of interest. The authors recognize four groups of cloud-specific vulnerabilities (Grobauer et al., 2011), as follows:

- Vulnerabilities intrinsic to or prevalent in a core cloud computing technology (web applications and services, virtualization and cryptography, etc.).
- Vulnerabilities that have their root cause in an essential cloud characteristic (unauthorized access to management interface, internet protocol vulnerabilities, data recovery vulnerability, metering and billing evasion, etc.).
- Defects in known security controls (insufficient network-based control, poor key management procedure, the fact that security metrics are not adapted to cloud infrastructure, etc.).
- Prevalent vulnerabilities in state-of-the-art cloud offerings.

The authors also define the cloud reference architecture, consisting of three main parts – supporting IT infrastructure, cloud-specific infrastructure and cloud service consumer – considering cloud-specific vulnerabilities in each of these components.

CLOUD COMPUTING IN EPU: ADVANTAGES AND RISKS

Advantages of Cloud Computing in EPUs

There are several benefits of moving traditional SCADA system as well as modern smart grid applications to the cloud (Inductive Automation, 2011; Manoj, Ashwini, & Vivekkant, 2017; Naveen, Wong, Kobina Danquah, Sidhu, & Abu-Siada, 2016):

- **Operating Expenses Optimization**: In the concept "pay-for-use", operation expenses are cheaper for a company than the costs of buying, installation and maintaining their own hardware and software.
- **On-demand Self-service**: Cloud computing supports elastic harmonization of resources to actual needs. When a company needs more resources, it doesn't need to buy and install new servers, databases, web servers, etc. Additional resource can be easily leased on a virtual cloud-based server.
- **Technical Staff Optimization**: The use of additional resources doesn't mean engagement of additional staff to provide support and maintenance of these resources.
- **Ease Sharing and Accessing Data Anywhere**: The data stored on a cloud server are available and accessible anywhere in the world.
- **Better Collaboration of Project's Participants**: Since information in the cloud is easily accessible, it enables better collaboration of multiple individuals at different levels of the company engaged on particular project.

- **Easy Upgrade and Adding New Applications**: Upgrading of existing applications and installing new ones is easy in the cloud environment. Once application is installed or upgraded, it is instantly available to everyone with access rights.

Risks of Cloud Computing in EPUs

Modern electric power utility systems are larger and more complex than earlier and impose requirements that can be met only through application of advanced technologies. Unfortunately, in spite of significant advantages of modern technology applications, EPU organizations are faced with challenges, which never existed before, particularly with those related to information security (Raković, Mandić Lukić, & Čukić, 2016). A large number of more sophisticated facilities increase their vulnerability to different attacks since the control systems are not isolated but are networked and remotely accessible. In addition, these systems consist of standard hardware and software components and open platforms (Ethernet, TCP/IP, web) that are widely applied; their solutions are well known, including their shortcomings, wireless technologies are increasingly applied, etc.

There are a great number of information security-related risks in cloud computing environment. Some of the most important ones are discussed here, with particular emphasis on EPU systems (Cloud Standards Customer Council [CSCC], 2017; Raković, 2018):

- **Loss of Governance Ownership**: In public cloud deployment model, the customers practically assign the control to a cloud service provider in a great number of issues. Business relationships are governed by a SLA, made between a customer and a service provider. However, there is no guarantee of full commitment of provider in practice to resolve all issues in compliance with customer interests, and there is a high probability of negligence in relation to information security. In EPU systems, regardless of whether the point in question is a real-time service or out of real-time service that requires a large volume of data processing, such loss of governance is not acceptable at all. It means that in these types of systems the only applicable deployment model should be either fully private cloud or hybrid solution, in which the customer i.e. EPU organization retains control over the most critical elements.
- **Responsibility Ambiguity**: Within SLA, information security-related responsibilities are commonly divided between the customer and the provider. In spite of intention of both parties to the agreement to precisely regulate all issues, there is a real risk that some issues will remain uncovered in the process of segregation of duties. Potential consequences of this type of problem depend on a cloud computing service model applied (SaaS, PaaS, IaaS). Sometimes, an imprecision is not evident in regular situations, but can be encountered in certain specific situations. In EPU systems such specific situations can cause catastrophic consequences.
- **Authentication and Authorization**: Access to sensitive cloud services from any point of the Internet requires highly reliable identification of participants (customers, employees, contractors, partners, etc.). In such conditions, it is necessary to establish a strong authentication (participant identification i.e. verification whether an entity is, in fact, what it declares itself to be) and authorization (what authorities the entity has when accessing to a resource i.e. what action is possible to perform –reading only or data change). In EPU systems this issue is critical because of significant consequences it may have on the security of people, equipment, facilities, as well as the system as a whole, in case of any security breach.

- **Isolation Failure**: When the same resource is shared among multiple tenants, a serious problem may occur in case of failure of mechanisms that isolate parts of a common resource, assigned to different customers (store, routing or switching resource, etc) because it could result in information leakage to the public. Such type of attack is known as "Guest –Hopping". In case of EPU systems such type of risk is unacceptable. It means that only deployment model of cloud computing applied can be private, or perhaps a hybrid one, with clear separation of data and other information from other customers, if any.

- **Compliance and Legal Risks**: While attempting to achieve a form of certification related to compliance of its system with industrial standards or regulatory requirements, the cloud computing customer may face the problem if a provider cannot submit an evidence of its own compliance with subject requirements, or if it does not allow the audit by the cloud customer's certification body. It is well known that EPU organizations often certify their management systems according to the valid management standards, in particular quality and information management standards, such as ISO 9001:2015 and ISO 27001:2013, respectively. An audit of such standards asks the organization to demonstrate fulfillment of requirements in many different forms (records, audit on site, business continuity testing, etc). In this auditing process, cooperation with the cloud service provider is required. Lack of this cooperation could affect the opportunity of EPU organizations to certify these systems and can cause serious harm to a company's reputation, which is of particular importance in market conditions.

- **Handling of Security Incidents**: Within SLA, a customer may decide to delegate detection, reporting and subsequent management of information security breaches to the provider, although these incidents have direct impacts on the customer itself. In such a case, the SLA should define precise rules related to timely notification of cloud computing customer of any information security incident as to enable the customer to take appropriate actions to eliminate, or at least mitigate the potential consequences. This segment of SLA should be the subject of particular attention in case of EPU systems, because any delay in notification of a security breach, or problem hush up, can have catastrophic consequences.

- **Management Interface Vulnerability**: In case of public cloud, resource management interfaces are accessible through the Internet, thus increasing the risks because they allow access to a large number of resources, particularly combined with remote access, taking into account vulnerability of web browsers. In case of EPU systems, any form of remote access, regardless of a deployment model applied (public, private, hybrid), should be implemented with due care, through the application of full set of controls, to avoid potential information leakage problems.

- **Application Protection**: Applications are usually protected using Defense-in-Depth solutions, which enable clear segregation of physical and virtual resources and application of Demilitarized zone (DMZ) concept. When it is necessary to decide to delegate infrastructure security responsibilities to a service provider, the customer should redefine perimeter security at the network level, applying necessary controls at the user, application and data level, enable these controls to also be applied in cloud services since the cloud plays a role of the traditional data center. In case of EPU systems, this segment should be carefully defined within SLA, having in mind always mentioned orientation to private or hybrid deployment models.

- **Data Protection**: It is evident that there are highly sensitive data, and any loss or unavailability of these data can cause significant problems to the customer. Therefore, handling these data represents a very difficult task for the cloud service provider. This problem is particularly visible in multiple data transfer (e.g., when the cloud service provider uses subcontractors in service provision). In case of EPU systems this issue is essential for the customer and it can be resolved by applying the private or hybrid cloud, in which the customer does not cede control over the data to the provider.

- **Personal Data Regulation**: Any personal data should be treated according to the requirements of laws and/or regulations. It includes not only the protection of such personal data, but also rights granted to the data subject to inspect, correct or delete their data, or to request that their data is transferred elsewhere.

- **Malicious Behavior of Insiders**: Malicious actions of people working within the organization can cause significant damage because of the access and authority they have. This issue is very complex in the cloud computing environment since such activity may occur within either the customer or the provider's organization or in both of them. Level of complexity and criticality is higher in case of EPU organizations, but, unfortunately, it cannot be resolved generally. The only way to handle it is appropriate checking of people nominated for these jobs, segregation of duties that does not delegate maximum authority to any participant, regular control of people and observance of procedures, logging person's activities within the system, etc.

- **Business Failure of the Provider**: In case of any business problems or bankruptcy of the provider, data and applications essential to the customer's business can be unavailable for an extended period of time. This problem can be very important in case of EPU systems, and it should be resolved by establishing alternative resources to represent a redundancy. With respect to consequences, such event in case of EPU system has a character of catastrophic one. It must necessarily be taken into account in defining business continuity plan, including "Disaster Recovery" location, where the essential data needed for recovery in case of catastrophic events (disasters) are stored.

- **Service Unavailability**: This can be caused by hardware, software or communication network failures. It is known that majority of services within EPU have reliability requirements expressed in several "nines" (e.g., 0.999). It means that, within SLA, it is necessary to explicitly point out to provider level of availability as an element of quality of service to be provided. There are several technical actions that enable such level of availability (main and stand by transmission routes, doubled central processing units, doubled power supply units etc.).

- **Vendor Lock-in**: Dependency on specific solutions applied within services of a particular cloud service provider could lead to the customer being tied to that provider, and there is a risk data or services to be unavailable in case of changing the provider. If there is no interoperability of interfaces associated with cloud services, it can also cause dependency of a particular provider and can make a problem to switch to another provider. In case of EPU system, this segment should clearly be defined within SLA with respect to technical solutions applied. It is necessary to avoid any proprietary solutions which cannot be applied by other providers.

- **Insecure or Incomplete Data Deletion**: When the contract with a provider is terminated for any reason, the critical issue is to provide deletion of the customer's data related to service provided, because it assumes deletion of data even at locations where they have been backed up. In case when these data are mixed on the same media with other customers' data, it is very difficult to erase them selectively. It means that multi-tenancy (the sharing of hardware resources) represents a higher risk to the customer than in case of dedicated hardware, although the second one has higher costs. In case of cloud computing arrangement for EPU systems it means that the only solution is to use a dedicated hardware in both the main and backup arrangements. In addition,

SLA should enable the customer to have full control over locations where these data are stored, to allow systematic and secure data deletion in case of termination of contract with the provider.

- **Visibility and Audit**: Every system faces the problems periodically. To protect themselves, users within organization sometimes create a "shadow", i.e. parallel systems without explicit approval of the organization. Key challenges for the security team are to know about all uses of cloud services within the organization (what resources are being used, for what purpose, to what extent, and by whom), understand what laws, regulations and policies may apply to such uses, and to understand consequences to information assets. In case of EPU systems, any parallel and unofficial systems are not acceptable and should be prevented with both technical and organizational actions.

All the above-mentioned risks should be taken into account in the choice of deployment model of cloud computing service, in the process of SLA preparation, and should be treated in a proper way to eliminate and/or mitigate its negative impact to information security.

TRANSITION FROM CLASSICAL TO CLOUD COMPUTING ENVIRONMENT

Transition from classical IT environment to cloud computing represents a very complex process that requires time, financial and human resources. From the point of view of the main topic of this chapter, it is very important to provide that information security is kept or improved, if possible. To enable the customers to assess the risks and to manage information security in this transition process, particular guide is defined (CSCC, 2017), consisting of ten global steps to include as follows:

Step 1: Ensure Effective Governance, Risk and Compliance Processes: This step applies to policies and procedures established within an organization related to information security and legal compliance. With respect to traditional IT environment the situation becomes more complex because the risks may be different for several reasons - shared responsibilities between the cloud computing customer and the provider (depending on what service model is used – IaaS, PaaS or SaaS), the fact that technical resources, as well as operation controls, belong to service provider, interface used by customer to access the cloud service, etc. The cloud computing customers should be aware of these risks and to decide what level of these risks is acceptable to them. These risks also include aspects related to specific laws and regulations applied, because some specific obligations can be imposed on both the customer and the provider. As mentioned earlier in this chapter, the general-purpose standard for information security management ISO 27001 (ISO, 2013) within Annex 1 defines 114 controls, and a particular ISO 27017 standard (ISO, 2015) defines in which level these controls are modified in case of the cloud computing environment, and defines 7 new controls, specific to this environment.

Step 2: Audit Operational and Business Processes: It is very important for the customer to provide audit of all provider's activities by engaging an independent auditor. This should be the subject of their mutual agreement (SLA). From the customer's point of view, it is essential to provide isolation of its applications and data in a shared, multi-tenant environment, protection of its assets from unauthorized access by the provider's staff and appropriate notification in case of any security breach without unnecessary delay.

Step 3: Manage People, Roles and Identities: The use of cloud computing assumes engagement of both the provider's employees that have an access to user data and applications and customer's employees that perform some operations within provider's system. It requires clear definition of rules who and in which way can access to resources, clear definition of roles of all participants and establishment of identity and access management functions including monitoring and logging of any access to customer data and applications. From the customer's point of view it is very important that the provider supports robust i.e. strong multi-factor authentication and, if necessary, biometric identity verification.

Step 4: Ensure Proper Protection of Data and Information: Distributed infrastructure and shared responsibilities within the cloud places particular emphasis on the security of data and information that are stored or transferred. The risks associated with data are very different -theft or unauthorized use of data, unauthorized handling or change of data, unavailability of data, etc. General approach to data security is defined through controls from ISMS standard (ISO, 2013) and specific controls for cloud environment given within sector-specific standard (ISO, 2015). The responsibility for application of these controls is different, depending on cloud computing service model applied. In IaaS arrangement the responsibility predominantly lies with the customer, in SaaS arrangement is predominantly placed on the provider, because the customer has no direct control over the data and applications, while in PaaS arrangement the responsibility is shared between the customer and the provider. Controls that should be implemented to provide security of data and applications in cloud computing environment include (CSCC, 2017) creating a data assets catalog, taking into consideration the forms of data, taking into account privacy requirements usually implying some limitations on the use and access to personal identifiable information, applying procedures which ensure confidentiality, integrity and availability of information, as well as applying identity and access management.

Step 5: Enforce Privacy Policies: At a global level, the privacy and protection of personal data are promoted through laws and regulations related to collection, processing and store of personally identifiable information (PII). This is the subject of particular ISO 27018 (ISO, 2019) standard. It is necessary to note that there is a difference between the security and the privacy. Security is related to protection of attacks, independently if they are oriented to theft of personally identifiable data or not. Privacy is predominantly oriented to personal data collected, processed and stored within an organization that could be threatened by unconscientious behavior of participants or software bugs, and not only by the activities of malicious persons. Three years ago, the European Union adopted a new regulation 679/2016 on the protection of personal data, known as the General Data Protection Regulation – GDPR, which entered into force in May 2016 and applies since 25 May 2018 (De Hert, Papakonstantinou, & Kamara, 2011; European Union, 2016). As per terminology of the GDPR, in cloud computing environment the customer plays a role of the data controller i.e. the responsibility for protecting the data remains with the customer even in arrangements when this responsibility may be shared with others. Even in cases when the organization relies on the third party in data handling, the data controller remains responsible for any loss, damage or misuse of the data. One of the most useful possibilities in cloud computing environment is to anonymize data before its use in the cloud service (so-called "pseudonymization") and to keep the relationship between the anonymous records with the real people in a separate database, not available within the cloud.

Step 6: Assess the Security Provisions for Cloud Applications: An organization (both the cloud service provider and the customer) should be proactive in the protection of all applications critical for its business activities to protect them from threats both outside and inside. Each service model (IaaS, PaaS, SaaS) requires particular considerations of protection aspects, taking into account that each level of protection has its own costs related to technology solutions, resources, auditing, etc. It is very important to establish appropriate balance between these costs and the benefits taking into account that any security breach can cause significant consequences related to potential liability or reputation loss of the organization.

Step 7: Ensure Security of Cloud Networks and Connections: Obligation of a cloud service provider is to ensure proceeding of legitimate traffic and to prevent any kind of malicious activity. The provider should ensure appropriate level of protection for all customers from both external and internal impacts. The controls related to external network impacts include (CSCC, 2017) traffic monitoring, protection from "denial-of-service" threat, detection and prevention of intrusion, event-related recording, etc. The controls related to internal network impacts should protect customers from each other, protect provider's network from customers (segregation) and monitor intrusion attempts within the network.

Step 8: Evaluate Security Controls on Physical Infrastructure and Facilities: This step is oriented towards expansion of requirements and controls from Annex A of the ISMS standard (ISO, 2013) to physical structure and equipment of provider, not only the customer (physical security in secure areas, control of the personnel working in secure areas, appropriate maintenance of supporting services as electricity supply, air conditioning, etc., particular protection regimes for the most critical equipment, including cabling, control of assets removal, as well as re-use of equipment, establishing backup, redundancy and business continuity plans, including disaster recovery location, etc).

Step 9: Manage Security Terms in the Cloud Service Agreement: Independently of deployment mode, two parties in cloud computing arrangement – the customer and the service provider – regulate their mutual obligations by an agreement. First, this agreement should define scope of work, roles and responsibilities of each party. Then, the service level parameters should be established, measurable and verifiable, if possible. Finally, security aspects should be carefully considered within the agreement. One of the most important obligations of the service provider is to notify the customers in a timely manner of any breach of its data or information occurred, taking actions to mitigate its consequences, performing forensic analysis to avoid undesired event recurrence, resolving of indemnity requirements, etc.

Step 10: Understand the Security Requirements of the Exit Process: It is necessary to define obligations of all parties in case of legitimate situation related to termination of cooperation. In such a case, two important issues should be resolved. The first is related to provider's obligations to permanently erase from the system all customer data after defined period of time, including backup copies of data along with data derived from them, etc. The second is transition of customer activities into new environment without any loss or breach of data that assumes retrieval of all data in a suitable secure form, retaining of backups for some period of time after termination of arrangement, event logs conducting for activities related to transition process, etc.

These ten steps are also generally applicable in EPU environment with some system specifics. Particular attention should be paid to steps 5 and 10. Attention related to step 5 is necessary because EPU systems, especially electricity distribution organizations, collect and store a set of data about their consumers, predominantly residential ones (address, names, owner identity, number of family members, distribution of consumption during the year, actual consumption, etc). For example, actual consumption or its distribution during a year provides information of habits and behavior of natural persons living in the house or flat, their presence or absence, etc. which represents a basis for profiling and misuse of this information. Attention to step 10 is necessary because any dependence of EPU organization on service provider should be treated very carefully, both from the point of view of quality of service provided and guaranteed level of information availability.

It is clear that cloud computing enables users to have higher level of services related to information security in comparison with situation of individual computer, because these activities require both the knowledge and experience. Decision related to transition towards cloud environment represents some kind of compromise between the advantages and disadvantages. It should be understood that the transition process is very complex, and includes technical and organizational, as well as economic and legal aspects.

FUTURE RESEARCH DIRECTIONS

It is evident that the cloud computing represents an emerging trend because of its numerous advantages, particularly in general-purpose systems. In January 2019, the traditional annual survey of actual trends in the cloud computing area was published (Flexera, 2019). As per this survey, several trends were reported. First, public cloud adoption is growing, while private cloud use is declining. Then, multi-cloud represents the preferred strategy among enterprises, with trend to apply hybrid solutions (combining public and private clouds). Finally, the number one priority in 2019 is cloud cost optimization.

In spite of limitations related to applicability of the cloud computing approach within corporate systems as is electric power utility, due to the recognized problems and risks, it is clear that above mentioned trend is very difficult to stop. In such conditions, it is very important to concentrate efforts on investigation of possibilities to decrease risks related to information security within these types of systems. This implies application of both technical and organizational actions, based on the standards and best practices. Particular attention should be paid to issues related to service level agreement between EPUs as the cloud computing users and the cloud computing providers. From the point of view of issues discussed within this chapter, it is evident that hybrid cloud is preferred deployment model, as a compromise between too expensive private clouds and security critical public ones. One of the most important organizational actions is education of people because all breach investigation reports point out that information security problems are predominantly caused by insiders' activities.

CONCLUSION

In spite of their orientation towards modern technologies, it is rather dangerous to mechanically apply cloud computing solutions, particularly within the infrastructure-related systems, where any oversight in the area of information security can have unforeseeable consequences for the security of people, facilities, equipment, as well as for the services provided to population. The fact that the cloud computing becomes more popular and has been increasingly applied in recent years shows that the advantages can overcome the risks and problems to which the cloud computing is exposed. Therefore, it can be concluded that only private or hybrid type of cloud computing is applicable within the electric power utilities since each particular solution enables appropriate level of control that a user can have over the data and information used.

REFERENCES

Bitzer, B. (2015). Application of cloud computing for power systems. Trivent Publishing. Retrieved November 10, 2019, from https://trivent-publishing.eu/pdfdownload/18.BertholdBitzer.pdf

Chaichi, N., Lavoie, J., Zarrin, S., Khalifa, R., & Sue, F. (2015). A comprehensive assessment of cloud computing for smart grid applications: A multi-perspectives framework. In *Proceedings of the PICMET 2015: Management of the Technology Age* (pp. 2541-2547). Portland, OR: Portland State University. 10.1109/PICMET.2015.7273227

Chen, Y., Chen, J., & Gan, J. (2015). Experimental study in cloud-computing-based electric power SCADA system. *ZTE Communications*, *13*(3), 33–41.

Church, P., Mueller, H., Ryan, C., Gogouvitis, S. V., Goscinski, A., & Tari, Z. (2017). Migration of a SCADA system to IaaS clouds – a case study. *Journal of Cloud Computing: Advances, Systems, and Application*, *6*(11), 1–12.

Cloud Standards Customer Council (CSCC). (2017). *Security for cloud computing – Ten steps to ensure success* (version 3.0). Retrieved November 10, 2019, from https://www.omg.org/cloud/deliverables/CSCC-Security-for-Cloud-Computing-10-Steps-to-Ensure-Success.pdf

De Hert, P., Papakonstantinou, V., & Kamara, I. (2014). *The new cloud computing ISO/IEC 27018 standard through the lens of the EU legislation on data protection* (Working Paper, vol. 1, no. 2). Brussels Privacy Hub. Retrieved November 10, 2019, from https://www.brusselsprivacyhub.eu/publications/wp12.html

European Union. (2016). *Protection of natural persons with regard to the processing of personal data and on the free movement of such data* (Regulation [EU] 2016/679). Retrieved November 10, 2019, from https://eur-lex.europa.eu/eli/reg/2016/679/oj

Flexera. (2019, February 27). Cloud computing trends: 2019 state of the cloud survey [Web log comment]. Retrieved November 10, 2019, from https://www.flexera.com/blog/cloud/2019/02/cloud-computing-trends-2019-state-of-the-cloud-survey

Grobauer, B., Walloschek, T., & Stocker, E. (2011). Understanding cloud computing vulnerabilities. *IEEE Security and Privacy*, *9*(2), 50–57. doi:10.1109/MSP.2010.115

Inductive Automation. (2011). *Cloud-based SCADA systems: The benefits & risks* (White Paper). Retrieved November 10, 2019, from https://www.controlglobal.com/assets/11WPpdf/111202-inductiveautomation-cloud.pdf

International Organization for Standardization (ISO). (2012). Annex SL: Proposals for management system standards. *ISO/IEC Directives Part 1, Consolidated ISO Supplement – Procedures specific to ISO*.

International Organization for Standardization (ISO). (2013). Information technology – Security techniques – Information security management systems – Requirements. *Standard ISO/IEC 27001:2013*.

International Organization for Standardization (ISO). (2015). Information technology – Security techniques – Code of practice for information security controls based on ISO/IEC 27002 for cloud services. *Standard ISO/IEC 27017:2015/ITU-T X.1631*.

International Organization for Standardization (ISO). (2017). Information technology – Security techniques – Information security controls for the energy utility industry. *Standard ISO/IEC 27019:2017*.

International Organization for Standardization (ISO). (2018). Information technology – Security techniques – Information security management systems – Overview and vocabulary. *Standard ISO/IEC 27000:2018*.

International Organization for Standardization (ISO). (2019). Information technology – Security techniques – Code of practice for personally identifiable information (PII) in public clouds acting as PII processors. *Standard ISO/IEC 27018:2019*.

International Telecommunication Union – Telecommunication Standardization Sector (ITU-T). (2015). Security framework for cloud computing. [Geneva, ITU-T.]. *ITU-T Recommendation, X*, 1601.

Manoj, H. R., Ashwini, R., & Vivekkant, J. (2017). Real time monitoring of substation by using cloud computing. *International Journal of Engineering Research and Application, 7*(9), 1–4.

Mell, P., & Grance, T. (2011). *The NIST definition of cloud computing (NIST Special Publication 800-145)*. Gaithersburg, MD: U.S. National Institute of Standards and Technology.

Naveen, P., Wong, K. I., Kobina Danquah, M., Sidhu, A. S., & Abu-Siada, A. (2016). Cloud computing for energy management in smart grid – an application survey. In *Proceedings of the IOP Conference Series*. Miri, Malaysia: IOP Publishing Ltd. *Materials Science and Engineering, 121*, 1–11.

Parthasarathy, S., & Karthika, M. (2017). Cloud computing support for smart grid applications. *International Journal on Advances in Computer and Electronics Engineering, 2*(11), 11–17.

Popeanga, J. (2012). Cloud computing and smart grids. *Database Systems Journal, 3*(3), 57–66.

Raković, R. (2017). *Bezbednost informacija – osnove i smernice* [*Information security: Fundamentals and guidelines*]. Belgrade, Serbia: Academic Mind.

Raković, R. (2018). Aspekti bezbednosti informacija u okruženju računarstva u oblaku [Information security aspects in cloud computing environment]. *InfoM, 17*(66), 26–30.

Raković, R., Mandić Lukić, J., & Čukić, N. (2016). Information security in electric power utilities' environment. In *Proceedings of South East Europe Regional Conference* (Paper P07). Portoroz, Slovenia: CIGRÉ.

Wilhoit, K. (2013, April 4). SCADA in the cloud – A security conundrum? *Trend Micro Incorporated* [Web log comment]. Retrieved November 10, 2019, from https://blog.trendmicro.com/trendlabs-security-intelligence/scada-in-the-cloud-a-security-conundrum/

ADDITIONAL READING

Choeichum, A., Ponyangnok, N., Krutgard, Y., & Inyoo, W. (2018). PEA SCADA online monitoring. *International Journal of Computer Electrical Engineering, 10*(3), 195–204. doi:10.17706/IJCEE.2018.10.3.195-204

Cloud Standards Customer Council. (2016). *Practical guide to hybrid cloud computing* [PowerPoint slides]. Retrieved November 10, 2019, from http://www.cloud-council.org/CSCC-Practical-Guide-to-Hybrid-Cloud-Computing-BrightTALK-4-21-16.pdf

Cloud Standards Customer Council. (2017). *Practical guide to cloud computing* (version 3.0). Retrieved November 10, 2019, from https://www.omg.org/cloud/deliverables/CSCC-Practical-Guide-to-Cloud-Computing.pdf

Diouani, S., & Medromi, H. (2018). Green cloud computing: Efficient energy-aware and dynamic resources management in data centres. *International Journal of Advanced Computer Science and Applications, 9*(7), 124–127. doi:10.14569/IJACSA.2018.090717

Firdaus, Z., Jamil, N., Qassim, Q. S., Rusli, M. E., Ja'affar, N., Maslina, D., & Hasan, H. C. (2018). A study on security vulnerabilities assessment and quantification in SCADA systems. *Journal of Engineering and Applied Sciences (Asian Research Publishing Network), 13*(6), 1338–1346.

Nasr, M. S., & Abdullah, A. N. (2017). Design and implementation of IoT cloud moveable SCADA supported by GSM for industrial applications. *Journal of Babylon University. Engineering and Science, 25*(2), 409–424.

Object Management Group (OMG). (2019, February). *Practical guide to cloud service agreements* (version 3.0) (Discussion Paper from the OMG Cloud Working Group). Retrieved November 10, 2019, from https://www.omg.org/cloud/deliverables/Practical-Guide-to-Cloud-Service-Agreements.pdf

Object Management Group (OMG). (2019, March). *Practical guide to cloud deployment technologies* (version 1.0) (Document mars/2019-03-03). Retrieved November 10, 2019, from https://www.omg.org/cloud/deliverables/Practical-Guide-to-Cloud-Deployment-Technologies.pdf

Perrons, R. K. (2015). How the energy sector could get it wrong with cloud computing. *Energy Exploration & Exploitation, 33*(2), 217–226. doi:10.1260/0144-5987.33.2.217

Zheng, L., & Yao, J. (2016). The construction of power cloud integrated with heterogeneous application service systems. In *Proceedings of the International Conference on Communications, Information, Management and Network Security* (pp. 345-348). Paris: Atlantis Press. 10.2991/cimns-16.2016.86

KEY TERMS AND DEFINITIONS

Authentication: The act of proving identity of a computer system user. Actually, this is a process of verifying that user (person, computer etc.) is what it claims to be. This process can be based on something the user knows (password, personal identification number – PIN, etc.), something the user has (ID card, security token, etc.) or something the user is (fingerprint, retinal pattern, signature, voice, face, etc).

Authorization: Process of verifying that user (person, computer etc.) is permitted to take an action within the system, usually after successful authentication. It consists of a predefined set of permissions and restrictions for the particular user (read-only rights, read/write rights, change rights, etc.).

Cloud Computing: The new concept in computing, in comparison with the traditional one. It assumes on-demand availability of computer system resources, particularly data storage and computing power, based on resource sharing and cost minimization, typically applying a "pay-as-you-go" model.

Cloud Computing Service Customer: An individual or an organization that uses cloud computing services from Cloud Providers.

Cloud Computing Service Provider: An individual or an organization responsible for making cloud computing services available to Cloud Customers.

Hybrid Cloud: Cloud environment that represents a combination of two or more clouds (private, community or public). It retains and respects the specifics of the customers in comparison with other ones that use benefits of sharing common resources.

Information Assets: Everything that has a value to the organization. It can generally be classified into six categories – data (in all forms), software (system, application, development), hardware (computers, servers, printers, plotters, etc.), services (computer and communication services, general services – electricity supply, heating, air-conditioning etc.), people (number and competence of employees) and non-material assets (reputation, image of organization, certificates and licenses, awards, etc.).

Information Security: Preservation of basic properties of information (confidentiality, integrity and availability), whereby other properties can also be involved (authenticity, accountability, non-repudiation, reliability, etc.).

Private Cloud: Cloud infrastructure operated solely for a single organization.

Service Level Agreement: The document that regulates the relationship between a cloud computing service provider and a cloud computing service customer, depending on the cloud computing service model applied (infrastructure, platform, software, communications or network as a service).The agreement defines mutual obligations of each party, parameters of the service provided, as well as the data and information security aspects of the arrangement.

Chapter 12

Energy Internet:
Architecture, Emerging Technologies, and Security Issues

Slavica V. Boštjančič Rakas

(iD) https://orcid.org/0000-0002-0551-3070

Mihailo Pupin Institute, University of Belgrade, Serbia

ABSTRACT

This chapter presents the development of the Energy Internet throughout the history as an evolutionary solution based on modern technological development and needs, with the respect of its architecture, key features, and key concepts, such as energy router, prosumer, and virtual power plant. The architecture of modern IT support for the electric power sector is considered, including its basic characteristics, the integration of contemporary information and communication technologies, such as cloud and fog computing, as well as the security and quality of service issues that arise with the application of these technologies. This chapter provides an overview of recent research related to the concept of Energy Internet and identifies gaps and directions for further research.

INTRODUCTION

Electric power industry is constantly evolving. Since the beginning of the use of electrical energy, i.e., the second industrial revolution, power utility systems have experienced four development phases, from decentralized system through centralized and distributed systems to intelligent and fully connected power utility system. The latest is also known as the Industry 4.0, which represents a part of the fourth industrial revolution.

Advanced technological development of sensor and metering equipment, as well as the trends toward more optimal integration of distributed energy resources (DERs) have influenced the creation of a platform for innovative form of power utility system, also known as Energy Internet, Internet of Energy or Smart Grid 2.0 (J. Cao & Yang, 2013; Jaradat, Jarrah, Bousselham, Jararweh, & Al-Ayyoub, 2015; K. Wang et al., 2017b; You, L. Jin, Zong, & Bindner, 2015). Such a system represents a wide area net-

DOI: 10.4018/978-1-7998-2910-2.ch012

work (WAN), which integrates energy flow with the business and operational data flows to provide for an intelligent management of the power utility system. Information and communication technologies (ICT), especially technologies such as cloud computing, Internet of Things (IoT), Big data analytics, mobile Internet, are becoming a part of electrical energy sector, in all of its segments, including generation, transmission, distribution and sale of electric power (Navigant, 2018). So Energy Internet, which integrates energy technology and ICT, represents a complex cyber-physical system. Such an integration also provides a detailed insight to generation and consumption of energy, as well as prediction of future activities in order to improve energy efficiency and reduce overall costs. According to some predictions, there will be soon more than 800 million of intelligent electronic devices installed worldwide (Jaradat et al., 2015). In order to enable more thorough tracking and planning, information should be collected in short time intervals (e.g., 15 seconds), which will produce around 77 billion of daily measurements. The IoT is used, in power utility systems, to collect and analyze real-time data for intelligent energy management with the purpose of increasing operational and communication efficiencies (Sani et al., 2019). It also improves visibility of system's objects, optimizes management of DERs, reduces energy losses and decreases overall costs.

However, the use of ICT technologies enhances the risk regarding cyber security attacks that could negatively affect the electrical power grid. The number of registered cyber attacks is increasing in the recent years, thus making the power utility systems much more exposed to security threats. These attacks can potentially put at risk a whole industrial process (Lamba, Simková, & Rossi, 2019; Macek, Dordevic, Timcenko, Bojovic, & Milosavljevic, 2014; Markovic-Petrovic, Stojanovic, & Bostjancic Rakas, 2019).

This chapter aims to present an overview of recent research related to the concept of Energy Internet, to assess their maturity for implementation in real networks, and to identify gaps and directions for further research. First, the development of the Energy Internet and introduction to the concepts such as prosumers, virtual power plants, microgrids, smart grids and energy router, are presented. In addition, heterogeneous DERs and increasing amount of data are combined to obtain more flexible, personalized, and efficient power utility systems. Further, application of cloud and fog computing in the Energy Internet has been considered. In order to handle a huge amount of data, a promising solution should be cloud computing, which can provide for the following facilities for intelligent power utility systems: data storage, management of DERs and development of virtual power plants. Despite these advantages, cloud computing introduces risks regarding cyber security and quality of service (QoS). Special attention is dedicated to security issues in cloud environment.

As a possible solution to overcome the security risks in cloud computing, fog computing, as an emerging technology, enables distributed management, reduced latency and improved security. Cyber security of fog computing environment as a part of Energy Internet has been addressed in more details. The chapter ends with the conclusions and guidelines for the future research directions in the area.

BACKGROUND

Energy Internet was first systematically discussed in 2011 as a new system for energy utilization that integrates renewable energy sources (RESs), distributed power plants and energy storage technologies based on Internet technology (Rifkin, 2011).

Since then many researchers tackled these issues by addressing different aspects of such a complex system. Zhong et al. (2016) proposed Software defined Energy Internet as a hierarchical energy control architecture. This architecture assumes separation of energy, data, and control planes, as well as the three types of energy routers. Control plane is in charge of decision making regarding the global energy management, data plane is responsible for decision making regarding energy-related data services, while energy plane with energy routers only keeps basic intelligence for energy control execution.

Energy Internet architecture constructed of six layers, namely Business Layer, Use Case Layer, Operation Layer, Communication Layer, Interface Layer and Appliance Layer, has been proposed in (Zhou, Ni, & Zhu, 2017). The architecture is built taking into account the Smart Grid Architecture Model by the European Commission, the Local Area Grid concept by US Consortium for Intelligent Management of Electric-power Grid, the US green energy grid infrastructure and National Institute of Standards and Technology framework for smart grid interoperability.

A prototype of China's first conceptual solar-based smart micro Energy Internet has been presented in (Mei et al., 2017), together with the energy management scheme that is based on engineering game-theory. It represents a distributed form of Energy Internet and is capable of multi-criteria self-approaching-optimum dispatch and control strategies based on engineering game-theory methods. Another Internet of Energy platform for management of smart microgrids has been proposed in (Marzal, Gonzáles-Medina, Salas-Puente, Garcerá, & Figueres, 2019) and it represents a flexible, distributed and embedded communication platform for collecting, processing and analyzing the data from microgrids for monitoring and control purposes. This communication platform is based on point-to-point communications that can work in synchronous and asynchronous modes. The authors also designed Internet of Energy protocol and routing algorithm for control and monitoring of smart microgrids.

A community Energy Internet is proposed by N. Liu et al. (2018), as an integration of electric and thermal networks, to improve the economy of energy system. This system introduces a framework for energy sharing for prosumers (heat or electricity prosumers).

Even though the concept of Energy Internet is still mostly discussed in academic circles, there are companies offering some specific Energy Internet applications, and also, different countries take part in the development of such a system through different projects financed by their governments.

Future Renewable Electric Energy Delivery and Management Systems (FREEDM) project was launched in the USA, in 2008, where the Energy Internet consists of plug and play interfaces, energy router and a dedicated operating system based on open standards (A. Huang, Crow, Heydt, Zheng, & Dale, 2011). In the same year, German Ministry for Economic Affairs and Energy started E-Energy project that is based on ICT and including the users in establishing the balance between energy generation and consumption (Block & Briegel, 2010). Digital Grid was presented in 2011 in Japan that uses Internet technology to reduce chain failures in large areas and to highly integrate renewable sources, with dividing big synchronized power utility network into several smaller local synchronized power utility networks (Abe, Taoka, & McQuilkin, 2011). Chinese electric power company (State Grid Corporation of China) proposed in 2015 a Global Energy Internet concept, i.e., globally connected, highly intelligent network that is based on high voltage network as a backbone, and is focused to transmission of clean (green) energy (H. Chen, Teng, & Bu, 2018).

The US company AutoGrid, founded at the Stanford University, offers Energy Internet platform that allows optimization and management of distributed energy sources, virtual power plant services and real-time management of energy storage (AutoGrid, n.d.). Silver Power Systems, a company from UK, offers Energy Management Platform for control and management of energy sources, storage and assets by using IoT and Big Data analytics. This four-layer software architecture also enables customized solutions according to specific customer's needs (Silver Power Systems, n.d.). Redgrid is working on a protocol named Internet of Energy, which can be a part of devices that generate, consume and storage electric energy. This protocol provides their mutual communication and it consists of two layers: communication and application layers (Redgrid, n.d.).

POWER UTILITY SYSTEMS' DEVELOPMENT THROUGH HISTORY

Since the second industrial revolution at the end of nineteenth century, technologies for generation and consumption of electrical energy went through four major development phases (Kumar & Gupta, 2018):

1. **Decentralized Power Utility System:** At the beginning of the use of electricity, in the second industrial revolution, technical level of electrical energy generation and consumption was relatively low. The demand for electricity was met by small generators with low technological level and low production. Such a system was isolated and not very efficient.
2. **Centralized Power Utility System:** In the era of accelerated industrialization, the technology of electricity generating has made great progress. The main sources of electrical energy were different interconnected power plants. Electric energy generation became independent and important industrial sector. Centralized production of great amount of electric energy has improved, to great extent, the efficiency of electricity supply. Centralized production, long-range power transmission and stable supply have decreased the costs intensively.
3. **Distributed Power Utility System:** As a part of the third industrial revolution and with increasing serious problems related to the necessary resources and negative impact on the environment due to use of certain types of power plants, it became very important to build a cleaner or environmentally-friendly power utility system (Lund, Mikkola, & Ypyä, 2015). Rapid development of technologies related to renewable energy sources, i.e., wind farms and solar power plants, allowed for development of distributed generation of electricity and microgrids. On one hand there was the tendency of less reliance on electricity obtained from fossil fuels and on the long distance transmission of electricity. On the other hand, the need for efficient distribution of electricity and reduction of costs for distributed energy sources increased. Therefore, it was very important to provide the balance between the supply and the demand of electricity, improve energy efficiency and to promote sustainable development. Distributed power utility system was complementary with the traditional centralized power utility system.
4. **Intelligent and Connected Power Utility System:** Is a part of the Industry 4.0. ICT technologies become, ever more, a part of the traditional industrial sectors, including power sector. With cloud computing, IoT, Big Data analytics, and mobile Internet, the traditional power utility system becomes more and more intelligent. Smart metering as well as acquisition and processing of large amount of data are of the key importance. Big Data analytics and emergence of targeted marketing strategies enabled two-way interaction and QoS improvement. New products, services and business models are emerging.

The main goal of evolution is a migration of power utility system towards Energy Internet, i.e., the creation of smart, efficient, safe, flexible, personalized and sustainable system for generation, transmission, distribution and consumption of electricity, that will enhance the quality of life and that will promote economic and social development.

Table 1. Characteristics of development phases of power utility systems

Decentralized	Centralized	Distributed	Intelligent and Connected
• Small. • Isolated. • Self-sufficient. • Inefficient. • Low technological level.	• Industrial sector. • Big. • Efficient. • Transmission network. • High level of pollution.	• Diverse. • Small range. • Renewable sources. • Ecological. • Flexible. • Low level of pollution.	• Intelligent. • Connected. • Digitalized. • Large amount of data. • Interactive. • Personalized. • Efficient.

Table 1 summarizes the main characteristics of power utility system development phases.

ENERGY INTERNET

Key Concepts

This subchapter provides a description of key Energy Internet concepts, such as prosumer, virtual power plant, microgrid, smart grid and energy router (Kumar & Gupta, 2018). The understanding of these concepts is important for recognition of business values and analysis of business innovations in the environment of Energy Internet.

Prosumer

In the electric power sector, rapid development and wide use of distributed generation and storage of electricity enabled that traditional electricity consumer can be not only a passive consumer, but also an independent electricity producer, a so called *prosumer*. There are three major roles of a prosumer, energy producer, energy consumer and energy seller (Zafar et al., 2018). They consume and produce electricity using RESs and can help address the environmental and economic concerns regarding the increasing energy demand.

Microgrid

Microgrid represents low-voltage and medium-voltage distribution systems, and is located at or near the sites of energy consumption. This is a small energy distribution system that provides the supply for consumers from several DERs, including distributed generators and distributed devices for energy storage (Lasseter, 2002). The main benefits of microgrids are:

1. Reliable operation.
2. Operation either connected or disconnected from the main grid, which is an advantage in case of emergency or power failure in the main grid.
3. Facilitation of integrating renewable energy resources (sun and wind) with no need for redesign of energy transmission and distribution systems.
4. Decreased pollution.

Virtual Power Plant

Virtual power plant is innovative operating concept of power utility system. It assumes integration of distributed generators, electric energy storage system, controllable loads and DERs (which are often renewable) with advanced technologies for management, measurement, communication etc., that are controlled as a whole from a single centralized control center. Therefore, virtual power plant represents a virtual whole that primarily relies on specific software and communication links, and it actually represents a service for the management of electricity production and consumption (Saletović, Salkić, & Softić, 2017). It gathers different types of small scale electrical energy sources, that combined can efficiently replace or complement traditional hydropower plants to cover peak consumption. Virtual power plant enables efficient management of increasing number of unpredictable renewable resources, electrical energy storage and consumption management.

Smart Grid

Smart grid represents an important concept in power utility system, which was created at the beginning of 21st century. Smart grid integrates electric energy and information flows by integration of ICT and traditional power grid (Tuballa & Abundo, 2016). Intelligent measuring devices and other advanced measuring infrastructure can collect a great amount of data about the consumption of electric energy in real time. Based on analysis of such data, smart grid becomes more stable and more economical. Energy Internet is actually an evolution of smart grid towards Internet-based environment to upgrade the performance of such a system.

Energy Router

Energy router represents the core of Energy Internet and it connects three subsystems, namely energy, information, and network subsystems. It enables energy and data flow forwarding and it is a fundamental and indispensable equipment to support the smart energy management (J. Cao & Yang, 2013). Xu et al. (2011) introduced a concept of energy router for dynamic scheduling of energy flows and communications between power devices in real time. Energy router integrated with four modules, such as solid state transformer module, intelligence control module, fault detection module and communication module, is proposed by L. Chen et al. (2015). A. Huang and Cockrell (2019) proposed how a solid-state transformer can be utilized as an energy router in the Energy Internet.

With its optimized intelligence control strategy, energy router has an important supporting role in the distribution network.

Architecture

Energy Internet assumes integration of power utility network and ICT system to improve management of power utility network, as well as development of new services. It represents a software platform that provides control, monitoring and management of the whole smart grid, with all power utility systems interconnected (Sani et al., 2019). Such a system requires high reliability, high speed data transmission and high bandwidth, low latency, as well as the balance between energy generation and consumption. As opposed to intelligent network, which is focused to optimize the energy supply, Energy Internet aims at the integration of distributed (renewable) energy sources and personalized use of electric energy in households (K. Wang et al., 2017b). An example of such a system is presented in Figure 1. It is a WAN network that connects different parts of power utility system, such as electrical energy sources (big power plants, distributed energy sources), transmission system, distribution system, electrical energy consumers (general public, industry, commercial consumers), energy storage system, monitoring and control system and data centers. WAN network consists of energy routers that allow information exchange and management of energy flow between different areas. These routers are responsible for allocation of electric energy, two-way control of electric power and electric energy flows as well as device grouping, i.e., real-time optimization of energy generation and consumption.

The main features of Energy Internet are as follows (J. Cao & Yang, 2013; Sani et al., 2019; Shakerighadi, Anvari-Moghaddam, Vasquez, & Guerrero, 2018):

1. Control and monitoring of all activities and functionalities of the power utility system through IoT.
2. Energy interoperability with the ability for all the elements to exchange information.
3. Integration of energy and information.
4. Intelligent energy networking to achieve fault self-diagnosis, self-healing, self-control, etc.
5. Enabling wide-area energy sharing and emerging of energy prosumer.
6. Leveraging renewable energy as a primary energy source.
7. Large-scale distributed power generation and energy storage.
8. Emission-awareness.

Renewable energy sources are of emission-aware nature and can play an important role in building an environmentally friendly energy supply system.

Even though there are similarities between the Energy Internet and smart grid, the main differences are as follows (Q. Sun, 2019; Surani, 2019; K. Wang et al., 2017a; K. Wang et al., 2017b):

*   Energy Internet integrates numerous power utility networks, real-time monitoring and control technology, as well as energy distribution technology, while the smart grid is a modernized electrical grid. Energy Internet mainly focuses on renewable DERs.
*   Energy Internet uses distributed control and electrical energy generators can have "plug and play" function. In smart grid, collecting of information and routing commands is centralized and each generator needs "permission" from the control center before it accesses the power system.
*   In Energy Internet information system and physical system are integrated, while in the smart grid these systems are separated.
*   Energy Internet provides bidirectional exchange of information and energy sharing, while smart grid supports one-way communication.
*   Energy Internet is dominated by Internet technologies, whereas smart grid is dominated by communication system and traditional industry.
*   Energy Internet encompasses different types of DERs, particularly the renewable and environmental-friendly energy, such as solar, wind, nuclear power, etc.
*   The objective of Energy Internet is to achieve energy balance between supply and demand based on the Internet, distributed intelligence, and big data analytics on a large-scale level. In smart grid, the energy coordination is usually enabled locally.

Figure 1. An example of energy internet architecture (adapted from K. Wang et al., 2017b)

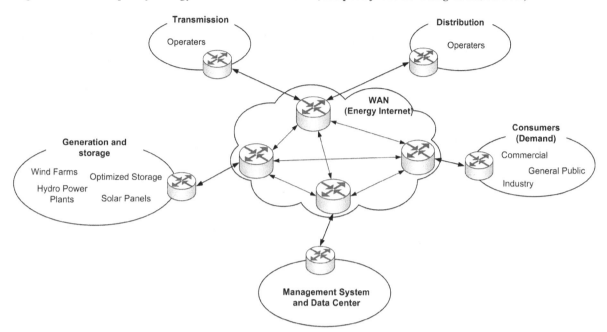

ICT as a Foundation for Energy Internet

Industrial sector has numerous benefits from the use of IoT in the sense of system automation, application of different types of sensors, efficiency improvement and revenue increase. IoT represents a dynamic network infrastructure that relies on interconnected self-configuring intelligent network nodes, such as sensors, actuators and mobile devices (Timčenko, Zogović, Jevtić, & Đorđević, 2017). The amount of data collected in such systems is measured in millions of gigabytes. Traditional information technologies cannot satisfy requirements for data analysis, latency, mobility, security, privacy and bandwidth. New ICT technologies are becoming more and more a part of power utility system in all of its parts (from generation, transmission, distribution and consumption), in order to optimize, personalize and enhance efficiency of electricity generation and consumption systems. Fog computing represents decentralized network architecture where the data storage, data processing and applications are distributed in a most efficient way between data sources and the cloud. Fog computing and cloud computing are similar in the sense of usage of computational, storage and network technologies. On the other hand, the most important difference is that fog computing is located near the end users, which is suitable for applications and services with stringent latency requirement. Only a portion of data is transmitted to the cloud for further processing, therefore the bandwidth utilization is better, and also location-awareness characteristic enables mobility support. Fog computing basically extends the cloud computing services to network edge, i.e., closer to consumers. Consequently, end users, fog computing and cloud computing encompass three-layered architecture, as shown in Figure 2.

The lowest layer refers to end-user devices, such as remote terminal units (RTUs), programmable logic controllers (PLCs), intelligent electronic devices (IEDs), intelligent measuring devices, different sensors and IoT devices.

Figure 2. Three-layered architecture of cloud/fog/IoT environment in power utility system

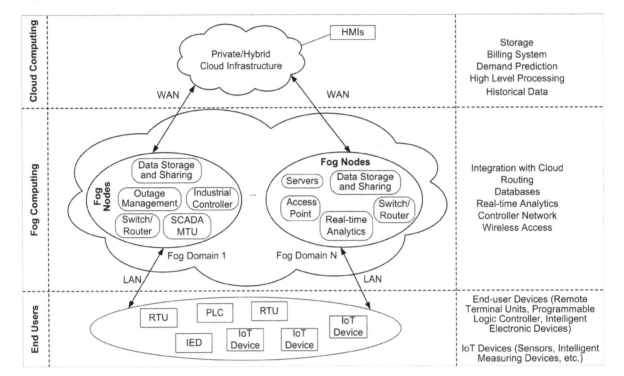

Middle layer encompasses one or more fog domains that are managed by the same or different providers. Fog domain consists of fog nodes, i.e., devices that enable data acquisition, processing and storage as well as network connections. Examples of such devices are industrial controllers, switches, routers, servers etc. Fog nodes enable integration with the higher layer (cloud), routing, storage, and data sharing, real-time data processing, outage management, management of end-user devices (RTUs, PLCs, IEDs), wireless access, etc. Fog nodes are virtualized networked data centers, which run atop access points (typically, wireless) at the edge of the access network, with main characteristics as follows (Naranjo, Baccarelli, & Scarpiniti, 2018):

1. Location awareness.
2. Low energy consumption.
3. Heterogeneity of the served devices.
4. Mobility support.
5. Device isolation.

Fog computing enables data processing in network elements (fog nodes) that are placed at the edge/ end of access network, i.e., between remote cloud and IoT devices. The aim is to enhance computational resources and bandwidth without significant impact on QoS provided for end users. The lowest and the middle layers are usually connected with wired or wireless local area network.

The highest layer is responsible for functions such as high level storage, billing system, demand forecasting, high level processing and archive data analysis. The communication between the middle and the highest level is provided through WAN connections.

CYBER SECURITY IN ENERGY INTERNET ENVIRONMENT

Security attacks on smart grid have increased over the last few years, which caused big economic losses and increased concerns regarding environment. Energy Internet should improve the cyber security of a smart grid. However, due to the complexity of Energy Internet, it is very difficult to design a fully secure and efficient framework for detection and prevention of attacks and vulnerabilities (Sani et al., 2019).

The main problems of implementation of Energy Internet are issues regarding complexity, efficiency, reliability, and information and network security. Such a system represents very complex infrastructure since it integrates ICT technologies, technologies for utilization of RESs and technologies for electricity storage, therefore modeling, analysis and design of appropriate communication infrastructure are a big challenge. Besides, integration of ICT with all parts of power utility system makes this system more vulnerable in the sense of cyber security, therefore very reliable and sophisticated security systems are needed.

Evolution of power utility system's communication infrastructure enabled new problems regarding information and network cyber security. Unlike public and corporate ICT systems, where information and network security has reached certain level of maturity, industrial systems require different and new solutions to be used in such an environment. The use of new ICT technologies brings new and specific information and network security issues. In the case of integration of power utility system with environments such as cloud computing and fog computing, special attention has to be paid to information security. In that sense, users can use a guide of ten basic steps for estimation of security level in cloud/fog computing environment (Cloud Standards Customer Council [CSCC], 2017; Raković, 2018).

Besides the threats that exist in available computing platforms and networks, cloud computing introduces additional ones, such as (Khan, Parkinson, & Qin, 2017):

- Attacks by other customers.
- Access control issues.
- Insider attacks.
- Shared technology issues.
- Failures in provider or customer security systems.
- Flawed integration of provider and customer security systems.
- Insecure application programming interfaces.
- Data loss or leakage.
- Account or service hijacking, etc.

Energy Internet integrated with cloud computing faces the same cyber security risks like any other system based on cloud computing technology. But there are some additional threats in such environment that additionally expose power utility systems to risk.

To assess the maturity grade of a particular cloud service the following criteria must be met:

1. Secure access for users.
2. Isolation of information flows originating from different applications.
3. Data encryption.
4. Automated distribution of software patches.
5. Continuous control and evaluation of security mechanisms in real time.
6. Continuous analysis of events, incidents, suspicious activities and anomalies.
7. Log files creation and analysis to detect attacks and to react to detected attacks in real time.
8. Consistent and reliable customer service.

Certain problems that come with the cloud computing environment can be resolved with the introduction of fog computing, where the protection is executed locally rather than in the cloud. This enables the use of corporate IT policies, control and procedures that are used in traditional power utility systems. In that way security level is increased compared to cloud computing. The majority of fog nodes has hardware root of trust that represents the base of three-layered security chain, from end users' devices, through fog computing layer to cloud computing layer. But, there are still missing standardized security solutions for fog computing unlike the cloud computing.

The use of IoT also raises certain issues, such as:

- Interoperability sssues - integration of new technologies from different vendors raise.
- How to efficiently use a great amount of data that is generated by different parts of power utility system to enhance system performance.
- Data and privacy security as additional challenge.

Security solutions for IoT and fog computing are generally similar to ones used in cloud computing, with the focus to the following techniques (Khan et al., 2017; Timcenko, 2014):

- **Authentication**: All messages and all entities need to be authenticated, with the use of different techniques, including public cryptography, biometric authentication, etc.;
- **Access Control**: All fog nodes need to provide an access control and authorization to secure operations like read and write data, program execution and sensors/actuators management;
- **Intrusion Detection and Prevention Techniques**: Generally used in cloud computing environment to detect possible incidents such as cyber attacks, violation of network security policies or standard security practices. In fog computing environment, intrusion detection and prevention systems can be implemented on user side as well as on the network side (fog), which provides double security, from internal attacks and attacks coming from the cloud. In the case of intrusion detection, fog nodes block malicious traffic and protect critical infrastructure. Sensitive data can be processed locally on the field site.
- **Privacy**: Fog nodes have to be secured with security techniques, since they are located close to or on the field sites, where they are gathering sensitive data.

The accuracy of collected data is critical for the normal and safe operation of the power system. The design of Energy Internet should encompass complex requirements regarding security system, taking into account different security issues on physical, software, and organizational level. Specific security policies should be determined to provide an adequate reaction in the case of failures and attacks and to provide information and network security (Conseil International des Grands Réseaux Électriques [CIGRÉ], 2007). The process of assessing the information and network infrastructure protection relies on different key factors: the specificity of the underlying system architecture; defined security requirements; and set of the detected security system failures (Saleem, Crespi, Rehmani, & Copeland, 2017; Sani et al., 2019). These policies define rules regarding main security requirements:

- **Availability**: As the most important security requirement regarding normal operation of critical infrastructure. The system must ensure reliable and timely use of and access to information.
- **Integrity**: As a protection against malicious modification or destruction of information.
- **Confidentiality**: As a protection of personal privacy and proprietary information from unauthorized access by entities, individuals, or processes.
- **Authorization**: As determination of levels of authority, for every authenticated user, to access resources controlled by the system.
- **Non-repudiation**: As the ability to prevent components from denying their involvement in an action that they participated in (a proof of entities' behavior).

QoS REQUIREMENTS

Besides security, QoS provisioning is also very important part of good network performance (Boštjančič Rakas & Stojanović, 2019; Đorđevic, Maček, & Timčenko, 2015; L. Huang, Y. Liu, J. Wu, G. Li, & J. Li, 2018). QoS provisioning represents a network ability to guarantee a particular level of performance or to provide different priorities to different applications (Stojanovic, Bostjancic Rakas, & Acimovic-Raspopovic, 2010). It mainly refers to network efficiency, network performance metrics, such as bandwidth, delay, jitter, error rate, etc., and fulfillment of service conditions from service level agreement (SLA). SLA specifies QoS attributes as well as QoS guarantees that the provisioned level of QoS meets the required one (Stojanovic & Bostjancic Rakas, 2013).

QoS requirements in Energy Internet network differ from the ones required in the traditional networks, due to real-time operating requirements, especially at the fieldbus and controller network layers. Most of the industrial applications have stringent performance requirements regarding delay, packet loss and bandwidth. Most of applications require response times from 250 microseconds to 1 millisecond, while less stringent processes pose response time requirements from 1 to 10 milliseconds (Galloway & Hancke, 2013). Higher layers tend to have progressively lower delay requirements, typically up to 1 second. The risk of not meeting the requirements is increased with the use of public cloud services, since the user does not have the control over network performance. Availability and reliability are very important as well. The loss of functionality of a particular part of critical infrastructure, even for a few seconds, can cause serious consequences to the industrial process. According to CIGRÉ recommendation, system availability in power utilities needs to be higher than 99.98% (CIGRÉ, 2004, p.23).

FUTURE RESEARCH DIRECTIONS

Although the Energy Internet is promising concept, there are still many key technical issues to be resolved, such as optimal coupling of multi-energy systems, advanced ICT systems for secure operation, more demonstration projects of new functionality for the large-scale Energy Internet, etc. (Y. Cao et al., 2018).

Since energy and information flows are tightly coupled, intensive research efforts are needed to resolve technical issues regarding information acquisition, secure communication and real-time control. However, energy interconnection and information interconnection are based on different physical laws; hence, the development of novel theoretical models and secure protocol standards are strongly encouraged.

Concern and special attention should be paid to cyber security as a main operational risk factor, which requires additional research work and stipulates gradual migration toward this complex cyber-physical system. A proper cyber security risk analysis should be conducted to each particular case, and there is a strong need to develop novel risk assessment methods for that purpose (Stojanovic, Bostjancic Rakas, & Markovic-Petrovic, 2019). In particular, fuzzy logic seems to be a promising method for cyber security risk assessment in all parts of Energy Internet system, because it represents a suitable tool to include both the objective component (based on the available technical information, e.g., historical data), and the subjective component, based on experience and professional opinions of relevant experts (Markovic-Petrovic et al., 2019). Taking into account the assessed risk, the cost increase is justified to provide secure communication services.

Finally, it should be noted that in most developing countries in the world, the electricity production remains monopolistic. Pricing policies are often determined with government intervention, in a way that protects the customers from paying too much for energy and to ensure that the utility companies don't make extraordinary profits. For that reason, the regulations and policies that were used previously would not apply to the new system. New regulations and policies are needed to ensure that producers and consumers are not being exploited.

CONCLUSION

Power utility systems have gone through four basic stages of technological development throughout the history, where, in line with the latest developments and requirements, the next phase should be an intelligent and connected power system based on the Internet technology. Due to demands for energy supply and energy efficiency, as well as the need for environmentally-friendly energy, technological advances create conditions for new intelligent power utility systems, which would allow optimal integration and use of DERs. Energy Internet with the concept of close integration of energy and information could provide for a cleaner and more efficient use of energy. It enables a two-way exchange of information and energy, with an integration of advanced ICT technology, intelligent terminals and systems that can upgrade traditional power grids into new intelligent platforms.

The importance of such systems is reflected through the financial support of governments of the most developed countries, primary by national and international projects that address different aspects of Energy Internet. Besides, Energy Internet becomes a constitutional part of the Industry 4.0 initiative that has been adopted and implemented in more than 40 countries worldwide.

The described Energy Internet system represents integration of power utility system with contemporary ICT system that improves management of electric power utility network and enables the development of new services. Although such a system brings numerous advantages, there are also big challenges and issues, especially when it comes to cyber security. These issues require paying special attention and developing the adequate security mechanisms.

ACKNOWLEDGMENT

This research was supported by the Serbian Ministry of Education, Science and Technological Development [grant number TR32025 and grant number TR32037].

REFERENCES

Abe, R., Taoka, H., & McQuilkin, D. (2011). Digital grid: Communicative electrical grids of the future. *IEEE Transactions on Smart Grid, 2*(2), 399–410. doi:10.1109/TSG.2011.2132744

AutoGrid. (n.d.). *AutoGrid Energy Internet Platform™*. Retrieved September 3, 2019, from https://www.auto-grid.com/platform/autogrid-energy-internet-platform/

Block, C., & Briegel, F. (Eds.). (2010). *Internet of Energy: ICT for energy markets of the future*. Berlin, Germany: Industrie-Förderung Gesellschaft mbH. Retrieved September 3, 2019, from https://www.iese.fraunhofer.de/content/dam/iese/en/mediacenter/documents/BDI_initiative_IoE_us-IdE-Broschuere_tcm27-45653.pdf

Boštjančič Rakas, S., & Stojanović, M. (2019). A centralized model for establishing end-to-end communication services via management agents. *Promet - Traffic & Transportation, 31*(3), 245-255.

Cao, J., & Yang, M. (2013). Energy Internet – Towards smart grid 2.0. In *Proceedings of the Fourth International Conference on Networking and Distributed Computing 2013* (pp. 105-110). New York: IEEE. 10.1109/ICNDC.2013.10

Cao, Y., Li, Q., Tan, Y., Li, Y., Chen, Y., Shao, X., & Zou, Y. (2018). A comprehensive review of Energy Internet: Basic concept, operation and planning methods, and research prospects. *Journal of Modern Power Systems and Clean Energy, 6*(3), 399–411. doi:10.100740565-017-0350-8

Chen, H., Teng, Y., & Bu, X. (2018). *Breaking into the 'Energy Internet' era in China: An analysis of China's Smart Grid development* (L.E.K. Consulting Executive Insights, Vol. XX, issue 5). Retrieved, September 03, 2019, from https://www.lek.com/insights/ei/breaking-energy-internet-era-china-analysis-chinas-smart-grid-development

Chen, L., Sun, Q., Zhao, L., & Cheng, Q. (2015). Design of a novel energy router and it's application in Energy Internet. In *Proceedings of the Chinese Automation Congress (CAC)* (pp. 1462-1467). New York: IEEE. 10.1109/CAC.2015.7382730

Cloud Standards Customer Council (CSCC). (2017). *Security for cloud computing – Ten steps to ensure success* (version 3.0). Retrieved September 3, 2019, from https://www.omg.org/cloud/deliverables/CSCC-Security-for-Cloud-Computing-10-Steps-to-Ensure-Success.pdf

Conseil International des Grands Réseaux Électriques (CIGRÉ). (2004). *Integrated service networks for utilities* (Technical Brochure TB 249, WGD2.07). Paris, France: CIGRÉ.

Conseil International des Grands Réseaux Électriques (CIGRÉ). (2007). *Security for information systems and intranets in electric power systems* (Technical Brochure 317, JWGD2/B3/C2.01). Paris, France: CIGRÉ.

Đorđevic, B., Maček, N., & Timčenko, V. (2015). Performance issues in cloud computing: KVM hypervisor's cache modes evaluation. *Acta Polytechnica Hungarica, 12*(4), 147–165.

Galloway, B., & Hancke, G. P. (2013). Introduction to industrial control networks. *IEEE Communications Surveys and Tutorials, 15*(2), 860–880. doi:10.1109/SURV.2012.071812.00124

Huang, A. Q., & Cockrell, D. D. (2019). Solid state transformers, the energy router and the energy Internet. In W. Su, & A. Q. Huang (Eds.), *The Energy Internet* (pp. 21–44). Cambridge, UK: Elsevier. doi:10.1016/B978-0-08-102207-8.00002-3

Huang, A. Q., Crow, M. L., Heydt, G. T., Zheng, J. P., & Dale, S. J. (2011). The future renewable electric energy delivery and management (FREEDM) system: The Energy Internet. *Proceedings of the IEEE, 99*(1), 133–148. doi:10.1109/JPROC.2010.2081330

Huang, L., Liu, Y., Wu, J., Li, G., & Li, J. (2018). Software-defined dynamic QoS provisioning for smart metering in Energy Internet using fog computing and network calculus. *IET Cyber-Physical Systems: Theory & Applications, 3*(3), 142–149.

Jaradat, M., Jarrah, M., Bousselham, A., Jararweh, Y., & Al-Ayyoub, M. (2015). The Internet of Energy: Smart sensor networks and big data management for smart grid. *Procedia Computer Science, 56*, 592–597. doi:10.1016/j.procs.2015.07.250

Khan, S., Parkinson, S., & Qin, Y. (2017). Fog computing security: A review of current applications and security solutions. *Journal of Cloud Computing: Advances, Systems and Applications, 6*(19), 1–22.

Kumar, R., & Gupta, V. (2018). Realization and concept of Energy Internet. *Indian Journal of Social Research, 17*(2), 6–11.

Lamba, V., Simková, N., & Rossi, B. (2019). Recommendations for smart grids security risk management. *Cyber-Physical Systems, 5*(2), 92–118. doi:10.1080/23335777.2019.1600035

Lasseter, R. H. (2002). Microgrids. In *Proceedings of the IEEE Power Engineering Society Winter Meeting* (pp. 305-308). New York: IEEE. 10.1109/PESW.2002.985003

Liu, N., Guo, B., Liu, Z., & Wang, Y. (2018). Distributed energy sharing for PVT-HP prosumers in community energy Internet: A consensus approach. *Energies, 11*(7), 1–18. doi:10.3390/en11071891

Lund, P. D., Mikkola, J., & Ypyä, J. (2015). Smart energy system design for large clean power schemes in urban areas. *Journal of Cleaner Production, 103*, 437–445. doi:10.1016/j.jclepro.2014.06.005

Macek, N., Dordevic, B., Timcenko, V., Bojovic, M., & Milosavljevic, M. (2014). Improving intrusion detection with adaptive support vector machines. *Elektronika ir Elektrotechnika, 20*(7), 57–60. doi:10.5755/j01.eee.20.7.8025

Markovic-Petrovic, J. D., Stojanovic, M. D., & Bostjancic Rakas, S. V. (2019). A fuzzy AHP approach for security risk assessment in SCADA networks. *Advances in Electrical and Computer Engineering*, *19*(3), 69–74. doi:10.4316/AECE.2019.03008

Marzal, S., Gonzáles-Medina, R., Salas-Puente, R., Garcerá, G., & Figueres, E. (2019). An embedded Internet of Energy communication platform for the future smart microgrids management. *IEEE Internet of Things Journal*, *6*(4), 7241–7252. doi:10.1109/JIOT.2019.2915389

Mei, S., Li, R., Xue, X., Chen, Y., Lu, Q., Chen, X., ... Chen, L. (2017). Paving the way to smart micro Energy Internet: Concepts, design principles, and engineering practices. *CSEE Journal of Power and Energy Systems*, *3*(4), 440–449. doi:10.17775/CSEEJPES.2016.01930

Naranjo, P. G. V., Baccarelli, E., & Scarpiniti, M. (2018). Design and energy-efficient resource management of virtualized networked Fog architectures for the real-time support of IoT applications. *The Journal of Supercomputing*, *74*(6), 2470–2507. doi:10.100711227-018-2274-0

Navigant. (2018). *Energy cloud 4.0 - capturing business value through disruptive energy platforms* (White Paper). Retrieved September 3, 2019, from https://www.navigant.com/-/media/www/site/insights/energy/2018/energy-cloud-4-capturing-business-value.pdf

Raković, R. (2018). Aspekti bezbednosti informacija u okruženju računarstva u oblaku [Information security aspects in cloud computing environment]. *InfoM*, *17*(66), 26–30.

Redgrid. (n.d.). *The Internet of Energy*. Retrieved September 3, 2019, from https://redgrid.io/

Rifkin, J. (2011). *The third industrial revolution: How lateral power is transforming energy, the economy, and the world*. New York: St. Martin's Griffin.

Saleem, Y., Crespi, N., Rehmani, M. H., & Copeland, R. (2017). Internet of Things-aided smart grid: Technologies, architectures, applications, prototypes, and future research directions. *IEEE Access: Practical Innovations, Open Solutions*, *7*, 62962–63003. doi:10.1109/ACCESS.2019.2913984

Saletović, J., Salkić, H., & Softić, A. (2017). Virtual power plants - Concept, perspectives, and challenges. In *Proceedings of the 13th Bosnian CIGRÉ* (Article C6, pp. 1-8). Sarajevo, Bosnia and Herzegovina: BH K CIGRÉ.

Sani, A. S., Yuan, D., Jin, J., Gao, L., Yu, S., & Dong, Z. Y. (2019). Cyber security framework for Internet of Things-based Energy Internet. *Future Generation Computer Systems*, *93*, 849–859. doi:10.1016/j.future.2018.01.029

Shakerighadi, B., Anvari-Moghaddam, A., Vasquez, J. C., & Guerrero, J. M. (2018). Internet of Things for Modern Energy Systems: State-of-the-Art, Challenges, and Open Issues. *Energies*, *11*(5), 1–23. doi:10.3390/en11051252

Silver Power Systems. (n.d.). *Energy management platform*. Retrieved September 3, 2019, from https://www.silverpowersystems.com/energy-management-platform

Stojanovic, M., & Bostjancic Rakas, S. (2013). Policies for allocating performance impairment budgets among multiple IP providers. *AEÜ. International Journal of Electronics and Communications*, *67*(3), 206–216. doi:10.1016/j.aeue.2012.08.001

Stojanovic, M., Bostjancic Rakas, S., & Acimovic-Raspopovic, V. (2010). End-to-end quality of service specification and mapping: The third-party approach. *Computer Communications*, *33*(11), 1354–1368. doi:10.1016/j.comcom.2010.03.024

Stojanović, M. D., Boštjančič Rakas, S. V., & Marković-Petrović, J. D. (2019). SCADA systems in the cloud and fog environments: Migration scenarios and security issues. *FACTA UNIVERSITATIS Series: Electronics and Energetics*, *32*(3), 345–358.

Sun, Q. (2019). *Energy Internet and We-Energy*. Singapore: Springer. doi:10.1007/978-981-13-0523-8

Surani, R. R. (2019). From smart grids to an Energy Internet: A review paper on key features of an Energy Internet. *International Journal Of Engineering Research & Technology*, *8*(4), 228–231.

Timčenko, V., Zogović, N., Jevtić, M., & Đorđević, B. (2017). An IoT business environment for multi objective cloud computing sustainability assessment framework. In *Proceedings of the 7th International Conference on Information Society and Technology ICIST 2017* (vol. 1, pp. 120-125). Belgrade, Serbia: Society for Information Systems and Computer Networks.

Timcenko, V. V. (2014). An approach for DDoS attack prevention in mobile ad hoc networks. *Elektronika ir Elektrotechnika*, *20*(6), 150–153. doi:10.5755/j01.eee.20.6.7289

Tuballa, M. L., & Abundo, M. L. (2016). A review of the development of smart grid technologies. *Renewable & Sustainable Energy Reviews*, *59*, 710–725. doi:10.1016/j.rser.2016.01.011

Wang, K., Hu, X., Li, H., Li, P., Yeng, D., & Guo, S. (2017a). A survey on energy Internet communications for sustainability. *IEEE Transactions on Sustainable Computing*, *2*(3), 231–254. doi:10.1109/TSUSC.2017.2707122

Wang, K., Yu, J., Yu, Y., Qian, Y., Zeng, D., Guo, S., ... Wu, J. (2017b). A survey on Energy Internet: Architecture, approach, and emerging technologies. *IEEE Systems Journal*, *12*(3), 2403–2416. doi:10.1109/JSYST.2016.2639820

Xu, Y., Zhang, J., Wang, W., Juneja, A., & Bhattacharya, S. (2011). Energy router: Architectures and functionalities toward Energy Internet. In *Proceedings of the IEEE International Conference on Smart Grid Communications* (pp. 31-36). New York: IEEE.

You, S., Jin, L., Zong, Y., & Bindner, H. W. (2015). The Danish perspective of energy Internet: From service-oriented flexibility trading to integrated design. *Zhongguo Dianji Gongcheng Xuebao*, *35*(14), 3470–3481.

Zafar, R., Mahmood, A., Razzaq, S., Ali, W., Naeem, U., & Shehzad, K. (2018). Prosumer based energy management and sharing in smart grid. *Renewable & Sustainable Energy Reviews*, *82*, 1675–1684. doi:10.1016/j.rser.2017.07.018

Zhong, W., Yu, R., Xie, S., Zhang, Y., & Tsang, D. H. K. (2016). Software defined networking for flexible and green energy Internet. *IEEE Communications Magazine*, *54*(12), 68–75. doi:10.1109/MCOM.2016.1600352CM

Zhou, Y., Ni, W., & Zhu, Z. (2017). Architecture of energy Internet and its technologies in application reviewed. *Journal of Clean Energy Technologies*, *5*(4), 320–327. doi:10.18178/JOCET.2017.5.4.391

ADDITIONAL READING

Cheng, L., Yu, T., Jiang, H., Shi, S., Tan, Z., & Zhang, Z. (2019). Energy Internet access equipment integrating cyber-physical systems: Concepts, key technologies, system development, and application prospects. *IEEE Access: Practical Innovations, Open Solutions*, 7, 23127–23148. doi:10.1109/ACCESS.2019.2897712

Faheem, M., Shah, S. B. H., Butt, R. A., Raza, B., Anwar, M., Ashraf, M. W., ... Gungor, V. C. (2018). Smart grid communication and information technologies in the perspective of Industry 4.0: Opportunities and challenges. *Computer Science Review*, 30, 1–30. doi:10.1016/j.cosrev.2018.08.001

Gui, Y., Siddiqui, A. S., & Saqib, F. (2018). Hardware based root of trust for electronic control units. [New York: IEEE.]. *Proceedings of the SoutheastCon*, 2018, 1–7.

Hussain, M., & Sufyan Beg, M. M. (2019). Fog computing for Internet of Things (IoT)-aided smart grid architectures. *Big Data and Cognitive Computing*, 3(8), 1–29.

Mell, P., & Grance, T. (2011). *The NIST definition of cloud computing (NIST Special Publication 800-145)*. Gaithersburg, MD: U.S. National Institute of Standards and Technology.

Muhanji, S. O., Flint, A. E., & Farid, A. M. (2019). *EIoT - The development of the Energy Internet of Things in energy infrastructure*. Cham, Switzerland: Springer International Publishing. doi:10.1007/978-3-030-10427-6

Nardelli, P. H. J., Alves, H., Pinomaa, A., Wahid, S., Tome, M. C., Kosonen, A., ... Carrillo, D. (2019). Energy Internet via packetized management: Enabling technologies and deployment challenges. *IEEE Access: Practical Innovations, Open Solutions*, 7, 16909–16924. doi:10.1109/ACCESS.2019.2896281

Qi, J., & Wu, D. (2018). Green energy management of the Energy Internet based on service composition quality. *IEEE Access: Practical Innovations, Open Solutions*, 6, 15723–15732. doi:10.1109/ACCESS.2018.2816558

Raptis, T. P., Passarella, A., & Conti, M. (2019). Data management in Industry 4.0: State of the art and open challenges. *IEEE Access: Practical Innovations, Open Solutions*, 7, 97052–97093. doi:10.1109/ACCESS.2019.2929296

Song, X. (2018). Research on security protection architecture of Energy Internet information communication. In *Proceedings of the 3rd International Conference on Circuits and Systems, MATEC Web of Conferences* (pp. 1-5). Paris: EDP Sciences. 10.1051/matecconf/201822802010

KEY TERMS AND DEFINITIONS

Cyber-Physical System: A large scale, geographically dispersed, aggregate, life-critical system that comprises sensors, actuators as well as control and networking components.

Energy Internet: A power system that integrates different types of energy resources, storage, and loads, and enables peer-to-peer energy delivery on a large scale. It is based on the existing energy infrastructure integrated with an advanced Internet technology and renewable energy power generation technology to achieve wide-area intelligent optimization of multiple energy sources.

Energy Router: A device that integrates power electronics, communications and automation technologies, as a support in realization of Energy Internet.

Industry 4.0: The subset of the fourth industrial revolution that concerns industry. It assumes automation and data exchange in manufacturing technologies and processes which include cyber-physical systems, the Internet of Things, industrial Internet of Things, cloud computing, fog computing and artificial intelligence.

Microgrid: A small network of electricity users with a local source of supply that is usually attached to a centralized national grid but is able to function independently.

Prosumer: A mixture of the words "producer" and "consumer". It denotes a person or company that acts as energy producer, energy consumer and energy seller, at the same time.

Root of Trust: A set of functions in the trusted computing module that is always trusted by the computer's operating system. Since cryptographic security assumes key-based encryption and functions such as generating/verifying digital signatures, root of trust schemes generally include an appropriate hardware module.

Smart Grid: It is an electricity network based on digital technology, which provides monitoring, analysis, control and communication within the supply chain. It improves efficiency, reduce energy consumption and cost, and maximize the transparency and reliability of the energy supply chain.

Virtual Power Plant: A distributed power plant that integrates distributed generators, electric energy storage system, controllable loads and distributed energy resources for the purposes of enhancing power generation, as well as trading or selling power on the electricity market.

Chapter 13
A Compressive Compilation of Cyber Security for Internet of Energy (IoE)

Gustavo Arroyo-Figueroa

https://orcid.org/0000-0003-0764-045X

Instituto Nacional de Electricidad y Energías Limpias, Mexico

Isai Rojas-Gonzalez

Instituto Nacional de Electricidad y Energías Limpias, Mexico

José Alberto Hernández-Aguilar

https://orcid.org/0000-0002-5184-0005

Universidad Autonoma del Estado de Morelos, Mexico

ABSTRACT

Internet of energy (IoE) is the natural evolution of Smart Grid incorporating the paradigm of internet of things (IoT). This complicated environment has a lot of threats and vulnerabilities, so the security challenges are very complex and specialized. This chapter contains a compilation of the main threats, vulnerabilities, and attacks that can occur in the IoE environment and the critical structure of the electrical grid. The objective is to show the best cybersecurity practices that can support maintaining a safe, reliable, and available electrical network complying with the requirements of availability, integrity, and confidentially of the information. The study includes review of countermeasures, standards, and specialized intrusion detection systems, as mechanisms to solve security problems in IoE. Better understanding of security challenges and solutions in the IoE can be the light on future research work for IoE security.

DOI: 10.4018/978-1-7998-2910-2.ch013

INTRODUCTION

In recent years, there has been a technological revolution in electricity grids mainly motivated by energy crisis, clean power generation, carbon emissions, ultra-high voltage, storage, distributed power generation and intelligent distribution networks. It is evident that these critical problems cannot be addressed with traditional electricity grid (World Energy Council, 2015).

The smart grid (SG) is the technological paradigm being proposed to satisfy the aforementioned challenges. SG aims to improve the reliability and quality of energy supply, incorporate clean energy sources and manage power plants efficiently; have fully automated distribution management; carry out the balance of the electrical system through the management of the demand and the storage of energy; allow customers to participate in the control of the conscious use of energy; incorporate distributed and connected energy storage; incorporate micro networks of connected communities; incorporate smart cities and electric vehicles; demand response through prices and contracts; and incorporate distributed generation schemes (Arroyo-Figueroa, Escobedo-Briones, & Santamaria-Bonfil, in press).

However, there still exist some gaps and limitations for the implementation of SG (K. Wang et al., 2018a). The electric infrastructure continues to move into a future where the modern grid driven by the combination of intelligent devices and high-speed communication with near real-time processing of the data (Carlson, 2019). This integration is called Internet of Energy (IoE) (Unterweger, 2018). The IoE is a new paradigm developing a revolutionary vision of smart grids into the Internet. IoE is perfecting the smart grid in an all-round manner, using wireless sensor networks, actuators, smart meters, and other components of the power grid together with information and communication technology (Ghasempour, 2019).

The aim of IoE is to collect, organize and make the information, from individual grid-edge devices across the network, available to all other grid management participants simply and quickly (Carlson, 2019). IoE technology includes utilizing smart sensors, common among other Internet of Things (IoT) technology applications, which allows such IoE-facilitated mechanics as power monitoring, distributed storage, and renewable energy integration. The fundamental issue is the volume of data and the time required to analyze the information. The data volume and scale can be overcome using secure communication networking of the devices, together with leading edge information technology (IT) like cloud computing. As device information is consumed by a cloud-based platform, the integration and sharing of information can be simplified using software applications running on top of the cloud platform. The cloud platform will become a data lake for different applications to utilize (Jaradat, Jarrah, Bousselham, Jararweh, & Al-Ayyoub, 2015).

The communication infrastructure is an essential component for implementing the IoE. A scalable and robust communication infrastructure is crucial in both operating and maintaining smart energy systems (Ebrahimy & Pourmirza, 2017). The growth and success of the IoE will rely on how we use cloud-based systems for integration and our willingness across the industry to co-create the systems and processes for management of the future grid. Achieving an IoE is not without its challenges. According to K. Wang et al. (2018b, p. 79276), one of the challenges that should be taken into account for the wide-scale implementation and development of IoE into smart energy applications is:

"**Cyber Security and Privacy-aware Data Management for IoE**: Among many applications in IoE, energy consumption data could be linked and mined to gain useful insights for optimization of energy utilization. At the same time, privacy and security concerns can prevent the information disclosure, energy waste and disaster. Further safeguards are needed to build trust in the data, which is instrumental for making critical decisions for the development of IoE".

The secure transmission and processing of data play a particularly important role in IoE; communication is essential to process large volumes of data and to better understand and perform real-time decision making of network operations. The goal is to make it impossible to falsify or manipulate grid data and maintain system integrity. To achieve this, modern cyber security technologies and standards must be applied to ensure a maximum degree of security at all levels.

Therefore, how to ensure the confidentiality, integrity and availability of the data in the IoE, has become an urgent problem and research hotspot. This chapter presents a comprehensive compilation of cyber security issues for the IoE. Mainly, it has the following aims:

- To show the architecture of IoE as the integration of SG and IoT.
- To provide a deep understanding of security vulnerabilities, threats and attacks of IoE via critical assets studies and network communication.
- To show countermeasures proposals based on secure communication protocols, secure information systems, standards and specialized intrusion detection systems (IDSs), as mechanisms to solve security problems in IoE.
- To discuss security challenges and the future research directions for the design of secure architectures and network protocols for IoE.

The structure of the chapter is as follows. The background section provides a discussion on the architecture and communications of smart grid and its evolution to Internet of Energy. The following section analyzes security and vulnerability threats in IoE, from a critical asset point of view. Further, the authors give a summary of security countermeasures used in IoE, based on standards for secure communication protocols, methodologies for the development of secure information systems, intrusion detection systems and security monitoring centers. The chapter ends with the main conclusions regarding challenges in the architectures, security, and applications in the IoE.

BACKGROUND

Internet of Energy Architecture

IoE can be defined as the evolution of smart grids into the web, perfecting the smart grid in an all-round manner. The architecture of IoE is the evolution of the architecture of SG. According to National Institute of Standards and Technology (NIST, 2012, p. 14), a SG can be defined as "a modernized grid that enables bidirectional flows of energy and uses two-way communication and control capabilities that will lead to an array of new functionalities and applications". The SG paradigm aims to improve the reliability and quality of the energy supplied, incorporate clean energy sources and efficiently manage power plants; have a fully automated distribution network; carry out the balance of the electrical system through demand management and energy storage; allow customers to participate in the control of the conscious use of energy; incorporate distributed and connected energy storage; incorporate micro networks of connected communities; incorporate smart cities and electric vehicles; demand response through prices and contracts; and incorporate distributed generation schemes. Figure 1 shows the main elements of SG (Arroyo-Figueroa et al., in press).

The architecture of SG is very complex regarding electrical and communications networks. A study reported by Aggarwal et al. (2010) show that there are over 2000 power distribution substations, about 5600 distributed energy facilities, and more than 130 million customers all over the US SG can be divided into systems and communications. In this section, an overview of the SG components – systems and communications, and the evolution to IoE are presented.

SG Systems

The SG combines several distributed and heterogeneous systems, technologies and infrastructures including microgrids, advanced metering infrastructure (AMI), substations, demand response, synchrophasor systems, supervisory control and data acquisition (SCADA) systems and electric vehicles (EV), home energy management (HEM), among others. Figure 2 shows the most important systems of SG. More information about other systems of SG is provided in (Cagri Gungor et al., 2013; Parra, Rodríguez, & Arroyo-Figueroa, 2014).

The AMI is responsible for collecting, measuring and analyzing energy and provides the two-way communication from the user to the utility. It is composed of three main components: smart meter, meter data management system (MDMS), and the communication network (Faisal, Aung, Williams, &

Figure 1. Main elements of smart grid

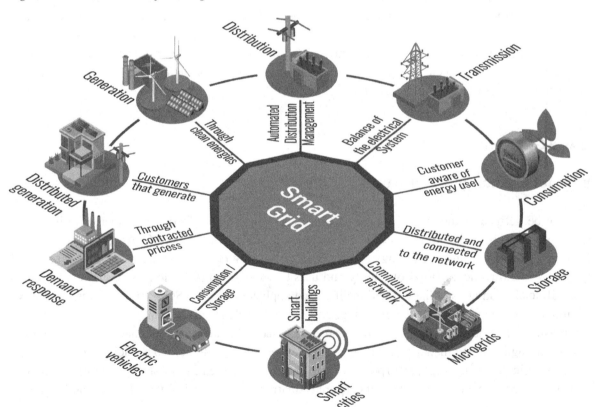

Figure 2. SG systems

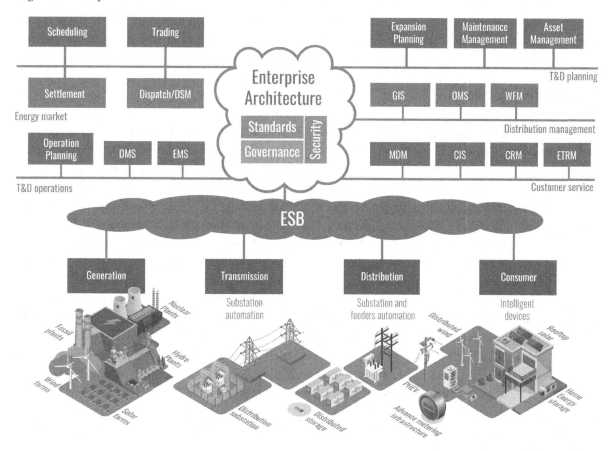

Sanchez, 2015). Smart meters are digital meters, consisting of microprocessors and a local memory, and they are responsible to monitor and collect the power consumption of home appliances and transmitting data in real time to the meter data management system. MDMS is responsible for storing the information provided by smart meters that belong in a specific geographic area. The communication between the smart meters, the home appliances, and the MDMS is defined through several communication protocols, some of the most used are Z-wave and Zigbee (Faisal et al., 2015).

A SCADA system has three main components: the remote terminal unit (RTU), master terminal unit (MTU) and human-machine interface (HMI) (Cherdantseva et al., 2016). RTU is a device composed of sensors, logic controller and communication network. It is responsible for collecting data from the measuring instruments, detecting abnormal behaviors and activating or deactivating technical components. MTU is a device responsible for controlling the RTU. The HMI is a graphic interface for the SCADA system operator. The communication network is based on industrial protocols, such as Modicon communication bus (Modbus), Distributed Network Protocol 3 (DNP3) and International Electrotechnical Commission (IEC) 61850 (Mohagheghi, Stoupis, & Z. Wang, 2009).

Synchrophasors have fast time-stamped device called phasor measurement units (PMUs) to constitute the basis of real-time monitoring and control. Additionally, it has a phasor data concentrator, a HMI and a communication network. A PMU consists of current transformers, potential transformers, and analog units, which execute various measurements from current/voltage waveforms, such as frequency, phase angle, active power and reactive power. PMUs have a GPS with them to time stamp the data and they are employed in electrical networks to collect the analog data for situational awareness. The communication networks are usually carried out through Institute of Electrical and Electronics Engineers (IEEE) C37.118.2 and IEC 61850 standards (Usman & Faruque, 2019).

SG Communications

The communication is the heart of the SG system by providing interconnections between all of the systems and devices. The telecommunication technology is used to enable the data digitization, intelligent applications, and increased reliability. Figure 3 illustrates the SG communication network architecture. The architecture of SG network communication consists of three main categories: home area network (HAN), neighborhood area network (NAN), and wide area network (WAN); for each network there are different kind of protocols. The three main tiers that are located between these three networks are the core backbone, back-haul distribution, and the access point (Cagri Gungor et al., 2013).

HANs support low-bandwidth communication between home electrical appliances and smart meters, home appliances use ZigBee and Z-wave; and recently the EEBus standard (EEBus Initiative, 2019). NAN can be described as the communication network for power distribution areas and includes distribution automation and control devices communicating over networks between individual service connections and backhaul points to the electric utilities, the devices are usually connected via IEEE 802.11, IEEE 802.15.4, or IEEE 802.16 standards. WAN provides communication between the electric utility and substations, several industrial protocols are used especially DNP3 and Modbus. Within the substation automation (SCADA), the protocol IEC 61850 is used (El Mrabet, Kaabouch, Has. El Ghazi, & Ham. El Ghazi, 2018). This section provides a brief introduction to three widely-used protocols in power systems: the Modbus, DNP3 and IEC 61850 (Al-Dalky, Abduljaleel, Salah, Otrok, & Al-Qutayri, 2014; Rodofile, Radke, & Foo, 2016; IEC, 2016).

Modbus is an open serial protocol that uses a Master/Slave technique to communicate between devices. Modbus is typically used to transmit data from control instrumentation to a logic controller or a system for archiving data. There are three types of Modbus: Modbus ASCII, Modbus RTU, and Modbus/TCP (Transmission Control Protocol). In the first one, messages are coded in hexadecimal. Though it is slow, it is ideal for radio links and telephone communications. The most basic difference between Modbus RTU and Modbus TCP is that Modbus TCP runs on an Ethernet physical layer and Modbus RTU is a serial level protocol based on Recommended Standard 232 (RS-232). With the introduction of Modbus TCP, everything was simplified and easier. With Modbus TCP, controllers can much more efficiently use the bandwidth on Ethernet to be the Master to hundreds of Modbus TCP slave devices, such as sensors, drivers, and programmable logic controllers (PLCs). Modbus is widely used in industrial architecture, because of its relative ease of use by communicating raw data without restriction of authentication, encryption, or any excessive overhead (Al-Dalky et al., 2014).

DNP3 was first designed for SCADA applications and is now widely used in electrical, water, oil, gas, and other industries. DNP3 was initially designed with four layers: physical, data link, transport, and application layers. The original physical layer was based on serial communication protocols, such as RS-232, RS-422, or RS-485 (Knapp & Samani, 2013). Today's DNP3 has been extended to work over Internet Protocol (IP) networks through the encapsulation of the TCP or User Datagram Protocol (UDP) packets, and thus can be regarded as a three-layer network protocol operating upon the TCP/IP layer to support end-to-end communication. DNP3 did not provide any security mechanism such as

Figure 3. SG communications

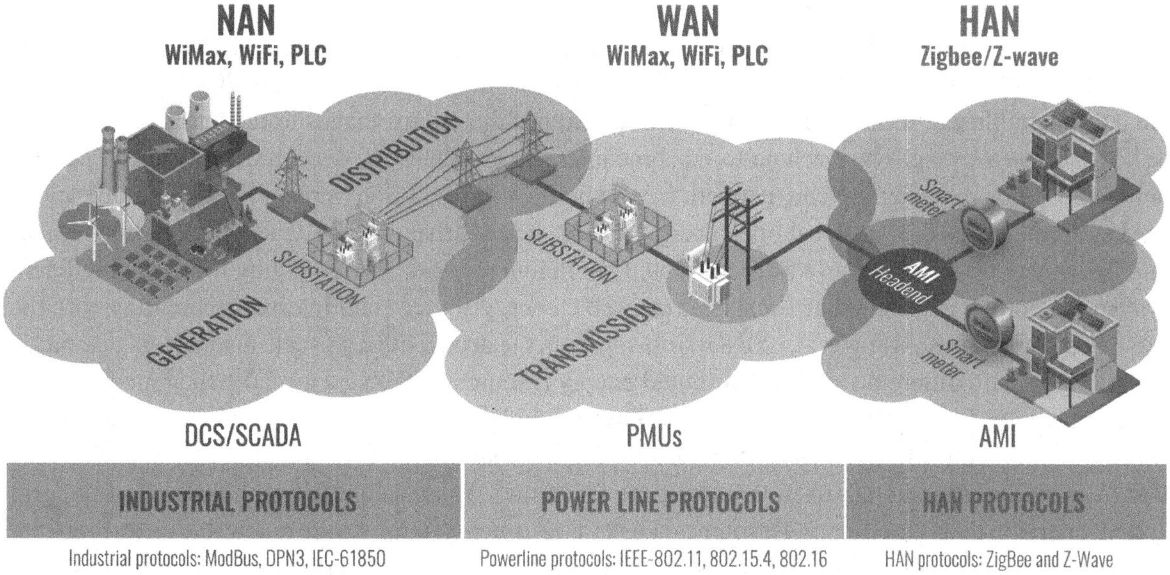

encryption or authentication, but this problem was fixed with a secure version of DNP3 called "DNP3 secure" (Rodofile et al., 2016).

IEC 61850 is a recent standard for Ethernet-based communications in modern power substation automation (IEC, 2016). IEC 61850 provides interoperability between intelligent electronic devices and better device-to-device communication. IEC 61850 supports a wide range of applications, including TCP/IP, UDP/IP, and an application directly-to-MAC stack for time-critical messages. In addition, IEC 61850 explicitly defines timing requirements for information and data exchange in power substations. For example, with the integration of the IEC 61850 protocol the latency can be between 3–10 ms. One of the main features of IEC 61850 is object-oriented data in the form of names, structures and formats representation. IEC 61850 also provides a Substation Configuration description Language (SCL), which is a standard file that documents the characteristics of the data exchange interface (DEI) communication parameters and uses an extensible markup language (XML) format.

IoE: The Evolution of SG

Internet of Energy (IoE) is the natural evolution de Smart Grid derived of the necessity of highly integrated grid of renewable energy, large-scale distribution generation (GD), distributed energy storage, smart metering monitoring, data sharing, real-time pricing, and market transaction. IoE is a new vision of SG that integrate Internet concept. Based on the concept of IoT, IoE will be a system that interrelates smart metering, intelligent devices, wearables and smart appliances, which are provided with unique identifiers and the ability to transfer data over a network without requiring human-to-human or human-to-computer interaction.

An IoE ecosystem consists of web-enabled smart devices that use embedded processors, sensors and communication hardware to collect, send and act on data they acquire from power network. IoE devices share the sensor data they collect by connecting to an IoE gateway or other edge device, in which data is sent to the cloud to be analyzed.

From point of view of internet communication paradigm, using IoE for the management of the SG networks would provide a rich set of advantages (Bui, Castellani, Casari, & Zorzi, 2012). For example, the interoperability of IoE will be possible with different ITs systems thanks to the harmonizing effect of IP-based networking. The machine-to-machine interactions enable the decentralization of the control procedures, thus relieving the core network from a high communication burden. Peer communications are key to the success of a global open energy market (transactive energy). The IoE paradigm makes intelligent networks evolve into a fully connected intelligent network. The emerging IoE is an intelligent system integrating distributed and scalable renewable energy sources and Internet technology with the existing smart grid (K. Wang et al., 2018a). IoE supports the access of large-scale distributed generation (DG) system with different types of distributed energy resources (DERs), especially the renewable and environmentally friendly energy, such as solar power, wind power, nuclear power, ocean power, etc. as well as distributed energy storage system access. Figure 4 shows the conceptual model of IoE. In the first level are the operational assets that make the SG: smart sensors and devices, bulk generation, grid system operator, distributed energy resources (DER), consumer systems, future renewable electric energy delivery and management (FREEDM) system, energy control center, electric vehicles, D&T grid, and so on. The second level are the energy systems in the cloud, the systems required for plan and operate the grid: planning, operation, customer, markets, assets management and communications and security. The third level are the energy services applications; these applications allow the necessary flexibility to support operational and analytical systems.

SECURITY CHALLENGES OF IoE

The IoE communication network is a mission critical network for information exchange in power grid. In general, the presence of communication nodes of IoE has rendered the energy sector more vulnerable to attacks. As IoE is the evolution of SG, it inherits the security challenges (vulnerabilities, threats, and attacks) of SG, in addition to those of IoT.

Vulnerabilities might allow an attacker to penetrate a network, gain access to control software, and alter load conditions to destabilize the grid in unpredictable ways. The vulnerabilities might allow attackers to access the network, break the confidentiality and integrity of the transmitted data, and make the service unavailable. Threats refer to the various possible actions that may be influenced either by artificial or natural means, against a SG. These threats do not represent failures but may result in failure if necessary actions are not taken. Hence the need to study the threats and challenges as well as a set objective is necessary for a well secured SG (Mendel, 2017).

IoE requires high level of security to protect the smart grid systems from any vulnerability and attack that may cause to access the network, break the confidentiality and integrity of the transmitted data, and make the service unavailable. To ensure secure and reliable operation, it is important to identify and understanding the cyber vulnerabilities, threats and attacks related with IoE in order to define the countermeasures needed to mitigate the risk of a successful cyber attack.

Several research works on SGs focus on threats, vulnerabilities and attacks. Otuoze et al. (2018) classify the threats and vulnerabilities in two types: technical and non-technical, where technical threats focus on infrastructural security, technical operational security and system data management security.

Figure 4. Conceptual model of IoE

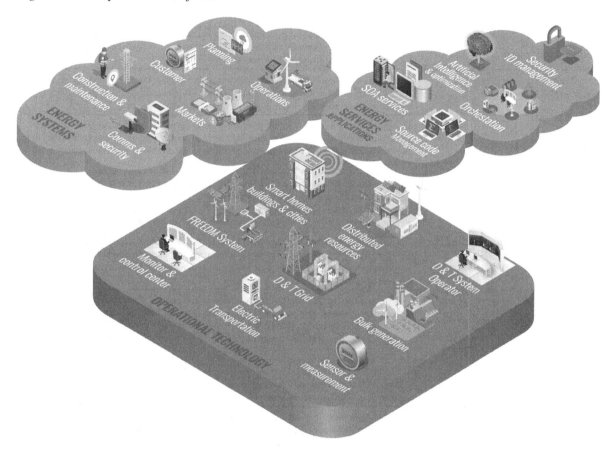

W. Wang and Lu (2013) provide an extensive analysis of network vulnerabilities under important use cases in the SG. They also analyze network vulnerabilities in the SG under denial of service (DoS) attacks, which can severely degrade the communication performance and further impair the operation of electronic devices. Aloul et al. (2012) propose eight most serious vulnerabilities in SG: customer security, greater number of intelligent devices, physical security, the lifetime of power systems, implicit trust between traditional power devices, different team's backgrounds, using IP and commercial off-the-shelf hardware and software and more stakeholders. Table 1 presents a classification of vulnerabilities in IoE.

The IoE will inherit physical and dynamic system threats as well as well-known communication and network threats such as those targeting its integrity and availability. Dari and Essaaidi (2015) classify the threats into three categories: people and policy, platform and network. Goel and Hong (2015) analyze the most prevalent threats to the operation and safety of the SG. The threats come from physical destruction of infrastructure, data poisoning, denial of services, malware and intrusion, and from the consumer due to breach of privacy of the data and malicious control of personal devices and appliances. Cagri Gungor et al. (2013) provide an in-depth analysis of vulnerability and threats of protocols: Bluetooth, Z-Wave, Zigbee, WiMAX, IEC 61850 protocol, and power line communication. Table 2 presents a list of the main threats in IoE.

Attackers could be script kiddies, elite hackers, terrorists, employees, competitors, or customers. W. Wang and Lu (2013) classify the attacks based on the impact of each attack on the information security:

Table 1. IoE issues: vulnerabilities

Issue	Comments
Customer information	The private consumer information that might be used to infer consumer's activities, devices being used, and times when the home is vacant.
Major attack surface	The attack surface is huge due to the large number of interconnected intelligent devices that are involved in managing both the electricity supply and network demand. These intelligent devices may act as attack entry points into the network.
Obsolescence of power systems	Many of these devices were not designed to support security mechanisms therefore they are vulnerable due to insecure defaults, lack of authentication/authorization; also they are susceptible to memory corruption, code injection and credential malicious management, among others.
Absence of identity verification between traditional power devices	Without mutual authentication the exchanged information between devices is exposed to be target of espionage or theft. Device-to-device communication in control systems is vulnerable to data spoofing where the state of one device affects the actions of another. For instance, a device sending a false state makes other devices behave in an unwanted way.
More users and stakeholders	There will be a large number of users, consumers, suppliers, generators, transporters, vendors, among many others. This increase the number of possible accidental and / or intentional security incidents
Compatibility of secure protocols	To guarantee the data confidentiality that are processed and exchanged into IoE, it is necessary to use secure protocols however not all of current devices are compatible, for example in industrial control system (ICS) system it is very common the use of Modbus protocol that is not designed with mechanisms of information security.
Convergence of network and systems	It is not a simple task to achieve stability in the convergence of IT, Operational Technologies (OT) and adding the IoT as a global platform for communications. In this context, there are different requirements for each field; response times, priorities, protocols, architectures and operation methodologies.
Lack of laws and international regulations	Laws, regulations and standards are necessary to establish what is allowed, what is prohibited, what are penalties, responsibilities, requirements, models, and best practices related to the SG and IoT cyber security in a cooperative context to aim for the best results
Software	Software suffers from a wide variety of vulnerabilities that include malwares. General purpose system suffers from a various well known vulnerabilities that should be patched to ensure that the system stay updated.

Table 2. IoE issues: threats

Issue	Comments
Cyberwar	The automation of the critical infrastructure processes in the countries, causes them to be attractive as a target of attack, that is why the war between the powerful countries in the world has moved to cyber space.
Terrorism	Terrorists who view the smart grid as an attractive target because the damages have a deep impact.
Hacktivism	They also find the Smart Grid a very attractive target but they only seek to direct attention to their political or social motives.
Fierce competition	Competitors could attack each other to get advantage in the business market including tactics like a sabotage, theft or espionage.
Malware spreading	The spread of malware continues to increase and it is an issue due to the absence of malware containment mechanisms in industrial control networks.

confidentiality, integrity, and availability (CIA) requirements. Rawat and Bajracharya (2015) classified attacks based upon the type of the network, namely, HAN, NAN and WAN. In addition, they presented the impact of each attack on the information security based on CIA. Bhatt et al. (2017) defined different types of attacks for the SG: data injection attacks (dias), deception attacks, denial of service attacks, replay attacks, time synchronization attacks, additional dynamic system attacks, SCADA attacks, smart meter attacks, physical layer attacks, network-based attacks. Aloul et al. (2012) define three main categories of attacks: component-wise, protocol-wise, and topology-wise. Other attacks were discussed in X. Wang and Yi (2011), and Mo et al., (2012), including: malware spreading, access through database links, compromising communication equipment, injecting false information, network availability, eavesdropping and traffic analysis, and Modbus security issue.

Flick and Morehouse (2010) classify the attackers into:

1. **Nonmalicious Attackers**: who view the security and operation of the system as a puzzle to be cracked. Those attackers are normally driven by intellectual challenge and curiosity.
2. **Consumers**: Driven by vengeance and vindictiveness towards other consumers making them figure out ways to shut down their home's power.
3. **Terrorists**: Who view the smart grid as an attractive target as it affects millions of people making the terrorists' cause more visible.
4. **Employees**: Disgruntled on the utility/customers or ill-trained employees causing unintentional errors.
5. **Competitors**: Attacking each other for the sake of financial gain.

In this context, inside of SG there are many components and systems that are susceptible to be vulnerated by taking advantage of their weaknesses, and that causes negative effects in the normal operations of power supply chain. Table 3 shows some of cyber attacks that could occur on the components and systems of the SG (El Mrabet et al., 2018):

It is clear that the security challenges in IoE are great and require multidisciplinary attention from different perspectives. In the following Section the main countermeasure and standards applied to IoE are shown.

Table 3. Likelihood of the attack to be performed and its associated severity

		Severity of the Attack		
		Low	**Medium**	**High**
Likelihood of the Attack to be Performed	High	• Traffic analysis • Privacy violation		• Virus, worms, Trojan horse • DoS • Backdoor
	Medium	• Social engineering • Scanning	• Man-In-The-Middle (MITM) • Replay attack	• Jamming channel • Masquerade attack • Integrity violation
	Low			• Popping the HMI

Table 4. Cyber attacks on smart grid (El Mrabet et al., 2018)

Attacking Cycle Step	Attack Category	Attack Example	Compromised Application/ Protocol in Smart Grid	Compromised Security's Parameter	Possible Countermeasures
Reconnaissance	• Traffic analysis	Sniffing	• Modbus protocol • DNP3 protocol	• Confidentiality	Secure DNP3, PKI (SKMA, SMOCK), TLS, SSL, encryption, authentication
	• Social engineering	Phishing			
		Password pilfering			
Scanning	• Scanning IP • Port • Service • Vulnerabilities	Modbus network scanning	• Modbus protocol	• Confidentiality	IDS, SIEM, automated security compliance checks
		DNP3 network scanning	• DNP3 protocol		
Exploitation	• Virus • Worms • Trojan horse	Stuxnet	• SCADA • PMU, • Control device	• Confidentiality • Integrity • Availability • Accountability	DLP, IDS, SIEM, antivirus, diversity technique
		Duqu	• SCADA		
	• DoS	Puppet attack	• AMI	• Availability	SIEM, IDS, flow entropy, signal strength, sensing time measurement, transmission failure count, pushback, reconfiguration methods
		Time delay switch (TDS)	• Instability of smart grid systems		
		Time synchronization attack (TSA)	• PMU • Smart grid equipment's GPS		
	• MITM	Eavesdropping attack	HMI, PLC	• Confidentiality • Integrity	Secure DNP3, PKI (SKMA, SMOCK), TLS, SSL, encryption, authentication
		Intercept / alter / inject	SCADA		
		Intercept / alter / inject	DNP3, SCADA		
		Intercept/alter	AMI		
	• Replay attack	Capture / alter / replay	IED, SCADA, PLC	• Confidentiality • Integrity	Secure DNP3, TLS, SSL, encryption, authentication PKI (SKMA, SMOCK)
		Capture / alter / replay	Authentication scheme in AMI		
	• Jamming channel	Flooding	PMU	• Availability	JADE, anti-jamming (FHSS, DSSS)
		Maximum attacking strategy using spoofing and Jamming (MAS-SJ)	CRN in WSGN		
	• Popping the HMI	Overheating	SCADA, EMS, substations.	• Confidentiality • Integrity • Availability • Accountability	DLP, IDS, SIEM, antivirus, automated security compliance checks
	• Masquerade attack	Unauthorized access through legitimate access identification	PLC	• Confidentiality • Integrity • Availability • Accountability	DLP, IDS, secure DNP3, SIEM, TLS, SSL, encryption, authentication, PKI (SKMA, SMOCK)
	• Integrity violation	Alter	Smart meter, RTU	• Integrity • Availability	DLP, IDS, SIEM, secure DNP3, TLS, SSL, encryption, authentication, PKI (SKMA, SMOCK)
		False data injection	EMS, SCADA, AMI		
	• Privacy violation	Unauthorized reading of private data	Demand Response program, Smart meters	• Confidentiality	Secure DNP3, PKI (SKMA, SMOCK), TLS, SSL, encryption, authentication
Maintaining access	• Backdoor	Hidden access door	SCADA	• Confidentiality • Integrity • Availability • Accountability	IDS, SIEM, anti-virus, diversity technique

Table 5. IoE countermeasures

Countermeasure	Technical Example	Non-technical Example	Challenges Example
Hardening access control	• Using a double factor mechanism for user identity verification • Mutual authentication techniques for devices that interoperate with each other, for example IPSec and TLS protocols	• Define access control policies • Define the authentication standards	• Update legacy and obsolete devices • To change the regulation so that the security schemes are enforceable from the design of smart devices
Malware prevention and protection	• Implement anti-malware protection into operational devices	• Implement anti-malware protection update program	• Protect legacy and obsolete devices. Some embedded systems are designed to only run software that is supplied by the manufacturer
Perimeter cyber security	• Firewall, Network Intrusion Prevention System (NIPS) and Network Intrusion Detection System (NIDS) technologies	• Define the rules of authorized network traffic	• IT has latency tolerance, OT requires real-time response
Vulnerability assessment program	• Use scanning vulnerability tools to detect flaws into the systems	• Implement a program for periodic scans that allows to detect and attend vulnerabilities	• Undesirable disruptions may occur in ICS networks when the vulnerability scans are running due high sensibility of OT devices in the face of unusual traffic that is generated
Awareness programs	N/A	• Courses, workshops, conferences and diffusion campaigns, all about cyber security best practices	• Resistance to change and negation by thoughts such as "It is not possible that will occur" or "It is just a science fiction" or "Our systems are secure because they are isolated and they are not connected to the Internet" or "Cybersecurity is expensive and only if something happens then we will see what to do"
The use of secure protocols	• IPSec, DNP3 (no encryption), TLS, HTTPS, among others	• Establish regulations that require the use of communications secure protocols to protect data exchange	• Compatibility and security in communication protocols for OT devices.
Implement and improve cryptography mechanisms	• Implement strong cryptographic algorithms to use secure Public Key Infrastructure (PKI)	• Establish an information classification schema to determine what information must be encrypted	• Traditional encryption mechanisms are not fully compatible with OT response times and current devices do not have enough processing power neither enough storage capability to perform advanced encryption and authentication techniques
Secure remote access	• Devices that support Virtual Private Network (VPN) architectures for secure communication	• Policy of access control that includes remote access privileges definition	• Compatibility of the legacy ICS network and devices with the current VPN architectures
Early visibility of cyber attacks	• Network monitoring tools with artificial intelligence that could allow detections and alerts almost immediately	• Promotion of culture for users to report cyber security anomalies and incidents	• To avoid that monitoring tools interfere with normal functions of operational networks
Attack Containment and Resilience	• Networks segmentation • Separate, as much as possible, corporate network and operational network • Decrease asset visibility	• Defense in depth scheme • Operations continuity plan • Disaster recovery plan • Define emergency response team	• Obsolescence of the legacy ICS network and devices
Strengthen the regulations and standardization of best cyber security practices	N/A	• Establish laws about cyber security in the Smart Grid • Define international cooperation agreements on cyber security • Develop the adequate standards to the Internet of Energy needs	• Laws, regulations and standards are necessary to establish what is allowed, what is prohibited, what are penalties, responsibilities, requirements, models, and best practices related with the SG cyber security in a cooperative context for aim the best results

Table 6. Standards of the International Electrotechnical Commission (IEC)

Standard	Description	Smart Grid Useful	IoT Useful
IEC 61400-25	The mappings specified in the part of IEC 61400-25 comprises a mapping to SOAP-based web services, OPC/XML-DA, IEC 61850-8-1 MMS, IEC 60870-5-104 and a mapping to DNP3.	X	X
IEC 61850-90-5	Communication networks and systems for power utility automation.	X	
IEC 62056-5-3	Electricity metering data exchange – The DLMS/COSEM suite.	X	
IEC 62351	Its focus is on data and communications security in power systems management.	X	X
IEC 62443 series	It is the worldwide standard for security of the ICSs in the OT domain of organizations.	X	X
IEC PAS 62559	IntelliGrid methodology for developing requirements for energy systems.	X	

Table 7. Standards of the Institute of Electrical and Electronics Engineers (IEEE)

Standard	Description	Smart Grid Useful	IoT Useful
IEEE 1711	Test standard of a cryptographic protocol for cyber security of serial link substations.	X	
P1915.1	Standard for software defined networking and network function virtualization security.	X	
IEEE 1686	Standard for intelligent electronic devices cyber security capabilities.	X	X
IEEE 1888.3-2013	Standard for ubiquitous green community control network: security.		X

SECURITY MECHANISM FOR IoE

Security Countermeasure for IoE

With the evolution of Smart Grid into Internet of Energy, challenges grow too, so we must consider that the Information Technology cyber security problems are now affecting the Operational Technology (OT) in the industrial control system (ICS) additionally the big challenges to secure the information when

Table 8. Standards of the National Institute of Standards and Technologies (NIST)

Standard	Description	Smart Grid Useful	IoT Useful
NISTIR 7628	Guidelines for smart grid cybersecurity.	X	X
NIST SP 800-53	Security and privacy controls for Information Systems and Organizations.	X	X
NIST SP 800-82	Guide to Industrial Control Systems (ICS) Security.	X	
NIST SP 800-160	Systems Security Engineering.	X	X
NIST FIPS 140-2	Security Requirements for Cryptographic Modules.	X	

Table 9. Standards of the International Organization for Standardization (ISO)

Standard	Description	Smart Grid Useful	IoT Useful
ISO/IEC 27000 series	The series contains the best practices in information security to develop, implement and maintain specifications for Information Security Management Systems (ISMS).	X	X
ISO/IEC 27001	It specifies the requirements for the implementation of the ISMS.	X	X
ISO/IEC 27002	Code of practice for information security controls.	X	X
ISO 15118	Road vehicles: Vehicle to grid communication interface.	X	X

using the web-based solutions from the IoT. Having overviewed the major vulnerabilities and security challenges, this section the recent security solutions based on countermeasures and standards. Table 5 presents a resume of the main IoE countermeasures.

Security Standards for IoE

The growing need for ubiquity of information has driven the evolution of Smart Grid technology towards a convergent approach with IoT technology. This entails significant cyber security challenges for the Internet of Energy agreement.

In this context, technological countermeasures of protection are required and countermeasures of a regulatory nature are required, such as standards, models, methodologies, and so on.

In an effort to unify the criteria and establish the necessary basis for strengthening the mechanisms of cyber security in the IoE, several standards have been published, both for the Smart Grid and for the IoT.

In the following, several of the existing standards are mentioned and it is important to highlight that research works and adjustments are being carried out by various international organizations for the standardization of cyber security in the SG (Tables 6–12).

Intrusion Detection and Prevention Systems (IDPS) for IoE

In addition to traditional intrusion prevention techniques, security standards and other countermeasures, it is necessary to have mechanisms to detect threats before they cause extensive damage in order to protect networks and systems from more sophisticated attacks and malware. An IDS system is a security mechanism that has the function to dynamically monitor the events that occur in a system or network and decides whether these events are symptomatic of an attack or an illegitimate use of the system. The

Table 10. Standards of the North American Electric Reliability Corporation (NERC)

Standard	Description	Smart Grid Useful	IoT Useful
NERC CIP 002-009	Set of eight standards (including cyber asset identification, security management controls, personnel and training, electronic security perimeters, physical security, system security management, incident reporting and response, and recovery plan for critical cyber assets), each of which is mandatory for electric power and utility companies.	X	

Table 11. Standards of other organizations

Organization/Protocols	Description	Smart Grid Useful	IoT Useful
The IoT Security Foundation	It provides knowledge and clear security best practices to those who specify, make, and use IoT products and systems.		X
The Open Web Application Security Project (OWASP)	OWASP has ten IoT security projects to help with this: IoT attack surface areas; IoT vulnerabilities; firmware analysis; ICS/SCADA software weaknesses; community information; IoT testing guides; IoT security guidance; principles of IoT security; IoT framework assessment, developer, consumer and manufacturer guidance; and design principles.		X
The Online Trust Alliance (OTA)	Aims to educate users and develop and advance best practices and tools to enhance users' security, privacy, and identity.		X
The Secure Technology Alliance	It is working to stimulate the understanding, adoption, and widespread application of secure solutions, including smart cards, embedded chip technology, and related hardware and software.		X
IoT IAP	It addresses security challenges related to IoT.		X
The Cloud Security Alliance (CSA)	It offers cloud security-specific research, education, certification, events, and products, including ones focused on IoT.		X
I am the Cavalry	Aims to ensure that technologies with the potential to impact public safety and human life are worthy of trust and focus on IoT.		X
The IoT Global Council	It focuses on IoT data and security.		X
The Internet Research Task Force	It has established important security works related with IoT.		X
The Industrial Internet Consortium (IIC)	It produced a specific cyber security framework for the IoT.		X
World Wide Web Consortium (W3C)	It explores ideas prior to standardization together with collaboration with external groups, e.g. standards development organizations and industry alliances.		X

presence of IDS system is vital for the reliable operation of IoE and mainly for ensuring the security requirements of CIA. The IDS can operate as a second line of defense in a communication network, by enhancing the operation of others security mechanisms.

The basic architecture of an IDS has four main modules (Kumar & Dutta, 2016): a *monitor* that collects audit data from the network or system; an *analysis engine* that processes the data to detect intrusive activity in accordance with intrusion models; *intrusion models* that represents the knowledge about of normal/abnormal behavior from the audit records; and a *reporting and response module* that generates the alerts only when an intrusion is detected by the intrusion recognition module. An IDS can be classified into two categories: Host-based IDS (HIDS), and Network-based IDS (NIDS). A HIDS monitors all

Table 12. Standards for protocols

Organization/Protocols	Description	Smart Grid Useful	IoT Useful
QUIC (Quick UDP Internet Connections, pronounced quick)	It was designed to provide security protection equivalent to TLS/SSL.		X
DTLS (Datagram Transport Layer)	It provides communications privacy for datagram protocols.		X
Content-Centric Networking (CCN)	Next-gen network architecture to solve challenges in content distribution scalability, mobility, and security.		X
AMQP (Advanced Message Queuing Protocol)	An open standard application layer protocol for message-oriented middleware that consider security.		X
LPWAN – Weightless	For exchanging data with high levels of security through wireless.		X
Telehash - JSON+UDP+DHT=Freedom	A secure wire protocol powering a decentralized overlay network for apps and devices.		X
Open Trust Protocol (OTrP)	A protocol to install, update, and delete applications and to manage security configuration in a Trusted Execution Environment (TEE).		X

or parts of the dynamic behavior and the state of a computer system. A NIDS monitors network traffic for particular network segments or devices and analyzes the network and protocol behavior to identify suspicious activities. In general, IDS fall into two categories according to the detection methods they use: misuse detection and anomaly detection. Misuse detection identifies intrusions by matching observed data with predefined descriptions of intrusive behavior. The anomaly detection constructs models for normal behavior and detects anomalies in the observed data noting the deviations of these models.

The presence of IDS in IoE is required, since the security policy violations in this ecosystem may cause dangerous situations and disastrous accidents. A significant advantage of these systems is that they possess the ability to recognize zero-day attacks by using artificial intelligence mechanisms. The intrusion models are the heart of the IDS and they are based on artificial intelligence (AI) algorithms. An extensive study of the use of computational intelligence is presented by Wu and Banzhaf (2010). Kathirvel et al. (2018) provide a study of various techniques of data mining and clustering applied to IDS and how they help to effectively detect the intrusion in network. Aziz et al. (2017) presented a comparison of classification techniques applied for network intrusion detection and classification; they show different classifiers and compare them to increase the detection accuracy and obtain more information on the detected anomalies. They also show an analysis of ensemble and hybrid techniques, considering both homogeneous and heterogeneous types of ensemble methods. This study shows that the AI techniques are associated to the types of network attacks – DoS, probe, user to root (U2R) and remote to user (R2U).

The traditional intrusion detection systems based on signature and anomaly techniques are no longer sufficient to protect IoE environment due to their new connectivity and management challenges. IoE requires security systems to render them resilient and protected through intrusion detection and prevention system (IDPS). In general, the rapid progress of computer networks necessitated the development of appropriate mechanisms that have the ability to automate the process of detecting or/and preventing possible security violations. Radoglou-Grammatikis and Sarigiannidis (2019) examine the contribution of IDPSs in the SG paradigm, providing an analysis of 37 cases. The study focused on the advanced metering infrastructure (AMI), SCADA systems, substations, and synchrophasors.

It is clear that IDPS systems are critical for any security system that is deployed in SG. Their role lies in further detecting whether an attacker has compromised grid systems and gained access to power grid networks. They should be capable of identifying threats and attacks in the whole SG, by having global visibility, while being able to access both power and information systems. Stand-alone IDPS has a number of desirable characteristics for optimized performance, maximum protection and minimum error that easily translates into a set of nonfunctional system requirements. Patel et al. (2017) define eight functional requirements of an IDPS for SG environment:

- **Support for Legacy Protocols and Systems**: SG is still largely dependent on legacy communication protocols and nodal systems composed of legacy hardware with limited computing resources, long maintenance cycles, and their stand-alone distributed placement. The IDPS should handle these systems and protocols without any degradation or effect on real-time performance.
- **Scalability**: Due to the extensive coverage of users in SG, an IDPS should be scalable to deal with the vast number of network communication nodes.
- **High Accuracy of Detection and Prevention Capability**: Due to the growth of attacks, complexity and unpredictability, it is necessary for the system to recognize any new attacks and their vulnerable intention to choose the best response according to the risk severity and proper prevention strategy without human intervention.
- **Standards Compliance**: The IDPS should accommodate established international ICT and SCADA standards as well as emerging SG standards.
- **Adaptive**: The architectural model of IDPSs should be able to handle any changes to the topology of the SG and allow the monitoring and control of network elements in real-time.
- **Accuracy**: Due to the critical mission of an SG, IDPS should not adversely affect the performance of the real-time processes and the underlying network, especially when network traffic changes. IDPS should be deterministic in its behavior.
- **Resistance to Compromise:** A Smart IDPS (SIDPS) must protect itself from unauthorized access or attacks. It should be capable of authenticating networked devices and other IDPSs mutually, authenticating the administrator and auditing his/her actions, protecting its data and blocking any loopholes that may create additional vulnerabilities.
- **Synchronization of Autonomous IDPSs:** A collaborative IDPS is a massive collaboration of a large number of autonomous IDPS where the information and activities of each IDPS is synchronized in order to recognize distributed and concurrent attacks, apply an appropriate response or modify a particular component system or the whole network configuration, and adopt proper prevention strategies through collaboration.

The diversity and complexity of communications that take place in IoE, and the huge volume of data generated by the operational systems characterize an environment with severe security gaps. Therefore, several projects have been developed around security across interdependent critical infrastructures (CI) in electric grid. Some examples are:

Figure 5. Conceptual architecture distributed heterogeneous framework structure within SG networks with CSIDPS (adapted from Patel et al., 2017)

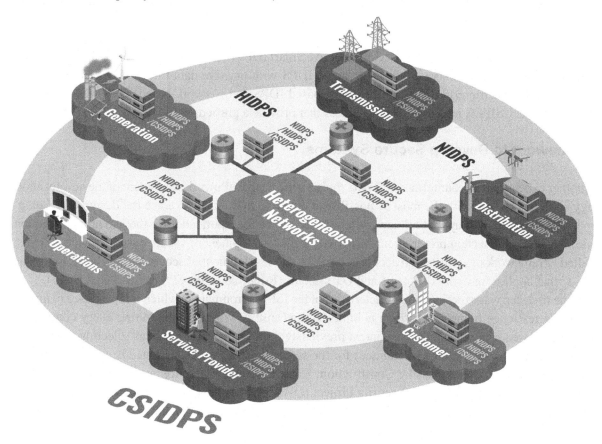

- MICIE project that developed an alerting system, which identifies, in real time, the level of possible threats induced on a given CI by undesired events that happened in such CI and/or other interdependent CIs (Castrucci et al., 2009).
- Situation AWare Security Operations Center (SAWSOC) project whose objective was the development of a SAWSOC center with holistic approach and enhanced awareness technology that allows dependable detection and diagnosis of attacks (SAWSOC, 2016).
- CRitical Infrastructure Security AnaLysIS (CRISALIS) project aims at providing new means to secure CI environments from targeted attacks. It is focuses on these two aspects: detection of vulnerabilities and attacks in CI environments (control systems based on SCADA protocols and the AMI) (CRISALIS Consortium, 2015).
- Cybersecurity on SCADA: risk prediction, analysis and reaction tools for Critical Infrastructures (CockpitCI) project's aim is to design and develop a system capable of detecting malicious network traffic which may disrupt the correct functioning of a SCADA system and tamper with its normal operation (Foglietta, Panzieri, Macone, Liberati, & Simeoni, 2013).
- Advanced Tools to assEss and mitigate the criticality of ICT compoNents and their dependencies over Critical InfrAstructures (ATENA) project aims at leveraging the outcomes from previous European projects, particularly from CockpitCI and MICIE projects, and pushes at innovating

them by exploiting advanced features of ICT and cyber security, to be tailored and validated in selected use cases, in order to be adopted at operational industrial maturity level (Adamsky et al., 2018).

These efforts scale IDPS to a set of Collaborative Smart IDPS (CSIDPS), as shown in Figure 5. Figure depicts the structure of a cooperative distributed IDPS with massive data traffic flows from multiple sources of the electric grid that combined Host-based IDPS and Network-based IDPS. The result is a homogeneous CSIPDS in every level of process that provide a unified view (Patel et al., 2017).

Framework to Develop Secure Systems

Another cyber security countermeasure is to apply a schema that allows development of the new technology solutions for IoE with the most as possible of cyber security aspects, since the design of development itself, in such a way that all new systems that will be incorporated have the adequate protection mechanisms. This section presents an alternative for the development of secure corporate web systems, called "Framework of security and access control for the development of secure Web systems for Smart Grid" that applies for both IT systems and OT systems (Rojas González & Sánchez Pérez, 2015).

The first step was to define the characteristics of the IoE environment in which it is proposed to implement the reference framework, which is important because it will allow delimiting every component of the proposed solution. Under the context previously defined, the next step was selecting a set of the most important and recognized techniques for the secure software development. Then were selected 4 techniques (CbyC: Correctness by Construction; CLASP: Lightweight Application Security Process; OWASP: Open Web Application Security Project (OWASP); CERT: Recommendations of CMU) that are of the most use due to their effectiveness and the prestige of institutions that created them (Figure 6).

Figure 6. Techniques for development secure systems, security principle and security concepts

Concepts identified	For each scheme, the principle of security related to the concept identified			
	CbyC	CERT	OWASP	CLASP
Easiness	☑ principle 6	☑ principle 4	☑ principle 9	⊟
Avoiding mistakes	☑ principle 1,2,5	☑ principle 2	☑ principle 5, 10	⊟
Validate inputs	⊟	☑ principle 1	⊟	☑ principle 9
Security by default	⊟	☑ principle 5	☑ principle 2	☑ principle 5
Principle of least privilege	⊟	☑ principle 6	☑ principle 3	☑ principle 7
Defense in depth	⊟	☑ principle 8	☑ principle 4	☑ principle 6
Reduce attack surfaces	⊟		☑ principle 1	☑ principle 4

With the knowledge obtained, the first concepts of the reference framework were established, regarding the components of denominated framework and nine security principles.

To define the security principles, a qualitative comparison was used, such as it was done with the framework concepts; in the comparison were considered advantages and disadvantages rescuing the most relevant concepts. The security principles must be considered every moment, even in all activities done before and after the development process. The security principles are the premises about how to carry out the activities that integrate the security practices.

1.   Keep yourself informed.
2.   Avoiding mistakes.
3.   Keep a schema simple.
4.   Validate the data inputs.
5.   Security by default.
6.   The least privilege.
7.   Defense in Depth.
8.   Develop incrementally.
9.   Ethical perspective of attacker.

To define the access control model, two existing models were considered: Role Based Access Control (RBAC) and Attribute Based Access Control (ABAC) models. Characteristics of these models are convenient for desired model of corporate web portals that require the use of the concepts of roles and attributes. In the case of recommendations for Single Sign On, the premises and concepts of the model

Figure 7. General representation of the framework for the development of secure web systems

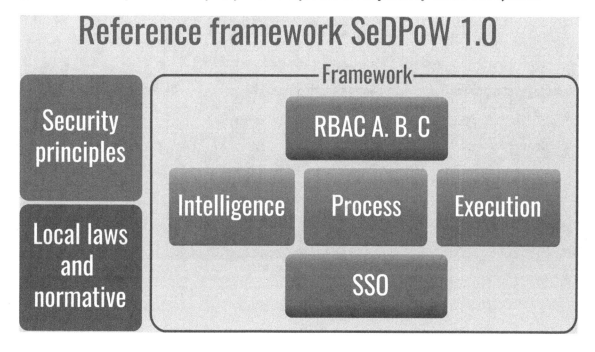

Figure 8. Domains and security practices with activities for the development of secure web systems.

INTELLIGENCE	PROCESS	EXECUTION
Training and guidance (TG)	**Initial planning (IP)**	**Operating configuration (OC)**
TG1. Train to the staff of software development in computer security	IP1. Include the participation of security advisors for the initial planning of the project	OC1. System final configuration
TG2. Promote culture of security	IP2. Identify all high-level IT&OT assets	OC2. Identify and gather security recommendations
	IP3. Classify information to be processed and stored in the portal	
	IP4. Obtain information about the threats and informatics attacks most relevant of the moment	
Continous improvement (CI)	**Secure Design (SD)**	**Transfer of responsability (TR)**
CI1. Identify and document each opportunity of improve the reference framework	SD1. Disseminate the information obtained in the IP4 activity among members of the development team	TR1. Establish formal agreements
CI2. Periodically analyze improvement opportunities	SD2. Perform a quick risk analysis of IT assets identified	TR2. Transfer the system control
	SD3. Determine what are the security requirements	TR3. Formally deliver the system
	SD4. Incorporate security requirements in the high-level design and architecture of the corporate portal	
	SD5. Define security tests for the portal in its totality	
	SD7. Define security test for each module	
Knowledge retention (KR)	**Secure construction (SC)**	**Obtaining knowledge (OK)**
KR1. Create knowledge repositories	SC1. Programming each module using best practices	OK1. Gathering empirical data
KR2. Keep repositories updated	SC2. Validate the programming of each module	
	SC3 Execute the security tests of each module	
	SC4. Execute security tests of the portal in its totality (global tests)	

were studied in order to take the most adequate ones to be incorporated in the reference framework according with the defined context.

Finally, the legal aspects were considered by the study of two laws of data personal protection in Mexico: "Ley Federal de Protección de Datos Personales en Posesión de Particulares" (Federal Law on Protection of Personal Data Held by Individuals) and "Ley Federal de Transparencia y Acceso a la Información Pública Gubernamental" (Federal Law of Transparency and Access to Public Government Information). From both laws were taken the precepts concerning, directly or indirectly, the information technologies.

Framework

Based on the knowledge gained and preset conditions of the application environment was defined the Framework for the development of secure web systems, Figure 7 shows the global representation of the framework.

The framework was integrated with three domains composed by nine security practices. the complete framework including the activities of each security practice, see Figure 8.

The framework of security and access control, for the development of corporate web portals, integrates a series of safety recommendations regarding the design and the construction of web systems. Using the reference framework will provide an extra value for web systems that are developed under this scheme. Its essence agile and light weight will facilitate that the development teams incorporate the recommendations into their software development processes. When a system is developed, mitigating security concerns is much less expensive if done in the early stages of its development.

FUTURE RESEARCH DIRECTIONS

IoE requires specialized security solutions designed specifically for operational network and web applications, the better understanding of security challenges and solutions in IoE can be the light on the future research work in this amazing and challenging environment of security. Future research directions are aimed at developing security mechanisms for operational networks based on computational intelligence:

- Modify the security schemes of operational legacy systems.
- Design the architecture of an intelligent security management center.
- Develop security policies in the national energy sector based on a framework.
- Finally, the implementation of a security framework for IoE in a power national utility.

CONCLUSION

In this chapter we presented a comprehensive survey of security issues and solutions in IoE. First, we introduced the IoE architecture as the evolution of SG. Then we defined security requirements and analyzed the security challenges in IoE; potential security vulnerabilities and threats for IoE environment and for critical infrastructure (SCADA, AMI, PMUs). As a result of this analysis, we propose a security framework-based countermeasures, standards, IDPS and development of secure software. The aim was to provide guidelines for the design and implantation of security solutions to achieve the requirements of confidentiality, integrity, and availability information delivery in IoE.

The IoE is a new power generation paradigm developing a revolutionary vision of smart grids into the Internet for new business models of energy. As we have reviewed, security challenges are still under development in IoE, especially because trust in the data must be taken into account when making critical decisions for the development of secure-IoE.

Due to distinct features of domains of IoE, a security solution may be potentially applicable to one domain but not the others. Many security methods and schemes could be applicable to IoE, especially in information networks domains that interact with customers and financial transactions based on Internet. The Generation/Transmission/Distribution domains require security solutions to not only protect information exchange, but also meet the requirements for data communication and processing. DoS attacks are the main security issue because they have an immediate impact on the availability, which is arguably the most important security requirement of power distribution and transmission.

REFERENCES

Adamsky, F., Aubigny, M., Battisti, F., Carli, M., Cimorelli, F., Cruz, T., ... Soua, R. (2018). Integrated protection of industrial control systems from cyber-attacks: The ATENA approach. *International Journal of Critical Infrastructure Protection*, *21*, 72–82. doi:10.1016/j.ijcip.2018.04.004

Aggarwal, A., Kunta, S., & Verma, P. K. (2010). A proposed communications infrastructure for the smart grid. In *Proceedings of the Innovative Smart Grid Technologies (ISGT)* (pp. 1-5). New York: IEEE. 10.1109/ISGT.2010.5434764

Al-Dalky, R., Abduljaleel, O., Salah, K., Otrok, H., & Al-Qutayri, M. (2014). A Modbus traffic generator for evaluating the security of SCADA systems. In *Proceedings of the 9th International Symposium on Communication Systems, Networks, & Digital Sign (CSNDSP)* (pp. 809-814). New York: IEEE. 10.1109/CSNDSP.2014.6923938

Aloul, F., Al-Ali, A. R., Al-Dalky, R., Al-Mardini, M., & El-Hajj, W. (2012). Smart grid security: Threats, vulnerabilities and solutions. *International Journal of Smart Grid and Clean Energy*, *1*(1), 1–6. doi:10.12720gce.1.1.1-6

Arroyo-Figueroa, G., Escobedo-Briones, G., & Santamaria-Bonfil, G. (in press). Development of technology infrastructure of big data analytics for smart grid. *IEEE Latin America Transactions*.

Aziz, A. S. A., Hanafi, S. E.-O., & Hassanien, A. E. (2017). Comparison of classification techniques applied for network intrusion detection and classification. *Journal of Applied Logic, 24* (Part A), 109-118.

Bhatt, T., Kotwal, C., & Chaubey, N. (2017). Survey on smart grid: Threats, vulnerabilities, and security protocol. *International Journal of Electronics, Electrical, and Computational System*, *6*(9), 340–348.

Bui, N., Castellani, A. P., Casari, P., & Zorzi, M. (2012). The Internet of Energy: A web-enabled smart grid system. *IEEE Network*, *26*(4), 39–45. doi:10.1109/MNET.2012.6246751

Cagri Gungor, V., Sahin, D., Kocak, T., Ergut, S., Buccella, C., Cecati, C., & Hancke, G. P. (2013). A survey on smart grid potential applications and communication requirements. *IEEE Transactions on Industrial Informatics, 9*(1), 28–42. doi:10.1109/TII.2012.2218253

Carlson, M. (2019, January 29). From a smart grid to the Internet of Energy. *Smart Energy International, 2019*(1), 22-23. Retrieved November 10, 2019, from http://spintelligentpublishing.com/Digital/SmartEnergy/SEI12019/index.html?r=65

Castrucci, M., Macone, D., Harpes, C. P., Aubigny, M., Aubert, J., Incoul, C., … Tanenbaum, D. (2009). MICIE ICT system requirements - Preliminary version. In M. Castrucci (Ed.), MICIE Project Deliverable D4.1.1. European Commission FP7.

Cherdantseva, Y., Burnap, P., Blyth, A., Eden, P., Jones, K., Soulsby, H., & Stoddart, K. (2016). A review of cyber security risk assessment methods for SCADA systems. *Computers & Security, 56*, 1–27. doi:10.1016/j.cose.2015.09.009

CRISALIS Consortium. (2015). *CRISALIS - CRitical Infrastructure Security AnaLysIS*. Retrieved October 15, 2019, from https://cordis.europa.eu/project/rcn/103538/factsheet/en

Dari, E. Y., & Essaaidi, M. (2015). An overview of smart grid cyber-security state of the art study. In *Proceedings of the 3rd International Renewable and Sustainable Energy Conference (IRSEC)* (pp. 1-7). New York: IEEE. 10.1109/IRSEC.2015.7455097

Ebrahimy, R., & Pourmirza, Z. (2017). Cyber-interdependency in smart energy systems. In *Proceedings of the 3rd International Conference on Information Systems Security and Privacy (ICISSP 2017)* (pp. 529-537). Setúbal, Portugal: SciTePress. 10.5220/0006262805290537

EEBus Initiative E. V. (2019). Retrieved November 10, 2019, from https://www.eebus.org/en/technology/

El Mrabet, Z., & Kaabouch, N. (2018). Cyber-security in smart grid: Survey and challenges. *Computers & Electrical Engineering, 67*, 469–482. doi:10.1016/j.compeleceng.2018.01.015

Faisal, M. A., Aung, Z., Williams, J. R., & Sanchez, A. (2015). Data-stream-based intrusion detection system for advanced metering infrastructure in smart grid: A feasibility study. *IEEE Systems Journal, 9*(1), 31–44. doi:10.1109/JSYST.2013.2294120

Flick, T., & Morehouse, J. (2010). *Securing the smart grid: Next generation power grid security*. Burlington, MA: Syngress.

Foglietta, C., Panzieri, S., Macone, D., Liberati, F., & Simeoni, A. (2013). Detection and impact of cyber attacks in a critical infrastructures scenario: The CockpitCI approach. *International Journal of System of Systems Engineering, 4*(3/4), 211–221. doi:10.1504/IJSSE.2013.057669

Ghasempour, A. (2019). Internet of Things in smart grid: Architecture, applications, services, key technologies, and challenges. *Inventions MDPI Journal, 4*(1). *Article, 22*, 1–12.

Goel, S., & Hong, Y. (2015). Security challenges in smart grid implementation. In S. Gaycken (Ed.), *SpringeBriefs in Cybersecurity. Smart grid security* (pp. 1–39). London, UK: Springer-Verlag.

International Electrotechnical Commission (IEC). (2016). Communication networks and systems in substations. *IEC Standard 61850-5.*

Jaradat, M., Jarrah, M., Bousselham, A., Jararweh, Y., & Al-Ayyoub, M. (2015). The Internet of Energy: Smart sensor networks and Big Data management for smart grid. *Procedia Computer Science, 56,* 592–597. doi:10.1016/j.procs.2015.07.250

Kathirvel, K., Ramachandran, C., & Sivarathy, N. (2018). A survey on IDs using clustering techniques in data mining. *International Journal of Pure and Applied Mathematics, 118*(8), 655–660.

Knapp, E. D., & Samani, R. (2013). *Applied cyber security and the smart grid: Implementing security controls into the modern power infrastructure.* Waltham, MA: Syngress.

Kumar, S., & Dutta, K. (2016). Intrusion detection in mobile ad hoc networks: Techniques, systems, and future challenges. *Security and Communication Networks, 9*(14), 2484–2556. doi:10.1002ec.1484

Mendel, J. (2017). Smart grid cyber security challenges: Overview and classification. *E-mentor, 68*(1), 55–66. doi:10.15219/em68.1282

Mo, Y., Kim, T. H.-J., Brancik, K., Dickinson, D., Lee, L., Perrig, A., & Sinopoli, B. (2012). Cyber-physical security of a smart grid infrastructure. *Proceedings of the IEEE, 100*(1), 195–209. doi:10.1109/JPROC.2011.2161428

Mohagheghi, S., Stoupis, J., & Wang, Z. (2009). Communication protocols and networks for power systems-current status and future trends. In *Proceedings of the IEEE/PES Power Systems Conference and Exposition* (pp. 1-9). New York: IEEE. 10.1109/PSCE.2009.4840174

National Institute of Standards and Technology (NIST). (2012). *NIST framework and roadmap for smart grid interoperability standards (NIST Special Publication 1108, Release 2.0).* Gaithersburg, MD: U.S. NIST.

Otuoze, A. O., Mustafa, M. W., & Larik, R. M. (2018). Smart grids security challenges: Classification by sources of threats. *Journal of Electrical Systems and Information Technology, 5*(3), 468–483. doi:10.1016/j.jesit.2018.01.001

Parra, I., Rodríguez, A., & Arroyo-Figueroa, G. (2014). Electric utility enterprise architecture to support the smart grid-enterprise architecture for the smart grid. In *Proceedings of 11th International Conference on Informatics in Control, Automation, and Robotics (ICINCO 2014)* (pp. 673-679). New York: IEEE. 10.5220/0005014006730679

Patel, A., Alhussian, H., Pedersen, J. M., Bounabat, B., Celestino, J. Jr, & Katsikas, S. (2017). A nifty collaborative intrusion detection and prevention architecture for smart grid ecosystems. *Computers & Security, 64,* 92–109. doi:10.1016/j.cose.2016.07.002

Radoglou-Grammatikis, P. I., & Sarigiannidis, P. G. (2019). Securing the smart grid: A comprehensive compilation of intrusion detection and prevention systems. *IEEE Access: Practical Innovations, Open Solutions, 7,* 46595–46620. doi:10.1109/ACCESS.2019.2909807

Rawat, D. B., & Bajracharya, C. (2015). Cyber security for smart grid systems: Status, challenges and perspectives. In *Proceedings of the SoutheastCon* (pp. 1-6). New York: IEEE. 10.1109/SECON.2015.7132891

Rodofile, N. R., Radke, K., & Foo, E. (2016). DNP3 network scanning and reconnaissance for critical infrastructure. In *Proceedings of Australasian Computer Science Week Multiconference* (Article 39). New York: ACM. 10.1145/2843043.2843350

Rojas González, I., & Sánchez Pérez, G. (2015). Framework for the development of secure web systems for electrical companies. In *Proceedings of 2015 CIGRÉ SCD2 Colloquium*. Paris, France: CIGRÉ.

Situation AWare Security Operations Center (SAWSOC). (2016). CORDIS, European Commission. Retrieved November 10, 2019, from https://cordis.europa.eu/project/rcn/110931/factsheet/it

Unterweger, M. (2018). *From the Internet of Things (IoT) to the Internet of Energy (IoE). (Technical Article)*. Siemens. Available from IoT-Siemens Download Center.

Usman, M., & Faruque, M. O. (2019). Applications of synchrophasor technologies in power systems. *Journal of Modern Power Systems and Clean Energy*, 7(2), 211–226. doi:10.100740565-018-0455-8

Wang, K., Yu, J., Yu, Y., Qian, Y., Zeng, D., Guo, S., ... Wu, J. (2018a). A survey on Energy Internet: Architecture, approach, and emerging technologies. *IEEE Systems Journal*, 12(3), 2403–2416. doi:10.1109/JSYST.2016.2639820

Wang, K., Zhang, Y., Guo, S., Dong, M., Hu, R. Q., & He, L. (2018b). IEEE Access special section editorial: The Internet of Energy: architectures, cybersecurity, and applications – part II. *IEEE Access: Practical Innovations, Open Solutions*, 6, 79276–79279. doi:10.1109/ACCESS.2018.2885242

Wang, W., & Lu, Z. (2013). Cyber security in the Smart Grid: Survey and challenges. *Computer Networks*, 57(5), 1344–1371. doi:10.1016/j.comnet.2012.12.017

Wang, X., & Yi, P. (2011). Security framework for wireless communications in smart distribution grid. *IEEE Transactions on Smart Grid*, 2(4), 809–818. doi:10.1109/TSG.2011.2167354

World Energy Council. (2015). *World-energy-resources*. Retrieved November 10, 2019, from https://www.worldenergy.org/assets/images/imported/2016/10/World-Energy-Resources-Full-report-2016.10.03.pdf

Wu, S. X., & Banzhaf, W. (2010). The use of computational intelligence in intrusion detection systems: A review. *Applied Soft Computing*, 10(1), 1–35. doi:10.1016/j.asoc.2009.06.019

ADDITIONAL READING

Cerra, A. (2019). *The cybersecurity playbook: How every leader and employee can contribute to a culture of security*. Hoboken, NJ: John Wiley & Sons, Inc.

Kabalci, E., & Kabalci, Y. (2019). *From smart grid to Internet of Energy*. Cambridge, MA: Academic Press.

Maleh, Y. (Ed.). (2018). *Security and privacy management, techniques, and protocols*. Hershey, PA: IGI Global. doi:10.4018/978-1-5225-5583-4

Muhanji, S. O., Flint, A. E., & Farid, A. M. (2019). eIoT: The development of the Energy Internet of Things in energy infrastructure. Cham, Switzerland: Springer International Publishing.

Patel, A., Taghavi, M., Bakhtiyari, K., & Celestino, J. Jr. (2013). An intrusion detection and prevention system in cloud computing: A systematic review. *Journal of Network and Computer Applications*, *36*(1), 25–41. doi:10.1016/j.jnca.2012.08.007

Scarfone, K., & Mell, P. (2007). *Guide to intrusion detection and prevention systems (IDPS) (NIST Special Publication 800-94)*. Gaithersburg, MD: U.S. National Institute of Standards and Technology.

Sikos, L. F. (Ed.). (2018). Intelligent systems reference library: Vol. 151. *AI in cybersecurity*. Cham, Switzerland: Springer International Publishing.

Siozios, K., Anagnostos, D., Soudris, D., & Kosmatopoulos, E. (Eds.). (2019). *IoT for smart grids: Design challenges and paradigms*. Cham, Switzerland: Springer International Publishing. doi:10.1007/978-3-030-03640-9

Wolf, M., & Serpanos, D. (Eds.). (. (2018). Safe and secure cyber–physical systems. [Special issue]. *Proceedings of the IEEE*, *106*(1). doi:10.1109/JPROC.2017.2781198

KEY TERMS AND DEFINITIONS

Collaborative IDPS (CIDPS): A collaborative IDPS is a massive collaboration of a large number of autonomous IDPSs where their information and activities synchronized in order to recognize distributed and concurrent attacks; and adopt proper prevention strategies through collaboration.

Computational Intelligence (CI): Is the development and application of biologically and linguistically motivated computational paradigms such as: Neural Networks, Fuzzy Systems and Evolutionary Computation.

Framework to Develop Secure Systems: Is a framework of security and access control for the development of secure Web systems for Smart Grid.

Internet of Energy (IoE): Is the implementation of Internet of Things (IoT) technology into energy grid to optimize the efficiency of energy infrastructure and reduce cost.

Internet of Things (IoT): Refers to the billions of physical devices around the world that are now connected to the internet, collecting and sharing data.

Intrusion Detection and Prevention System (IDPS): Is a system for the detection and prevention of attacks in networks or device.

Smart Grid (SG): Is an electricity supply network that uses digital communications technology to detect and react to local changes in usage.

Chapter 14
Cloud–Based Dynamic Line Rating:
Architecture, Services, and Cyber Security

Valentina V. Timčenko
https://orcid.org/0000-0002-6667-2155
Mihailo Pupin Institute, University of Belgrade, Serbia

ABSTRACT

Introduction of the Dynamic Line Rating (DLR) concept has an important role in implementing smart grids in the power utility's transmission network. DLR assumes real-time control of the overhead transmission line, based on the continuous evaluation of the actual thermal and other operating conditions, and further estimation of the maximum transmission line's load and other relevant parameters that determine operational limitations. This chapter presents cloud-based DLR systems in terms of architecture, cloud services, and cyber security issues. DLR systems are explored with regards to cloud computing in industry, applicable cloud services and infrastructures, and communication system's performance. Security and privacy of cloud-based DLR systems have been addressed in terms of public and private services. A secure hybrid cloud-based architecture to support DLR is proposed.

INTRODUCTION

Advanced information and communication technologies (ICT) such as cloud computing, Internet of Things (IoT), big data, mobile Internet are gradually being deployed in the industrial sector. In the power industry, such a trend is continuing toward smart grids, Industrial IoT (IIoT) and the Internet of Energy (IoE). These new technologies should be used in production, transmission and distribution of electric power, thus constituting an intelligent electric power system (Zhou, Yang, & Shao, 2016).

Most of countries have experienced restructuring of their electric utility companies, due to the liberalization of the electricity market, as well as the rapid and continuous development of technologies for production of electric energy. Probably, the most significant changes relate to the use of distributed and renewable energy sources (Vezzoli et al., 2018, pp. 23-39). These processes caused an increase in

DOI: 10.4018/978-1-7998-2910-2.ch014

electricity trading on the energy commodities exchange. The deregulated energy market forced fundamental changes in the investment and operational decisions regarding transmission lines. All these facts have strongly influenced the research, development and implementation of Dynamic Line Rating (DLR) systems.

Introduction of the DLR concept allows for a real-time control of the transmission line, based on the continuous evaluation of the actual thermal and other operating conditions, and further estimation of the acceptable transmission line's load and other relevant parameters that determine operational limitations. DLR systems detect additional available capacities and, in this way, provide advantageous conditions for power system management procedures.

DLR system can be implemented as a stand-alone solution, but it is commonly integrated with the power utility's Supervisory Control And Data Acquisition (SCADA) system (Bostjancic Rakas, Timcenko, A. Kabovic, & M. Kabovic, 2016; Uski-Joutsenvuo & Pasonen, 2013). Information obtained from the DLR system can further be processed by the utility Energy Management System (EMS) or Distribution Management System (DMS).

DLR systems perform continuous data acquisition and analysis and based on that provide energy optimization, prevention from the conductor overheating, and enhance the overall security and reliability of the power system. Since DLR operation relies strongly on receiving accurate data in real time, the information security is of the most importance and should be implemented with special care. Actually, implementation of the DLR system requires a proper level of information and network infrastructure security. Some recent initiatives were raised towards the proper and full assessment of the DLR data application in the operating environment (Federal Energy Regulatory Commission [FERC], 2019; U.S. Department of Energy, 2019). These reports define and analyze the impact of DLR systems on the availability of transmission line capacity, the optimization and accuracy in the process of the DLR protocol implementation, interoperability and cyber security capabilities, as well as the financial and environmental impacts.

DLR plays an important role in implementing the smart grids in the transmission network, thus allowing for prompt response in the case of detected incidents (Budka, Deshpande, & Thottan, 2014, pp. 209-225; National Association of State Energy Officials [NASEO], 2011). Cloud computing is a prospective model for support of smart grid applications due to its advanced computing and data storage capabilities, flexibility, provision for big data analytics, as well as cost savings (Dileep, 2020; Markovic, Zivkovic, Branovic, Popovic, & Cvetkovic, 2013). At the same time, cloud computing brings in some risks, primary in terms of security and reliability (Yigit, Gungor, & Baktir, 2014).

The objectives of this chapter are: (1) to provide a survey of technical capabilities for implementing DLR systems using cloud computing services and (2) to assess advantages and disadvantages of cloud-based DLR solutions with particular focus on cyber security, as a main risk factor.

The rest of the chapter is organized as follows. The background section presents general architecture of DLR systems as well as a brief overview of cloud computing. The following section deals with general security issues in cloud computing environment. After that, cloud-based DLR systems are explored, including general considerations about cloud computing in industry, discussion on cloud services and infrastructures that are applicable to DLR systems, and communication system's performance. Next, security and privacy of cloud-based DLR systems have been addressed in terms of public and private services. Additionally, a secure hybrid cloud-based architecture to support DLR is proposed. Suggestions for the future research and final conclusions close the chapter.

BACKGROUND

DLR Systems

Traditionally, power utilities have evaluated the operation of overhead transmission lines by static thermal rating, which is normally based upon the worst-case weather assumptions and specific conductor parameters. Proliferation of renewable energy generation sources worldwide causes that power generation is becoming highly dependent on the weather and climate conditions. Power generation from most renewable energy sources, such as wind farms and solar panels, is a direct function of the onsite meteorological conditions (Michiorri et al., 2015). Hydro-power is also dependent on weather conditions, but with different, less variable dynamics (Ramos, Castelletti, Pulido-Velazquez, & Gustafsson, 2016).

With the introduction of DLR concept, a considerable improvement was gained, since it enables dynamic increase of power lines' transmission capacity and improves power grids' operating security (McCall, & Goodwin, 2015). DLR system performs real-time management of the overhead transmission lines, i.e., it continuously estimates permissible carrying capacity (ampacity) of the transmission line, taking into actual thermal and operating conditions. The main goal of the DLR system is to properly respond to transmission line capacity limit, while preserving system's reliability, availability, and security.

There are two main categories of methods for calculation of DLR ratings, which use either direct or indirect monitoring sensors. Direct monitoring sensors allow observation of different conductor's variables, such as line tension, line sag, line vibrations, conductor temperature, etc., while the indirect monitoring sensors measure weather parameters, such as wind speed, wind direction, solar radiation, ambient temperature, air pressure (A. Kabovic, M. Kabovic, Bostjancic Rakas, & Timcenko, 2018; Estanqueiro et al., 2018; Uski-Joutsenvuo & Pasonen, 2013).

Every DLR system that uses such measurements for determining conductor ampacity has three main parts: sensor unit, communication system, and system for data acquisition, processing and distributing. The sensor unit is installed on or near the conductor line. It represents an embedded system using wireless communication, such as Universal Mobile Telecommunications System (UMTS) and/or Long-Term Evolution (LTE), for sending the data to the nearby communication device (usually located on the transmission line tower) or directly to the central acquisition server, through appropriate Wide Area Network (WAN) links. The exact location of the sensor unit is determined taking into account the minimal wind speed and minimal ground clearance (the distance between the transmission line and the object on the ground). The data from sensor units is collected in real time every 1 to 10 minutes, depending on the type of the sensor and conditions of the transmission line's load.

A general architecture of the DLR system is presented in Figure 1. It consists of the three main parts: a measuring unit, a DLR server, and workstations. *The measuring unit* encompasses a sensor unit and weather station. The sensor unit (SU) measures conductor temperature, tension and/or sag, and it is mounted on the transmission line. The weather station (WS) is located right next to the sensor unit or on the specific distances from the sensor unit, and it measures ambient parameters (air temperature, wind speed and direction, solar radiation). Measuring units can be directly connected to field devices as well, such as remote terminal units (RTUs). Data collected from measuring units is send to *DLR server*, a server for acquisition and processing of the obtained data. DLR server determines the conductor ampacity, taking into account the actual conditions of the transmission line and ambient. All collected data is stored in appropriate database. Processed data is sent to the control system (SCADA). *Work stations* are used for real time monitoring of particular transmission line's temperature and ampacity, as well as for maintenance and configuration of measuring units.

The DLR server can be configured to send messages to the electric utility's SCADA system, using some of standard or proprietary telecontrol protocols. These messages are then processed by EMS or DMS, for display and calculations.

The main benefits of the DLR system are as follows:

- Increase of the transmission system efficiency, i.e., more efficient utilization of transmission line's load.
- Operational flexibility of the transmission system.
- Improved utilization of the existing assets, which decreases overall costs.
- Greenhouse gas emissions reduction, through integration of renewable energy resources.
- Improvement of the security of power grid's operation in normal operating conditions.

In order to get the full benefit of the DLR system, it is also necessary to use the methods for short term (few hours) and long term (up to two days) forecasting. Short term forecasting allows for the dispatchers to make the right decision in case of unpredictable situations or variations in energy generation from wind farms. Long term forecasting helps with the energy trading, particularly if renewable energy resources are deployed (Ardito, Procaccianti, Menga, & Morisio, 2013; Aznarte & Siebert, 2017).

Figure 1. A general architecture of the DLR system

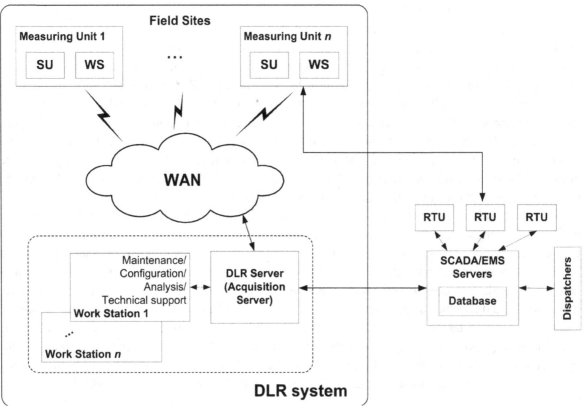

In addition to the fact that allows maximization of transmitted energy, DLR system with the long-term forecasting can predict the amount of energy obtained from the wind farms. Therefore, DLR system represents an important part of the energy management system. Such a complex system operates with large number of data in real time, thus requiring significant computing resources.

Basic Features of Cloud Computing

The U.S. National Institute of Standards and Technology (NIST) defines cloud computing as "a model for enabling ubiquitous, convenient, on-demand network access to a shared pool of configurable computing resources (e.g., networks, servers, storage, applications, and services) that can be rapidly provisioned and released with minimal management effort or service provider interaction" (Mell & Grance, 2011, p. 2).

A cloud infrastructure is the collection of hardware and software that enables the following five essential characteristics of cloud computing: on-demand self-service, broad network access, resource pooling, rapid elasticity and measured service (Mell & Grance, 2011, p. 2). It can be public, private or hybrid. With the public cloud, ICT services are delivered across the Internet. The services may be free, subscription-based or freemium (a mix of the words "free" and "premium"; a basic service is provided free of charge, but additional features are charged). Private cloud refers to an infrastructure that is owned or leased by a single organization. The data center resources may be located on-premises or operated by a third-party vendor. Hybrid cloud is a mix of private and public cloud infrastructures, which are connected by standard or proprietary technology that allows portability of data and applications. The resources are typically coordinated as an integrated infrastructure environment.

Basically, cloud computing offers to end users computer resources and storage capacities hosted on the Internet rather than on a local server or personal computer. The users may access to cloud resources through web browsers or computer applications, while their data and applications remain on cloud servers, at a remote location.

According to Mell and Grance (2011), there are three basic cloud service models:

1. **Software as a Service (SaaS):** Offers the authorized consumers to use provider's applications (through various client interfaces) running on a cloud infrastructure. Consumers are allowed to control only a limited set of user-specific application configuration settings.
2. **Platform as a Service (PaaS):** Enables the authorized consumers to deploy their own or the acquired applications using software development environments (platforms) supported by the cloud service provider. Consumers retain control over applications and some platform configuration settings, while cloud provider controls everything else (network, servers, operating systems, storage).
3. **Infrastructure as a Service (IaaS):** Assumes the lease of computing infrastructure in terms of virtual servers, storage capacities and other basic computer resources. The consumers can deploy and run arbitrary software, including operating system and applications. They retain control over operating systems, middleware, and deployed applications and, in some cases, some networking components such as host firewalls.

Besides the three aforementioned cloud service models (categories), the International Telecommunication Union – Telecommunication Standardization Sector (ITU-T, 2014) defines four additional categories:

- **Communications as a Service (CaaS):** Offers the consumers real time interaction and collaboration.
- **Compute as a Service (CompaaS):** Offers the consumers the use of processing resources needed to deploy and run their own software.
- **Data Storage as a Service (DSaaS):** Enables the consumers the use of data storage and related capabilities.
- **Network as a Service (NaaS):** Offers the consumers the transport connectivity and related network capabilities.

The emerging cloud service categories encompass: Database as a Service, Desktop as a Service, Email as a Service, Management as a Service, and Security as a Service (ITU-T, 2014).

CLOUD SECURITY

Cloud security encompasses a broad set of policies, controls, procedures and technologies that are used to protect data, applications, and infrastructures involved in cloud computing.

Security risks in the cloud are usually considered as shared responsibility between the cloud provider and the customer. In other words, the provider cares about security of the cloud itself, while the customers deal with security of what they put in the cloud, depending on the type of cloud service. In every cloud service, the customers are responsible for securing access and protecting their data from security threats. Table 1 summarizes shared responsibilities for security in the basic cloud service models (Stojanovic, Bostjancic Rakas, & Markovic-Petrovic, 2018).

Ravi Kumar et al. (2018) provide a comprehensive survey of cloud security issues. They identify the four major categories of data security issues and discuss possible solutions under each of these categories:

- Confidentiality, integrity and availability (CIA triad) related security issues.
- Authentication and access control (AAC) related security issues.
- Broken authentication, session and access control.
- Other minor data-related security issues, which can occur through data location, multi-tenancy and backup in the cloud.

Table 1. Shared responsibility for security in basic cloud service models

Feature	Responsibility		
	IaaS	PaaS	SaaS
• User access.	• Customer.	• Customer.	• Customer.
• Data.	• Customer.	• Customer.	• Customer.
• Applications.	• Customer.	• Customer.	• Cloud provider.
• Middleware.	• Customer.	• Cloud provider.	• Cloud provider.
• Operating system.	• Customer.	• Cloud provider.	• Cloud provider.
• Virtualization.	• Cloud provider.	• Cloud provider.	• Cloud provider.
• Servers.	• Cloud provider.	• Cloud provider.	• Cloud provider.
• Storage.	• Cloud provider.	• Cloud provider.	• Cloud provider.
• Networking.	• Cloud provider.	• Cloud provider.	• Cloud provider.

Cloud vulnerabilities also depend on the type of service model. Therefore, SaaS security issues are similar to those of web service, PaaS is particularly susceptible to shared technology issues, while IaaS is disposed to all of the threats that are well known from the traditional ICT infrastructure.

Finally, most of international standardization bodies adopted (or are adopting) standards for cloud security. Common standards for management of the information security are adopted by the International Organization from Standardization (ISO) and the International Electrotechnical Commission (IEC), and belong to the ISO/IEC 27000-series. The standard ISO/IEC 27017 (ISO, 2015) provides enhanced controls for cloud service providers and cloud service customers. It clarifies both party's roles and responsibilities and also deals with the issues such as the removal/return of assets when a contract is terminated, protection and separation of the customer's virtual environment, virtual machine configuration, administrative operations and procedures associated with the cloud environment, cloud customer monitoring of activity within the cloud, virtual and cloud network environment alignment. This standard is also adopted by the ITU-T, in its recommendation X.1631.

CLOUD-BASED DLR SYSTEMS

Cloud Computing in Industry

In the past few years, cloud computing is being progressively focused to corporate systems. Cost savings, scalability, centralized data storage, efficient system configuration and maintenance are some reasons that make migration to cloud environment interesting to companies. Cloud service providers adopt a "pay as you go" or OpEx (operational expenditure) model, which allows customers to pay only for what they use. Leasing of computing resources and access to them are performed on-demand, at a less price than buying, installing and maintaining their own ICT equipment. Consequently, the number of technical staff is also being reduced.

The most popular public cloud service providers, such as Amazon Web Services, Google Cloud Platform, or Microsoft Azure, are making intensive efforts toward the "Industry cloud", i.e., cloud solutions that will meet the needs of organizations with business operations in industries (Sanders, 2019). Examples of specialized industry cloud service providers include NTT DATA, SAP, Veeva Systems, NCR, Shopify, etc. These industry-oriented services extend general-purpose cloud services, particularly SaaS offerings, with customer relationship management (CRM) and enterprise resource planning (ERP) services. They also include PaaS and IaaS service categories.

Industry cloud is not limited to public services; hybrid and private industry cloud infrastructures can be deployed with the assistance of system integration companies specialized in cloud design and implementation.

In the electric power industry, cloud computing is typically applied for information management and distributed energy management (Yigit et al., 2014). As already mentioned, cloud computing offers several benefits for smart grid applications. Particularly, it provides hardware and software resources needed to support big data analytics (Benhaddou et al., 2015). In addition, scalability and elasticity provided by cloud computing services contribute to continuity and accuracy of dynamic smart grid operations such as prediction, load management, as well as optimization of demand and consumption (Ardito et al., 2013).

Electrical distribution systems are another important application area of industry cloud computing. The web-based cloud platforms provide consumers the real-time information about energy usage and cost of energy. This helps residents to organize their energy consumption and reduce bills. Besides, such applications can help users to select an optimal tariff plan according to their consumer profile.

Cloud Services and Infrastructures Applicable to DLR Systems

Since the DLR system is typically integrated with the SCADA/EMS system, as explained in the background section, migration of SCADA toward cloud environment may impact the cloud-based DLR system architecture. Stojanovic et al. (2018) discuss migration scenarios of SCADA systems to the cloud, and distinguish public and private/hybrid cloud computing environments.

Following such an approach, in the public cloud scenario, the DLR server is running on company's premises, and is directly connected to sensor elements. It transfers data to the cloud where they can be stored and distributed toward remote work stations. In the private/hybrid cloud scenario, a distributed DLR application is completely executed in the cloud environment, and is remotely connected to sensor elements, via WAN links.

Figure 2 illustrates possible applications of cloud computing in DLR systems in terms of different cloud services and different types of cloud infrastructure. Typical applications of cloud computing in DLR systems encompass:

1. Storage of big data that are being collected over a long term period from the large number of sensor elements, as well as the relevant meteorological data. Such databases can be implemented using the following cloud services:
   a. **DaaS**: Enables data management and optimization in the cloud. It is typically offered as a public cloud service.
   b. **CompaaS**: Assumes cloud processing resources (e.g., virtual machines), needed to deploy and run utility's own software for database management. It can be offered as a public cloud service or implemented in the private cloud.
2. Processing of the collected data using a set of various algorithms for short term and long term prediction of the maximum transmission line's load. Such algorithms can be implemented using the following cloud services:
   a. **PaaS**: Provides platforms for big data analysis and visualization of results.
   b. **IaaS**: Provides infrastructure resources needed for data storage, web hosting, network performance monitoring, and high performance computing.

Technically, both services can be deployed in the public and private/hybrid cloud environments; however, security makes a great difference, which is discussed in the next section.

3. SaaS-based DLR Solution is offered as SaaS-based DLR Solution as a public cloud service, which enables weather forecasting at any location of the weather station (e.g., using geospatial data) and managing the data collected from weather stations (Gentle, 2016). Such a service enables the users to track changes of current load in a real time, and to take the appropriate actions based on that information.

Communication System's Performance

Most of industrial applications require strict guarantees for quality of service (QoS) in terms of throughput, delay and packet loss rate. Regarding DLR, in many cases the data sent every minute to DLR system must be reliably transmitted with moderate delay requirements (Vasseur & Dunkels, 2010). Application of public cloud services increases the risk that such guarantees will not be fulfilled, particularly because the network performance is out of users' control (Đorđević, Maček, & Timčenko, 2015). Before making a decision to lease cloud services, each company should take into account consequences of QoS degradation on the industrial process. Increased and unpredictable delay is particularly critical, since it can block operation of the whole real-time system.

System's availability and reliability are possible problems of all systems that use cloud services, because cloud servers are placed at locations that are neither known nor accessible to customers. For that reason, before migration of the industrial system to cloud environment, the company should carefully consider the consequences of data loss (in intervals from several minutes to several hours) to the industrial process.

SECURITY AND PRIVACY OF CLOUD-BASED DLR SYSTEMS

Cyber security and privacy are the most important issues in DLR-based cloud systems. While cyber security denotes the practice of defending information and infrastructure from malicious attacks, privacy relates to company's rights to control confidential information and the way it is used.

Figure 2. Applications of cloud computing in DLR systems: Cloud services and different types of cloud infrastructure

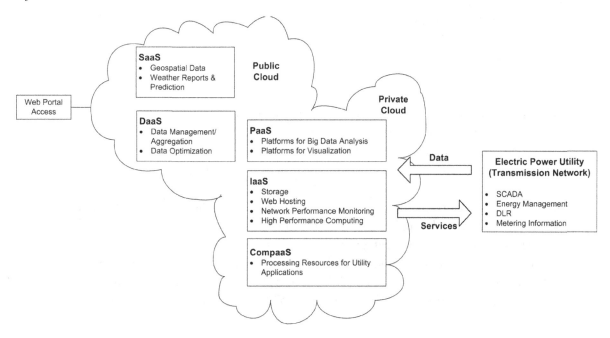

Information and infrastructure security of the industrial systems typically require solutions that are tailored to the control environment. Security management assumes definition and implementation of the appropriate security policies, risk assessment, design of the overall security architecture, as well as selection and implementation of the appropriate security mechanisms.

Due to the need for reliable DLR data acquisition in a real time, protection of information and equipment assumes a number of measures such as implementation of the access control, installing the antivirus software, the use of intrusion detection and prevention systems (IDPSs), data encryption and the use of firewalls (Ardito et al., 2013; Fang et al., 2016).

Security of Public Cloud Services

The most important question concerns the choice of cloud service provider. The choice depends on the offered service maturity, which is assessed according to a set of criteria such as level of QoS guarantees, mutual isolation of applications/traffic originating from different sources, data encryption, level of customer's control regarding changes in the provider's infrastructure, software updating on a regular basis, continuous assessment of security mechanisms efficiency, capability of detecting intrusions in real time, response to detected attacks, etc.

An efficient way to ensure secure services is to establish well-defined service level agreement (SLA) between the customer and the provider (Stojanovic et al., 2018; Yigit et al., 2014). SLA is a contract (agreed and signed by both the cloud provider and the customer) that may include many components, from definition of services to termination of agreement. It typically encompasses technical part (QoS parameters, availability, reliability, specification of security solutions), financial part (e.g., tariffs and billing principles), as well as legal part (rights and obligations of both parties, as well as consequences in the case of contract violation).

Another useful method is to introduce secure service oriented product line, i.e., to integrate security activities in the service oriented product line process, with the objective to proactively produce secure services (Achour, Labed, & Ben Ghezala, 2015).

Cloud-based DLR systems suffer from the same cyber security risks as general-purpose cloud services, described in the background section. Still, several threats in cloud environments might make DLR systems more vulnerable:

- Various forms of Denial of Service (DoS) and Distributed DoS (DDoS), and man-in-the-middle (MITM) attacks such as active eavesdropping, protocol spoofing, etc.
- Insecure network connections between DLR systems and the cloud.
- Lack of protection for some proprietary protocols used in the electric utility.
- The use of commercial off-the-shelf solutions (instead of manufacturing execution systems).

With regards to taxonomy of cloud security issues, presented earlier in this chapter, the following cyber security solutions can be applied for cloud-based DLR systems.

Ensuring Data Confidentiality, Integrity and Availability: In DLR systems, input and output data differ in terms of requirements for confidentiality. Namely, a part of input data is publicly available, e.g., weather reports, weather forecast, etc., while the output information (estimated ampacity) is strictly confidential. Strong encryption algorithms should be applied, including asymmetric cryptographic algorithms such as Rivest–Shamir–Adleman (RSA) and symmetric algorithms such as Advanced Encryption Standard (AES) (Khanezaei & Hanapi, 2014).

Data availability and data integrity are of the key importance for both input and output data (Akyol, 2012). The input data should be unmodified and available in a real time, since they are the basis for estimation of the maximum transmission line's load. Similar considerations stand for the DLR output data, which provide inputs to SCADA/EMS facilities.

The main prerequisite for efficient protection is to classify the data, identify the sensitive data, define security policies, and define appropriate access methods for different types of data. Further, policies for data storage and destroy of data should be specified. This means that physical and logical security protection should be ensured for data storage, together with the backup and recovery plan. Next, it is necessary to identify which type of data can be shared, and to define the appropriate data sharing policy. A corrective action plan should be predefined, in the case of data corruption or hacking. SLA should encompass methods for enforcement of the aforementioned security policies (Ravi Kumar et al., 2018).

Authentication and access control: In the cloud environment, authentication is applied to both the persons and the equipment. Automated actions like online backup, patching and updating operating systems and remote monitoring need to be authorized. Strong authentication techniques are needed, because the cloud services are accessed through various devices and interfaces. These techniques may include username and password, Mobile Trusted Module (MTM), multifactor, Public Key Infrastructure (PKI), single sign-on and biometric authentication (Babaeizadeh, Bakhtiari, & Mohammed, 2015; Farooq, 2017).

Other mechanisms include firewalls, IDPS solutions that are tailored to the industry environment (Hu, A. Yang, H. Li, Y. Sun, & L. Sun, 2018; Macek, Dordevic, Timcenko, Bojovic, & Milosavljevic, 2014), as well as clear distinction of responsibilities between the cloud provider and the user. These mechanisms can be implemented at different network and cloud layers.

Prevention of Breaking Authentication, Session and Access Control: This group of measures encompasses establishing and implementing a well-defined set of strong authentication and session management controls, checking access from unknown/untrusted sources, automated verification of authentication deployment, etc.

Other Useful Security Measures: This group encompasses a number of preventive measures. For example, the customer should be aware of the logical and the physical location of the data in the cloud. Intelligent data segregation techniques should be used by the cloud service provider to mutually isolate data from different users. Finally, strong encryption techniques should also be applied for the backup data to avoid data leakage.

Security of Private Cloud Services

Achieving security in the private cloud infrastructure is much easier, because network owner is responsible for the overall security solutions and functions, including definition of security policies, design of security architecture as well as selection of the appropriate security mechanisms. The main benefits of the private cloud as compared to the public cloud, which contribute to improving the overall security, are as follows:

- Better flexibility in terms of virtualization, e.g., the ability to manage multiple groups of virtual machines with separate administrators.

- No limitations for selection of the operating systems templates and versions, as well as configuration options.
- Ability to implement specific security controls.
- Visibility of security logs, real-time security threats, and other activities.
- Detailed real-time view into cloud operating, statistics, metering, and performance.
- Ability to specify where data is stored.

All these advantages are particularly expressed in private PaaS and IaaS solutions. The private PaaS software can be set up on any type of infrastructure and allows power utility to deploy and manage its business and operational applications while also meeting strict security and privacy requirements. Private IaaS is a unique instance of the cloud service; hence, power utility can customize it to a much greater degree than the public cloud service. The situation is slightly different with the private SaaS, which actually represents SaaS applications delivered on a single tenant architecture hosted in a highly secure network environment. However, cost savings that are the main benefit of public SaaS model are almost neutralized with the private cloud.

Proposal of Secure Hybrid Cloud-based Architecture to Support DLR

Achieving high level of security and privacy assumes implementation of previously described security measures regarding data confidentiality, integrity and availability; authentication and access control; prevention of breaking authentication, session and access control, etc. A secure architecture of the DLR system using hybrid cloud is proposed based on previous analysis, and illustrated in Figure 3. Such architecture can easily be extended to support other smart grid applications.

DLR application is distributed in the private cloud using private PaaS in terms of:

- Collecting measured data from sensor units regarding transmission line's parameters.
- Data aggregation, storage and management, including database management and file hosting service.
- Processing of the assembled data using a set of algorithms for short term and long term prediction of the ampacity.
- Sending the output data to the control system (SCADA) using standard or proprietary telecontrol protocol. Protocol converter is used to achieve the interoperability between the DLR and SCADA systems.

Public SaaS is used to provide publicly available information regarding weather reporting and forecasting at the selected locations.

The four inline network-based IDPSs are collocated with firewalls and installed at network's vulnerability points to cyber attacks. They monitor the traffic in particular network segments and examine the activities of network and application layer protocols in order to identify and stop suspicious activities. Besides events monitoring and analysis, IDPS typically records information about the events, notifies the administrator about important events through warnings and alarms, and generates appropriate reports.

Hybrid cloud infrastructure can take advantage from cost efficiency of public cloud services and the high level of security for critical applications that are running in the private cloud. Besides, private

Figure 3. An architecture of the DLR system using cloud services: public SaaS and private PaaS

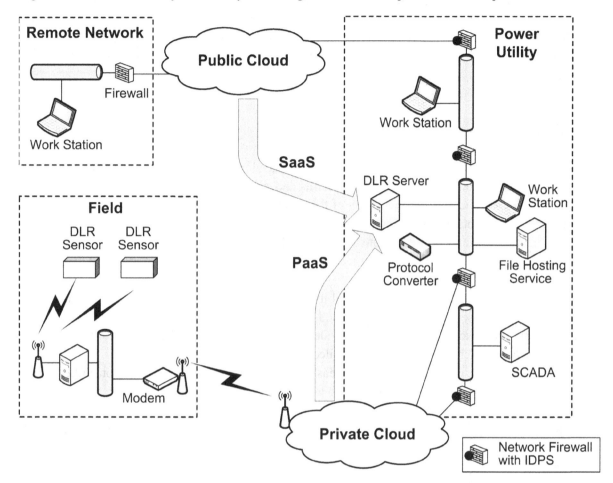

PaaS enables support of different software platforms that are tailored to other critical applications in the power utility.

FUTURE RESEARCH DIRECTIONS

Although smart grids have been widely addressed in the literature, insufficient attention has been paid to cloud-based DLR systems. Hence, additional research work is needed to properly address this important topic. The most relevant future research directions include (but are not restricted to) the following issues.

First, public cloud service providers should make additional efforts to develop a set of secure industry-oriented PaaS and IaaS services. Particularly, secure IaaS might be attractive to power utilities because it provides a high level of customer's control.

Second, the applicability of Security as a Service cloud model to securing DLR systems (and the other parts of smart grid) should be investigated in more details. In this model, cloud service provider may integrate its security services into a corporate infrastructure more cost effectively than the power utility can provide on its own.

Third, a comprehensive cyber security risk analysis should be conducted before making decision to migrate the DLR system toward cloud environment. Therefore, new methods for cyber security risk assessment in smart grids using cloud services should be developed.

Finally, additional work is needed to enhance security mechanisms such as cloud-based IDPS, which must meet the stringent requirements of power utilities operations.

CONCLUSION

Migration of power utility systems to cloud environment is a relatively new business strategy that requires in-depth analysis and thorough evaluation of benefits and risks.

DLR systems and methods for prediction of the maximum transmission line's load, as a functional part of smart grids, contribute to efficient load management in power utility network and optimization of electric energy distribution. Taking into account that DLR system collects and processes in real time massive amount of data, cloud computing technologies can provide sufficient computing and storage resources.

Since DLR systems are a part of the critical infrastructure, they are disposed to additional security threats and vulnerabilities, introduced by the cloud. With public cloud services, one of the most sensitive issues concerns the choice of cloud service provider. For that reason, it is of key importance to establish well-defined SLA, which should include a detailed specification of security controls.

Securing the private cloud infrastructure is easier, because power utility takes responsibility for the overall security of its system, while maintaining technical benefits of cloud computing. Such solutions require a comprehensive cost-benefit analysis.

Finally, hybrid cloud infrastructures are a promising solution because they can benefit from cost efficiency of public cloud services, while retaining high level of security for critical applications that are executed in the private cloud.

ACKNOWLEDGMENT

This research was supported by the Serbian Ministry of Education, Science and Technological Development [grant number TR 32037].

REFERENCES

Achour, I., Labed, L., & Ben Ghezala, H. (2015). Proposition of secure service oriented product line. In *Proceedings of the 6th International Conference on Information Systems and Economic Intelligence* (pp. 52-59). New York: IEEE. 10.1109/ISEI.2015.7358724

Akyol, B. A. (2012). Cyber security challenges in using cloud computing in the electric utility industry (Pacific Northwest National Laboratory Report PNNL-21724). Retrieved August 1, 2019 from https://www.pnnl.gov/main/publications/external/technical_reports/PNNL-21724.pdf

Ardito, L., Procaccianti, G., Menga, G., & Morisio, M. (2013). Smart grid technologies in Europe: An overview. *Energies*, *6*(1), 251–281. doi:10.3390/en6010251

Aznarte, J. L., & Siebert, N. (2017). Dynamic line rating using numerical weather predictions and machine learning: A case study. *IEEE Transactions on Power Delivery*, *32*(1), 335–343. doi:10.1109/TPWRD.2016.2543818

Babaeizadeh, M., Bakhtiari, M., & Mohammed, A. M. (2015). Authentication methods in cloud computing: A survey. *Research Journal of Applied Sciences, Engineering and Technology*, *9*(8), 655–664. doi:10.19026/rjaset.9.1451

Benhaddou, D., Abid, M. R., Achahbar, O., Khalil, N., Rachidi, T., & Al Assaf, M. (2015). Big Data processing for smart grids. *IADIS International Journal on Computer Science and Information Systems*, *10*(1), 32–46.

Bostjancic Rakas, S., Timcenko, V., Kabovic, A., & Kabovic, M. (2016). Cyber security issues in conductor temperature and meteorological measurement based DLR system. In *Proceedings of the Mediterranean Conference on Power Generation, Transmission, Distribution and Energy Conversion* (pp. 1-7). New York: IEEE.

Budka, K. C., Deshpande, J. G., & Thottan, M. (2014). *Computer Communications and Networks. Communication networks for smart grids: Making smart grid real*. London, UK: Springer Verlag. doi:10.1007/978-1-4471-6302-2

Dileep, G. (2020). A survey on smart grid technologies and applications. *Renewable Energy*, *146*, 2589–2625. doi:10.1016/j.renene.2019.08.092

Đorđević, B., Maček, N., & Timčenko, V. (2015). Performance issues in cloud computing: KVM hypervisor's cache modes evaluation. *Acta Polytechnica Hungarica*, *12*(4), 147–165.

Estanqueiro, A., Ahlrot, C., Duque, J., Santos, D., Gentle, J. P., & Abboud, A. W., … Kanefendt, T. (2018). DLR use for optimization of network design with very large wind (and VRE) penetration. In *Proceedings of the 17th Wind Integration Workshop* (Article 263). Darmstadt, Germany: Energynautics GmbH.

Fang, B., Yin, X., Tan, Y., Li, C., Gao, Y., Cao, Y., & Li, J. (2016). The contributions of cloud technologies to smart grid. *Renewable & Sustainable Energy Reviews*, *59*, 1326–1331. doi:10.1016/j.rser.2016.01.032

Farooq, H. (2017). A Review on cloud computing security using authentication techniques. *International Journal of Advanced Research in Computer Science*, *8*(2), 19–22.

Federal Energy Regulatory Commission (FERC). (2019). *Managing transmission line ratings* (Docket No. AD19-15-000). Retrieved September 25, 2019, from https://www.ferc.gov/CalendarFiles/20190823124451-Managing%20Transmission%20Line%20Ratings_Staff%20Paper.pdf

Gentle, J. P. (2016). *Operational and strategic implementation of dynamic line rating for optimized wind energy generation integration* (Technical Report No. INL/EXT-16-40751; TRN: US1702282). Retrieved September 25, 2019, from https://www.osti.gov/servlets/purl/1364098

Hu, Y., Yang, A., Li, H., Sun, Y., & Sun, L. (2018). A survey of intrusion detection on industrial control systems. *International Journal of Distributed Sensor Networks*, *14*(8), 1–14. doi:10.1177/1550147718794615

International Organization for Standardization (ISO). (2015). Information technology – Security techniques – Code of practice for information security controls based on ISO/IEC 27002 for cloud services. *Standard ISO/IEC 27017:2015/ ITU-T X.1631.*

International Telecommunication Union – Telecommunication Standardization Sector (ITU-T). (2014). *Information technology – Cloud computing – Overview and vocabulary. ITU-T Recommendation Y.3500.* Geneva, Switzerland: ITU-T.

Kabovic, A., Kabovic, M., Bostjancic Rakas, S., & Timcenko, V. (2018). Models for short-term forecasting of parameters used for calculation of the overhead line ampacity. In *Proceedings of the 26th Telecommunications forum TELFOR 2018* (pp. 687-690). New York: IEEE. 10.1109/TELFOR.2018.8612136

Khanezaei, N., & Hanapi, Z. M. (2014). A Framework based on RSA and AES encryption algorithms for cloud computing services. In *Proceedings of the IEEE Conference on Systems, Process and Control* (pp. 58-62). New York: IEEE. 10.1109/SPC.2014.7086230

Macek, N., Dordevic, B., Timcenko, V., Bojovic, M., & Milosavljevic, M. (2014). Improving intrusion detection with adaptive support vector machines. *Elektronika ir Elektrotechnika, 20*(7), 57–60. doi:10.5755/j01.eee.20.7.8025

Markovic, D. S., Zivkovic, D., Branovic, I., Popovic, R., & Cvetkovic, D. (2013). Smart power grid and cloud computing. *Renewable & Sustainable Energy Reviews, 24,* 566–577. doi:10.1016/j.rser.2013.03.068

McCall, J. C., & Goodwin, T. (2015). Dynamic Line Rating as a means to enhance transmission grid resilience. In *Proceedings of the CIGRÉ Colloquium – Grid of the Future* (Article 49). CIGRE U.S. National Committee.

Mell, P., & Grance, T. (2011). *The NIST definition of cloud computing (NIST Special Publication 800-145).* Gaithersburg, MD: U.S. National Institute of Standards and Technology.

Michiorri, A., Nguyen, H.-M., Alessandrini, S., Bjørnar Bremnes, J., Dierer, S., Ferrero, E., ... Uski, S. (2015). Forecasting for dynamic line rating. *Renewable & Sustainable Energy Reviews, 52,* 1713–1730. doi:10.1016/j.rser.2015.07.134

National Association of State Energy Officials (NASEO). (2011). *Smart grid and cyber security for energy assurance* (Technical Report). Retrieved September 25, 2019, from https://www.naseo.org/data/sites/1/documents/publications/NASEO_Smart_Grid_and_Cyber_Security_for_Energy_Assurance_rev_November_2011.pdf

Ramos, M. H., Castelletti, A., Pulido-Velazquez, M., & Gustafsson, D. (2016). Weather and climate services for hydropower management. In *Proceedings of the Hydropower and Environmental Sustainability.* Paris, France: Société Hydrotechnique de France (SHF).

Ravi Kumar, P., Herbert Rajb, P., & Jelcianac, P. (2018). Exploring data security issues and solutions in cloud computing. *Procedia Computer Science, 125,* 691–697. doi:10.1016/j.procs.2017.12.089

Sanders, J. (2019, August 1). Guide to industry cloud: What businesses need to know. *ZDNet.* Retrieved September 25, 2019, from https://www.zdnet.com/article/guide-to-industry-cloud-what-businesses-need-to-know/

Stojanović, M. D., Boštjančič Rakas, S. V., & Marković-Petrović, J. D. (2018). Cloud-based SCADA systems: Cyber security considerations and future challenges. In *Proceedings of the 4th Virtual International Conference on Science, Technology and Management in Energy – eNergetics 2018* (pp. 253-260). Nis, Serbia: Research and Development Center "ALFATEC", and Complex System Research Center.

U.S. Department of Energy. (2019). *Dynamic line rating* (Report to Congress). Retrieved September 25, 2019, from https://www.energy.gov/sites/prod/files/2019/08/f66/Congressional_DLR_Report_June2019_final_508_0.pdf

Uski-Joutsenvuo, S., & Pasonen, R. (2013). *Maximising power line transmission capability by employing dynamic line ratings – technical survey and applicability in Finland* (Research Report VTT-R-01604-1). Retrieved September 25, 2019, from http://sgemfinalreport.fi/files/D5.1.55%20-%20Dynamic%20line%20rating.pdf

Vasseur, J.-P., & Dunkels, A. (2010). *Interconnecting smart objects with IP: The next Internet*. Burlington, MA: Morgan Kaufmann.

Vezzoli, C., Ceschin, F., Osanjo, L., M'Rithaa, M. K., Moalosi, R., Nakazibwe, V., & Diehl, J. C. (2018). *Designing sustainable energy for all*. Cham, Switzerland: Springer. doi:10.1007/978-3-319-70223-0

Yigit, M., Gungor, V. C., & Baktir, S. (2014). Cloud computing for smart grid applications. *Computer Networks*, *70*, 312–329. doi:10.1016/j.comnet.2014.06.007

Zhou, K., Yang, S., & Shao, Z. (2016). Energy Internet: The business perspective. *Applied Energy*, *178*, 212–222. doi:10.1016/j.apenergy.2016.06.052

ADDITIONAL READING

Alvarez, D. L., Rosero, J. A., da Silva, F. F., Bak, C. L., & Mombello, E. E. (2016). Dynamic line rating – Technologies and challenges of PMU on overhead lines: A survey. In *Proceedings of the 51st International Universities Power Engineering Conference UPEC* (pp. 1-6). New York: IEEE. 10.1109/UPEC.2016.8114069

Beres, A., Genge, B., & Kiss, I. (2015). A brief survey on smart grid data analysis in the cloud. *Procedia Technology*, *19*, 858–865. doi:10.1016/j.protcy.2015.02.123

Buyya, R., Vecchiola, C., & Thamarai Selvi, S. (2013). *Mastering cloud computing: Foundations and applications programming*. San Francisco, CA: Morgan Kaufmann Publishers Inc.

Estanqueiro, A., Ahlrot, C., Duque, J., Santos, D., Gentle, J. P., & Abboud, A. W., … Kanefendt, T. (2018). DLR use for optimization of network design with very large wind (and VRE) penetration. In *Proceedings of the 17th Int'l Wind Integration Workshop* (pp. 1-8). Stockholm, Sweden: KTH Royal Institute of Technology.

Hari Krishna, B., Kiran, S., Murali, G., & Pradeep Kumar Reddy, R. (2016). Security issues in service model of cloud computing environment. *Procedia Computer Science*, *87*, 246–251. doi:10.1016/j.procs.2016.05.156

International Organization for Standardization (ISO). (2013a). Information technology – Security techniques – Information security management systems – Requirements. *Standard ISO/IEC 27001:2013*.

International Organization for Standardization (ISO). (2013b). Information technology – Security techniques – Code of practice for information security controls. *Standard ISO/IEC 27002:2013*.

Kabovic, A. V., Kabovic, M. M., Bostjancic Rakas, S. V., & Timcenko, V. V. (2017). Short-term wind forecasting based on time series data for Dynamic Line Rating. In *Proceedings of the 25th Telecommunications forum TELFOR 2017*. New York: IEEE. 10.1109/TELFOR.2017.8249456

Lindsey. (n.d.). *SMARTLINE-TCF: Transmission capacity forecasting and dynamic line rating platform*. Retrieved September 25, 2019, from http://lindsey-usa.com/dynamic-line-rating/

Velumadhava Rao, R., & Selvamani, K. (2015). Data security challenges and its solutions in cloud computing. *Procedia Computer Science*, *48*, 204–209. doi:10.1016/j.procs.2015.04.171

KEY TERMS AND DEFINITIONS

Ampacity: The current carrying capacity of an overhead line (expressed in amperes) that a conductor can carry continuously without overheating (a mix of the words "ampere" and "capacity").

Cloud Security: A set of policies, controls, procedures and technologies utilized to protect data, applications, and infrastructures involved in cloud computing.

Data Availability: The process of ensuring that the information is available to end users and applications, on request.

Data Confidentiality: The process of ensuring that the information is not exposed to unauthorized persons, entities and processes.

Data Integrity: The process of ensuring the overall accuracy, completeness, and consistency of data, i.e., a guarantee that the information has not been modified in an unauthorized way.

Dynamic Line Rating (DLR): A real-time control of the transmission line that assumes continuous monitoring of the actual operating conditions, and estimation of the acceptable transmission line's load and other relevant parameters that determine operational limitations.

Industry Cloud: A set of cloud solutions that will meet the needs of organizations with business operations in industries; refers to both public and private cloud infrastructures.

Intrusion Detection and Prevention System (IDPS): A software system that monitors the events occurring in a computer system or network and analyzes them in order to detect possible incidents, to block detected incidents, and to prevent occurring of similar malicious events.

Operational Expenditure (OpEx): The costs for a company to run its business operations on a daily basis.

Chapter 15
Cyber Security in Health:
Standard Protocols for IoT and Supervisory Control Systems

Bruno J. Santos
Instituto Federal de São Paulo, Brazil

Rachel P. Tabacow
Instituto Federal de São Paulo, Brazil

Marcelo Barboza
Instituto Federal de São Paulo, Brazil & Escola Politécnica da Universidade de São Paulo, Brazil

Tarcisio F. Leão
Instituto Federal de São Paulo, Brazil

Eduardo G. P. Bock
Instituto Federal de São Paulo, Brazil

ABSTRACT

Cyber security in Healthcare is a growing concern. Since it has been a proliferation of IoT devices, data breaches from the healthcare industry are increasing the concern about how cyber security can protect data from connected medical devices. Recent years have seen numerous hacking and IT security incidents. Many healthcare organizations are facing problems to defend their networks from cybercriminals. In the current digital era, the physical world has a cyber-representation. Both the real and virtual worlds are connected in areas, such as informatics and manufacturing. Health 4.0 (H4.0) refers to a group of initiatives aiming to improve medical care for patients, hospitals, researchers, and medical device suppliers. Increasing collaboration in terms of medical equipment, artificial organs, and biosensors is a way to facilitate H4.0. As a result, cyber security budgets have increased, new technology has been purchased, and healthcare organizations are improving at blocking attacks and keeping their networks secure.

DOI: 10.4018/978-1-7998-2910-2.ch015

INTRODUCTION

In contemporary society, information is one of the most valuable resources. It does not matter if it is an eastern or western society, information is fundamental in the decision-making process or in the creation of new products and in competitiveness in the healthcare industry. Information enables successful treatments to be distance replicated independently and it turns possible to minimize human errors. New healthcare treatment techniques are created and assimilated with this information. As a valuable asset data is highly protected, redoubling precautions because it is critical in relation to patients' lives. Digital cyber security operates with the objective of protecting this information, privacy and well-being of patients, minimizing risks, establishing controls and establishing an information security policy (Castells, 1997).

Cyber security in Healthcare is a growing concern for further steps towards technological growth of society, especially when it comes to digital threats and data protection. Since there is a proliferation of Internet of Things (IoT) devices, healthcare industry is increasing the concern about how cyber security can protect data from connected medical devices. The United States designed a law to provide privacy standards and to protect medical records that took effect on April 14, 2003. This law also complies with other health information provided by patients, usage and disclosure with health insurance companies, hospitals and even doctors. According to Health Insurance Portability and Accountability Act (HIPAA), last years have seen numerous hacking and information technology (IT) security incidents. Many healthcare organizations are facing problems to defend their network of cybercriminals not just in US but in the whole world. The General Data Protection Regulation (GDPR) is a European Union Regulation accepted on April 27, 2016 (Scholl et al., 2008; Torres, Campos, Martins, & Bock, 2019).

Cybercrime emerged in the late 1970s as the computer IT industry took shape. Even in 2015, healthcare suffered cyberattacks and industry data were compromised in more than 113 million records. More patient records were exposed or stolen in 2015 than in previous 6 years combined (Scholl et al., 2008; Von Solms & Van Niekerk, 2013). Data breaches are growing and cybercriminals are developing sophisticated tools to attack, to gain access to data and to hold data and networks. This book chapter aims to cover the best technologies and academic background to protect healthcare industry with effective policies, standards and procedures (Baheti & Gill, 2011; Bock et al., 2017; Zhou, Thieret, Watzlaf, DeAlmeida, & Parmanto, 2019).

BACKGROUND

An increase in attacks and invasions on medical devices has caused regulators to take notice; Food and Drugs Administration (FDA) issued a safety communication in June 2013 entitled "Cybersecurity for Medical Devices and Hospital Networks". The working group, involving representatives of the FDA, the Office of the National Coordinator for Health Information Technology, and the Federal Communications Commission, has released a report calling for increased private-sector involvement and a risk-based regulatory framework. But the problem is that they did not define the framework, and burdensome with regulation could greatly increase emerging threats. Cyberattack is a clear and present threat in healthcare; thus it is time to organize, convene, and focus in protection of patient data. Since technology has unquestionably improved healthcare, it is mandatory to ensure that the promised benefits continue to be delivered safely (Baheti & Gill, 2011).

An important related topic is Telehealth, an approach that aims to provide high quality health services to people who cannot easily access these services. When it comes to cyber threats and frequently reported health data breaches, many people may be hesitant to use Telehealth-based services. The HIPAA protocol includes comprehensive details that are not always specific to telehealth and is therefore difficult for telehealth professionals to use (Zhou et al., 2019).

The term Industry 4.0 first appeared in Germany in 2011 proposing the beginning of the 4th Industrial Revolution by the combination of technology and intelligent data processing. Due to exponential advance of computers processing capacity, the immense amount of digitized information in networks requires new strategies of industrial innovation and security (Cavalheiro et al., 2011b; Santos et al., 2018).

Industry 4.0 is consolidated by complementing industrial information technology and industrial automation technologies such as: Wireless, Radio Frequency Identification (RFID), Service Oriented Architecture (SOA), Cognitive Computing and Cloud (Perakslis, 2014; Santos et al., 2018). The main pillars of Industry 4.0 are: capacity for decision making and modification of production processes in real time; virtualization of the productive process; decentralization of decision-making processes; modularity in subunits of productive system and interoperability with communication capacity between cyber-physical systems, sensors, actuators and humans. One of the main sectors impacted by Industry 4.0 is the healthcare industry with the common term Health 4.0 (Coventry & Branley, 2018; Tabacow, Bock, & Nakamoto, 2018).

STANDARD PROTOCOLS FOR IOT

The Reconfigurable Platform of Assistive Technology (RPAT) was built based on Computer Integrated Manufacturing (CIM) approach. RPAT can be essentially considered, for all intents and purposes, as a case study presented here, illustrative, didactic and an exploratory experimental research. Even though it is not exactly a production process, RPAT adopts a local driver integration and real-time demand supervision system for all operating system resources and information, for data use, computing, and automation.

The concept of CIM emerged in 1973 as a suggestion for the development of industrial enterprises, proposing an optimization not by increasing the enterprise efficiency in context, but as interdependent, information-driven manner. According to the CIM concept, the main obstacle to the exercise of development functions is the lack of integration between departments, activities, and systems. The global state and greater capacity and adaptability merged into a coordinated, rapid and flexible manner, according to the characteristics of two information sources:

- **External:** Orders and changes or the market/customers.
- **Internal:** The anticipated and unexpected events from the company and the shop floor.

Systems control tools do not use the Distributed Hierarchical Control System (DHCS) concept. As control actions are carried out by the combination of decision-making machines, they are geographically distributed, autonomous and self-contained, by the combination of advanced, work for the implementation of the global control task.

The CIM Hierarchical Structure is the total set of functions that are implemented by a distributed control system, which presents the high level of performance and action index. Thus, actions can be applied at various hierarchical levels, having the specific temporary and temporal characteristics of each level.

A structure of the CIM is made by four levels: machine, cell, sector and factory, where each level is organized hierarchically as shown in Figure 1.

The CIM structure was adapted to the reality of RPAT, being modeled as:

1. **Machine**: Area of operation of local controllers, based on the command and acquisition system of actuators and sensors.
2. **Cell:** Organization of local controllers operations, aiming at a responsive flow of commands.
3. **Sector:** Responsible for the intelligent control of RPAT, based on cognition of operation data, specialist diagnosis and patient treatment evolution.
4. **Factory:** Responsible for RPAT's customization capability for the clinical application of a specific patient even though RPAT comes from an industrial production process.

Industry 4.0 and Health 4.0

Health 4.0 is characterized by high connectivity of devices and equipment, so digital security has become a key element with the expansion of communication networks (Perakslis, 2014). In a Health 4.0 scenario, there is the integration of industry, hospitals, patients and IoT devices, through an intelligent central. Alternatively, systems can count with Artificial Intelligence algorithms, Big Data processing and cloud computing services. A key to ensuring security is access protection. From protecting physical and logical access to devices, the healthcare industry can establish monitoring services and policies to minimize threats (Cavalheiro et al., 2011b).

The security policies are based on the three pillars of prevention procedures: integrity, availability and confidentiality. Integrity guarantees that information has not been unduly altered or unauthorized. If information tampering occurs, it is important to have mechanisms that signal such occurrence. Availability is the guarantee that information will be available whenever necessary. Confidentiality is the certainty that access to information will be made only by those who have the right. It is important to emphasize that the objective is not to deny access to information, but to prevent information from becoming available to undue persons, while ensuring that those who are authorized can access it (Kruse, Frederick, Jacobson, & Monticone, 2017; Perakslis, 2014).

IoT and Collaborative Control Theory

The IoT, or as it may be called, Web of Things (WoT), is a concept that has gained fame and recognition in modern western society. However, while many people can already see the impacts of an interconnected network of smart products connected to the internet, there are several steps that are still being defined in the history of civilization.

One of the points being discussed is the concept of sustainable mobility. Sustainable mobility is one of the main goals of an Intelligent City. Thus, the development of intelligent transport and parking systems is a key aspect in achieving this goal. Among many facilities and benefits to society, security is also an aspect that can guarantee police tracking, speed control policies and fines.

One of the impacts to be measured is the transformation of conventional markets impacting the way people hire and provide services. The business impact of intelligent equipment connected to large databases goes beyond simply connecting people and objects through gadgets.

Figure 1. A structure of CIM and its four levels: machine, cell, sector and factory

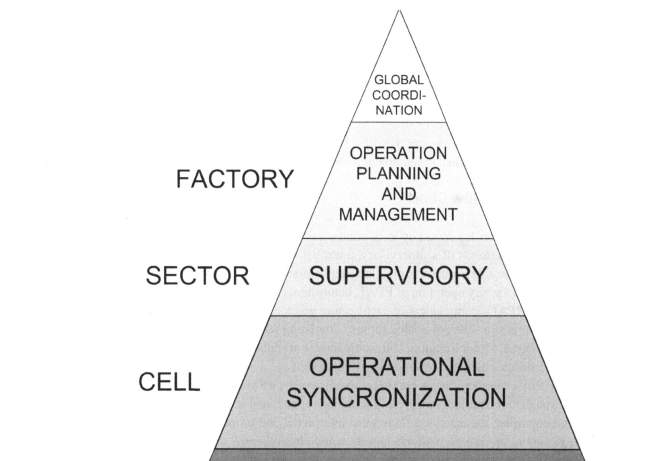

But, as discussed since the beginning of this chapter, a very relevant aspect is the increase in security vulnerabilities and the difficulty of attesting the cyber security linked to the use of IoT, its technical and ethical challenges.

Thus, several IoT protocols focus on the use of security and reciprocity concepts for the protection of critical data. The most commonly used protocols today are: IEEE 802.15.4; IPv6 over Low-Power Wireless Personal Area Networks (6LoWPAN) and Routing Protocol for Low-Power and Lossy Networks (RPL); Message Queuing Telemetry Transport (MQTT); Constrained Application Protocol (CoAP); Data Distribution Service (DDS) and other proprietary protocols.

A discussion regarding future trends in health equipment, artificial organs and biosensors is required for collaborations aiming to improve medical care for patients, change the business practices of hospitals and create new insight for researchers and medical device manufacturers (Sousa Sobrinho et al., 2018).

In fact, in some industries, this practice, which is called digital and cyber convergence, has already been established, and the IoT is the main technology used. IoT is the basis of Industry 4.0 (I4.0) in manufacturing and digital convergence in informatics. These technologies can be studied under collaborative control theory (CCT) ("Cyber crime timeline," n.d.).

Collaboration enables the improvement of any natural or artificial system (Sannino, De Falco, & De Pietro, 2019). Collaboration can be achieved by sharing information, resources, and responsibilities by distributing agents to plan, create and analyze activities required to achieve individual and common goals ("Cyber crime timeline," n.d.).

Based on the Industry 4.0 concept, Health 4.0 (H4.0) has been derived according to the health domain. H4.0 has been established based on collaboration control theory (Sousa Sobrinho et al., 2018).

RPAT Operational Flow Chart

In RPAT, linear actuators are driven by local controllers with acquisition and actuation routines following the operating commands of a supervisory controller incorporated in Health 4.0. In addition, local controllers are responsible for the sensors' data acquisition such as temperature, humidity, RPAT slope and others. For satisfactory operation of RPAT, controllers should have efficient and organized priority communication. RPAT's communication architecture was validated in virtual environment where local controllers interpreted a series of analog inputs, simulating possible sensors (Temperature, Humidity, Load, Applied Force, Motor Rotation, Ultrasonic) and sent status flags (operations, assistance or safety operations in extreme cases) to the supervisory controller.

In supervisory controller, flags were first authenticated by a Structured Query Language (SQL) database, and through the compiled compare and actuation routine, sent actuation flags to the local controller. In the local controller, the actuation flags were interpreted and proportionally triggered the actuators (heating, vibration, movement, platform elevation and physiotherapy routines). During actuation, state data was sent to the supervisory controller, which in turn stored the data in memory and sent it to Big Data, which was simulated by server programs. The structure of RPAT counts with linear actuators, where their association allows the maintenance of RPAT in three different positions:

- Horizontal Execution: Aiming to assist the patient and the physiotherapist in the physiotherapy session.
- Verticalized Execution: Aiming to aid in blood circulation.
- Mixed Execution: Aiming to assist in the transition of a patient with limited movement.

RPAT operations flowcharts are presented at hardware (Figure 2), software (Figure 3), and data (Figure 4) levels.

Figure 2 shows the RPAT operational hardware flowchart and what happens in each predetermined state. In the "zero" state, it can be seen that RPAT is flat like a table or a bed in Physiotherapy Clinic. The state "one" represents the tipping for patient reception. In state "two", RPAT adapts to the curvature of the patient's spine opening option, in state "three" for physiotherapy or recreation.

Figure 3 represents the Human Machine Interface and the operational flowchart. As soon as the zero state routine is started, there is a choice of A (Artificial Intelligence) or B (Cloud Storage), when the decision making impacts on actuators and sensors interacting for each following states (one, two or

Figure 2. RPAT hardware operational flowchart showing states and positions

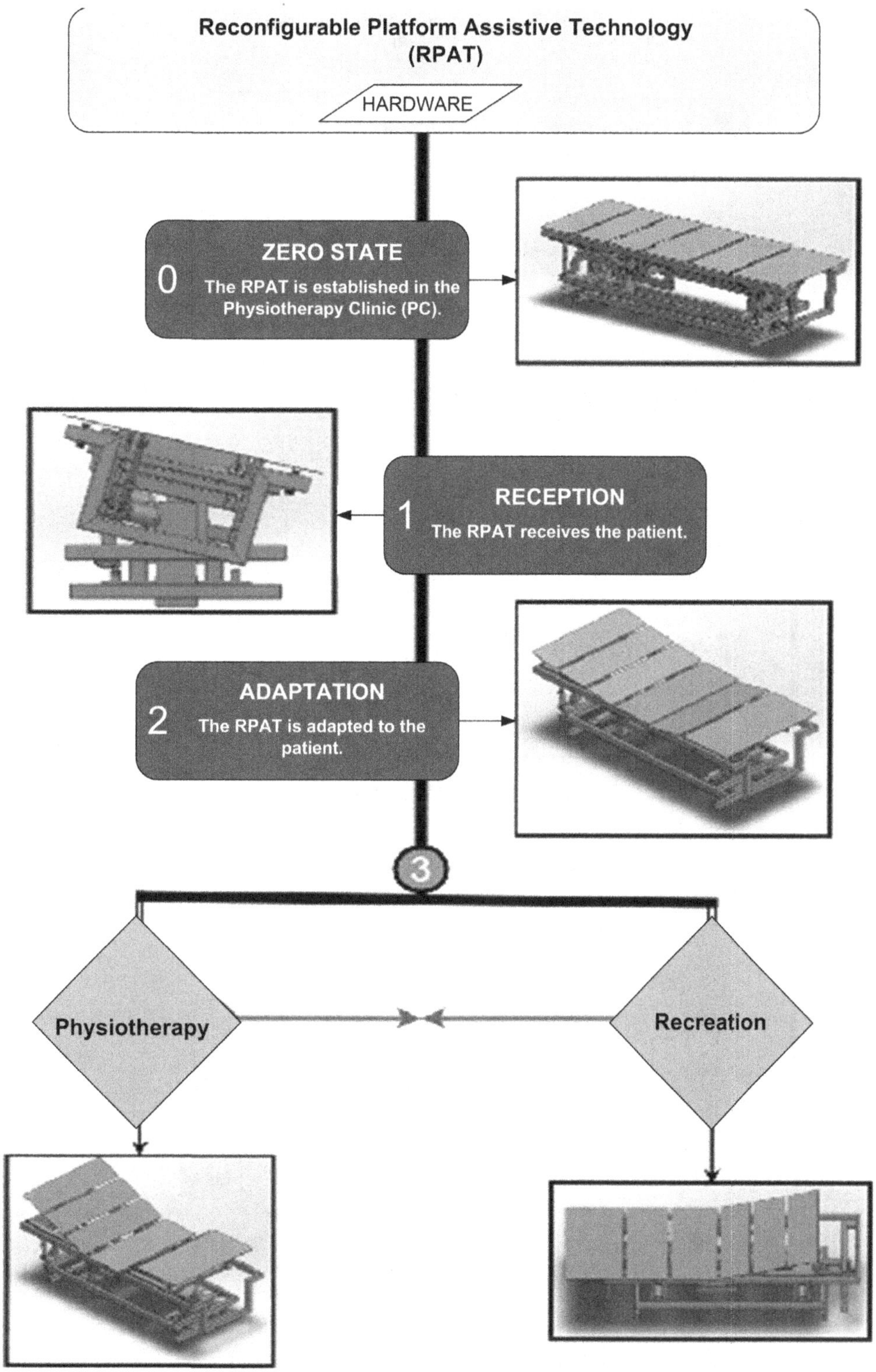

Figure 3. RPAT software interface and operational flowchart

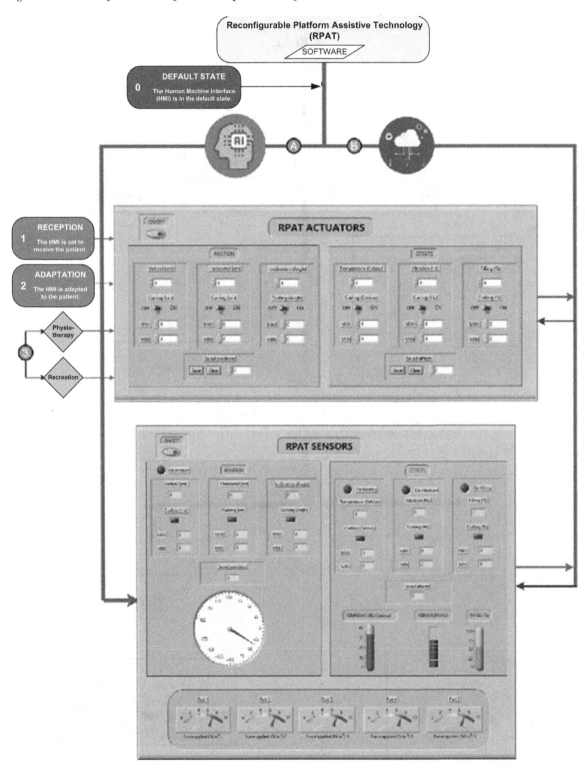

three) option. Each software change is followed by confirmations in the network communication protocol to validate the actual state of the physical mode. Only then, software parameters changes can be made.

The RPAT data flowchart can be seen in Figure 4, showing the actuators, sensors, human-machine interface (HMI), cloud data processing, artificial intelligence (AI), local and supervisory control. For each set of actuators and sensors there is a local control that takes decisions and interacts with supervisory control under a predefined hierarchy. The emergency routine, for example, takes precedence over the demands of local controls and network communication.

Figure 4. RPAT data flowchart showing actuators, sensors, HMI, cloud, AI, local and supervisory control

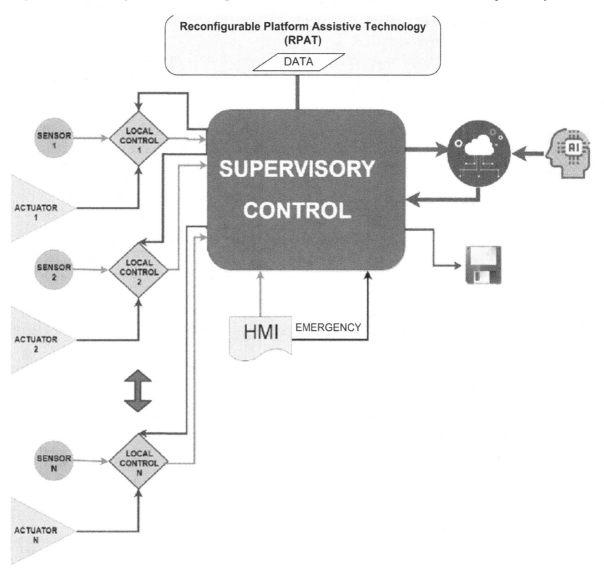

RAMI 4.0 and Supervisory Control Systems

The most commonly used reference architecture model during the third industrial revolution was ISA 95 (Araki et al., 2018). This model is also known as the automation pyramid. The ISA 95 model is hierarchical and centralized in such a way that it is proposed that each layer only communicates with its neighboring layers (Araki et al., 2018; Lu, Morris, & Frechette, 2016; Otto, Campos, De Souza, Martins, & Bock, 2018; Zezulka, Marcon, Vesely, & Sajdl, 2016).

The concept of a Supervisory Control and Data Acquisition (SCADA) does apply with graphics and batch processing parallel with Safety Instrumented System (SIS) as it can be seen in the example illustrated in Figure 5.

In this application, RPAT was modeled with Collaborative Control Theory in order to allow IoT devices hierarchy and assured cyber security. In this case, security and safety are comprised by SIS interaction.

Data acquisition and future implementation algorithms are shown in the third layer (at the top) of Figure 5. First layer is composed by the main RPAT and the three other peripheral subsystems. Each system has its own drivers and controls. Second layer is mainly an adaptation for the Local Control physically management of events with SIS.

In the fourth industrial revolution, to deploy an autonomous, distributed production system that narrows the relationship between real and virtual world, ISA 95 reference architecture is no longer sufficient.

Figure 5. Control architecture and Supervisory Control System based on three layers applied in Reconfigurable Platform of Assistive Technology (adapted from Bock et al., 2017)

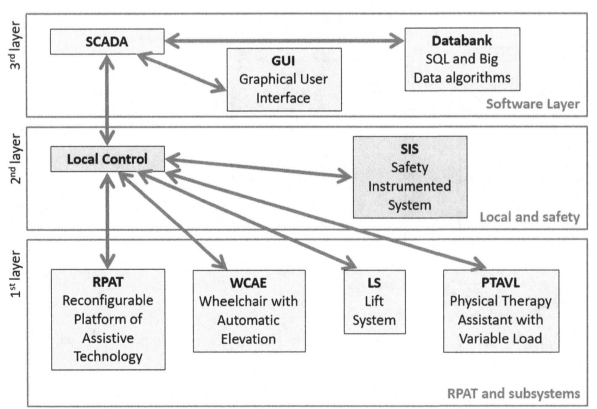

Therefore, Reference Architectural Model for Industry 4.0 (RAMI 4.0) was created (Araki et al., 2017; Leão et al., 2014; Otto et al., 2018; Zezulka et al., 2016). RAMI 4.0 is a reference architecture model for industry 4.0. This model was first presented at the Hannover Fair in 2015 (Adolphs et al., 2015).

RAMI 4.0 was created from the following standards adopted by the International Organization for Standardization (ISO) and the International Electrotechnical Commission (IEC): ISO/IEC 62264, IEC 62541, IEC 61512 and IEC 62890. It proposed a three-dimensional model to provide a basic reference architecture for I4.0 systems. Thus, CIM architecture for healthcare systems can be built from ISO/IEC standards to identify cyber threats at various levels (Bock et al., 2011b; Kagermann, Wahlster, & Helbig, 2013; Uebelhart et al., 2013).

SOLUTIONS AND RECOMMENDATIONS

As can be seen in this chapter, while IoT technologies play important roles in people's daily lives, their incorporation into health systems may leave them vulnerable to threats. This is due to the fact that medical devices are connected and provide easy access. In addition, outdated systems and lack of emphasis on cyber security can make the system and the network unsafe. As the focus of this work is to seek solutions for improving patient safety and health, it should be noted that IoT health technologies contain large amounts of valuable and sensitive data. Other attacks can be motivated by political gains, even by the cyber war itself between countries. An attack can result in the loss of critical equipment functioning within hospitals and intensive care units. The escalation of ransomware attacks in hospitals can paralyze entire health systems (Bock et al., 2011a; Bock et al., 2011c; Bock et al., 2008; Cavalheiro et al., 2011a; Fonseca et al., 2008; Leão et al., 2012).

Critical health systems can be protected by the technologies presented here, and thus, when attacked, human lives will not be at risk.

It is mentioned in the introduction that this work is focused and delimited on the application of standard protocols for IoT and Supervisory Control Systems in 4.0 Health, as we consider that the focus is on applying a technology to control systems without extending the problem to the creation or programming of codes for cyber threats in security systems. The healthcare industry is an attractive target for criminals and digital threats for two key reasons, it is a rich source of valuable data and its defenses are currently weak. Cyber security breaches include health information theft and ransomware attacks in hospitals and may include attacks on deployed medical devices. Therefore, the technological advancement of systems based on safe protocols is fundamental for patient safety (Henriksen, Burkow, Johnsen, & Vognild, 2013; Lutes, 2000; Uwizeyemungu, Poba-Nzaou, & Cantinotti, 2019).

FUTURE RESEARCH DIRECTIONS

Due to the emergence and consolidation of HIPAA, a lot of research work has been done in the field of cyber security in health. Various forms of threats and protections are constantly appearing and evolving, thus making an incessant technological race. Nevertheless, as proposed in this work, a very delicate and subtle theme is the practical use in embedded equipments and IoT devices, which may be implantable. With the methodology proposed in RPAT, a solid foundation has been consolidated for deployment of secure systems according to what is expected for future developments in Industry 4.0. Although not all forms of cyber threats have been addressed, the adopted protocols allow the platform to deploy different security mechanisms and update them over time.

CONCLUSION

In the quest for greater independence for people with disabilities and to improve the results of long-term therapies within the hospital or home, assistive technologies are increasingly being studied and developed. In them, more and more automations are present, being essential the development of a supervisory system that is responsible for the control of the various local control systems and their integration with the cyber security in health.

Some lessons can be drawn from what has been exposed in this chapter. Among the main threats to the health of patients it can be included the rapid technological advance and the evolution of security policies. As the healthcare IT infrastructure faces new technology and security protocols, the industry is a major target for stealing medical information. While examples have been illustrated here and reports have been made of security and government efforts to reduce the prevalence of cyberattacks, the health sector is lagging behind other leading industries in protecting vital data.

Healthcare must continually adapt to changing cyber security trends and threats, such as ransomware, where critical infrastructure is tapped and valuable patient data is extracted for the benefit of the intruder. It is imperative that time and funding need to be invested in researching data safety models, as well as maintaining and ensuring the protection of healthcare technology and the confidentiality of patients' information from unauthorized access (Kruse et al., 2017). In future works, more emphasis will be placed on power consumption issues as this is an important factor IoT handling devices.

With the presentation of these facts, the concern has further increased with the identification of health technology security weaknesses by the 'White Hacker' (the hacker who assumes the doctor's credential). This suggests that remote manipulation of medical devices, such as artificial hearts and insulin pumps, is an unnerving possibility for the possibility of killing a person from a distance.

Cyber security is an essential part of maintaining patient safety, privacy and trust. More money and effort should be invested to ensure the safety of healthcare technologies and patient information. Security should be designed from product design to avoid future cyber attack issues. Cyber security praxis must become part of the patient care culture (Coventry & Branley, 2018).

Internet of Things in parallel with Assistive Technologies can promote greater independence for people with disabilities and improve long-term therapies results inside the hospital. The proposed control architecture for Cyber Security in Health based on protocols (as illustrated in Figure 1) also allows big data analysis, a potential source for clinical discoveries in future. Cloud computing can provide the infrastructure for IoT integrating monitoring devices, storage devices, analytics tools, visualization platforms and client delivery. Since Cyber Security remains one of the most important issues that baffle the development and applications of IoT, a taylor-made designed SIS methodology is a promising part in Supervisory Systems Architecture.

ACKNOWLEDGMENT

This research was supported by Brazilian Funding Agencies: Coordination for the Improvement of Higher Education Personnel [grant number CAPES PGPTA 88887.123938/2014-00]; National Council for Scientific and Technological Development [grant number CNPq 310085/2015-2]; and The São Paulo Research Foundation [grant number FAPESP PIPE/PITCHGOV 2017/25233-9].

REFERENCES

Adolphs, P., Bedenbender, H., Dirzus, D., Ehlich, M., Epple, U., Hankel, M., . . . Wollschlaeger, M. (2015). *Referenzarchitekturmodell Industrie 4.0 (RAMI4.0)* [*Reference architecture model Industrie 4.0* (RAMI 4.0)] (Status Report). Frankfurt am Main, Germany: ZVEI & Düsseldorf, Germany: VDI. Retrieved October 30, 2019, from https://www.zvei.org/fileadmin/user_upload/Themen/Industrie_4.0/ Das_Referenzarchitekturmodell_RAMI_4.0_und_die_Industrie_4.0-Komponente/pdf/Statusreport-Referenzmodelle-2015-v10.pdf

Araki, S. Y., Florentino, P., Bock, E., Saito, M., Hernandes, M., & Fuentes, L. ... De Arruda, A. C. F. (2018). Automatic elevation system of a wheelchair. In J. C. M. Carvalho, D. Martins, R. Simoni, & H. Simas (Eds.), Mechanisms and Machine Science: Vol. 54. Multibody mechatronic systems. (pp. 474-484). Cham, Switzerland: Springer International Publishing.

Araki, S. Y., Florentino, P., Saito, M., Hernandes, M., Bock, E., & Fuentes, L., ... De Arruda, A. C. F. (2017). Computational modelling of an automatic wheelchair lift system for assistive technology. In *Proceedings of the 3rd International Conference on Control, Automation and Robotics (ICCAR)* (pp. 448-452). New York: IEEE. 10.1109/ICCAR.2017.7942736

Baheti, R., & Gill, H. (2011). Cyber-physical systems. In T. Samad, & A.M. Annaswamy (Eds.), The impact of control technology, 161-166. New York: IEEE Control Systems Society.

Bock, E., Andrade, A., Dinkhuysen, J., Arruda, C., Fonseca, J., Leme, J., ... Nosé, Y. (2011a). Introductory tests to in vivo evaluation: Magnetic coupling influence in motor controller. *ASAIO Journal (American Society for Artificial Internal Organs), 57*(5), 462–465. doi:10.1097/MAT.0b013e31823005dc PMID:21841468

Bock, E., Antunes, P., Leão, T., Uebelhart, B., Fonseca, J., Leme, J., ... Arruda, C. (2011b). Implantable centrifugal blood pump with dual impeller and double pivot bearing system: Electromechanical actuator, prototyping, and anatomical studies. *Artificial Organs, 35*(5), 437–442. doi:10.1111/j.1525-1594.2011.01260.x PMID:21595708

Bock, E., Antunes, P., Uebelhart, B., Leão, T., Fonseca, J., & Cavalheiro, A. ... Arruda, C. (2011c). Design, manufacturing and tests of an implantable centrifugal blood pump. In L. M. Camarinha-Matos (Ed.), IFIP Advances in Information and Communication Technology: Vol. 349. Technological innovation for sustainability – DoCEIS 2011 (pp. 410-417). Berlin, Germany: Springer.

Bock, E., Araki, S., Souza, R., Ronei, D., Hernandes, M., & Frantz, J., ... Campos, A. (2017). Integrated supervisory system to control a reconfigurable platform of assistive technology. In *Proceedings of the 3rd International Conference on Control, Automation, and Robotics (ICCAR)* (pp. 444-447). New York: IEEE. 10.1109/ICCAR.2017.7942735

Bock, E., Ribeiro, A., Silva, M., Antunes, P., Fonseca, J., Legendre, D., ... Andrade, A. (2008). New centrifugal blood pump with dual impeller and double pivot bearing system: Wear evaluation in bearing system, performance tests, and preliminary hemolysis tests. *Artificial Organs*, *32*(4), 329–333. doi:10.1111/j.1525-1594.2008.00550.x PMID:18370949

Castells, M. (1997). *End of millennium: The information age: Economy, society and culture.* Cambridge, MA: Blackwell Publishers.

Cavalheiro, A., & Santos, Fo. D., Andrade, A., Cardoso, J. R., Bock, E., Fonseca, J., & Miyagi, P. E. (2011a). Design of supervisory control system for ventricular assist device. In L. M. Camarinha-Matos (Ed.), IFIP Advances in Information and Communication Technology: Vol. 349. Technological innovation for sustainability – DoCEIS 2011 (pp. 375-382). Berlin, Germany: Springer.

Cavalheiro, A. C. M., Santos Fo, D. J., Andrade, A., Cardoso, J. R., Horikawa, O., Bock, E., & Fonseca, J. (2011b). Specification of supervisory control systems for ventricular assist devices. *Artificial Organs*, *35*(5), 465–470. doi:10.1111/j.1525-1594.2011.01267.x PMID:21595713

Coventry, L., & Branley, D. (2018). Cybersecurity in healthcare: A narrative review of trends, threats and ways forward. *Maturitas*, *113*, 48–52. doi:10.1016/j.maturitas.2018.04.008 PMID:29903648

Cyber crime timeline. (n.d.). CW Jobs. Retrieved October 30, 2019, from https://www.cwjobs.co.uk/careers-advice/it-glossary/cyber-crime-timeline

Fonseca, J., Andrade, A., Nicolosi, D. E. C., Biscegli, J. F., Legendre, D., Bock, E., & Lucchi, J. C. (2008). A new technique to control brushless motor for blood pump application. *Artificial Organs*, *32*(4), 355–359. doi:10.1111/j.1525-1594.2008.00554.x PMID:18370953

Henriksen, E., Burkow, T. M., Johnsen, E., & Vognild, L. K. (2013). Privacy and information security risks in a technology platform for home-based chronic disease rehabilitation and education. *BMC Medical Informatics and Decision Making*, *13*(1), 85. doi:10.1186/1472-6947-13-85 PMID:23937965

Kagermann, H., Wahlster, W., & Helbig, J. (2013). *Recommendations for implementing the strategic initiative INDUSTRIE 4.0 securing the future of German manufacturing industry (Final Report of the Industrie 4.0 Working Group).* Berlin, Germany: Forschungsunion.

Kruse, C. S., Frederick, B., Jacobson, T., & Monticone, D. K. (2017). Cybersecurity in healthcare: A systematic review of modern threats and trends. *Technology and Health Care*, *25*(1), 1–10. doi:10.3233/THC-161263 PMID:27689562

Leão, T., Fonseca, J., Bock, E., Sá, R., Utiyama, B., & Drigo, E., ... Andrade, A. (2014). Speed control of the implantable centrifugal blood pump to avoid aortic valve stenosis: Simulation and implementation. In *Proceedings of the 5th RAS/EMBS International Conference on Biomedical Robotics and Biomechatronics* (pp. 82-86). New York: IEEE. 10.1109/BIOROB.2014.6913756

Leão, T. F., Bock, E., Fonseca, J., Andrade, A., Cavalheiro, A., & Uebelhart, B., … Campo, A. (2012). Modeling study of an implantable centrifugal blood pump actuator with redundant sensorless control. In *Proceedings of the 44th Southeastern Symposium on System Theory (SSST)* (pp. 174-178) New York: IEEE. 10.1109/SSST.2012.6195148

Lu, Y., Morris, K. C., & Frechette, S. P. (2016). Current standards landscape for smart manufacturing systems (NIST Interagency/Internal Report [NISTIR] 8107). Gaithersburg, MD: U.S. National Institute of Standards and Technology.

Lutes, M. (2000). Privacy and security compliance in the E-healthcare marketplace. *Healthcare Financial Management, 54*(3), 48–50. PMID:10847915

Otto, T. B., Campos, A., De Souza, M. A., Martins, D., & Bock, E. (2018). Online posture feedback system aiming at human comfort. In F. Rebelo, & M. Soares (Eds.), Advances in Intelligent Systems and Computing: Vol. 777. Advances in ergonomics in design (pp. 924-935). Cham, Switzerland: Springer. doi:10.1007/978-3-319-60582-1_93

Perakslis, E. D. (2014). Cybersecurity in health care. *The New England Journal of Medicine, 371*(5), 395–397. doi:10.1056/NEJMp1404358 PMID:25075831

Sannino, G., De Falco, I., & De Pietro, G. (2019). A continuous non-invasive arterial pressure (CNAP) approach for Health 4.0 systems. *IEEE Transactions on Industrial Informatics, 15*(1), 498–506. doi:10.1109/TII.2018.2832081

Santos, B., Leão, T., Tabacow, R., Souza, J., Campos, A., & Martins, D. … Bock, E. (2018). Controle de uma plataforma reconfigurável de tecnologia assistiva incorporada a Saúde 4.0 [Control of a reconfigurable platform of assistive technology incorporated to Health 4.0]. In F. O. Medola, & L. C. Paschoarelli (Eds.), Tecnologia assistiva – Pesquisa e conhecimento II (pp. 93-102). Bauru, Brazil: Canal 6 Editora.

Scholl, M., Stine, K., Hash, J., Bowen, P., Johnson, A., Smith, C. D., & Steinberg, D. I. (2008). *An introductory resource guide for implementing the health insurance portability and accountability act (HIPAA) security rule (NIST Special Publication 800-66 Rev. 1).* Gaithersburg, MD: U.S. National Institute of Standards and Technology. doi:10.6028/NIST.SP.800-66r1

Sobrinho, J. R. S., Legaspe, E., Drigo, E., Dias, J. C., Dias, J. C., Barboza, M., … & Santos Filho, D. J. (2018, May). Supervisory control system associated with the development of device thrombosis in VAD. In L. M. Camarinha-Matos, K. O. Adu-Kankam, & M. Julashokri (Eds.), IFIP Advances in Information and Communication Technology: Vol. 521. Technological innovation for resilient systems (pp. 90-97). Cham, Switzerland: Springer International Publishing.

Tabacow, R. P., Bock, E. G. P., & Nakamoto, F. Y. (2018). Modelagem em Redes de Petri do sistema de controle local da plataforma de tecnologia assistive [Modeling in Petri Nets of the local control system of the assistive technology platform]. *The Academic Society Journal, 2*(3), 173–178. doi:10.32640/tasj.2018.3.173

Torres, E. C., Campos, A. A., Martins, D., & Bock, E. (2019). Robotic system for active-passive strength therapy. In T. Ahram, W. Karwowski, & R. Taiar (Eds.), Advances in Intelligent Systems and Computing: Vol. 876. Human systems engineering and design (pp. 987-993). Cham, Switzerland: Springer International Publishing. doi:10.1007/978-3-030-02053-8_150

Uebelhart, B., Da Silva, B. U., Fonseca, J., Bock, E., Leme, J., Da Silva, C., ... Andrade, A. (2013). Study of a centrifugal blood pump in a mock loop system. *Artificial Organs*, *37*(11), 946–949. doi:10.1111/aor.12228 PMID:24237361

Uwizeyemungu, S., Poba-Nzaou, P., & Cantinotti, M. (2019). European hospitals' transition toward fully electronic-based systems: Do information technology security and privacy practices follow? *JMIR Medical Informatics, 7*(1), e11211, 1-32.

Von Solms, R., & Van Niekerk, J. (2013). From information security to cyber security. *Computers & Security*, *38*, 97–102. doi:10.1016/j.cose.2013.04.004

Zezulka, F., Marcon, P., Vesely, I., & Sajdl, O. (2016). Industry 4.0–An introduction in the phenomenon. *IFAC-PapersOnLine*, *49*(25), 8–12. doi:10.1016/j.ifacol.2016.12.002

Zhou, L., Thieret, R., Watzlaf, V., DeAlmeida, D., & Parmanto, B. (2019). A telehealth privacy and security self-assessment questionnaire for telehealth providers: Development and validation. *International Journal of Telerehabilitation*, *11*(1), 3–14. doi:10.5195/ijt.2019.6276 PMID:31341542

ADDITIONAL READING

Dubgorn, A., Kalinina, O., Lyovina, A., & Rotar, O. (2018). Foundation architecture of telemedicine system services based on Health 4.0 concept. In *SHS Web of Conferences, 44* (00032, pp. 1-10). EDP Sciences.

Ferrer-Roca, O., & Méndez, D. G. (2012). Health 4.0 in the i2i Era. *International Journal of Reliable and Quality E-Healthcare*, *1*(1), 43–57. doi:10.4018/ijrqeh.2012010105

Health Insurance Portability and Accountability Act (HIPAA) compliance checklist. (2018-2019). *HIPAA Journal*. Retrieved October 30, 2019, from https://www.hipaajournal.com/hipaa-checklist-download/

Moghaddam, M., & Nof, S. Y. (2018). Collaborative service-component integration in cloud manufacturing. *International Journal of Production Research*, *56*(1-2), 677–691. doi:10.1080/00207543.2017.1374574

U.S. Department of Health & Human Services. *Cyber security guidance material*. (n.d.). Retrieved October 30, 2019 from, https://www.hhs.gov/hipaa/for-professionals/security/guidance/cybersecurity/index.html

U.S. Department of Health & Human Services. (n.d.). *Ransomware guidance – fact sheet: Ransomware and HIPAA*. Retrieved October 30, 2019, from https://www.hhs.gov/sites/default/files/RansomwareFactSheet.pdf?language=es

U.S. National Institute of Standards and Technology. (2018). *Framework for improving critical infrastructure cybersecurity* (Version 1.1). Retrieved October 30, 2019, from https://nvlpubs.nist.gov/nistpubs/CSWP/NIST.CSWP.04162018.pdf

Zhong, H., Levalle, R. R., Moghaddam, M., & Nof, S. Y. (2015). Collaborative intelligence - definition and measured impacts on internetworked e-work. *Management and Production Engineering Review*, 6(1), 67–78. doi:10.1515/mper-2015-0009

KEY TERMS AND DEFINITIONS

Artificial Intelligence (AI): An area of computer science that emphasizes the creation of intelligent machines that work and react like humans.

Big Data: Extremely large data sets that may be analyzed computationally to reveal patterns, trends, and associations, especially relating to human behavior and interactions.

Collaborative Control Theory (CCT): A collection of principles and models for supporting the effective design of collaborative e-Work systems.

Computer Integrated Manufacturing (CIM): The manufacturing approach of using computers to control entire production process. This integration allows individual processes to exchange information with each other and initiate actions.

Distributed Hierarchical Control System (DHCS): A form of control system in which a set of devices and governing software are arranged in a hierarchical tree.

Food and Drugs Administration (FDA): The American agency is separated into divisions that oversee a majority of the organization's obligations involving food, drugs, cosmetics, animal food, dietary supplements, medical devices, biological goods, and blood products.

Health 4.0 (H4.0): Since Industry 4.0 extends further the IoT model with the inclusion of robotics and automation, H4.0 is the application of the I4.0 paradigm to the healthcare sector.

Health Insurance Portability and Accountability Act (HIPAA): The Health Insurance Portability and Accountability Act of 1996 (HIPAA) is an American federal law that requires employers to protect employee medical records as confidential. HIPAA includes regulations that cover how employers must protect employees' medical privacy rights and the privacy of their health information.

Internet of Things (IoT): A system of interrelated computing devices, mechanical and digital machines, objects, animals or people that are provided with unique identifiers (UIDs) and the ability to transfer data over a network without requiring human-to-human or human-to-computer interaction.

Radio Frequency Identification (RFID): A form of wireless communication that incorporates the use of electromagnetic or electrostatic coupling in the radio frequency portion of the electromagnetic spectrum to uniquely identify an object, animal or person.

Compilation of References

2017 *cyberattacks on Ukraine*. (n.d.). In Wikipedia. Retrieved November 01, 2019, from https://en.wikipedia.org/wiki/2017_cyberattacks_on_Ukraine

Aazam, M., Zeadally, S., & Harras, K. A. (2018). Deploying fog computing in Industrial Internet of Things and Industry 4.0. *IEEE Transactions on Industrial Informatics*, *14*(10), 4674–4682. doi:10.1109/TII.2018.2855198

Abe, R., Taoka, H., & McQuilkin, D. (2011). Digital grid: Communicative electrical grids of the future. *IEEE Transactions on Smart Grid*, *2*(2), 399–410. doi:10.1109/TSG.2011.2132744

Achour, I., Labed, L., & Ben Ghezala, H. (2015). Proposition of secure service oriented product line. In *Proceedings of the 6th International Conference on Information Systems and Economic Intelligence* (pp. 52-59). New York: IEEE. 10.1109/ISEI.2015.7358724

Adamsky, F., Aubigny, M., Battisti, F., Carli, M., Cimorelli, F., Cruz, T., ... Soua, R. (2018). Integrated protection of industrial control systems from cyber-attacks: The ATENA approach. *International Journal of Critical Infrastructure Protection*, *21*, 72–82. doi:10.1016/j.ijcip.2018.04.004

Adolphs, P., Bedenbender, H., Dirzus, D., Ehlich, M., Epple, U., Hankel, M., . . . Wollschlaeger, M. (2015). *Referenzarchitekturmodell Industrie 4.0 (RAMI4.0)* [Reference architecture model Industrie 4.0 (RAMI 4.0)] (Status Report). Frankfurt am Main, Germany: ZVEI & Düsseldorf, Germany: VDI. Retrieved October 30, 2019, from https://www.zvei.org/fileadmin/user_upload/Themen/Industrie_4.0/Das_Referenzarchitekturmodell_RAMI_4.0_und_die_Industrie_4.0-Komponente/pdf/Statusreport-Referenzmodelle-2015-v10.pdf

Aggarwal, A., Kunta, S., & Verma, P. K. (2010). A proposed communications infrastructure for the smart grid. In *Proceedings of the Innovative Smart Grid Technologies (ISGT)* (pp. 1-5). New York: IEEE. 10.1109/ISGT.2010.5434764

Ahmad Khan, M. (2016). A survey of security issues for cloud computing. *Journal of Network and Computer Applications*, *71*, 11–29. doi:10.1016/j.jnca.2016.05.010

Akella, R., Tang, H., & McMillin, B. M. (2010). Analysis of information flow security in cyber-physical systems. *International Journal of Critical Infrastructure Protection*, *3*(3-4), 157–173. doi:10.1016/j.ijcip.2010.09.001

Akyol, B. A. (2012). Cyber security challenges in using cloud computing in the electric utility industry (Pacific Northwest National Laboratory Report PNNL-21724). Retrieved August 1, 2019 from https://www.pnnl.gov/main/publications/external/technical_reports/PNNL-21724.pdf

Alcaraz, C., & Zeadally, S. (2015). Critical infrastructure protection: Requirements and challenges for the 21st century. *International Journal of Critical Infrastructure Protection*, *8*, 53–66. doi:10.1016/j.ijcip.2014.12.002

Al-Dalky, R., Abduljaleel, O., Salah, K., Otrok, H., & Al-Qutayri, M. (2014). A Modbus traffic generator for evaluating the security of SCADA systems. In *Proceedings of the 9th International Symposium on Communication Systems, Networks, & Digital Sign (CSNDSP)* (pp. 809-814). New York: IEEE. 10.1109/CSNDSP.2014.6923938

Aleksandrova, M. (2019). Industrial IoT security: How to protect smart manufacturing. Retrieved October 8, 2019, from https://easternpeak.com/blog/industrial-iot-security-how-to-protect-smart-manufacturing/

Ali, S., & Li, Y. (2019). Learning multilevel auto-encoders for DDoS attack detection in smart grid network. *IEEE Access: Practical Innovations, Open Solutions*, 7, 108647–108659. doi:10.1109/ACCESS.2019.2933304

Almalawi, A., Tari, Z., Khalil, I., & Fahad, A. (2013). SCADAVT – A framework for SCADA security testbed based on virtualization technology. In *Proceedings of the 38th Conference on Local Computer Networks (LCN 2013)* (pp. 639-646). New York: IEEE. 10.1109/LCN.2013.6761301

Aloul, F., Al-Ali, A. R., Al-Dalky, R., Al-Mardini, M., & El-Hajj, W. (2012). Smart grid security: Threats, vulnerabilities and solutions. *International Journal of Smart Grid and Clean Energy*, 1(1), 1–6. doi:10.12720gce.1.1.1-6

Al-rimy, B. A. S., Maarof, M. A., & Shaid, S. Z. M. (2017). A 0-day aware crypto-ransomware early behavioral detection framework. In F. Saeed et al. (Eds.), Lecture Notes on Data Engineering and Communications Technologies: Vol. 5. Recent Trends in Information and Communication Technology (pp. 758-766). Cham, Switzerland: Springer.

American National Standards Institute/International Society of Automation (ANSI/ISA). (2018). *Security for industrial automation and control systems. ANSI/ISA-62443 Series of standards*. Washington, DC: ANSI.

Anton, S. D., Fraunholz, D., Lipps, C., Pohl, F., Zimmermann, M., & Schotten, H. D. (2018). Two decades of SCADA exploitation: A brief history. In *Proceedings of the IEEE Conference on Applications, Information and Network Security* [New York: IEEE.]. *Anästhesiologie, Intensivmedizin, Notfallmedizin, Schmerztherapie*, *2017*, 98–104.

Aragó, A. S., Martinez, E. R., & Clares, S. S. (2014). SCADA laboratory and test-bed as a service for critical infrastructure protection. In *Proceedings of the 2nd International Symposium on ICS & SCADA Cyber Security Research* (pp. 25-29). New York: ACM. 10.14236/ewic/ICSCSR2014.4

Araki, S. Y., Florentino, P., Bock, E., Saito, M., Hernandes, M., & Fuentes, L. … De Arruda, A. C. F. (2018). Automatic elevation system of a wheelchair. In J. C. M. Carvalho, D. Martins, R. Simoni, & H. Simas (Eds.), Mechanisms and Machine Science: Vol. 54. Multibody mechatronic systems. (pp. 474-484). Cham, Switzerland: Springer International Publishing.

Araki, S. Y., Florentino, P., Saito, M., Hernandes, M., Bock, E., & Fuentes, L., … De Arruda, A. C. F. (2017). Computational modelling of an automatic wheelchair lift system for assistive technology. In *Proceedings of the 3rd International Conference on Control, Automation and Robotics (ICCAR)* (pp. 448-452). New York: IEEE. 10.1109/ICCAR.2017.7942736

Ardito, L., Procaccianti, G., Menga, G., & Morisio, M. (2013). Smart grid technologies in Europe: An overview. *Energies*, 6(1), 251–281. doi:10.3390/en6010251

Ariyaluran Habeeb, R. A., Nasaruddin, F., Gani, A., Targio Hashem, I. A., Ahmed, E., & Imran, M. (2019). Real-time big data processing for anomaly detection: A survey. *International Journal of Information Management*, 45, 289–307. doi:10.1016/j.ijinfomgt.2018.08.006

Arnaert, M., & Antipolis, S. (2016). Modeling vulnerable Internet of Things on SHODAN and CENSYS: An ontology for cyber security. In *Proceedings of the Tenth International Conference on Emerging Security Information, Systems and Technology SECURWARE 2016* (pp. 299-302). Wilmington, DE: IARIA.

Arroyo-Figueroa, G., Escobedo-Briones, G., & Santamaria-Bonfil, G. (in press). Development of technology infrastructure of big data analytics for smart grid. *IEEE Latin America Transactions*.

ATENA Consortium. (2016). A European H2020 Project – ATENA. Retrieved November 10, 2019, from https://www.atena-h2020.eu/

Atzori, L., Iera, A., & Morabito, G. (2010). The Internet of Things: A survey. *Computer Networks: The International Journal of Computer and Telecommunications Networking*, *54*(15), 2787–2805. doi:10.1016/j.comnet.2010.05.010

AutoGrid. (n.d.). *AutoGrid Energy Internet Platform™*. Retrieved September 3, 2019, from https://www.auto-grid.com/platform/autogrid-energy-internet-platform/

Awad, R. A., Beztchi, S., Smith, J. M., Lyles, B., & Prowell, S. (2018). Tools, techniques, and methodologies: A survey of digital forensics for SCADA systems. In *Proceedings of the Annual Industrial Control System Security (ICSS) Workshop*. New York, NY: ACM. 10.1145/3295453.3295454

Aziz, A. S. A., Hanafi, S. E.-O., & Hassanien, A. E. (2017). Comparison of classification techniques applied for network intrusion detection and classification. *Journal of Applied Logic, 24* (Part A), 109-118.

Aznarte, J. L., & Siebert, N. (2017). Dynamic line rating using numerical weather predictions and machine learning: A case study. *IEEE Transactions on Power Delivery*, *32*(1), 335–343. doi:10.1109/TPWRD.2016.2543818

Babaeizadeh, M., Bakhtiari, M., & Mohammed, A. M. (2015). Authentication methods in cloud computing: A survey. *Research Journal of Applied Sciences, Engineering and Technology*, *9*(8), 655–664. doi:10.19026/rjaset.9.1451

Babić, B. M., Milić, S. D., & Rakić, A. Ž. (2017). Fault detection algorithm used in a magnetic monitoring system of the hydrogenerator. *IET Electric Power Applications*, *11*(1), 63–71. doi:10.1049/iet-epa.2016.0232

Baheti, R., & Gill, H. (2011). Cyber-physical systems. In T. Samad, & A.M. Annaswamy (Eds.), The impact of control technology, 161-166. New York: IEEE Control Systems Society.

Bahrami, S., & Sheikhi, A. (2016). From demand response in smart grid toward integrated demand response in smart energy hub. *IEEE Transactions on Smart Grid*, *7*(2), 650–658.

Bai, W., Yang, H., Yu, A., Xiao, H., He, L., Feng, L., & Zhang, J. (2018). Eavesdropping-aware routing and spectrum allocation based on multi-flow virtual concatenation for confidential information service in elastic optical networks. *Optical Fiber Technology*, *40*, 18–27. doi:10.1016/j.yofte.2017.10.004

Baker, T., Mackay, M., Shaheed, A., & Aldawsari, B. (2015). Security-oriented cloud platform for SOA-based SCADA. In *Proceedings of the 15th IEEE/ACM International Symposium on Cluster, Cloud and Grid Computing* (pp. 961-970). New York: IEEE. 10.1109/CCGrid.2015.37

Barabási, A. L., Albert, R., & Jeong, H. (2000). Scale-free characteristics of random networks: The topology of the world-wide web. *Physica A*, *281*(1-4), 69–77. doi:10.1016/S0378-4371(00)00018-2

Bawany, N. Z., Shamsi, J. A., & Salah, K. (2017). DDoS attack detection and mitigation using SDN: Methods, practices, and solutions. *Arabian Journal for Science and Engineering*, *42*(2), 425–441. doi:10.100713369-017-2414-5

Bediako, P. K. (2017). *Long short-term memory recurrent neural network for detecting DDoS flooding attacks within TensorFlow implementation framework*. (Doctoral dissertation). Retrieved November 15, 2019, from http://urn.kb.se/resolve?urn=urn:nbn:se:ltu:diva-66802

Benhaddou, D., Abid, M. R., Achahbar, O., Khalil, N., Rachidi, T., & Al Assaf, M. (2015). Big Data processing for smart grids. *IADIS International Journal on Computer Science and Information Systems*, *10*(1), 32–46.

Benzel, T. V., Braden, B., Faber, T., Mirkovic, J., Schwab, S. J., Sollins, K. R., & Wroclawski, J. (2009). Current developments in DETER cybersecurity testbed technology. In *Proceedings of the Cybersecurity Applications & Technology Conference for Homeland Security* (pp. 57-70). New York: IEEE. 10.1109/CATCH.2009.30

Benzel, T. V., Braden, R., Kim, D., Neuman, C., Joseph, A. D., & Sklower, K. (2006). Experience with DETER: A testbed for security research. In *Proceedings of the 2nd International Conference on Testbeds and Research Infrastructures for the Development of Networks and Communities, 2006. TRIDENTCOM 2006* (pp. 379-388). New York: IEEE. 10.1109/TRIDNT.2006.1649172

Berbakov, L., Anton-Haro, C., & Matamoros, J. (2013). Optimal transmission policy for cooperative transmission with energy harvesting and battery operated sensor nodes. *Signal Processing*, *93*(11), 3159–3170. doi:10.1016/j.sigpro.2013.04.009

Berbakov, L., Anton-Haro, C., & Matamoros, J. (2014). Joint optimization of transmission policies for collaborative beamforming with energy harvesting sensors. *IEEE Transactions on Wireless Communications*, *13*(7), 3496–3509. doi:10.1109/TWC.2014.2323268

Berbakov, L., Jovanović, Č., Svetel, M., Vasiljević, J., Dimić, G., & Radulović, N. (2019). Quantitative assessment of head tremor in patients with essential tremor and cervical dystonia by using inertial sensors. *Sensors (Basel)*, *19*(19), 1–16. doi:10.339019194246 PMID:31574913

Bergman, D. C., Jin, D., Nicol, D. M., & Yardley, T. M. (2009). The virtual power system testbed and inter-testbed integration. In *Proceedings of the 2nd Conference on Cyber Security Experimentation and Test*. New York: ACM.

Bhatt, T., Kotwal, C., & Chaubey, N. (2017). Survey on smart grid: Threats, vulnerabilities, and security protocol. *International Journal of Electronics, Electrical, and Computational System*, *6*(9), 340–348.

Bilar, D., Cybenko, G., & Murphy, J. P. (2013). Adversarial dynamics: The conficker case study. In S. Jajodia et al. (Eds.), Advances in Information Security: Vol. 100. Moving Target Defense II (pp. 41-71). New York: Springer.

Bitzer, B. (2015). Application of cloud computing for power systems. Trivent Publishing. Retrieved November 10, 2019, from https://trivent-publishing.eu/pdfdownload/18.BertholdBitzer.pdf

Block, C., & Briegel, F. (Eds.). (2010). *Internet of Energy: ICT for energy markets of the future*. Berlin, Germany: Industrie-Förderung Gesellschaft mbH. Retrieved September 3, 2019, from https://www.iese.fraunhofer.de/content/dam/iese/en/mediacenter/documents/BDI_initiative_IoE_us-IdE-Broschuere_tcm27-45653.pdf

Bock, E., Antunes, P., Uebelhart, B., Leão, T., Fonseca, J., & Cavalheiro, A. … Arruda, C. (2011c). Design, manufacturing and tests of an implantable centrifugal blood pump. In L. M. Camarinha-Matos (Ed.), IFIP Advances in Information and Communication Technology: Vol. 349. Technological innovation for sustainability – DoCEIS 2011 (pp. 410-417). Berlin, Germany: Springer.

Bock, E., Araki, S., Souza, R., Ronei, D., Hernandes, M., & Frantz, J., … Campos, A. (2017). Integrated supervisory system to control a reconfigurable platform of assistive technology. In *Proceedings of the 3rd International Conference on Control, Automation, and Robotics (ICCAR)* (pp. 444-447). New York: IEEE. 10.1109/ICCAR.2017.7942735

Bock, E., Andrade, A., Dinkhuysen, J., Arruda, C., Fonseca, J., Leme, J., ... Nosé, Y. (2011a). Introductory tests to in vivo evaluation: Magnetic coupling influence in motor controller. *ASAIO Journal (American Society for Artificial Internal Organs)*, *57*(5), 462–465. doi:10.1097/MAT.0b013e31823005dc PMID:21841468

Bock, E., Antunes, P., Leão, T., Uebelhart, B., Fonseca, J., Leme, J., ... Arruda, C. (2011b). Implantable centrifugal blood pump with dual impeller and double pivot bearing system: Electromechanical actuator, prototyping, and anatomical studies. *Artificial Organs*, *35*(5), 437–442. doi:10.1111/j.1525-1594.2011.01260.x PMID:21595708

Bock, E., Ribeiro, A., Silva, M., Antunes, P., Fonseca, J., Legendre, D., ... Andrade, A. (2008). New centrifugal blood pump with dual impeller and double pivot bearing system: Wear evaluation in bearing system, performance tests, and preliminary hemolysis tests. *Artificial Organs, 32*(4), 329–333. doi:10.1111/j.1525-1594.2008.00550.x PMID:18370949

Boštjančič Rakas, S., & Stojanović, M. (2019). A centralized model for establishing end-to-end communication services via management agents. *Promet - Traffic & Transportation, 31*(3), 245-255.

Boštjančič Rakas, S., & Stojanović, M. (2019). A centralized model for establishing end-to-end communication services via management agents. *Promet – Traffic & Transportation, 31*(3), 245-255.

Boštjančič Rakas, S. (2020). Energy Internet: Architecture, emerging technologies and security issues. In M. Stojanovic, & S. Bostjancic Rakas (Eds.), *Cyber security of industrial control systems in the Future Internet environment.* Hershey, PA: IGI Global.

Bostjancic Rakas, S., Timcenko, V., Kabovic, A., & Kabovic, M. (2016). Cyber security issues in conductor temperature and meteorological measurement based DLR system. In *Proceedings of the Mediterranean Conference on Power Generation, Transmission, Distribution and Energy Conversion* (pp. 1-7). New York: IEEE.

Boyes, H., Hallaq, B., Cunningham, J., & Watson, T. (2018). The Industrial Internet of Things (IIoT): An analysis framework. *Computers in Industry, 101*, 1–12. doi:10.1016/j.compind.2018.04.015

Brown, G. G., Carlyle, W. M., Salmerón, J., & Wood, K. (2005). Analyzing the vulnerability of critical infrastructure to attack and planning defenses. *Tutorials in Operations Research,* 102-123.

Budka, K. C., Deshpande, J. G., & Thottan, M. (2014). *Computer Communications and Networks. Communication networks for smart grids: Making smart grid real.* London, UK: Springer Verlag. doi:10.1007/978-1-4471-6302-2

Bui, N., Castellani, A. P., Casari, P., & Zorzi, M. (2012). The Internet of Energy: A web-enabled smart grid system. *IEEE Network, 26*(4), 39–45. doi:10.1109/MNET.2012.6246751

Buratti, C., Stajkic, A., Gardasevic, G., Milardo, S., Abrignani, M., Mijovic, S., ... Verdone, R. (2016). Testing protocols for the Internet of Things on the EuWIn platform. *IEEE Internet of Things Journal, 3*(1), 124–133. doi:10.1109/JIOT.2015.2462030

Butun, I., Sari, A., & Österberg, P. (2019). Security implications of fog computing on the Internet of Things. In *Proceedings of the International Conference on Consumer Electronics* (pp. 1-6). New York: IEEE. 10.1109/ICCE.2019.8661909

Byers, C. (2018). Fog computing for industrial automation. Retrieved October 8, 2019, from https://www.controleng.com/articles/fog-computing-for-industrial-automation/

Cagri Gungor, V., Sahin, D., Kocak, T., Ergut, S., Buccella, C., Cecati, C., & Hancke, G. P. (2013). A survey on smart grid potential applications and communication requirements. *IEEE Transactions on Industrial Informatics, 9*(1), 28–42. doi:10.1109/TII.2012.2218253

Cao, J., & Yang, M. (2013). Energy Internet – Towards smart grid 2.0. In *Proceedings of the Fourth International Conference on Networking and Distributed Computing 2013* (pp. 105-110). New York: IEEE. 10.1109/ICNDC.2013.10

Cao, Y., Li, Q., Tan, Y., Li, Y., Chen, Y., Shao, X., & Zou, Y. (2018). A comprehensive review of Energy Internet: Basic concept, operation and planning methods, and research prospects. *Journal of Modern Power Systems and Clean Energy, 6*(3), 399–411. doi:10.100740565-017-0350-8

Carlin, S., & Curran, K. (2013). Cloud computing security. In K. Curran (Ed.), *Pervasive and Ubiquitous Technology Innovations for Ambient Intelligence Environment* (pp. 12–17). Hershey, PA: IGI Global. doi:10.4018/978-1-4666-2041-4.ch002

Carlson, M. (2019, January 29). From a smart grid to the Internet of Energy. *Smart Energy International, 2019*(1), 22-23. Retrieved November 10, 2019, from http://spintelligentpublishing.com/Digital/SmartEnergy/SEI12019/index.html?r=65

Castells, M. (1997). *End of millennium: The information age: Economy, society and culture.* Cambridge, MA: Blackwell Publishers.

Castrucci, M., Macone, D., Harpes, C. P., Aubigny, M., Aubert, J., Incoul, C., … Tanenbaum, D. (2009). MICIE ICT system requirements - Preliminary version. In M. Castrucci (Ed.), MICIE Project Deliverable D4.1.1. European Commission FP7.

Cavalheiro, A., & Santos, Fo. D., Andrade, A., Cardoso, J. R., Bock, E., Fonseca, J., & Miyagi, P. E. (2011a). Design of supervisory control system for ventricular assist device. In L. M. Camarinha-Matos (Ed.), IFIP Advances in Information and Communication Technology: Vol. 349. Technological innovation for sustainability – DoCEIS 2011 (pp. 375-382). Berlin, Germany: Springer.

Cavalheiro, A. C. M., Santos Fo, D. J., Andrade, A., Cardoso, J. R., Horikawa, O., Bock, E., & Fonseca, J. (2011b). Specification of supervisory control systems for ventricular assist devices. *Artificial Organs, 35*(5), 465–470. doi:10.1111/j.1525-1594.2011.01267.x PMID:21595713

Chabukswar, R., Sinópoli, B., Karsai, G., Giani, A., Neema, H., & Davis, A. (2010). Simulation of network attacks on SCADA systems. *First Workshop on Secure Control Systems. Cyber Physical Systems Week.* Retrieved November 05, 2019, from https://ptolemy.berkeley.edu/projects/truststc/pubs/693/SCS%20Paper.pdf

Chaichi, N., Lavoie, J., Zarrin, S., Khalifa, R., & Sue, F. (2015). A comprehensive assessment of cloud computing for smart grid applications: A multi-perspectives framework. In *Proceedings of the PICMET 2015: Management of the Technology Age* (pp. 2541-2547). Portland, OR: Portland State University. 10.1109/PICMET.2015.7273227

Chavan, P., Patil, P., Kulkarni, G., Sutar, R., & Belsare, S. (2013). IaaS cloud security. In *Proceedings of the 2013 International Conference on Machine Intelligence and Research Advancement* (pp. 549-553). New York: IEEE.

Cheminod, M., Durante, L., Seno, L., & Valenzano, A. (2018). Performance evaluation and modeling of an industrial application-layer firewall. *IEEE Transactions on Industrial Informatics, 14*(5), 2159–2170. doi:10.1109/TII.2018.2802903

Chen, H., Teng, Y., & Bu, X. (2018). *Breaking into the 'Energy Internet' era in China: An analysis of China's Smart Grid development* (L.E.K. Consulting Executive Insights, Vol. XX, issue 5). Retrieved, September 03, 2019, from https://www.lek.com/insights/ei/breaking-energy-internet-era-china-analysis-chinas-smart-grid-development

Chen, L., Sun, Q., Zhao, L., & Cheng, Q. (2015). Design of a novel energy router and it's application in Energy Internet. In *Proceedings of the Chinese Automation Congress (CAC)* (pp. 1462-1467). New York: IEEE. 10.1109/CAC.2015.7382730

Chen, Y., Chen, J., & Gan, J. (2015). Experimental study in cloud-computing-based electric power SCADA system. *ZTE Communications, 13*(3), 33–41.

Chen, Y., Chen, J., & Gan, J. (2015). Experimental study on cloud computing based electric power SCADA system. *ZTE Communications, 13*(3), 33–41.

Cherdantseva, Y., Burnap, P., Blyth, A., Eden, P., Jones, K., Soulsby, H., & Stoddart, K. (2016). A review of cyber security risk assessment methods for SCADA systems. *Computers & Security, 56*, 1–27. doi:10.1016/j.cose.2015.09.009

Christodoulopoulos, K., Tomkos, I., & Varvarigos, E. (2011). Elastic bandwidth allocation in flexible OFDM based optical networks. *Journal of Lightwave Technology, 29*(9), 1354–1366. doi:10.1109/JLT.2011.2125777

Church, P., Mueller, H., Ryan, C., Gogouvitis, S. V., Goscinski, A., & Tari, Z. (2017). Migration of a SCADA system to IaaS clouds – a case study. *Journal of Cloud Computing: Advances, Systems, and Application, 6*(11), 1–12.

Church, P., Mueller, H., Ryan, C., Gogouvitis, S. V., Goscinski, A., & Tari, Z. (2017). Migration of a SCADA system to IaaS clouds – a case study. *Journal of Cloud Computing: Advances, Systems, and Applications, 6*(11), 1–12.

Cimpanu, C. (2016, March 9). *Korean energy and transportation targets attacked by OnionDog APT*. Retrieved November 01, 2019, from https://news.softpedia.com/news/korean-energy-and-transportation-targets-attacked-by-oniondog-apt-501534.shtml

Cimpanu, C. (2019, March 9). Georgia county pays a whopping $400,000 to get rid of a ransomware infection. *ZDNet*. Retrieved November 10, 2019, from https://www.zdnet.com/article/georgia-county-pays-a-whopping-400000-to-get-rid-of-a-ransomware-infection/

CISA - Cyber+Infrastructure. (2017). *ICS Archive Information Products* [Number of vulnerable products used in different industries]. Retrieved, November 10, from https://www.us-cert.gov/ics/ics-archive

Cloud Standards Customer Council (CSCC). (2017). *Security for cloud computing – Ten steps to ensure success* (version 3.0). Retrieved November 10, 2019, from https://www.omg.org/cloud/deliverables/CSCC-Security-for-Cloud-Computing-10-Steps-to-Ensure-Success.pdf

Cloud Standards Customer Council (CSCC). (2017). *Security for cloud computing – Ten steps to ensure success* (version 3.0). Retrieved September 3, 2019, from https://www.omg.org/cloud/deliverables/CSCC-Security-for-Cloud-Computing-10-Steps-to-Ensure-Success.pdf

Cockpit, C. I. Consortium. (2012). A European FP7 Project – CockpitCI. Retrieved November 10, 2019, from https://cockpitci.itrust.lu/

Colbert, E. J., & Hutchinson, S. (2016). Intrusion detection in industrial control systems. In E. J. Colbert, & A. Kott (Eds.), *Cyber-security of SCADA and other industrial control systems* (pp. 209–237). Cham, Switzerland: Springer. doi:10.1007/978-3-319-32125-7_11

Conklin, W. A. (2006). Cyber defense competitions and information security education: An active learning solution for a capstone course. In *Proceedings of the 39th Annual Hawaii International Conference on System Sciences (HICSS'06)* (vol. 9, pp. 220b-220b). New York: IEEE. 10.1109/HICSS.2006.110

Conseil International des Grands Réseaux Électriques (CIGRÉ). (2004). *Integrated service networks for utilities* (Technical Brochure TB 249, WGD2.07). Paris, France: CIGRÉ.

Conseil International des Grands Réseaux Électriques (CIGRÉ). (2007). *Security for information systems and intranets in electric power systems* (Technical Brochure 317, JWGD2/B3/C2.01). Paris, France: CIGRÉ.

Contreras, L. M., Lopez, V., Gonzalez de Dios, O., Tovar, A., Munoz, F., Azanon, A., & Fernandez-Palacios, J. P. (2012). Toward cloud-ready transport network. *IEEE Communications Magazine, 50*(9), 48–55. doi:10.1109/MCOM.2012.6295711

Cook, K., Shaw, T., Hawrylak, P. J., & Hale, J. (2016). Scalable attack graph generation. In *Proceedings of the 11th Annual Cyber and Information Security Research Conference* (Article 21). New York: ACM. 10.1145/2897795.2897821

Cook, A., Nicholson, A., Janicke, H., Maglaras, L., & Smith, R. (2016). Attribution of cyber attacks on industrial control systems. *EAI Transactions on Industrial Networks and Industrial Systems, 3*(7), 1–15.

Costin, A. (2016). Security of CCTV and video surveillance systems: Threats, vulnerabilities, attacks, and mitigations. In *Proceedings of the 6th international workshop on trustworthy embedded devices* (pp. 45-54). New York: ACM. 10.1145/2995289.2995290

Coventry, L., & Branley, D. (2018). Cybersecurity in healthcare: A narrative review of trends, threats and ways forward. *Maturitas, 113*, 48–52. doi:10.1016/j.maturitas.2018.04.008 PMID:29903648

CRISALIS Consortium. (2015). *CRISALIS - CRitical Infrastructure Security AnaLysIS*. Retrieved October 15, 2019, from https://cordis.europa.eu/project/rcn/103538/factsheet/en

Cruz, T., Barrigas, J., Proenca, J., Graziano, A., Panzieri, S., Lev, L., & Simoes, P. (2015). Improving network security monitoring for industrial control systems. In *Proceedings of the IFIP/IEEE International Symposium on Integrated Network Management, IM 2015* (pp. 878-881). New York: IEEE. 10.1109/INM.2015.7140399

Cruz, T., Rosa, L., Proenca, J., Maglaras, L., Aubigny, M., Lev, L., ... Simões, P. (2016). A cybersecurity detection framework for supervisory control and data acquisition systems. *IEEE Transactions on Industrial Informatics*, *12*(6), 2236–2246. doi:10.1109/TII.2016.2599841

Cusack, B., & Tian, Z. (2017). Evaluating IP surveillance camera vulnerabilities. In *Proceedings of the 15th Australian Information Security Management Conference* (pp. 25-32). Perth, Australia: Edith Cowan University.

Cyber crime timeline. (n.d.). CW Jobs. Retrieved October 30, 2019, from https://www.cwjobs.co.uk/careers-advice/it-glossary/cyber-crime-timeline

Dari, E. Y., & Essaaidi, M. (2015). An overview of smart grid cyber-security state of the art study. In *Proceedings of the 3rd International Renewable and Sustainable Energy Conference (IRSEC)* (pp. 1-7). New York: IEEE. 10.1109/IRSEC.2015.7455097

Dawson, L. A., Lamb, C., & Carbajal, A. J. (2018). *Industrial control systems cyber security risk candidate methods analysis (No. SAND2018-7592)*. Albuquerque, NM: Sandia National Lab. doi:10.2172/1463794

Dayal, A., Deng, Y., Tbaileh, A., & Shukla, S. (2015). VSCADA: A reconfigurable virtual SCADA test-bed for simulating power utility control center operations. In *Proceedings of the IEEE Power & Energy Society General Meeting* (pp. 1-5). New York: IEEE. 10.1109/PESGM.2015.7285822

Dayarathna, M., & Perera, S. (2018). Recent advancements in event processing. *ACM Computing Surveys*, *51*(2), 1–36. doi:10.1145/3170432

De Donno, M., Dragoni, N., Giaretta, A., & Spognardi, A. (2017). Analysis of DDoS-capable IoT malwares. In *Proceedings of the Federated Conference on Computer Science and Information Systems* (pp. 807-816). New York: IEEE.

De Hert, P., Papakonstantinou, V., & Kamara, I. (2014). *The new cloud computing ISO/IEC 27018 standard through the lens of the EU legislation on data protection* (Working Paper, vol. 1, no. 2). Brussels Privacy Hub. Retrieved November 10, 2019, from https://www.brusselsprivacyhub.eu/publications/wp12.html

December 2015 Ukraine power grid cyberattack. (n.d.). In Wikipedia. Retrieved October 08, 2019, from https://en.wikipedia.org/wiki/December_2015_Ukraine_power_grid_cyberattack

Demertzis, K., & Iliadis, L. (2019). Cognitive web application firewall to critical infrastructures protection from phishing attacks. *Journal of Computations & Modelling*, *9*(2), 1–26.

Derbyshire, R., Green, B., Prince, D., Mauthe, A., & Hutchison, D. (2018). An analysis of cyber security attack taxonomies. In *Proceedings of the IEEE European Symposium on Security and Privacy Workshops* (pp. 153-161). New York: IEEE. 10.1109/EuroSPW.2018.00028

Develder, C., De Leeheer, M., Dhoedt, B., Pickavet, M., Colle, D., De Turck, F., & Demeester, P. (2012). Optical networks for grid and cloud computing applications. *Proceedings of the IEEE*, *100*(5), 1149–1167. doi:10.1109/JPROC.2011.2179629

Dileep, G. (2020). A survey on smart grid technologies and applications. *Renewable Energy*, *146*, 2589–2625. doi:10.1016/j.renene.2019.08.092

Ding, D., Han, Q. L., Xiang, Y., Ge, X., & Zhang, X. M. (2018). A survey on security control and attack detection for industrial cyber-physical systems. *Neurocomputing*, *275*, 1674–1683. doi:10.1016/j.neucom.2017.10.009

Dogaru, D. I., & Dumitrache, I. (2019). Cyber attacks of a power grid analysis using a deep neural network approach. *Journal of Control Engineering and Applied Informatics*, *21*(1), 42–50.

Dondossola, G., Garrone, F., Szanto, J., Deconinck, G., Loix, T., & Beitollahi, H. (2009). ICT resilience of power control systems: experimental results from the CRUTIAL testbeds. In *Proceedings of the IEEE/IFIP International Conference on Dependable Systems & Networks* (pp. 554-559). New York: IEEE. 10.1109/DSN.2009.5270292

Đorđevic, B., Maček, N., & Timčenko, V. (2015). Performance issues in cloud computing: KVM hypervisor's cache modes evaluation. *Acta Polytechnica Hungarica*, *12*(4), 147–165.

Doshi, R., Apthorpe, N., & Feamster, N. (2018). Machine learning DDoS detection for consumer internet of things devices. In *Proceedings of the IEEE Security and Privacy Workshops (SPW)* (pp. 29-35). New York: IEEE. 10.1109/SPW.2018.00013

Ebrahimy, R., & Pourmirza, Z. (2017). Cyber-interdependency in smart energy systems. In *Proceedings of the 3rd International Conference on Information Systems Security and Privacy (ICISSP 2017)* (pp. 529-537). Setúbal, Portugal: SciTePress. 10.5220/0006262805290537

EEBus Initiative E. V. (2019). Retrieved November 10, 2019, from https://www.eebus.org/en/technology/

El Mrabet, Z., & Kaabouch, N. (2018). Cyber-security in smart grid: Survey and challenges. *Computers & Electrical Engineering*, *67*, 469–482. doi:10.1016/j.compeleceng.2018.01.015

Estanqueiro, A., Ahlrot, C., Duque, J., Santos, D., Gentle, J. P., & Abboud, A. W., ... Kanefendt, T. (2018). DLR use for optimization of network design with very large wind (and VRE) penetration. In *Proceedings of the 17th Wind Integration Workshop* (Article 263). Darmstadt, Germany: Energynautics GmbH.

European Union Agency for Cybersecurity (ENISA). (2017). *Communication network dependencies for ICS/SCADA systems*. Retrieved November 10, 2019, from https://www.enisa.europa.eu/publications/ics-scada-dependencies

European Union. (2016). *Protection of natural persons with regard to the processing of personal data and on the free movement of such data* (Regulation [EU] 2016/679). Retrieved November 10, 2019, from https://eur-lex.europa.eu/eli/reg/2016/679/oj

Faisal, M. A., Aung, Z., Williams, J. R., & Sanchez, A. (2015). Data-stream-based intrusion detection system for advanced metering infrastructure in smart grid: A feasibility study. *IEEE Systems Journal*, *9*(1), 31–44. doi:10.1109/JSYST.2013.2294120

Falco, G., Caldera, C., & Shrobe, H. (2018). IIoT cybersecurity risk modeling for SCADA systems. *IEEE Internet of Things Journal*, *5*(6), 4486–4495. doi:10.1109/JIOT.2018.2822842

Fang, B., Yin, X., Tan, Y., Li, C., Gao, Y., Cao, Y., & Li, J. (2016). The contributions of cloud technologies to smart grid. *Renewable & Sustainable Energy Reviews*, *59*, 1326–1331. doi:10.1016/j.rser.2016.01.032

Farooq, H. (2017). A Review on cloud computing security using authentication techniques. *International Journal of Advanced Research in Computer Science*, *8*(2), 19–22.

Farooq, M. U., Waseem, M., Khairi, A., & Mazhar, S. (2015). A Critical analysis of the security concerns of Internet of Things (IoT). *International Journal of Computers and Applications*, *111*(7), 1–6. doi:10.5120/19547-1280

Federal Energy Regulatory Commission (FERC). (2019). *Managing transmission line ratings* (Docket No. AD19-15-000). Retrieved September 25, 2019, from https://www.ferc.gov/CalendarFiles/20190823124451-Managing%20Transmission%20Line%20Ratings_Staff%20Paper.pdf

Fink, G. A., Best, D. M., Manz, D. O., Popovsky, V., & Endicott-Popovsky, B. (2013). Gamification for measuring cyber security situational awareness. In D. D. Schmorrow, & C. M. Fidopiastis (Eds.), Lecture Notes in Computer Science: Vol. 8027. *Foundations of Augmented Cognition*. Berlin, Germany: Springer. doi:10.1007/978-3-642-39454-6_70

Flexera. (2019, February 27). Cloud computing trends: 2019 state of the cloud survey [Web log comment]. Retrieved November 10, 2019, from https://www.flexera.com/blog/cloud/2019/02/cloud-computing-trends-2019-state-of-the-cloud-survey

Flick, T., & Morehouse, J. (2010). *Securing the smart grid: Next generation power grid security*. Burlington, MA: Syngress.

Foglietta, C., Panzieri, S., Macone, D., Liberati, F., & Simeoni, A. (2013). Detection and impact of cyber attacks in a critical infrastructures scenario: The CockpitCI approach. *International Journal of System of Systems Engineering*, *4*(3/4), 211–221. doi:10.1504/IJSSE.2013.057669

Fok, M. P., Wang, Z., Deng, Y., & Prucnal, P. R. (2011). Optical layer security in fiber-optic networks. *IEEE Transactions on Information Forensics and Security*, *6*(3), 725–736. doi:10.1109/TIFS.2011.2141990

Fonseca, J., Andrade, A., Nicolosi, D. E. C., Biscegli, J. F., Legendre, D., Bock, E., & Lucchi, J. C. (2008). A new technique to control brushless motor for blood pump application. *Artificial Organs*, *32*(4), 355–359. doi:10.1111/j.1525-1594.2008.00554.x PMID:18370953

Forum of Incident Response and Security Teams (FIRST). (2015). *Common vulnerability scoring system v3.0: Specification document*. Retrieved November 01, 2019, from https://www.first.org/cvss/v3.0/specification-document

Foundation, O. P. C. (2018). *Practical security recommendations for building OPC UA applications* (White Paper). Retrieved August 1, 2019, from https://opcfoundation.org/wp-content/uploads/2017/11/OPC-UA-Security-Advise-EN.pdf

Freitas, M. B., Rosa, L., Cruz, T., & Simões, P. (2019). SDN-enabled virtual data diode. In S. K. Katsikas & ... (Eds.), Lecture Notes in Computer Science: Vol. 11387. *Computer Security* (pp. 102–118). Cham, Switzerland: Springer. doi:10.1007/978-3-030-12786-2_7

Frost, L., & Tajitsu, N. (2017, May 15). Renault-Nissan is resuming production after a global cyberattack caused stoppages at 5 plants. *Reuters*. Retrieved November 01, 2019, from https://www.businessinsider.com/renault-nissan-production-halt-wannacry-ransomeware-attack-2017-5?IR=T

Furdek, M., Skorin-Kapov, N., Bosiljevac, M., & Sipus, Z. (2010). Analysis of crosstalk in optical couplers and associated vulnerabilities. In *Proceedings of the 33rd International Convention MIPRO* (pp. 461-466). New York: IEEE.

Galloway, B., & Hancke, G. P. (2013). Introduction to industrial control networks. *IEEE Communications Surveys and Tutorials*, *15*(2), 860–880. doi:10.1109/SURV.2012.071812.00124

Gao, J., Liu, J., Rajan, B., Nori, R., Fu, B., Xiao, Y., ... Chen, C. L. P. (2014). SCADA communication and security issues. *Security and Communication Networks*, *7*(1), 175–194. doi:10.1002ec.698

Garcia-Morchon, O., Kumar, S., & Sethi, M. (2019). Internet of things (IoT) Security: State of the Art and Challenges. *IETF RFC 8576 (Informational)*. Retrieved October 8, 2019, from https://www.rfc-editor.org/search/rfc_search.php

García-Teodoro, P., Díaz-Verdejo, J., Maciá-Fernández, G., & Vázquez, E. (2009). Anomaly-based network intrusion detection: Techniques, systems, and challenges. *Computers & Security*, *28*(1-2), 18–28. doi:10.1016/j.cose.2008.08.003

Gardašević, G., Veletić, M., Maletić, N., Vasiljević, D., Radusinović, I., Tomović, S., & Radonjić, M. (2017). The IoT architectural framework, design issues and application domains. *Wireless Personal Communications*, *92*(1), 127–148. doi:10.100711277-016-3842-3

Gartner, Inc. (2017). *Gartner says worldwide IoT security spending to reach $348 million in 2016.* Retrieved November 10, 2019, from https://www.gartner.com/en/newsroom/press-releases/2016-04-25-gartner-says-worldwide-iot-security-spending-to-reach-348-million-in-2016

Gavrovska, A. M., Milivojević, M. S., Zajić, G., & Reljin, I. (2016). Video traffic variability in H. 265/HEVC video encoded sequences. In *Proceedings of the 13th Symposium on Neural Networks and Applications (NEUREL)* (pp. 1-4). New York: IEEE. 10.1109/NEUREL.2016.7800130

Gavrovska, A. M., Zajić, G. J., Milivojević, M. S., & Reljin, I. S. (2018). Machine-learning based blind visual quality assessment with content-aware data partitioning. In *Proceedings of the 14th Symposium on Neural Networks and Applications (NEUREL)* (pp. 1-5). New York: IEEE. 10.1109/NEUREL.2018.8587018

Gavrovska, A., Zajić, G., Reljin, I., & Reljin, B. (2013). Classification of prolapsed mitral valve versus healthy heart from phonocardiograms by multifractal analysis. *Computational and Mathematical Methods in Medicine*, *2013*, 1–10. doi:10.1155/2013/376152 PMID:23762185

Genç, Z. A., Lenzini, G., & Ryan, P. Y. A. (2018). No random, no ransom: A key to stop cryptographic ransomware. In C. Giuffrida, S. Bardin, & G. Blanc (Eds.), *Vol: 10885. Detection of Intrusions and Malware, and Vulnerability Assessment* (pp. 234–255). Lecture Notes in Computer Science. Cham, Switzerland: Springer. doi:10.1007/978-3-319-93411-2_11

Gentle, J. P. (2016). *Operational and strategic implementation of dynamic line rating for optimized wind energy generation integration* (Technical Report No. INL/EXT-16-40751; TRN: US1702282). Retrieved September 25, 2019, from https://www.osti.gov/servlets/purl/1364098

Ghaeini, H., & Tippenhauer, N. (2016). Hamids: Hierarchical monitoring intrusion detection system for industrial control systems. In *Proceedings of the 2nd ACM Workshop on Cyber-Physical Systems Security and Privacy (CPS-SPC'16)* (pp. 103-111). New York, NY: ACM. 10.1145/2994487.2994492

Ghasempour, A. (2019). Internet of Things in smart grid: Architecture, applications, services, key technologies, and challenges. *Inventions MDPI Journal*, *4*(1). Article, *22*, 1–12.

Ghosh, S., & Sampalli, S. (2019). A survey of security in SCADA networks: Current issues and future challenges. *IEEE Access: Practical Innovations, Open Solutions*, *7*. doi:10.1109/ACCESS.2019.2926441

Giraldo, J., Sarkar, E., Cardenas, A. A., Maniatakos, M., & Kantarcioglu, M. (2017). Security and privacy in cyber-physical systems: A survey of surveys. *IEEE Design Test*, *34*(4), 7–17. doi:10.1109/MDAT.2017.2709310

Godfrey, M., & Zulkernine, M. (2013). A server-side solution to cache-based side-channel attacks in the cloud. In *Proceedings of the International Conference on Cloud Computing (CLOUD)* (vol. 6, pp. 163-170). New York: IEEE. 10.1109/CLOUD.2013.21

Goel, S., & Hong, Y. (2015). Security challenges in smart grid implementation. In S. Gaycken (Ed.), *SpringeBriefs in Cybersecurity. Smart grid security* (pp. 1–39). London, UK: Springer-Verlag.

Goldenberg, N., & Wool, A. (2013). Accurate modeling of Modbus/TCP for intrusion detection in SCADA systems. *International Journal of Critical Infrastructure Protection*, *6*(2), 63–75. doi:10.1016/j.ijcip.2013.05.001

Graveto, V., Rosa, L., Cruz, T., & Simões, P. (2019). A stealth monitoring mechanism for cyber-physical systems. *International Journal of Critical Infrastructure Protection*, *24*, 126–143. doi:10.1016/j.ijcip.2018.10.006

Grobauer, B., Walloschek, T., & Stocker, E. (2011). Understanding cloud computing vulnerabilities. *IEEE Security and Privacy*, *9*(2), 50–57. doi:10.1109/MSP.2010.115

Gruschka, N., & Iacono, L. (2009). Vulnerable cloud: SOAP message security validation revisited. In *Proceedings of the International Conference on Web Services* (pp. 625-631). New York: IEEE. 10.1109/ICWS.2009.70

Gunes, V., Peter, S., Givargis, T., & Vahid, F. (2014). A survey on concepts, application, and challenges in cyber-physical systems. *Transactions on Internet and Information Systems (Seoul)*, *8*, 4242–4268.

Gupta, A., Kumar, M., Hansel, S., & Saini, A. K. (2013). Future of all technologies - The cloud and cyber physical systems. *International Journal of Enhanced Research in Management & Computer Applications*, *2*(2), 1–6.

Han, S., Xie, M., Chen, H.-H., & Ling, A. Y. (2014). Intrusion detection in cyber- physical systems: Techniques and challenges. *IEEE Systems Journal*, *8*(4), 1052–1062. doi:10.1109/JSYST.2013.2257594

Hari Krishna, B., Kiran, S., Murali, G., & Pradeep Kumar Reddy, R. (2016). Security issues in service model of cloud computing environment. *Procedia Computer Science*, *87*, 246–251. doi:10.1016/j.procs.2016.05.156

Harnik, D., Pinkas, B., & Shulman-Peleg, A. (2010). Side channels in cloud services: Deduplication in cloud storage. *IEEE Security and Privacy*, *8*(6), 40–47. doi:10.1109/MSP.2010.187

Hashizume, K., Rosado, D. G., Fernandez-Medina, E., & Fernandez, E. B. (2013). An analysis of security issues for cloud computing. *Journal of Internet Services and Applications*, *4*(1), 1–13. doi:10.1186/1869-0238-4-5

Hawrylak, P. J., Hartney, C., Haney, M. A., Hamm, J. K., & Hale, J. (2013). Techniques to model and derive a cyber-attacker's intelligence. In B. Igelnik, & J. M. Zurada (Eds.), *Efficiency and Scalability Methods for Computational Intellect* (pp. 162–180). Hershey, PA: IGI Global. doi:10.4018/978-1-4666-3942-3.ch008

Hawrylak, P. J., Louthan, G., Daily, J. S., Hale, J. W., & Papa, M. (2012). Attack graphs and scenario driven wireless computer network defense. In M. Khosrow-Pour (Ed.), *Crisis Management: Concepts, Methodologies, Tools, and Applications* (pp. 774–791). Hershey, PA: IGI Global.

Hay, A., Cid, D., & Bray, R. (2008). *OSSEC host-based intrusion detection guide*. Burlington, MA: Syngress Publishing.

Hemsley, K. E., & Fisher, R. E. (2018). *History of industrial control system cyber incidents* (Idaho National Laboratory Technical Report INL/CON-18-44411-Revision-2). Retrieved October 15, 2019, from https://www.osti.gov/servlets/purl/1505628

Henriksen, E., Burkow, T. M., Johnsen, E., & Vognild, L. K. (2013). Privacy and information security risks in a technology platform for home-based chronic disease rehabilitation and education. *BMC Medical Informatics and Decision Making*, *13*(1), 85. doi:10.1186/1472-6947-13-85 PMID:23937965

Heritage, I. (2019). Protecting Industry 4.0: Challenges and solutions as IT, OT and IP converge. *Network Security*, *2019*(10), 6–9. doi:10.1016/S1353-4858(19)30120-5

Hermann, M., Pentek, T., & Otto, B. (2015). *Design principles for Industrie 4.0 scenarios: A literature review*. Retrieved November 10, 2019, from http://www.snom.mb.tu-dortmund.de/cms/de/forschung/Arbeitsberichte/Design-Principles-for-Industrie-4_0-Scenarios.pdf

Howard, P. D. (2015). *A security checklist for SCADA systems in the cloud*. Retrieved October 8, 2019, from https://gcn.com/articles/2015/06/29/scada-cloud.aspx

Huang, A. Q., & Cockrell, D. D. (2019). Solid state transformers, the energy router and the energy Internet. In W. Su, & A. Q. Huang (Eds.), *The Energy Internet* (pp. 21–44). Cambridge, UK: Elsevier. doi:10.1016/B978-0-08-102207-8.00002-3

Huang, A. Q., Crow, M. L., Heydt, G. T., Zheng, J. P., & Dale, S. J. (2011). The future renewable electric energy delivery and management (FREEDM) system: The Energy Internet. *Proceedings of the IEEE, 99*(1), 133–148. doi:10.1109/JPROC.2010.2081330

Huang, L., Liu, Y., Wu, J., Li, G., & Li, J. (2018). Software-defined dynamic QoS provisioning for smart metering in Energy Internet using fog computing and network calculus. *IET Cyber-Physical Systems: Theory & Applications, 3*(3), 142–149.

Huang, Y., Wang, X., Wang, K., Zhang, D., & Dai, B. (2017). A novel optical encoding scheme based on spectral phase encoding for secure optical communication. In *Proceedings of the International Conference on Optical Communications and Network (ICOCN)* (vol. 16, pp. 1-3). New York: IEEE. 10.1109/ICOCN.2017.8121476

Humayed, A., Lin, J., Li, F., & Luo, B. (2017). Cyber-physical systems security – A survey. *IEEE Internet of Things Journal, 4*(6), 1802–1831. doi:10.1109/JIOT.2017.2703172

Hu, P., Dhelim, S., Ning, H., & Qiu, T. (2017). Survey on fog computing: Architecture, key technologies, applications and open issues. *Journal of Network and Computer Applications, 98*, 27–42. doi:10.1016/j.jnca.2017.09.002

Hurttila, A. (2019). *Cybersecurity in SCADA engineering.* Retrieved November 15, 2019, from https://www.theseus.fi/bitstream/handle/10024/170574/Hurttila%2C%20Antti.pdf?sequence=2&isAllowed=y

Hu, Y., Yang, A., Li, H., Sun, Y., & Sun, L. (2018). A survey of intrusion detection on industrial control systems. *International Journal of Distributed Sensor Networks, 14*(8), 1–14. doi:10.1177/1550147718794615

Hwang, R. H., Peng, M. C., Nguyen, V. L., & Chang, Y. L. (2019). An LSTM-based deep learning approach for classifying malicious traffic at the packet level. *Applied Sciences, 9*(16), 3414. doi:10.3390/app9163414

Hylving, L., & Schultze, U. (2013). Evolving the modular layered architecture in digital innovation: The case of the car's instrument cluster. In *Proceedings of the International Conference on Information Systems (ICIS 2013): Reshaping Society Through Information Systems Design* (vol. 2, article 13). Red Hook, NY: Curran Associates.

Ibarra, J., Javed Butt, U., Do, A., Jahankhani, H., & Jamal, A. (2019). Ransomware impact to SCADA systems and its scope to critical infrastructure. In *Proceedings of 12th International Conference on Global Security, Safety, and Sustainability, ICGS3 2019* (pp. 1-12). New York: IEEE. 10.1109/ICGS3.2019.8688299

Indian Institute of Technology. Kanpur. (2019). *Interdisciplinary center for cyber security and cyber defense of critical infrastructures.* Retrieved, November 02, 2019, from https://security.cse.iitk.ac.in

Inductive Automation. (2011). *Cloud-based SCADA systems: The benefits & risks* (White Paper). Retrieved November 10, 2019, from https://www.controlglobal.com/assets/11WPpdf/111202-inductiveautomation-cloud.pdf

Industrial Control Systems Cyber Emergency Response Team (ICS-CERT). (2016a). *ICS-CERT annual vulnerability coordination report.* Retrieved November 10, 2019, from https://www.hsdl.org/?abstract&did=804703

Industrial Control Systems Cyber Emergency Response Team (ICS-CERT). (2016b). *Recommended practice: Improving industrial control system cybersecurity with Defense-in-Depth strategies.* Retrieved November 10, 2019, from https://www.hsdl.org/?abstract&did=797585

Industrial Control Systems Cyber Emergency Response Team (ICS-CERT). (2019). *ICS advisory* (ICSA-19-150-01). Retrieved, November 02, 2019, from https://www.us-cert.gov/ics/advisories/ICSA-19-150-01

Industrial Internet Consortium (IIC). (2016). Industrial Internet of Things Volume G4: Security Framework. Document IIC:PUB:G4:V1.0:PB:20160919. Retrieved October 8, 2019, from https://www.iiconsortium.org/pdf/IIC_PUB_G4_V1.00_PB.pdf

Industrial Internet Consortium (IIC). (2019). The Industrial Internet of Things Volume G1: Reference Architecture, Version 1.9. Retrieved October 8, 2019, from https://www.iiconsortium.org/pdf/IIRA-v1.9.pdf

Inoubli, W., Aridhi, S., Mezni, H., Maddouri, M., & Mephu Nguifo, E. (2018). An experimental survey on big data frameworks. *Future Generation Computer Systems*, *86*, 546–564. doi:10.1016/j.future.2018.04.032

Institute of Electrical and Electronics Engineers (IEEE). (2011). IEEE Standard for local and metropolitan area networks - Part 15.4: Low-rate wireless personal area networks (LR-WPANs). *Standard 802.15.4-11.*

Institute of Electrical and Electronics Engineers (IEEE). (2017). *Artificial intelligence and machine learning applied to cybersecurity.* Retrieved November 10, 2019, from https://www.ieee.org/content/dam/ieee-org/ieee/web/org/about/industry/ieee_confluence_report.pdf?utm_source=lp-link-text&utm_medium=industry&utm_campaign=confluence-paper

International Electrotechnical Commission (IEC). (2016). Communication networks and systems in substations. *IEC Standard 61850-5.*

International Organization for Standardization (ISO). (2012). Annex SL: Proposals for management system standards. *ISO/IEC Directives Part 1, Consolidated ISO Supplement – Procedures specific to ISO.*

International Organization for Standardization (ISO). (2013). Information technology – Security techniques – Information security management systems – Requirements. *Standard ISO/IEC 27001:2013.*

International Organization for Standardization (ISO). (2014). Asset management – Overview, principles and terminology. *Standard ISO, 55000,* 2014.

International Organization for Standardization (ISO). (2015). Information technology – Security techniques – Code of practice for information security controls based on ISO/IEC 27002 for cloud services. *Standard ISO/IEC 27017:2015/ ITU-T X.1631.*

International Organization for Standardization (ISO). (2015). Information technology – Security techniques – Code of practice for information security controls based on ISO/IEC 27002 for cloud services. *Standard ISO/IEC 27017:2015/ ITU-T X.1631.*

International Organization for Standardization (ISO). (2017). Information technology – Security techniques – Information security controls for the energy utility industry. *Standard ISO/IEC 27019:2017.*

International Organization for Standardization (ISO). (2018). Information technology – Security techniques – Information security management systems – Overview and vocabulary. *Standard ISO/IEC 27000:2018.*

International Organization for Standardization (ISO). (2019). Information technology – Security techniques – Code of practice for personally identifiable information (PII) in public clouds acting as PII processors. *Standard ISO/IEC 27018:2019.*

International Telecommunication Union – Telecommunication Standardization Sector (ITU-T). (2014). *Information technology – Cloud computing – Overview and vocabulary. ITU-T Recommendation Y.3500.* Geneva, Switzerland: ITU-T.

International Telecommunication Union – Telecommunication Standardization Sector (ITU-T). (2015). Security framework for cloud computing. [Geneva, ITU-T.]. *ITU-T Recommendation, X,* 1601.

Iturbe, M., Garitano, I., Zurutuza, U., & Uribeetxeberria, R. (2017). Towards large-scale, heterogeneous anomaly detection systems in industrial networks: A survey of current trends. *Security and Communication Networks*, *2017*, 1–17. doi:10.1155/2017/9150965

Jakšić, M., Rakićević, J., & Jovanović, M. (2018). Sustainable technology and business innovation framework: A comprehensive approach. *Amfiteatru Economic, 20*(48), 418–436. doi:10.24818/EA/2018/48/418

Jansen, W. A. (2011). Cloud hooks: Security and privacy issues in cloud computing. In *Proceedings of the 44th International Conference on System Science* (vol. 44, pp. 1-10). New York: IEEE. 10.1109/HICSS.2011.103

Jaradat, M., Jarrah, M., Bousselham, A., Jararweh, Y., & Al-Ayyoub, M. (2015). The Internet of Energy: Smart sensor networks and big data management for smart grid. *Procedia Computer Science, 56*, 592–597. doi:10.1016/j.procs.2015.07.250

Jiang, Y., Yin, S., & Kaynak, O. (2018). Data-driven monitoring and safety control of industrial cyber-physical systems: Basics and beyond. *IEEE Access: Practical Innovations, Open Solutions, 6*, 47374–47384. doi:10.1109/ACCESS.2018.2866403

Jinno, M., Takara, H., Kozicki, B., Tsukisima, Y., Sone, Y., & Matsuoka, S. (2009). Spectrum-efficient and scalable elastic optical path network: Architecture, benefits, and enabling technologies. *IEEE Communications Magazine, 47*(11), 66–73. doi:10.1109/MCOM.2009.5307468

John, R. I., & Mendel, J. M. (2009). Fuzzy logic, type-2 and uncertainty. In R. A. Meyers (Ed.), *Encyclopedia of Complexity and System Science*. New York: Springer. doi:10.1007/978-0-387-30440-3_235

Johnson, B. D. (2017). *A widening attack plain*. West Point, NY: Army Cyber Institute.

Junejo, K., & Goh, J. (2016). Behaviour-based attack detection and classification in cyber physical systems using machine learning. In *Proceedings of the 2nd ACM International Workshop on Cyber-Physical System Security (CPSS'16)* (pp. 34-43). New York, NY: ACM. 10.1145/2899015.2899016

Kaaniche, N., & Laurent, M. (2014). A secure client side deduplication scheme in cloud storage environments. In *Proceedings of the International Conference on New Technologies, Mobility, and Security (NTMS)* (vol. 6, pp. 1-7). New York: IEEE. 10.1109/NTMS.2014.6814002

Kabovic, A., Kabovic, M., Bostjancic Rakas, S., & Timcenko, V. (2018). Models for short-term forecasting of parameters used for calculation of the overhead line ampacity. In *Proceedings of the 26th Telecommunications forum TELFOR 2018* (pp. 687-690). New York: IEEE. 10.1109/TELFOR.2018.8612136

Kagermann, H., Wahlster, W., & Helbig, J. (2013). *Recommendations for implementing the strategic initiative INDUSTRIE 4.0 securing the future of German manufacturing industry (Final Report of the Industrie 4.0 Working Group)*. Berlin, Germany: Forschungsunion.

Kalluri, R., Mahendra, L., Kumar, R. K., & Prasad, G. L. (2017). Simulation and impact analysis of denial-of-service attacks on power SCADA. In *Proceedings of the National Power Systems Conference (NSPC)*. New York: IEEE.

Kamble, A., & Bhutad, S. (2018). Survey on Internet of Things (IoT) – security issues & solutions. In *Proceedings of the Second International Conference on Inventive Systems and Control (ICISC 2018)*, (pp. 307-312). New York: IEEE. 10.1109/ICISC.2018.8399084

Kannus, K., & Ilvonen, I. (2018). Future prospects of cyber security in manufacturing: findings from a Delphi study. In *Proceedings of the 51st Hawaii International Conference on System Sciences* (pp. 4762-4771). Waikoloa Village, HI: Curran Associates. 10.24251/HICSS.2018.599

Kao, D. Y., & Hsiao, S. C. (2018). The dynamic analysis of WannaCry ransomware. In *Proceedings of 20th International Conference on Advanced Communication Technology ICACT* (pp. 159-166).New York: IEEE

Karnik, N. N., Mendel, J. M., & Liang, Q. (1999). Type-2 fuzzy logic systems. *IEEE Transactions on Fuzzy Systems, 7*(6), 643–658. doi:10.1109/91.811231

Karri, R., Rajendran, A. J., Rosenfeld, K., & Tehranipoor, M. (2010). Trustworthy hardware: Identifying and classifying hardware trojans. *Computer*, *43*(10), 39–46. doi:10.1109/MC.2010.299

Kathirvel, K., Ramachandran, C., & Sivarathy, N. (2018). A survey on IDs using clustering techniques in data mining. *International Journal of Pure and Applied Mathematics*, *118*(8), 655–660.

Khan, A., & Turowski, K. (2016). A survey of current challenges in manufacturing industry and preparation for Industry 4.0. In A. Abraham, S. Kovalev, V. Tarassov, & V. Snášel (Eds.), *Advances in Intelligent Systems and Computing: Vol 450. Proceedings of the First International Scientific Conference "Intelligent Information Technologies for Industry (IITI'16)* (pp. 15-26). Cham, Switzerland: Springer.

Khanezaei, N., & Hanapi, Z. M. (2014). A Framework based on RSA and AES encryption algorithms for cloud computing services. In *Proceedings of the IEEE Conference on Systems, Process and Control* (pp. 58-62). New York: IEEE. 10.1109/SPC.2014.7086230

Khan, S., Parkinson, S., & Qin, Y. (2017). Fog computing security: A review of current applications and security solutions. *Journal of Cloud Computing: Advances, Systems and Applications*, *6*(19), 1–22.

Khan, S., Parkinson, S., & Qin, Y. (2017). Fog computing security: A review of current applications and security solutions. *Journal of Cloud Computing: Advances, Systems, and Applications*, *6*(19), 1–22.

Kilpatrick, H. (2018). *Five infamous IoT hacks and vulnerabilities.* Retrieved November 10, 2019, from https://www.iotsworldcongress.com/5-infamous-iot-hacks-and-vulnerabilities/

Kim, J., Shin, N., Jo, S. Y., & Kim, S. H. (2017). Method of intrusion detection using deep neural network. In *Proceedings of the IEEE International Conference on Big Data and Smart Computing (BigComp)* (pp. 313-316). New York: IEEE.

Klinkowski, M., & Walkowiak, K. (2013). On the advantages of elastic optical networks for provisioning of cloud computing Traffic. *IEEE Network*, *27*(6), 44–51. doi:10.1109/MNET.2013.6678926

Knapp, E. D., & Samani, R. (2013). *Applied cyber security and the smart grid: Implementing security controls into the modern power infrastructure.* Waltham, MA: Syngress.

Kostic-Ljubisavljevic, A., & Mikavica, B. (2018). Vertical integration between providers with possible cloud migration. In M. Khosrow-Pour (Ed.), *Encyclopedia of Information Science and Technology* (Vol. II, pp. 1164–1173). Hershey, PA: IGI Global. doi:10.4018/978-1-5225-2255-3.ch100

Kourai, K., Azumi, T., & Chiba, S. (2012). A self-protection mechanism against stepping-stone attacks for IaaS clouds. In *Proceedings of the International Conference on Ubiquitous Intelligence Computing and International Conference on Autonomic Trusted Computing* (vol. 9, pp. 539-546). New York: IEEE. 10.1109/UIC-ATC.2012.139

Kruse, C. S., Frederick, B., Jacobson, T., & Monticone, D. K. (2017). Cybersecurity in healthcare: A systematic review of modern threats and trends. *Technology and Health Care*, *25*(1), 1–10. doi:10.3233/THC-161263 PMID:27689562

Kumar, R., & Gupta, V. (2018). Realization and concept of Energy Internet. *Indian Journal of Social Research*, *17*(2), 6–11.

Kumar, S., & Dutta, K. (2016). Intrusion detection in mobile ad hoc networks: Techniques, systems, and future challenges. *Security and Communication Networks*, *9*(14), 2484–2556. doi:10.1002ec.1484

Kushalnagar, N., Montenegro, G., & Schumacher, C. (2015). IPv6 over low-power wireless personal area networks (6LoWPANs): Overview, assumptions, problem statement, and goals. *IETF RFC 4919 (Informational)*. Retrieved November 10, 2019, from https://datatracker.ietf.org/doc/rfc4919/

Kwon, C., Liu, W., & Hwang, I. (2013). Security analysis for Cyber-Physical Systems against stealthy deception attacks. In *Proceedings of the 2013 American Control Conference* (pp. 3344-3349). New York: IEEE. 10.1109/ACC.2013.6580348

Lamba, V., Simková, N., & Rossi, B. (2019). Recommendations for smart grids security risk management. *Cyber-Physical Systems*, *5*(2), 92–118. doi:10.1080/23335777.2019.1600035

Lasseter, R. H. (2002). Microgrids. In *Proceedings of the IEEE Power Engineering Society Winter Meeting* (pp. 305-308). New York: IEEE. 10.1109/PESW.2002.985003

Leander, B., & Causevic, A. (2019). Applicability of the IEC 62443 standard in Industry 4.0/IIoT. In *Proceedings of the 14th International Conference on Availability, Reliability and Security*, (Article 101, pp. 1-8). Canterbury, UK: ACM. 10.1145/3339252.3341481

Leão, T. F., Bock, E., Fonseca, J., Andrade, A., Cavalheiro, A., & Uebelhart, B., ... Campo, A. (2012). Modeling study of an implantable centrifugal blood pump actuator with redundant sensorless control. In *Proceedings of the 44th Southeastern Symposium on System Theory (SSST)* (pp. 174-178) New York: IEEE. 10.1109/SSST.2012.6195148

Leão, T., Fonseca, J., Bock, E., Sá, R., Utiyama, B., & Drigo, E., ... Andrade, A. (2014). Speed control of the implantable centrifugal blood pump to avoid aortic valve stenosis: Simulation and implementation. In *Proceedings of the 5th RAS/EMBS International Conference on Biomedical Robotics and Biomechatronics* (pp. 82-86). New York: IEEE. 10.1109/BIOROB.2014.6913756

Lee, R. M., Assante, M. J., & Conway, T. (2014). *Cyber attack on German steel mill* (Case Study Paper). SANS Institute. Retrieved November 01, 2019, from https://ics.sans.org/media/ICS-CPPE-case-Study-2-German-Steelworks_Facility.pdf

Lee, R., Assante, M., & Conway, T. (2016). Analysis of the cyber attack on the Ukrainian power grid. Washington, DC: Electricity Information Sharing and Analysis Center (E-ISAC).

Lei, H., Chen, B., Butler-Purry, K. L., & Singh, C. (2018). Security and reliability perspectives in cyber-physical smart grids. In *Proceedings of the IEEE Innovative Smart Grid Technologies-Asia (ISGT Asia)* (pp. 42-47). New York: IEEE. 10.1109/ISGT-Asia.2018.8467794

Li, H., Ota, K., & Dong, M. (2018). Learning IoT in edge: Deep learning for the Internet of Things with edge computing. *IEEE Network*, *32*(1), 96–101. doi:10.1109/MNET.2018.1700202

Li, M., Yu, S., Ren, K., Lou, W., & Hou, Y. (2013). Toward privacy-assured and searchable cloud data storage services. *IEEE Network*, *27*(4), 56–62. doi:10.1109/MNET.2017.1600280

Lin, B., Chen, W., & Chu, P. (2015). Mergers and acquisitions strategies for industry leaders, challengers, and Niche players: Interaction effects of technology positioning and industrial environment. *IEEE Transactions on Engineering Management*, *62*(1), 80–88. doi:10.1109/TEM.2014.2380822

Liu, B., Zhang, L., Xin, X., & Wang, Y. (2014). Physical layer security in OFDM-PON based on dimension-transformed chaotic permutation. *IEEE Photonics Technology Letters*, *26*(2), 127–130. doi:10.1109/LPT.2013.2290041

Liu, F., Ren, L., & Bai, H. (2014). Mitigating cross-VM side channel attack on multiple tenants cloud platform. *Journal of Computers*, *9*(4), 1005–1013. doi:10.4304/jcp.9.4.1005-1013

Liu, F., Tong, J., Mao, J., Bohn, R., Messina, J., Badger, L., & Leaf, D. (2011). *NIST cloud computing reference architecture (NIST Special Publication 500-292)*. Gaithersburg, MD: U.S. National Institute of Standards and Technology.

Liu, N., Guo, B., Liu, Z., & Wang, Y. (2018). Distributed energy sharing for PVT-HP prosumers in community energy Internet: A consensus approach. *Energies*, *11*(7), 1–18. doi:10.3390/en11071891

Liu, Y., Dong, M., Ota, K., Li, J., & Wu, J. (2018). Deep reinforcement learning based smart mitigation of DDoS flooding in software-defined networks. In *Proceedings of the IEEE 23rd International Workshop on Computer Aided Modeling and Design of Communication Links and Networks (CAMAD)* (pp. 1-6). New York: IEEE. 10.1109/CAMAD.2018.8514971

Li, W., Xie, L., Deng, Z., & Wang, Z. (2016). False sequential logic attack on SCADA system and its physical impact analysis. *Computers & Security, 58*, 149–159. doi:10.1016/j.cose.2016.01.001

Li, X., Wan, P., Zhang, H., Li, M., & Jiang, Y. (2018). The application research of Internet of Things to oil pipeline leak detection. In *Proceedings of the 2018 15th International Computer Conference on Wavelet Active Media Technology and Information Processing (ICCWAMTIP)* (pp. 211-214). New York: IEEE. 10.1109/ICCWAMTIP.2018.8632561

Li, X., Zhou, C., Tian, Y.-C., & Qin, Y. (2018). A dynamic decision-making approach for intrusion response in industrial control systems. *IEEE Transactions on Industrial Informatics, 15*(5), 2544–2554. doi:10.1109/TII.2018.2866445

Long, M., Wu, C.-H., & Hung, J. Y. (2005). Denial of service attacks on network-based control systems: Impact and mitigation. *IEEE Transactions on Industrial Informatics, 1*(2), 85–96. doi:10.1109/TII.2005.844422

Lu, Y., Morris, K. C., & Frechette, S. P. (2016). Current standards landscape for smart manufacturing systems (NIST Interagency/Internal Report [NISTIR] 8107). Gaithersburg, MD: U.S. National Institute of Standards and Technology.

Lundbohm, E. (2017). Understanding nation-state attacks. *Network Security, 2017*(10), 5–8. doi:10.1016/S1353-4858(17)30101-0

Lund, P. D., Mikkola, J., & Ypyä, J. (2015). Smart energy system design for large clean power schemes in urban areas. *Journal of Cleaner Production, 103*, 437–445. doi:10.1016/j.jclepro.2014.06.005

Lutes, M. (2000). Privacy and security compliance in the E-healthcare marketplace. *Healthcare Financial Management, 54*(3), 48–50. PMID:10847915

Lu, Y. (2017). Industry 4.0: A survey on technologies, applications and open research issues. *Journal of Industrial Information Integration, 6*, 1–10. doi:10.1016/j.jii.2017.04.005

Lu, Y., & Xu, L. D. (2018). Internet of Things (IoT) cybersecurity research: A review of current research topics. *The Internet of Things Journal, 6*(2), 2103–2115. doi:10.1109/JIOT.2018.2869847

Macek, N., Dordevic, B., Timcenko, V., Bojovic, M., & Milosavljevic, M. (2014). Improving intrusion detection with adaptive support vector machines. *Elektronika ir Elektrotechnika, 20*(7), 57–60. doi:10.5755/j01.eee.20.7.8025

MacKay, M., Baker, T., & Al-Yasiri, A. (2012). Security-oriented cloud computing platform for critical infrastructures. *Computer Law & Security Review, 28*(6), 679–686. doi:10.1016/j.clsr.2012.07.007

Mackintosh, M., Epiphaniou, G., Al-Khateeb, H., Burnham, K., Pillai, P., & Hammoudeh, M. (2019). Preliminaries of orthogonal layered defence using functional and assurance controls in industrial control systems. *Journal of Sensor and Actuator Networks, 8*(1), 14. doi:10.3390/jsan8010014

Maglaras, L. A., Cruz, T., & Jiang, J. (2014). Integrated OCSVM mechanism for intrusion detection in SCADA systems. *Electronics Letters, 50*(25), 1935–1936. doi:10.1049/el.2014.2897

Maglaras, L., Ferrag, M. A., Derhab, A., Mukherjee, M., & Janicke, H. (2019). Cyber security: From regulations and policies to practice. In A. Kavoura, E. Kefallonitis, & A. Giovanis (Eds.), *Springer Proceedings in Business and Economics. Strategic innovative marketing and tourism* (pp. 763–770). Cham, Switzerland: Springer International Publishing. doi:10.1007/978-3-030-12453-3_88

Mahan, R. E., Fluckiger, J. D., Clements, S. L., Tews, C., Burnette, J. R., Goranson, C. A., & Kirkham, H. (2011). *Secure data transfer guidance for industrial control and SCADA systems*. Richland, WA: Pacific Northwest National Lab. doi:10.2172/1030885

Mahmoud, M. S., Hamdan, M. M., & Baroudi, U. A. (2019). Modeling and control of cyber-physical systems subject to cyber attacks: A survey of recent advances and challenges. *Neurocomputing*, *338*(21), 101–115. doi:10.1016/j.neucom.2019.01.099

Mahoney, W., & Gandhi, R. A. (2011). An integrated framework for control system simulation and regulatory compliance monitoring. *International Journal of Critical Infrastructure Protection*, *4*(1), 41–53. doi:10.1016/j.ijcip.2011.03.002

Mamdani, E. H. (1977). Application of fuzzy logic to approximate reasoning using linguistic synthesis. *IEEE Transactions on Computers*, *C-26*(12), 1182–1191. doi:10.1109/TC.1977.1674779

Mamdani, E. H., & Gaines, B. (Eds.). (1981). *Fuzzy reasoning and its applications*. New York: Academic Press.

Manoj, H. R., Ashwini, R., & Vivekkant, J. (2017). Real time monitoring of substation by using cloud computing. *International Journal of Engineering Research and Application*, *7*(9), 1–4.

Mantere, M., Sailio, M., & Noponen, S. (2013). Network traffic features for anomaly detection in specific industrial control system network. *Future Internet*, *5*(4), 460–473. doi:10.3390/fi5040460

Marković, D. R., Gavrovska, A. M., & Reljin, I. S. (2016). 4K video traffic analysis using seasonal autoregressive model for traffic prediction. In *Proceedings of the 24th Telecommunications Forum (TELFOR)* (pp. 1-4). New York: IEEE. 10.1109/TELFOR.2016.7818885

Markovic, D. S., Zivkovic, D., Branovic, I., Popovic, R., & Cvetkovic, D. (2013). Smart power grid and cloud computing. *Renewable & Sustainable Energy Reviews*, *24*, 566–577. doi:10.1016/j.rser.2013.03.068

Markovic-Petrovic, J. D., Stojanovic, M. D., & Bostjancic Rakas, S. V. (2019). A fuzzy AHP approach for security risk assessment in SCADA networks. *Advances in Electrical and Computer Engineering*, *19*(3), 69–74. doi:10.4316/AECE.2019.03008

Markovic-Petrovic, J., & Stojanovic, M. (2013). Analysis of SCADA system vulnerabilities to DDoS attacks. In *Proceedings of the 11th International Conference on Telecommunications in Modern Satellite Cable and Broadcasting Services - TELSIKS 2013* (vol. 2, pp. 591-594). New York: IEEE. 10.1109/TELSKS.2013.6704448

Markovic-Petrovic, J., & Stojanovic, M. (2014). An improved risk assessment method for SCADA information security. *Elektronika ir Elektrotechnika*, *20*(7), 69–72. doi:10.5755/j01.eee.20.7.8027

Marrone, S. (2017). Towards a unified definition of cyber and physical vulnerability in critical infrastructures. In *Proceedings of 2nd IEEE European Symposium on Security and Privacy Workshops, EuroS and PW 2017*. New York: IEEE 10.1109/EuroSPW.2017.67

Martin, G., Martin, P., Hankin, C., Darzi, A., & Kinross, J. (2017, July 6). Cybersecurity and healthcare: How safe are we? *BMJ (Online)*. Retrieved November 10, 2019, from https://www.bmj.com/content/358/bmj.j3179

Marzal, S., Gonzáles-Medina, R., Salas-Puente, R., Garcerá, G., & Figueres, E. (2019). An embedded Internet of Energy communication platform for the future smart microgrids management. *IEEE Internet of Things Journal*, *6*(4), 7241–7252. doi:10.1109/JIOT.2019.2915389

Marz, N., & Warren, J. (2015). *Big Data: Principles and best practices of scalable realtime data systems*. New York: Manning Publications

Matherly, J. (2016). *Complete guide to Shodan: Collect. Analyze. Visualize. Make Internet intelligence work for you.* British Columbia, Canada: Leanpub.

Mayne, M. (2018, February 15). First confirmed cryptocurrency attack on SCADA network [Web log comment]. Retrieved October 31, 2019, from https://www.immuniweb.com/blog/first-confirmed-cryptocurrency-attack-on-scada-network.html

Mazurczyk, W., & Szczypiorski, K. (2011). Is cloud computing steganography-proof? In *Proceedings of the International Conference on Multimedia Information Networking and Security* (vol. 3, pp. 441-442). New York: IEEE.

McCall, J. C., & Goodwin, T. (2015). Dynamic Line Rating as a means to enhance transmission grid resilience. In *Proceedings of the CIGRÉ Colloquium – Grid of the Future* (Article 49). CIGRE U.S. National Committee.

McDermott, C. D., Majdani, F., & Petrovski, A. V. (2018). Botnet detection in the internet of things using deep learning approaches. In *Proceedings of the International Joint Conference on Neural Networks (IJCNN)* (pp. 1-8). New York: IEEE. 10.1109/IJCNN.2018.8489489

Meidan, Y., Bohadana, M., Mathov, Y., Mirsky, Y., Shabtai, A., Breitenbacher, D., & Elovici, Y. (2018). N-BaIoT – Network-based detection of IoT botnet attacks using deep auto-encoders. *IEEE Pervasive Computing*, *17*(3), 12–22. doi:10.1109/MPRV.2018.03367731

Mei, S., Li, R., Xue, X., Chen, Y., Lu, Q., Chen, X., ... Chen, L. (2017). Paving the way to smart micro Energy Internet: Concepts, design principles, and engineering practices. *CSEE Journal of Power and Energy Systems*, *3*(4), 440–449. doi:10.17775/CSEEJPES.2016.01930

Mell, P., & Grance, T. (2011). *The NIST definition of cloud computing (NIST Special Publication 800-145).* Gaithersburg, MD: U.S. National Institute of Standards and Technology.

Mendel, J. (2017). Smart grid cyber security challenges: Overview and classification. *E-mentor*, *68*(1), 55–66. doi:10.15219/em68.1282

Mendel, J. M. (2014). General type-2 fuzzy logic systems made simple: A tutorial. *IEEE Transactions on Fuzzy Systems*, *22*(5), 1162–1182. doi:10.1109/TFUZZ.2013.2286414

Mendel, J. M., Hagras, H., Tan, W.-W., Melek, W. W., & Ying, H. (2014). *Introduction to type-2 fuzzy logic control: Theory and applications.* Hoboken, NJ: John Wiley & Sons. doi:10.1002/9781118886540

Mendel, J. M., & John, R. I. B. (2002). Type-2 fuzzy sets made simple. *IEEE Transactions on Fuzzy Systems*, *10*(2), 117–127. doi:10.1109/91.995115

Menon, V. K., Sajith Variyar, V., Soman, K. P., Gopalakrishnan, E. A., Kottayil, S. K., Almas, M. S., & Nordström, L. (2019). A Spark™ based client for synchrophasor data stream processing. In *Proceedings of the Conference on the Industrial and Commercial Use of Energy, ICUE* (pp. 1-9). New York: IEEE.

Michiorri, A., Nguyen, H.-M., Alessandrini, S., Bjørnar Bremnes, J., Dierer, S., Ferrero, E., ... Uski, S. (2015). Forecasting for dynamic line rating. *Renewable & Sustainable Energy Reviews*, *52*, 1713–1730. doi:10.1016/j.rser.2015.07.134

MICIE Consortium. (2011). *MICIE - Tool for systemic risk analysis and secure mediation of data exchanged across linked CI information infrastructures.* Retrieved October 15, 2019, from https://cordis.europa.eu/project/rcn/88359/factsheet/en

Mikavica, B., & Kostic-Ljubisavljevic, A. (2016). Interconnection contracts between service and content provider with partial cloud migration. *Elektronika ir Elektrotechnika*, *22*(6), 92–98. doi:10.5755/j01.eie.22.6.17230

Mikavica, B., Markovic, G., & Kostic-Ljubisavljevic, A. (2018). Lightpath routing and spectrum allocation over elastic optical networks in content provisioning with cloud migration. *Photonic Network Communications, 36*(2), 187–200. doi:10.100711107-018-0788-2

Milić, S., & Srećković, M. (2008). A stationary system of non-contact temperature measurement and hot box detecting. *IEEE Transactions on Vehicular Technology, 57*(5), 2684–2694. doi:10.1109/TVT.2008.915505

Milic, S., Vulevic, B., & Stojic, Dj. (2019). A fuzzy-measurement algorithm for assessing the impact of EMF on health. *Nuclear Technology & Radiation Protection, 34*(2), 129–137. doi:10.2298/NTRP190121018M

Milić, S., Žigić, A., & Ponjavić, M. (2013). On-line temperature monitoring, fault detection and a novel heat run test of water-cooled rotor of hydrogenerator. *IEEE Transactions on Energy Conversion, 28*(3), 698–706. doi:10.1109/TEC.2013.2265262

Miloslavskaya, N., & Tolstoy, A. (2019). Internet of Things: Information security challenges and solutions. *Cluster Computing, 22*(1), 103–119. doi:10.100710586-018-2823-6

Mirian, A., Ma, Z., Adrian, D., Tischer, M., Chuenchujit, T., Yardley, T., ... Bailey, M. (2016). An Internet-wide view of ICS devices. In *Proceedings of the 14th Annual Conference on Privacy, Security, and Trust, PST 2016* (pp. 96-103). New York: IEEE. 10.1109/PST.2016.7906943

Misović, D., Milić, S., & Đurović, Ž. (2016). Vessel detection algorithm used in a laser monitoring system of the lock gate zone. *IEEE Transactions on Intelligent Transportation Systems, 17*(2), 430–440. doi:10.1109/TITS.2015.2477352

MITRE. (2019). *Common vulnerabilities and exposures (CVE)*. Retrieved November 10, 2019, from https://cve.mitre.org/data/downloads/index.html

Mohagheghi, S., Stoupis, J., & Wang, Z. (2009). Communication protocols and networks for power systems-current status and future trends. In *Proceedings of the IEEE/PES Power Systems Conference and Exposition* (pp. 1-9). New York: IEEE. 10.1109/PSCE.2009.4840174

Mohammadpourfard, M., Sami, A., & Seifi, A. R. (2017). A statistical unsupervised method against false data injection attacks: A visualization-based approach. *Expert Systems with Applications, 84*, 242–261. doi:10.1016/j.eswa.2017.05.013

Moon, D., Im, H., Kim, I., & Park, J. (2017). DTB-IDS: An intrusion detection system based on decision tree using behavior analysis for preventing APT attacks. *The Journal of Supercomputing, 73*(7), 2881–2895. doi:10.100711227-015-1604-8

Morris, T., & Gao, W. (2013). Classifications of industrial control system cyber attacks. In *Proceedings of the 1st International Symposium for ICS & SCADA Cyber Security Research* (pp. 22-29). Leicester, UK: British Computer Society.

Mouradian, C., Naboulsi, D., Yangui, S., Glitho, R. H., Morrow, M. J., & Polakos, P. A. (2018). A comprehensive survey on fog computing: State-of-the-art and research challenges. *IEEE Communications Surveys and Tutorials, 20*(1), 416–464. doi:10.1109/COMST.2017.2771153

Mouratidis, H., & Diamantopoulou, V. (2018). A security analysis method for Industrial Internet of Things. *IEEE Transactions on Industrial Informatics, 14*(9), 4093–4100. doi:10.1109/TII.2018.2832853

Mo, Y., Kim, T. H.-J., Brancik, K., Dickinson, D., Lee, L., Perrig, A., & Sinopoli, B. (2012). Cyber-physical security of a smart grid infrastructure. *Proceedings of the IEEE, 100*(1), 195–209. doi:10.1109/JPROC.2011.2161428

Muthusenthil, B., & Kim, H. S. (2018). CCTV surveillance system, attacks and design goals. *Iranian Journal of Electrical and Computer Engineering, 8*(4), 2072.

Nagaraja, S., Mittal, P., Hong, C., Caesar, M., & Borisov, N. (2010). BotGrep: Finding P2P bots with structured graph analysis. In *Proceedings of the 19th USENIX conference on Security*. New York: ACM.

Nakamoto, S. (2008). *Bitcoin: A peer-to-peer electronic cash system* [White Paper]. Retrieved November 10, 2019, from https://bitcoin.org/bitcoin.pdf

Naranjo, P. G. V., Baccarelli, E., & Scarpiniti, M. (2018). Design and energy-efficient resource management of virtualized networked Fog architectures for the real-time support of IoT applications. *The Journal of Supercomputing, 74*(6), 2470–2507. doi:10.100711227-018-2274-0

Natalino, C., Schiano, M., Di Giglio, A., Wosinska, L., & Furdek, M. (2018). Field demonstration of machine-learning-aided detection and identification of jamming attacks in optical networks. In *Proceedings of the 2018 European Conference on Optical Communication (ECOC)* (pp. 1-3). New York: IEEE. 10.1109/ECOC.2018.8535155

National Association of State Energy Officials (NASEO). (2011). *Smart grid and cyber security for energy assurance* (Technical Report). Retrieved September 25, 2019, from https://www.naseo.org/ data/sites/1/documents/publications/NASEO_Smart_Grid_and_Cyber_Security_for_Energy_Assurance_rev_November_2011.pdf

National Institute of Standards and Technology (NIST). (2012). *Guide for conducting risk assessments (NIST Special Publication 800-30 Rev. 1)*. Gaithersburg, MD: U.S. NIST.

National Institute of Standards and Technology (NIST). (2012). *NIST framework and roadmap for smart grid interoperability standards (NIST Special Publication 1108, Release 2.0)*. Gaithersburg, MD: U.S. NIST.

Naveen, P., Wong, K. I., Kobina Danquah, M., Sidhu, A. S., & Abu-Siada, A. (2016). Cloud computing for energy management in smart grid – an application survey. In *Proceedings of the IOP Conference Series*. Miri, Malaysia: IOP Publishing Ltd. *Materials Science and Engineering, 121*, 1–11.

Navigant. (2018). *Energy cloud 4.0 - capturing business value through disruptive energy platforms* (White Paper). Retrieved September 3, 2019, from https://www.navigant.com/-/media/www/site/insights/energy/2018/energy-cloud-4-capturing-business-value.pdf

Nazir, S., Patel, S., & Patel, D. (2017). Autonomic computing architecture for SCADA cyber security. *International Journal of Cognitive Informatics and Natural Intelligence, 11*(4), 66–79. doi:10.4018/IJCINI.2017100104

Negi, R., Kumar, P., Ghosh, S., Shukla, S. K., & Gahlot, A. (2019). Vulnerability assessment and mitigation for industrial critical infrastructures with cyber physical test bed. In *Proceedings of the IEEE International Conference on Industrial Cyber Physical Systems (ICPS)* (pp. 145-152). New York: IEEE. 10.1109/ICPHYS.2019.8780291

Nicholson, A., Webber, S., Dyer, S., Patel, T., & Janicke, H. (2012). SCADA security in the light of cyber-warfare. *Computers & Security, 31*(4), 418–436. doi:10.1016/j.cose.2012.02.009

North American Energy Reliability Committee (NERC). (2010). *NERC-CIP Reliability Standards (CIP-002 through CIP-009)*. Retrieved November 2019, from https://www.nerc.com/pa/Stand/Pages/CIP0024RI.aspx

Ntalampiras, S. (2016). Automatic identification of integrity attacks in cyber-physical systems. *Expert Systems with Applications, 58*, 164–173. doi:10.1016/j.eswa.2016.04.006

Nugent, E. (2017, November/December). How cloud and fog computing will advance SCADA systems. *Manufacturing Automation, 32*(7), 22–24.

O'Hare, J., MacFarlane, R., & Lo, O. (2019). Identifying vulnerabilities using internet-wide scanning data. In *Proceedings of the 12th International Conference on Global Security, Safety and Sustainability, ICGS3 2019*. New York: IEEE. 10.1109/ICGS3.2019.8688018

Obregon, L. (2015). *Secure architecture for industrial control systems*. SANS Institute. Retrieved November 16, 2019, from https://www.sans.org/reading-room/whitepapers/ICS/secure-architecture-industrial-control-systems-36327

Ogie, R. I. (2017). Cyber security incidents on critical infrastructure and industrial networks. In *Proceedings of the 9th International Conference on Computer and Automation Engineering* (pp. 254-258). New York: ACM. 10.1145/3057039.3057076

Otto, T. B., Campos, A., De Souza, M. A., Martins, D., & Bock, E. (2018). Online posture feedback system aiming at human comfort. In F. Rebelo, & M. Soares (Eds.), Advances in Intelligent Systems and Computing: Vol. 777. Advances in ergonomics in design (pp. 924-935). Cham, Switzerland: Springer. doi:10.1007/978-3-319-60582-1_93

Otuoze, A. O., Mustafa, M. W., & Larik, R. M. (2018). Smart grids security challenges: Classification by sources of threats. *Journal of Electrical Systems and Information Technology*, *5*(3), 468–483. doi:10.1016/j.jesit.2018.01.001

Pacheco, A., Cano, P., Flores, E., Trujillo, E., & Marquez, P. (2018). A smart classroom based on deep learning and osmotic IoT computing. In *Proceedings of the Congreso Internacional de Innovación y Tendencias en Ingeniería (CONIITI)* (pp. 1-5). New York: IEEE. 10.1109/CONIITI.2018.8587095

Pajouh, H. H., Dehghantanha, A., Khayami, R., & Choo, K. K. R. (2018). A deep recurrent neural network based approach for Internet of Things malware threat hunting. *Future Generation Computer Systems*, *85*, 88–96. doi:10.1016/j.future.2018.03.007

Palisse, A., Le Bouder, H., Lanet, J. L., Le Guernic, C., & Legay, A. (2017). Ransomware and the legacy crypto API. In F. Cuppens, N. Cuppens, J.-L. Lanet, & A. Legay (Eds.), Lecture Notes in Computer Science: Vol. 10158. *Risks and Security of Internet and Systems* (pp. 11–28). Cham, Switzerland: Springer. doi:10.1007/978-3-319-54876-0_2

Parra, I., Rodríguez, A., & Arroyo-Figueroa, G. (2014). Electric utility enterprise architecture to support the smart grid-enterprise architecture for the smart grid. In *Proceedings of 11th International Conference on Informatics in Control, Automation, and Robotics (ICINCO 2014)* (pp. 673-679). New York: IEEE. 10.5220/0005014006730679

Parthasarathy, S., & Karthika, M. (2017). Cloud computing support for smart grid applications. *International Journal on Advances in Computer and Electronics Engineering*, *2*(11), 11–17.

Patel, A., Alhussian, H., Pedersen, J. M., Bounabat, B., Celestino, J. Jr, & Katsikas, S. (2017). A nifty collaborative intrusion detection and prevention architecture for smart grid ecosystems. *Computers & Security*, *64*, 92–109. doi:10.1016/j.cose.2016.07.002

Patel, S., & Zaveri, J. (2010). A risk-assessment model for cyber attacks on information systems. *Journal of Computers*, *5*(3), 352–359. doi:10.4304/jcp.5.3.352-359

Perakslis, E. D. (2014). Cybersecurity in health care. *The New England Journal of Medicine*, *371*(5), 395–397. doi:10.1056/NEJMp1404358 PMID:25075831

Phillips, L. R., Richardson, B. T., Stamp, J. E., & LaViolette, R. A. (2009). Final report: impacts analysis for cyber attack on electric power systems (National SCADA Test Bed FY08) (Technical Report No. SAND2009-1673). Albuquerque, NM: Sandia National Laboratories.

Poolsappasit, N., Dewri, R., & Ray, I. (2012). Dynamic security risk management using Bayesian attack graphs. *IEEE Transactions on Dependable and Secure Computing*, *9*(1), 61–74. doi:10.1109/TDSC.2011.34

Popeanga, J. (2012). Cloud computing and smart grids. *Database Systems Journal*, *3*(3), 57–66.

Posirca, O. (2017, May 13). Dacia production in Romania, partially crippled by cyber-attack | WannaCry infection suspected. *Business Review*. Retrieved, November 02, 2019, from http://business-review.eu/news/dacia-production-in-romania-partially-crippled-by-cyber-attack-wannacry-infection-suspected-137678

Pramod, T. C., & Sunitha, N. R. (2018). SCADA: Analysis of attacks on communication protocols. In *Proceedings of the International Symposium on Sensor Networks, Systems and Security* (pp. 219-234). Cham, Switzerland: Springer. 10.1007/978-3-319-75683-7_17

PRECYSE Consortium. (2015). *PRECYSE - Prevention, protection and REaction to CYber attackS to critical infrastructures*. Retrieved October 2019, from https://cordis.europa.eu/project/rcn/102446/factsheet/en

Qassim, Q. S., Jamil, N., Daud, M., Ja'affar, N., Yussof, S., Ismail, R., & Kamarulzaman, W. A. (2018). Simulating command injection attacks on IEC 60870-5-104 protocol in SCADA system. *IACSIT International Journal of Engineering and Technology*, 7(2), 153–159. doi:10.14419/ijet.v7i2.14.12816

Qiu, T., Chen, N., Li, K., Atiquzzaman, M., & Zhao, W. (2018). How can heterogeneous Internet of Things build our future: A survey. *IEEE Communications Surveys and Tutorials*, 20(3), 2011–2027. doi:10.1109/COMST.2018.2803740

Queiroz, C., Mahmood, A., & Tari, Z. (2011). SCADASim – A framework for building SCADA simulations. *IEEE Transactions on Smart Grid*, 2(4), 589–597. doi:10.1109/TSG.2011.2162432

Radoglou-Grammatikis, P. I., & Sarigiannidis, P. G. (2019). Securing the smart grid: A comprehensive compilation of intrusion detection and prevention systems. *IEEE Access: Practical Innovations, Open Solutions*, 7, 46595–46620. doi:10.1109/ACCESS.2019.2909807

Raković, R. (2017). *Bezbednost informacija – osnove i smernice [Information security: Fundamentals and guidelines]*. Belgrade, Serbia: Academic Mind.

Raković, R., Mandić Lukić, J., & Čukić, N. (2016). Information security in electric power utilities' environment. In *Proceedings of South East Europe Regional Conference* (Paper P07). Portoroz, Slovenia: CIGRÉ.

Raković, R. (2018). Aspekti bezbednosti informacija u okruženju računarstva u oblaku [Information security aspects in cloud computing environment]. *InfoM*, 17(66), 26–30.

Ramos, M. H., Castelletti, A., Pulido-Velazquez, M., & Gustafsson, D. (2016). Weather and climate services for hydropower management. In *Proceedings of the Hydropower and Environmental Sustainability*. Paris, France: Société Hydrotechnique de France (SHF).

Raposo, D., Rodrigues, A., Sinche, S., Sá Silva, J., & Boavida, F. (2019). Security and fault detection in In-node components of IIoT constrained devices. *IEEE Local Computer Networks Conference (LCN)*. New York: IEEE.

Ravi Kumar, P., Herbert Rajb, P., & Jelcianac, P. (2018). Exploring data security issues and solutions in cloud computing. *Procedia Computer Science*, 125, 691–697. doi:10.1016/j.procs.2017.12.089

Rawat, D. B., & Bajracharya, C. (2015). Cyber security for smart grid systems: Status, challenges and perspectives. In *Proceedings of the SoutheastCon* (pp. 1-6). New York: IEEE. 10.1109/SECON.2015.7132891

Redgrid. (n.d.). *The Internet of Energy*. Retrieved September 3, 2019, from https://redgrid.io/

Repository of industrial security incidents (RISI) online incident database . (2015). Retrieved October 08, 2019, from https://www.risidata.com/Database/event_date/asc

Rettig, L., Khayati, M., Cudre-Mauroux, P., & Piorkowski, M. (2015). Online anomaly detection over Big Data streams. In *Proceedings of the IEEE International Conference on Big Data* (pp. 1113-1122). New York: IEEE. 10.1109/BigData.2015.7363865

Rifkin, J. (2011). *The third industrial revolution: How lateral power is transforming energy, the economy, and the world*. New York: St. Martin's Griffin.

Ritala, P., Olander, H., Michailova, S., & Husted, K. (2015). Knowledge sharing, knowledge leaking and relative innovation performance: An empirical study. *Technovation*, *35*, 22–31. doi:10.1016/j.technovation.2014.07.011

Roberts, P. (2018, March/April). This is what happens when bitcoin miners take over your town. *Politico Magazine*. Retrieved November 10, 2019, from https://www.politico.com/magazine/story/2018/03/09/bitcoin-mining-energy-prices-smalltown-feature-217230

Rodenas-Herraiz, D., Garcia-Sanchez, A., Garcia-Sanchez, F., & Garcia-Haro, J. (2013). Current trends in wireless mesh sensor networks: A review of competing approaches. *Sensors (Basel)*, *13*(5), 5958–5995. doi:10.3390130505958 PMID:23666128

Rodofile, N. R., Radke, K., & Foo, E. (2016). DNP3 network scanning and reconnaissance for critical infrastructure. In *Proceedings of Australasian Computer Science Week Multiconference* (Article 39). New York: ACM. 10.1145/2843043.2843350

Rodrigues, J., De Rezende Segundo, D., Junqueira, H., Sabino, M., Prince, R., Al-Muhtadi, J., & De Albuquerque, V. H. C. (2018). Enabling technologies for the Internet of Health Things. *IEEE Access: Practical Innovations, Open Solutions*, *6*, 13129–13141. doi:10.1109/ACCESS.2017.2789329

Rojas González, I., & Sánchez Pérez, G. (2015). Framework for the development of secure web systems for electrical companies. In *Proceedings of 2015 CIGRÉ SCD2 Colloquium*. Paris, France: CIGRÉ.

Rosa, L., Alves, P., Cruz, T., & Simões, P. (2015). A comparative study of correlation engines for security event management. In *Proceedings of the 10th International Conference on Cyber Warfare and Security (ICCWS 2015)*. Kruger National Park, South Africa: ACPI Press.

Rosa, L., Freitas, M., Mazo, S., Monteiro, E., Cruz, T., & Simoes, P. (2019). A comprehensive security analysis of a SCADA protocol: From OSINT to mitigation. *IEEE Access: Practical Innovations, Open Solutions*, *7*, 42156–42168. doi:10.1109/ACCESS.2019.2906926

Rosa, L., Proença, J., Henriques, J., Graveto, V., Cruz, T., Simões, P., ... Monteiro, E. (2017). An evolved security architecture for distributed industrial automation and control systems. In *Proceedings of the 16th European Conference on Information Warfare and Security, ECCWS 2017*. Dublin, Ireland: ACPI.

Rubio, J. E., Alcaraz, C., Roman, R., & Lopez, J. (2019). Current cyber-defense trends in industrial control systems. *Computers & Security*, *87*, 1–12. doi:10.1016/j.cose.2019.06.015

Sabaliauskaite, G., Ng, G. S., Ruths, J., & Mathur, A. (2017). A comprehensive approach, and a case study, for conducting attack detection experiments in cyber-physical systems. *Robotics and Autonomous Systems*, *98*, 174–191. doi:10.1016/j.robot.2017.09.018

Sadeghi, A.-R., Wachsmann, C., & Waidner, M. (2015). Security and privacy challenges in industrial Internet of Things. In *Proceedings of the 52nd ACM/EDAC/IEEE Design Automation Conference* (pp. 1-6). New York: IEEE. 10.1145/2744769.2747942

Sajid, A., Abbas, H., & Saleem, K. (2016). Cloud-assisted IoT-based SCADA systems security: A review of the state of the art and future challenges. *IEEE Access: Practical Innovations, Open Solutions*, *4*, 1375–1384. doi:10.1109/ACCESS.2016.2549047

Saleem, Y., Crespi, N., Rehmani, M. H., & Copeland, R. (2017). Internet of Things-aided smart grid: Technologies, architectures, applications, prototypes, and future research directions. *IEEE Access: Practical Innovations, Open Solutions*, *7*, 62962–63003. doi:10.1109/ACCESS.2019.2913984

Saletović, J., Salkić, H., & Softić, A. (2017). Virtual power plants - Concept, perspectives, and challenges. In *Proceedings of the 13ᵗʰ Bosnian CIGRÉ* (Article C6, pp. 1-8). Sarajevo, Bosnia and Herzegovina: BH K CIGRÉ.

Salim, M. M., Rathore, S., & Park, J. H. (2019). Distributed denial of service attacks and its defenses in IoT: A survey. *The Journal of Supercomputing*, 1–44.

Samčović, A. (2016). Security Issues in Internet of Things Environment. In *Proceedings of the Eighth International Conference on Business Information Security* (pp. 59-65). Belgrade, Serbia: Metropolitan University.

Samčović, A. (2019). Multimedia Services in Cloud Computing Environment. In *Proceedings of the International Scientific Conference on Information Technology and Data Related Research - Sinteza 2019* (pp. 176-183). Belgrade, Serbia: Singidunum University.

Sanders, J. (2019, August 1). Guide to industry cloud: What businesses need to know. *ZDNet*. Retrieved September 25, 2019, from https://www.zdnet.com/article/guide-to-industry-cloud-what-businesses-need-to-know/

Sandikkaya, M. T., & Harmanci, A. E. (2012). Security problems of Platform-as-a-Service (PaaS) clouds and practical solutions to the problems. In *Proceedings of the IEEE 31st Symposium on Reliable Distributed Systems* (pp. 463-468). New York: IEEE. 10.1109/SRDS.2012.84

Sani, A. S., Yuan, D., Jin, J., Gao, L., Yu, S., & Dong, Z. Y. (2019). Cyber security framework for Internet of Things-based Energy Internet. *Future Generation Computer Systems*, *93*, 849–859. doi:10.1016/j.future.2018.01.029

Sannino, G., De Falco, I., & De Pietro, G. (2019). A continuous non-invasive arterial pressure (CNAP) approach for Health 4.0 systems. *IEEE Transactions on Industrial Informatics*, *15*(1), 498–506. doi:10.1109/TII.2018.2832081

Santos, B., Leão, T., Tabacow, R., Souza, J., Campos, A., & Martins, D. … Bock, E. (2018). Controle de uma plataforma reconfigurável de tecnologia assistiva incorporada a Saúde 4.0 [Control of a reconfigurable platform of assistive technology incorporated to Health 4.0]. In F. O. Medola, & L. C. Paschoarelli (Eds.), Tecnologia assistiva – Pesquisa e conhecimento II (pp. 93-102). Bauru, Brazil: Canal 6 Editora.

Scarfone, K., & Mell, P. (2007). *Guide to intrusion detection and prevention systems (IDPS) (NIST Special Publication 800-94)*. Gaithersburg, MD: U.S. National Institute of Standards and Technology.

Scholl, M., Stine, K., Hash, J., Bowen, P., Johnson, A., Smith, C. D., & Steinberg, D. I. (2008). *An introductory resource guide for implementing the health insurance portability and accountability act (HIPAA) security rule (NIST Special Publication 800-66 Rev. 1)*. Gaithersburg, MD: U.S. National Institute of Standards and Technology. doi:10.6028/NIST.SP.800-66r1

Schwab, W., & Poujol, M. (2018). The state of industrial cybersecurity 2018. Retrieved October 8, 2019, from https://ics.kaspersky.com/media/2018-Kaspersky-ICS-Whitepaper.pdf

SecureWorks, Inc. (2015, April 8). Vulnerability assessments versus penetration tests [Web log comment]. Retrieved June 23, 2019, from https://www.secureworks.com/blog/vulnerability-assessments-versus-penetration-tests

Shakerighadi, B., Anvari-Moghaddam, A., Vasquez, J. C., & Guerrero, J. M. (2018). Internet of Things for Modern Energy Systems: State-of-the-Art, Challenges, and Open Issues. *Energies*, *11*(5), 1–23. doi:10.3390/en11051252

Sha, L., Gopalakrishnan, S., Liu, X., & Wang, Q. (2008). Cyber-physical systems: A new frontier. In *Proceedings of the IEEE International Conference on Sensor Networks, Ubiquitous, and Trustworthy Computing* (pp. 1-9). New York: IEEE.

Shelby, Z., Hartke, K., & Bormann, C. (2014). The constrained application protocol (CoAP). *IETF RFC 7252 (Standards Track)*. Retrieved November 10, 2019, from https://datatracker.ietf.org/doc/rfc7252/

Shone, N., Ngoc, T. N., Phai, V. D., & Shi, Q. (2018). A deep learning approach to network intrusion detection. *IEEE Transactions on Emerging Topics in Computational Intelligence*, *2*(1), 41–50. doi:10.1109/TETCI.2017.2772792

Sicari, S., Rizzardi, A., Grieco, L. A., & Coen-Porisini, A. (2015). Security, privacy and trust in Internet of Things: The road ahead. *Computer Networks*, *76*, 146–164. doi:10.1016/j.comnet.2014.11.008

Silver Power Systems. (n.d.). *Energy management platform*. Retrieved September 3, 2019, from https://www.silverpowersystems.com/energy-management-platform

Simões, P., Cruz, T., Proença, J., & Monteiro, E. (2015). Specialized honeypots for SCADA systems. In M. Lehto, & P. Neittaanmäki (Eds.), Intelligent Systems, Control and Automation: Science and Engineering: Vol. 78. Cyber Security: Analytics, Technology, and Automation (pp. 251-269). Cham, Switzerland: Springer. doi:10.1007/978-3-319-18302-2_16

Singh, S. K., Bziuk, W., & Jukan, A. (2016). Balancing Data Security and Blocking Performance with Spectrum Randomization in Optical Networks. In *Proceedings of the IEEE Global Communications Conference (GLOBECOM)* (pp. 1-7). New York: IEEE. 10.1109/GLOCOM.2016.7841622

Singh, V. K., Ebrahem, H., & Govindarasu, M. (2019). Security evaluation of two intrusion detection systems in smart grid SCADA environment. In *Proceedings of the 2018 North American Power Symposium, NAPS 2018*. New York: IEEE.

Sisinni, E., Saifullah, A., Han, S., Jennehag, U., & Gidlund, M. (2018). Industrial Internet of Things: Challenges, opportunities, and directions. *IEEE Transactions on Industrial Informatics*, *14*(11), 4724–4734. doi:10.1109/TII.2018.2852491

Situation AWare Security Operations Center (SAWSOC). (2016). CORDIS, European Commission. Retrieved November 10, 2019, from https://cordis.europa.eu/project/rcn/110931/factsheet/it

Skorin-Kapov, N., Furdek, M., Zsigmond, S., & Wosinska, L. (2016). Physical layer security in evolving optical networks. *IEEE Communications Magazine*, *54*(8), 110–117. doi:10.1109/MCOM.2016.7537185

Sobrinho, J. R. S., Legaspe, E., Drigo, E., Dias, J. C., Dias, J. C., Barboza, M., ... & Santos Filho, D. J. (2018, May). Supervisory control system associated with the development of device thrombosis in VAD. In L. M. Camarinha-Matos, K. O. Adu-Kankam, & M. Julashokri (Eds.), IFIP Advances in Information and Communication Technology: Vol. 521. Technological innovation for resilient systems (pp. 90-97). Cham, Switzerland: Springer International Publishing.

Soufiane, S., & Halima, B. (2017). SaaS cloud security: Attacks and proposed solutions. *Transactions on Machine Learning and Artificial Intelligence*, *5*(4), 291–301. doi:10.14738/tmlai.54.3194

Sridhar, S., Hahn, A., & Govindarasu, M. (2012). Cyber-physical system security for the electric power grid. *Proceedings of the IEEE*, *100*(1), 210–224. doi:10.1109/JPROC.2011.2165269

Stapleton, M., Maamoun, K., & Mouftah, H. T. (2018). Implementing CoS in EON protection and restoration schemes to preserve network resources. In *Proceedings of the 20th International Conference on Transparent Optical Networks (ICTON)* (pp. 1-4). New York: IEEE. 10.1109/ICTON.2018.8473666

Steitz, C., & Auchard, E. (2016, April 26). German nuclear plant infected with computer viruses, operator says. *Reuters*. Retrieved October 08, 2019, from https://www.reuters.com/article/us-nuclearpower-cyber-germany/german-nuclear-plant-infected-with-computer-viruses-operator-says-idUSKCN0XN2OS

Stewart, W. (2018, February 9). Illegal Bitcoin mining factory sparks massive blaze thanks to overheating computers used to create cryptocurrency. *The Sun*. Retrieved November 10, 2019, from https://www.thesun.co.uk/news/5538526/bitcoin-mining-factory-cryptocurrency-illegal-russia-fire-overheating-computers/

Stojanović, M. D., Boštjančič Rakas, S. V., & Marković-Petrović, J. D. (2018). Cloud-based SCADA systems: Cyber security considerations and future challenges. In *Proceedings of the 4th Virtual International Conference on Science, Technology and Management in Energy – eNergetics 2018* (pp. 253-260). Nis, Serbia: Research and Development Center "ALFATEC", and Complex System Research Center.

Stojanović, M. D., Boštjančič Rakas, S. V., & Marković-Petrović, J. D. (2019). SCADA systems in the cloud and fog environments: Migration scenarios and security issues. *FACTA UNIVERSITATIS Series: Electronics and Energetics*, *32*(3), 345–358.

Stojanovic, M., & Bostjancic Rakas, S. (2013). Policies for allocating performance impairment budgets among multiple IP providers. *AEÜ. International Journal of Electronics and Communications*, *67*(3), 206–216. doi:10.1016/j.aeue.2012.08.001

Stojanovic, M., Bostjancic Rakas, S., & Acimovic-Raspopovic, V. (2010). End-to-end quality of service specification and mapping: The third-party approach. *Computer Communications*, *33*(11), 1354–1368. doi:10.1016/j.comcom.2010.03.024

Stojanovic, M., Kostic-Ljubisavljevic, A., & Radonjic-Djogatovic, V. (2013). SLA-controlled interconnection charging in next generation networks. *Computer Networks*, *57*(11), 2374–2394. doi:10.1016/j.comnet.2013.04.013

Stouffer, K., Pillitteri, V., Lightman, S., Abrams, M., & Hahn, A. (2015). *Guide to industrial control systems (ICS) security (NIST Special Publication 800-82 Rev. 2)*. Gaithersburg, MD: U.S. National Institute of Standards and Technology. doi:10.6028/NIST.SP.800-82r2

Subashini, S., & Kavita, V. (2011). A survey on security issues in service delivery models of cloud computing. *Journal of Network and Computer Applications*, *34*(1), 1–11. doi:10.1016/j.jnca.2010.07.006

Sugeno, M., & Takagi, A. (1983). A new approach to design of fuzzy controller. In P. P. Wang (Ed.), *Advances in fuzzy sets, possibility theory and applications* (pp. 325–334). New York: Plenum Press. doi:10.1007/978-1-4613-3754-6_20

Sui, X., Wu, J., Yin, W., Zhou, D., & Gong, Z. (2010). MALsim: A functional-level parallel simulation platform for CMPs. In *Proceedings of the 2nd International Conference on Computer Engineering and Technology (ICCET):* Vol. 2. New York: IEEE.

Sun, Q. (2019). *Energy Internet and We-Energy*. Singapore: Springer. doi:10.1007/978-981-13-0523-8

Surani, R. R. (2019). From smart grids to an Energy Internet: A review paper on key features of an Energy Internet. *International Journal Of Engineering Research & Technology*, *8*(4), 228–231.

Tabacow, R. P., Bock, E. G. P., & Nakamoto, F. Y. (2018). Modelagem em Redes de Petri do sistema de controle local da plataforma de tecnologia assistive [Modeling in Petri Nets of the local control system of the assistive technology platform]. *The Academic Society Journal*, *2*(3), 173–178. doi:10.32640/tasj.2018.3.173

Takagi, T., & Sugeno, M. (1985). Fuzzy identification of systems and its applications to modeling and control. *IEEE Transactions on Systems, Man, and Cybernetics*, *15*(1), 116–132. doi:10.1109/TSMC.1985.6313399

Tang, B., Chen, Z., Hefferman, G., Pei, S., Wei, T., He, H., & Yang, Q. (2017). Incorporating intelligence in fog computing for big data analysis in smart cities. *IEEE Transactions on Industrial Informatics*, *13*(5), 2140–2150. doi:10.1109/TII.2017.2679740

Tang, J., Sun, D., Liu, S., & Gaudiot, J. L. (2017). Enabling deep learning on IoT devices. *Computer*, *50*(10), 92–96. doi:10.1109/MC.2017.3641648

Teixeira, M., Salman, T., Zolanvari, M., Jain, R., Meskin, N., & Samaka, M. (2018). SCADA system testbed for cybersecurity research using machine learning approach. *Future Internet*, *10*(8), 76. doi:10.3390/fi10080076

Ten, C. W., Manimaran, G., & Liu, C. C. (2010). Cybersecurity for critical infrastructures: Attack and defense modeling. *IEEE Transactions on Systems, Man, and Cybernetics. Part A, Systems and Humans, 40*(4), 853–865. doi:10.1109/TSMCA.2010.2048028

Thames, L., & Schaefer, D. (2016). Software-defined cloud manufacturing for industry 4.0. *Procedia CIRP, 52*, 12–17. doi:10.1016/j.procir.2016.07.041

Timčenko, V., Zogović, N., Jevtić, M., & Đorđević, B. (2017). An IoT business environment for multi objective cloud computing sustainability assessment framework. In *Proceedings of the 7th International Conference on Information Society and Technology ICIST 2017* (vol. 1, pp. 120-125). Belgrade, Serbia: Society for Information Systems and Computer Networks.

Timcenko, V. V. (2014). An approach for DDoS attack prevention in mobile ad hoc networks. *Elektronika ir Elektrotechnika, 20*(6), 150–153. doi:10.5755/j01.eee.20.6.7289

Tom, R. J., & Sankaranarayanan, S. (2017). IoT based SCADA integrated with fog for power distribution automation. In *Proceedings of the 12th Iberian Conference on Information Systems and Technologies* (pp. 1-4). New York: IEEE. 10.23919/CISTI.2017.7975732

Torres, E. C., Campos, A. A., Martins, D., & Bock, E. (2019). Robotic system for active-passive strength therapy. In T. Ahram, W. Karwowski, & R. Taiar (Eds.), Advances in Intelligent Systems and Computing: Vol. 876. Human systems engineering and design (pp. 987-993). Cham, Switzerland: Springer International Publishing. doi:10.1007/978-3-030-02053-8_150

Tuballa, M. L., & Abundo, M. L. (2016). A review of the development of smart grid technologies. *Renewable & Sustainable Energy Reviews, 59*, 710–725. doi:10.1016/j.rser.2016.01.011

Tung, Y., Tseng, S., Shih, J., & Shan, H. (2014). W-VST: A testbed for evaluating web vulnerability scanner. In *Proceedings of the 14th International Conference on Quality Software* (pp. 228-233). New York: IEEE. 10.1109/QSIC.2014.50

Tuptuk, N., & Hailes, S. (2018). Security of smart manufacturing systems. *Journal of Manufacturing Systems, 47*, 93–106. doi:10.1016/j.jmsy.2018.04.007

U.S. Department of Energy. (2019). *Dynamic line rating* (Report to Congress). Retrieved September 25, 2019, from https://www.energy.gov/sites/prod/files/2019/08/f66/Congressional_DLR_Report_ June2019_final_ 508_0.pdf

Uebelhart, B., Da Silva, B. U., Fonseca, J., Bock, E., Leme, J., Da Silva, C., ... Andrade, A. (2013). Study of a centrifugal blood pump in a mock loop system. *Artificial Organs, 37*(11), 946–949. doi:10.1111/aor.12228 PMID:24237361

Unterweger, M. (2018). *From the Internet of Things (IoT) to the Internet of Energy (IoE). (Technical Article)*. Siemens. Available from IoT-Siemens Download Center.

Uski-Joutsenvuo, S., & Pasonen, R. (2013). *Maximising power line transmission capability by employing dynamic line ratings – technical survey and applicability in Finland* (Research Report VTT-R-01604-1). Retrieved September 25, 2019, from http://sgemfinalreport.fi/files/D5.1.55%20-%20Dynamic%20line%20rating.pdf

Usman, M., & Faruque, M. O. (2019). Applications of synchrophasor technologies in power systems. *Journal of Modern Power Systems and Clean Energy, 7*(2), 211–226. doi:10.100740565-018-0455-8

Uwizeyemungu, S., Poba-Nzaou, P., & Cantinotti, M. (2019). European hospitals' transition toward fully electronic-based systems: Do information technology security and privacy practices follow? *JMIR Medical Informatics, 7*(1), e11211, 1-32.

Vanier, D. J. (2001). Why industry needs management tools. *Journal of Computing in Civil Engineering, 15*(1), 35–43. doi:10.1061/(ASCE)0887-3801(2001)15:1(35)

Vasiljević, D., & Gardašević, G. (2019). Packet aggregation scheduling in 6TiSCH networks. In *Proceedings* of the *IEEE EUROCON 2019: 18th International Conference on Smart Technologies* (pp. 1-5). New York: IEEE.

Vasseur, J.-P., & Dunkels, A. (2010). *Interconnecting smart objects with IP: The next Internet.* Burlington, MA: Morgan Kaufmann.

Velasco, L., Riuz, M., Christodoulopoulos, K., Varvarigos, M., Zotkiewicz, M., & Pioro, M. (2016). Routing and spectrum allocation. In V. Lopez, & L. Velasco (Eds.), *Elastic optical networks: Architecture, technologies, and control* (pp. 55–81). Cham, Switzerland: Springer.

Vezzoli, C., Ceschin, F., Osanjo, L., M'Rithaa, M. K., Moalosi, R., Nakazibwe, V., & Diehl, J. C. (2018). *Designing sustainable energy for all.* Cham, Switzerland: Springer. doi:10.1007/978-3-319-70223-0

VIKING Consortium. (2011). *VIKING - Vital Infrastructure, networKs, INformation and control systems manaGement.* Retrieved October 15, 2019, from https://cordis.europa.eu/project/rcn/88625/factsheet/en

Vilajosana, X., Watteyne, T., Vučinić, M., Chang, T., & Pister, K. (2019). TiSCH: Industrial performance for IPv6 Internet-of-Things networks. *Proceedings of the IEEE, 107*(6), 1153–1165. doi:10.1109/JPROC.2019.2906404

Vishwakarma, R., & Jain, A. K. (2019). A survey of DDoS attacking techniques and defense mechanisms in the IoT network. *Telecommunication Systems,* 1–23.

Vitali, T., David, T., Ofer, B., Michal, F., Aubigny, M., Panzieri, S., & Simões, P. (2017). *D7.1 – Validation plan.* AT-ENA Project Document.

Von Solms, R., & Van Niekerk, J. (2013). From information security to cyber security. *Computers & Security, 38,* 97–102. doi:10.1016/j.cose.2013.04.004

Waagsnes, H., & Ulltveit-moe, N. (2018). Intrusion detection system test framework for SCADA systems. In *Proceedings of the 4th International Conference on Information Systems Security and Privacy* (pp. 275-285). Madeira, Portugal: ScitePress. 10.5220/0006588202750285

Wang, K., Hu, X., Li, H., Li, P., Yeng, D., & Guo, S. (2017a). A survey on energy Internet communications for sustainability. *IEEE Transactions on Sustainable Computing, 2*(3), 231–254. doi:10.1109/TSUSC.2017.2707122

Wang, K., Yu, J., Yu, Y., Qian, Y., Zeng, D., Guo, S., ... Wu, J. (2017b). A survey on Energy Internet: Architecture, approach, and emerging technologies. *IEEE Systems Journal, 12*(3), 2403–2416. doi:10.1109/JSYST.2016.2639820

Wang, K., Zhang, Y., Guo, S., Dong, M., Hu, R. Q., & He, L. (2018b). IEEE Access special section editorial: The Internet of Energy: architectures, cybersecurity, and applications – part II. *IEEE Access: Practical Innovations, Open Solutions, 6,* 79276–79279. doi:10.1109/ACCESS.2018.2885242

Wang, W., & Lu, Z. (2013). Cyber security in the Smart Grid: Survey and challenges. *Computer Networks, 57*(5), 1344–1371. doi:10.1016/j.comnet.2012.12.017

Wang, X., & Yi, P. (2011). Security framework for wireless communications in smart distribution grid. *IEEE Transactions on Smart Grid, 2*(4), 809–818. doi:10.1109/TSG.2011.2167354

Wan, J., Suo, H., Yan, H., & Liu, J. (2011). A general test platform for cyber-physical systems: Unmanned vehicle with wireless sensor network navigation. *Procedia Engineering, 24,* 123–127. doi:10.1016/j.proeng.2011.11.2613

Wei, J., Zhang, X., Ammons, G., Bala, V., & Ning, P. (2009). Managing security of virtual machine images in a cloud computing. In *Proceedings of the ACM Workshop on Cloud Computing Security (CCSW '09)* (pp. 91-96). New York: ACM.

Wilhoit, K. (2013, April 4). SCADA in the cloud – A security conundrum? *Trend Micro Incorporated* [Web log comment]. Retrieved November 10, 2019, from https://blog.trendmicro.com/trendlabs-security-intelligence/scada-in-the-cloud-a-security-conundrum/

Winkler, T., & Rinner, B. (2013). Privacy and security in video surveillance. In P. K. Atrey, M. S. Kankanhalli, & A. Cavallaro (Eds.), *Intelligent Multimedia Surveillance* (pp. 37–66). Berlin, Germany: Springer. doi:10.1007/978-3-642-41512-8_3

Winter, T., Thubert, P., Brandt, A., Hui, J., Kelsey, R., & Levis, P. … Alexander, R. (2012). RPL: IPv6 routing protocol for low-power and lossy networks. *IETF RFC 6550 (Standards Track)*. Retrieved November 10, 2019, from https://datatracker.ietf.org/doc/rfc6550/

Wollschlaeger, M., Sauter, T., & Jasperneite, J. (2017). The future of industrial communication: Automation networks in the era of the Internet of Things and Industry 4.0. *IEEE Industrial Electronics Magazine*, *11*(1), 17–27. doi:10.1109/MIE.2017.2649104

World Energy Council. (2015). *World-energy-resources*. Retrieved November 10, 2019, from https://www.worldenergy.org/assets/images/imported/2016/10/World-Energy-Resources-Full-report-2016.10.03.pdf

Wueest, C. (2014). *Targeted attacks against the energy sector*. San Diego, CA: Symantec Corporation.

Wu, H., Zhou, F., Zhu, Z., & Chen, Y. (2016). Interference-and-security-aware distance spectrum assignment in elastic optical networks. In *Proceedings of the 21st European Conference on Networks and Optical Communications (NOC)* (vol. 21, pp. 100-105). New York: IEEE. 10.1109/NOC.2016.7506993

Wu, S. X., & Banzhaf, W. (2010). The use of computational intelligence in intrusion detection systems: A review. *Applied Soft Computing*, *10*(1), 1–35. doi:10.1016/j.asoc.2009.06.019

Xuan, H., Wang, Y., Hao, S., Xu, Z., Li, X., & Gao, X. (2016). Security-aware routing and core allocation in elastic optical network with multi-core. In *Proceedings of the International Conference on Computational Intelligence and Security (CIS)* (vol. 12, pp. 294-298). New York: IEEE. 10.1109/CIS.2016.0073

Xu, H., Qiu, X., Sheng, Y., Luo, L., & Xiang, Y. (2018). A QoS-driven approach to the cloud service addressing attributes of security. *IEEE Access: Practical Innovations, Open Solutions*, *6*, 34477–34487. doi:10.1109/ACCESS.2018.2849594

Xu, H., Yu, W., Griffith, D., & Golmie, N. (2018). A survey on Industrial Internet of Things: A cyber-physical systems perspective. *IEEE Access: Practical Innovations, Open Solutions*, *6*, 78238–78259. doi:10.1109/ACCESS.2018.2884906

Xu, Y., Zhang, J., Wang, W., Juneja, A., & Bhattacharya, S. (2011). Energy router: Architectures and functionalities toward Energy Internet. In *Proceedings of the IEEE International Conference on Smart Grid Communications* (pp. 31-36). New York: IEEE.

Yang, H., Cheng, L., & Chuah, M. C. (2019). Deep-learning-based network intrusion detection for SCADA systems. In *Proceedings of the IEEE Conference on Communications and Network Security (CNS)*. New York: IEEE. 10.1109/CNS.2019.8802785

Yang, H., Qin, G., & Ye, L. (2019). Combined wireless network intrusion detection model based on deep learning. *IEEE Access: Practical Innovations, Open Solutions*, *7*, 82624–82632. doi:10.1109/ACCESS.2019.2923814

Yang, Y., McLaughlin, K., Sezer, S., Littler, T., Im, E. G., Pranggono, B., & Wang, H. F. (2014). Multiattribute SCADA-specific intrusion detection system for power networks. *IEEE Transactions on Power Delivery*, *29*(3), 1092–1102. doi:10.1109/TPWRD.2014.2300099

Yigit, M., Gungor, V. C., & Baktir, S. (2014). Cloud computing for smart grid applications. *Computer Networks, 70*, 312–329. doi:10.1016/j.comnet.2014.06.007

Yin, C., Zhu, Y., Fei, J., & He, X. (2017). A deep learning approach for intrusion detection using recurrent neural networks. *IEEE Access: Practical Innovations, Open Solutions, 5*, 21954–21961. doi:10.1109/ACCESS.2017.2762418

You, S., Jin, L., Zong, Y., & Bindner, H. W. (2015). The Danish perspective of energy Internet: From service-oriented flexibility trading to integrated design. *Zhongguo Dianji Gongcheng Xuebao, 35*(14), 3470–3481.

Yuan, X., Li, C., & Li, X. (2017). DeepDefense: Identifying DDoS attack via deep learning. In *Proceedings of the IEEE International Conference on Smart Computing (SMARTCOMP)* (pp. 1-8). New York: IEEE. 10.1109/SMART-COMP.2017.7946998

Zaddach, J., Bruno, L., Francillon, A., & Balzarotti, D. (2014). Avatar: A framework to support dynamic security analysis of embedded systems' firmwares. In *Proceedings of the Network and Distributed System Security (NDSS) Symposium*. Internet Society.

Zadeh, L. A. (1965). Fuzzy sets. *Information and Control, 8*(3), 338–353. doi:10.1016/S0019-9958(65)90241-X

Zadeh, L. A. (1999). From computing with numbers to computing with words. From manipulation of measurements to manipulation of perceptions. *IEEE Transactions on Circuits and Systems, 46*(1), 105–119. doi:10.1109/81.739259

Zafar, R., Mahmood, A., Razzaq, S., Ali, W., Naeem, U., & Shehzad, K. (2018). Prosumer based energy management and sharing in smart grid. *Renewable & Sustainable Energy Reviews, 82*, 1675–1684. doi:10.1016/j.rser.2017.07.018

Zajić, G., Gavrovska, A., Reljin, I., & Reljin, B. (2019). A video hard cut detection using multifractal features. *Multimedia Tools and Applications, 78*(5), 6233–6252. doi:10.100711042-018-6420-8

Zeng, Y., Qiu, M., Zhu, D., Xue, Z., Xiong, J., & Liu, M. (2019). DeepVCM: A deep learning based intrusion detection method in VANET. In *Proceedings of the IEEE 5th Intl Conference on Big Data Security on Cloud (Big Data Security), IEEE Intl Conference on High Performance and Smart Computing (HPSC) and IEEE Intl Conference on Intelligent Data and Security (IDS)* (pp. 288-293). New York: IEEE. 10.1109/BigDataSecurity-HPSC-IDS.2019.00060

Zezulka, F., Marcon, P., Vesely, I., & Sajdl, O. (2016). Industry 4.0–An introduction in the phenomenon. *IFAC-PapersOnLine, 49*(25), 8–12. doi:10.1016/j.ifacol.2016.12.002

Zhang, N. (2018). Smart logistics path for cyber-physical systems with Internet of Things. *IEEE Access: Practical Innovations, Open Solutions, 6*, 70808–70819. doi:10.1109/ACCESS.2018.2879966

Zhang, Y., Juels, A., Reiter, M. K., & Ristenpart, T. (2014). Cross-tenant side-channel attacks in PaaS clouds. In *Proceedings of the ACM SIGSAC Conference on Computer and Communications Security* (pp. 990-1003). New York: ACM.

Zhong, W., Yu, R., Xie, S., Zhang, Y., & Tsang, D. H. K. (2016). Software defined networking for flexible and green energy Internet. *IEEE Communications Magazine, 54*(12), 68–75. doi:10.1109/MCOM.2016.1600352CM

Zhou, X., Xu, Z., Wang, L., Chen, K., Chen, C., & Zhang, W. (2018). Behavior based anomaly detection model in SCADA system. In *Proceedings of the MATEC Web of Conferences* (vol. *173*, Article 01011). EDP Sciences. 10.1051/matecconf/201817301011

Zhou, F., Goel, M., Desnoyers, P., & Sundaram, R. (2011). Scheduler vulnerabilities and coordinated attacks in cloud computing. In *Proceedings of the International Symposium on Network Computing and Applications (NCA)* (vol. 10, pp. 123-130). New York: IEEE. 10.1109/NCA.2011.24

Zhou, K., Yang, S., & Shao, Z. (2016). Energy Internet: The business perspective. *Applied Energy*, *178*, 212–222. doi:10.1016/j.apenergy.2016.06.052

Zhou, L., Guo, H., & Deng, G. (2019). A fog computing based approach to DDoS mitigation in IIoT systems. *Computers & Security*, *85*, 51–62. doi:10.1016/j.cose.2019.04.017

Zhou, L., Thieret, R., Watzlaf, V., DeAlmeida, D., & Parmanto, B. (2019). A telehealth privacy and security self-assessment questionnaire for telehealth providers: Development and validation. *International Journal of Telerehabilitation*, *11*(1), 3–14. doi:10.5195/ijt.2019.6276 PMID:31341542

Zhou, X., Xu, Z., Wang, L., & Chen, K. (2017). What should we do? A structured review of SCADA system cyber security standards. In *Proceedings of the 4th International Conference on Control, Decision, and Information Technologies* (pp. 605-614). New York: IEEE. 10.1109/CoDIT.2017.8102661

Zhou, Y., Ni, W., & Zhu, Z. (2017). Architecture of energy Internet and its technologies in application reviewed. *Journal of Clean Energy Technologies*, *5*(4), 320–327. doi:10.18178/JOCET.2017.5.4.391

Zhu, J., Zhao, B., Lu, W., & Zhu, Z. (2016). Attack-aware service provisioning to enhance physical-layer security in multi-domain EONs. *Journal of Lightwave Technology*, *34*(11), 2645–2655. doi:10.1109/JLT.2016.2541779

Zimba, A., Chen, H., & Wang, Z. (2019). Bayesian network based weighted APT attack paths modeling in cloud computing. *Future Generation Computer Systems*, *96*, 525–537. doi:10.1016/j.future.2019.02.045

Zimba, A., & Chishimba, M. (2019). On the economic impact of crypto-ransomware attacks: The state of the art on enterprise systems. *European Journal for Security Research*, *4*(1), 3–31. doi:10.100741125-019-00039-8

Zimba, A., Wang, Z., & Chen, H. (2018). Multi-stage crypto ransomware attacks: A new emerging cyber threat to critical infrastructure and industrial control systems. *ICT Express*, *4*(1), 14–18. doi:10.1016/j.icte.2017.12.007

Zimba, A., Wang, Z., Chen, H., & Mulenga, M. (2019). Recent advances in cryptovirology: State-of-the-art crypto mining and crypto ransomware attacks. *Transactions on Internet and Information Systems (Seoul)*, *13*(6), 3258–3279.

Zimba, A., Wang, Z., Mulenga, M., & Odongo, N. H. (in press). Crypto mining attacks in information systems: An emerging threat to cyber security. *Journal of Computer Information Systems*.

Zou, X., Cao, J., Sun, W., Guo, Q., & Wen, T. (2019). Flow data processing paradigm and its application in smart city using a cluster analysis approach. *Cluster Computing*, *22*(2), 435–444. doi:10.100710586-018-2839-y

About the Contributors

Mirjana Stojanović received her B.Sc. (1985) and M.Sc. (1993) degrees in electrical engineering and her Ph.D. degree (2005) in technical sciences, all from the University of Belgrade, Serbia. She is currently full professor in Information and Communication Technologies at the Faculty of Transport and Traffic Engineering, University of Belgrade. Previously, she held research position at the Mihailo Pupin Institute, University of Belgrade, and was involved in developing telecommunication equipment and systems for regional power utilities and major Serbian corporate systems. Prof. Stojanovic participated in the CIGRÉ D2 international projects concerning operational services using IP virtual private networks and integrated management information in utilities. She published a number of book chapters, journal articles, and conference papers in her field. Her research interests include communication protocols, cyber security, service and network management, and QoS solutions in the next-generation Internet.

Slavica Boštjančič Rakas received her B.Sc. (2004) and M.Sc. (2007) degrees in traffic engineering and her Ph.D. degree (2011) in technical sciences, all from the University of Belgrade, Serbia. Dr. Boštjančič Rakas joined Mihailo Pupin Institute in Belgrade in 2005, where she is currently research fellow in the area of telecommunication networks. She has participated in several research projects and studies concerning the design of next-generation networks, quality of service and network management systems. As author or coauthor, she published more than 40 papers at national and international journals, books and conferences. Her research interests include quality of service architectures, network management in the future Internet, and security issues in industrial control systems.

* * *

Gustavo Arroyo-Figueroa is a researcher in the Technologies Information at Instituto Nacional de Electricidad y Energías Limpias. Gustavo Arroyo-Figueroa completed his Ph.D. at Monterrey Institute of Technology and his undergraduate studies at the Celaya Institute of Technology. He is head of research area of Information Technologies. His research includes Artificial Intelligence applications in the energy sector (automation and processes control, intelligent management of data, intelligent training and computer security schemes based on AI). His subjects of interest are Automated Learning, Big Data and Analytics, Predictive Analysis, Forecast Models, Ensemble Methods and Hybrid Systems.Dr. Arroyo-Figueroa has published over 80 journal papers and has presented a similar number of papers in international conferences. He is a reviewer for several international journals and has held various roles in scientific committees of various organizations and meetings. He is member of National Research System of Mexico and board of the Mexican Society of Artificial Intelligence and national member of CIGRE.

Marcelo Barboza is an Electrical Engineer, Master in Control and Automation, PhD in Mechatronics by Poli / USP, with main research in control of ventricular assist devices through artificial neural networks. Marcelo is also Murrelektronik Innovation and Marketing Manager and founder of Industrial Automation Meetup. He has 20 years of experience in departments such as Technical Support, Application Engineering and Product Management.

Lazar Berbakov is Research Associate at the Mihailo Pupin Institute, University of Belgrade, Serbia. He received the M.Sc. degree in telecommunications engineering from the Faculty of Technical Sciences, Novi Sad, Serbia, in 2007, and the Ph.D. degree in signal theory and telecommunications from the Polytechnic University of Catalonia, Barcelona, Spain, in 2013. From 2008 to 2013, he was part of the Ph.D. program at the Centre Tecnològic de Telecomunicacions de Catalunya, Castelldefels, Spain, and a recipient of the FPU Ph.D. scholarship granted by the Spanish Ministry of Education. In 2014, he joined Mihailo Pupin Institute, where he serves as a Researcher in the area of telecommunications and signal processing. His main research interests include signal processing in wireless sensor networks and biomedical signals. He takes part at international conferences and journals and works as a paper reviewer.

Eduardo Guy Bock holds a degree in Mechanical Engineering from Sao Judas Tadeu University (2003), master's and doctorate degrees in Mechanical Engineering from Campinas State University - Unicamp (2007) and (2011). He is associate professor (class D-IV) of the Bioengineering and Biomaterials Laboratory (BIOENG) www.labbioeng.com and of the Department of Mechanics of the Federal Institute of Education Science and Technology of São Paulo. He has experience in Biomedical Engineering, focusing on Bioengineering, acting on the following subjects: biomaterials, tribology, numerical simulation, artificial organs, artificial heart, circulatory assistance, left ventricular assistance and extracorporeal circulation.

Filipe Caldeira is an Adjunct Professor at the Polytechnic Institute of Viseu, Portugal. He obtained his PhD degree in Informatics Engineering from the Faculty of Sciences and Technology of the University of Coimbra. He is a researcher at the CI&DETS research centre of the Polytechnic Institute of Viseu and at the Centre for Informatics and Systems of the University of Coimbra. His main research interests include ICT security, namely, trust and reputation systems, Smart Cities and Critical Infrastructure Protection. His research papers were published in various international conferences, journals and book chapters. He has also been recently involved in some international and national research projects. He serves on the Technical Program Committee of several International and national conferences and as a reviewer for some international peer-reviewed journals. Since 2005 he is regularly invited to act as invited expert evaluator and project reviewer for the European Commission - Research Executive Agency.

Tiago Cruz received the Ph.D. degree in informatics engineering from the University of Coimbra, Coimbra, Portugal, in 2012. He has been an Assistant Professor in the Department of Informatics Engineering, University of Coimbra, since December 2013. His research interests include areas such as management systems for communications infrastructures and services, critical infrastructure security, broadband access network device and service management, Internet of Things, software-defined networking, and network function virtualization (among others). He is the author of more than 40 publications, including chapters in books, journal articles, and conference papers. Dr. Cruz is a member of the IEEE Communications Society.

Miguel Freitas received the M.Sc. degree in chemical engineering from the Technical University of Lisbon, in 2016, and the M.Sc. degree in informatics engineering from the University of Coimbra, in 2018, where he is currently a Junior Researcher with the Center for Informatics and Systems. His research interests include software-defined networking, cybersecurity, and critical infrastructure protection.

Gordana Gardašević received the BSc, MSc, and PhD degrees in Electrical Engineering (with specialization in Telecommunications) from the Faculty of Electrical Engineering (FEE), Banja Luka, Bosnia and Herzegovina, in 1995, 2001, and 2008, respectively. She awarded the scholarship granted by the Greek Government and was a PhD Research Fellow at School of Electrical and Computer Engineering, National Technical University of Athens (NTUA), Greece, from 2006 to 2008. For the academic year 2013-2014, she was a Postdoctoral Fellow at the University of Bologna. She is currently working as Associate Professor and Chief of Telecommunications Department at FEE, Banja Luka. Prof. Gardašević published three books and one monograph, as well as more than 70 scientific papers in international journals and conference proceedings. She has participated in a number of international and national research teams and projects. Key research interests are radio-communications, wireless sensor networks, Industrial Internet of Things architectures and applications, next-generation network architectures and applications, cross-layer protocol design.

Ana Gavrovska is currently Assistant Professor at School (Faculty) of Electrical Engineering (from 2017), University of Belgrade. She received her dipl.ing (five year university) degree in electrotechnical engineering in 2007, and her PhD degree in electrotechnical engineering and computer science at the Department of Telecommunications and information technologies, at School (Faculty) of Electrical Engineering, University of Belgrade. Her research interest include linear and nonlinear methods, multimedia, television and telemedicine systems, signal and image processing, video technologies, and telecommunications. She is the author of more than hundred research publications and a book.

Abraham Habib is a graduate student at The University of Tulsa.

John Hale is a Professor in the Tandy School of Computer Science and a faculty researcher in the Institute for Information Security (iSec) at The University of Tulsa. He received his Bachelor of Science in 1990, Master of Science in 1992 and doctorate degree in 1997, all in computer science from the University of Tulsa. Dr. Hale has overseen the development of one of the premier information assurance curricula in the nation while at iSec. In 2000, he earned a prestigious National Science Foundation CAREER award for his education and research initiatives at iSec. His research interests include cyber attack modeling, analysis and visualization, enterprise security management, secure operating systems, distributed system verification and policy coordination.

Anand Handa is working as a Project Executive Officer in the Interdisciplinary Center for Cyber Security and Cyber Defense of Critical Infrastructure (C3i Center) at IIT Kanpur. His current research areas include malware analysis, memory forensics, and intrusion detection systems (IDS). Anand Handa has a total of 11 years of experience in academia and research. At C3i, his main focus is to work closely on projects having malware analysis and IDS as a significant component. Anand Handa also contributes to C3i, IIT Kanpur, in the training activities organized for security professionals belonging to different organizations from various countries as an exchange program. He also presented and published research work at multiple conferences in CSCML (Israel), AsiaJCIS (Japan), SPACE (India), etc.

Peter Hawrylak, Ph.D. received the B.S. degree in computer engineering, the M.S. degree in electrical engineering, and the Ph.D. in electrical engineering from the University of Pittsburgh, Pittsburgh, PA, USA, in 2002, 2004, and 2006 respectively. He is an Associate Professor in the Department of Electrical and Computer Engineering, with a joint appointment in the Tandy School for Computer Science, at The University of Tulsa, Tulsa, OK, USA.

João Henriques is a PhD candidate in Science and Information Technology at the University of Coimbra (UC) and Assistant Professor at the Department of Informatics Engineering at the Polytechnic Institute of Viseu (IPV). His research interests at the Center for Informatics and Systems (CISUC) at UC includes forensic and audit compliance for critical infrastructures protection. He also remains as Software Engineer in the private sector.

Jose Alberto Hernández obtained a PhD in Engineering and Applied Sciences from the Autonomous University of the State of Morelos. During 2017 he carried out a postdoctoral research stay at the National Institute of Electricity and Clean Energy. He is a full-time research professor at the Faculty of Accounting, Administration and Information Technology (FCAeI) of the UAEMor. His scientific interests include data mining, big data analytics and computer security.

Ryan Irvin is an undergraduate student at the University of Tulsa in his junior year. He has been researching in cybersecurity since his freshman year. He is majoring in Electrical and Computer Engineering with a minor in Computer Science. He hopes to continue his work in cybersecurity for the rest of his time in college and after college.

Aleksandra Kostić Ljubisavljević is currently employed as Associate Professor at the University of Belgrade - Faculty for Transport and Traffic Engineering. She received her B.Sc. (1999.), M.Sc. (2005.) and Ph.D (2011.) degrees in telecommunication traffic engineering at the University of Belgrade. She published more than 150 papers regarding her scientific area of interest: economical and technical aspects of telecommunication networks integration, optical communication networks, visible light communication, intelligent transportation systems (communication systems), and telecommunication network regulation.

Douglas Kunda is Dean of the School of Science, Engineering and Technology of Mulungushi University in Kabwe, Zambia. He holds a Doctorate degree in Computer Science from the University of York, UK. He is Fellow of the ICT Association of Zambia and Member of Association for Computing Machinery (ACM). He worked as the Project Manager for the Integrated Financial Management Information System (IFMIS) project for the Ministry of Finance in Zambia. He has presented papers at various International Conferences and published several articles in different journals. He is certified SAP ERP Solution Manager Consultant with experience in Java, C++, PHP/ MySQL web platforms, Microsoft products including SQL Server databases, Oracle and PostgreSQL databases, Linux, CISCO networking, PRINCE2 and Moodle.

Tarcisio Leão holds PhD in Sciences from the Dante Pazzanese Institute of Cardiology - Associate Entity of the University of São Paulo in the Medicine / Technology and Intervention in Cardiology program (2015). Master in Automation and Process Control and graduated in Industrial Automation Technology from the Federal Institute of Education, Science and Technology of São Paulo (2012). He is currently Professor at the Federal Institute of Education, Science and Technology of São Paulo and collaborating researcher at the Dante Pazzanese Institute of Cardiology. He is professor / Board Member of the Graduate Program Professional Master in Automation and Process Control. He has experience in Mechanical / Electronic Engineering, focusing on Bioengineering, acting on ventricular assist devices. At IFSP he is a lead researcher at the Life Automation Laboratory (LAV) and coordinator of the Control and Automation Engineering course. Tarcisio Leão has experience in the Industrial area, in the measurement of water and natural gas flow and in the development of metering systems / products.

Jasna Marković-Petrović received her B.Sc. (1992) and M.Sc. (2011) degrees in electrical engineering and Ph.D. (2018) in technical sciences, all from the University of Belgrade, Serbia. She is currently with the Public Enterprise "Electric Power Industry of Serbia", Serbia. Her activities involve implementation of the technical information system, participation in projects concerning upgrading the remote control system of the hydropower plant, and implementation of the SCADA security system. She is a member of the Serbian National CIGRÉ Study Committee D2. Her main research interests involve smart grids, SCADA and industrial control systems security, and cyber risk management.

Aleksandar Mastilović received the BSc and MSc degrees in Electrical Engineering – Telecommunications from the University of Sarajevo, Faculty of Electrical Engineering (Bosnia and Herzegovina), in 2009 and 2016, respectively. He received the EU Marie Curie Fellowship for the research and Ph.D. project in 2014, when he has started working at the University of Novi Sad, Faculty of Technical Sciences (Serbia) on the EU FP7 project ADVANTAGE. His research focus is the modern telecommunications system, the Internet of Things and Machine-to-Machine applications e.g. Smart Cities, computer networks and cybersecurity. He is currently employed at the Communications Regulatory Agency Bosnia and Herzegovina as the Advisor to the Director. Aleksandar Mastilović is the governance and executive boards member in the IEEE (Publications Services and Products Board, Conferences Committee, Young Professionals Committee, IoT Standards Steering Committee), member of the ITU working group on cybersecurity, G20 Global Solutions member of Young Global Changers, as well as many international technical and policy-making organizations. He is also the co-author of the IEEE trend paper AI and ML on Cybersecurity.

Branka Mikavica received her B.Sc. (2011), M.Sc. (2013) and Ph.D. (2019) degrees in telecommunication traffic engineering from the University of Belgrade – Faculty of Transport and Traffic Engineering, where she is currently teaching and research assistant. As author or coauthor, she published more than 40 papers in national and international journals, books and conferences. Her research interests include networks integration, cloud computing and elastic optical networking.

Saša Milić was born in Belgrade in Serbia, on July 11, 1967. He received the B.Sc.E.E., M.Sc.E.E, and Ph.D. in 1993, 2000 and 2008, from the University of Belgrade, respectively. Since 1994, he has been an R&D engineer in electrical measurements at the Department of Electrical Engineering of Nikola Tesla Institute, University of Belgrade. He is currently engaged as leader of the research team in the optoelectronic and magnetic laboratory. He is also currently engaged in the research in several National Projects in Industrial and Science. His research interests include measurements of temperature and displacement measurement by optical methods such as infrared principles and lasers, respectively.

Rohit Negi is currently the lead engineer and security operation center lead of C3i center, IIT Kanpur, India. Also, he is challenge lead for embedded security challenge, CSAW. He is an ICS security research scholar with 7+ years of experience specializing in cyber defense of industrial automation and operational technologies. He has international IEEE transactions and contributed chapters for cyber security. He has been speaker in Nullcon, Techkriti, CSAW, etc. He has organized workshops in a few large events like Nullcon and Techkriti. He has delivered training sessions to participants enrolled from more than 15 different countries under the ITEC Programme of the Ministry of External Affairs.

Pedro Quitério received the M.Sc. degree in informatics engineering from the University of Coimbra, in 2018, where he is currently a Junior Researcher with the Center for Informatics and Systems. His research interests include web development, data visualization, event management and critical infrastructure protection.

Radoslav Raković graduated from the Faculty of Electrical Engineering, University of Belgrade, received his M.Sc.E.E. degree at the same faculty in the area of telecommunications, and his Ph.D. degree at the Faculty of Organizational Sciences, University of Belgrade, in the area of software engineering. He has more than thirty years of experience in design and implementation of telecommunication systems in Electric Power Utilities in Serbia and abroad. His areas of engagement are telecommunication and information systems and networks, project management, business excellence, integrated management systems as well as information security. He has published more than 160 scientific and specialized papers and 8 books. Four years (2008-2012) he was professor of the Project Management College, Belgrade. He is a member of several professional organizations (CIGRE, YUPMA, FQCE) and Full member and vice-president of the Engineering Academy of Serbia. He is currently the Head of IMS Department in Energorpojekt Entel plc, Belgrade.

Rujit Raval is motivated and independent Computer Science professional with almost 2 years of research experience and about 1.5 years of experience in the industry in the field of software development and security. He has proven track record as a successful project leader while leading a multidisciplinary team at Enterprise Security Lab (ESL) at The University of Tulsa. He also has 4+ years of hands-on software development experience with Python, Java, PHP, and C#. He has good experience with Django, a high-level Python Web framework and frameworks like Tornado and Flask. Rujit Raval is experienced in WAMP (Windows, Apache, MYSQL, and Python/PHP) and MVC Struts. He has sound knowledge on RDBMS concepts with Oracle and SQL Server 2012, MySQL.

Isai Rojas-Gonzalez holds master degree in Security Engineering and Information Technology from the National Polytechnic Institute, Mexico. He is engineer in Computational Systems by the Technological Institute of Zacatepec. He joined the INEEL in 2003 to the Management team of Information Technology. He has participated in various research and development projects of corporate computer systems, in topics such as cybersecurity, web portals, knowledge management, collaboration systems, and systems for planning and strategic management, all oriented to the Energy Sector in Mexico. He currently participates in technological projects as a specialist in information security, leading activities to implement cybersecurity strategies for companies in the National Electric Sector in Mexico. He is the coordinator of the Computer Security Practice Community at INEEL. He has published paper of technological dissemination and has imparted several conferences on cybersecurity, for example the paper presented at the CIGRÉ Tutorial & Colloquium in Lima, Peru and the conference imparted at the 14th Mexican International Conference on Artificial Intelligence in Mexico.

Luis Rosa received the M.Sc. degree in informatics engineering from the Higher School of Technology and Management, Polytechnic Institute of Coimbra, Coimbra, Portugal, in 2013. He is currently pursuing the Ph.D. degree in informatics engineering with the University of Coimbra, where he is also a Junior Researcher at the Centre for Informatics and Systems and participates in several research projects in those fields. His research interests include security, event management, and critical infrastructure protection.

Andreja Samčović is a Professor of Information and Communication Technologies at the University of Belgrade, Serbia. His areas of expertise include: Multimedia signal processing (audio, image, video), Multimedia compression, Multimedia communications and Information security. He has been a visiting professor and scholar worldwide (universities in numerous countries, such as Germany, England, Austria, Slovakia…). He has taught a number of courses, seminars, tutorials, invited lectures, such as master course in Saint-Etienne (France), as well as at the summer school on Cyprus. He has published more than 150 papers in peer-reviewed journals and conference proceedings. Also, he participated in national and international projects (COST, bilateral projects). Additionally, his activities include reviews in international journals and conferences.

Bruno Santos is master student in Mechanical Engineering from the Federal Institute of Education, Science and Technology of São Paulo - Campus São Paulo; Graduating in Electronic Engineering from the Federal Institute of Education, Science and Technology of São Paulo - Campus São Paulo; Graduated in Industrial Automation at the Federal Institute of Education, Science and Technology of São Paulo - Campus São Paulo; student researcher at the Laboratory of Automation for Life (LAV) by the Federal Institute of Education, Science and Technology of São Paulo - Campus São Paulo; student researcher at the Bioengineering Laboratory (Bioeng) by the Federal Institute of Education, Science and Technology of São Paulo - Campus São Paulo; Full Domain Software: Matlab, Simulink, AutoCAD, Solid Works, Lab View, Proteus (Electronic Circuit Simulation), Eagle (Integrated Circuit Design), Ladder (PLC Programming), EdgeCam, FluidSIM (Hydraulic, Pneumatic and Electro-Pneumatic Installation Simulation), SinapGRID (Electrical Distribution Network Load and Loss Simulation), Windows, Linux, and Platforms: Google Cloud Platform, Xamarin, Azure, Bluemix, Build. me, Visual Basics, Code Composer Studio, Arduino IDE, CodeBreak, Android Studio, and App Inventor. Programming language: C, C, C #, Assembly, Java, JavaScript, HTML5 and Python. Full Domain Hardware: Frequency Drives (Specifically WEG CFW - 08), PLCs (Specifically WEG CLIC - 02), Soft-Starters (Specifically WEG SSW - 07), Integrated Circuits and Signal Processors, Data Acquisition Equipment data and FPGAs (National Instruments and Xilinx) and microcontrollers / microprocessors: Arduino, Raspberry, Texas Instruments and Intel 8051. Work experience and published work in Mechatronics, Automation, and Assistive Technology.

Sandeep Shukla is currently the Head of Computer Science and Engineering Department, Indian Institute of Technology, Kanpur, India. He is currently the Editor-in-Chief of ACM Transactions on Embedded Systems, and associate editor for ACM transactions on Cyber Physical Systems. Professor Sandeep K. Shukla is an IEEE fellow, an ACM Distinguished Scientist, and served as an IEEE Computer Society Distinguished Visitor during 2008-2012, and as an ACM Distinguished Speaker during 2007-2014. In the past, he has been associate editors for IEEE Transactions on Computers, IEEE Transactions on Industrial Informatics, IEEE Design & Test, IEEE Embedded Systems Letters, and many other journals. He was a faculty at the Virginia Tech, Virginia, USA between 2002 and 2015. Professor Sandeep K. Shukla also has been a visiting faculty at INRIA, France and University of Kaiserslautern, Germany.

Paulo Simões is Associate Professor at the Department of Informatics Engineering of the University of Coimbra, Portugal, from where he obtained his doctoral degree in 2002. He is also senior researcher at the Centre for Informatics and Systems of the University of Coimbra and regularly leads technology transfer projects for industry partners such as telecommunications operators and energy utilities. He has been involved in many European research projects, with technical and managerial duties. His research interests include Future Internet, Network and Infrastructure Management, Security, Critical Infrastructure Protection and Virtualization of Networking and Computing Resources. He has over 150 publications in refereed journals and conferences, and he regularly serves on program committees of international conferences of these areas. He is IEEE senior member.

Rachel Tabacow holds post graduation in polymer engineering from Oswaldo Cruz College (2015), and bachelor degree in Technology in Production Processes by IFSP (2012). She worked as a substitute professor at the Federal Institute of São Paulo. Currently, she works with equipment for the Plastic Industry (robots). She has research experience in Mechanics, focusing on production processes.

Valentina Timčenko received her B.Sc. (2004) and M.Sc. (2010) degrees in Electrical Engineering, both from the University of Belgrade. She is with the Mihailo Pupin Institute, University of Belgrade, since 2004, where her current position is research assistant in telecommunications. Ms. Timčenko has participated in several research projects and studies concerning next generation networks design and management systems. Her research interests include network design and implementation, and particularly cyber security in general-purpose and industrial systems. She is currently pursuing Ph.D. degree in computer science at the School of Electrical Engineering, University of Belgrade, Serbia.

Aaron Zimba is lecturer at Mulungushi University and obtained his PhD in Network and Information Security at the University of Science and Technology Beijing in the Department of Computer Science and Technology. He received his Master and Bachelor of Science degrees from the St. Petersburg Electrotechnical University in St. Petersburg in 2009 and 2007 respectively. He is also a member of the IEEE. His main research interests include Network and Information Security, Network Security Models, Cloud Computing Security and Malware Analysis.

Index

L

M

N

O

P

Q

R

S

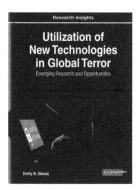

Ensure Quality Research is Introduced to the Academic Community

Become an IGI Global Reviewer for Authored Book Projects

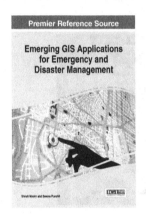 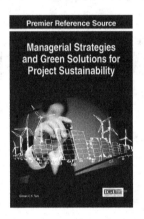  

The overall success of an authored book project is dependent on quality and timely reviews.

In this competitive age of scholarly publishing, constructive and timely feedback significantly expedites the turnaround time of manuscripts from submission to acceptance, allowing the publication and discovery of forward-thinking research at a much more expeditious rate. Several IGI Global authored book projects are currently seeking highly-qualified experts in the field to fill vacancies on their respective editorial review boards:

Applications and Inquiries may be sent to:
development@igi-global.com

Applicants must have a doctorate (or an equivalent degree) as well as publishing and reviewing experience. Reviewers are asked to complete the open-ended evaluation questions with as much detail as possible in a timely, collegial, and constructive manner. All reviewers' tenures run for one-year terms on the editorial review boards and are expected to complete at least three reviews per term. Upon successful completion of this term, reviewers can be considered for an additional term.

If you have a colleague that may be interested in this opportunity,
we encourage you to share this information with them.

IGI Global Proudly Partners With eContent Pro International

Receive a 25% Discount on all Editorial Services

Editorial Services

IGI Global expects all final manuscripts submitted for publication to be in their final form. This means they must be reviewed, revised, and professionally copy edited prior to their final submission. Not only does this support with accelerating the publication process, but it also ensures that the highest quality scholarly work can be disseminated.

English Language Copy Editing

Let eContent Pro International's expert copy editors perform edits on your manuscript to resolve spelling, punctuaion, grammar, syntax, flow, formatting issues and more.

Scientific and Scholarly Editing

Allow colleagues in your research area to examine the content of your manuscript and provide you with valuable feedback and suggestions before submission.

Figure, Table, Chart & Equation Conversions

Do you have poor quality figures? Do you need visual elements in your manuscript created or converted? A design expert can help!

Translation

Need your documjent translated into English? eContent Pro International's expert translators are fluent in English and more than 40 different languages.

Email: customerservice@econtentpro.com   **www.igi-global.com/editorial-service-partners**

Publisher of Peer-Reviewed, Timely, and
Innovative Academic Research Since 1988

IGI Global's Transformative Open Access (OA) Model:
How to Turn Your University Library's Database Acquisitions Into a Source of OA Funding

In response to the OA movement and well in advance of Plan S, IGI Global, early last year, unveiled their OA Fee Waiver (Offset Model) Initiative.

Under this initiative, librarians who invest in IGI Global's InfoSci-Books (5,300+ reference books) and/or InfoSci-Journals (185+ scholarly journals) databases will be able to subsidize their patron's OA article processing charges (APC) when their work is submitted and accepted (after the peer review process) into an IGI Global journal.*

How Does it Work?

1. When a library subscribes or perpetually purchases IGI Global's InfoSci-Databases including InfoSci-Books (5,300+ e-books), InfoSci-Journals (185+ e-journals), and/or their discipline/subject-focused subsets, IGI Global will match the library's investment with a fund of equal value to go toward subsidizing the OA article processing charges (APCs) for their patrons.

   Researchers: Be sure to recommend the InfoSci-Books and InfoSci-Journals to take advantage of this initiative.

2. When a student, faculty, or staff member submits a paper and it is accepted (following the peer review) into one of IGI Global's 185+ scholarly journals, the author will have the option to have their paper published under a traditional publishing model or as OA.

3. When the author chooses to have their paper published under OA, IGI Global will notify them of the OA Fee Waiver (Offset Model) Initiative. If the author decides they would like to take advantage of this initiative, IGI Global will deduct the US$ 1,500 APC from the created fund.

4. This fund will be offered on an annual basis and will renew as the subscription is renewed for each year thereafter. IGI Global will manage the fund and award the APC waivers unless the librarian has a preference as to how the funds should be managed.

Hear From the Experts on This Initiative:

"I'm very happy to have been able to make one of my recent research contributions, 'Visualizing the Social Media Conversations of a National Information Technology Professional Association' featured in the *International Journal of Human Capital and Information Technology Professionals*, freely available along with having access to the valuable resources found within IGI Global's InfoSci-Journals database."

– Prof. Stuart Palmer,
Deakin University, Australia

For More Information, Visit: www.igi-global.com/publish/contributor-resources/open-access or contact IGI Global's Database Team at eresources@igi-global.com.

Printed in the United States
By Bookmasters